WORKS OF
RICHARD SIBBES

Works of
RICHARD SIBBES
Volume 3

An Exposition of 2nd Corinthians
Chapter One

EDITED BY
Alexander B. Grosart

THE BANNER OF TRUTH TRUST

THE BANNER OF TRUTH TRUST
3 Murrayfield Road, Edinburgh EH12 6EL
P.O. Box 621, Carlisle, Pennsylvania 17013, U.S.A.

*

The Complete Works of Richard Sibbes first published in
seven volumes 1862-64
This reprint of volume 3 first published by the Banner of
Truth Trust 1981
ISBN 0 85151 329 8

*

Printed in U.S.A. by offset lithography by
Fairfield Graphics, Fairfield, PA

EXPOSITION OF 2ᴰ CORINTHIANS CHAPTER I.

EXPOSITION OF SECOND CORINTHIANS CHAPTER I.

NOTE.

The 'Exposition' of 2d Corinthians chapter i., was published in a handsome folio, under the editorial supervision of Dr Manton. The original title-page is given below.* Prefixed to the volume is a very fine portrait of Sibbes, after the same original evidently with that earlier engraved for 'Bowels Opened,' and other works, in quarto and smaller size, but in the style of Hollar. The admirers of Puritan literature will find it no less interesting than rewarding, to compare the present 'Exposition' of Sibbes with that of a man of kindred intellect and character, viz., Anthony Burgesse, 'Pastor of Sutton-Coldfield, in Warwickshire.' His 'sermons' on the same portion of Holy Scripture bear the following title, 'An Expository Comment, Doctrinal, Controversal [sic], and Practical, upon the whole First Chapter of the Second Epistle of St Paul to the Corinthians' (London, folio, 1661). Our copy has the rare autograph of the excellent Bishop Beveridge, on the title-page, with a note of its price, '*pret* 12. s.'   **G.**

* Original title :—

A Learned
COMMENTARY
OR
EXPOSITION
UPON

The first CHAPTER of the Second Epistle of *S. Paul*
to the *CORINTHIANS*.

BEING

The Substance of many SERMONS formerly
Preached at *Grayes-Inne, London,*
By that Reverend and Judicious Divine,
RICHARD SIBBS, D.D.
Sometimes Master of *Catherine Hall*, in *Cambridge*, and Preacher
to that Honourable Society.
Published for the Publick Good and Benefit of the Church
of *CHRIST*.
By *Tho. Manton*, B. D. and Preacher of the Gospel at *Stoake-
Newington*, near *London*.
———————— *Vivit post funera virtus.*
Psalm 112. 6.
The Righteous shall be in everlasting remembrance.
2 Pet. 1. 15.
*Moreover, I will endeavour that you may be able after my decease, to have these
things always in remembrance.*
LONDON,
Printed by *F. L.* for *N. B.* and are to be sold by *Tho. Parkhurst*, at his Shop
at the sign of the three Crowns over against the Great Conduit, at
the Lower end of Cheapside. 1655.

TO THE READER.

Good Reader,—There is no end of books, and yet we seem to need more every day. There was such a darkness brought in by the fall, as will not thoroughly be dispelled till we come to heaven; where the sun shineth without either cloud or night. For the present, all should contribute their help according to the rate and measure of their abilities. Some can only hold up a candle, others a torch; but all are useful. The press is an excellent means to scatter knowledge, were it not so often abused. All complain there is enough written, and think that now there should be a stop. Indeed, it were well if in this scribbling age there were some restraint. Useless pamphlets are grown almost as great a mischief as the erroneous and profane. Yet 'tis not good to shut the door upon industry and diligence. There is yet room left to discover more, above all that hath been said, of the wisdom of God and the riches of his grace in the gospel; yea, more of the stratagems of Satan and the deceitfulness of man's heart. Means need to be increased every day to weaken sin and strengthen trust, and quicken us to holiness. Fundamentals are the same in all ages, but the constant necessities of the church and private Christians, will continually enforce a further explication. As the arts and slights of besieging and battering increase, so doth skill in fortification. If we have no other benefit by the multitude of books that are written, we shall have this benefit: an opportunity to observe the various workings of the same Spirit about the same truths, and indeed the speculation is neither idle nor unfruitful.

There is a diversity of gifts as there is of tempers, and of tempers as there is of faces, that in all this variety, God may be the more glorified. The penmen of Scripture, that all wrote by the same Spirit, and by an infallible conduct, do not write in the same style. In the Old Testament, there is a plain difference between the lofty, courtly style of Isaiah, and the priestly, grave style of Jeremiah. In Amos there are some marks of his calling* in his prophecy. In the New Testament, you will find John sublime and seraphical, and Paul rational and argumentative. 'Tis easy to track both by their peculiar phrases, native elegances, and distinct manner of expression. This variety and 'manifold grace,' 1 Pet. iv. 10,† still

---

* That is, a 'herdsman.'—G.

† Ubi Vulgat. Dispensatio multiformis gratiæ. The more accurate rendering from the Vulgate is, 'Unusquisque, sicut accepit gratiam, in alterutrum illam administrantes, sicut boni dispensatores multiformis gratiæ Dei.'—Ed. Paris, 2 vols. 12mo. 1851.—G.

continueth. The stones that lie in the building of God's house are not all of a sort. There are sapphires, carbuncles, and agates, all which have their peculiar use and lustre, Isa. liv. 12.* Some are doctrinal, and good for information, to clear up the truth and vindicate it from the sophisms of wretched men ; others have a great force and skill in application. Some are more evangelical, their souls are melted out in sweetness ; others are sons of thunder, more rousing and stirring, gifted for a rougher strain, which also hath its use in the art of winning souls to God. 'Twas observed of the three ministers of Geneva, that none thundered more loudly than Farel, none piped more sweetly than Viret, none taught more learnedly and solidly than Calvin.† So variously doth the Lord dispense his gifts, to shew the liberty of the spirit, and for the greater beauty and order of the church ; for difference with proportion causeth beauty ; and to prevent schism, every member having his distinct excellency. So that what is wanting in one, may be supplied by another ; and all have something to commend them to the church, that they may be not despised ; as in several countries they have several commodities to maintain traffic between them all. We are apt to abuse the diversity of gifts to divisions and partialities, whereas God hath given them to maintain a communion.‡ In the church's vestment there is variety, but no rent. *Varietas sit, scissura non sit.*

All this is the rather mentioned, because of that excellent and peculiar gift which the worthy and reverend author had in unfolding and applying the great mysteries of the gospel in a sweet and mellifluous way; and therefore was by his hearers usually termed *The Sweet Dropper*, sweet and heavenly distillations usually dropping from him with such a native elegance as is not easily to be imitated. I would not set the gifts of God on quarrelling, but of all ministries, that which is most evangelical seemeth most useful. ' The testimony *of Jesus* is the spirit of prophecy,' Rev. xix. 10. 'Tis spoken by the angel to dissuade the apostle from worshipping him. You that preach Jesus Christ and him crucified and risen from the dead, have a like dignity with us angels that foretell things to come, your message is ' the spirit of prophecy ; ' as if he had said, This is the great and fundamental truth wherein runneth the life, and the heart-blood of religion.

The same spirit is breathing in these discourses that are now put into thy hand, wherein thou wilt find much of the comforts of the gospel, of the sealing of the Spirit, and the constant courses of God's love to his people, fruitfully and faithfully improved for thy edification.

---

* Varia gemmarum genera propter varia dona quæ sunt in Ecclesia.—Sanct[ius].

† Gallica mirata est Calvinum Ecclesia nuper ; quo nemo docuit doctius. Est quoque te nuper mirata Farelle tonantem ; quo nemo tonuit fortius. Et miratur adhuc fundentem mella Viretum ; quo nemo fatur dulcius. Scilicet aut tribus his servabere testibus olim, aut interibis Gallia.—*Beza.* (Poemata et Epigrammata, p. 90, 32mo, Ludg. Bat., 1614).—G.

‡ Tunc bene multiformis Dei gratia dispensatur, quando acceptum donum etiam ejus qui hoc non habet, creditur, quando propter eum cui impenditur sibi datum putatur.—*Gregor.* Moral., lib. xxviii., c. 6.

Let it not stumble thee that the work is *posthume*,* and cometh out so long after the author's death. It were to be wished that those who excel in public gifts would, during life, publish their own labours, to prevent spurious obtrusions upon the world, and to give them their last hand and polishment, as the apostle Peter was careful to ' write before his decease,' 2 Pet. i. 12–14. But usually the church's treasure is most increased by legacies. As Elijah let fall his mantle when he was taken up into heaven, so God's eminent servants, when their persons could no longer remain in the world, have left behind them some worthy pieces as a monument of their graces and zeal for the public welfare. Whether it be out of a modest sense of their own endeavours, as being loath upon choice, or of their own accord to venture abroad into the world, or whether it be that being occupied and taken up with other labours, or whether it be in a conformity to Christ, who would not leave his Spirit till his departure, or whether it be out of an hope that their works would find a more kindly reception after their death, the living being more liable to envy and reproach (but when the author is in heaven the work is more esteemed upon earth), whether for this or that cause, usually it is, that not only the life, but the death of God's servants hath been profitable to his church, by that means many useful treatises being freed from the privacy and obscureness to which, by modesty of the author, they were formerly confined.

Which, as it hath commonly fallen out, so especially in the works of this reverend author, all which (some few only excepted†) saw the light after the author's death, which also hath been the lot of this useful comment; only it hath this advantage above the rest, that it was perused by the author during life, and corrected by his own hand, and hath the plain signature and marks of his own spirit, which will easily appear to those that have been any way conversant with his former works. This being signified (for further commendation it needeth none), I ' commend thee to God, and to the word of his grace,' which is able to build thee up, and to give thee an inheritance among the sanctified, remaining

Thy servant in the Lord's work,

Thomas Manton.‡

---

* That is, 'posthumous.'—G.

† ' Some few only excepted,' viz., those which form vol. I. of this collective edition of his works.—G.

‡ It were supererogatory to annotate a name so illustrious in the roll of Puritans as is that of Thomas Manton. His memoir will appear as an introduction to his works in the present series, by one admirably qualified for doing it justice. But it may be here noticed that he was born at Lawrence-Lydiard (now Lydeard, St Lawrence), Somersetshire, in 1620, and died on October 18. 1677. Consult ' Life,' by Harris, prefixed to Sermons on 119th Psalm, and ' Nonconformists' Memorial,' i., pp. 175–179, 426–431. He was one of the ' ejected' of 1662.—G.

A COMMENTARY

UPON

THE FIRST CHAPTER OF THE SECOND EPISTLE OF ST PAUL TO THE CORINTHIANS.

Paul, an apostle of Jesus Christ, by the will of God, and Timothy our brother, unto the church of God which is at Corinth, with all the saints which are in all Achaia: Grace be to you, and peace, from God our Father, and from the Lord Jesus Christ.—2 Cor. I. 1, 2.

THE preface to this epistle is the same with other prefaces. Our blessed apostle had written a sharp epistle to the Corinthians, especially reproving their tolerating of the incestuous person.* That, his first epistle, took effect, though not so much as he desired, yet it prevailed so far, with them, that they excommunicated the incestuous person, and likewise reformed divers abuses. Yet notwithstanding, it being a proud, factious, rich city, where there was confluence of many nations, being an excellent port, and mart-town,† there were many proud, insolent teachers, which thought basely of St Paul; and thereupon he writes this second epistle: the scope whereof is partly apologetical, partly exhortatory.

(1.) Apologetical—to defend himself. Exhortatory—to instruct them in several duties, as we shall see in the passages of it.

The general scope of it is this, to shew that the ministerial labour is ' *not in vain in the Lord,*' 1 Cor. xv. 58. The fruit of the first Epistle to the Corinthians is seen in this second ; the first Epistle took effect. Therefore we should not be discouraged, neither we that are ministers of the church, or those that are ministers in their own families, as every man should be. Be not discouraged at unlikelihood. There is alway some success to encourage us, though not so much as we look for in this world, because there is a reprobate generation that are alway set upon cavilling, and opposing ; yet some success there will be, as there was here.

A second thing in general out of the whole scope is this, to teach us *to vindicate our credit, when the truth may be wounded through us,* as the apostle stands here upon his reputation, and labours to free, and to clear himself from all imputations. But especially he doth this by his life, for that is the best apology. But because that would not serve, it would not speak loud enough, therefore he makes an excellent apology in this epistle. But to come to the particulars.

* Cf. 1 Cor. v. 1, *seq.*—G. † That is, ' market-town' =commercial city.—G.

'*Paul, an apostle of Jesus Christ, by the will of God, and Timothy our brother.*' This chapter is *apologetical*, especially after the preface. He stands in defence of himself against the imputations : first, *that he was a man neglected of God*—he was so persecuted, and oppressed with so many afflictions. And the second is the imputation of *inconstancy*—that he came not to them when he had made a promise to come. This chapter is especially in defence of these two.

In an excellent heavenly wisdom, he turns off the imputation of afflictions, and inverts the imputation the clean contrary way. And he begins with thanksgiving, ' Blessed be God, the Father of our Lord Jesus Christ, the Father of mercies, the God of all comfort, who hath comforted us in all our tribulations : ' as if God had done him a great favour in them, as we shall see when we come to those words.

For the preface, it is common with all his epistles, therefore we make it not a principal part of the chapter. Yet because these prefaces have the seeds of the gospel in them, the seeds of heavenly comfort and doctrine, I will speak something of it. Here is an inscription, and a salutation.

In the inscription, there are the parties from whom this epistle was written, ' Paul, an apostle of Jesus Christ by the will of God, and Timothy our brother.' And the persons to whom : ' To the church of God at Corinth, and all the saints in Achaia.'

The salutation : ' Grace and Peace ;' in the form of a blessing, ' Grace and peace.'

From whom : ' From God the Father, and from our Lord Jesus Christ.'

'*Paul an apostle,*' &c. In this inscription he sets down his office, ' an apostle,' and ' an apostle of Jesus Christ.' How apostles differ from other ministers, it is an ordinary point. St Paul was called to be an apostle by Christ himself, 1 Cor ix. 1. ' Am I not an apostle ? have I not seen Christ ?' It was the privilege of the apostles to see Christ. They were taught immediately by Christ, and they had a general commission to teach all, and they had extraordinary gifts. All these were in St Paul eminently. And this was his prerogative, that he was chosen by Christ in heaven, in glory. The other were chosen by Christ when he was in abasement, in a state of humiliation. ' Paul an apostle of Jesus Christ.'

'*By the will of God.*' By the appointment of God, by the designment[*] of Christ ; for every man in his particular calling is placed in it ' by the will of God. St Paul saith, he was an apostle ' by the will of God, not by the will of man.' This is the same word as is in the beginning of the Epistle to the Philippians.[†]

In a word, it teacheth us this first observation, *That we should think ourselves in our standings and callings to be there by the will of God.*

And therefore should serve him by whose will we are placed in that standing. Let every man consider, who placed me here ? God. If a hair cannot fall from my head without his providence, Mat. x. 30, much less can the disposing of my calling, which is a greater matter ; therefore I will seek his glory, and frame myself and courses answerable to the will of him by whose will I am in this place.

Men have not their callings only to get riches, and to get preferment. Those are base ends of their own to serve themselves. God placeth us in our particular callings, not to serve ourselves, but to serve him ; and he

---

[*] That is, ' designation.'—G.   [†] This is a slip for Ephesians.—G.

will cast in those riches, honour, preferment, dignity, and esteem, so much as is fit for us in the serving of him in our places.

The other party* in the inscription, from whom the epistle is, is,

' *Timothy our brother.*' He sends his Epistle from Timothy as well as from himself. This he doth to win the more acceptance among the Corinthians, by the consent of so blessed a man as Timothy was, who was an evangelist. Unity by consent is stronger. And there is a natural weakness in men to regard the consent and authority of others, more than the things themselves. And indeed, if God himself in heavenly love and mercy condescend to help our weakness, much more should all that are ' led by the Spirit of God,' Gal. v. 18. We are subject to call in question the truths of God. Therefore he helps us with sacraments, and with other means and allurements ; and although that be truth that he saith, yet because he would undermine our distrustful dispositions by all means, he useth those courses. So St Paul, that they might respect what he wrote the more, as from a joint spirit, he writes, ' Paul, and Timothy our brother.'

It was an argument of much modesty and humility in this blessed apostle, that he would not of himself seem, as it were, to monopolize their respect, as if all should look to him, but he joins Timothy with him ; so great an apostle joins an inferior.

There is a spirit of singularity in many; they will seem to do all themselves, and carry all themselves before them ; and they will not speak the truths that others have spoken before them without some disdain. As a proud critic said, ' I would they had never been men that spake our things before we were, that we might have had all the credit of it' (*a*). Oh, no ! Those that are led with the Spirit of God, they are content in modesty and humility to have others joined with them ; and they know it is available† for others likewise ; they will respect the truth the more.

And thus far we yield to the papists when we speak of this, whether the church can give authority to the word of God or no. In regard of us, the church hath some power, in regard of our weakness ; but what is that power ? It is an inducing power, an alluring power, a propounding power, to propound the mysteries of salvation. But the inward work, the convincing power, is from the evidence of the Spirit of God, and from the Scripture itself. All that the church doth is to move, to induce, and to propound this, *quoad nos*. It hath some power in the hearts of men.

The church thus far gives authority to the Scriptures in the hearts of men, though it be an improper phrase to say it gives authority; for, as the men said to the woman of Samaria, ' Now we believe it ourselves, not because thou toldest us,' &c., John iv. 42. The church allures us to respect the Scriptures ; but then there is an inward power, an inward majesty in the Scriptures, and that bears down all before it.

Again, here is a ground why St Paul alleged human authority sometimes in his epistles, and in his dealing with men ; because he was to deal with men, that would be shamed the more with them. Anything that may strengthen the truth in regard of the weakness of those with whom we have to deal, may be used in a heavenly policy. ' One of your own prophets,' saith St Paul, towards the end, i. 12. And so in the Acts of the Apostles, xvii. 28, he quotes a saying out of an atheist (*b*).

---

* This use of ' party ' = person, which is not uncommon in Sibbes and his contemporaries, shews that it is not the modern vulgarism (so-called) which precisians would make it.—G.   † That is, ' advantageous.'—G.

'*Timothy our brother.*' '*Brother:*' he means not only by grace but by calling. As we know in the law and other professions, those of the same profession are called before brethren; so Timothy was St Paul's brother, not only by grace, but by calling; and two bonds bind stronger. Here is a treble bond, nature, grace, calling. They were men, they were fellow Christians, and they were teachers of the gospel. Therefore he saith, '*Timothy our brother.*' Timothy was an evangelist, yet notwithstanding it was a greater honour to him to be a brother to St Paul than to be an evangelist. An hypocrite may be an evangelist; but a true brother of St Paul none but a true Christian can be. All Christians are brethren. It is a word that levels all; for it takes down the mountains, and fills up the valleys. The greatest men in the world, the mountains, if they be Christians, they are brethren to the lowest. And it fills up the valleys. The lowest, if they be Christians, are brethren to the highest; howsoever in worldly respects, they cease in death; as personal differences, and differences in calling, they all cease in death. All are brethren; therefore he useth it for great respect. St Paul was a great apostle; Timothy an inferior man, yet both brethren, '*Timothy our brother.*'

'*To the church of God at Corinth.*' We have seen the persons from whom, '*Paul and Timothy.*' Now here are the persons to whom, '*to the church of God at Corinth.*' Corinth was a very wicked city, as, where there is a great confluence of many people, there is a contagion of many sins of the people; and yet notwithstanding in this Corinth there was a church. For as Christ saith, '*No man can come to me, except my Father draw him,*' John vi. 44; so where the Father will draw, who can draw back? Even in Corinth God hath his church. He raiseth up a generation of men, a church, which is a company of creatures differing as much from the common, as men do from beasts. And yet such is the power and efficacy of the blessed gospel of salvation, having the Spirit of God accompanying it, that even in Corinth, a wretched city, this word and this Spirit raised up a company of men, called here by the name of a church, and saints. And such power indeed hath the word of God with the Spirit, not only in wicked places, but in our wicked hearts too.

Let a man have a world of wickedness in him, and let him come and present himself meekly and constantly to the means of salvation, and God in time by his Spirit will raise a new frame of grace in his heart, he will make a new creation. As at the first he created all out of nothing, order out of confusion; so out of the heart, which is nothing but a chaos of confusion, of blindness, and darkness, and terror (there is a world of confusion in the heart of man); God by his creating word (for his word of the gospel is creating, as well as his word was at the first in the creation of the world; it hath a creating power) he raiseth an excellent frame in the heart of a man, he scatters his natural blindness, he sets in order his natural confusion, that a man becomes a new creature, and an heir of a new world.

Let no people despair, nor no person; for God hath his church in '*Corinth.*'

But what is become of this church now? Why, alas! it is under the slavery of the Turks, it is under miserable captivity at this day. At the first, Corinth was overthrown by Numeus,* a Roman captain, for the abusing the Roman ambassadors; it was ruinated for the unfit carriage to the ambassadors, who would not suffer themselves to be contemned, nor the

* Qu. 'Mummius?'—ED.

majesty of the Roman empire. But Augustus Cæsar afterwards repaired it (c). And now for neglecting of God's ambassadors, the preachers of the gospel, it is under another misery, but spiritual; it is under the bondage, I say, of that tyrant.

What is become of Rome, that glorious city? It is now 'the habitation of devils, a cage of unclean birds,' Rev. xviii. 2. What is become of those glorious churches which St John wrote those epistles to in his Revelation? and which St Paul wrote unto? Alas, they are gone! the gospel is now come into the western parts. And shall we think all shall be safe with us, as the Jews did, crying, ' The temple of the Lord, the temple of the Lord?' Jer. vii. 4. No, no! unless we respect Christ's blessed gospel of salvation, except we bring forth fruits worthy of it, except we maintain and defend it, and think it our honour and our crown, and be zealous for it. If we suffer the insolent enemies of it to grow as vipers in the very bosom of the church, what is like to become of us? If there were no foreign enemies to invade us, we would let slip the glorious gospel of salvation. God will not suffer this indignity to this blessed jewel, his truth; he will not suffer the doctrine of the gospel to be so disrespected. You see the fearful example of the church of Corinth. Let those whom it may concern, that have any advantage and authority, let them put in for God's cause, put in for the gospel, labour to propagate and to derive* this blessed truth we enjoy to posterity, by suppressing as much as they may the underminers of it. It is an acceptable service. ' To the church of God at Corinth.'

' *And all the saints in Achaia.*' Corinth was the city, Achaia the country wherein Corinth was. There were then saints, holy men in all Achaia. And St Paul writes to ' all saints,' to weak saints, to strong saints, to rich saints, to poor saints; because every saint hath somewhat that is lovely and respective† in them, somewhat to be respected. The least grace deserves respect from the greatest apostle. And all have one head, all have one hope of glory, all are redeemed with the same ' precious blood of Christ,' 1 Pet. i. 19 (and so I might run on). The many privileges agree to all. Therefore, all should have place in our respect. ' To *all* saints,' that the least should not think themselves undervalued. Weakness is most of all subject to complaining if it be disrespected. Therefore, in heavenly wisdom and prudence, the apostle puts in ' *all* saints,' in all Achaia whatsoever. Besides the mother city, the metropolis of that country, which was Corinth, there were saints scattered. God in heavenly wisdom scatters his saints. As seed, when it is scattered in the ground, it doth more good than when it is on heaps in the barn; so God scatters his saints as jewels, as the lights of the world. Here he will have one to shine and there another. Here he will have one fruitful to condemn the wicked world where they are, and by their good example, and their heavenly and fruitful conversation, to draw out of the wicked estate of nature those with whom they are. Therefore he will have them scattered here and there, not only at Corinth, but ' saints in all Achaia,' besides scattered in other places.

But we must know, by the way, that these saints had reference to some particular church: for though it be sufficient to make a Christian to have union with Christ (there is the main, the head); yet notwithstanding, he must be a branch, he must be a member of some particular congregation. Therefore we have it in Acts ii. 47: ' God added *to the church* such as should be saved.' Those that are added to salvation must be added to the

* That is, 'transmit.'—G.   † That is, ' respect-worthy.'—G.

church; a man must be a member of some particular church. So, though these were scattered, they were members of some church. God's children are as stones in some building; and there is an influence of grace comes from Christ, the Head, to every particular member, as it is in the body. God quickens not straggling members, that have no reference to any particular church. That I note by the way. ' To the church of God at Corinth, and all the saints in Achaia.'

'*Saints.*' *Quest.* The apostle calls them saints. All believers are called saints. Are they so? Are all in the visible church saints? Yes, say some, and therefore they say that our church is not a true visible church; because many of them are not saints, say some that went out from among us.

Ans. I answer, *all are, or should be saints.* St Paul wrote here to those that were sacramental* saints, and such as by outward covenant and profession were saints; not that they were all of them inwardly so; but all should be so done. He calls them so, to put them in mind of their duty. To clear this point a little.

1. Sometimes the church of God in the Scripture hath its name *from the commixtion of good and bad in it.* So it is called a field where there is a mixture of good and bad seed, Mat. xiii. 19, 20; so it is called a house wherein there are vessels of honour and vessels of dishonour, 2 Tim. ii. 20; because there is such a mixture in the visible church.

2. Sometimes the church hath the name from the better part, and so it is the spouse of Christ, the love of Christ, ' a peculiar people,' ' an holy nation,' 1 Pet. ii. 9, and ' saints,' as it is here. Not that all are so, but it hath the denomination from the better part; all should be so, and the best are so, and it is sufficient that the denomination of a company be from the better part. As we say of gold ore: though there be much earth mixed with it, yet in regard of the better part we call it gold, we give it that name; so, in regard that the best are saints, and that all should be so, therefore he calls them all saints.

Quest. Should all in the visible church be saints by profession, and by sacrament? Should all that are baptized, and receive the communion, enter into a profession of sanctity? What say you then to a profane, atheistical generation, that, forsooth, make a show of holiness, and therefore we must look for none of them?

Ans. I say all profane persons are gross hypocrites. Why? for are you members of the church or no? Yes, will every one say; will you make me an infidel? will you make me a pagan? Well, take your own word then. What is it to be a member of the church but to be a saint? Must thou be a saint? Doth not thy profession, as thou art a member, bind thee to be a saint? In baptism, was not thy promise to ' renounce the devil, the world, and the flesh?' In renewing thy covenant in the communion, dost not thou purpose to cleave to God in all things? Thou that takest liberty, therefore, in the church of God, under the profession of religion, to live as a libertine, thou art a gross hypocrite, and this aggravates thy sin, and makes it worse than a pagan's. Thou which art in the bosom of the church, in the kingdom of saints, as it is in Dan. vii. 18, ' the people of the saints of the Most High,' the people of God in the church wherein thou art a professed member; and yet dost thou take liberty grossly to offend God?

Quest. What doth make a saint?

Ans. In a word, to the constitution of a true saint, there is

* That is, ' professed.' ' avowed.'—G.

A separation, dedication, qualification, conversation.

1. There is a *separation* presently. When a man is a saint, he is separate from the confused company of the world, from the kingdom of Satan. Therefore those that have all companies alike, that carry themselves indifferently in all companies, as men that profess a kind of civility, that are taken up with the complement* of the times, men that learn the language of the times, that are for all sorts, they know not what belongs to the high profession of Christianity.

There is a due to all, I confess ; there is a benevolence and a beneficence to all ; but there is a kind of complacency, a sweet familiarity, and amity which should be reserved to a few, only to those in whom we see the evidences and signs of grace. If there be not a separation in respect of grace, there is no holiness at all ; a saint must be separated. Not locally, but in regard of amity, in regard of intimate friendship. As we see it is in outward things, in some of our houses. There is a court where all come, poor and rich ; and there is the house where those of nearer acquaintance come ; and then there is the innermost room, the closet, where only ourselves and those which are nearest to us come. So it is in the passages of the soul. There are some remote courtesies that come from us, as men, to all, be they what they will ; there are other respects to others that are nearer, that we admit nearer, that are of better quality ; and there are other that are nearest of all, that we admit even into the closet of our hearts : and those are they with whom we hope to have communion for ever in heaven, the blessed people of God, termed here 'saints.' It is an evidence of our translation from a cursed estate to a better when we love such. 'Hereby we know,' saith St John, 'that we are translated from death to life, because we love the brethren,' 1 John iii. 14. There must be a separation.

2. And withal there must be a *dedication of ourselves to the service of God.* A Christian, when he knows himself by the word of truth and by the work of the Spirit, to be God's child, he dedicates himself to better services than before. He thinks himself too good, he thinks too highly of himself to be a base blasphemer, or swearer, to be a filthy person. He considers himself as 'the temple of the Holy Ghost,' 1 Cor. iii. 16, and he useth himself to better purposes, to better studies, to do good.

3. And then with dedication, there is *an inward qualification* to inable† him with light never to forget the image of God. Herein this saintship stands, especially in this inward qualification, whereby we resemble Christ the King of saints. All our sanctification comes from him. As Aaron's ointment went down from his head to his beard, and so to his skirts, Ps. cxxxiii. 2, so all our sanctification is from Christ. Every saint is qualified from the Spirit of Christ. 'Of his fulness,' John i. 16, we receive this inward qualification, that we have another judgment of things than this world hath ; what is good and what is bad, what is true and what is false, what is comfortable and what tends to discomfort. He hath another conceit of things. He hath another light than he had before, and than other carnal men have. He hath a heavenly light. He hath another language. He gives himself to prayer and to thanksgiving. He is given to savoury discourse. He hath other courses in his particular calling and in his general calling than other refuse‡ company have, or than himself had before his calling. This is from his qualification.

4. And this qualification and *conversation go together.* He hath a new

---

* That is, 'compliment' = fine manners.—G.   † That is, 'enable' = endow.—G.
‡ That is, 'worthless.'—G.

conversation. He carries himself even like to him that ' hath called him out of darkness into marvellous light,' 1 Pet. ii. 9. So a true saint, as every professor of religion ought to be, he is dedicate to God, and he is qualified in some degree, as Christ was, by his Holy Spirit. He is a new creature. ' He that is in Christ is a new creature,' 2 Cor. v. 17, and he shews this by his conversation, or else he is no saint.

Quest. How shall we know a saint from a mere civil* man ? (as there be many that live and die in that estate, which is to be pitied ; and one main end of our calling is not only to reduce profane men to a better fashion of life, but to shew civil men their danger.)

Ans. A mere civil man looks to the second table. He is smooth in his carriage and conversation with men, but negligent in his service to God. A civil man he looks to his outward carriage, but he makes no conscience of secret sins. He is not ' holy in all manner of conversation,' as St Peter saith, 1 Pet. i. 15. ' Be ye holy in all manner of conversation,' in private, in public, in your retired carriage. He makes no conscience of his thoughts, of his speeches, of all.

You may know an hypocrite so, that carries himself smoothly and acceptably in the eye of the world ; but he makes no conscience of his thoughts, he makes no conscience of his affections, of his desires, of his lusts, and such things. He makes no conscience of lesser oaths, nor perhaps of rotten discourses. No ; they are all for this, that they may pass in the world, that they may carry themselves with acceptance. As for what belongs to the ' new creature,' to saints, they care not ; for they have vain conceits of these, and judge them as hypocrites. Because such a one knows himself should be an hypocrite, if he should do otherwise than he doth, therefore he thinks that others that are above his pitch are hypocrites, and they make a show of that that is not in them ; because if he should make show of that, his heart would tell him that he were an hypocrite.

A true saint differs from an hypocrite in many respects ; but in this one mainly, that a true saint of God is altered in the inward frame and qualification of his soul. He is a ' new creature.' Therefore there is a spring of better thoughts, of better desires, of better aims in him than in other men. And he labours more after the inward frame of his heart than after his outward carriage. What he is ashamed to do, he is ashamed to think, he is ashamed to lust after. What he desires to do, he desires to love in his heart. He labours that all may be true in the inward man ; because grace, as well as nature, begins from the heart, from the inward parts.

An hypocrite never cares for that. All his care is for the outward parts. He is sale-work. So his carriage be acceptable to others, all his care is taken. He lives to the view. Therefore he looks not to the substance and the truth, but to the shadow and appearance.

Now I come to the salutation itself.

VERSE 2.

' *Grace be unto you,*' &c. ' Grace ' doth enter into the whole conversation of a Christian, and doth sweeten his very salutations. Which I observe, because many men confine their religion to places, to actions, and to times. There is a relish of holiness in everything that comes from a Christian ; in his salutations and courtesies. St Paul salutes them,

* That is, ' moral.'—G.

' Grace and peace from God,' &c. And the use of holy salutations are *to shew* [*and*] *win love.*

To shew love and respect. Therefore he salutes them ; and by shewing love, to gain love ; for there is a loadstone in love. And thirdly, the use of salutations is by them to convey some good. For these salutations are not mere wishes, but prayers, nay, blessings. God's people are a blessed people, and they are full of blessing. They carry a blessing in their very speeches.

Quest. What is a blessing ?

Ans. A blessing is a prayer, with the application of the thing prayed for. It is somewhat more than a prayer, ' Grace be with you, and peace.' It is not only a mere wish, I desire it ; nay, my desire of it is with an applying of it. ' Grace shall be with you, and peace,' and the more because I heartily wish it to you. It is no light matter to have the benediction and salutation of a holy man, especially those that are superiors ; for the superiors bless the inferiors. There is a grace goes even with the very salutations, with the common prayers of a holy man. It is a comfortable sign when God doth enlarge the heart of a holy man to wish well to a man.

And surely the very consideration of that should move us to let them have such encouragement from our carriage and demeanour, that they may have hearts to think of us to the throne of grace, to give us a good wish, to give us a good desire. For every gracious desire, every prayer, hath its effect when it comes from a favourite of God, especially from such a man as St Paul was ; from a minister, a holy man in a calling, a man of God. They have their efficacy with them. They are not empty words, ' grace and peace.'

The popes think it a great favour when they bestow their apostolical benediction and blessing. Their blessing is not much worth. Their curse is better than their blessing. But surely the blessing of a man rightly called, those that are true ministers of Christ, they are clothed with power and efficacy from God. ' Grace be with you, and peace ;' it is no idle compliment.

And here you see likewise what should be the manner of the salutation of Christians. As they ought to salute, to shew love, and to gain love, so all their salutations should be holy. There is a taking the name of God in vain in salutations ofttimes, ' God save you,' &c., and it must be done with a kind of scorn ; and if there be any demonstration of religion, it becomes them not, that which should become them most. What should become a saint, but to carry himself saint-like ? And yet men must do it with a kind of scorn, with a kind of graceless grace. That which in the religious use of it is a comfortable and sweet thing, and is alway with a comfortable and gracious effect in God's children ; either it hath effect, and is made grace to them to whom it is spoken, or returns to them that speak it. As Christ saith to his disciples, ' When you come into a house, pronounce peace to them ; and if the house be not worthy, your peace shall return to you,' Mat. x. 13. So the salutations of a good man, if they be not effectual to the parties, if they be unworthy, rebellious creatures, they return again to himself ; they have effect one way or other. Let it not be done, therefore, with a taking the name of God in vain in a scornful manner, but with gravity and reverence, as becometh a holy action. There is some limitation and exception of this. Salutations, in some cases, may be omitted.

1. *As in serious business,* ' salute no man by the way,' as Christ saith to his apostles, Luke x. 4. A neglect sometimes is good manners, when

respect is swallowed up in a greater duty. As it was good manners for David to dance and to carry himself, as it were, unseemly before the ark, 2 Sam. vi. 14 ; because he was to neglect respect to meaner persons, to forget the respect he was to shew to men. Being altogether taken up with higher matters, it was a kind of decency and comeliness. And overmuch scrupulousness and niceness in lesser things, when men are called to greater, is but unmannerly manners. In these cases, these lesser must give way and place to the greater. ' Salute no man by the way.' Despatch the business you are about ; that is, if it may be a hindrance in the way, salute not. This is in respect of time.

2. And as for time, *so for persons.* A notorious, incorrigible heretic, salute not. To salute such a one would be, as it were, a connivance or an indulgence to him. ' Salute him not' (*d*). The denying of a salutation many times hath the force of a censure. The party neglected may think there is somewhat in him for which he is neglected in that manner. In these cases, salutations may be omitted sometimes. But I go unto the particulars.

' *Grace be unto you and peace.*' These are the good things wished. We see the apostle, a blessed man, that had been ' in the third heaven' rapt up, 2 Cor. xii. 2, that had been taught of Christ what things were most excellent, and had himself seen ' excellent things which he could not utter,' 2 Cor. xii. 4, when he comes to wishes, we see out of heavenly wisdom and experience he draws them to two heads, all good things to ' grace and peace.' If there had been better things to be wished, he would have wished them, but grace and peace are the principal things.

Quest. What is meant by grace here ?

Ans. Grace, in this place, *is the free favour and love of God from his own bowels ;* not for any desert, or worth, or strength of love of ours. It is his own free grace and love, which is shed by the Holy Ghost, and springs only from his own goodness and loving nature, and not from us at all. This is grace. It must be distinguished from the fruits of it ; as the apostle doth distinguish them, ' grace, and the gifts of grace,' Rom. v. 15. There is favour and the gifts of favour, which is grace inherent in us. Here especially is meant the fountain and spring of all the favour of God, with the manifestation of it, with the increase of it, with the continuance of it. He wisheth these things, the favour of God, with the manifestation of it to their souls ; that God would be gracious to them, so that he would shew his grace ; that he would discover it, and shine upon them ; and to that end that he would give them his Holy Spirit, to shed ' his love into their hearts,' Rom. v. 5. This shining of God into the heart, this shedding of the love of God into the heart, is the grace here meant ; God's favour, with the manifestation of it to the soul, and with the continuance of it, and the increase of it still. ' Grace unto you.' As if he should have said, I wish you the favour of God, and the report of it to your souls ; that as he loves you through his Christ, so he would witness as much by his Holy Spirit to your souls. And I wish you likewise the continuance of it, and the increase of it, and the fruits of it likewise (for that must not be excluded), all particular graces, which are likewise called graces. They have the name of favours, because they come from favour ; and favour is the chief thing in them. What is the chief thing in joy, in faith, in love ? They are graces. They cannot be considered as qualifications, as earthly things in us. They proceed from the grace and love of God, and have their especial value from thence. So I wish you the manifestation, the continuance and increase of favour, with all the fruits of God's favour, especially such as concern a better life. The word is easily understood after the common sense. Grace is the loving and free respect of a superior to an inferior ; the respect of a magistrate to such as are under him. Such a one is in grace with the prince, we say. We mean not any inherent thing, but free grace. So in religion it is not any inherent, habitual thing, grace ; but it is free favour, and whatsoever issues from free favour. This must be the rather observed, this phrase, against the papists. We say we are justified by grace, and so do they. What do they mean by being justified by grace ? That is, by inherent grace. We say, No ; we are justified by grace ; that is, by the free favour of God in Jesus Christ. So is the acception * of the word.

But, to come to the point, that which I will now note is this, that

Doct. A Christian, though he be in the state of grace and favour with God, yet still he needs the continuance of it.

He stands in need of the continuance of God. St Paul here prays for grace and peace, to those that were in the state of grace already. Why ? The reason of it is, that we run into new breaches every day, of ourselves. As long as there is a spring of corruption in us, a cursed issue of corruption, so long there will be some actions, and speeches, and thoughts, that will issue, that would of themselves break our peace with God, or at least hinder the sweet sense of it. Therefore, we have continual occasion to renew our desires of the sense and feeling of the favour of God, and to renew our pardon every day, to take out a pardon of course, as we have now the liberty to do. So oft as we confess our sins, ' he is merciful to forgive us,' 1 John i. 9. And to win his favour, we have need every day still of grace. I list not to join in conflict here with the papists concerning their opinion. I will but touch it by the way, to shew the danger of it. They will not have all of mere grace. But Christians are under grace while they are in this world, as St Paul saith, all is grace, grace still : nay, at the day of judgment, ' The Lord shew mercy to the house of Onesiphorus at that day,' 2 Tim. i. 16, at the day of judgment. Grace and mercy must be our plea, till we come to heaven. They stand upon grace to enable † us to the work ; and then by the work we may merit our own salvation, and so they will not have it of grace, of gift ; but as a stipend, a thing of merit, directly contrary to St Paul, Rom. vi. 23, Eternal life is χάρισμα. The word comes of χάρις, of gift. ' The gift of God, a free gift through Jesus Christ our Lord.' So from the first grace, to eternal life, which is the complement of all, all is grace.

As for the New Testament, it is the covenant of grace. The whole carriage of our salvation is called the covenant of grace ; because, God of grace doth enter into covenant with us. He sent Christ of grace, who is the foundation of the covenant. The fulfilling of it, on our part, is of grace. He gives us faith. ' Faith is the gift of God,' Eph. ii. 8. ' He puts his fear in our hearts that we should not depart from him,' Jeremiah xxxii. 40. And when he enters into covenant with us, it is of grace and love. It was of grace that he sent Christ to be the foundation of the covenant ; that in the satisfying of his justice he might be gracious to us, without disparagement to his justice. Of grace he fulfils the condition on our part. We are no more able to believe than we are to fulfil the law ; but he enables us by his word and Spirit, attending upon the means of salvation, to fulfil the covenant. And when we have done all, he gives us of grace, eternal life ; all is of grace.

* That is, ' acceptation.'—G.　　　　† That is, ' qualify.'—G.

There is nothing in the gospel but grace. Therefore in the Ephesians, i. 6, it is stood upon by the apostle, ' To the praise of the glory of his rich grace.' From election to glorification, all is to the glory of his grace.

We ought to conceive of God as a gracious Father, withholding his anger, which we deserve to be poured upon us; by the intercession of Christ, withholding that anger, and the fruits of it. And, notwithstanding we are in grace, if we neglect to seek to God the Father, if we neglect to seek to Christ, who makes intercession for us, then, though we be in the first grace still, we are not cast away yet; we are *filii sub ira*, sons under wrath; we are under anger, though not under hatred.

Therefore, every day we should labour to maintain the grace of God with the assurance of it. It is a great matter to carry ourselves so, as we may be under the sense and feeling of the grace of God. It is not sufficient to be in the grace of God, but to have the report of it to our own hearts, have it to shine upon us.

Quest. How should we carry ourselves so, that we may be in [a] state of grace ? that is, in such a state as we may find the sweet evidence and comfortable feeling continually, that we are God's children.

Ans. First of all, there must be *a perpetual, daily practice of abasing ourselves, of making ourselves poor;* that is, every day to see the vanity of all things in the world out of us; to see the weakness of grace in us; to see the return of our corruptions that foil us every day ; that so we may see in what need we stand of the favour of God : considering that all comforts without are vanity, and that all the graces in us are stained with corruption ; considering, besides the stains of our graces, that there is a continual issue of corruption. These things will make our spirits poor, and make us hunger and thirst after the sense and feeling of free pardon every day. This will enforce us to renew our patent, to renew our portion in the covenant of grace, to have daily pardon. This should be our daily practice, to enter deeper and deeper into ourselves.

This is to ' live by faith,' Gal. ii. 20. As God is continually ready to shew us favour in Christ, not only at the first in acquitting us from our sins, but continually doth shew us favour upon all occasions, and is justifying and pardoning, and speaking peace continually to us ; so there must be an action answerable in us, that is depending upon God by faith, living by faith. This we do by seeing in what need we stand of grace. ' God resists the proud, but gives grace to the humble,' James iv. 6.

2. Then, again, that we may walk in the grace of God, and in the sense of it, let us every day labour *to have our souls more and more enriched with the endowments and graces of God's Spirit,* that we may be objects of God's delight. Let us labour to be affected to things as he is affected. Two cannot ' walk together except they be agreed,' Amos iii. 3. Let us hate that which God hates, and delight in that which God delights in, that we may have a kind of complacency, and be in love with the blessed work of the Spirit of God more and more. Let us labour to delight in them that grow in grace, as the nearer any one comes to our likeness, the more we grow in familiarity with them. Labour also to preserve a clear soul, that God may shine upon us. God delights not in strangeness to us. His desire is that we may walk in the sense and assurance of his grace and favour.

Quest. How shall we know that we are in a state of grace with God ?

Ans. I answer, that we do not deceive ourselves ;

1. We must look *to the work of God's grace.* God's grace is a fruitful grace. His favour is fruitful. It is not a barren favour; it is not a winter sun.

The sun in the winter, it carries a goodly countenance, but it heats not to any purpose; it doth not quicken. But God's grace, it carries life and heat where it comes. Therefore, if we be in a state of grace and favour with God, we may discern it.

But in times of desertion, though a person be in grace and favour with God, yet many times he thinks he is not so.

It is true. Then, we must not always go to our feeling at such times, and the enlargement of our hearts by the Spirit of comfort, but go to the work of grace. For,

2. Where grace and favour is, there are *the graces of the Spirit*. As it is not a bare favour in regard of comfort, so it is not a barren favour in regard of graces; for every heart that is in favour with God hath some graces of the Spirit. God enriches the soul where he shews favour. His love-tokens are some graces. Therefore, if the witness and comfort of the Spirit cease in case of desertion, let us go to the work of the Spirit, and by that we may know if we be in grace with God. For God's people are a ' peculiar people:' and God's children have always some peculiar grace. Some ornaments, some jewels the spouse of Christ hath, which others have not.

Therefore, examine thy heart, what work of God there is, and what desire thou hast after better things, what inward hatred against that which is ill, what strength thou hast against it. Go to some mark of regeneration, of the ' new creature,' and these will evidence that we are in a state of grace with God, because these are peculiar favours. And though we feel not the comfort, yet there is a work, and that work will comfort us more than the comfort itself will do.

3. And this is one thing whereby we may know we are in favour with God, when we can comfort ourselves, *and can go to the throne of grace through Christ. When we can go boldly to God it is a sign of favour.* When we can call upon him, when we can go in any desertion to prayer, when in any affliction we can have enlarged hearts, it is a sign of favour with God. A mere hypocrite, or a man that hath not this peculiar grace, he trusts to outward things; and when they are gone, when he is in trouble, he hath not the heart to go to God. His heart is shut up, he sinks down, because he relied upon common matters. He did not rely upon the favour of God and the best fruit of it, which are graces, but upon common favours. Therefore, he sinks in despair.

But a sound Christian, take him at the worst, he can sigh to God, he can go to him, and open his soul to him. ' By Christ we have an entrance to the Father,' Eph. ii. 18; ' We have boldness through faith,' Eph. iii. 12. Every Christian hath this in the worst extremity, he hath a spirit of prayer. Though he cannot enlarge himself, yet he can sigh and groan to God, and God will hear the sighs of his own Spirit; they are loud in his ears. David, at the worst, he prays to God; Saul, at the worst, he goes to the witch, 1 Sam. xxviii. 7, *seq.*, and from thence to his sword's point, 1 Sam. xxxi. 4. But usually, the usual temper and disposition of a man in the state of grace is joy; for, as one saith, grace is the begetter of joy; for they both have one root in the Greek language. There is the same root for favour and for joy (*e*). So favour is usually and ordinarily with a sweet enlargement of heart. We may thank ourselves else, that do not walk so warily and so jealously as we should.

The reward that God gives his children that are careful is a spirit of joy. ' Being justified by faith, we have peace with God, and joy in tribulation,' Rom. v. 1. For, even as it is in human matters, the favour and countenance of the king, it is as a shower of rain after a drought, it comforts his subjects. There is a wondrous joy in the favour and grace of great persons alway; and as the favourable aspect of the heavens upon inferior bodies promiseth good things,* and men promise themselves from that favour and good, so the favour and grace of God enlarge the soul with joy and comfort. And there is that measure of joy in those that are in the free favour of God, that they will honour God freely, to cast themselves upon his mercy.

And it is with a disesteem of all things in the world besides. It is such a joy as works in the soul a base esteem of all things else. St Paul esteemed all dross, ' in comparison of the knowledge of Christ,' Philip. iii. 8, and the favour of God in Christ. So in Ps. iv., David saith of some, ' There be many that will say, Who will shew us any good?' ver. 6. *Any* good! It is no matter. But saith the Holy Spirit in David, ' Lord, lift up the light of thy countenance upon me,' ver. 6. He goes to prayer. He saith not, ' Who will shew us any good?' It is no matter what, or how we come by it, any earthly good worldly men desire. No; saith he, ' Lord, shew us the light of thy countenance.' He desires that above all things, so he saith, ' The lovingkindness of the Lord is better than life itself,' Ps. lxiii. 3. Life is a sweet thing, the sweetest thing in the world; but the grace and favour of God is better than that. For in this, when all comforts fail, the children of God have assurance, that ' neither life, nor death, nor things present, nor things to come, nor anything, can separate us from the love of God in Christ,' Rom. viii. 38, which shews itself better than life itself. When life fails, this favour shall never fail. Nothing shall be able to separate us from the favour of God in Christ. It is an everlasting favour, and therefore everlasting because it is free. If it were originally in us, it would fail when we fail; but it is an everlasting favour because it is free. God hath founded the cause of love to us in himself. So much for that, ' Grace be unto you.'

' *And peace.*' All that I will say of peace in this place is this, to shew, *Obs.* That *true peace issues from grace.*

It is to be had thence. Peace, we take here for that sweet peace with God, and peace of conscience, and likewise peace with all things, when all things are peaceable to us, when there is a sweet success in all business, with a security in a good estate. It is a blessed thing when we know that all will be well with us. This quiet and peaceable estate issues from grace, peace of conscience especially. I observe it the rather [because] it hath been the error of the world to seek peace where it is not, to seek peace in sanctification, to seek it in the work of grace within a man, not to speak of worldly men, that seek peace in outward contentments, in recreations, in friends, and the like. Alas! it is a poor peace. But I speak of religious persons that are of a higher strain. They have sought peace, but not high enough. True peace must be selected from grace, the free favour in Christ. This will quiet and still the clamours of an accusing conscience. God reconciled in Christ will pacify the conscience; nothing else will do it. For if our chief peace were fetched from sanctification,' as many fetch it thence in error of judgment, alas! the

* That is, according to (the now exploded, but in time of Sibbes accredited system of) astrology. Even Bacon and Milton believed in the influence of the stars. —G.

conscience would be dismayed, and always doubt whether it had sanctification enough or no. Indeed, sanctification and grace within is required as a qualification, to shew that we are not hypocrites, but are in the state and covenant of grace. It is not required as a foundation of comfort, but as a qualification of the persons to whom comfort belongs. Therefore, David, and St Paul, and the rest, that knew the true power and efficacy of the gospel, they sought for peace in the grace and free favour of God.

Let us lay it up to put it in practice in the time of dissolution, in the time of spiritual conflict, in the time when our consciences shall be awakened, and perhaps upon the rack, and Satan will be busy to trouble our peace, that we may shut our eyes to all things below, and see God shining on [us] in Christ; that we may see the favour of God in Christ, by whose death and passion he is reconciled to us, and in the grace and free favour of God in Christ we shall see peace enough.

It is true, likewise, besides peace of conscience, of all other peace, peace of success and peace of state. That all creatures and all conditions are peaceable to us, whence is it? It is from grace. For God, being reconciled, he reconciles all. When God himself is ours, all is ours. When he is turned, all is turned with him. When he becomes our Father in Christ, and is at peace with us, all are at peace besides. So that all conditions, all estates, all creatures, they work for our good. It is from hence, when God is turned, all are turned with him. He being the God of the creature, that sustains and upholds the creature, in whom the creature hath his being and working, he must needs therefore turn it for the good of them that are in covenant with him. All that are joined in covenant with him, he fills them with peace, because they are in grace with him.

This should stir up our hearts, above all things in the world, to pray for grace, to get grace, to empty ourselves of self-confidence, that we may be vessels for grace, to make grace our plea, to magnify the grace of God.

We must never look in this world for a peace altogether absolute. That is reserved for heaven. Our peace here is a troubled peace. God will have a distinction between heaven and earth. But when our peace is interrupted, when the waters ' are come into our souls,' Ps. lxix. 1, what must be our course? When we would have peace, go to grace, go to the free promise of grace in Christ. ' Grace and peace.'

' *From God our Father, and the Lord Jesus Christ.*' The spring of grace and peace are here mentioned.

After the preface, he comes to the argument which he intends; and begins with blessing.

One part of the scope of this blessed apostle is, to avoid the scandal* of his sufferings; for he was a man of sorrows, if ever man was. Next Christ, who was a true man of sorrow, the blessed apostle was a man of miseries and sorrow. Now, weak, shallow Christians thought him to be a man deserted of God. They thought it was impossible for God to regard a man so forlorn, so despicable as this man was. What doth he? Before he comes to other matters, he wipes away this imputation and clears this scandal. You lay my crosses, and sufferings, and disgraces in the world to my shame! It is your weakness. That which you account my shame is a matter of praise. I am so far from being disheartened or discouraged from what I suffer, that,

* That is, ' to take away the stumblingblock.'—G.

VERSE 3.

'*Blessed be God, the Father of Christ, the Father of mercies,*' *&c.*
That which to the flesh is matter of scandal and offence, that to the
spirit and to a spiritual man is matter of glory, so contrary is the flesh
and the spirit, and so opposite is the disposition and the current of the
fleshly man to the spiritual man. Job was so far from cursing God for
taking away, that he saith, ' Blessed be the name of God,' not only for
giving, but for taking away too, Job i. 21.

What ground there is in troubles and persecutions to bless God we shall
see in the current and passages of the chapter.

To come, then, to the very verse itself, where there is a blessing and
praising of God first; and in this praising consider

The act, object, reasons.

1. *The act,* ' Blessed be God,' which is a praising.

2. *The object* is ' God the Father.

3. *The reasons* are enwrapped in the object, ' Blessed be God the Father
of our Lord Jesus Christ.'

(1.) Because he is the God and Father of Jesus Christ, therefore blessed
be he. Another reason is,

(2.) Because he is the ' Father of mercies.' Another reason is,

(3.) From the act of this disposition of mercy in God, he is the ' God of
all comfort,' and as he is comfortable, so he doth comfort. ' Thou art
good and doest good,' saith the psalmist, Ps. cxix. 68. Thou art a God of
comfort, and thou dost comfort. For as he is, so he doth. He shews his
nature in his working, ' Blessed be God, the Father of our Lord Jesus
Christ, the Father of mercies, and God of comfort,' of which I shall speak
when I come to them.

' *Blessed be God, the Father,*' *&c.* We see here the heart of the blessed
apostle, being warmed with the sense and taste of the sweet mercy of God,
stirs up his tongue to bless God; a full heart and a full tongue. We
have here the exuberancy, the abundance of his thankfulness breaking
forth in his speech. His heart had first tasted of the sweet mercies and
comforts of God before he praiseth God. The first thing that we will observe hence is, that

*It is the disposition of God's children, after they have tasted the sweet mercy
and comfort and love of God, to break forth into the praising of God and to
thanksgiving.*

It is as natural for the new creature to do so as for the birds to sing in
the spring. When the sun hath warmed the poor creature, it shews its
thankfulness in singing; and that little blood and spirits that it hath being
warmed after winter, it is natural for those creatures so to do, and we delight in them.

It is as natural for the new creature, when it feels the Sun of righteousness warming the soul, when it tastes of the mercy of God in Christ, to shew
forth itself in thankfulness and praise; and it can no more be kept from it,
than fire can keep from burning, or water from cooling. It is the nature
of the new creature so to do.

The reason is, every creature must do the work for which God hath
enabled* it, to the which God hath framed it. The happiness of the

* That is, ' qualified.'—G.

creature is in well-doing, in working according to its nature. The heathen could see that. Now all the creatures, the new creature especially, is for the glory of God in Christ Jesus. All the new creature, and what privileges it hath, and what graces it hath, all is, that God may have the glory of grace. Why then, it must needs work answerable to that which God hath created it for. Therefore it must shew forth the praise and glory of God. ' Blessed be God,' saith the apostle, Eph. i. 3 ; and the blessed apostle Peter begins his epistle, ' Blessed be the Father of our Lord Jesus Christ, who hath begotten us to an inheritance immortal and undefiled, which fadeth not away, reserved for us in heaven,' 1 Pet. i. 3.

I shall not need to set down with the exposition of the word ' blessed :' how God blesseth us, and how we bless God. His blessing is a conferring of blessing ; our blessing is a declaring of his goodness. It is a thing well enough known. Our blessing of God is a praising of God, a setting out what is in him.

Only one thing is to be cleared. What good can we do to God in blessing of him ? He is blessed, though we bless him not ; and he is praised, whether we praise him or no. He had glory enough before he made the world. He contented himself in the Trinity, the blessed Trinity in itself, before there were either angels, or men, or other creatures to bless him ; and now he can be blessed enough, though we do not bless him.

It is true he can be so ; and he can have heaven, though thou hast it not, but be a damned creature ; and he will be blessed, whether thou bless him or no.

1. Our blessing of him *is required as a duty*, to make us more capable of his graces, ' To him that hath shall be given,' Mat. xiii. 12. To him that hath, and useth that he hath to the glory of God, shall be given more. We give nothing.

The stream gives nothing to the fountain. The beam gives nothing to the sun, for it issues from the sun. Our very blessing of God is a blessing of his.

It is from his grace that we can praise his grace ; and we run still into a new debt, when we have hearts enlarged to bless him.

We ought to have our hearts more enlarged, that we can be enlarged to praise God.

2. *And to others it is good*, for others are stirred up by it. God's goodness and mercy is enlarged in regard of the manifestation of it to others, by our blessing of God.

3. Yea, this good *comes to our souls*. Besides the increase of grace, we shall find an increase of joy and comfort. That is one end why God requires it of us. Though he himself, in his essence, be alway alike blessed, yet he requires that we should be thankful to him alway ; that we should bless and praise him even in misery and affliction. And why, then ?

1. *Because, if we can work upon our hearts a disposition to see God's love, and to praise and bless him, we can never be uncomfortable.* We have some comfort against all estates and conditions, by studying to praise God, by working of our hearts to a disposition to praise and bless God ; for then crosses are light, crosses are no crosses then. That is the reason that the apostles and holy men so stirred up their hearts to praise and thanksgiving, that they might feel their crosses the less, that they might be less sensible of their discomforts. For undoubtedly, when we search for matter of praising God in any affliction, and when we see there is some mercy yet reserved, that we are not consumed, the consideration that there is alway

some mercy, that we are yet unthankful for, will enlarge our hearts ; and God, when he hath thanks and praise from us, he gives us still more matter of thankfulness, and the more we thank him and praise him, the more we have matter of praise.

This being a truth, that God's children, when they have tasted of his mercy, break forth into his praise, it being the end of his favours; and nature being inclined thereto, this should stir us up to this duty. And that we may the better perform this holy duty, let us take notice of all God's favours and blessings. Knowledge stirs up the affections. Blessing of God springs immediately from an enlarged heart, but enlargement of heart is stirred up from apprehension. For as things are reported to the knowledge, so the understanding reports them to the heart and affections. Therefore it is a duty that we ought to take notice of God's favours, and with taking notice of them,

2. *To mind them, to remember them, forget not all his benefits.* ' Praise the Lord, O my soul, and forget not all his benefits,' Ps. ciii. 2, insinuating that the cause why we praise not God is the forgetting of his benefits.

Let us take notice of them, let us register them, let us mind them, let us keep diaries of his mercies and favours every day.* He renews his mercies and favours every day, and we ought to renew our blessing of him every day. We should labour to do here, as we shall do when we are in heaven, where we shall do nothing else but praise and bless him. We ought to be in heaven, while we are on the earth, as much as we may. Let us register his favours and mercies.

Quest. But what favours ?

Ans. Especially spiritual, nay, first spiritual favours, without which we cannot heartily give thanks for any outward thing. For the soul will cast with itself, till it feel itself in covenant with God in Christ, that a man is the child of God.

Indeed I have many mercies and favours. God is good to me. But perhaps all these are but favours of the traitor in the prison, that hath the liberty of the tower, and all things that his heart can desire ; but then he looks for an execution, he looks for a writ to draw him forth to make him a spectacle to all. And so this trembling for fear of a future ill which the soul looks for, it keeps the soul from thankfulness. It cannot be heartily thankful for any mercy, till it can be thankful for spiritual favours.

Therefore first let us see that our state be good, that we are in Christ, that we are in covenant of grace, that though we are weak Christians, yet we are true, [that] there is truth in grace wrought in us. And then, when we have tasted the best mercies, spiritual mercies ; when we see we are taken out of the state of nature (for then all is in love to us), when we have the first mercy, pardoning mercy, that our sins are forgiven in Christ, then the other are mercies indeed to us, not as favours to a condemned man.

And that is the reason that a carnal man, he hath his heart shut, he cannot praise God, he cannot trust in God ; because he staggers in his estate, because he is not assured. He thinks, it may be God ' fattens me against the day of slaughter,' Jer. xii. 3. Therefore I know not whether I should praise him for this or no. But he is deceived in that. For if he had his heart enlarged to bless God for that, God would shew further favour still ; but the heart will not yield hearty praise to God, till it be persuaded of God's love. For all our love is by reflection. ' We love him, because he

* ' Diaries.' As a fine specimen of, and counsels in regard to, this kind of diary, see Beadle's ' Diary of a Thankful Christian,' 12mo, 1656.

loved us first,' 1 John iv. 19, and we praise and bless him, because he hath blessed us first in heavenly blessings in Christ.

Let us take notice of his favours, let us remind them, let us register them, especially favours and mercies in Christ. Let us after* think how we were pulled out of the cursed estate of nature, by what ministry, by what acquaintance, by what speech, and how God hath followed that mercy with new acquaintance, with new comfort to our souls, with new refreshings; that by his Spirit he hath repressed our corruptions, that he hath sanctified us, made us more humble, more careful, that he hath made us more jealous, more watchful. These mercies and favours will make others sweet unto us.

And then learn to prize and value the mercies of God, which will not be unless we compare them with our own unworthiness. Lay his mercies together with our own unworthiness, and it will make us break forth into blessing of God, when we consider what we are ourselves, as Jacob said, ' less than the least of God's mercies,' Gen. xxxii. 10.

We forget God's mercies every day. He strives with our unthankfulness. The comparing of his mercies with our unworthiness, and our desert on the contrary, will make us to bless God for his goodness and patience, that he will not only be good to us, in not inflicting that which our sins have deserved. ' Blessed be God, the Father of our Lord Jesus Christ.'

And, to name no more but this one, above all, *beg of God his Holy Spirit*. For this blessing of God is nothing else but a vent from the Spirit. For as organs and wind instruments do never sound except they be blown, they are dead and make no music till there be breath put into them; so we are dead and dull instruments. Therefore it is said, we are ' filled with the Holy Ghost,' Acts ix. 17. All God's children, they are filled with the Spirit before they can praise God. The Spirit stirs them up to praise him, and as it gives them matter to praise him; for so it gives the sacrifice of praise itself. God gives to his children both the benefits to bless him for, and he gives the blessing of a heart to bless him. And we must beg both of God; beg a heart able to discern spiritual favours, to taste and relish them, and to see our own unworthiness of them; and beg of God his Holy Spirit to awaken, and quicken, and enlarge our dead and dull hearts to praise his name.

Let us stir up our hearts to it, stir up the Spirit of God in us. Every one that hath the Spirit of God should labour to stir up the Spirit. As St Paul writes to Timothy, 2 Tim. i. 6, and as David stirs up himself, ' Praise the Lord, O my soul: and all that is within me, praise his holy name,' Ps. ciii. 1, *seq.*, so we should raise up ourselves, and stir up ourselves, to this duty.

And *shame ourselves*. What! hath God freed me from so great misery? And hath he advanced me to so happy an estate in this world? Doth he put me in so certain a hope of glory in the world to come? Have I a certain promise to be carried to salvation? that neither ' things present, nor things to come, shall be able to separate me from the love of God in Christ Jesus'? Rom. viii. 38. Doth he renew his mercies every day upon me? And can I be thus dead, can I be thus dull-hearted? Let us shame ourselves. And certainly if a man were to teach a child of God a ground of humiliation, if a child of God that is in the state of grace should ask how he might grow humble and be abased more and more, a man could

* Qu. ' often?'—ED.

give no one direction better than this, to consider how God hath been good continually; how he hath been patient and good, and upon what ground we hope that he will be so; and to consider the disposition of our own drooping, drowsy souls. If this will not abase a soul that hath tasted the love and mercy of God, nothing in the world will do it. There never was a child of God of a dull temper and disposition, but he was ashamed that, being under such a covenant of favour, that he should yet not have a heart more enlarged to bless God.

To stir us up to this duty, for arguments to persuade us, what need we use many?

1. It should be our duty in this world *to be as much in heaven and heavenly employment*. ' Our conversation is in heaven,' saith the apostle, Phil. iii. 20. How can we be in heaven more than by practising of that which the saints and angels, and the cherubins and seraphins, spend all their strength in there? How do they spend all that blessed strength with cheerfulness and joy, that are in that place of joy? How do they spend it but in setting forth the praise of God, the wonderful goodness of God, that hath brought them to that happiness? Certainly that which we shall do for ever in heaven, we ought to do as much as we may do on earth.

2. And it is, as I said before, in all afflictions and troubles the only special way to mitigate them, *to work our hearts to thankfulness for mercies and favours that we enjoy*. We have cause indeed at the first to be abased and humbled; but we have more cause to rejoice in working our hearts to comfort, in blessing of God. It will ease the cross, any cross whatsoever. I will not dwell further upon the point. I shall have occasion oft to digress upon this duty.

The object of praise here is God, clothed with a comfortable description; not God simply, for, alas! we have no hearts to praise God, take God only armed with justice, clothed with majesty. Consider God thus, indeed he deserves glory and praise, but the guilty soul will not praise him thus considered, and abstracted from mercy, and goodness, and love. Therefore saith he, 'Blessed be God.' God how considered? ' Blessed be God, the Father of our Lord Jesus Christ.'

First, he is Father of Christ, and then Father of mercies, and God of comfort. God, so considered, be blessed!

Obs. God, as he is to be prayed unto, so he is to be praised, and only God.

This sacrifice, this perfume, this incense, it must not be misspent upon any creature. We have all of his grace, and we should return all to his glory. That is a duty. But consider him as he is described here, first, ' the Father of Christ,' and then the ' Father of mercies, and God of all comfort.' And it is not to be omitted, that first begins with this.

1. ' *Blessed be God, the Father of our Lord Jesus Christ.*' Not the Father of our Lord Jesus Christ only as he is God, but the Father of our Lord Jesus Christ as he is man. For God being the Father of whole Christ, being Father of the person, he is Father of the manhood, taken into unity with that person. So he is Father both of God and man. They cannot be divided in Christ. He being the Father of whole Christ, he is the Father of God and man. And he is first the Father of Christ, and then the Father of us, and the Father of mercies. For, alas! unless he had been the Father of Christ, God and man, mediator, he could never have been the Father of such cursed creatures as we are. But because he is the Father of Christ, of that blessed manhood, which Christ hath taken into

unity of person with the Godhead, therefore he is the Father of us, who by union are one with Christ.

The point then is, that,

Doct. God, thus considered, as the Father of Jesus Christ, is to be praised.

Here is the reason of blessing and praising him, in this, that he is the Father of Jesus Christ, for thence he comes to be our Father. It is a point that we think not oft enough on, but it is the ground of all comfort; for we have all at the second hand. Christ hath all first, and we have all from him. He is the first Son, and we are sons. He is the first beloved of God, and we are beloved in him. He is filled first with all grace, and we are filled from him : ' of his fulness we receive grace for grace,' John i. 16. He was first acquitted of our sins, as our surety, and then we are justified, because he was justified from our sins, being our surety. He is ascended into heaven, we shall ascend. He sits at the right hand of God, and we sit with him in heavenly places. He judgeth, we shall judge.* Whatsoever we do, Christ doth it first. We have it in Christ, and through Christ, and from Christ. He is the Father of Christ, and our Father.

Use 1. Therefore we ought to bless God for Christ, that he would predestinate Christ to be our Head, to be our Saviour; that he would take the human nature of Christ and make it one person with his divine nature, and so predestinate us, and elect, and choose us to salvation in him. Blessed be God, that he would be the Father of Jesus Christ !

Use 2. And as this should stir us up to bless God for Jesus Christ, so likewise *it should direct us to comfortable meditations, to see our nature in Christ first, and then in ourselves.* See thy nature abased in Christ, see thy nature glorified in Christ, see thy nature filled with all grace in Christ, and see this, that thou art knit to that nature, thou art flesh of Christ's flesh, and bone of his bone, and thou shalt be so as he is. In that Christ's nature was first abased, and then glorified, this nature shall first be abased to death and dust, and then be glorified. Christ died, ' and rose again,' Rom. xiv. 9. Thou art predestinated to be conformable to Christ. For as his flesh was first humbled and then glorious, so thine must be first humble, and then glorious. His flesh was holy, humble, and glorious, and so must ours be. Whatsoever we look for in ourselves, that is good, we must see it in Christ first.

And when we hear in the gospel, in the articles of the creed, of Christ crucified, of Christ dying, of Christ rising, ascending, and sitting at the right hand of God ; let us see ourselves in him, see ourselves dying in him, and rising in him, and sitting at the right hand of God. For the same God that raised Christ natural, will raise Christ mystical. He will raise whole Christ ; for he is not glorified by pieces. As whole Christ natural, in his body and members, was raised, so shall whole Christ mystical be. Therefore in every article of the creed bless God, bless God for abasing of Christ, bless God for raising him up, bless God for raising us up. ' Blessed be God, who hath raised us up to an immortal hope, by the resurrection of Christ,' saith St Peter, 1 Peter i. 3. Bless God for the ascension of Christ, that our head is in heaven. Let us bless God, not for personal favours only, but go to the spring. Bless God for shewing it to Christ, and to us in him.

This point the apostle had learned well. Therefore he begins with praise, ' Blessed be God, the Father of our Lord Jesus Christ.' If the Virgin Mary thought herself blessed, ' and all generations should call her blessed,' Luke i. 48, for bearing our Saviour in her womb, and so being his mother, then

* ' Him' is added here, an evident misprint.—G.

all generations must needs do this duty to call God blessed, because he is the Father of Christ. So God the Father is to be blessed as the spring of favours ; for he gave Christ. All generations call the Virgin Mary blessed, because she was the mother of Christ : but that was in a lower degree than God was his Father. This point ought to take up our meditations, to think we have all in Christ first. To think of ourselves in Christ, it is comfortable ; and Christ shall have more glory by it. God the Father and the Son shall have glory by it, and we shall have comfort.

The second consideration of God is, not only as he is the Father of Christ, but as he is

2. '*The Father of mercies.*' God is the Father of Christ, and our Father, ' and the Father of mercies.' But as I said before in this method, he is first the Father of Christ, and then our Father, and then ' the Father of mercies.' For he could never be the Father of mercies to us, except he were the Father of Christ. For mercy must see justice contented.* One attribute in God must not devour another. All must have satisfaction. His justice must have no wrong. Nor it hath not now. It is fully satisfied by Christ.

Therefore God is the Father of Christ, that Christ in our nature might die for us, and so he might be our Father notwithstanding our sins, having punished our sins in our surety, Christ. So being the Father of Christ, and our Father, he is the Father of mercies ; his justice hath no loss by it.

If God had not found out a way, out of the bowels of his mercy, how he might shew good to us, by reconciling mercy and justice in the mediator Christ, in punishing him for our sins, to set us free, he had never been a Father of mercy; if he had not been the Father of Christ first. For we being in such contrary terms as God and we were, he being holiness, and we nothing but a mass of sin and corruption ; without sufficient satisfaction of an infinite person there could be no reconciliation. Therefore he is the Father of Christ, who died for us. He took our nature upon him to satisfy God's justice, and then Father of us, and so Father of mercy to us.

He may well be the Father of mercies now, being the Father of Christ, of our nature in Christ : for, as I said, he is the Father of Christ as man, as well as he is God. Being the Father of our nature, being taken into the unity with his own Son's nature, for both make one Christ, he becomes ' the Father of mercies.' He is a Father to him by nature, to us by grace and adoption. ' The Father of Christ, and Father of mercies.' It is a necessary method, for God out of Christ is a fountain indeed, but he is a ' fountain sealed up.' He is a God merciful and gracious in his own nature, but there is sin that stops the fountain, that stops the current of the mercy. There must be therefore satisfaction to his justice and wrath, before there can be reconciliation, before there can any mercy flow from him. He is first the Father of Christ, and then the ' Father of mercies.' We have all from Christ. If he were not the Father of Christ, he should be the Father of nobody ; for immediately† no man is able to appear before God without a mediator.

' Father of mercies.' By Father, which is a kind of hebraism (*f*), is meant he is the original, the spring of mercies, he is the ' Father of mercies.' He doth not say the Father of one mercy, but the ' Father of mercies.' His mercy is one ; it is his nature, it is himself. As he is one, so mercy in him is one. It is one in the fountain, but many in the streams. It is one

* That is, 'satisfied.'—G.   † That is, ═ ' in himself.'—G.

in him, one nature, and one mercy. But because we have not one sin, but many sins, we have not one misery, but many, that lies upon this frail nature of ours. Therefore according to the exigencies of us wretched creatures, according to our sins and miseries, his mercies stream out. They are derived* and run out to all kind of sin and misery whatsoever.

'The Father of mercies.' If all mercies were lost, they must be found in him. He is 'the Father of mercies.' They are his bowels, as it were, and mercy pleaseth him as a man is pleased with his own natural child.† 'The Father of mercies.' He doth not say the Author of mercies, but the Father of them. He gives them the sweetest name that can be. He doth not say the Father of revenge, or of judgment, though he be the Father of them too; but to his children the Father of mercies. A sweet name under which none should despair!

But to shew some reasons why he is so styled.

1. There is good reason. Being the Father of Christ, *his justice being fully contented*, sin being taken away that stopped the current of his mercies, he being naturally merciful, his mercies run freely. 'Father of Christ, and Father of mercies.' It follows well. He is the Father of mercies, because he is the Father of Christ; and because his justice is satisfied in him, and he being naturally merciful, what hinders but that mercy may run amain, freely, and abundantly upon those that are in covenant with him in Chrst, that are members of Christ. That is one reason, because his justice is satisfied.

2. And because he is *naturally merciful*, therefore he is the 'Father of mercies.' The sea doth not more naturally flow, and is moist, and the sun doth not more naturally shine, the fire doth not more naturally burn, heavy bodies do not more naturally sink to the centre, than God doth naturally shew pity and mercy where his justice is satisfied; for it is his nature, it is himself.

The apostle doth not name other attributes, for, alas! other attributes would scare us. As, for example, if the guilty conscience consider him as a God of justice, it will reason thus: What is this to me? I am a sinner, and he will be just in punishing. If he consider he is a God of wisdom, the conscience considers he is the more wise to find out my windings and turnings from him, and my covering of my sins; he is the more wise to find me out in my courses, and to shame me. He doth not say, he is a God of power, the father of power. The guilty conscience then would reason, he is the more able to crush me and to send me to hell.

Indeed, there is no attribute of God, but it is matter of terror, being secluded from mercy; but considering God the Father of mercies, then we may consider sweetly and comfortably of all other attributes. He is merciful and good to me; therefore his wisdom, that shall serve to do me good, to devise good things for me; his power shall serve to free me from mine enemies; his justice to revenge my quarrel; and so all other attributes shall be serviceable to my comfort. They may be thought upon sweetly, where mercy is laid claim unto before. Therefore, here he is called 'the Father of mercies,' and not the Father of other attributes.

'*Of mercies.*' To unfold the word a little, 'mercy' is here the same with grace to a person in misery. Mercy is but free favour shewed to a miserable person. Grace shews the freeness of it, and mercy shews the state of

* That is, 'transmitted.'—G.

† That is, = 'marriage-born, not in the modern sense, in Scotland, of illegitimate.'—G.

the person to whom it is shewn. Alway where mercy is, either there is present or else possible misery.

There was mercy shewed to angels that stood, to free them, to give them grace to stand. They might have fallen as the devils did when they were angels. None are the subjects of mercy, but such as either are in misery, or are possible to fall into misery. Now, when God keeps and upholds the creature from falling into that which he is subject to fall into (he being a creature taken out of nothing, and therefore subject to fall to nothing without assistance), to hold him from that whereto he would fall without being upheld, this makes him the object of mercy, whatsoever the misery be, spiritual or outward.

Thus God is the Father of mercy; he upholds his children from that which else they would fall into continually. He is ' the Father of mercy,' before conversion, offering and enjoining mercy to them, that as they will be good to their souls, they would receive mercy. He joins his glory and his mercy together, that he will be glorified in shewing mercy; and he presseth it upon us. What a mercy is this, that he should press mercy upon us for our own good ? ' Why will ye die, O house of Israel,' Jer. xxvii. 13. And, ' Come unto me, all ye that are weary and heavy laden,' Mat. xi. 28. There is mercy before conversion. And there is mercy in prolonging his wrath, in not punishing; and there is mercy in pardoning sin freely, in pardoning all sin, the punishment and the guilt, and all. And when we are in the state of grace, and have our sins pardoned, still it is his mercy to forbear the punishments due to us, in mitigating his corrections, and in seasonable corrections. For it is a mercy for God to correct his children seasonably. ' Therefore we are corrected of God, that we should not be damned with the world,' 1 Cor. xi. 32.

It is a mercy to have seasonable correction. It is a mercy to have correction mitigated and sweetened with some comforts. It is a mercy after we are in the state of grace, besides this, to have the continuance of outward blessings.

God renews his mercies every day. His mercies fail not,' Lament. iii. 22. His mercies are renewed continually upon us.

So he is Father of all kind of mercies; privative* mercies, in freeing us from ill; and positive mercies, in bestowing good. Pardoning mercies, healing mercies, preserving mercies, all mercies come from this Father of

I will not stand to unfold them in particular; for indeed every thing that comes from God to his children, it is a mercy. It is as it were dipt in mercy before it comes to us. It is a mercy, that is, there is a freedom in it, and a pity to his creature. For the creature is alway in some necessity and in some dependence. We are in a state of necessities in this life, in some misery or other, and that, as I said, is the object of mercy.

Besides, we are dependent for the good we have. It is at God's mercy to continue or to take away any comfort that he gives us. Every thing is a mercy. And in every thing we take from God we ought to conceive a mercy in it, and to think this is a mercy from God. If we have health, it is a mercy; if we have strength, it is a mercy; if we have deliverance, it is a mercy. It comes in the respect and relation of a mercy, all that comes from God. He is not said to be the father of the thing; but the ' Father of mercies.' There is a mercy contained in the thing. They come from the pity and love of God, and that is the sweetest. Therefore, he is said to be the ' Father of mercies.'

* That is, = ' negative.'—G.

Quest. What use may we make of this, that God is the ' Father of mercies ' ?

Ans. It is a point full of sweet and comfortable uses, to those that are not in the state of grace, and to those that are in the state of grace.

Use 1. *To those that are not in the state of grace, they should see here a haven to flee to ; a city of refuge to flee unto.* Do but consider, thou wretched soul, how God is styled a ' Father of mercies' to thee, a God of bounty. All is to allure thee to repentance, to allure thee to come in. He is not merciful by accident, but he is naturally merciful in himself. He hath bowels of mercy in himself. ' Mercy pleaseth him,' Micah vii. 18.

Therefore, despair not, thou drooping soul, whosoever thou art that are under the guilt of sin ! come to the Father of mercies ! cast thyself into this sea of his mercy ! hide thyself in these bowels ! be not an enemy to thine own mercy ! As Jonah saith, ' Refuse not thy own mercy,' Jonah ii. 8, that is offered. There is mercy pressed upon thee, mercy with threatening if thou believe not mercy, now thou art called to receive it. The wrath of God hangs over thee as a weight, or as a sword ready to fall upon thee. As Christ saith, ' The wrath of God hangs over us,' John iii. 36, if we do not receive mercy offered us.

Allege not thy sins against mercy. Thy sins are the sins of a creature ; God is the ' Father of mercies.' He is infinite. Christ thy Saviour hath made an infinite satisfaction, and thy sins are finite, and in that respect there is mercy for thee if thou wilt come in, if thou apprehend and receive mercy.

' One deep calls upon another deep,' Ps. xlii. 7. The depth of thy sins and misery draws unto it, and calls upon the depth of mercy. ' The mercy of God is above all his works,' Ps. cxlv. 9. It is not only above all his works to cover them all, and under them to uphold them, but it is beyond them all. His mercy exceeds all other attributes to the creature. It is above his works, and upon his works, and under his works, and it is above thy works too. He is more glorious in his mercy than in any other attribute. He doth all for the glory of his mercy, both in the creation and in the gospel. His mercy, therefore, is above his own works, and above thy works if thou come in.

Oil is of a kingly nature. It swims above all other liquids. So the mercy of God, like oil, it swims above all other attributes in him, and above all sin in thee, if thou wilt receive it.

' Father of mercies.' In a corrupt estate the special mercy is forgiving mercy. If it were not for forgiving mercies, all other gifts and mercies were to little purpose. For it were but a reserving of us to eternal judgment, but a feeding the traitor to the day of execution, a giving him the liberty of the prison, which is nothing unless his treason be pardoned. So the forgiving mercy leads to all the rest. Now these forgiving mercies, they are unlimited mercies, there is no bounds of them. For he being the Father of Christ, who is an infinite person, and having received an infinite satisfaction from an infinite Person, he may well be infinitely merciful ; and himself is an infinite God. His mercies are like himself. The satisfaction whereby he may be merciful is infinite. Hereupon it is that he may pardon, and will pardon all sin without limitation, if they be never so great never so many.

This I observe, the rather to appease the conscience of a sinner when it is suppressed* with terror and fear of the greatness of his sins. Consider

* Qu. ' oppressed ?—G.

how God hath set down himself, and will be known and apprehended of us, not only as merciful, but a ' Father of mercies,' and not of one mercy, but of all mercies, not only giving, but, forgiving especially, ' Which forgiveth all thy sins, and healeth all thy infirmities,' Ps. ciii. 3. This I observe against a proneness in us to despair. We are not now proner in the time of peace to presume, than when conscience is awakened, to despair; we are prone to both alike. For here is the poison of man's corruption. Is God so merciful? Surely, I may go on in sin, and cry God mercy, and there is an end. God is merciful, nay, the Father of mercies.

Now, in the time of peace, sin is nothing with us. Swearing is nothing, rotten discourse is nothing, going beyond others in our dealing and commerce is nothing, getting an estate by fraud and deceit is nothing. ' The bread of deceit is sweet,' Prov. xx. 17. Loose, licentious, libertine life, is nothing. And those that do not follow the same excess, and are [not] dissolute, it is a strange matter with us, they are strange people. We think it strange that others do not so, and if they be better than we, it is but hypocrisy. Men measure all by themselves. So all is nothing. Great, gross swearing is nothing. Men glory in it, and to make scruple of it, it is thus and thus. They have terms for it. And what is the bawd* for all this? Oh! God is merciful, and Christ he is wondrous merciful; he took our nature that he might die for us, &c.

It is true indeed. But when the conscience is awakened, then the conscience will tell thee another lesson. The conscience will set God as just, and Satan will help conscience with accusations and aggravations. It is true, it is too true. The conscience will take part with God and with his word. It is true thou hast done thus and thus. These are thy sins, and God is just.

And especially at the hour of death, when earthly comforts fail, and there is nothing but sin set before a man's eyes, the comforts that are set before him can do him no good. Then the conscience will hardly† receive any comfort: especially the consciences of such as have gone on in a course of sin, in spite of good means. A conscience of such a man as either refuseth or rejects the means, because it would favour itself in sin; or a conscience that being under means, having had its sins discovered to it, that conscience will hardly admit of any comfort. And there is none, but they find it another manner of matter than they think it. Sin is a blacker thing than they imagine. Their oaths that they trifle with, and their dissolute and their rotten discourse, when they should be better affected‡, upon the Sabbath, and such like. Therefore we ought to look to it.

Well! to press this point of presumption a little further, now I am in it, we are wondrous prone to abuse this mercy to presumption, and after to despair.

I consider this beforehand, that however God's mercy be unlimited, as iudeed it is in itself, it is so unlimited to those that repent, and to those that receive and embrace mercy, and mercy in one kind as well as another. It is so to those that repent of their sins. For God is so the ' Father of mercy,' as that he is the ' God of vengeance ' too, Deut. xxxii. 5. He is a just God too.

The conscience will tell you this well enough, when the outward comforts, that now you dally with and set as gods in the room of God, and drown yourselves in sensuality and idolatry with the creature, and put them

---

* *Sic* Qu. ' bode ?' = bid, meaning bait.—G.

† That is, ' affectioned' = disposed.—G.   ‡ That is, ' with difficulty.'—G.

in the place of God,—when they are taken away, conscience will tell you that God is merciful indeed ; but he is just to such that refuse mercies.

Therefore, though his mercy be unlimited to such as are broken-hearted to such as repent of their sins (for he will glorify his mercy as he may glorify his other attributes), he is wisely merciful. If he should be merciful to such as go on in sin, he should not be wisely merciful.

Who among men, if he be wise, would be merciful to a child or servant without acknowledgment of the fault ?

Was not David over-merciful to Absalom ? Yes ; it was his fault. Yet, out of wisdom, he would not admit him into his presence till he was humbled for his fault and made intercession, though he doated upon him, 2 Sam. xiv. 28. God is infinitely wise, as he is merciful. Therefore, he will not be merciful to him that goes on in wickedness and sin. This cannot be too often pressed, for the most of the auditors, wheresoever we speak, the devil hath them in this snare, that God is merciful, &c. And doth he not know how to use it ? He is so indeed, but it is to repentant souls that mean to break off their course of sin.

Otherwise, if the mercy of God work the other way, hearken to thy doom, ' He that blesseth himself,' saith God by Moses, and saith, ' These curses shall not come to me,' he that blesseth himself and saith, Oh, all shall be well, God is merciful, &c., ' my wrath shall smoke against him,' Deut. xxix. 16, 20, and I will not be merciful to him that goes on in his sins. God will ' wound the hairy scalp of him that goes on in sin,' Ps. lxviii. 21. As the apostle saith, he that abuseth the bounty and patience of God, that should lead him to repentance, ' he treasureth up wrath against the day of wrath,' Rom. ii. 5. The Scripture is never in any case more terrible than this way. In Isa. xxviii. 15, ' You have made a covenant with hell and death,' with God's judgments ; but hell and death hath not made a covenant with you. You make a covenant, and think you shall do well ; but God is terrible to such. His wrath shall smoke against such as make a covenant with his judgments, and treasure up wrath against the day of wrath.

Take heed. If the proclamation of mercy call thee not in, if thou stand out as a rebel and come not in, but go on still, then justice lays hold on thee, God's wrath shall smoke against thee, as we see in Prov. i. 26, ' I will laugh at your destruction,' speaking of those that would not come in and as * it is in Isa. xxvii. 11, ' He that formed them and made them will have no mercy on them, nor shew them favour.' He will have no delight in them. They are ignorant sots, and will not labour to know God and his will, to do and obey it. ' He that made them will have no delight in them, and he that formed them will reject them.' It is a pitiful thing when God, that made them and formed them in their mother's womb, whose creatures they are, shall have no delight in them ; when he that made them, his heart shall not pity them, Ezek. xviii. 18. He that goes on in a course of sin presumptuously and doth not repent, God's eye shall not pity him. ' He that made him will have no delight in him.'

Therefore the apostle, because we are disposed and prone to abuse the goodness and longsuffering of God and the mercies of Christ, he saith, ' Be not deceived, be not deceived ' (he oft presseth this), ' for neither the covetous nor licentious persons shall enter into heaven,' 1 Cor. vi. 10.

Though God be merciful, if thou live in these sins, be not deceived,

* By a strange misprint, the words ' and as,' appear in the unmeaning form of ' Chidas,' in the folio. It is plain that ' and as' was intended by Sibbes.—G.

thou shalt never enter into heaven. God will not be merciful to the most of those that even now live in the bosom of the church, because they make mercy a band to their sinful courses. God will harden himself. He will not bless such. He hath no mercy for such. To such he is a God of vengeance.

His mercy is to such as are weary of their sinful courses. As I said, he is merciful, but so as he is wise.

What prince will prostitute a pardon to one that is a rebel, and yet thinks himself a good subject all the while? He is no rebel; cares he for a pardon? and shall he have a pardon when he cares not for it? Those that are not humbled in the sight and sense of their sins, that think themselves in a good estate, they are rebels, that have not sued out their pardon. There is no mercy to them yet. ' He that made them will not pity them,' because they are ignorant, hardened wretches, that live in blasphemy, in swearing, in corrupt courses, in hardness of heart, that live in sins, that their own conscience and the conscience of others about them know that they are sins, devouring sins, that devour all their comfort; and yet, notwithstanding, they dream of mercy. Mercy! Hell is their portion, and not mercy, that make an idol of God.

Thus it is with us; we are prone to presume upon God's mercy. I speak this that we should not surfeit of this sweet doctrine, that God is the ' Father of mercies.' He is so to repentant sinners, to those that believe. To those mercy is sweet. We know oil is above all liquors. God's mercy is above all his own works and above our sins. But what is the vessel for this oil? This oil of mercy, it is put in broken vessels; it is kept best there. A broken heart, a humble heart, receives and keeps mercy.

As for proud dispositions, as all sinners that go on in a course of sin, the psalmist terms them proud men; he is a proud man that sets his own will against God's command. ' God resists the proud,' James iv. 6. It is the humble, yielding heart, that will be led and lured by God, that is a vessel to receive mercy. It must be a deep vessel, it must be a broken vessel, deep with humiliation, broken by contrition, that must receive mercy. And it must be a large vessel laid open, capable to receive mercy, and all mercy, not only pardoning mercy, but healing mercy, as I said out of that psalm, ' That forgiveth all thy sins, and healeth all thy transgressions,' Ps. ciii. 3.

Therefore those that have not grace and mercy, to heal their corruptions, to dry up that issue in some comfortable measure, they have no pardoning mercy; and those that desire not their corruptions to be healed, they never desire heartily their corruptions to be pardoned. Those mercies go together.

He is not the ' Father of mercy,' but of all mercies that belong to salvation, and he gives them every one, and he that desires the one, desires the other.

Let us consider how the sweet descriptions of God, and how his promises work upon us. If they work on us to make us presume, it is a fearful case. It is as bad a sign as may be, to be ill, because God is good, ' to turn the grace of God into wantonness,' Jude ver. 4.

But as we are thus prone to presume; so when conscience is awaked we are as prone to despair. Therefore if they work with us this way, ' there is mercy with God, therefore I will come in;' ' therefore I will cast down my weapons at his feet,' ' I will cease to resist him,' ' I will come in, and take

terms of peace with him,' ' I will yield him obedience for the time to come;'
' therefore I will fear and love so good a God.' If it work thus, it is a
sign of an elect soul, of a gracious disposition. And then if thou come
in, never consider what thy sins have been; if thou come in, God will
embrace thee in his mercy. Thy sins are all as a spark of fire that falls
into the ocean, that is drowned presently. So are thy sins in the ocean of
God's mercy.

There is not more light in the sun, there is not more water in the sea,
than there is mercy in the ' Father of mercy,' whose bowels are opened to
thee if thou be weary of thy sinful courses, and come in, and embrace
mercy.

In the tabernacle, we know, there was a mercy-seat. We call it a propitiatory. In the ark, which this mercy-seat covered, was the law. Now
in the law there were curses against all sinners.

The mercy-seat was a type of Christ, covering the law, covering the
curse. Though thou be guilty of the curse a thousand times, God in
Christ is merciful. Christ is the mercy-seat. Come to God in Christ.
There is mercy in Israel notwithstanding thy great sins. If we cast away a
purpose of living in sin, and cast away our weapons, and submit ourselves
to him, he is the Father of mercies. That is, he is merciful from himself,
he is the spring of them, and hath them from his own bowels. They are
free mercies, because he is the Father of them.

For he is just by our fault, he is severe from us, he takes occasion from
our sins; but he is merciful from his own bowels. He is good from himself. We provoke him to be severe and just. Therefore be we never so
miserable in regard of sin, and the fruits of sin, yet he is the Father of
mercy, of free mercy; mercy from himself. ' Mercy pleaseth him,' Micah
vii. 18. He is delighted in it.

Now that which is natural comes easily, as water from the fountain
comes without violence, and heat from the fire comes without any violence,
because it is natural. A mother pities her child, because it is natural.
There is a sweet instinct of nature that moves and pricks forward nature to
that affection of love that she bears to her child. So it is with God. It is
nature in him to be merciful to his, because they are his. Mercy is his
nature. We are his. We being his, his nature being merciful, he will be
merciful to all that are his, to such as repent of their sins, and lay hold of
his mercy by a true faith.

His word shews likewise his mercy. There is not one attribute set down
more in Scripture than mercy. It is the name whereby he will be known,
Exod. xxxiv. 6, where he describes it, and tells us his name. What is the
name of God? His longsuffering, and mercy, &c. There is a long description of God in that place. David, in Ps. iii., besides that which is in
every prophet almost, hath the same description of God, to comfort God's
people in his time. In Ps. lxxxvi., ciii., cxlv., there is the same description of God as there is in Moses. He is merciful and longsuffering, &c.
He describes himself to be so, and his promises are promises of mercy.
At what time soever a sinner repents, and without limitation of sins, all
sins shall be forgiven. ' The blood of Christ purgeth us from all sin,'
1 John i. 7.

If there be no limitation of persons whomsoever, of sins whatsoever,
or of time whensoever, here is a ground that we should never despair.
' God is the Father of mercies.'

It is excellent that the prophet hath, to prevent the thoughts of a dejected soul, ' Let the wicked forsake his way, and the unrighteous man his thoughts, and return to the Lord, and he will have mercy upon him, and to our God, for he will abundantly pardon,' Isa. lv. 7.

Obj. Aye, but I have abused mercy a long time; I have lived in sin, and committed great sins. Well, notwithstanding that, see how he answers it : ' My thoughts are not your thoughts.' You are vindictive. If a man offend you, you are ready to aggravate the fault, and to take revenge, &c. ' But my thoughts are not as your thoughts, nor my ways as your ways,' saith the Lord; ' for as far as the heaven is above the earth, so are my thoughts above your thoughts, and my ways above your ways,' Ps. ciii. 11. We have narrow, poor thoughts of mercy, because we ourselves are given to revenge, and we are ready, when we think of our sins, to say, Can God forgive them? can God be merciful to such? &c. ' My thoughts are not as your thoughts, nor my ways as your ways.'

It is good to consider this, and it is a sweet meditation; for the time undoubtedly will come, that unless God's mercy and God's thoughts should be, as himself is, infinite, unless his ways should be infinitely above our ways, and his thoughts infinitely above ours in mercy, certainly the soul would receive no comfort.

The soul of a Christian acquainted with the word of God knows that God's mercy is, as himself is, infinite, and his thoughts this way are, as himself is, infinite. Therefore the Scripture sets down the mercies of God by all dimensions. There is the depth of wisdom, but when he comes to speak of love and mercy, as it is in Eph. iii. 18, ' Oh, the depth, and breadth, and height of this ! '

Indeed, for height, it is higher than the heavens; for depth, it fetcheth the soul from the nethermost deep. We have deep misery, ' Out of the deep I cried to thee,' Ps. cxxx. 1; yet notwithstanding, his mercy is deeper than our misery. O the depth of his mercy! There is a depth of mercy deeper than any misery or rebellion of ours, though we have sunk deep in rebellion. And for the extent of them, as I said before, ' his mercy is over all his works,' Ps. cxlv. 9. It extends to the utmost parts of the earth. The Scripture doth wonderfully enlarge his mercy beyond all dimensions whatsoever. These things are to good purpose; and it is a mercy to us that he sets forth himself in mercy in his word, because the soul, sometime or other when it is awakened, as every one that God delights in is awakened, first or last, it needs all that is, it is all little enough.

God is merciful to those that are heavy laden, that feel the burden of their sins upon their souls. Such as are touched with the sense of their sins, God still meets them half-way. He is more ready to pardon than they are to ask mercy. As we see in the prodigal, when he had wasted all, when he was as low as a man could be, when he was come to husks, and when he had despised his father's admonition, yet upon resolution to return, when he was stung with the sense of his sins, his father meets him and entertains him; he upbraids him not with his sin, Luke xv. 20, *seq.*

Take sin, with all the aggravations we can, yet if we repent and resolve upon new courses, there is comfort, though we relapse into sin again and again. If we must pardon ten times seven-times, as Christ saith, Luke xvii. 4,* certainly there cannot be more mercy in the cistern than there is

---

* With reference to a former note (vol. I. page 231), Sibbes's phrase should have been printed 'seventy seven-times.' The question to our Lord was, ' till seven-times ?' ' Yes,' he replied, ' till seventy seven-times,' which is = seventy times seven. Sibbes's quotation above is a slip.—G.

in the fountain; there cannot be more mercy in us than there is in the
' Father of mercies,' as God is.

Take sin in the aggravations, in the greatness of it, Manasseh's sin,
Peter's denying of his Master, the thief on the cross, and Paul's persecution! Take sin as great as you will, he is the ' Father of mercies.' If we
consider that God is infinite in mercy, and that the Scripture reveals him
as the ' Father of mercies,' there is no question but there is abundance, a
world of comfort to any distressed soul that is ready to cast itself on God's
mercy.

Use 2. For those that are converted, that are in the state of grace—Is God
' the Father of mercies ?' *let this stir us up to embrace mercy, every day to
live by mercy, to plead mercy with God in our daily breaches;* to love and fear
God, because there is mercy with him that ' he might be feared,' Ps. cxxx. 4.
It is a harder matter to make a daily sweet use of this than it is taken
for. Those that are the fittest subjects for mercy, they think themselves
furthest off from mercy. Come to a broken soul, who is catched in the
snare; whose conscience is on the rack, he thinks, alas! there is no mercy
for me! I have been such a sinner, God hath shewed me mercy before, and
now I have offended him again and again. Those that are the subjects of
mercy, that are the nearest to mercy, when their conscience is awakened,
they think themselves furthest off, and we have need to press abundance of
mercy, and all little enough to set the soul in frame. There is none of us
all, but we shall see a necessity of pressing this one time or other, before
we die. David when he had sinned, he knew well enough that God was
merciful. Oh, but it was not a slight mercy that would satisfy him, as we
see, Ps. li., how he presseth upon God for mercy, and will a little serve
him? No! ' according to thy abundant mercy,' ver. 1. He presseth
mercy, and abundance of mercy, a multitude of mercies; and unless he had
seen infinite mercy, abundant mercy in God, when his conscience was
awaked with the foulness of his sin (there being such a cry for vengeance,
his sin called and cried); if the blood of Christ had not cried above it,
' Mercy, mercy,' and abundance of mercy, multitudes of compassion, the
soul of David would not have been stilled.

So other saints of God, when they have considered the foulness of sin,
how odious it is to God, they could not be quieted and comforted, but that
they saw mercy, and abundance of mercy. As the apostle St Peter saith,
' Blessed be God, the Father of our Lord Jesus Christ, who, of his abundant
mercy, hath begotten us again to a lively hope, by the resurrection of Jesus
Christ, to an inheritance, immortal,' &c., 1 Pet. i. 3.

' God is the Father of mercies.' For faith will not have sufficient footing,
but in infinite mercy. In the time of despair, in the time of torment of
conscience, in the time of desertion, it must be mercy, and ' the Father of
mercies,' and multitudes of compassions, and bowels of love; and all little
enough for faith to fix on, the faith of a conscience on the rack. But when
faith considers of God set out—not as Satan sets him forth, a God of vengeance, a ' consuming fire,' Heb. xii. 29,—when faith considers God pictured
out in the gospel, it sees him the Father of Christ and our Father, and the
Father of mercies and God of comfort, faith seeing infinite mercy in an
infinite God; and seeing mercy triumph against justice, and all other attributes, here faith hath some footing, and stays itself, or else the converted,
sanctified soul, seeing the odiousness of sin, and the clamorousness of sin, such
that it will not be satisfied, but with abundant mercy; and God must be presented to it as a ' Father of mercy' and compassion, before it can have peace.

Therefore, if so be at any time our conscience be awakened, and the devil lays hard to us, let us think of God as he hath made himself known in his word, as a ' Father of mercies and God of comfort,' represent him to our souls, as he represents himself in his word. Times of desertion, when we seem to be forsaken of God, will enforce this. Times of desertion will come, when the soul will think God hath forgotten to be merciful, and hath shut up his love in displeasure. Oh, no! he is the Father of mercy, he never shuts up his bowels altogether, he never stops the spring of his mercy. He doth to our feeling, but it is his mercy that he doth that; it is his mercy that he hinders the sense of mercy. He doth that in mercy. It is to make us more capable of mercy afterward.

Therefore, saith the Father, when he comes to us in his love, and the sense of it, it is for our good; and when he takes the sense of his love from us, it is for our good. For when he takes away the sense of his love from us, it is to enlarge our souls to be more capable of mercy after, to prize it more, to walk warily, and jealously, to look to our corruptions better. Therefore in the time of desertion think of this, when God seems to forget us. ' Can a mother forget her child?' Isa. xlix. 15. Suppose she should be so unnatural as to do it, which can hardly be believed, that a mother should forget her child, ' Yet notwithstanding I will not forget you;' you are ' written upon the palms of my hands,' ver. 16, that is, I have you alway in my eye. So that if there were no mercies to be found in nature, no bowels to be found in a mother (where usually they are most abundant), yet notwithstanding there is mercy to be found in ' the Father of mercies' still. Therefore in such times let us make use of this.

And another thing that we ought to learn hence is this, if God be so in Christ Jesus, for we must alway put that in, for he is merciful with satisfaction. And yet it is his mercy that he would admit of satisfaction. His mercy devised a way to content justice. His mercy set all on work. Mercy is above justice in the work of salvation. Justice hath received contentment from mercy. But that by the way, to make us have higher thoughts of mercy, than any other attribute of God in the doctrine of the gospel, in that kingdom of Christ. It is a kingdom of grace *and mercy,* if we have hearts to embrace it.

Let this encourage us to come to God, and to cast ourselves into the arms of this merciful Father. If we have lived in other courses before, let the mercy of God work upon our souls. In Rom. ii. 4, it is pressed there excellently. ' This mercy of God should lead us to repentance,' it should encourage us. What makes a thief or a traitor come in, when there is proclamation out against him? If there be a pardon sent after him, it makes him come in, or else he runs out still further and further, while the hue and cry pursues him. But hope of mercy and pardon will bring him in again. So it is that that brings us in again to God, the very hope of mercy and pardon. If we be never so ill, or have been never so ill, do not put off, but take this day now; ' Now is the time,' now, ' while it is called to-day,' Ps. xcv. 7, 8, take the present time. Here is our error, if God be ' the Father of mercy,' I will cry him mercy at the hour of death. Aye, thou mayest go to hell with mercy in thy mouth. He is merciful to those that truly repent. But how dost thou know that thy repentance on thy deathbed will be true? It is not sorrow for sickness, and grief for death, and fear of that. But there must be a hatred of sin. And how shall conscience tell thee now thou hast repented, that it is a hating of thy sinful courses, rather than the fear of damnation? that is rather from the sense of grief. Conscience will hardly be comforted in this, for it will upbraid. Aye, now, now you would have mercy.

We see by many that have recovered again, that have promised great matters in their sickness, that it is hypocritical repentance, for they have been worse after than they were before (f*). It is not a sufficient matter to yield thee comfort, that thou art much humbled in thy sickness, and at the hour of death; for it is hard for thee to determine whether it be true repentance, or mere sorrow for sin as it brings judgment. Fear of damnation is not sufficient to bring a man to heaven. Thy nature must be changed before thou come to heaven. Thou must love righteousness because it is righteousness. Thou must love God because he is good. Thou must hate sin because it is sin.

How canst thou tell, when thou hast been naught before affliction, whether affliction have wrought this, that thou repentest only out of hatred of judgment, to shun that, or out of hatred of sin, because it is sin? Therefore now a little repentance in thy health, and in the enjoying of thy prosperity, a little hatred of ill ways now, will more comfort thee than a thousand times more prayer and striving will then. Although, if thou canst do it truly then, yet the gate of mercy is open, but thy heart will scarce say it is truly done, because it is forced.

Then, again, perhaps thou shalt not have the honour of it, thou shalt not have the mercy. Thou that hast refused mercy, and lived in a loose, profane course, thou that hast despised mercy all the while, God will not honour thee so much as to have a good word, or a sorrowful word, that even very grief shall not extort it from thee. But as thou hast forgotten God in thy life, and wouldst not own his admonitions, thou shalt forget thyself in death, and be taken away suddenly, or else with some violent disease that shall take away the use of the parts that God hath given thee, as inflammation of the spirits, or the like, that shall take away the use of sound reason. It is madness, and no better, to live as the most live, to cry God is merciful, &c. Thou mayest go to hell for all that. Repentance must be from a true hatred of sin; and that that must comfort thee, must be a disposition for the present, for then it is unforced.

Therefore all these sweet comforts are to you that come in and leave your wicked courses. If you have been swearers, to swear no more; if you have been deceivers, to deceive no more; if you have been licentious, to be so no more, but to break off the course of your sins as God shall enable you. Or else this one thing, think of it, that you now daub your conscience withal, and go on in sin with that, will be most terror to you, even mercy. Nothing will vex you so much as mercy afterward. Then thou shalt think with thyself, I have heard comfortable [tidings] of the promises, and of the nature of God, but I put off and despised all, I regarded my sinful courses more than the mercy of God in Christ, they were sweeter to me than mercy. I lived in sins, out of the abundance of profaneness that did me no good; I lived in sins, out of the superfluity of profaneness that I had neither profit nor pleasure by, and neglected mercy. The consideration of mercy neglected, with the continuing in a wretched course, it will more aggravate the soul's torment.

Let us be encouraged to come in. Such as intend to leave their sinful courses, let them remember that then they come to a Father of mercy that is more ready to pardon than you are to ask it, as you see in the prodigal son, which I instanced in before; it is a notable, sweet story. I have a Father, saith he, when he had spent all, and was come to husks, Luke

xv. 16. Affliction is a notable means to make us to taste and relish mercy. I have a Father, and there is plenty in his house; and he comes and confesseth his sin. He had no sooner resolved, but his Father, he doth not stay for him, but he meets him, and kisseth him, Luke xv. 20, *seq.*

Let us consider of this description of God, the Father of mercy. It should move any that are in ill and lewd courses before, ' In my Father's house there are good things,' and in his heart there are bowels of mercy. I have a Father, and a Father of mercy. I will go home, and submit myself to him, and say to him, I have been thus and thus, but I will be so no more. You shall find that God, by his Spirit, will be readier to meet you than you are to cast yourselves at the feet of his mercy, and into the arms of his mercy. He will come and meet you, and kiss you. You shall find much comfort upon your resolution to come in, if it be a sound resolution.

The son fears his father's displeasure; but saith the father, 'My thoughts are not as your thoughts.' Oh! I fear he will not receive me! Yes, yes, he is willing to embrace you. Mercy pleaseth him; ' and why will you perish, O house of Israel?' Jer. xxvii. 13.

Again, ' God is the Father of mercies ' This should stir us up to an imitation of this our gracious Father; for every father begets to his own likeness, and all the sons of this Father are like the Father. They are merciful. ' The kings of Israel are merciful kings,' 1 Kings xx. 31, saith the heathen king Benhadad; and the God of Israel is a merciful God, and all that are under God are merciful. His sons are ' merciful as their heavenly Father is merciful, Luke vi. 36. Therefore, if we would make it good to our own hearts, and the opinion and judgment of others of us, that we are children of this merciful Father, we must put on bowels of mercy ourselves as in Col. iii. 12, ' Now, therefore, as the elect of God,' as you will make it good that God hath elected you, ' put on the bowels of mercy.' Whatsoever we have from God, it comes in the respect of a mercy, and so it should do from God's children. Everything that comes from them to them that are in misery, it should be a mercy. They should not only bestow the thing, but a sweet mercy with the thing. A child of God he pours out his bowels to his brother, as Isaiah saith, ' Pour out thy bowels,' &c., Isa. lxiii. 15. There is some bowels, that is, there is an affection in God's children. They give not only the thing, the relief, but mercy with it, that hath a sweet report to the soul. There is pity, that more comforts a sanctified soul than the thing itself. We must not do works of mercy proudly (*g*). It is not the thing that God stands on, but the affection in the thing. His benefits are with a fatherly pity. So should ours be with a pitiful respect, with a tender heart. ' The very mercies of the wicked are cruel,' Prov. xii. 10. If they be merciful, there is some pride of spirit, there is some taste of a hard heart, of an hypocritical spirit. Somewhat is not as it should be. Their mercies are not mercies. We must in our mercy imitate the Father of mercies.

Alas! it is the fault of our time. There is little mercy to those that are in misery. What a cruel thing is it that so many, I would I could say Christian souls, I cannot say so, but they are a company of men that have the image of God upon them, men that live miserable poor, such as, for aught I know, God's mercy hath purchased with the blood of his Son, and may belong to God's kingdom. They have the image of God upon them, yet they live without laws, without church, without commonwealth, irregular persons, that have no order taken for them, or not executed at the least, to repress the sturdy of them, and to relieve those that are to be relieved for age or impotency (*g**).

It is a pitiful thing and a foul blemish to this commonwealth, and will bring some ill upon wealth, and plague it from such irregular persons.   He will plague the commonwealth for such enormities.   How do they live ?   As beasts, and worse.   They submit themselves to no orders of the church.   They have none, and submit to none.   Here is an object of mercy to those that it concerns.

And likewise, mercy ought to be shewed to the souls of men, as well as to their miserable and wretched estates.   Is popery antichristian ?   What mercy is it to suffer poisoners ?   What a mercy were it in a commonwealth to suffer men that are incendiaries to have liberty to do what mischief they would ?   or men that should poison fountains, and all that should refresh and nourish men ?   Were this any policy for the body ?   And is it any policy to suffer those to poison the judgments of people with heresies to God, and treason to their prince ?   to draw the affections of men from religion and the state, where is mercy all the while ?

Oh ! is it a mercy to them not to restrain them ?   Mercy !   Is it mercy to the sheep to let the wolves at liberty ?   No.   If you will be merciful, to shew mercy to the souls of these men is to use them hardly, that they may know their error.   They may now impute the liberty they have to the approbation of their cause ; and so they are cruel, not only to others, but to their own souls.

I speak this the rather, [that] it may be a seasonable speech at this time, to enforce good laws this way.   It is a great mercy.   Mercy to the soul, it is the greatest mercy ; and so cruelty to the soul is the greatest cruelty that can be.

What should I speak of mercy to others ?   Oh, that we would be merciful to our own souls !   God is merciful to our souls.   He sent his Son to ' visit us from on high,' in bowels of compassion.   He sent Christ, as Zacharias saith, Luke i. 68, and yet we are not merciful to ourselves.   How many sinful, wretched persons pierce their hearts through with covetousness, and other wicked courses, that are more dangerous to the soul than poison is to the body !   They stab their souls with cares, and lusts, and other such kind of courses.   What a mockery is this of God, to ask him mercy, when we will not be merciful to our own souls !   and to entreat others to pray for us, when we will not be merciful to ourselves ! .   Shall we go to God for mercy, when we will not shew mercy to ourselves ?   Shall we desire him to spare us, when we will not spare ourselves ?   It is a mocking of God to come and offer our devotions here, and come with an intent yet to live in any sin.   God will not hear us, if we purpose to live in sin.   ' If I regard iniquity in my heart, God will not hear my prayer,' Ps. lxvi. 18.   As we ought to be merciful to the souls of others, and to the estates of others, so we should to our own souls.

How can they reform evils abroad, those that are governors, when they do not care to reform themselves ?   Can they be merciful to the souls of others, that are cruel to their own ?   They cannot.   Let mercy begin at home.

This is that that the Scripture aims at.   Mercy and the right use of it, is the way to come to salvation ; and the abuse of it is that that damns ; and they are damned most that abuse mercy.   Oh, the sins against the gospel will lie upon the conscience another day.   The sins against the law, they help, with the gospel, to see mercy ; but sins against mercy prefer our sins above mercy ; and in temptations to despair, to extenuate mercy, hereafter it will be the very hell of hell, that we have sinned against mercy, that we have not embraced it with faith, that we have not repented to be capable of it.

Use 3. But to end the point with that which is the most proper use of all, which is *an use of comfort in all estates, to go to God in all.* 'He is the Father of mercy.' And when all is taken from us in losses and crosses, to think, well, our fathers may die, and our mothers may die, and our nearest and dearest friends that have most bowels of pity, may die ; but we have a Father of mercy, that hath eternal mercy in him. His mercies are tender mercies, and everlasting mercies, as himself is. We are everlasting. Our souls are immortal. We have an everlasting Father, that is the 'Father of mercies.' When all are taken away, God takes not himself away. He is the Father of mercy still.

Now that we may make ourselves still capable of mercy, still fit for mercy, let us take this daily course.

1. Let us labour every day, *to have broken and deep souls.* As I said before, it is the broken heart that is the vessel that contains mercy, a deeper heart that holds all the mercy. We need, therefore, to empty ourselves by confession of our sins, and search our own thoughts and ways, and afflict our souls by repentance ; and when* we shall be fit objects for God the Father of mercy to shed mercy into misery. It is the loadstone of mercy, misery left discerned and complained of. Let us search and see our misery, our spiritual misery especially ; for God begins mercy to the soul in his children, he begins mercy there especially. General mercy he shews to beasts, to all creatures ; but special mercy begins at the soul. Now, I say, misery being the loadstone of mercy, let us lay before God by confession and humiliation, the sores and sins of our souls. And then make use of this mercy every day ; for God is not only merciful in pardoning mercy at the first, in forgiving our sins at the first, but every day he is ready to pardon new sins, as it is Lam. iii. 23, 'He renews his mercies every day, every morning.' God renews his mercies not only for body, but for soul. There is a throne of grace and mercy every day open to go to, and a sceptre of mercy held out every day to lay hold on, and a 'fountain for Judah and Jerusalem to wash in every day,' Zech. xiii. 1. It is never stopped up, or drawn dry. The fountain is ever open, the sceptre is ever held forth, and the throne is ever kept.

God keeps not terms. Now the Court of Chancery is open, and now it is shut. But he keeps court every day. Therefore Christ in the gospel enjoins us to go to God every day. Every day we say the Lord's prayer, 'forgive us our trespasses,' Luke xi. 4, insinuating that the court of mercy is kept every day to take out our pardon. Every day there is a pardon of course taken out, 'at what time soever a sinner repents,' &c., 1 Kings viii. 38, *seq.*

Quest. How shall we improve this mercy every day ?

Ans. 1. Do this ; when thou hast made a breach in thy conscience, every day believe this, that God is 'the Father of mercies,' and he may well be merciful now, because he hath been sufficiently satisfied by the death of Christ. 'He is the Father of Christ, and the Father of mercies.' This do every day.

2. And withal consider our condition and estate is a state of dependence. 'In him we live and move and have our being,' Acts xvii. 28. This will

* Qu. ' then ? '—ED.

force us to mercy, that he would hold us in the same estate we are in, and go on with the work of grace, that he would uphold us in health, for that depends upon him ; that he would uphold us in peace, for that depends upon him : he is ' the God of peace,' 1 Cor. xiv. 33, that he would uphold us in comfort and strength, to do good and resist evil. We are in a dependent state and condition in all good of body and soul. He upholds the whole world, and every particular. Let him take away his hand of merciful protection and sustaining from us, and we sink presently.

3. And every day consider how we are environed with any danger. Remember, we have compassing mercies, as we have compassing dangers, as it is, ' Mercy compasseth us round about,' Ps. xxxii. 10. Every day, indeed, we have need of mercy. That is the way to have mercy. Here is a fountain of mercy, ' the Father of mercy,' bowels opened. The only way to use it is to see what need we have of mercy, and to fly to God ; to see what need we have in our souls, and in regard of outward estate, and to see that our condition is a dependent condition.

Use 4. And lastly, *to make a use of thankfulness*, ' Blessed be God, the Father of mercy,' *we have the mercy of public continued peace, when others have war*, and their estates are consumed. ' Blessed be God, the Father of mercy, we sit under our own vines, and under our own fig-trees,' Micah iv. 4. If we have any personal mercies, ' Blessed be God, the Father of mercies,' this way. If he shew mercy to our souls, and pardon our sins, ' Blessed be God, the Father of mercies,' in this kind ; that he hath taken us and redeemed us out of that cursed estate, that others walk in that are yet in their sins. Oh ! it is a mercy, and for this we should have enlarged hearts.

And withal consider the fearful estate of others, that God doth not shew mercy to, and this will make us thankful. As for instance, if a man would be thankful, that hath a pardon, let him see another executed, that is, broken upon the wheel or the rack, or cut in pieces and tortured, and then he will think, I was in the same estate as this man is, and I am pardoned. Oh ! what a gracious Sovereign have I ! The consideration of the fearful estate out of mercy, what a fearful estate those are in that live in sins against conscience, that they are ready to drop into hell when God strikes them with death ; if they die so, what a fearful estate they are in ! and that God should give me pardon and grace to enter into another course of life ; that though I have not much grace, yet I know it is true I am the child of God ; the consideration of the misery of others, in part in this world without repentance, and especially what they shall suffer in hell ; to consider the torment of the souls that are not in the state of grace, this will make us thankful for mercies, for pardoning and forgiving mercies, for protecting mercies, that God hath left thousands in the course of nature, going on in a wilful course of sin. This is that that the apostle here practiseth. ' Blessed be God, the Father of mercies.' The other style here is,

' *The God of all comfort.*' The life of a Christian is a mystery ; as in many respects, so in this, that whereas the flesh in him, though he be not altogether flesh, thinks him to be a man disconsolate, the spirit finds matter of comfort and glory. From whence the world begins discouragement and the flesh upbraiding, from thence the Spirit of God in holy St Paul begins matter of glory. They thought him a man neglected of God, because he was afflicted. No ! saith he, ' blessed be the God of all comfort.' Our comforts are above our discomforts. As the wisdom of the flesh is enmity to God and his Spirit in all things, so in this, in the judgment of the cross; for that which is bitterest to the flesh is sweetest to the spirit. St Paul therefore opposeth his comforts spiritual to his disgraces outward; and because it is unfit to mention any comfort, any good from God without blessing of him, that is the spring and fountain from whence we have all, he takes occasion, together with the mention of comfort, to bless God, ' the God of all comfort.'

The verse contains a wise prevention of scandal at the cross. St Paul was a man of sorrows if ever any was, next to Christ himself, and that [he] might prevent all scandal at his crosses, and disgraceful afflicted usage, he doth shew his comforts under the cross, which he would not have wanted to have been without his cross. Therefore he begins here with praising of God.

We praise God for favours, and indeed the comforts he had in his crosses were more than the grievance he had by them; therefore had cause to bless God; 'Blessed be God,' &c.

' The God of all comfort.' ' The God of comfort, and the God of all comfort.' We must give St Paul leave to be thus large, for his heart was full; and a full heart, a full expression. And he speaks not out of books, but from sense and feeling. Though he knew well enough that ' God was the Father of mercy and God of all comfort,' that way; yet these be words that come from the heart, come from feeling rather than from the tongue. They came not from St Paul's pen only. His pen was first dipped in his heart and soul when he wrote this. ' God is the Father of mercy, and God of all comfort.' I feel him so; he comforts me in all tribulations.

' The God of all comfort.' To explain the word a little. Comfort is either the thing itself, a comfortable outward thing, a blessing of God wherein comfort is hid, or else it is reasons; because a man is an understanding creature, reasons from which comfort is grounded; or it is a real comfort, inward and spiritual, by the assistance and strength of the Spirit of God, when perhaps there is no outward thing to comfort. And perhaps reasons and discourse are not present at that time, yet there is a presence of the Spirit that comforts, as we see ofttimes a man is comforted with the very sight of his friend, without discourse. To a man endued with reason, whose discomforts are spiritual, for the most part, in the soul, the very presence of a man that he loves puts much delight into him. What is God then? ' The God of comfort.' His very presence must needs comfort. Comfort is taken many other ways, but these are the principal, to this purpose.

1. First, *comfort is the thing itself.* There is comfort in every creature of God, and God is the God of that comfort. In hunger, meat comforts; in thirst, drink comforts; in cold, garments comfort; in want of advice, friends comfort, and it is a sweet comfort. ' God is the God of *all* comfort;' of the comfortable things. But besides the necessary things, every sense hath somewhat to comfort it. The eye, besides ordinary colours, hath delightful colours to behold; and so the ear, besides ordinary noise and sounds, it hath music to delight it; the smell, besides ordinary savours, it hath sweet flowers to refresh it; and so every part of the body, besides that which is ordinary, it hath somewhat to comfort it. Because God is nothing but comfort to his creature, if it be as it should be, he is God of these comforts, ' the God of all comfort,' of the comfort of outward things, of friends, &c.

2. So he is the God of the second comfort, *of comfortable reasons and arguments*. For a man, especially in inward troubles, must have grounds of comfort from strong reasons. God ministereth these. He is the God of these. For he hath given us his Scriptures, his word; and the comforts that are fetched from thence are strong ones, because they are his comforts. It is his word. The word of a prince comforts, though he be not there to speak it. Though it be a letter, or by a messenger, yet he whose word it is, is one that is able to make his word good. He is Lord and Master of his word. The word of God is comfortable, and all the reasons that are in it, and that are deduced from it, upon good ground and consequence, they are comfortable, because it is God's word. He is the God of all. And those comforts in God's word, and reasons from thence, they are wonderful in the variety of them. There is comfort from the liberty of a Christian laid out there, that he hath free access to the throne of grace; comfort from the prerogatives of a Christian, that he is the child of God, that he is justified, that he is the heir of heaven, and such like; comforts from the promises of grace, of the presence of God, of assistance by his presence. These things out of the word of God are wondrous plentiful. Indeed, the word of God is a breast of comfort, as the prophet calls it: 'Suck comfort out of the breasts of comfort,' Isa. lxvi. 11.

The books of God are breasts of comfort, wells of comfort. There are springs of comfort.

God's word is a paradise, as it were. In paradise, there were sweet streams that ran through; and in paradise stirred the voice of God, not only calling, 'Adam, where art thou?' terrifying of him, but the voice of God promising Adam the blessed seed, Gen. iii. 9.

So in the word of God, there is God rousing out of sin, and there is God speaking peace to the soul. There is a sweet current of mercy runs from the paradise of God; and there is the 'tree of life,' Rev. ii. 7, Christ himself, and trees of all manner of fruit, comforts of all sorts whatsoever. And there is no angel there, to keep the door and gate of paradise with a fiery, flaming sword. No! this paradise is open for all. And they are cruel tyrants that stop this paradise, that stop this fountain, as the papists do. As God is the God of comfort, so he is the God of comfort in that respect.

But this is not enough, to make him the God of comfort. We may have the word of God, and all the reasons from thence, from privileges and prerogatives, and examples, and yet not be comfortable, if

3. We have not the God of comfort, with the word of comfort, *the Spirit of God*, that must apply the comfort to the soul, and be the God of comfort there.

For there must be application, and working of comfort out of God's word upon the soul, by the Spirit. The Spirit must set it on strongly and sweetly, that the soul may be affected.

You may have a carnal man—he for fashion or custom reads the Scriptures, and he is as dead-hearted when he hath done as when he began. He never looks to the Spirit of comfort. There must be the Spirit of God, to work, and to apply comfort to the heart, and to teach us to discourse and to reason from the word; not only to shew the reasons of the word, but to teach us to draw reasons from the word, and to apply them to our particular state and condition. The Spirit teacheth this wisdom. And therefore it is well called the Comforter. 'I will send you the Comforter,' John xiv. 26. The poor disciples had many comforts from Christ, but because the Comforter was not come, they were not comfortable, but heavy. What was the reason? Because 'the Comforter was not come.' When the Holy Ghost was come, after the resurrection and ascension of Christ, when he had sent the Comforter, then they were so full of comfort, that they rejoiced that they 'were thought worthy to suffer anything for Christ,' Acts v. 41; and the more they suffered, the more joyful, and comfortable, and glorious they are.

You see what a comfort is. It is the things themselves, and the word, and reasons from it, and likewise the Spirit of God with the reasons, and with presence. Sometimes without any reasons, with present strength, God doth establish the soul. Together with reasons, there is a strengthening power of the Spirit, a vigour that goes with the Spirit of God, that joins with the spirit of the afflicted person. So whether it be the outward thing, as reasons and discourse, or the presence of the Spirit, God joining with our spirit, God is the God of that comfort, the 'God of all comfort.'

A comfort is anything that allays a malady, that either takes it away, or allays and mitigates it. A comfort is anything that raiseth up the soul. The comforts that we have in this life, they are not such as do altogether take away sorrow and grief, but they mitigate them. Comfort is that which is above a malady. It is such a remedy as is stronger to support the soul from being cast down over much with the grievance, whether it be grievance felt, that we are in the sense of such a grievance as is feared. When the soul apprehends anything, to set against the ill we fear that is stronger than it; when the soul hath somewhat that it can set against the present sense of the grievance that is stronger than it, though it do not wholly expel it, but the discomfort remains still in some degree, it may be said well to be a comfort.

The reason why I speak of this mitigation is, because in this life God never so wholly comforts his children, but there will be flesh left in them; and that will murmur, and there will be some resistance against comfort. While there are remainders of sin, there will be ground of discomfort, by reason of the conflict between the flesh and spirit.

For instance, a man hath some cross on him: what saith the flesh? God is mine enemy, and I will take such and such courses. I will not endure this. This is the voice of the flesh, of the 'old man.' What saith the spirit? Surely God is not mine enemy. He intends my good by these things. So while these fight, here is the 'flesh against the spirit,' Gal. v. 17. Yet here is comfort, because the spirit is predominant. But it is not fully comfort, because there is the 'old man' in him, that withstands comfort in the whole measure of comfort.

Therefore we must take this degree. We cannot have the full comfort till we come to heaven. There all tears shall be wiped from our eyes. In this world we must be content to have comfort with some grief. The malady is not wholly purged.

Sometimes God removes the outward grievance more fully. God helps many times altogether, as in sickness to health perfectly. But I speak not of that. Comfort is that which is opposite to misery, and it must be stronger, for there is no prevailing but by a stronger. When the agent is not above the patient, there is no prevailing. There is a conflict till one have got the mastery.

'The God of all comfort.' 'All,' that is, of all comfortable things, and of all divine reasons. It must be most substantial comfort. The soul in some maladies will not be comforted by philosophical reasons. Saith the heathen, ' The disease is stronger than the physic,' when he considers Plato's comforts and the like. So we may say of the reasons of philosophical men, Romanists, and moralists. When they come to terror of conscience, when they come to inward grievances, inward stings that are in a man, from a man's conscience (as all discomforts usually when they press hard, it is with a guilty conscience), what can all such reasons do? To say it is the state of other men, and it is in vain to murmur, and I know not what, such reasons as Seneca and Plato and others have, it will scarce still the conscience for a fit. They are ignorant of the root. Alas! how can they tell the remedy, when they know not the ground of the malady?

It must be God, it must be his word, his truth. The conscience must know it to be God's truth, and then it will comfort. God is the God of comfort, of the things, and of the reasons. They must be his reasons.

And he also is the author of that spiritual presence; he is with his children. When ' they are in the fire, he goes with them into the water,' as it is in Isa. xliii. 2. He is with them ' in the valley of death,' Ps. xxiii. 4. They shall find God with them to comfort them. So there is a kind of presence with God's comforts, and a banishing of all discomfort.

And this comfort is as large as the maladies, as large as the ills are. He is a God of comfort against every particular ill. If there be diverse ills, he hath diverse comforts; if they be long ills, he hath long comforts; if there be strong ills, he hath strong comforts; if there be new ills, he hath new comforts. Take the ills in what extent and degree you will, God hath somewhat to set against them that is stronger than they, and that is the blessed estate of God's children. He is the ' God of all comfort.'

St Chrysostom, an excellent preacher, yields me one observation upon this very place (*h*). It is the wisdom of a Christian to see how God describes himself, there being something in God answerable to whatsoever is ill in the world. The Spirit of God in the Scripture sets forth God fitting to the particular occasions. Speaking here of the misery and the disgraceful usage of St Paul, being taught by the Spirit of God, he considereth God as a ' Father of mercies' and a ' God of comfort.' Speaking of the vengeance on his enemies, the psalmist saith, ' Thou God of vengeance, shew thyself,' Ps. xciv. 1. In God there is help for every malady.

Therefore the wisdom of a Christian is to single out of God what is fitting his present occasion. In crosses and miseries, think of him as a ' Father of mercies;' in discomforts, think of him as a ' God of comfort;' in perplexities and distress, think of him as a God of wisdom; and oppression of others, and difficulties which we cannot wade out of, think of him as a God and Father Almighty, as a God of vengeance; and so every way to think of God appliable to the present occasion. And though many of us have no great affliction upon us for the present, yet we should. lay up store against the evil day; and therefore it is good to treasure up these descriptions of God, ' the Father of mercies, and God of all comfort.'

To explain the word a little. What doth he mean by ' God ' in this place?

That he is the God of comfort, that hath a further comfort in it, in the very title that is called the God of comfort. In that he is called the *God* of comfort, it implies two things.

1. First, it shews that *he is a Creator of it;* that he can work it out of what he will, out of nothing.

2. And then, that he can *raise it out of the contrary*, as he raised light out of darkness in the creation, and in the government of this world he raiseth his children out of misery. As he raised all out of nothing, order out of

confusion, so in his church he is the God of comfort. He can raise comfort out of nothing ; out of nothing that is likely to yield comfort. Put the case that there be neither medicine, nor meat, nor drink, nor nothing to comfort us in this world, as we shall have none of these things in heaven, he is the God of comfort that shall supply all our wants. As he shall then be all in all, so in this world, when it is by the manifestation of his glory. When Moses was forty days in the mountain, he wanted outward comforts ; but he had the God of comfort with him, and he supplied the want of meat and drink and all other comforts, because he is the God of all comfort. In him are all comforts originally and fundamentally ; and if there be none, he can create and make them of nothing.

God, as a God properly, makes something of nothing. That is to be a God ; for nothing but God can make something of nothing. Gods upon earth call men their creatures, in a kind of imitation of God ; but that is but a phrase that puffs them up. They are but gods in a kind of sense, and the other are but creatures in a kind of sense ; because, perhaps they have nothing in them, and in that sense, deservedly creatures. But it is proper to God, to make somewhat of nothing ; and so he is the ' God of comfort.' Where there is no comfort at all, he can raise comfort, as he made the world of nothing by his very word.

And which is more, it is the property of God as God, it is peculiar to God to make comfort out of that which is contrary. Therein he shews himself most to be a God of all. He can raise comfort out of discomfort, life out of death. When Christ had been three days in the grave, he raised him. As it is with the head of comfort, with the head of believers, so it is with every particular Christian. He raiseth them out of death. Those that sow in sorrow, they reap in joy. What cannot he do that can raise comfort out of discomfort ? and discomforts oftentimes are the occasions of the greatest comforts. Let a Christian go back to the former course of his life, and he shall find that the greatest crosses that ever he suffered will yield him most comfort, and who did this ? Certainly it must be God, that can raise all out of nothing, and that can make comfort not only out of comfortable creatures that are ordained for comfort ; but he can draw honey out of the lion's belly. ' Out of the eater came meat, and out of the strong came sweetness,' saith Samson in his riddle, Judges xiv. 14. When a honeycomb shall come out of the lion's belly, certainly this is a miracle, this may well be a riddle. This is the riddle of Christianity, that God who is the God of comfort, he raiseth comforts out of our chiefest discomforts. He can create it out of that which is contrary.

Therefore Luther's speech is very good, ' All things come from God to his church, especially in contraries ;' as he is righteousness, but it is in sin felt. He is comfort, but it is in misery. He is life, but it is in death. We must die before we live. Indeed, he is all, but it is in nothing, in the soul that feels itself to be nothing. There is the foundation for God to work on. Therefore the God of comfort can create comfort. If none be, he can make comfort. If the contrary be, he can raise contraries out of contraries. He is the ' God of all comfort.' Every word hath emphasis and strength in it.

' The God of all comfort.' Amongst divers other things that flow from hence, mark the order. He is the ' God and Father of Christ' first, and then the ' Father of mercy,' and ' the God of comfort.'

Take him out of this order, and think not of him as a God of comfort, but as a ' consuming fire,' Heb. xii. 29. But take the method of the text, now he is the ' God of comfort after he is the Father of Christ.' This being laid as a ground, the text itself as a doctrine, what subordinate truths arise hence ?

First of all, if God be ' God of all comfort,' there is this conclusion hence ; that, *whatsoever the means of comfort be, God is the spring of it.*

Christ is the conduit next to God ; for he is close to God. God is the God of Christ, and the Holy Ghost is usually the stream. The streams of comfort come through Christ the conduit ; from God the Father, the fountain, by the graces of the Spirit. But I speak of outward comforts. ' Blessed be God the Father, Son, and Holy Ghost.' All are comforters ! God the Father is the father of comfort ; the Holy Ghost is the comforter ; Christ Jesus likewise is the God of comfort. Whatsoever the outward means be, yet God the Father, Son, and Holy Ghost are the comforters. Take them together. That is the conclusion hence.

I observe it the rather, to cure a disposition to atheism in men that look brutishly to the thing. They look to the comfort, and never look to the comforter, even for outward comforts. Wicked men, their bellies are filled with the comforts of God, but it is with things that are comfortable, that are abstracted from the comforter. They care not for the root, the favour and mercy of God. So they have the thing, they care not.

Therefore they are not thankful to God, nor in their wants, they go not to the God of comfort. Why ? They think they have supply enough, they have friends, they have riches, that ' are their stronghold,' Ps. lxxxix. 40, and if they have outward necessaries to supply and comfort them, that is all they care for. As for the ' *God* of comfort,' they trouble not their hands* with him.

A Christian, whatsoever the comfort be, if it be outward, he knows that the God of comfort sends it, and that is the reason he is so thankful for all outward comforts. If they be the necessaries for this life, in meat he tastes the comfort of God, in drink he tastes the comfort of God, in the ornaments of this life he tastes the comfort of God. It is God that heats him with fire, it is God that clothes him with garments, it is God that feeds him with meat, it is God that refresheth his senses in these comforts.

Therefore the heathen, out of their ignorance, they made every thing a god that was comfortable, out of which they received comfort. They made a god of the fire, and of the water. These are but instruments of the God of comfort, but the heathen made gods of them. A Christian doth not so, but he sees God in them, and drives† these streams from the fountain. God is seen to be the God of comfort in them all.

Again, considering that God is ' the God of all comfort,' this should teach us as thankfulness to God, so prayer in the want of any comfort, that he would both give the thing, and the comfort of the thing. We may have the thing and the wrath of God with it. But thou that art the God of comfort, vouchsafe the outward comforts to us, and vouchsafe comfort with them. Thou that art the God of every thing, and of the comfort of the thing, vouchsafe both.

Again, if God be the God of all comfort whatsoever, then here is a ground of divers other truths ; as, for instance, that if we look for any comfort from the things, or from reasons and discourse, or from God, we should go to God in the use of the thing, before the use, after the use, at all times. Before the use, that God would suggest, either by reading, or hearing, &c.,

* Qu. ' heads.'—G. † Qu. ' derives ? ' = traces.—G.

reasons of comfort. In the use, that he would settle and seal comfort to our souls. Lord, I hear many sweet things. I read many comfortable things. These would affect a stone almost; yet unless thou set them on my soul, they will never comfort me. Thou art the God of comfort. The materials are from thee. But except with revelation and discovery thou join application, all will not comfort, unless with revelation and application thou open my soul to join with these comforts.

3. In the third place, *There must be a discovery and application, and an opening of the soul to them.* As there be divers flowers that open and shut with the sun, so the soul, by the Spirit of God, it opens to comforts. Though comforts be put close to the soul, if that do not open to them, there is no comfort given; for all is in the application. There is a double application, of the thing to the soul, and of the soul to the thing. God must do all.

Quest. What is the reason that many hear sermons, and read sweet discourses, and yet when they come to suffer crosses and afflictions they are to see ? *

Ans. They go to the stream, they cut the conduits from the spring, they go not to the well head, they see not the derivation of comfort. It is necessary for the deriving of comfort to the soul, to take the scales from the eye of the soul. They see not the necessity of a divine presence to apply it, and to lay it close to the soul, and to open the soul, to join the soul to those comforts. ' God is the God of all comfort.' If anything will stir up devotion much to pray to God, undoubtedly this will be effectual, that whatsoever the comfort be, whether it be outward things or reasons and discourses whatsoever, we may go to God that he would give it.

Well, this being so, if God be the ' God of all comfort,' the well of comfort, the Father of comfort, and hath remedies for every malady, then you see here whither to go. You see a Christian in all estates hath ground of comfort, for he is in covenant with the God of comfort.

Quest. You will say to me, What is the reason that Christians are no more comfortable, having the ' God of comfort' for their God ?

Ans. I answer: 1. It is partly *from ignorance.* We have remainders of ignorance, that we know not our own comfort. Satan doth veil the eye of the soul in the time of trouble, that we cannot see that there is a well of comfort. Poor Hagar, when she was almost undone for thirst, yet she had a fountain of water near hand; but she saw it not, she was so overtaken with grief, Gen. xxi. 15, *seq.* Ignorance and, 2, *passion* hinder the sight of comfort. When we give way so much to the present malady, as if there were no God of comfort in heaven, as if there were no Scripture that hath breasts of comfort, that is as full as a breast that is willing to discharge itself of comfort. As if there were no matter of comfort, they feed upon grief, and delight to flatter theirselves in grief, as Rachel, ' that mourned, and would not be comforted,' Mat. ii. 18. So out of a kind of ignorance, and passion, and wilfulness they will not be comforted.

And again, 3, *aggravating the grievance.* As Bildad saith, ' Are the comforts of God light to thee ?' Job xv. 11. These are good words, but my discomforts are greater, my malady is greater. So the comforts of the Holy Ghost, the comforts of God's Spirit, seem light to them. Ignorance, and passion, and dwelling too much, makes us neglect comfort. It makes us to see comfort to be no comfort in a manner. Mary, when Christ was before her eyes, they were so blubbered with tears, with fear that her Lord

* Qu. 'seek.'—G.

was lost, that she could not see him, even when he was before her, John xx. 15. So grief and passion hinder the soul so much from seeing God's comforts, that we see them not when they are before us, when they are present. So men are guilty of their own discomfort. It is their own fault.

4. Again, ofttimes *forgetfulness.* As the apostle saith, 'Have ye forgotten the consolation that speaks?' Heb. xii. 5. Have ye forgotten that every son that God chastiseth not is a bastard? Have ye forgotten? Insinuating that, if they had remembered this, it would have comforted them. 'Have ye forgotten?'

5. And then one especial cause is, that I spake of before, *the looking to things present,* forgetting the spring, the well-head of comfort, God himself; the looking too much to the means. Oh! say some, if they be in distress, if I had such a book, if I had such a man to comfort me, certainly it would be otherwise with me, I should be better than I am. Put case he were with thee, alas! he is not at the spring! It is the God of comfort that must comfort thee, man, in all thy distresses whatsoever. Therefore if thou attribute not more to God than to the creature, nay, than to an angel, if he were to comfort thee, thou shalt find no comfort. 'I, even I, am he that comforts thee,' Isa. li. 12. I am he that pardons thy sins, which is the cause of all discomfort. That is comfort! That is the sting of all. 'I am he that pardons thy sins.'

We, as criers, may speak pardon to the soul; but God must give it. We may speak comfort, but God must give it. He must say to the soul, 'I am thy salvation,' Ps. xxxv. 3. When men idolise any discourse in books, or any particular man over much (though we may value those that are instrumental above others, there may be a difference of gifts, but), the resting too much in the creature, it is an enemy to comfort; and some grow to that wilfulness in that kind, that they will neglect all because they have not that they would have, whereas if they would look to God, meaner means would serve the turn ofttimes, if they would go to the God of comfort.

VERSE 4.

' *Who comforteth us in all tribulation.*' Afflictions and crosses, as they are irksome in suffering, so they are likewise disgraceful; and as it was in the cross of Christ, there were * two things, torment and shame. The one he felt himself, the other he had from others; those two. Disgrace is proper to the cross. So it is in all the crosses that we suffer, there is some disgrace with it. Therefore St Paul, to prevent the scandal and disgrace of the cross, as I said before, he doth here begin with praising God even for crosses in the midst of them. 'Blessed be God, the Father of mercies, the God of all comfort; who comforteth us in all tribulations,' &c.

' Who comforteth us in all tribulation.' These words contain a making good of the former title, 'He is a God of comfort, and doth comfort; he is good, and doth good.' He fills up his name by his works. He shews what he is. The Scripture doth especially describe God, not in all things as he is in himself; but as he is, and works to his poor church. And they are useful terms, all of them. He is 'the Father of mercy,' because he is so to his church. He is the ' God of comfort,' because he

* Misprinted 'was.'—G.

is so to his people. Therefore he saith here, as he is ‘the God of comfort;’ so he doth comfort us in all tribulation. He doth not say, who keeps us out of misery. Blessed be the God of comfort, that never suffers us to fall into discomfort! No! but ‘blessed be the God of comfort, that comforts us *in all tribulation*.’ It is more to raise good out of evil, than not to suffer evil to be at all. It shews greater power, it manifests greater goodness, to triumph over ill, when it [is] suffered to be, and so not to keep ill from us, but to comfort us in it.

He doth not say for the time past, which hath comforted us, or which can comfort us if it please him. No! He doth it. It is his use.* He doth it alway. It springs from his love. He never at any instant or moment of time forgets his children. And he saith not, he doth comfort us in one or two, or a few tribulations; but he comforteth us in ‘*all tribulations*,’ of what kind or degree soever.

Obj. It may be objected, to clear the sense a little, he doth not alway comfort: for then there could be no time of discomfort.

Ans. I answer: He doth alway comfort in some degree; for take a Christian at the lowest, yet he hath so much comfort as to keep him from sinking. When he is at the depth of misery, there is a depth of mercy lower than he. ‘Out of the deep have I cried unto thee, Lord,’ Ps. cxxx. 1; and this is a comfort that he hath in the midst of discomforts, that he hath a spirit of prayer; and if not a spirit of prayer, yet a spirit of sighing and groaning to God, and God hears the sighs and groans of his own Spirit in his children. When they cannot distinctly pray, there is a spirit to look up to God. ‘Though thou kill me, yet will I trust in thee,’ saith Job, Job xiii. 15, in the midst of his miseries. So though God, more notoriously to the view of the world, sometime doth comfort before we come to trouble, that we may bear it the better, and sometime he doth comfort more apparently after we come out; yet notwithstanding, in the midst of discomforts, he doth alway comfort so far as that we sink not into despair. There is somewhat to uphold the soul. For when Solomon saith, ‘A wounded spirit, who can bear?’ Prov. xviii. 14; that is, none can bear it; it is the greatest grief. Then I would know, what keeps a wounded spirit from sinking that it doth not despair? Is it not a spirit stronger than the wounded spirit? It is† not God that is greater than the wounded conscience? Yes! Then there is comfort greater than the discomfort of a wounded conscience, that keeps it from despair. Those that finally despair, they are none of God’s. So that, take the words in what regard or in what sense you will, yet there is a sweet and comfortable sense of them, and the apostle might well say, he is the ‘God of all comfort, that doth comfort us in all tribulation.’

It is here a ground supposed, that *God’s children are subject to tribulation.*

We are subject here to tribulation of all kinds, for God comforts us in all our tribulations. We are here in a state, therefore, needing comfort, because we are in tribulation.

And the second is that God doth answer our state. *God doth comfort his children in all tribulation.*

And the ground is from himself. ‘He is the God of comfort.’ He doth but like himself, when he doth it. The God of comfort shews that he is so, by comforting us in all tribulations.

First, It is supposed that *in this world we are in tribulations.*

Indeed, that I need not be long in. We must, at one time or other, be

---

* That is, his ‘wont.’—G.   † Qu. ‘is it?’—Ed.

in tribulation, some or other. For though, in regard of outward afflictions, we are free from them sometimes, we have a few holidays, as we say; yet notwithstanding, there is in the greatest enlargements of God's children in this world, somewhat that troubles their minds. For either there is some desertion, God withholds comfort from them in some measure, he shews himself a stranger, which humbles them much; or else they have strong temptations of Satan, to sin by prosperity, &c., which grieves them as much as the outward cross; or else their grievance is, that they cannot serve God with that cheerfulness of spirit. Is there nothing, whoever thou art, that troubles thee as much as the cross in the day of affliction? Certainly there is somewhat or other that troubleth the soul of a Christian. He is never out of one grievance or other.

The life of a Christian is as a web, that is woven of good and ill. He hath good days and ill days; he hath tribulations and comforts. As St Austin saith very well, between these two, tribulation on our part, and comfort on God's part, our life runs between these two. Our crosses and God's comforts, they are both mingled together.

There is no child of God, but knows what these things mean, troubles either from friends or enemies, or both, domestical or personal, in body or mind, one way or other. That is supposed, and it were not an unproper argument to the text; for when he saith 'in all tribulations,' it is laid as a ground that every man suffers tribulation one way or other. But I shall have fitter occasion after to enlarge this.

Again we see here, that *God comforts his children in all tribulation.*

And his comforts are answerable to their discomforts, and beyond them. They are stronger to master all opposites whatsoever, and all grievances. There could be no comfort else. Alas! what are all discomforts, when God sets himself to comfort? When he will be a God of comfort, one look, one glance of his fatherly countenance in Jesus Christ, will banish all terrors whatsoever, and make even a very dungeon to be a paradise. 'He comforteth us in all tribulation.'

And this he doth, as you may perceive by the unfolding of the words, either by some outward thing applied to the outward want or cross, or by some inward reasons, that are opposite to the inward malady, or by an inward presence. His comforts are appliable to the tribulation, and to the strength, and length, and variety of it. We may know it by his course in this life. What misery are we subject to in this life! but we have comfort fit for it? So good is God.

We may reason thus very well. If so be that in our pilgrimage here, in this life of ours, which is but the gallery, as it were, to heaven; if in this short life, which is but a way or passage, we have, both day and night, so many comforts: in the very night, if we look up to heaven, we see what glorious things there are towards the earth here, on this side the heaven, the stars of the light,* &c. And if so be upon the earth there be such comforts, especially in the spring and summer time, if the very earth, the basest dregs of the world, yield such comfort and delights to all the senses, then a man may reason very strongly, what comforts shall we have at home? If God by the creatures thus comforts us in our outward wants, what are the inward comforts of his Spirit here to his children? and what are the last comforts of all, the comforts reserved at home, when God 'shall be all in all?' 1 Cor. xv. 28.

Now there are some drops of comfort conveyed in smells, some in gar-

* Qu. 'the light of the stars?'—ED.

ments, some in friends, some in diet; here a drop, and there a drop. But when we shall have immediate communion there with the God of comfort himself, what comforts shall we have there? God comforts us here, by providing for us, and giving us things that are comfortable.

Or by giving reasons and grounds of comfort, which are stronger than the reasons and grounds of discomfort, reasons from the privileges and prerogative of Christians, &c. The Scripture is full of them.

But likewise, which is the best of all, and most intended, the inward inspring of comfort, with the reasons and grounds, he inwardly conveys comforts to the soul, and strengtheneth and supports the soul. And he doth this not only by the application of the reasons, and the things that we understand, to the soul, but by opening the soul to embrace them. For sometime the soul may be in such a case as it may reject comfort, that ' the consolation of the Almighty,' Job xv. 11, may seem light to it. Sometime there may be such a disposition of soul, that the chiefest comforts in Scripture yield it no comfort. They are not embraced. The soul is shut to them. God provides reasons and grounds of comfort, and likewise he applies these comforts by his Spirit to the soul, and he inwardly warms and opens the soul to embrace comfort. He opens the understanding to understand, and the will and affections to embrace, or else there will be no comfort.

Many are like Rachel. Her children were gone, and it is said of her, ' She would not be comforted,' Mat. ii. 18. God is the ' God of comfort.' As he gives the matter and ground of comfort, and reasons out of his holy word above all discomforts; so by his Spirit he frames and fits the heart to entertain these, to take the benefit of them.

' He comforts us in all tribulation.' To comfort is to support the soul against the grievance past, or felt, or feared.

There may be some remainders of grief for what is past. Grief present presseth most, and grief feared. Now God comforteth, whatsoever the grievance is, by supporting the soul against it, as I said before.

We are in tribulation in this life, and yet in all tribulations God doth comfort us. To add to that I said before of this point, let us therefore go to God in all the means of comfort, because he is the God of it, and he must comfort us.

Therefore, when we send for divines, or read holy books, for we must use all means, we must not set God against his means, but join them together: to add that caution by the way.

We may not, therefore, necessitate the God of comfort, that because he comforts us, therefore we will neglect reading and prayer, and conference with them that God hath exercised in the school of Christ, who should speak comfort to the weary soul by their office.

No, no! *God and his means must be joined together.* We must trust God, but not tempt him. To set God against his means is to tempt him; that because he is the God of comfort, therefore we will use no means, no physician for the body or for the soul. This is absurd. He is the God of comfort in the means. He comforts us ' in all tribulation,' by means, if they be to be had.

If there be no means to be had, he is the God of comfort, he can create them; and if it be so far that there be no means, but the contrary, he is a God that can comfort out of discomfort, and can, as I said, make the greatest grounds of comfort out of the greatest discomforts. But he is a God of the means, if they be to be had. If there be none, then let us go to him, and say, Thou God of comfort, if thou do not comfort, none can comfort; if thou help not, none can help; and then he will help, and help strongly. It is necessary to look to God, whatever the means be. It is he that comforts by them. Therefore let him have the praise. If we have any friend, any comfort of the outward man, or any solace of the inward man, by seasonable speech, &c., blessed be the ' God of comfort' who hath sent this comforter; who hath sent me comfort by such, and such, let him have the praise. Whatsoever the means be, the comfort is his.

And that is the cause that many have no more comfort. They trust to the means over much, or neglect the means.

Again, if ' God comfort in all tribulation,' let Christians be ashamed to be overmuch disconsolate, that have the ' God of comfort' for their God, ' who comforteth in all tribulation.' ' Why art thou so cast down?' Ps. xlii. 11. ' Is there no balm in Gilead for thee? Jer. viii. 22. ' Is there not a God in Israel?' 1 Sam. xvii. 46. It is the fault of Christians; they pore too much on their troubles, they look all one way. They look to the grievance, and not to the comfort.

There is a God of comfort that answers his name every way in the exercise of that attribute to his church. Therefore Christians must blame themselves if they be too much cast down; and labour for faith to draw near to this God of comfort.

It should make them ashamed of themselves that think it even a duty, as it were, to walk drooping, and disconsolately, and deadly, to have flat and dead spirits. What! is this beseeming a Christian that is in covenant with God, that is the ' God of comfort,' and that answers his title in dealing with his children, that is ready to comfort them in all tribulation? What if particular comforts be taken from thee, is there not a God of comfort left? he hath not taken away himself. What if thou be restrained, and shut up from other comforts, can any shut up God's Spirit? can any shut up God and our prayers?

Is not this a comfort, that we may go to God alway? and he is with us in all estates and in all wants whatsoever? So long as we are in covenant with the ' God of comfort,' why should we be overmuch cast down?' ' Why art thou so troubled, O my soul?' Ps. xlii. 11. David checks his soul thrice together for distrust in God. He is thy God, the God of all comfort.

Quest. What course shall we take that we may derive to ourselves comfort from this God of comfort, who comforteth us in all our tribulations?

Ans. 1. Let us consider *what our malady and grievance is*, especially let us look to our spiritual grievance and malady, sin: for sin is the cause of all other evils. Therefore it is the worst evil. And sin makes us loathed of God, the fountain of good. It drives us from him, when other evils drive us to him; and therefore it is the worst evil in that sense too.

2. Again, in the second place, *look to the discomforts of sin*, especially in the discomforts of conscience of those that are awakened; and Satan useth that as a means to despair in every cross.

(1.) Therefore let us search and try our souls *for our sins;* for our chief discomforts are from sin. For, alas! what are all other comforts? and what are all other discomforts? If a man's conscience be quiet, what are all discomforts? and if conscience be on the rack, what are all comforts? The disquiet and vexation of sin is the greatest of all; because then we have to deal with God. When sin is presented before us, and the judgments of God, and God as an angry judge, and conscience is awaked and on the rack, what in the world can take up the quarrel and appease conscience, when we and God are at difference, when the soul speaks nothing but discomfort ?

In this case remember that God doth so far prevent objections in this kind from the accusations of conscience, that he reasons that he will comfort us, from that that conscience reasons against comfort. He doth this in the hearts of his children to whom he means to shew mercy : as we see in the poor publican. ' Lord, be merciful to me a sinner,' saith he, Luke xviii. 13. God taught him that reasoning. Nature would have taught him to reason as Peter did, ' Lord, depart from me, I am a sinful man,' Luke v. 8, and therefore I have nothing to do with God.

So our Saviour Christ, ' Come unto me, all ye that are weary and heavy laden,' Mat. xi. 28. They think, of all people they ought to run from God, they are so laden with sin, they have nothing to do with God. ' Oh, come unto me,' saith Christ. Therefore, when thy conscience is awakened with the sense of sin, remember what is said in the gospel, ' Be of good comfort, he calleth thee,' Mark x. 49 ; be thou of good comfort, thou art one that Christ calls, ' Come unto me, ye that are weary and heavy laden ;' and ' Blessed are those that mourn,' Mat. v. 4.

That which thou and the devil with thy conscience would move thee to use as an argument to run away, our Saviour Christ in the gospel useth as an argument to draw thee forward. He comes for such, ' to seek, and to save the lost sinners.' This is a faithful saying, saith St Paul, that ' Christ came to save sinners.' Therefore, believe not Satan. He presents God to the soul that is humbled, and terrified in the sight of sin, as cruel, as a terrible judge, &c. He hides the mercy of God from such. To men that are in a sinful course he shews nothing but mercy. Aye, but now there is nothing but comfort to thee that art cast down and afflicted in the sense of thy sins ; for all the comforts in the gospel of forgiveness of sins, and all the comforts from Christ's incarnation, the end of his coming in the flesh, the end of his death, and of all, is to save sinners.

Look thou, therefore, to the throne of mercy and grace, when thy conscience shall be awakened with the sense of sin, and Satan shall use that as an argument to draw thee from God. Consider the Scripture useth this as an argument to drive me to God, to allure me to him. ' Come unto me, all ye that are weary and heavy laden.' And ' Christ came to seek and to save that which was lost.' Luther, a man much exercised in spiritual conflicts, he confessed this was the balm that did most refresh his soul, ' God hath shut up all under sin, that he might have mercy upon all,' Rom. iii. 19. He shut up all under sin as prisoners, to see themselves under sin, and under the curse, that he might ' have mercy upon all ;' upon all those that are convinced with the sense and sight of their sins. He hath shut up all under sin, that he might have mercy upon all those that belong to him.

This raised up that blessed man. Therefore, let us not be much discomforted, but ' be of good comfort, Christ calls us.'

For such as are sinners, that are given to the sins of the tongue, and of the life, to rotten discourse, to swearing and such like, to such as mean to be so, and think their case good. Oh ! God is ' the God of comfort !' To such, as I said before, I can speak no comfort, nor the word of God speaks none. They must have another word and another Scripture ; for this word speaks no comfort to such that are sinful and wretched, and will be so, and justify themselves to be so.

All the judgments in the Scripture are theirs. Hell and damnation and wrath, that is their portion to drink.

We can speak no comfort to such, nor the word of God that we unfold. It hath not a drop of comfort for them. God will not be merciful to such as go on in wicked, rotten, scandalous courses, that because hell hath not yet taken them, they may live long, and so make a ' covenant with hell and death,' Isa. xxviii. 18, and bless themselves.

Oh ! but thou hast made no covenant with God, nor he hath made none with thee ; and hell and death have made no covenant with thee, though thou hast made one with them. But there are two words go to a covenant. Death and hell shall seize upon thee, notwithstanding thy covenant.

Those that will live in sin in despite of the ministry, in spite of afflictions, there is no comfort to such. I speak only to the broken heart, which are fit vessels for comfort. God is ' the God of comfort' to such. What shall we say, then, to such as, after they have had some evidence of their good estate, that they are Christians, are fallen into sin ? Is there any comfort for such ?

Yes. Doth not St Paul, in 2 Cor. v. 20, desire such to be ' reconciled to God ?' ' We are, as ambassadors of Christ, desiring you to be reconciled,' if you have sinned. So God hath comfort for those that have sinned. Christ knew that we should every day run into sins unawares. Therefore, he teaches us in the Lord's prayer to say every day, ' Forgive us our debts, our trespasses,' Mat. vi. 12. There is ' balm in Gilead,' there is mercy in Israel, for such daily trespasses as we run into.

Therefore, let none be discouraged, but fly presently to the ' God of comfort and Father of mercies.' And think not that he is weary of pardoning, as man is, for he is infinite in mercy ; and though he be the party offended, yet he desires peace with us.

Caution. But yet, notwithstanding that we shall not love to run into his books, he doth, with giving the comfort of the pardon of sin, when we fall into it, add such sharp crosses, as we shall wish we had not given him occasion to correct us so sharply. We shall buy our comfort dear. We had better not have given him occasion.

God forgave the sin of David after he had repented, though he were a good man before ; but David bought the pleasure of his sin dear. He wished a thousand times that he had never given occasion to God to raise good out of his evil, to turn his sin to his comfort. Yet God will do this, because God would never have us in a state of despair.

2. For *other grievances* besides sin, the comforts that we are to apply are more easy, and they are infinite, if we could reckon the particular comforts that God comforts his children withal.

It is good to have general comforts ready for all kind of maladies and grievances, and* this poor, wretched life of ours, in our absence from God, is subject to.

(1.) As, for instance, that general comfort, *the covenant of grace.* That is a spring of comfort, that God is our God and Father in Christ. What can come from a gracious and good God in covenant with us but that which is good ?—nothing but what is favourably good, I mean. For the covenant is everlasting. When God takes once upon him to be our Father in covenant, he is so for ever. *Dum castigas pater, &c.* While he corrects, he is a Father ; and when he smiles upon us, he is a Father.

God in the covenant of grace takes upon him a relation that ever holds.

* Qu. ' that ?'—ED.

As he is for ever the Father of Christ, so he is for ever the Father of those that are members of Christ; and whatsoever comes from the Father of mercy, whether he correct or smile, whatsoever he doth, is in mercy.

(2.) Again, in the midst of any grievance remember *the gracious promise of mitigation*, 1 Cor. x. 13. 'God will not suffer us to be tempted above our strength, but he will give an issue to the temptation.' He will give a mitigation, and either he will raise our strength to the temptation, or he will bring the temptation and trial to our strength. He will fit them, and this is a comfort.

(3.) There is comfort, likewise, in all troubles whatsoever, *of the presence of God*. God will be present with us if once we be in covenant with him. He will be present in all trials to assist us, to strengthen us, to comfort us, to raise our spirits. And if God be present, he will banish all discomforts; for God is light, and where light is, darkness vanisheth. Now God, being the Father of light, that is, of all comfort, where he is present he banisheth discomfort in what measure he is pleased to banish it. Therefore David often reasoneth from the presence of God to the defiance of all troubles, Ps. iii. 6, 'If God be with me, I will not fear ten thousand that are against me.' And in Ps. xxiii. 4, 'Though I walk in the valley of the shadow of death, I will not fear, for thou art with me.' And 'if God be with us, who can be against us?' Rom. viii. 33, 34. 'And when thou passest through the fire, I will be with thee,' &c., Isa. xliii. 2. I will be with thee, not to keep thee out, but to uphold thee, as he did the martyrs. There was a fire of comfort in them above that fire that consumed their bodies; and, as we see, he was with the three children. There was 'a fourth, like the Son of God,' Dan. iii. 25.

So in all tribulations there is another with us, that is, the Spirit of God, that comforts us in all, and is present with us in all. The goldsmith, when he puts the wedge into the fire, he stands by till the dross be consumed. So God is with his children in the furnace of affliction. He brings them into affliction; he continues with them in affliction; and he brings them at last out of affliction. The presence of God is a main and a grand comfort in all tribulation.

(4.) Besides, in all that befalls us whatsoever, *consider the end*. All is for a good end. 'All things work together for the best to them that love God,' saith St Paul, Rom. viii. 28. Why do we endure physic? Because we know the physician is wise, and he is our friend, and he doth it to carry away burdensome, hurtful humours. We shall be better and lighter afterwards. Do we do this in our common course in the things of this life? Grace will much more certainly teach us to do it; to reason, It is from a father, and it is for my good. Let us look whence it comes and what it tends to, with the promise of mitigation and of God's presence in our troubles. These are main comforts, if we could think of them, if the devil did not take them out of our memory.

(5.) And for the fifth * ground of comfort that God doth comfort us withal in all tribulations, it is the promise of *final deliverance and final comfort* for ever. If none will raise our souls, that will, when we shall consider that it will not be long.

'The short afflictions in this world bring an eternal weight of glory,' 2 Cor. iv. 17. There will be a final deliverance. Life itself, that is, the subject that receives affliction, that is short. Our life is but a moment, 2 Cor. iv. 17. Therefore, our afflictions must be short.

* Misprinted 'first.'—G.

Life is longer than discomforts. There is but a piece of our life subject to miseries; and if that be but a vapour, but a moment, and as a point between eternity before and eternity after, what are the miseries of this life? Certainly they are but for a moment.

Therefore, the promise of final deliverance, when all tears shall be wiped from our eyes, this should comfort us, if nothing else would. This is the way, therefore, whereby God usually comforts, by suggesting the heads and springs of comfort.

And, indeed, there is a daily method of comforting, whereby we may comfort ourselves in all crosses, if we would use that daily method and order of comfort. As there is a kind of diet to keep the body in temper, so there is a kind of spiritual diet to keep the soul in temper, in a course of comfort, unless it be when God takes liberty to cast down for some special end, as we see in Job.

Therefore, let us take this course; for God, as he comforteth us, so he comforts us as understanding creatures, he useth our understanding to consider how we should comfort ourselves; and after we are once in a state of comfort, if we be not wanting to ourselves, there is no great difficulty to keep our comfort. There are means to keep daily comfort. God hath provided them, and he will be present to make good all his comforts. Grant it, therefore, that we are in the covenant of grace, that God is our Father in Christ, and we take him to be our God, to be all-sufficient, then, to keep ourselves in a daily temper for comfort,

[1.] Every day *keep our souls tender*, that we may be capable of comfort; keep the wound open, that we may receive balm, that there grow not a deadness upon the heart, considering that while we live here there is alway some sin in us, that must be wrought out by some course or other. Let us try and search our souls, what ill is in the wound; let us keep it open and tender, that there may be a fitness for mercy, to receive the balm of comfort, which will not be if we slubber over. Certainly it is an excellent course every day to search our hearts and ways, and presently to apply the balm of comfort, the promise of pardon. Take the present, when we have searched the wound, to get pardon and forgiveness daily. As we sin daily, Christ bids us ask it daily.

This will make us fit for comfort, by discerning the estate of our souls, and the remainders of corruption. That which sharpens appetite and makes the balm of God to be sweet indeed, is the sense of, and the keeping open of our wound. A daily search into our wants and weaknesses, a daily fresh sight of the body of sin in us, and experience how it is fruitful in ill thoughts, and desires, and actions, this will drive us to a necessity of daily comfort.

And certainly a fresh sight of our corruptions, it is never without some fresh comfort. We see St Paul, Rom. vii., he sets himself to this work, to complain of his indisposition, by reason of sin in him; and how doth he end that sight and search into his own estate? He ends in a triumphing manner, ' Thanks be to God, through Jesus Christ our Lord: There is no condemnation to them that are in Christ Jesus,' verse 25; after he had complained, ' Oh, miserable man that I am! who shall deliver me from this body of death?' There can be no danger in a deep search into our ways and hearts, if this be laid as a ground before, that there is more supply and heavenly comfort in God, and the promises of God, than there can be ill in our souls. Then the more ill we find in ourselves, the more we are disposed to fetch grounds of comfort from God.

[2.] And together with this searching of our souls, and asking daily pardon, let us for the time to come *renew our covenant with God*, that we may have the comfort of a good conscience to get pardon for our sins past, and renew our resolutions for the time to come.

[3.] And withal, that we may use an orderly course of comfort, let us every day *feed on Christ*, the food of life; let us every day feed upon something in Christ. Consider the death of Christ, the satisfaction he hath made by his death, his intercession in heaven. His blood runs afresh, that we may every day feed on it.

We may run every day into new offences against the law, to new neglect of duty, into new crosses; let us feed upon Christ. He came into the world ' to save sinners,' 1 Tim. i. 15, to make us happy, with peace of conscience here, and with glory afterward. Let us feed on Christ daily. As the body is fed with cordials, so this feeds, and comforts, and strengthens the soul.

This is to live by faith, to lead our lives by faith, to feed on Christ every day.

[4.] And likewise, if we will keep our souls in a perpetual temper of comfort, let us every day *meditate of some prerogatives of Christians*, that may raise our souls; let us single out some or other. As for example, that excellent prerogative to be the ' sons of God,' 1 John iii. 2. What love! saith the apostle, that we, of rebels and traitors, in Christ should be made the sons of God! That of slaves, we should be made servants; of servants, sons; of sons, heirs; and of heirs, fellow-heirs with Christ: what prerogative is this, that God should give his Son to make us, that were rebels, sons, heirs, and fellow-heirs with Christ! Gal. iv. 7. And to consider what follows upon this liberty, that we have from the curse of the law, to go to God boldly, to go to the throne of grace through Christ, our elder Brother, by prayer; to think of eternal life as our inheritance; to think of God above as our Father. Let us think of our prerogatives of religion, adoption, and justification, &c.

Upon necessity we are driven to it, if we consider the grievances of this world, together with our corruptions. Our corruptions, and afflictions, and temptations, and desertions, one thing or other, will drive us to go out of ourselves for comfort, to feed on the benefits by Christ. And consider what he hath done. It is for us, the execution of his office, and all for us; what he is, what he did, what he suffered, what procured, all is for us. The soul delighting itself in these prerogatives, it will keep the soul in a perpetual estate of comfort. Therefore the Scripture sets forth Christ by all terms that may be comfortable. He is the door to let us in. ' He is the way, the truth, and the life,' John xiv. 6, the water and the bread, &c. In sin, he is our righteousness; in death, he is our life; in our ignorance, he is our way; in spiritual hunger and thirst, he is the bread and water of life: he is all in all. And if we cannot think of some prerogative of Christianity, then think of some promise. As I said before, think of the covenant of grace. There is a spring of comfort in that, that God in Christ is our God to death, and for ever; and that promise I speak of, that ' All things shall work for the best,' Rom. viii. 28.

Let us every day think of these things, and suggest them to our own souls, that our souls may be affected with them, and digest them, that our souls and they may be one, as it were.

[5.] And every day stir up our hearts *to be thankful*. A thankful heart can never want comfort; for it cannot be done without some comfort and cheerfulness. And when God receives any praise and glory, he answers it with comfort. A thankful heart is alway comfortable.

[6.] And let us stir up our hearts *to be fruitful in the holy actions.* The reward of a fruitful life is a comfortable life. Besides heaven, God alway in this life gives a present reward to any good action. It is rewarded with peace of conscience. Besides, it is a good foundation against the evil day. Every good action, as the apostle saith to Timothy, it ' lays up a good foundation,' 1 Tim. vi. 19. The more good we do, the more we are assured that our faith is not hypocritical, but sound and good, and will hold out in the time of trial. It will be a good foundation that we have had evidence before, that we have a sound and fruitful faith.

What do wicked men, careless, sinful creatures, that go on in a course of profaneness and blasphemy, &c.? They lay a ground of despair, a ground of discomfort, to be swallowed up in the evil day. Then conscience will be awaked at the last, and Satan will be ready to join with conscience, and conscience will seal all the accusations that Satan lays against them ; and where is the poor soul then ? As it is with them, so, on the contrary, the Christian soul that doth good, besides the present comfort of a good conscience, it lays a good foundation against the time to come ; for in the worst times, it can reason with itself, My faith is not fruitless, I am not an hypocrite. Though the fruits of it be weak, and mixed with corruptions, yet there is truth in them. This will comfort us when nothing else will.

Therefore let us every day be setting ourselves in some good way ; for comfort is in comfortable courses, and not in ill courses. In God's ways we shall have God's comforts. In those ways let us exercise the spiritual strength we have ; let us pray to God, and perform the exercise of religion with strength, shew some zeal in it ; let us shew some zeal against sin, if occasion be, if it be in God's work, in God's way. Let a man set himself upon a good work, especially when it is in opposition ; for the honour of God, and the peace of his conscience. Presently there is comfort upon it.

[7.] And that we may not be discouraged with the imperfection of our performances, one way of daily comfort is, *to consider the condition of the covenant of grace between God and us.* In the covenant of grace, our performances, if they be sincere, they are accepted ; and it is the perfection of the gospel, sincerity. Sincerity will look God in the face with comfort, because he is with the upright. So much truth in all our dealings, so much comfort.

[8.] And with sincerity labour *for growth*, to grow better and better. God in the gospel means to bring us to perfection in heaven by little and little. In the law there was present perfection required ; but in the gospel God requires that we should come to perfection by little and little, as Christ by little and little satisfied for our sins, and not all at once. In the condition of the covenant of grace, we must live and grow by grace, by little and little, and not all at once. The condition of the covenant of grace is not to him that hath strength of grace in perfection. But if we believe and labour to walk with God, if there be truth of grace, truth goes for perfection in the covenant of grace. We should labour for sound knowledge of the covenant of grace, that now we are freed from the rigour, as well as from the curse of the law ; that though we have imperfections, yet God will be our Father, and in this condition of imperfection he will be a pardoning Father, and looks on our obedience, though it be feeble, and weak, and imperfect, yet, being the obedience of children in the covenant of grace, and he accepts of what is his own, and pardons what is ours.

[9.] And every day labour *to preserve the comforts of the Spirit* that we have, not to grieve the Spirit; for comfort comes with the Spirit of God, as heat accompanies the fire. As wheresoever fire is, there is heat; so wheresoever the Spirit of God is, there is comfort; because the Spirit of God is God, and God is with comfort. Wheresoever comfort is, God is; and wheresoever God is, there is comfort. If we would have comfort continually every day, let us carefully watch that we give way to the Spirit of God, by good actions, and meditations, and exercises.

And by no means grieve the Spirit, or resist the Spirit, for then we resist comfort. If we speak any thing that is ill, we lose our comfort for that time. Conscience will check us. We have grieved the Spirit. If we hear any thing with applause, and are not touched with it, we lose our comfort; conscience will tell us we are dead-hearted, and not affected as we should be. There is a great deal of flesh and corruption that is affected with such rotten discourse. And so if we venture upon occasions, we shall grieve the Spirit, either if we speak somewhat to satisfy others that are nought,* or if we hear somewhat that is ill from others. Want of wisdom in this kind, doth make us go without comfort many times : want of wisdom to single out our company, or else [if we be with such, to do that that may please them, and grieve the Spirit, and hinder our own comfort.

[10.] These and such like directions, if we would observe, we might walk in a course of comfort. The God of comfort hath prescribed this *in the book of comfort.* These are the courses for God's children, to walk in a comfortable way, till they come to heaven. More especially, if we would at any time take a more full measure of comfort, then take the *book of God into your hand.* Those are comforts that refresh the soul. Single out some special portion of Scripture, and there you shall have a world of comfort, as, for example, let a man single out the Epistle to the Romans. If a man be in any grievance whatsoever, what a world of comfort is there, fitting for every malady! There is a method how to come to comfort.

There St Paul, in the beginning, first strips all men of confidence of any thing in themselves, and tells them that no man can be saved by works, Jews nor Gentiles, but all by the righteousness of God in Christ. ‘All are deprived of the glory of God,’ Rom. iii. 19, Jews, and Gentiles, everybody. And when we are brought to Christ, he tells us, in the latter end of the third chapter, that by Christ we have the forgiveness of all our former sins whatsoever. ‘ He is the propitiation for our sins.’ In the fourth chapter he comforts us by the example of Abraham and David, that they were justified without works by faith, not by works of their own, but by laying hold of the promises of comfort and salvation merely by Christ. And all that St Paul saith is ‘ written for us,’ 1 Cor. x. 11. But in the first chapter especially, because all the miseries of this life come from the ‘ first Adam.’ Because we are children of the ‘ first Adam,’ death and misery comes from that. He opposeth the comfort in the ‘ second Adam,’ and he shews that there is more comfort by the second Adam, than there is discomfort by the first. Righteousness in the second Adam ‘ reigns to life everlasting,’ Rom. v. 17, and glory. Sin and misery came by the first, but there is the pardon of all sin by the second Adam. He doth excellently oppose them in the latter end of that chapter. In the beginning of the fifth chapter he shews there the method, and descent of joy, ‘ Being justified by faith, in Christ, we have peace with God,’ Rom. v. 1. Considering that by the righteousness of Christ we are freed from sin, ‘ We have peace with

* Qu. ‘ naught ? ’—ED.

God through Jesus Christ our Lord,' Rom. v. 1. And ' we have boldness to the throne of grace, and we rejoice in tribulation : knowing that tribulation brings forth patience ; and patience, experience ; and experience, hope,' Rom. v. 4. He sets himself there of purpose to comfort in all tribulation, and he saith, in these things we rejoice, ' We rejoice in tribulation.'

Aye, but for our sins after our conversion, after we are in the state of grace, what comfort is there for them ? There is excellent comfort in the fifth of the Romans. ' If when we were enemies he gave his Son for us :' if he saved us by the death of Christ when we were enemies, much more, Christ being alive, and in heaven, he will keep it for us ; and keep us to salvation now, when we are friends, seeing he died for us when we were enemies. Aye, but the remainders of corruption in this world trouble us. That troubles our comfort, the combat between the flesh and the Spirit. Would you see comfort for that ? You shall see it in Romans vii. 24, 25. ' Oh, miserable man, who shall deliver me from this body of death ? Thanks be to God through Jesus Christ our Lord.' So he shews there what way to have comfort in the combat between the flesh and the spirit, to search into our corruptions, to lay them open to God by confession.

And then, in the beginning of the eighth chapter, saith he, ' There is no condemnation to them that are in Christ Jesus,' ver. 1. Though there be sin, yet there is no condemnation ; though there be this conflict between the flesh and the spirit. So he comforts them. And for the afflictions that follow our corruptions in this life, there is a treasure of comfort against them in that chapter ; for doth he not say, ' if we suffer with him, we shall reign with him,' ver. 17. And the same ' Spirit helps our infirmities, and teacheth us how to pray ?' ver. 26. We can never be uncomfortable if we can pray ; but there is a promise of the Spirit that stirs up sighs, and ' groans that cannot be expressed,' ver. 26, and a Christian hath alway a spirit of prayer, at the least of sighs and groans ; and God hears the sighs of his own Spirit.

And what a grand comfort is that, that I named before, verse 28, ' All things work for the best to them that love God.' And ' if God be with us, who can be against us.' ver. 33. And he sends us to Christ. If Christ be dead, ' or rather risen again, who shall lay anything to our charge ?' Christ is ' ascended to heaven, and makes intercession at the right hand of God,' ver. 34. Though Satan lay our sins to our charge, Christ makes intercession in heaven at the right hand of God. He makes continual intercession for our continual breaches with God. Who shall lay anything to our charge ? Aye, but all that power of hell and sin ! and all labour to separate us from God, to breed division between God and us. In the latter end of that chapter he bids defiance to all, what shall ' separate us from the love of God in Christ ?' ver. 35. It shall separate his love from Christ first. God's love is found in Christ. He shall cease to love Christ if he cease to love us. Aye, but we may afterward fall into an uncomfortable case. For that he saith, ' neither things present, nor things to come, shall be able to separate us,' ver. 38.

What an excellent spring of comfort is there in that reasoning, verse 32, ' If God spared not his own Son, but gave him to death for us all, how shall he not with him give us all things else.' How many streams may be drawn from that spring ! ' If God spared not his own Son, but gave him to death for us all, how shall he not with him give us all things else' in this world necessary, grace, provision, and protection, till he have brought us to heaven ? If he have given Christ, he will give all. Whatsoever is written, is written for our comfort. I name * this epistle, because I would name one instance for all. ' All is written for our comfort,' as he saith after in the same epistle, xv. 4. The written word, or the word unfolded ; the end of preaching, is especially to comfort. The chirurgeon opens a wound, and the physician gives a purge, but all is to restore at the last. All that the chirurgeon aims at, is to close up the wound at the last. So all our aim is to comfort. We must cast you down, and shew you your misery that you are in, and shew you, that if you continue in that course, hell and damnation belongs to you. But this is to make you despair in yourselves, and to fly to the God of comfort. The law is for the gospel. All serve to bring the soul to comfort.

Therefore go to the word of God, any portion, the Psalms or any special part of the Scripture ; and that, by the Spirit of God, will be a means to raise the soul. The Spirit in the word, joining with the Spirit in us, will make a sweet close together, and comfort us in all tribulation.

[11.] And *have recourse daily to common principles.* All the principles of religion serve for comfort, especially the articles of the creed. ' I believe in God the Father Almighty.' What a spring of comfort is in that ! What can befall from a father, but it shall turn to good, and by a Father Almighty ? Though he be never so strongly opposed, yet he will turn it to good. He is a ' Father Almighty.' And the articles of Christ, every article hath ground of daily comfort, of his abasement. In Christ, I see myself. He is my surety, ' the second Adam.' I see my sins crucified with him. This is the way to reap comfort when the conscience is disquieted. When I look upon my sins, not in my own conscience, but take it out there, and see it in Christ dying, and crucified, in the articles of abasement to see our sin, and misery, all in Christ.† For he stood there as surety, as a public person for all. What a comfort is this ! When I see how Christ was abased, I see my own comfort, for he was my surety. If my sins being laid on him, who was my surety, could not condemn him, or keep him in the grave, but overcame sin that was laid to his charge, surely‡ I shall overcome my corruptions. Nothing that I have shall overcome me, because it could not overcome Christ my surety. His victory is mine.

And so, if the soul be in any desolation and discomfort, all the articles of his ' glorification and exaltation.' His rising again acquits the soul. Therefore my sins are satisfied for, because my surety is out of prison. And his ascending into heaven shews my triumph. He led captivity captive. And the enemies that are left are for the trial of my faith, and not to conquer me. For Christ hath ' led captivity captive,' Ps. lxviii. 18, and is ascended into heaven. He led all in triumph, and sits at the right hand of God, to rule his church to the end of the world. He sits for me to overcome my enemies, as St Paul saith excellently, Rom. viii. 33, ' Who shall lay anything to the charge of God's people ? It is Christ that died, or rather, that is risen again, who sits at the right hand of God.'

And if we be troubled for the loss of a particular friend, there is comfort in that article of the ' communion of saints.' There are those that have more grace, and that is for me. If my own prayers be weak, ' I believe the communion of saints,' and have the benefit of their prayers. Every one that saith ' Our Father' brings me in, if I be in the covenant of grace, and of the communion of saints. If I have weaknesses in myself, ' I believe in the Holy Ghost,' the comforter of God's elect, and my comforter. If I

---

* Misprinted ' mean'.—G.   † Articles I. and IV., and *infra* IX.—G.
‡ That is, ' assuredly.'—G.

fear death, ' I believe the resurrection of the body.' If I fear the day of judgment, ' I believe that Christ shall be my judge.' He shall come to judge the quick and the dead. In all the miseries of this life, considering that they are but short, ' I believe the life everlasting.' So that indeed if we would dig to ourselves springs of comfort, let us go to the articles of our faith, and see how there are streams of comfort from every one answerable to all our particular exigencies and necessities whatsoever.

And to close up this point, remember, whatsoever means we use, what prerogative soever we think of, whatsoever we do, remember we go to the God of comfort, and desire him to bless his word in the ministry, and desire him to work in the communion of saints, with his Spirit to warm our hearts. Alway remember to carry him along in all, that we may have comfort from ' the God of comfort, who comforteth in all tribulations.'

Next words are,

' *That we may able to comfort them which are in any trouble.*' These words shew the end why God doth comfort us in all tribulation. One main end is, *that we should be comforted in ourselves.* That is the first. And then, that we, being comforted ourselves, from that ability *should be able to derive* comfort to others.* ' We are comforted in all tribulations, *that we should be able to comfort them that are in any tribulation.*'

It is not St Paul's case only, and great men in religion, ministers and the like. It is not their lot and portion alone to be persecuted and troubled, but

Obs. We are all in this life subject to disquiets and discomforts.

Every one, ' whosoever will live godly in Christ Jesus, must suffer persecution,' 2 Tim. iii. 12. Therefore the apostle saith not only our† tribulation ; but that ' we may be able to comfort them that are in any trouble.' Trouble is the portion of all God's children one with another. I do but touch that by the way. But that which I shall more stand upon, it is the end, one main end why God comforteth, especially ministers: it is, *that they should be able to comfort others* with the comforts that God hath comforted them withal. ' That we may be able,' &c. Now you must conceive that this ability, it is not ability alone without will and practice, as if he meant, God hath given me comfort that I might be able to comfort others if I will. That is not God's end only, that we may be able, but that we may exercise our ability, that it may be ability in exercise ; as God doth not give a rich man riches to that end that he may be able to relieve others if he will. No ! But if thou be a child of God, he gives thee ability and will too, he gives an inward strength. So the meaning here is, not that we may be able to comfort others if we will, but that we may be both able and willing to comfort others.

And to comfort others not only by our example, that because we have been comforted of God, so they shall be comforted. It is good, but it is not the full extent of the apostle's meaning ; for then the dead examples should comfort as well as the living. And indeed that is one way of comfort, to consider the examples of former times. But the apostle's meaning is, that I should comfort them not only by my example of God's dealing with me, that they should look for the like comfort. That is but one degree. His meaning is further therefore, that we should be able to comfort them by sympathizing with them ; as indeed it is a sweet comfort to those that are in distress when others compassionate their estate.

* That is, ' communicate.'—G   † Qu., ' one ?'—ED.

And not only so, by our example and sympathy with them, but likewise that we may be able to comfort them by the inward support, and strength, and light that we have found by the Spirit of God in ourselves. That is that that will enable us to comfort others, from that very support and inward strength that we have found from God ; by those graces, and that particular strength and comfort that we have had. When there is a sweet expressing of our inward comfort to them, shewing something in our comfort that may raise them up, in the like troubles that we were in, then the comfort will not be a dead comfort, when it comes from a man experienced. Personated comfort, when a man takes upon him to comfort, that only speaks comfort, but feels not what he speaks, there is little life in it. We are comforted that we may comfort others, with feeling, having been comforted ourselves before, with feeling, and comfortable apprehensions in ourselves. The point considerable in the first place, to make way to the rest, is this, that

Doct. God's children, they have all of them interest in divine comforts.

St Paul was comforted, that he might comfort others. Divine comforts belong to all. They are the portion of all God's people. The meanest have interest, as well [as] the greatest. There is the same spiritual physic for the poorest subject, and the greatest monarch. There is the same spiritual comfort for the meanest, and for the greatest Christian in the world. St Paul hath the same comfort as St Paul's children in the faith. What is the reason that they are communicable thus to all ? that they lie open to all ?

Reason 1. God is the God and Father of *all light and comfort.* Christ is the Saviour of all. All the privileges of religion belong to all equally. All are sons and heirs, and all are alike redeemed. ' The brother of low degree, and the brother of high degree,' James i. 9. They may differ in the references and relations of this life, but in Christ all are alike.

Reason 2. Besides, *it is the nature of spiritual privileges and blessings.* They are communicable to all alike without impairing. The more one hath, the less another hath not. All have an equal share. Every one hath interest entire ; every one hath all, without loss or hindrance to others. As for instance, the sun, every particular man hath all the good the sun can do, as well as all the world hath. It is peculiarly and entirely every man's own. Every man *in solidum* hath the use of it. The sun is not one man's more than another. As a public fountain or conduit, every man hath as much right in it as another. So in religion, the graces, and privileges, and favours, they lie open as the prerogatives and privileges of all God's children ; and that is the excellency of them. In the things of this life it is not so. They are not common to all alike. There is a loss in the division. The more one hath, the less another hath. And that is the reason why the things of this life breed a disposition of pride and envy. One envies another, because he wants that that another hath ; and one despiseth another, because he hath more than another hath ; but in the comforts of God's Spirit, and the prerogatives that are the ground of those comforts, all have interest alike.

Only the difference is in the vessels they bring. If one man bring a large vessel, a large faith, he carries more ; and another that brings a less faith carries less, but it lies open to all alike. As St Cyprian saith, we carry as much from God as we bring vessels. But all have interest alike in divine comforts.

Therefore among Christians there is little envy, because in the best things, which they value best, all may have alike ; and that which one desires, another may have as much as he. He knows he hath never the less.

Use. The point is *comfortable to all, even to the meanest,* and to them especially, that howsoever there be a difference between others and them in . outward things, that cease in death (for all differences shall cease ere long between us and others), yet the best things are common. In this life those things that are necessary, they are common, as the light, and the elements, fire, and water, &c. ; and those are necessary* that are not common. But especially in spiritual things, the best things are common. Let no man be discomforted, if he be God's child. Comfort belongs to him, as well as to the greatest apostle. The chiefest comforts belong to him as well as to the chiefest Christian. Therefore, let us envy none, nor despise none in this respect.

In the next place, we may observe here, hence, that *though these comforts be common, yet God derives these comforts commonly by the means of men.*

This is God's order in deriving these comforts to the soul. He comforts one, that another may be comforted. Not that the comforts themselves that join with our spirits come from men, but that, together with the speech and presence of men whom we love and respect, and in whom we discern the appearance of the Spirit of God to dwell, together with the speech of persons in whom the Spirit is strong and powerful, the Spirit of God ioins, and the Spirit raiseth the soul with comfort. So the Spirit comforteth, by comforting others, that they may comfort us.

This is not only true of ministers, but it is true of Christians, as Christians. For St Paul must be considered, in something as an apostle, in something as a Christian, in something as a minister of Christ. As an apostle, he had the care of ' all the churches,' &c., 2 Cor. xi. 28. As a Christian, he comforted and exhorted others. One Christian ought to comfort another. Therefore he would have done it as a Christian, if he had not been an apostle. And in something he is to be considered as a minister of Christ, as a teacher and ambassador of Christ, a teacher of the gospel. He was somewhat as an apostle, somewhat as a minister, somewhat as a Christian. Therefore it concerns us all to consider how to comfort one another as Christians. We are all members of the same body whereof Christ is the head. Therefore whatsoever comfort we feel, we ought to communicate.

The celestial bodies will teach us this. Whatsoever light or influence the moon and the stars receive, they bestow it on these inferior bodies. They have their light from the sun, and they reflect it again upon the creatures below. In the fabric of man's body, those official parts, as we call them, those parts and members of the body, the heart and the liver, which are both members and official parts, that do office and service to other parts, they convey and derive the spirits and the blood to all other parts. They receive strength, partly for themselves first, and then to convey it to other members. The liver is fed itself with some part of the blood, and it conveys the rest to the veins, and so to the whole body. The heart is nourished itself of the purest nourishment, the spirits are increased, and those spirits are spread through the arteries.

The stomach feeds itself with the meat it digests, and with the strength it hath. Being an official part, it serves other parts, and strengtheneth other parts ; and if there be a decay in it, there is a decay in all the parts of the body. So a Christian ought to strengthen himself, and then strengthen others. No man is for himself alone. And although whatso-

* Qu., ' not necessary ?'—ED.

over the means be, the comfort comes from God, yet he will have comfort to be conveyed to us by men this way.

Reason 1. Partly *to try our obedience,* whether we will respect his ordinance. He will have us go to men like ourselves. Now, if we will have comfort, we must look to his ordinance, we must have it of others, and not altogether from ourselves. And that is the reason why many go all their lifetime with heavy, drooping spirits. Out of pride and neglect, they scorn to seek it of others. They smother their grief, and bleed inwardly ; because they will not lay open the state of their souls to others. Although God be ' the God of comfort,' he hath ordained this order, that he will comfort us by them that he hath appointed to comfort us. He comforteth others, that they may comfort us. Though God be the God of comfort, yet he conveys it, for the most part, by the means of others. I say for the most part ; for he ties not himself to means, though he tie us to means, when we have means. Occasion may be, when a man is shut from all earthly comforts, as in contagious diseases, and restraint, &c. A man may be shut from all intercourse of worldly comforts ; but even then, a Christian is never in such an estate, but he hath one comfort or other. Then God comforts immediately, and then he comforts more sweetly and strongly ; then the soul cleaves to him close, and saith, Now thou must comfort or none, now the honour is all thine.

Now the nearer the soul is to the fountain of comfort, the more it is comforted, but the soul is never so near to God as in extremity of affliction. When all means fail, then the soul goes to the fountain of comfort, and gives all the glory to him. But I say, when there is means, God hath appointed to derive his comfort by means ; when we may have the benefit, of the communion of saints, of the word, &c. God will not comfort us immediately in the neglect of the means. ' He comforteth us, that we might comfort others.' And as he doth it to try our obedience,

Reason 2. So partly, *to knit us in love one to another.* For is not this a great bond to knit us one to another, when we consider that our good is hid in another ? The good that is derived to us, it is hid in others. And this makes us to esteem highly of others. How sweet are the looks and sight of a friend ! and more sweet the words of a friend, especially of an experienced friend, that hath been in the furnace himself.

Thus God, to knit us one to another in love, hath ordained that the comfort that he conveys, it should be conveyed by the means of others. Other reasons there may be given, but these are sufficient.

Use. If this be so, then we ought from hence to learn, *that whatsoever we have we are debtors of it to others,* whatsoever comfort we have, whether it be outward or inward comfort.

And even as God hath disposed and dispensed his benefits and graces to us, so let us be good stewards of it. We shall give account of it ere long. Let every man reason with himself, why have I this comfort that another wants ? I am God's steward ; God hath not given it to me to lay up, but to lay out. To speak a little of outward comforts. It is cursed atheism in many rich persons, that think they are to live here only to scrape an estate for them and their children ; when in the mean time their neighbours want, and God's children want, that are as dear to God as themselves, and perish for want of comfort. If they were not atheists in this point, they would think I am a steward, and what comfort shall I have of scraping much ? That will but increase my account. Such a steward were mad that would desire a great account. The more my account is, the more I have to answer for, and the more shall be my punishment if I quit not all well.

Now men out of atheism, that do not believe a day of judgment, a time of account, they engross comforts to them and theirs, as if there were not a church, as if there were not an afflicted body of Christ. They think not that they are stewards. Whereas the time will come, when they shall have more comfort of that that they have bestowed, than of that that they shall leave behind them to their children. That which is wisely dispensed for the comfort of God's people, it will comfort us, when all that we shall leave behind will not, nay, perhaps it will trouble us, the ill getting of it.

And so whatsoever inward comforts we have, it is for the comfort of others. We are debtors of it. Whatsoever ability we have, as occasion is offered, if there be a necessity in those that are of the same body with ourselves, we ought to regard them in pity and compassion. If we should see a poor creature cast himself into a whirlpool, or plunge himself into some desperate pit, were we not accessory to his death, if we should not help him! if we would not pull one out of the fire? Oh, yes! and is not the soul in as great danger? and is not mercy to the soul the greatest mercy? shall we see others ready to be swallowed up in the pit of despair, with heaviness of spirit? shall we see them dejected, and not take it to heart? But either we are unable to minister a word of comfort to them, or else unwilling : as if we were of Cain's disposition, that we would look to ourselves only; ' we are none of their keepers,' Gen. iv. 9.

It is a miserable thing to profess ourselves to be members of that body whereof Christ is the head, to profess the communion of saints, and yet to be so dead-hearted in these particular exigencies and occasions. It lies upon us as a duty, if God convey comforts to us from others ; and his end in comforting us any way, of putting any comfort in our hands outward or inward, it is to comfort others. If we do it not, we are liable to sin, to the breach of God's command, and we frustrate God's end.

But if this lie upon us as a duty to comfort others, then it concerns us to know how to be able to do it.

That we may be able to comfort others, let us,

(1.) Be ready *to take notice of the grievance of others;* as Moses went to see the afflictions of his brethren, and when he saw it, laid it to heart, Ex. iv. 31.

It is a good way to go to ' the house of mourning,' Eccles. vii. 2, and not to balk and decline our Christian brethren in adversity. God ' knows our souls in adversity, Ps. xxxi. 7 ; so should we do the souls of others, if they be knit to us in any bond of kindred, or nature, or neighbourhood, or the like. That bond should provoke us; for bonds are as the veins and arteries to derive comfort. All bonds are to derive good, whether bonds of neighbourhood, or acquaintance, &c. A man should think with himself, I have this bond to do my neighbour good. It is God's providence that I should be acquainted with him, and do that to him that I cannot do to a stranger. Let us consider all bonds, and let this work upon us : let us consider their grievance is a bond to tie us.

(2.) And withal let us labour *to put upon us the bowels of a father and mother,* tender bowels, as God puts upon him bowels of compassion towards us. So St Paul, being an excellent comforter of others, in 1 Thess. ii. 7, he shews there how he carried himself as a father, or mother, or nurse to them. Those that will comfort others, they must put upon them the affections of tender creatures as may be. They must be patient, they must be tenderly affected, they must have love, they must have the graces of communion.

What be the graces of communion? The graces of Christian communion to fit us in the communion of saints to do good, they are a loving, meek, patient spirit. Love makes patient. As we see mothers and nurses, what can they not endure of their children, because they love them? And they must be likewise wise and furnished. They that will comfort others must get wisdom and ability. They must get humility, they must abase themselves that they may be comfortable to others, and not stand upon terms. These be the graces of communion that fit us for the communion of saints.

What is the reason that many are so untoward to this duty, and have no heart to it, that they cannot indeed do it?

The reason is, they consider not their bonds: they do not ' consider the poor and needy,' Ps. xli. 1. They have not the graces of communion, they want loving spirits, they want ability, they are empty, they are not furnished, they have not knowledge laid up in store, they want humble spirits. The want of these graces makes us so barren in this practice of the communion of saints. Therefore we should bewail our own barrenness when we should do such duties, and cannot. And beg of God the spirit of love and wisdom, that we may do things wisely, that we may speak that which is fit. ' A word in season is as apples of gold with pictures of silver,' Prov. xxv. 11. And let us beg a humble spirit, that we may be abased to comfort others. As Christ in love to us he abased himself, he became man, and when he was man, he became a servant, he abased himself to wash his disciples' feet, talk with a silly woman, and such base offices. And if the Spirit of Christ be in us, it will abase us to offices of love, to support one another, to bear one another's burthens,' Gal. vi. 2.

(3.) Again, if we would comfort others as we should, let us labour *to get experience of comfort in ourselves.* God comforteth us that we might be able to comfort others. He will easily kindle others that is all on fire himself, and that is comforted himself. He can easily comfort others with that comfort he feels himself. Those that have experience can do it best.

As we see in physicians, if there be two physicians, whereof the one hath been sick of the disease that he is to cure in another; the other perhaps is more excellent than he otherwise, but he hath never been sick of it; the patient will sooner trust himself with the experienced physician than with the other; for undoubtedly he is better seen in that than the other, though perhaps the other may be a greater booked* physician than he. As it is with the physicians of the body, so it is with the physician of the soul: the experienced physician is the best. What is the reason that old men, and wise men, are the mercifulest of all? Because they have had experience of many crosses and miseries. A wise man knows what crosses are; he understands them best.

The way, then, to comfort others, is to get experience of divine comforts ourselves. And that we may get experience of God's comforts, let us mark what was said before of the rules of comfort, and work upon our own hearts whatsoever may be comfortable to others; that we may not be empty trunks to speak words without feeling.

He that is well may speak very good things to a sick man, but the sick man sees that he speaks without pity and compassion. Those that have

* That is, 'book-learned.'—G.

been sick of the same disease, when they come to comfort, they do it with a great deal of meekness and mildness. Those that are fit to comfort others must be spiritual themselves first, as the apostle saith, Gal. vi. 1. Saith the wise and holy apostle, ' If any man be overtaken,' as, alas! we are all overtaken with some corruption or other, ' ye that are spiritual, restore such a one,' set him in joint, as the word is (*i*), ' with the spirit of meekness, knowing that thou thyself mayest be tempted.'

The Spirit of God is a Spirit of comfort. The more we have of the Spirit, the fitter we are to comfort others. We see many men will speak very good things, but they do but personate sorrow, and personate comfort. It comes from them without feeling. As he saith, If thou didst believe these things that thou speakest, wouldst thou ever say them so ? He that speaks good things without experience, he speaks as if he did never believe them. Those that speak things with experience, that have wrought them upon their hearts and spirits, there is such a demonstration in the manner of their speaking, of a spirit of love and meekness, and compassion, that it prevails marvellously. It is so true that our Saviour Christ himself, that he might have the more tender bowels of compassion towards us, he made it one end of his incarnation, as it is pressed again and again in Heb. ii. and Heb. iv. The apostle dwells upon it, ' It became him to be man, to take upon him our infirmities, that he might be a merciful Redeemer, a merciful high priest,' Heb. ii. 17. It was one end of his incarnation that he might not only save us, but that he might be a merciful Redeemer, that he might have experience of our infirmities. Of persecution, he was persecuted himself; of want, he wanted himself; of temptation, he was tempted himself; of wrath, he felt it himself, ' My God, my God, why hast thou forsaken me ?' Mark xv. 34.

Here is the comfort of a Christian soul, that Christ hath begun to him in all. Therefore it became him to be man, not only to redeem us, but to be a merciful high priest, a comfortable high priest.

The way, then, you see, how to comfort others, is, to get our own hearts sensible of spiritual comfort. Two irons, if they be both hot, do close together presently, but unless both be hot, they do not join together handsomely. So that that makes us join together strongly is, if two spirits meet, and both be warm ; if one godly man comfort another godly man ; if one holy man labour to breed an impression of heat in another, there is a knitting of both spirits, they join strongly together. Therefore we ought to labour to get experience, that we may comfort others, seeing none can comfort so well as experimental Christians.

Quest. Why is experience such an enabling to spiritual comfort ?

Ans. 1. I answer, *because it brings the comfort home to our own souls.* The devil knows comfort well enough, but he feels none. Experience helps faith, it helps all other knowledge. Our Saviour Christ is said to learn by experience, for ' he learned obedience in that he suffered,' Heb. v. 8. Experience is such a means of the increasing of knowledge, as that it bettered the knowledge of Christ, that had all knowledge in him. He had knowledge by looking upon God, being the ' wisdom of God,' 1 Cor. i. 30, yet he learned somewhat by the experience, he bettered himself by experience. He knew what to bear the cross was by experience. He knew what infirmities were by experience. He knew what he could suffer by experience. So it added to his knowledge as man. And so the angels themselves are continual students in the mysteries of the gospel. They get experimental knowledge to the knowledge that they have inbred, and that knowledge that

they have by the presence of God. To that they add experimental knowledge.

So then, if it bettered the knowledge of our blessed Saviour, and increased
it, [if] it was a new way increased by experience, and it adds to the knowledge of the angels, much more to ours.

2. Then, again, *it gains a great confidence in the speaker;* for what we
speak with experience, we speak with a great deal of boldness.

3. Again, experimental comforts, those that we have felt ourselves, and
have felt likewise the grievance, *we speak them with such expressions as no
other can do,* in the apprehension of the party whom we comfort, so well
as an experienced person. For he goes about the work tenderly and gently
and lovingly, because he hath been in the same himself. And that is the
reason that the apostle St Paul, in the place I named before, Gal. vi. 1,
presseth this duty upon spiritual men, especially because themselves have
been tempted, and may be tempted. Those that have been tempted, and
think they may be afterward, this doth wondrously fit them for this work
of comforting others. But to add a little in this point, to shew how to
comfort others by our own experience and skill, I spake before of an art of
comforting ourselves. There is a skill likewise in comforting others.
Even as we comfort ourselves, in that method we must comfort others.
When we comfort ourselves, we must first consider our need of comfort,
search our wounds, our maladies, have them fresh in our sight, that so we
may be forced to seek for comfort; and as we ought to do this daily, so when
we are to comfort others,

(1.) We ought not only to comfort them, *but to search them as much as
we can,* what sin is in them, and what misery is upon them, and acquaint
them with their own estate that they are in, as far as we can discern. We
may judge of them partly by ourselves. For we must not prostitute comforts to persons that are indisposed, till we see them fitted. God doth
comfort, but it is the abject. Christ heals, but [it] is the wounded spirit.
He came to seek, but it is those that are lost. He came to ease, but it
is those that are 'heavy laden.' Therefore, that we may comfort them to
purpose, we ought to shew, and discover to them, what estate they are in,
that we may force them to comfort, if they be not enemies to comfort and
to their own souls.

He is an unwise physician that administers cordials before he gives pre-
paratives to carry away the noisome humours. They will do little good.
We ought therefore to prepare them this way, if we intend to do them good.

(2.) And then when we see what need they stand in, *bring them to Christ
and the covenant of grace.* That is the best way to comfort them, to bring
them to see that God is their Father, when we discern some signs of grace
in them. For this is the main stop in all comfort, that there is none but
they shall find by experience. They are ready to say, You teach wondrous
comforts, that there is an inheritance in heaven that God hath provided;
and on earth, there is an issue of all for good, and there is a presence of
God in troubles! This is true; but how shall I know this belongs to me?
This is the cavil of flesh and blood, that turns the back to the most heavenly
comforts that are. The main and principal thing therefore in dealing with
others, and with our own hearts, is to let them see that there are some signs
and evidences that they are in the covenant of grace, that they belong to
God. Unless we see that, all the comfort we can give them is to tell them
that they are not yet sunk into hell, and that they have space to repent.
But as long as men live in sinful courses, that they are not in a state of

grace, we can tell them no comfort, except they will devise a new Scripture, a new Bible. If they do so, they may have comfort. But this word of God, God herein speaks no comfort to persons that live in sin, and will do so. We should labour therefore to discern some evidence that they are in the state of grace.

And ofttimes those are indeed most entitled to comfort that think it furthest from them. Therefore we should acquaint them with the conditions of the covenant of grace, that God looks to truth. Therefore if we discern any true, broken, humble spirit, a hungering and a thirsting after righteousness, and a desire of comfort, 'Blessed are those that hunger and thirst,' Mat. v. 6 ; it belongs to them, we may comfort them. If we see spiritual poverty, that they see their wants, and would be supplied, 'Blessed are the poor in spirit,' Mat. v. 3 ; 'Be of good comfort,' Christ calls such, Mat. x. 49. If they see and feel the burden of their sins, we may comfort them. Christ calls them, 'Come unto me, ye that are weary and heavy laden,' Mat. xi. 28. If we discern spiritual and heavenly desires to grow in grace and overcome their corruptions, if we discover and discern this in their practice and obedience, 'God will fulfil the desires of them that fear him,' Ps. cxlv. 19. And he accepts the will for the deed.

There is a desire of happiness in nature that comforts not a man. It is no sign of grace to desire to be free from hell and to be in heaven. It is a natural desire. Every creature wishes well to heaven. But if there be a desire of the means that tend to heaven, a desire of grace, these are evidences of grace. These are the pulses that we may find grace by ; when they see their infirmities, and groan under them, and would be better, and complain that they are not better, and are out of love with their own hearts. There is a combat in their hearts, they are not friends with themselves. When we see this inward conflict, and a desire to better, and to get victories against their corruptions, though there be many corruptions and weaknesses, a man may safely say, they are in a state of grace, they are on the mending hand. For 'Christ will not break the bruised reed, nor quench the smoking flax,' Mat. xii. 20. 'And where he hath begun a good work, he will perfect it to the day of the Lord,' Philip. i. 6. He will cherish these weak beginnings, therefore we may comfort them on good ground.

(3.) Then, besides that, in our dealing with them, when we have discovered, by some evidence, that they belong to the covenant, that we see, by some love to good things, and to God's image in his children, and by other evidences, then we may comfort them boldly ; *and then to fetch from our own experience*, what a comfort will it be to such ! When we can say, My estate was as yours is ; I found those corruptions that you groan under ; I allowed not myself in them as you do not. When a man can say from his own experience, that notwithstanding these I have evident signs of God's Spirit that I am his, then he can comfort others by his own experience.

(4.) And what a comfort is it *to go to the experiments** of Scripture!* It is an excellent way. As now, let a man be deserted of God, David will comfort him by his experience, Ps. lxxvii. 2, 8, 10, where he saith he found God as his enemy ; and as Job saith, 'the terrors of God drank up his spirit,' Job vi. 4. Be of good comfort ! David would come and comfort thee if he were alive. If the terror of God be against thee for sin, that thy conscience is awakened, be of good comfort ! Christ, if he were on earth,

* That is, 'experiences' = examples.—G.

would shew thee by his own example that he endured that desertion on the cross: 'My God, my God, why hast thou forsaken me?' Mark xv. 34. If thou be molested and vexed with Satan, Job will comfort thee by his example. His book is most of it combating and comfort. And so for all other grievances, go to the Scriptures. Whatsoever is 'written, is written for our learning,' Pray to God, and he will hear thee as he did Elias.

Obj. Oh! but Elias was an excellent man.

Ans. The Scripture prevents* the objection: 'he was a man subject to infirmities,' James v. 17. If God heard him, he will hear thee. Believe in Christ, as Abraham did, 'the father of the faithful,' in the promised Messiah, and he will forgive thee all thy sins.

Obj. Oh! but he had a strong faith.

Ans. What hath the Scripture to take away this objection? In Rom. iv. 23, 'This was not written for Abraham only, but for those that believe with the faith of Abraham.'

Obj. Aye, but I am a wretched sinner, there is little hope of me.

Ans. Yes! St Paul will come and comfort thee by his example and experience: 'This is a faithful saying, that Jesus Christ came into the world to save sinners, of whom I am the chief,' 1 Tim. i. 15.

Obj. Aye, he came to save such sinners as St Paul was.

Ans. Aye, saith St Paul, 'and that I might be an example to all that shall believe in Christ, to the end of the world,' 1 Tim. i. 16. He takes away that objection. And the apostle is so heavenly wise, that where he speaks of privileges, he enlargeth it to others. 'There is no condemnation to them that are in Christ Jesus,' Rom. viii. 1. 'And what shall separate us from the love of God?' ver. 35. But when he speaks of matter of abasement, that we may see that he was, in regard of his corruptions, as much humbled as we, then he speaks in his own person: 'O wretched man that I am! who shall deliver me from this body of death?' Rom. vii. 24. Therefore his comforts belong to thee. Now, as these examples in Scripture, and the experiences of God's children there, be applicable to us, so much more the experience of God's children that are alive. Therefore we should be willing to do offices of comfort in this kind.

Those that are of ability, either men or women, they will have in their houses somewhat to comfort others, they will have strong waters, and cordials, and medicines; and they account it a glory to have somewhat that their neighbours may be beholden to them for. And though they bestow it freely, yet they think and account it a sufficient recompence that they can be beneficial to others. People do this for things of this life, and think they deserve a great deal of respect for their goodness in this kind. Surely, if we consider, there is a life that needs comfort more than this fading life, and there are miseries that pinch us more than the miseries of the body! Every one should labour to have in the house of his soul somewhat, some strong waters of comfort, that he may be able to tell others, This refreshed my soul, this hath done me good; I give you no worse than I took myself first. This wondrously commends the comfort in the party that gives it, and it commends it to the party that receives it, to take benefit by the comforts of other men. For is it not a strengthening to our case when another shall say to our comfort, It was my case? Is it not sealed by the evidence of two? Surely it is a great assurance when we have another to tell us his experience.

Use 1. Again, if this be God's order, that he will convey comfort to us

* That is, 'anticipates.'—G.

by others, then *we ought to depend upon God's ordinance*, we ought to expect comfort one from another, especially from the ministers, who are messengers of comfort. I speak it the rather, because in what degree we neglect any one means that God hath ordained to comfort us, though he be the God of comfort, yet in that measure we are sure to want comfort. And this is one principal ordinance, the ministry, and the communion of saints.

Some there be that will neglect the means of salvation. They have dead spirits, and live and die so, for the most part. They have much ado to recover comfort. Those men that retire themselves, that will work all out of the flint themselves, they are commonly uncomfortable. God hath ordained one to help another, as in an arch one stone strengtheneth another. The ministry especially is ordained for comfort.

2. And likewise God hath ordained *one Christian to comfort another*, as well as the ministers. Let us therefore regard much the communion of saints. Let one Christian labour to comfort another, and every one labour to be fit to receive comfort from others, labour to have humble and willing spirits. It is so true that God doth convey comfort, even by common Christians as well as the ministers, that St Paul himself, Rom. i. 12 ; he desires to see the Romans, ' that he might receive mutual comfort from them.' For a minister may have more knowledge and book-learning perhaps than another Christian that may have better experience than he, especially in some things ; and there is not the meanest Christian but he may comfort the greatest clerk in the world, and help him by his experience that God hath shewed to him, by declaring how God shewed him comfort at such a time, and upon such an occasion. The experience of God's people, the meanest of them may help the best Christians. Therefore he will have none to be neglected.

There is never a member of Christ's body, but hath some ability to comfort another ; for Christ hath no dead members. God will have it so, because he will have one Christian to honour another, and to honour them from the knowledge of the use and necessity that one hath of another. If God should not derive comfort from one to another in some degree, and from the meanest to the greatest, one would despise another. But God will not have it so. He will have the communion of saints valued to the end of the world. What will one Christian regard another, what would weak Christians regard the strong, and what would strong Christians regard the weak, if there were not a continual supply one from another? Therefore God hath ordained that by the ministry, and by the communion of saints, we should comfort one another.

Let us not think that this doth not concern us. It concerns us all. Therefore when we have any trouble in mind, let us regard the communion of saints, let us regard acquaintance. And let us know this, that God will hold us in heaviness till we have used all the means that he hath appointed. If one help not, perhaps another will; perhaps the ministry will help, perhaps acquaintance will help. But if we find not comfort in one, let us go over all. And, would you have more ? Christ himself, did he not take two disciples into the garden with him when his spirit was heavy ? Did not he know that God had ordained one to comfort another ? ' Two are better than one,' Eccles. iv. 9. If one be alone, he shall be a-cold, but if there be two, they heat one another. If there be one alone, there can hardly be true spiritual heat. If two be together, if one fall, ' the other may raise him up,' Eccles. iv. 10, but if one be alone and fall, who shall raise him up? It is meant spiritually, as well as bodily and outwardly by Solomon.

We cannot have a better president* than our blessed Saviour. Solitariness in such times in spiritual desertion ' it is the hour of temptation.' When did the devil set on Christ? When he was alone. It was the fittest time to tempt him when Christ was severed. So the devil sets on single persons when they are alone, and tempts them, and presseth them with variety of temptations. ' Woe to him that is alone,' Eccles. iv. 10. Christ sent his disciples by two and two, that one might comfort another, and one might strengthen another, Mark vi. 7.

Now, though in particular it belong to ministers in a more eminent sort ; yet let every one lay it to heart, you ought to have abilities to comfort others, and to receive comfort of others. And consider it is an angelical work to comfort others. We imitate God himself, and the most excellent creatures the angels, whose office is to comfort. Even our very Saviour, they came to comfort him in his greatest extremity. A man is a god to a man when he comforts. When he discomforts, and directs, and withdraws, he is a devil to a man. Men are beasts to men, devils to men, that way. But he that is an instrument to convey comfort, he is a god to a man. God is the God of comfort. Thou art in the place of God to a man when thou comfortest him, thou shalt save thyself and others. God honours men with his own title when they comfort. Not only ministers, but others save men. Thou shalt ' gain thy brother,' by thy admonition and reproof. What greater honour can ye have than God's own title, to be saviours one of another? It is the office, I say, of angels. They were sent to comfort Christ. It is their duty to pitch their tents about God's children, to suggest holy thoughts, as the devil suggests evil, and to be about us, though we think not of it. Nay, it is not only an angelical work, but it is the work of God's Spirit. The sweetest style of the Holy Ghost is to be a ' comforter.'

What shall we think of cursed spirits that insult over others' misery, that give them gall to eat, and vinegar to drink, that add affliction to the afflicted? What shall we say to barren spirits, that have not a word of comfort to say, but come in a profane and dead manner, I am sorry to see you thus, and I hope you will better. Barren soul, as the wilderness ! What ! a member of Christ, of the communion of saints, and no way furnished, no word of comfort to a distressed soul ! We may know the comfort we have ourselves to be comfort indeed, and from the grace and favour of God, when we have hearts enlarged to do good to others with it.

How do gifts and grace differ, to add that useful distinction? And a man may have a great many gifts and be proud, and full of envy, and have a devilish poisonful spirit to draw all to himself, and not be good, but be carried with self-love, and die a devil, notwithstanding his excellent parts. Why? Here are such gifts, and parts, but there is a bitter root of self-love to draw all to himself, to deify himself, to make an idol of himself. But grace with gifts works otherwise. That turns all by a spirit of love and humility to the good of others.

There is no envy in a gracious heart. So far forth as it is gracious there is no pride, no scorn to do good to others. How shall we distinguish men of excellent parts, whether they be Christians or not Christians? They have both of them wit and memory, they have both courage. Aye, but whether of them improve their parts and abilities most to the good of others? Whether of them hath the most humble spirit, the most loving

* That is, ' precedent.'—G.

spirit, the most discreet spirit, to be witty to do good to others upon all advantages. There is the Christian that hath God's grace with his gifts. But for the other, ' Knowledge puffeth up,' saith the apostle, 1 Cor. viii. 1. What edifies and builds us ? ' Love edifieth,' 1 Cor. viii. 1. Knowledge gathers many materials, stone, and timber, &c. What builds the house, the body of Christ ? It is a loving and humble spirit.

Therefore let us think that we have nothing in Christianity, by any parts we have, of memory or wit, or reading, &c., unless we have a humble spirit, that we can deny ourselves and debase ourselves to do good to others upon all the best advantages ; or else we have not the spirit of Christ, that sweet spirit of Christ that denied himself to do good to us.

Where grace is established once, and is in the right nature, there is a public mind ; and it is one of the best signs of a heart that is fashioned to the image of Christ, who denied himself, and became all in all to us, to have a public mind, to have self-love killed, to think I have nothing to purpose as I should have, except I can make use of it to the good of others. Therefore let us be willing to do good in this kind.

And as I said, let us make use of comfort from others. Think that they are reserved to the times and place where thou livest, that thou mightest make use of them. Therefore those that need comfort should not flatter themselves in their grief, but humbly depend upon the means that God hath ordained. And let every man think, what if God have hid my comfort in another man? What if he have given him ' the tongue of the learned,' Isa. l. 4, to speak a word in season unto me? Let no man think to master his trouble and grief by himself. We are members of the body, and the good that God will convey to us, must be from and by others. Therefore it is a mutual duty. Those that have comfort ought to comfort others ; and those that do need comfort, ought to repair to others. It is the ordinance of God, as Job saith, for one of ' a thousand to shew a man his righteousness,' Job xxxiii. 23. Though a man be never so wise, yet sometimes he knows not his own comfort. He knows not that portion of comfort that belongs to him, till some others discover it to him. Physicians will have others to heal themselves, to judge of their diseases; and certainly one reason why persons that are excellent in themselves, have passed their days in darkness, it hath been this, that they think to overmaster their heaviness and distraction of spirit with their own reason, &c., which will not be. God, what he will do, he will do by his own means and ordinance.

Use 3. Let us therefore learn, hence, *to see the goodness of God*, that besides the ministry that he hath ordained, and the salvation that he keeps for us, and the promises that he hath given us, and the angels that attend us, &c., he doth even ordain others, that are men, and have bodies with ourselves, other fellow-Christians, to be instruments to convey comfort. He trains them up, that they may be able to comfort, and do good to us ; and he hides the good he intends to us in them, and conveys it to us by them. It is a special goodness of God, that everything should tend to our good. Thus all things are for us. The sufferings of others tend to increase our comfort, and the comfort of others is for our comfort. There is such a sweet prudence in directing us to heaven, that God makes everything help ; not only our own troubles that we suffer ourselves, but he doth sweetly turn the troubles of others, and the comforts of others to our good.

It ministereth an argument of praising and blessing of God ; and that we should answer him in the like, that as he hath devised all the ways that may be of comforting us, of turning all to our good, that that we suffer ourselves, and that that others suffer ; so we should study by all means and ways to set forth his glory, and no way to grieve the Spirit of so gracious a God, that thus every way intends our comfort.

VERSE 5.

'*For as the sufferings of Christ abound in us, so our consolations also abound by Christ.*' Here the blessed apostle shews the reason why his heart was so enlarged, as we see in ver. 3, in the midst of his troubles and persecutions, to bless God. There was good reason ; for as his afflictions, so his consolations abounded. It is a reason, likewise, of his ability to comfort others, the reason why he was fitted to comfort others, because he found comfort abound in himself in his sufferings. So they have a double reference to the words before. But to take the words in themselves,

'*As the sufferings of Christ abound,*' *&c*. It is an excellent portion of Scripture, and that which I should have a great deal of encouragement to speak of, if the times and disposition of the hearers were for it ; for it is a text of comfort for those that suffer persecution, that suffer affliction for the gospel. Now, because we do not suffer, or at least we suffer not any great matter (except it be a reproach, or the like, which is a matter of nothing, but a chip of the cross, a trifle), therefore we hear these matters of comfort against the disgrace of the cross of Christ, with dead hearts. But we know not what we are reserved to ; therefore we must learn somewhat to store up, though we have not present use of it. The several branches of divine truths, that may be observed from these words, are first this, *That the sufferings of Christians may abound.* They are many in this world, and they may be more still. 'For as the sufferings of Christ abound in us,' &c.

Secondly, *what we ought to think of those sufferings, what judgment we are to have of them.* 'They are the sufferings of Christ.'

Thirdly, that being the sufferings of Christ, *he will not destitute* us of comfort* ; but we have our comfort increased in a proportion answerable to our troubles. 'So our consolations,' &c.

The fourth point is, *by whom and in whom all this is.* This strange work is by Christ. The balancing of these two so sweetly together, crosses and comforts, they come both from one hand, both from one spring, 'the sufferings of Christ,' and the comforts of Christ, and both abound. Our troubles are for him, and our comforts are by him. So here is sufferings and comfort, increase of suffering, increase of comfort, sufferings for Christ, and comfort by Christ. You see them balanced together, and you see which weighs down the balance. Comfort by Christ weighs down sufferings for Christ. The good is greater than the ill. It is a point of wondrous comfort. The ark, you know, mounted up as the waters mounted up, when the waters overflowed the world. So it is here in this verse. There is a mounting of the waters, a rising of the waters above the mountains. Afflictions increase, and grow higher and higher ; but be of good comfort, here is the ark above the waters, here is consolation above all. As our sufferings for Christ increase, so our consolations, likewise, by Christ increase.

For the first, I will be very short in it.

Doct. The sufferings of Christ abound in us.

* That is, 'deprive.'—G.

There is nobody in this world, but first or last, if they live any long time, they must suffer; and as a man is in degrees of goodness, so his sufferings must abound. The better man, the more sufferings. Sufferings abounded in St Paul. It doth not abound in all. That was personal in St Paul, to abound in sufferings. It doth not go out of the person of St Paul, and such as St Paul was. All must suffer, but not in a like measure. There are several cups. All do not abound in sufferings, as all do not abound in grace and strength. Those that are of a higher rank, their sufferings abound more. God doth not use an exact proportion in afflictions, but that which we call geometrical, a proportion appliable to the strength of the sufferer. Christ, as he had more strength than any, so he suffered more than any; and St Paul, having an extraordinary measure of strength, he suffered more than all the apostles. The sufferings of Christ abounded in him; but all must suffer.

What is the reason of it? What is the reason that troubles abound thus? Surely if we look to God, the devil, the world, ourselves, we shall see reasons enough.

Reason 1. If we look to *God and Christ, we are ordained to be conformable to Christ*. We must be conformable to Christ in sufferings first, before we be in glory. It is God's decree, we are called to sufferings, as well as to be believing. We must answer God's call. Every Christian must resolve to take up his cross every day, some degree of the cross or other. Reproach for Christ's sake is a suffering. The scorn of the world is the rebuke of Christ. We are called to suffering, as well as to glory. It is part of our effectual calling, it is an appendix, an accessory thing to the main. We must take grace with suffering, and it is well we may have it so too. It is well that we have the state of grace here, and glory hereafter, with suffering.

Reason 2. If we look *to the devil, there must be suffering*. Satan is the prince of the world. He is the prince of an opposite kingdom.

Reason 3. If we consider *what place we live in when we are taken out of the world to the blessed estate of Christians*, to be members of Christ and heirs of heaven. The world is strange to us, and we are strangers to it. Crosses and afflictions are necessary for them that are travellers. We would think else that we were at home, and forget our country. Considering the condition we live in, we must have sufferings. If we consider the disposition of the parties among whom we live, they are people of an opposite spirit. Therefore they malign us, because we are taken from among them; and though there be no opposition shewed to them, yet it upbraids enough their cursed estate when they see others taken from them. That speaks loud enough that their course is naught, that they see others mislike it. The world, that is led by the spirit of Satan, maligns them that are better than themselves. There is opposition between the seed of the serpent and the seed of the woman. So long as there are wicked men, that are instruments and organs of the devil, God's children must be opposed. While there is a devil suffered to be 'the god of the world,' 2 Cor. iv. 4, and so long as he hath so strong a faction in the world as he hath, 'the children of disobedience,' Eph. v. 6, in whom he rules, God's children shall never want suffering.

Reason 4. If we *regard ourselves*, we have always in ourselves good and bad. That which is good, we have need of sufferings to exercise it and to know it; for if there were no sufferings, how should we know what good we have?

(1.) Is it not a great comfort to a Christian, when he knows by suffering that he hath more patience than he looked for, that he hath more faith than he thought ne had, that he hath more love to God, that he can endure to suffer more for God than ever he thought he could, that he hath more resigning of his heart and giving up of himself than he thought of, that he can deny the world, which he thought he could not have done? What a comfort is it to a Christian when he knows by suffering what he can do and what he cannot do. It is good, therefore, and necessary in regard of ourselves, that we may know our strength.

(2.) In regard, likewise, of the evil that is in us, suffer we must. For there must be a daily purging; and the best instruments to scour us are wicked men, the devil's instruments. It is unfit for God's children to take that base office on them, for one Christian to fall upon another. It is good there should be an opposite faction in the world, that there should be wicked men, in regard of the ill that is in us. There is somewhat to be scoured and purged out. So we see, whether we look upward or downward, to God, or to the devil, or to the faction of the devil in the world, or to ourselves, for good or evil, it is necessary that there should be some afflictions.

And to speak a little more home to us, there must be sufferings in this regard, because the church alway hath corruption and soil, especially in prosperity. If a man look to the churches in Germany, that have suffered much of late,* and mark what reports hath been given of them, how cold and dull they were in the possession of the gospel, how indifferent they were, how they valued not that invaluable pearl, a man shall see that suffering was needful to scour them. If a man look to the state of this city, though there be many good people (the Lord increase the number of them), yet, if a man consider with what cold affections the blessed truth of God is entertained, which I say is above all, what is all that we enjoy? What is our peace to the gospel of peace? What is our prosperity, and what is all, to the blessed truth of salvation? If we had not that, wherein were not the Turks as good as we? For all other things, were not other nations as good as we? Certainly yes. For policy, and other beauty, and ornaments, and rarities, what have we to lift up our excellency but the continuance of the blessed doctrine of salvation, whereby our souls are begotten to God, to 'an inheritance immortal, undefiled, reserved in the heavens?' 1 Peter i. 4. Now, the cold esteem of this certainly will enforce in time a national suffering, unless there be a national repentance. It is true of every particular Christian. As we see, when the rain and the heat join together, they breed as well weeds as corn, so prosperity and the blessings of God, they have brought up in us much weeds as well as good corn; and there must be a time of weeding and purging in regard of our state in this world. We are gathering soil every day. There must be a suffering one time or other.

Obj. But some will say, What! do you talk of suffering? Now is a time of peace. We live among Christians, and not pagans and Turks; and for our adversaries, though they be many, yet they do not shew themselves.

Ans. St Austin answers this in himself. Do but begin to live as a Christian should, and see if thou shalt not be used unchristianly of them that are Christians in name, but not in deed. A suffering from Christians is more sharp than that of enemies. Those that are fleshly will be ready to be injurious; those that are carnal, formal professors, will be ready to offer some disgrace or other to those that are more spiritual than themselves.

There is a threefold suffering in the church since Christ's time. The first was of doctrine concerning the natures of Christ. There was persecution about that; for there were Arians that denied the Godhead, and others

* That is, 1624-5. Cf. note o*.—G.

that denied the manhood of Christ,* and such like great enemies of the church. Afterward, in popery, they set on Christ's offices, and divided his kingly and priestly and prophetical office, to the pope, to saints, to works, and such like, encroaching upon them, and persecuting with fire and faggot all those that gave all to Christ, and did not sacrilegiously give anything to the creature.

But there is a persecution as ill as any of these, where the nature and offices of Christ are well enough understood, where the power of religion is opposed by others, when so much religion as is necessary to bring a man to heaven is opposed; for it is not the knowledge of the nature, and offices, and benefits by Christ, but it is a knowledge that hath obedience with it that must bring us to heaven, a knowledge with self-denial, a knowledge with selling and parting with all our lusts and wicked courses, that will not stand with the gospel.

Now, where this is, this cannot be brooked by any means, and it goes under as great disgrace, as heresies did in former times. So that it is matter of reproach to have so much religion as is necessarily required of a man before he can be saved. That which the world disgraces is necessary to every man before he can be saved, that is, a strict giving up of himself to God, and a watching over his ways as much as human frailty will permit, a conscionable † endeavour in all things to please God, out of conscience and thankfulness to God. We must not think to come to heaven without that. It will not be. ' Without holiness none shall see God.' This despised holiness, this maligned holiness, is that which is necessary to bring us to heaven, and so much as is necessary to bring us to heaven is disgraced everywhere.

Those that resolve to be Christians in good earnest, and would have comfort on their deathbed and in the times of persecution, they must endure to be set light by, to bear the reproach of Christ. They must resolve on this beforehand, that when these things come to pass, we be not offended.

Use. Well, then, to make a little use of this. Since there must be troubles and crosses, and they must increase if we will be Christians, let this teach us *to judge aright of those that are ill thought on in the world ofttimes*, when we see nothing but good in their carriage. Oh, what imputations are laid on them! You may see what an indiscreet man he was, you may see that he lacked wisdom and policy, else he might have kept himself out of this trouble. I would ask such a party, Had not Christ as much wisdom as thee? He was the ' wisdom of the Father.' Did he keep out of reproaches? Was he not reproached as a troublesome man, as an enemy to Cæsar, and taxed for base things, as a ' winebibber,' &c., Mat. xi. 19, and one that ' had a devil,' Mat. xi. 18, and many other ways? Was not St Paul as discreet as we are, who in our understanding and conceit are ready to conceive distastefully of men that suffer anything for the gospel? And yet, notwithstanding, all his wisdom kept him not from the cross, ' but the cross abides me,' saith he, ' everywhere,' 2 Cor. i. 5. The devil and the cross follow God's children wheresoever they go. All their wisdom and holiness cannot keep them from it, because God hath decreed it and called them to it, and they must be conformable to Christ.

Therefore, let us take heed that we do not suffer men to suffer in our conceits, when they suffer in a good cause, the cross of Christ, reproachful things, base death, &c. Afflictions are therefore called the cross, because there is a kind of baseness with them, and as it is so, so carnal men esteem it.

* That is, the Gnostics.—G.   † That is, ' conscientious.'—G.

Presently with the suffering there goes a taint, and an abasing in their conceit, of those men that suffer in a good cause. There is a diminishing conceit goes in carnal men of that which should be their glory. ' Our crosses abound,' 2 Cor. i. 5. But what ought we to judge of these crosses?

Doct. They are the sufferings of Christ.

Quest. Why? Christ suffers nothing; he is in heaven, in glory. How can he suffer? This is to disparage his glorious estate, to make him suffer anything.

Ans. I answer, the sufferings of Christ, they are twofold. The sufferings of Christ's person, that which he suffered himself, which were propitiatory and satisfactory* for our redemption; and the sufferings of Christ in his mystical body, which likewise is called Christ. For Christ in Scripture is taken either for Christ himself, or for the members of Christ. ' Why persecutest thou me?' saith he to Saul, Acts ix. 4 ; or for the whole body mystical with the head, 1 Cor. xii. 27. ' So is Christ.' Christ, Head and members, is called Christ. Now, when he calls the sufferings of the church the sufferings of Christ, he means not the sufferings of Christ in his own person; for he suffers nothing; he is out of all the malice of persecutors ; they cannot reach to heaven to Christ; but he means the sufferings of Christ in his mystical body. These are called ' the sufferings of Christ.'

Quest. Why are these called the sufferings of Christ?

Ans. (1.) Partly, because they are the *sufferings of mystical Christ*, the body of Christ, the church. For the church, the company of true believers, are the fulness of Christ, they make up the mystical body of Christ. Therefore when they suffer, he that is the head suffers.

(2.) Again, they are called the sufferings of Christ, those that his members and children suffer, *because they are for Christ*, they are in his quarrel, they are for his truth, for his cause, and by his appointment he calls us to suffering. It is for his cause. In our intendment we intend to suffer for Christ, to maintain his cause. They are the sufferings of Christ likewise in the intent of the opposites and enemies. They persecute us for some goodness they see in us. They persecute the cause and truth of Christ in us. So they are the sufferings of Christ both ways.

(3.) Especially, they are the sufferings of Christ *by way of sympathy;* because Christ doth impute them to himself. ' The sufferings of Christ.' It is a phrase that springs from the near union that is between Christ and his members, the church; which is as near or nearer than any natural union between the head and members. Hereupon it comes that we are said to suffer with him, to die with him, to be crucified with him, to ascend with him, to sit in heavenly places with him, to judge the world with him, to do all with him by reason of this union. And he is said to suffer with us, to be afflicted in us, to be reproached with us. He was stoned in Stephen, he was persecuted by Saul, he was beheaded in Paul, he was burned with the martyrs, he was banished with the Christians, and he suffers in all his children. Not that he doth so in his own person, but because it pleaseth him, by reason of the near communion that is between him and us, to take that which is done to his members, as done to himself. Therefore they are called ' the sufferings of Christ.' He suffers when we suffer, and we suffer when he suffers.

The difference is, all the comforts in our sufferings, it comes from communion in his sufferings, because he is our surety. For why are we encouraged to suffer by way of sympathy and communion with him? Be-

* That is, ' satisfying.'—G.

cause he in love died for us, and was crucified for us, and abased for us, and shamed for us. And when is the soul encouraged to suffer afflictions for Christ? When it hath a little felt the wrath of God that Christ suffered for it. Oh, how much am I beholden to God for Christ, that endured the whole wrath of God? They are 'the sufferings of Christ.' This is a wondrous comfortable point; and it is a notion that doth sweeten the bitterest crosses, that they are the sufferings of Christ. Not only that we are conformable to Christ in them, we suffer as he did, but they are 'the sufferings of Christ,' he imputes them as done to him, he suffers with us.

(4.) And another reason, why they are the sufferings of Christ, it is because he not only takes it as done to himself, *but he is present with them.* He was with St Paul in the dungeon, he was with the three young men in the fiery furnace. There were three put in, and there was a fourth, which was Christ, the Son of God (*j*). He goes with the martyrs to the prison, to the stake. He is with them till he has brought them to heaven. He is present with them when they suffer.

Here I must, before I come to make use of it, distinguish between the crosses, and sufferings of Christ, and of ordinary sufferings as men.

[1.] Something in this vale of misery *we suffer as creatures:* as being subject to mutability and change, because this is a world of changes. In this sublunary world there is nothing but changes. Thus we suffer as creatures. All creatures are subject to vanity, and complain and groan under it.

[2.] Somewhat we suffer *as men.* It is the common condition of men. This nature of ours, since the fall, is subject to sicknesses, to crosses, and pain, and casualties. Every day brings new crosses with it. This we suffer as men.

[3.] Now the sufferings of Christians, *as religious holy men,* those are here meant, those are 'the sufferings of Christ.' Yet notwithstanding the sufferings as men, by the Spirit of God, help our conformity to Christ, by them the flesh is purged, and the Spirit strengthened, and weaning from the world is wrought, and a desire to heaven.

By the daily crosses we suffer as men, not for religion, we are much bettered; and those in some sort may be called the sufferings of Christ, because by them we are conformed to Christ more in holiness. We grow more out of love with the world, and more heavenly minded. This distinction is necessary to know which are best, the sufferings of Christians as good men.

Use. It is a point, I say, of wondrous comfort. That we should be conformable in our sufferings with our head Christ Jesus, our glorified head in heaven, is it not a wondrous comfort? Nay, is it not a glory? It is a wondrous glory that God will set us apart to do any thing, that God will take any thing of us, much more that he will single us out to be champions in his quarrel, and more, that he will triumph in us, that the comfort shall abound.

To give an instance. If a monarch should redeem a slave, a traitor from prison, and take him to fight in the quarrel of his own son, to be his champion, were it not an honour? So the very sufferings for Christ are an encouragement. The disgraces, and whatsoever they are that we suffer in a good cause, they are ensigns of honour, they are badges of honour of Christian knighthood. If a golden fleece, or a garter,* or such things, be accounted so highly of and glorified in, because they are favours, &c., much more should the sufferings for Christ be glorified in, as ensigns of the love of God, and of our Christian profession. When we fight under Christ's

* That is, the knightly 'orders' so designated.—G.

banner, we are like to Christ. We are conformable to him. He went before, and we follow his steps; ' and if we suffer with him, we shall be glorified with him,' Rom. viii. 17.

Therefore be not discouraged. That which we think to be matter of discouragement, it should be our crown. It is our crown to suffer reproach in a good cause. It is a sign God favours us, when he takes our credit, our goods, or our life to honour himself by. Is it not an honour to us? Doth he take anything from us but he gives us better? He takes our goods, but he gives us himself. He takes our liberty, but he gives us enlargement of conscience. He takes our life, but he gives us heaven. If he take anything from us, for to seal his truth, and stand out in his quarrel, as Christ saith, he ' gives an hundredfold' in this world, that is a gracious spirit of contentment and comfort.

We have God himself. Hath not he more that hath the spring than he that hath twenty cisterns? Those that have riches, and place, and friends, they have cisterns; but he that suffers for God, and for Christ, he hath Christ, he hath God, he hath the spring to go to. If all be taken from him, he hath God the spring to go to. If all particular beams, he hath the sun. It is durable, wondrous comfort to suffer for Christ's sake.

Therefore, let it encourage us in a good course, notwithstanding all the opposition we meet with in the world; let us here learn what is our duty. Let the malicious world judge, or say, or do what they will; if God be on our side, ' who can be against us?' Rom. viii. 33, 34. And if we suffer anything for Christ, he suffers with us, and in us, and he will triumph in us over all these sufferings at last.

I will add no more, to set an edge upon that I have said, than this, [as] ' they are the sufferings of Christ,' we should be many ways encouraged to suffer for him. For did not he suffer for us that, which if all the creatures in heaven and earth had suffered, they would have sunk under it, the wrath of God? And what good have we by his sufferings? Are we not freed from hell and damnation? and have we not title to heaven? Hath he suffered in his person so much for us, and shall not we be content to suffer for him, and his mystical body, that in his own body suffered so much for us?

Again, when we suffer in his quarrel, we suffer not only for him that suffered for us, but we suffer for him that sits at the right hand of God, that is glorious in heaven, ' the King of kings, and Lord of lords.' Our sufferings are sufferings for him that hath done so much for us, and for him that is so able now to over-rule all, to crush our enemies; for him that is so able now to minister comfort by his Spirit. This is a notable encouragement, that they are the sufferings of Christ, that is, so glorious as he is, and that will reward every suffering, and every disgrace. We shall be paid well for every suffering. We shall lose nothing.

And will not this encourage us likewise to suffer for Christ's sake, because he will be with us in all our sufferings. He will not leave us alone. It is his cause, and he will stand by his own cause. He will maintain his own quarrel. He will cause comfort to increase. Is it not an encouragement to defend a prince's quarrel in his own sight, when he stands by to abet us? It would encourage a dull mettle. When we suffer for Christ's cause, we have Christ to defend us. He is with us in all our sufferings to bear us up. He puts his shoulder under, by his Holy Spirit, to support us.

We cannot live long in this world. We owe God a death. We owe nature a death. The sentence of death is passed upon us. We cannot enjoy the comfort of this world long. And for favour and applause of the world, we must leave it, and it will leave us, we know not how soon. And this meditation should enforce us to be willing, however it go with us, for anything here, for life, or goods, or friends, or credit and reputation, or whatsoever, to be willing to seal the cause of Christ with that which is dearest to us. 'If we suffer with him, we shall be glorified with him,' Rom. viii. 17.

The very sufferings of Christ are better than the most glorious day of the greatest monarch in the world that is not a Christian. It is better to suffer with Christ, than to joy with the world. The very abasement of St Paul was better than the triumph of Nero. Let Moses be judge. He judged it the best end of the balance, Heb. xi. 26. The very sufferings and reproach of Christ, and of religion, is better than the best thing in the world. The worst thing in Christianity, is better than the best thing out of Christ. The best thing out of Christ is the honour of a king, the honour of a prince, to be a king's son, &c. But the reproach of Christ for a good cause is better than the best thing in the world. I say, let Moses be judge, if we will not believe it ourselves till we feel it. The worst day of a Christian is better than the best day of a carnal man ; for he hath the presence of God's Spirit to support him in some measure.

Therefore let us not be afraid beforehand. 'Fear nothing,' saith the apostle, 'that thou shalt suffer,' Acts xxvii. 24. And with Moses, let 'us not be ashamed of the rebuke of Christ,' Heb. xi. 26 ; but 'let us go out of the camp with Christ, bearing our reproach,' Heb. xiii. 13. And because we know not what God may call us to, let us entertain presently a resolution to endure whatsoever in this world God calls us to ; to pass through thick and thin, to pass through all kinds of ways to the 'hope of our glorious calling,' Philip. iii. 14 ; if by any way, by any means,' saith St Paul, 'I may attain the resurrection of the dead,' Philip. iii. 11 : if by any means I may come to heaven, by fair death, or by violent death. He scorned reproach, if by any means he might be happy.

And for others, it is a wondrous quailing to the spirits of men that offer any wrong, if it be but a disgrace. A scoff is a persecution to a Christian for a good cause. When wicked men oppose a Christian in a good cause and course, let us learn what they do, they 'kick against the pricks,' Acts ix. 5. Do they know what they do ? When they reproach Christians, it is the 'reproach of Christ,' Heb. xi. 26. What was Ishmael's scorning ? A persecution, Gal. iv. 29 Christ is scorned in his members. Will he endure this at their hands ? When good causes are opposed, Christ is opposed, and Christ is scoffed. This doth enable* our suffering, being an abasing of itself, that Christ accounts it done to him.

Base men of the world, they think when they scoff at goodness, and wrong the image of God in his children, they think they deride and despise a company of weak creatures, that they scoff at silly persons meaner than themselves. But they are deceived. They scoff Christ in them, and he takes it so, 'Saul, Saul, why persecutest thou me ?' Acts ix. 4. The foot is trod on the earth, and the head speaks from heaven. It is the reproach of Christ ; and it will be laid to thy charge at the day of judgment, that thou hast scoffed, and persecuted, and reproached Christ in his members. It will be a heavy indictment. Men should not regard what they conceive of things ; but what he that must be their judge will conceive of things ere long ; and he interprets it as done to his own person. It is true both of good and ill. Whatsoever good we do to a Christian as a Christian, to a disciple in the name of a disciple, Christ takes it as done to himself,

* That is, 'strengthen us in suffering.'—G.

'Inasmuch as you have done it to these, you have done it to me,' Mat. xxv. 40.

It should animate us to do good offices to those that are Christ's. What we do to them, we do to Christ. Let us be willing to refresh the bowels of Christ in his members, at home or abroad, as occasion serves; to maintain the quarrel of Christ as much as we can, to relieve Christ. He comes to us in the poor, and asks relief. He that shed his blood for us, he that died for us, he that hath given us all, asks a little pittance for himself; that we for his sake would be so good to him in his members, as to do thus and thus; that for Jonathan's sake we would regard poor, lame Mephibosheth, his son, 2 Sam. ix. 1, *seq.* Christ, though he be gone, he hath some Mephibosheths, some poor, weak members; and what offices we do them, he accounts done to himself. It runs on his score. He will be accountable for every good word we speak in his cause, for every defence, for every act of bounty. It is a point of large meditation to consider, that the crosses and afflictions of Christians, they are the sufferings of Christ.

Do but consider the Spirit of God intended in this phrase, to dignify all disgraces and indignities that are put upon us in a good cause and quarrel. Could he have said more in few words? He calls them not disgraces, or losses, or death; but he puts such a comfortable title upon them, that might make us in love with suffering anything, and set us on fire to endure anything in a good cause. They are the 'sufferings of Christ.'

'As the sufferings of Christ abound, so our consolations,' &c. The third general point is, *that our consolations are proportionable to our sufferings.* ' Our consolations abound.' We suffer in this world. That is hard. Aye, but they are the sufferings of Christ. There is sweetness. And then another degree is, our consolations abound as our sufferings abound. Consolation is, as I shewed before in the unfolding of the word, an inward support of the soul against trouble felt or feared; and it must be stronger than the grievance, or else the action of comfort will not follow. There is a disproportion between the agent and the patient, in all prevailing actions, or else there is no prevailing. If the comfort be not above the malady, it is no comfort. And therefore no comforts but divine comforts will stand at length, because in all other comforts *sedet medicinum morbo,*[*] the malady is above the remedy. They make glorious pretences, as the philosophers do, Plutarch and Seneca, and the rest. But they are as apothecaries' boxes. They have goodly titles, but there is nothing within.

Alas! when there is trouble in the conscience, awakened with the sight of sin, and the displeasure of God, what can all those precepts compose and frame the soul in petty troubles? They have their place; and surely the neglect of them many times is that that makes the cross heavier. But alas! in divine troubles, in terror of conscience, it must be divine comfort. It must be of like nature, or else the effect of comfort will never follow; and those be the comforts that he means here. As our troubles and afflictions abound, so our consolations, our divine supports, they abound. The point is this, that

Doct. Our comforts are proportionable to our sufferings.

What did I say, proportionable? It is above all proportion of suffering. As it is said, 'the afflictions of this life are not worthy of the glory that shall be revealed,' Rom. viii. 18. And indeed in this life the consolations abound as the sufferings abound. For God keeps not all for the life to come. He gives us a taste, a grape of Canaan, before we come to Canaan.

---

[*] Qu. '*cedit medicina morbo?*'—ED.

As the Israelites, they sent for grapes to taste the goodness of the land, and they had them brought to them by the spies, by which they might guess of the fruitfulness and sweetness of the land itself. So the taste and relish that God's children have of that fulness which is reserved in another world, it is answerable and proportionable to their sufferings; and in the proportion, the exceeding part is of comfort. There is an exceeding, if not for the present, yet afterwards. The ark did rise together with the water, and comforts rise together with matter of suffering.

But what is the reason of the proportion? Why the greatest comforts follow the greatest sufferings? What is the ground of it? They are many.

Reason 1. To name some: first of all, this is a ground *that the more capable the soul is of comfort, the more comfort it receives.* But great troubles bring a capacity and capableness of soul, fitting it to receive comfort. How is that? Troubles do humble the soul, and humility is a grace, and the vessel of all grace, and of comfort too. A low and meek spirit is a deep spirit, and the lower and deeper, and the larger the spirit is, the more capable it is to contain heavenly comfort. We know the more empty a man is of himself, the more fit he is for comfort; but crosses and afflictions empty us of ourselves, to see that there is nothing in us, that what we are we must be out of ourselves; and the less we are in ourselves, the more we are in God. And that is the reason that St Austin saith, that nothing is more strong than a humble, empty spirit; because it makes the creature to go out of itself to him that is strength itself, and comfort itself. Now, that which makes us go out of ourselves to strength, that is strong. But this doth crosses and afflictions. That is the main reason why the proportion holds.

Reason 2. Again, another reason is this, *troubles, and afflictions, and crosses do exercise graces;* and the more grace is exercised, the more comfort is derived, for comfort follows graces. The comforts of the Spirit follow the graces of the Spirit, as the heat follows the fire, or as the shadow follows the body. Now, the more grace, the more comfort; the more affliction, the more exercise of grace; the more exercise of grace, the more grace itself; as we see, the deeper the root the higher the tree. After the sharpest winter usually there is the sweetest spring, and the fruitfulest summer and autumn; because in the sharpest winter the ground is mellowed most, and the seed sinks the deepest; and the ground is inwardly warmed, the soil, the earth is prepared for it; and thereupon, when the outward heat comes to draw it forth, it comes to be abundantly fruitful. We see it in nature, that that we call *antiperistasis,*⁎ the environing of one contrary with another increaseth the contrary. Whatsoever is good is increased, being environed by the contrary ill, because they are put to the conflict.

So it is with the soul. It is the showers of affliction that bring the sweet flowers of comfort after. The soul is prepared and manured for them. The soul is exercised, and enlarged, and fitted for them every way. ' In the multitude of my sorrows, thy comforts refreshed my soul,' saith David, Ps. xciv. 19. Answerable to our discomforts, God's comforts refresh our souls.

Reason 3. And *God is so wise, that before we enter to suffer any great matter, he will give us more grace answerable to the greatness of our suffering,* and after great suffering he will give great comfort. God is so infinitely loving and wise, that he will not call us to suffer great troubles till he give us some grace answerable. As a captain will not set a fresh-water soldier in a

* That is, ' ἀντιπερίστασις, opposition or counteraction of the surrounding parts; in rhetoric as explained above.'—G.

sharp brunt, but some experienced man. Whatsoever wisdom is in man, it is but a drop in regard of that infinite wisdom that is in God. He proportions our strength before we suffer, and in suffering he doth increase it; and after suffering, then comfort comes following amain. Indeed, especially after a little while waiting, for God's time is the best time.

Reason 4. And we shall have most experience *of the presence of Christ and his Holy Spirit* at such times. The nearer to the spring of comfort, the more comfort. But in the deepest and sharpest afflictions, we are near to God. Therefore the more comfort.

How is this proved? The more we are stripped of outward comforts, the more near we are to God, who is styled the 'God that comforteth the abject,' Job xxix. 25; and the nearer to God, the nearer to comfort itself. For all comfort springs from him; and when outward means fail that should convey comfort to us, then he conveys it immediately by himself. I confess he is present at all times; but when the comfort is conveyed by the creature, by man, it is not so sweet as when God joins with the soul immediately, as in great crosses he doth. Such occasion, and such extremity may be, that none can comfort a man but God, by his Spirit. When Christ comes to the soul immediately, what abundance of comfort is there then! As a king that doth not send a messenger, but comes immediately in his own person to visit one in misery, what a grace is it! So what a grace is it to a soul afflicted and deserted, to have Christ immediately present! As the martyrs found, when no other creature could comfort them, there was a fire within above all the outward fire and torment, which abated and allayed the torments that were without. The divinest comforts are kept for the harshest and the worst times. We shall have the presence of Christ in the absence of all other creatures, and he will minister comfort. They may keep outward comforts from us, they can never keep the God of comfort from us; and so long as a Christian soul and God can close together, it cannot want comfort.

Reason 5. Another reason why comforts increase, *because we pray most then*. When we pray most, we are most happy. But in our greatest sufferings we pray most, and most ardently. Therefore then we feel most comfort. When God and a Christian soul can talk together, and have communion, though he cannot speak to God with his tongue, yet he can sigh and groan to God. He can pour forth his spirit to God, and as long as we can pray we can never be miserable; as long as the heart can ease itself into the bosom of God, there will alway be a return of a sweet answer. Of all the exercises of religion, that exercise that hath most immediate communion with God is prayer. Then we speak familiarly to God in his own language and words, and call upon him by his own promises. We allege those to him, and this cannot be, we cannot speak, and confer, and converse with the God of comfort without a great deal, without a world, of comfort. Great crosses drive us to this, and therefore then we have great comfort.

Use 1. What use may we make of this? First, for ourselves, *we should* * *not fear nor faint, neither faint in troubles nor fear troubles.* Faint not in them. We shall have comfort proportionable; and let us not fear troubles before they come, or any measure of them. Proportionable to the measure of our afflictions shall be our comfort. Let us not fear anything we shall suffer in this world in a good cause; for as we suffer so we shall receive from God. We fear our own good. For it is better to have the comfort we shall have in suffering anything for a good cause, than to be exempted

* Mis rinted 'would.'—G.

from the suffering and to want the comfort. There is no proportion. The choice is much better, to have comfort with grievance than to want the comfort together with the grievance. St Paul would not have chosen immunity from suffering, he would not have been exempted from the cross to have wanted his comfort.

For the disproportion is wide and great. The comforts are inward and sweet, the crosses, for the most part, are outward. What are all the crosses and sufferings in this world? Set aside an afflicted conscience, it is but brushing of the garment, as it were; some outward thing in the outward man, but the comforts are inward and deep.

But what if there be inward grievances too? Then we have deeper comforts than they. The cross is never so deep but the comfort is deeper. 'Oh the depth of the wisdom and love of God!' Rom. xi. 23. There is the part and dimension of God's love, the depth of it! There is a depth in crosses. 'Out of the deep have I cried to thee,' Ps. cxxx. 1. But there is a deeper depth of comfort, there is a hand under to fetch us up at the lowest. 'Thy right hand is upon me, and thy left hand is under me,' Song of Sol. ii. 6, saith the church to God. There is comfort lower and deeper than the grievance, though it be inward, spiritual grievance. Nay, of all grievances (I know what I speak a little of mine own experience, and it is true in the experience of all ministers and Christians, that) there is none that have more help than they that are exercised with spiritual temptations of conscience. They are forced to search for deep comforts. Shallow comforts will not serve their turn! And when they have them, they keep them, and make much of them. They have more retired and deep thoughts of Christ, and of comforts than other people, who as they are strangers to their crosses, so they are strangers to their comfort. There is no degree of proportion between the crosses and the comforts. The crosses are momentary, the comforts are growing. The crosses make us not a whit the worse, and the comforts make us better. Fear nothing therefore; but go on in the ways of religion, and never be discouraged to suffer in a good cause for fear of men, to think, Oh this will come, and that will come. No, no; if the sufferings grow, the comforts shall grow with it, be of good comfort.

Use 2. Again, another use may be, *that we judge aright of those that are disgraced in the world, if their cause be good;* that we should not have distasteful conceits of them, as indeed suffering breeds distaste naturally in men. They love men in a flourishing estate, and distaste them suffering; but that is corruption of men. But God is the nearest to them then, nearer than ever he was, and their comforts increase with their crosses. In the conjunction between the sun and the moon, as by experience we see, in the space between the old and new moon, there is a time of conjunction. We think the moon to be lost in that time, because we see her not; but the moon is more enlightened then, than ever she was in herself. But here is the reason, the light part of the moon is turned to the sunward, to heavenward, and the dark part is turned toward the earth. So a Christian in crosses and abasement seems to be a dark creature, but he is more enlightened then, than ever before? Why? His light part is to Godward, it is not seen of the world. The world sees his crosses, but they do not see his comforts. And as the moon is nearer the sun at that time than at other times; so the soul hath to deal with God in afflictions. It is nearer to God, and his dark side is toward the world. As the world sees the moon's eclipse, so the world sees our darkness, but not our inward comfort. Therefore we should judge aright of others in this case.

Use 3. Another use shall be *of thankfulness to God*, that besides the comforts of heaven (which are not to be spoken of, and which we shall not know till we come to feel them), besides the great comfort we have to be free from hell, that we have a measure of comfort here in this world, in our pilgrimage, and absence from heaven, such a measure of comfort, as may carry us with comfort along. We ought to be thankful to God, not only for redemption and glorification, but that God comforts us in our pilgrimage, that he mingles crosses with comforts; nay, that in this world our comforts are more than our crosses.

Obj. Some may object, Aye, but my crosses are more than my comforts?

Ans. Are they so? Dost thou suffer in a good cause or no? If thou dost, thy comforts are more than thy crosses, if there be not a fault in thee.

Quest. What shall I do therefore?

First, Take this direction in suffering, *pull out the sting of sin*, though we suffer in never so good a cause, for in one suffering, God aims at divers things. God in thy suffering aims at thy correction, as well as at the exercise of thy grace and at thy comfort. Therefore, let affliction have the correcting and amending part first, and then the comforting part will follow. Though the cause be good, yet God's children ofttimes want comfort till afterward. Why? They have not renewed their repentance, and cleansed their souls. They have not pulled out the sting. When they have repented of their personal sins that lie upon them, and gone back to the sins of their youth, and then renewed their covenant with God, and their purposes for the time to come, then comes comfort, and not before. Therefore it is no disparagment to a good cause, that sometimes Christians find not present comfort. They have personal sins that hang on them, that are not repented of, which God intends to amend them of, as well as to honour them by suffering in his cause.

Second. Again, if God's children complain, that their sufferings are above their strength, and above measure, and desire God to weigh their afflictions, they are so great, as Job saith,—*it is the speech of sense and not of faith*, it is the speech of the fit, and not of the state. There is a fit and a state. It is no matter what they say in their fit, then the flesh and sense speak, and not grace and faith at that time. If they judge by sense, then they judge so, but we know that reason corrects the errors of sense, and faith corrects the errors of reason. But what do they say in their constant state? Their comforts are answerable to their crosses, either in suffering or afterwards, though not alway at the same time. So much for that.

But this will be abused by carnal persons. We speak of abundance of comfort, but it is to those that have interest in it. The book of God speaks no comfort to persons that live in sin, and will do so. We speak comfort to those that are broken-hearted for their sins, that are content to endure the reproach of religion in despite of the world, that will bear the cross of Christ. For the other, as their jollity increaseth in the world, so their crosses and troubles shall increase. As it is said, Rev. xviii. 17, of mystical Babylon, the Church of Rome, that hath flourished in the world a great while, and sat as a queen and blessed herself, ' As she glorified herself, and lived deliciously, so much torment and sorrow give her.' So it is true of every wicked man that is in an evil course, and will be, and as the Scripture phrase is, ' blesseth himself in an evil course,' they shall be sure of the curse of God, and not of comfort. For in what proportion they have delighted themselves in this world in sin, in that proportion they shall have torment of conscience, if conscience be awaked in this world; and in that proportion they shall have torment in the world to come. As sin is growing, so rods are growing for them. Wicked men, saith St Paul, ' they grow worse and worse,' 2 Tim. iii. 13. The more they sin, the more they may. They sink in rebellion, and the more they sink in rebellion, the more they sink in the state of damnation. They fill up the measure of their sins, and treasure up the wrath of God against the day of wrath. Whosoever thou art that livest in a sinful course, and will do so in spite of God's ordinance, in spite of the motions of the Spirit, that hast the good motions of the Spirit knocking at thy soul, and yet wilt rather refuse comfort than take comfort, together with direction, go on still in this thy wicked course, but remember, as thy comforts increase in this world, so thy torment is increasing. And here is the disproportion between God's children and others. They have their sufferings first, and their comfort afterward; but others have their pleasure first, and their torment after. Theirs are for a time, but others for ever. Thus we see what we may comfortably observe from this, that comforts increase as crosses increase.

A word of the fourth and last point.

How comes this to pass, that *as our afflictions abound, so our consolations abound?*

Doct. They abound by Christ, saith the apostle, God the Father, he is the God of comfort; the Holy Ghost is the comforter. But how comes this to pass, that we that are not the objects of comfort, but of confusion, should have God the Father to be the ' God of comfort,' and the Holy Ghost ' to be our comforter?' Oh, it is that Jesus Christ, the great peace-maker, hath satisfied God, and procured the Holy Ghost; for the Holy Ghost is procured by the satisfaction and death of Christ, and he was sent after the resurrection and ascension of Christ. Therefore Christ is called ' the consolation of Israel,' Luke ii. 25, and those that waited for Christ waited for the consolation of Israel. All comfort is hid in Christ. He is the storehouse of comfort. ' We have it through him, and by him, and in him.' For that God is the ' Father of comfort,' it is because Christ is our mediator and intercessor in heaven; that the Holy Ghost is ' the comforter,' it is because Christ sent him. And the comforts of the Holy Ghost are fetched from Christ, from the death of Christ, or the ascension of Christ, from some argument from Christ. Whatsoever comforteth the soul, the Holy Ghost doth it by fetching some argument from Christ, from his satisfaction, from his worth, from his intercession in heaven. Something in Christ it is. So Christ by his Spirit doth comfort, and the reasons fetched by the Spirit are from Christ. Therefore it is by Christ.

What is the reason that a Christian soul doth not fear God as ' a consuming fire,' Heb. xii. 29, but can look upon him with comfort? It is because God hath received satisfaction by Christ. What is the reason that a Christian soul fears not hell, but thinks of it with comfort? Christ hath conquered hell and Satan. What is the reason that a Christian fears not death? Christ by death hath overcome death, and him that had the power of death, the devil. Christ is mine, saith the Christian soul. Therefore I do not fear it, but think of it with comfort, because a Christian is more than a conqueror over all these. What is the reason that a Christian is not afraid of his corruptions and sins? He knows that God, for Christ's sake, will pardon them, and that the remainder of his corruptions will work to his humiliation, and to his good. ' All shall work for the best to them that love God,' Rom. viii. 28. What is the reason that there is not any thing in the world but it is comfortable to a Christian? When he thinks of God, he thinks of him as a Father of comfort ; when he thinks of the Holy Ghost, he thinks of him as a Spirit of comfort; when he thinks of angels, he thinks of them as his attendants ; when he thinks of heaven, he thinks of it as of his inheritance; he thinks of saints as a communion whereof he is partaker. Whence is all this ? By Christ, who hath made God our Father, the Holy Ghost our comforter, who hath made angels ours, saints ours, heaven ours, earth ours, devils ours, death ours, all ours, in issue.

For God being turned in love to us, all is turned. Our crosses are no curses now, but comforts ; and the bitterest crosses yield the sweetest comforts. All this is by Christ, that hath turned the course of things, and hid blessings in the greatest crosses that ever were. And this he did in himself, before he doth it in us. For did not his greatest crosses tend to his greatest glory ? who ever in the world was abased as our head Christ Jesus was ? that made him cry, ' My God, my God, why hast thou forsaken me ?' Mat. xv. 34. All the creatures in the world would have sunk under the sufferings that Christ endured. What abasement to the abasement of Christ ? and what glory to the glory of Christ ? ' He humbled himself to the death of the cross; wherefore God gave him a name above all names, that at the name of Jesus every knee should bow, both of things in heaven, and things in earth, and things under the earth,' Phil. ii. 8. Now as it was in our head, his greatest abasement ushered in his greatest glory ; so it shall be in us,—our greatest crosses are before our greatest comforts. He is our president.* He is the exemplary cause as well as the efficient working cause. It is by Christ all this, that consolations abound in us. It was performed first in him, and shall be by him, by his Spirit to the end of the world.

Use. The use that we are to make of this is, that in all our sufferings, before we come to heaven, *we should look to Christ.* He hath turned all things. Let us study Christ, and fetch comfort from him. Our flesh was abased in him. Our flesh is glorified in him now in heaven, in his person. And so it must be in our own persons. Our flesh must be abased, and then as he is glorious in heaven, so shall we be in ourselves. That very Spirit that raised and advanced him at the lowest, that very Spirit (there being but one Spirit in the head and members) in our greatest abasement shall vouchsafe us the greatest advancement that we can look for, to sit at the right hand of God, to reign with Christ ; ' for if we suffer with him, we shall reign with him,' Rom. viii. 17.

And hence you may have a reason likewise why Christians have no more comfort. They do not study Christ enough. They consider not Christ, and the nearness wherein Christ is to them, and they to Christ, that both make one Christ. They do not consider how Christ hath sweetened all. He hath turned God, and turned all to us. He hath made God our Father, and in him all things favourable unto us. So that now the fire is our friend, the stone, and the gout, and all diseases, disgrace and temptation, all are at peace and league with us; all is turned in the use and issue to good, to the help and comfort of God's children (k). ' All things are yours, and you are Christ's, and Christ is God's,' 1 Cor. iii. 23. There is not the worst thing but it is at peace with us; because the malignant power it hath, in order to damnation, is taken away. Now it doth not hurt us, but there is a sovereign curing power to turn it to good.

I confess God's children are discomforted, but then they wrong their principles, they wrong their grounds, their religion, their Saviour. They

* That is, ' precedent' = exemplar.—G.

wrong all the comforts they have interest in, because they do not improve them when occasion serves, as Job is checked, ' Hast thou forgot the consolations of the Almighty ?' Job xv. 11, or why dost thou forget them ? So if we have consolations and forget them, and doat and pore upon our grievance, it is just with God to leave us comfortless ; not that we want any comfort, but we flatter our grievance and forget our comfort. Let us change our object, and when we have looked upon our grievance, and been humbled in the sight of our sins, let us look upon the promises, let us look upon Christ in glory, and see ourselves in heaven triumphing with him.

What can terrify a soul ? not death itself, when it sees itself in Christ triumphing. Faith sees me as well triumphing in heaven, and sitting at the right hand of God, as it doth Christ, for it knows I am a member of Christ, and whatsoever is between me and that happiness, that is reserved for me in heaven, I shall triumph over it.

Christ triumphed in his own person over death, hell, sin, the grave, the devil, and he will triumph in me his mystical body. What he hath done in himself, he will do in me. This faith will overcome the world, and the devil, and hell, and all that is between us and heaven. A Christian that sees himself sitting at the right hand of God with Christ, triumphing with him, he is discouraged at nothing ; for faith that makes things to come present, it sees him conquering already.

Let us be exhorted to joy, ' Rejoice, and again I say rejoice,' Philip. iv. 4. We have reason to do so, if we look to our grounds. But when we yield to Satan, and our own flesh, we rob God of his glory and ourselves of comfort, but we may thank ourselves for it.

But I come to the sixth verse, wherein the apostle enlargeth himself, by shewing the end of his sufferings in regard of them, by setting down both parts, both affliction and comfort.

VERSE 6.

' *Whether we be afflicted, it is for your consolation and salvation: or whether we be comforted, it is for your consolation and salvation.*' It is much in everything, how the mind is prepared to receive what is spoken. The apostle, therefore, to make way for himself in their hearts, he removes scandal from his sufferings, and he shews that it was so far that they should take offence at it, that they ought to do as he did, to bless God for it ; for as the sufferings of Christ abounded in him, so his comfort abounded. And because they should think themselves no way hurt by his sufferings and base usage in the world, he tells them in the verse that all was for their good. No man should be offended at his own good. They had no reason to take scandal at that which was for their good ; but, saith he, if you think basely of me for my sufferings, you think basely of your own comfort : for my sufferings are for your good, and my comforts are for your good. Whether I suffer or be comforted, it is for you.

The cross is a distasteful thing to us, and likewise the cross in others is a distasteful thing, not only distasteful and bitter to us, but shameful. St Paul knowing this, because he would, as I said, work himself into their good conceit, that he might prevail with them for their good, saith he, you ought not to think a whit the worse of me for this, for all is for you. So you see the scope of the words, ' Whether we be afflicted, it is for your consolation,' &c,

But first he speaks of affliction alone, and then of comfort alone. If we be afflicted, it is for your good; and if we be comforted, it is for your good. His reason is, because sometimes afflictions appear without comfort. Therefore he saith not, ' If we be comforted only, it is for your good ;' but ' If we be afflicted, it is for your good.' Sometimes comfort is before our afflictions. That we may endure it the better, God cheers us to it. Sometimes God sheds his Spirit in affliction, that there is abundance of comfort in it. But for the most part it comes after, after we have waited ; but in it there is always such a measure of comfort that supports us, that we sink not. Yet the special degree of comfort usually comes after. Therefore he speaks of affliction in the first place. ' If I be afflicted, it is for you,' &c.

The point is easy, that

Doct. The afflictions of the saints are for the good of others.

The afflictions of God's church are God's people's, especially the afflictions of pastors and leaders of God's army. God singles out some to suffer for the good of others ; the good especially of consolation and salvation, for these two goods.

Quest. How can this be, that the afflictions of God's people are for the consolation and salvation of others ?

Ans. I answer, many ways, as we shall see afterwards more particularly : but only now to make way.

1. Afflictions are for the good and comfort of others, *because we have their example in suffering, to train us up how to suffer.* Example is a forcible kind of teaching. Therefore, saith the apostle, our afflictions are for you, to lead and teach you the way how to suffer. Words are not enough, especially in matter of suffering. There must be some example. Therefore Christ from heaven came, not only to redeem us, but to teach us, not only by words, but by example, how to do, and suffer willingly, and cheerfully, and stoutly, in obedience to God, as he did.

2. Again, afflictions do good to others, *by ministering occasion to them to search deeper into the cause.* When they see the people of God are so used, they take occasion hereby to inquire what is the cause, and so take occasion to be instructed deeply in matters of religion ; for man's nature is inquisitive, and grace takes the hint off anything. What is the matter that such and such endure such things ? Hereupon, I say, they come to be better grounded in the cause, and little occasions ofttimes are the beginnings of great matters ; by reason that the spirit as well as wit is of a working nature, and will draw one thing from another. We see what a great tree riseth of a little seed ! how a little thing, upon report, worketh conversion. Naaman the Assyrian had a servant, and she told him that there was a prophet in Jewry that was a famous man, that did great matters, and if he would go to him, he should be cured of his leprosy. That little occasion being ministered, Naaman comes to the prophet, and he was cured of a double leprosy, both of soul and body, and went home a good man, 2 Kings v. 1, *seq.* So by way of ministering occasion of inquisition, the sufferings of others do good.

3. And then, seeing the constant and resolute spirits of those that suffer, it *doth them good, and comforts them :* for, first, it makes them conceive well of the cause: certainly these men that suffer constantly, and cheerfully, it is a good cause that they suffer for, when they see the cause is such a resolution and courage in the sufferers. And it makes them in love with, and begin to think well of, the persons, when they can deny themselves. Surely these men care not for the pleasures and vanities of the world, that can endure to suffer these. So Justin Martyr saith when he

saw Christians suffer ; he thought they were men that cared not for pleasures ; for if they had, they would not suffer these things *(l)*.

4. Besides, *they can gather from the presence of God's Spirit emboldening
the sufferers, what they may hope for themselves if they should suffer.* They
may reason thus : Is God by his Spirit so full and so strong in these that
are flesh and blood as we are ? Is he so strong in women, in young men,
in aged men, that neither their years, nor their sex, nor their tenderness,
can any kind of way hinder them from these kind of abasements and sharp
sufferings ? Surely the same Spirit of God will be as strong in me, if I
stand out in the same cause, and carry myself as they do. And there is
good reason, for God is the same God, the Spirit is the same Spirit, the
cause is the same cause. Therefore it is no false reasoning. I may, upon
a good presumption, hope for the presence and assistance of the Spirit of
God to enable and strengthen me as he did them ; for the same Spirit of
God will be strong in all.

5. And this is partly likewise *in the intent of them that suffer.* There is
a double intent. It is the intent of God to single them out to suffer for the
good of others ; and it is their intent to suffer that others may have good.
This is one reason why they are willing rather to suffer shame, or bodily
punishment, than they will hinder others of the good they may take by
their suffering. So it is God's end, and their end. It is for your consolation, in God's intent, and in my intent and purpose, and in the event itself.
Thus you see how afflictions, suffered in good cause, help for the consolation and salvation even of others. The example of those that suffer flow
into the mind, and insinuate into the judgment and affection, of the beholders
many ways.

And this the factors of antichrist know very well ; for if ever there be
any persecution again, we shall hardly have fire and faggot, that they may
not give example. They will come to gunpowder plots and massacres, and
such violent courses, to sweep away all. They know if it come to matter
of example once, the grace of God in his children, and the presence of his
Spirit, that shall appear to others, it is of a wondrous working force. They
are wise enough to know that. The devil teacheth them that wit, when he
hath been put by all his other shifts.

If it be so that the sufferings of God's children are for the good of others,
then to make some use of it.

Use 1. Let us not take offence at the cause of religion for suffering. We
ought not to have an ill conceit of a cause for suffering, but rather think the
better of it. I speak it in this regard, we have many that will honour
the martyrs that are dead, that are recorded in the book, but if any suffer
in the present view, before their eyes, they are disgraceful to them. This
should not be. For, first of all, if the cause be good, the end of good men
(by the help of the Spirit of God) is for thy good. Was it not a cruel thing
in Saul to strike at David when he played on his harp, when he sought his
good and easement ? 1 Sam. xviii. 10, 11. To kill a nightingale in singing,
it is a barbarous thing. God's children, by all that they suffer, intend the
good of others. Now, to hurt and malign them in doing good, to persecute
them that endure ill for our good, or that labour and do anything for our
good, it is a barbarous, savage thing. All is for the elect. ' I suffer not*
for the elect's sake,' saith St Paul in 2 Tim. ii. 10 ; so my sufferings are
for you. We may know we are elected of God, if we take good by the
sufferings of others ; if we take no scandal and offence, and do not add

* Qu. ' all ?'—ED.

affliction to the afflicted, for all is in God's intent, and in their intent, for
our good.

For instance (a little to enlighten the point, because it is not usually stood
on, and it is a notion that may help our conceits of the excellent estate of
God's children), reprobation, to go as high as we may, it is for their good,
to shew mercy to them, to set by and neglect so many, and to single them
out. The creation of the world is for their sakes. God's providence
directs all for their good. For why doth he suffer wicked men? It is that
they may be instruments to exercise them that are good. It is by reflection,
or some way for the cause of the good, that the wicked are suffered to be
upon the earth. The administration of the world, it is not for the rebels that
are in it, it is for those that are God's children; and he tosseth and tumbleth
empires and monarchies. The great men of the world, they think they do
great matters; but, alas! all this is for the exercise of the church, this is
reductive to the church, by God's providence. All their attempts are for
the little flock, for a few that are a despised company, that he means to
save, if we had eyes to see it.

So likewise his ordinances are to gather this church, which he hath
chosen from all the world to himself. The ordinances of the ministry,
and of the sacraments, the suffering of ministers, the doing and suffering
of Christians, all is for their good, as we see in this place, ' I suffer for
your consolation and comfort.' Heaven and earth stands for them. The
pillars of heaven and earth would be taken asunder, and all would come to
a chaos, an end would be of all, if the number of them were gathered that
are the blessed people of God, for whom all things are. The doings and
sufferings of God's people, we do not know indeed, that are ministers, who
belong to God and who do not, but our intent is to do good to those that
are God's, and the issue proves so. The rest God hath his end in it to
harden them, and bring them to confusion, to take excuse from them; but
the real good of all our pains and suffering is the elect's.

Let us examine what good we take by ordinances of God, and by
the sufferings of the present church, and the sufferings of the former
church. Do their examples animate, and quicken, and encourage us to
the like courses? It is a sign we are elected of God. There is no greater
sign of a good estate in grace, than a gracious heart, to draw good out of
the examples of others, and to draw good out of everything that befalls us,
because God's end in election, and his manner of providence, is to guide all
to their good.

Use 2. Again, we learn another thing likewise, *how God overrules in his
providence the projects of carnal men, of the devil and his instruments, and
agents and factors.* God overrules all things, that which in itself is ill, and
in the intendment* of the inflicter is ill, yet God turns it to the good of
others, and the good of them that suffer too. Satan intends no such matter,
as it is said, Isa. x. 5. Nebuchadnezzar thinks no such thing. ' Asshur,
the rod of my wrath,' he intends no such matter. They intend not the
consolation of God's when they wrong the saints of God, and so exercise
their patience and grace. No! they intend their hurt and confusions. It
is no matter what they intend; but God at the first created light out of
darkness, and in his providence doth great matters by small means. In his
providence over his church, he doth raise contraries out of contraries; he
turns the wicked projects of men to contrary ends, and makes all serviceable to his own end.

* That is, ' intention.'—G.

In state policy, he is accounted the wisest man that can make his enemies instrumental to his own purpose, that can make others serve his own
turn, to work his own ends by others that are his opposites; and he had
need of a great reaching head that can do so. The great providence of
heaven doth thus. God is the wisest politician in the world. All other
policy is but a beam from that Sun. He can make instrumental and serviceable to him his very enemies. And this is the torment of Satan, that
God overshoots him in his own bow. He overreacheth him in his own
policy. Where he thinks to do most harm he doth most good. In those
afflictions whereby he thinks to quell the courage of the church, God doth
exceeding good to them, and enlargeth the bounds of the church this way.

It is an ordinary speech, 'The blood of the martyrs is the seed of the
church' (*m*). The word of God is the seed of the church; how then is the
blood of the martyrs and sufferers the seed of the church? Thus the
word of God is the seed of the church, how? As it is in the Bible, in the
book? No! As it is published in preaching, much more as it is published
in confession, and much more as it is published and sealed in martyrdom,
by suffering. The word of God is so laid open, as not only spoken but
confessed and practised in life; and not only so, but sealed by enduring
anything. Thus it is the seed, and works strongly.

God overrules all inferiors. Though they have contrary motions in
their own intent to his, yet he brings them about to his end. As we see
the heavens have a contrary motion to the first heaven, that carries the
rest, the *primum mobile*, yet they are turned about by another motion, contrary to the bent of themselves. They go one way, and are carried another.*
As we see in the wheels of the clock, one runs one way, another another;
all make the clock strike, all serve the intent of the clockmaker; so one
runs one way, and another, another. Carnal men offer disgrace and disparagement to God's people; their intent is to otherthrow all, to disgrace
and to trample on the cause of religion; but God useth contrary wheels,
to make the clock strike. All turns in the issue to his end. Therefore
though we say in our common speech, that the devil is the god of this world,
it is the Scripture phrase, 2 Cor. iv. 4; and it is so in regard of the wicked
that are under him, yet he is a god under a God. There is but one monarch
of the world. He is a god that hath not power over swine further than he
is suffered, Mat. viii. 30, *seq*. It is a point of wondrous comfort, that
though we be thus used, yet there is an active providence, there is one
monarch, one great king, that rules all.

It is a ground of patience and contentment in whatsoever we suffer, not
to look to the next instrument, but [to] look to the overruling cause, that
will turn all in the issue to our good. This Joseph comforted his brethren
with. You sent me, and of an ill mind too; but God turned it to good.
It was no thank to them, yet it was no matter. He comforted them in this,
that God turned their malice to his good, and to their good too, for he was
sent as a steward to provide for them.

And it is one ground why to think more moderately in regard of anger,
fierceness, against wicked men, it is ground of pitying of them; for, alas!
poor souls, what do they! Though they intend it of malice, they are but
instruments, and shall be overruled to do good contrary to their meaning,
as St Paul saith here, 'Whether I be afflicted, it is for your consolation
and salvation.' The worst intents and designs of the enemies of religion,

* This frequently-recurring illustration is drawn from the Cartesian system of
astronomy, which Newton's discoveries had not yet superseded.—G.

was for the consolation and salvation of the Corinthians. It is good to
think of this beforehand. It is a ground of patience; and not only so,
but of comfort and joy, which is a degree above patience. God overrules
all thus. Therefore we should quietly cast ourselves wholly upon him,
willing to do and suffer whatsoever he will have us, knowing that he will
direct all to the good of the church, to our comfort, and his own glory.

Use 3. Again, a further use may be this, *to teach us to communicate our
estate to others, because it is for their good.* Good is diffusive, saith St Paul.
All that I do or suffer, it is for your good, to join comfort and suffering together. ' If I be comforted,' it is for you; and if I suffer, it is for you. It
must be by their taking notice of it, and that is not all that they ought to
take notice, but we ought to let them take notice as much as we can, ' Come,
children, and I will teach you the fear of the Lord,' Ps. xxxiv. 11. ' Come
and I will tell you what the Lord hath done for my soul.' ' The righteous
shall compass me about,' saith David, Ps. cxlii. 7. As when a man hath
some great matter to tell, there will be a ring of people about him, desirous
to hear what he saith ; so saith David, the righteous shall compass me
about. When David had sweet matter of experience, to tell what God had
done for him; how he had been with him in his affliction, and delivered him,
' the righteous shall compass me about,' I will declare it to others. For
God's children make others' case their own. They comfort them as they
would be comforted of them again.

As they ought to do so, so we should take notice of their troubles and
deliverances, how God sanctifies them to them. These things tend to
edification. There is the same reason to one saint of God as to all, and
God is the same to all in the like case. Experiments are made much of in
other things in physic, and judged cases in law, and such like. Tried
things in all professions are good. So tried truths should be valued. Now
when a man teacheth another his experiment,* it is a judged case, a tried
truth. It is not every truth that will stay the soul in the time of a great
temptation, but a truth proved, a tried truth. Therefore it is good for
parents and governors, for friends and for all degrees of men, to make it
one way to spend their time fruitfully, to discourse with others of the blessed
experiments which they have had of God's gracious providence, in the passages
of their life. ' Abraham will teach his children,' Gen. xviii. 19, I will tell
it to him therefore, saith God. It is a means for God to reveal many
things sweetly to us, when he knows we are of a communicative, spreading
disposition. God gains by that means. His glory is spread. Our grace
is increased. The good of others is multiplied.—To go on.

' *It is for your consolation and salvation.*' Whether we be afflicted, or
whether we be comforted, all is for your consolation and salvation. I will
not trouble you here with the diverse readings of copies. Some Greek
copies want the word salvation, but the most that the translations follow
have both consolation and salvation. Some have consolation and salvation
in the first, but they repeat it not in the second. ' Whether we be comforted, it is for your consolation and salvation.' But because the more
current have both, therefore we will join both, ' it is for your consolation
and salvation' (*n*).

For *huper*† in the Greek it hath a double force. It signifies either to
merit ; *hupon*,‡ to procure and merit salvation ; and so we do not under-

* That is, ' experience.'—G.   † That is, ὑπερ = over, above.—G.
‡ Apparently a misprint.—ED.

stand it. Or *huper***** for your good, a final cause. It includes either a meritorious deserving cause, or a final cause. ' Whether I be afflicted, it is for your consolation and salvation,' not by merit and desert;—so Christ's suffering was—but to help it forward in the execution of it.

I speak this to cut the sinews of a popish point, as I meet it, which is a cozening point of their religion, which indeed is not a point of religion, but a point of Romish policy, a point of cozenage; as most of their religion is but a trick for the belly. They have devices forsooth of the pope's treasury. He being the treasurer of the church, hath a treasury; and what must that be filled with ? With the merits of saints, with the superabundance. For they can deserve and procure heaven for themselves, and more than obey. There is an overplus of obedience. The superabundance of that is laid in a treasury. And who should have the benefit of that but the treasury of the church and the pope ? But how shall the church come by this abundant satisfaction and merit ? They must buy them by pardons, and they come not to have pardons for nought, but by purchasing of them, and hence come popish indulgences. That is nothing but a dispensing of the satisfaction and merits of the saints, which they did, say they, for the church, abusing such phrases as these. When they had more than their own obedience, they did good to others, and others had benefit by it.

A shameful opinion, bred in the dark night of popery, when the Scriptures were hid, and when people did lie in ignorance; and it was merely to advantage their own selves. For indeed the Scripture saith that God's children did suffer for the church ; but that was not for satisfaction for the church, but for the good of the church. Only Christ's death was satisfactory. Christ is the only treasury of the church, and the satisfaction of Christ. They think they merit by their sufferings, when they suffer for their merits. And they think they merit not only for themselves, but for others too, which is a diabolical sarcasm. The devil mocks them that way ; he makes them ignorant of themselves. Alas ! that a silly, sinful man should think to do enough for himself, and more than enough, enough for others ! The wise virgins had but oil enough for themselves ; they had none for others. But these wise virgins have more than for themselves ; they have for others too. It is not worth the standing on, to hinder better and more comfortable things. The phrase runs in this sense, when it is meant of Christ. Christ suffered for our satisfaction, for our redemption. And Leo the pope, one of the best of their popes, and in his rank, a holy man in his time, he saith excellent well for this, *sanctorum preciosa mors, &c.* The death of the saints is precious ; but the death of no saint is a propitiation for others. Their death is sanctified, but not propitiatory to others. Therefore *singularis singulis*. All the saints, their death was for themselves. It is an excellent speech *solus Christus, &c.* (*o*). Every other besides Christ, their death was singular. It went not out of their persons to do others good, otherwise than by an exemplary course, as St Paul speaks here. But only Christ it is, in whom all died, in whom all are crucified, in whom all are raised, in whom all ascend, in whom all are glorified. As public Adam, his death was for all. He was not considerable in his death, as one man, but as a ' second Adam,' who by his public obedience, as the first public person, by his disobedience infected all; so he by his obedience and satisfaction, by his passive obedience, especially when he shut up his obedience in death, all died in him. It was as much as if all had died, as if all

* That is, ὑπερ = for the realization of.—G.

had been crucified, and risen in him. The meaning is therefore, ' Whether we be afflicted, it is for your consolation and salvation,' to help it forward, to help forward your comfort, by way of example, and not by way of satisfaction and merit any kind of way.

Do but consider this one reason, and so I will end the point. There was no saint that ever merited heaven by his own satisfaction, therefore he could not do good to others by way of satisfaction. How do you prove that? By that excellent speech, in Rom. viii. 18, ' The sufferings of this world are not worthy of the glory that shall be revealed.' All that they suffered was not worthy of the glory to be revealed; therefore they could not by any satisfaction of their own merit heaven for themselves. What should we speak of others then, to do any good to others, I mean, by way of satisfaction? But he shews this in the next words more clearly, how good is done to others, ' Whether we be afflicted, it is for your consolation and salvation.'

' *Which is effectual in enduring the same sufferings that we also suffer.*' It is read in the margin, and most go that way, and the oldest interpreters too (*p*). Some translators have a word as fit in the margin as in the text oft-times, and they leave it to the readers to take which they will. It is good and useful both ways, but the most go that way, and it is more clear. The meaning is this, 'Whether we be afflicted, it is for your consolation and salvation,' which salvation of yours is wrought out, ' in enduring the same sufferings that we also suffer.' If it be read ' effectual,' as it is in the text, and not in the margin, then it is thus, ' If we be afflicted, it is for your consolation and salvation, the assurance whereof in you is effectual, to make you endure the sufferings that we suffer.'

Now here must be a thing clear.

How salvation is wrought by affliction?

I answer, salvation is wrought by Christ, by way of merit and procurement, and purchase and satisfaction to divine justice; but salvation, in regard of the profession of it, is wrought by afflictions, that is, we come to have it by this way. We might consider salvation in purchase and title, and salvation in possession and investing into it. Salvation in title and purchase is wrought by the death and sufferings of Christ, who hath this pre-eminence, to be called and styled a Saviour; but though it be gotten by him, it is not possessed but by a certain way and course. That salvation, the title whereof we have by Christ, it is not possessed or entered into, but by a course of suffering and doing. God hath measured out so many holy actions for every Christian to do, and so many things for every Christian to suffer, so many grievances, if he be of years of discretion. God hath a way to save children which lean to his wisdom, but this way God saveth men. They have a cup measured to them, they have so many afflictions to suffer, before they be possessed of that which Christ hath purchased. So it is wrought in regard of possession, in suffering the same afflictions that others suffer.

There are two ways, doing good, and suffering for good, that are the beaten way to obtain salvation, which salvation is wrought by the satisfaction of Christ. Mark here, he saith our sufferings tend to your comfort and salvation. How? Because it helps you to endure the same suffering. By seeing others suffer, and by enduring the like, we come to the possession of salvation in the end, because by seeing them suffer, we are encouraged to suffer. The point hence is this, that,

Doct. Whatsoever good we take by the sufferings of any, it is by stirring up and strengthening some grace in us.

Whatsoever good we take by any,—set Christ aside, from whom we take good likewise by way of example, as well as merit; but in a singular respect by way of merit,—but for others, whatsoever good we take, it is not direct, it is not immediate, but only by stirring up some grace, by strengthening some grace in us.   There is no good derived from others to me but by confirming and strengthening some grace.   So I come to have good by them, saith St Paul here, ' My sufferings increase your salvation.' But it is because my sufferings stir you up to suffer the same afflictions. You learn of me by my carriage and example to suffer, and so by suffering that which I suffer you come to salvation.

This is sufficient to convince that idle opinion that I spoke of before, that the sufferings of the saints are not conveyed by way of pardon to the ignorant people, that know not what saint, or pardon, or suffering, or merit is.   But the way of comfort by the suffering of others, is by confirming and strengthening some grace, of patience, or comfort, &c., in them.   All the good that is in the father cannot help the son, except he tread in his father's steps. If we go not in the same way as others do to heaven, in the same graces, all their sufferings will do us no good, but serve to condemn us.   The point is clear ; because it serves to enlighten other points, I do but name it. But that which I will a little more stand on is, that salvation is wrought by suffering.

Doct. We come to the possession of salvation by patience.

Faith of salvation by Christ stirs us up to suffer, till we come to the possession of that that we have title to.   Mark how these hang together. First, a Christian knows that God will save him by the merits, and satisfaction, and obedience of Christ, his surety.   The assured persuasion of this salvation that he hath title to by Christ, because the possession of it is deferred till the next world, and there is a distance of time, and that time is encumbered with afflictions, hereupon comes a necessity of some special grace to carry us along till we be fully invested into that that we have title to by Christ.   There must be some grace between faith and the possession of heaven.   I am assured of the possession of heaven in my first conversion ; but I am not invested into it.   It is deferred.   There is a distance of time which is afflictive ; for hope deferred maketh the heart faint. A thing that we have right and title to, deferred, afflicts the soul, and the deferring of good hath the respect of ill.   Good deferred puts upon it the consideration of ill ; for it is a grievance to want a good I have a right unto. Now it is not only deferred, but my life is an exercised life, with many actions and sufferings.   What grace must bear me up between me and heaven, and in the tediousness of the time prolonged ? Especially the grace of enduring.   Therefore faith in Christ, by which I have a title to heaven, that stirs up hope, and hope stirs up patience, and that helps me in the way to heaven.   It helps me to bear crosses and afflictions, and likewise to endure the tediousness and length of time till I come to heaven.   So salvation is wrought by suffering.   We come not to the possession of it but by suffering and enduring.   ' You have need of patience,' saith the apostle, Heb. x. 36.

Give me leave to clear the point a little.   How doth patience enter into this great work of helping our salvation ?   Patience in enduring affliction, it helps many ways.

1. *They work salvation, not by way of merit, for that were to disable the*

title we have by Christ, but by way af evidence. It helps the evidence of the title. For I have title by Christ. But how do I know that my evidence to that title is good? Afflictions, and the patient suffering of them. Not afflictions alone, but afflictions joined with the grace of patience to endure them; for else they do no good. Afflictions are evil in themselves. For thus it increaseth my evidence. Every heir is a son. For heaven is the inheritance of sons; and every son must be corrected; and I am corrected and afflicted in this life; and God doth give me grace to endure them, and to see my good in them. These afflictions, therefore, mingled with patient enduring of them, do evidence that I am not a bastard. In Heb. xii. 8, the apostle proves this. Every one that hath not some affliction or other, ' he is a bastard and not a son.' It increaseth my evidence that I am the child of God, especially if I suffer for a good cause. ' If we suffer with him, we shall reign with him,' Rom. viii. 17. Here the evidence is increased. By this I know I am in the way which is strewed with crosses and afflictions. We must enter into heaven this way. I know it for the way, so it furthers my salvation. It gives me assurance that my evidence is good.

It is the Scripture's manner to say things are done, when the knowledge of the thing is increased: as to say we are saved, when we know more assuredly that we shall be saved; to say we are in the kingdom of heaven when we know we are in the state of the kingdom of heaven, as in 2 Pet. iii. 18. Saith he, ' grow in grace,' &c., for by this means, ' a further entrance shall be ministered unto you, into the kingdom of God,' 2 Pet. i. 11. The knowledge of a man's estate in grace is a further entrance into the kingdom of God, that is begun here in this life. The knowledge that I am an heir of heaven, is to be in heaven before my time. Thus afflictions joined with patience help salvation, because they help the evidence of salvation. They shew that we are sons, and not bastards. It is an evidence of our adoption.

2. And then sufferings, joined with the grace of enduring, *help forward salvation by way of qualification.* There is a qualification and disposition of soul, which is necessary before we come to heaven; ' because no unclean thing shall ever come to heaven,' Rev. xxi. 27.

Now suffering, joined with patience, having a mighty and blessed work this way, to purge us of that soil that we cannot carry to heaven with us. We may not think to carry our unmortified pride and lusts, and base earthly affections, and our pleasures and riches ill gotten, to heaven with us. Oh, no! the presence of heaven is a more pure presence than so, and the place will not endure such defilements. We must be cleansed therefore.

Now, because afflictions endured with patience, have a blessed power to subdue that which by nature is powerful in us, to purge out those base affections, that are contrary to the glorious estate we look for; therefore they help us to heaven, they help the qualification of the person, not the merit and desert of it.

They help likewise the qualification, by removing that which corruption feeds on; for affliction endured removes that which corruption works on, and strengthens itself by. Affliction is either in removing riches, or honours, or pleasures, somewhat that corruption feeds on; for all corruption is about those idols, greatness, or pleasure, or profit of the world. Now sufferings crossing us in our reputation, or estates, or body, one way or other, they withdraw the fuel that feeds our corruptions, and so help mortification and purgation, and so fit us for heaven. They help our repentance. They make the favour of God sweet, and sin bitter. It is a bitter thing to offend God. We feel it by the afflictions that are laid on us.

3. Again, *many positive graces are required before we come to heaven.* Affliction endured helps all graces whatsoever. The only time for grace to thrive in is the time of affliction, for affliction endured helps our zeal, our love. We have experience of the patience of God, and they stir up prayer. All graces are set on work in affliction. ' Out of the deep have I cried,' Ps. cxxx. 1. Prayers are cries in affliction. They are not cold dull things, but set on fire ; they set the spirit on work to cry to God with earnest, frequent, and fervent prayer.

4. Then again, *afflictions endured, they work salvation and help us to heaven, because they whet and sharpen our desire of heaven ;* for when we find ill usage here below in our pilgrimage, we have a great desire to be at home at rest ; and that is one main end why God sends afflictions, to help salvation this way by sharpening our desires. For were it not for afflictions, and the enduring of them, would we ever say, ' Come, Lord Jesus, come quickly ' ? Rev. xxii. 20. Would we not be of Peter's mind, ' It is good for us to be here ' ? Mark ix. 5. Would we ever be weary of the world, before we be fired out of it and pulled out of it, as Lot out of Sodom ? No. They help our desire and earnestness. The creature groans, Rom. viii. 21, 22. ' Those that have received the first fruits of the Spirit, they wait for the adoption of the sons of God.' Those that have the beginnings of grace, they wait for the accomplishment. What makes this but afflictions and troubles of the world ? They desire a state wherein all tears shall be wiped from their eyes.

So we see, these and many other ways, but these are the principal, how afflictions, endured as they should be, they help salvation, they work our salvation. Though they work not the title of it, yet they help us in the way.

First, because they assure us that we are the sons of God, and so have evidence that we are in a good state ; and then they remove the hindrances and purge us of our sins. And then they help us in all graces, they cherish all graces, and they sharpen and whet the edge of our desires to be out of this world.

And all this must be in every Christian before he come to heaven ; for God never brings a man of years to heaven but he gives him cause to see why he would be out of this world, either by long sickness or affliction, or by one thing or other. He makes them see that it is better to be there than here ; and if it were not for crosses, who would be of that mind ?

Therefore, have we not cause to suspect ourselves that we are in smooth ways and find no crosses ? God doth give respite to his children. They have breathing times. They are not alway under crosses. He is merciful. Perhaps they have not strength enough. He will not bring them to the lists,* to the stage, because they are not enabled, they have not strength enough. But they that have a continual tenor of prosperity may well suspect themselves. If one have direction to such a place, and they tell him there are such ways, deep waters, that except he take heed he will be drowned, and step into holes, and they are craggy ways ; and if he meet with none of these, he may well think he is not in his way. So the way to heaven, it is through afflictions. We must endure many afflictions, saith the apostle here, ' Salvation is wrought by enduring the same afflictions

* That is, ' barriers.' Cf. Richardson, *sub voce*—G.

that you see in us.' Now, if I suffer and endure nothing, if I cannot endure so much as a filip, a disgrace, a frown, a scorn for Christ, if the way be over-smooth, it is not the way to heaven certainly. The way is not strewed with roses. We must have our feet ' shod with the preparation of the gospel,' Eph. vi. 15. They must be well shod that go among thorns ; and they had need to be well fenced that go the way to heaven. It is a thorny, rugged way. But it is no matter what the way be, so it brings us to heaven ; but certainly, if the way be too smooth, we ought to suspect ourselves.

Now, because it may be objected, many will say, alas ! What do we suffer ? and, therefore, our case is not good.

I answer, every Christian suffers one of these ways at one time or other, nay, at all times, either by sympathy with the church [or otherwise.]

1. Put the case we have no afflictions of our own, do we not *sympathise with the church beyond the seas ?* When thou hearest ill news, if thou be glad to hear it, certainly thy case is bad. There is a suffering by sympathy, and that suffering is ours.

2. Then again, there are afflictions and sufferings *that arise upon scandals*, that men run into before our eyes, which is a great grief. ' Mine eyes gush out with rivers of waters, because men keep not thy law,' saith David, Ps. cxix. 136. Is it not a matter of suffering to a Christian soul to see that he would not see, and to hear blasphemies and oaths that he would not hear ? to have the understanding forced to understand that he would not, living in a world of iniquity, in the kingdom of the devil ? It is a great grievance. ' Woe is me that I am forced to dwell in Meshech, and to have my habitation with the tents of Kedar,' Ps. cxx. 5. It is a pitiful affliction to the saints of God, to him that hath the life of grace in his heart, to have the wicked as ' goads and thorns,' as the Scripture saith the Jebusites should be to the Israelites, Num. xxxiii. 55 ; to have thoughts forced upon us and things forced upon our souls that we would not see nor think nor hear of, that which shall never be in heaven.

3. Again, *every one suffers the burden of his calling*, which is a great suffering. A man need not to whip himself, as the Scottish papists do (*q*), if he be but faithful in his calling. It is a notable means of mortification. God keeps a man from persecution many times because he hath burdens in his calling to exercise him. He hath many crosses in his calling. God hath joined sweat to labour, and trouble, and pains ; and there is no man that is faithful in his calling as he should be, but he shall find many crosses.

4. And then, that which afflicts most of all, the affliction of all afflictions, *the inward combat between the flesh and the spirit*, which God usually takes up in persecution and outward troubles. God's dear children in persecution find little molestation from their corruptions, because God will not lay more upon them than he will give them strength to bear ; and now, when he singles them out to outward crosses, he subdues their corruptions, that they do not vex them as before.

In the time of peace he lets loose their corruptions, sometimes anger, sometimes pride, sometimes one base affection, sometimes another ; and think you this is no grief to them ? Oh, yes ; it grieves them, and humbles them more than any cross would do. St Paul was grieved more at this than at all his sufferings. It made him cry out, ' Oh, wretched man that I am, who shall deliver me from this body of death ?' Rom. vii. 24. He doth not say, Oh, wretched man, who shall deliver me from crosses and afflictions ? Though they made him wretched in the eye of the world, yet he rejoiced in those. But his grief was, that he could not do the good that he would; and that made him cry out, ' O wretched man that I am,' &c. It is God that ties up our corruptions, that they run not so violently on the soul at one time as they do at another, for he hath the command of them by his Spirit. There is no Christian but one of these ways he suffers in the greatest time of peace. Especially this way God exerciseth them, that he makes them weary of their lives by this spiritual conflict. If they know what the life of grace means, he makes them know what it is to be absent from heaven. He makes them know that this life is a place of absence; and all this is to help our disposition to salvation, by helping mortification and by helping our desire to heaven. Those that go on in a smooth course, that know not what this inward combat means, and are carried away with their sins, they are so far from taking scandals to heart, that if they see evil men, they are ready to join with them, to join with blasphemers and wicked persons; and instead of sympathising with the church of God, they are ready to join with them that censure them, and so add affliction to the afflicted.

But to proceed.

' *Whether we be comforted, it is for your consolation and salvation.*' Of ' comfort ' I spake in the former verse. Only that note that I will briefly commend you to is this, that

Doct. God's children, hap how it will, they do good.

Cast them into what estate you will, they do good. They are good, and do good. If they be afflicted, they do good by that; if they have comfort, they do good to others by that. No estate is amiss to God's children; and that is the reason of their perfect resignation. The child of God perfectly resigns himself into God's hand. Lord, if thou wilt have me suffer, I will suffer; if thou wilt have me afflicted, I yield myself; if thou wilt have me enjoy prosperity, I will. I know it shall be for my good, and for the good of others.

There is an intercourse in the life of a Christian. He is now afflicted, and now comforted, not for his own sake only, but for the good of others; and when he shall be afflicted, and how long, and what comfort he shall have, how much, he leaves it to the wisdom of God. It is a blessed estate, if we could think of it, to be a Christian, that we need to care for nothing but to serve God. We need to care for nothing, but study to keep a good conscience. Let God alone with all our estate; for God will enable us to want and to abound in our own persons, and likewise he will sanctify our estate for the good of others.

And a Christian will be willing to be tossed, and to be ' changed from vessel to vessel,' Jer. xlviii. 11, from state to state, for the good of others. If his afflictions may do good to the church, he is content that God should withdraw his blessings from him, and humble him with crosses. If his example may be good to others, he is likewise joyful; when God gives him rest, and causeth an inward comfort, he knows that this is good for others. He hath learned in his first entrance into Christianity, self-denial, not to live to himself, but for the glory of God and the good of others, as much as he may.

Use. We should labour therefore to content ourselves in all conditions, knowing that all is for the best, not only to ourselves, and God's glory, but for the good of others. God, when he takes things from us, and afflicts us, and when he comforts us, he intends the comfort of others. So we should reason when we endure anything, and when we are comforted, certainly

God intends the good of others by this; therefore I will have a special care in suffering, to carry it decently and exemplarily, knowing that the eyes of many are upon me. I will carry myself so, that God may have glory, and others may have edification and comfort, knowing that I am but God's steward, to convey this to others, that are of the same body with myself. Therefore in our communion we have with others, upon any good occasion, we ought to express the blessed experience of the comfort of God upon us. This is the practice of holy men in their meeting with others, to shew them the comforts of God to their souls. ' Come, and I will shew you what God hath done for my soul,' Ps. cxlii. 7, saith the psalmist. All are the better for a good man. He doth good to all; and therefore Solomon saith, ' When a righteous man is advanced, the city rejoiceth,' Prov. xi. 10. They have cause, for he hath a public mind. Nothing doth more characterise, and is a better stamp of a true Christian, than a public mind.

A carnal man out of self-love may grieve at his own sins, and may labour to comfort himself; but a Christian thinks others shall take good by me. It is the mind of Christ, and it is the mind of all the members of Christ, when a man thinks he hath nothing, except he have it to improve for the good of others.

A dead, sullen, reserved spirit, is not a Christian's spirit. If by nature we have such, we must labour to help it with grace; for grace is a diffusive, communicating thing, not only in the ministers of God, but in every Christian. Grace will teach them to make savoury their conversation to others, this way, that whatsoever they are, or whatsoever they can do, or whatsoever they suffer, they study to improve all to the good of others.

And mark the extent of the loving wisdom and providence of God, how many things he doth at once. For in the same affliction ofttimes, he corrects some in his children, in the same affliction he tries some grace, in the same affliction he witnesseth to his truth in them, in the same affliction he doth good to others besides the good he doth to them. In the same affliction that others inflict, he hasteneth the ruin of them that offer it; at one time, and in one action, he hasteneth the destruction of the one, by hastening the good of the other; he ripens grace in his children, making them exemplary to others, and all in the same action, so large is the wise providence of God.

It should teach us likewise to follow that providence, and to see how many ways anything we suffer any kind of way may extend, that if one way will not comfort, another may. When we suffer, and are grieved, let us consider withal that he that doth the wrong, he hastens his ruin and judgment. As Pharaoh, when he hastened the overthrow of the children of Israel, he hastened his overthrow in the Red Sea. So a pit is digged for the wicked, when they dig a pit for the godly, Ps. vii. 15. And consider, to comfort thyself, thou hast some sin in thee, and God intends not only to witness this truth, but to correct some sin in thee, and thou must look to that. Thou hast some grace in thee, and he intends the trial of that. Look to these things. This shews strong heavenly-mindedness, when there is self-denial. Let us consider what God calls us to; for God looks to many things in the same act. Wherefore doth God give us reason and discourse, but to be able to follow him in his dealing, as far as we can reach to?

But I go on to the next verse.

VERSE 7.

' *And our hope of you is stedfast, knowing that as you are partakers of the suffering, so you shall be also of the consolation.*' This verse is nothing but a strengthening of what he said before. He had told them that whatsoever he suffered, it was for their comfort too ; and now he repeats it again, and sets a seal upon it, ' Our hope of you is stedfast, knowing that as you are partakers of the sufferings, so you shall also be of the consolation.' In these words he shews that they shall share in the good with him as well as in the ill; that the Spirit of God in them should help them to take all the good they could, both by his sufferings and by his comfort. For as he by the help of the Spirit of God intended the public good, intended their good and comfort in all, whether he were afflicted or comforted ; so he saith here, he was assured that as they were partakers of his sufferings, so they should be of his comforts likewise.

Here is the truth, and the seal of the truth.

The truth, that they were ' partakers of his sufferings,' and should be ' partakers of his consolations.'

And *the seal* is in the manner of affirming these truths, ' Our hope of you is stedfast.' And in this order I will speak of them. First,

Doct. God's children are partakers of the sufferings of others.

The Corinthians were partakers of the sufferings of St Paul.

God's children are partakers of the sufferings of others many ways.

First. By way of sympathy, taking to heart the estate of the church and children of God abroad. It grieved the Corinthians to hear that St Paul was afflicted ; for even as it is in the natural body, so likewise in the mystical body, there is a sympathy between the members.

Second. Likewise they partake of the sufferings of others *by way of proportion.* They suffered in their kind and proportion as he suffered; though perhaps not in the same very individual kind. There is a portion of suffering in the church. Some suffer one way, and others another; but all partake of sufferings in some degree or other.

3. Then again, they did partake of St Paul's sufferings *in preparation and disposition of mind.* Howsoever now they did not suffer as much as he, yet, saith he, I know as far as the Spirit of God is in you, you are prepared to suffer ; and what we are prepared to do, that we do. Christ saith we ' sell all for the gospel,' when upon serious examination of our hearts we find we can part with it. When we set ourselves to examination, what cannot I part with for Christ ? Can I part with my goods ? Can I part with my life ? If we can once come to resolution, it is done, as Abraham is said to sacrifice his son, because he resolved to do it, Heb. xi. 17 ; and David is said to build the temple, because he intended to do it, 1 Kings viii. 18. God looks upon us in our resolutions and preparations. What we resolve to do, that is done. So, saith he, you are partakers of my sufferings, not only by sympathy, and in proportion of sufferings, but you are prepared, he speaks charitably and lovingly, to suffer whatsoever I suffer, if God call you to it.

Reason. And the ground of Christians partaking of the sufferings one of another, it is the *communion that is between Christians.* They are all members of one body. If the hand suffer, the head suffers. The head thinks itself wronged when the hand or the foot is wronged, by reason of the sympathy between the members, as I said ; and so it is in the mystical body of Christ.

There are these three unions which depend one upon another.

1. *The union of Christ with our nature,* which is inseparable. It is an eternal union. He never lays that blessed mass of our flesh aside which he took, which is the ground of all our comfort; for God is now at one with us, because God hath taken our nature on him, and satisfied the wrath of God his Father.

2. Next the union of Christ with our nature, *is the union of Christ mystical.* Christ and his members when they suffer, Christ suffers. Their sufferings are the sufferings of Christ.

3. The third *is the union of one member with another,* that what one member suffers, another doth suffer. Therefore the Corinthians were partakers of Christ, because their sufferings were the sufferings of Christ; and they were partakers of St Paul's sufferings, because his sufferings were their sufferings.

They were partakers of Christ's sufferings, because of the communion between the head and the members ; and they were partakers of St Paul's sufferings, because of the communion of one member with another. And surely there is not a heart that was ever touched with the Spirit of God, but when he hears of any calamity of the church, whether it be in the Palatinate (*r*), in France, in the Low countries, or in any country in the world, if he hears that the church hath a blow, it strikes to the heart of any man that hath the Spirit of God in them, by a sympathetical suffering. It is one good sign to know whether a man be of the mystical body or no, to take to heart the grievance of the church. As good Nehemiah did ; he would not take comfort in the pleasures of a court, in the king of Babylon's court, when it went not well with his country. When the church was in distress, he took their grievance to heart. So Moses, the very joys of Pharaoh's court could not please him, when he considered the abasement of his countrymen, and he joined with them; and it is called the 'rebuke' of Christ.

So it is with all the people of God. There is a communication of sufferings. 'As you are partakers of the sufferings, so you shall be also of the consolation.'

Wherein two things are observable.

First, *that a necessary precedent condition of comfort is sufferings.*

And then the consequent of this, *that those that suffer as they should are sure of comfort.* These two things unfold the meaning of the Spirit of God here.

Before there be comfort, there must be suffering ; for God hath established this order. Even as in nature, there must be a night before the day, and a winter before a summer ; so in the kingdom of Christ, in his ruling of the church, there is this divine policy, there must be suffering before comfort. God will sooner break the league and the covenant between day and night, than this league of suffering and comfort : the one must be before the other. It was so in our head, Christ. He suffered, and then entered into his glory. So all his members must be conformable* to him in suffering, and then enter into their glory.

The reasons of this are divers.

Reason 1. First of all, this method and order is, first, suffering, and then comfort, *because God finds us in a corrupt estate ;* and something must be wrought out of us, before we can be vessels to receive comfort. Therefore there must be a purgation one way or other, either by repentance, or if not,

* Misprinted, ' comfortable.'—G.

by repentance, by affliction, to help repentance. There must be suffering before comfort. The soul is unfit for comfort.

Secondly, *this order commends and sweetens comfort to us.* For fire is sweet after cold, and meat is sweet after hunger ; so comfort is sweet after suffering. God fits us to comfort by this, by purging out what is contrary to comfort. And he endears comfort by this. Those that have felt the cross, comfort is comfort indeed to them. Heaven is heaven indeed to him that hath had a hell in his conscience upon earth, that hath been afflicted in conscience, or outwardly persecuted. It set a price and value upon comfort.

Partly likewise to sharpen our desire of comfort ; for suffering breeds sense, and sense that stirs up desire, and desire is eager. Now suffering, it makes comforts precious, and sets us in a wondrous strong desire after them.

And by this means, likewise, God comes to his own end, which is that our comforts may be eternal. Therefore we have that which is ill, in the first place. Woe to us, if it should be said to us, as to Dives in the gospel, ' Son, son, thou hadst thy good here, and now thou must have thy ill,' Luke xvi. 25. God intends not to deal so with his children; but they taste the worst wine first, and better afterward. Because he intends eternal happiness to them, he observes this method, first ill, and then good, the best at last.

Use 1. If this be so, *then why should we be offended at God's order ?* Why should we not take it, not only gently and meekly, but joyfully, the afflictions that God sends to prepare and fit us for happiness, to sharpen our desire to happiness, to make it precious to us ? Certainly it is a ground, not only of patience and meekness, but of joy and comfort, in all the things we suffer. Will a patient be angry with his chirurgeon for searching of his wound ? He knows that that is the way to cure him. Will any man take offence at the goldsmith for purging his mass ? They know that is the way to purify it, and fetch out the dross.

This is the method in nature. The ground must be ploughed and prepared, and then comes the harvest. Let us be content with this method, and rejoice in any suffering, knowing it will have a blessed issue ; and not to think much at suffering anything for a good cause in ourselves, or by way of sympathy or support with others, because this is the highway to a better estate. If we suffer with the church, or for the church, any kind of way, we shall be comforted with the church. It is that which sweetens the cross, that we are under hope of better still. Who would not endure a little grievance in the way, to have honour in the end ? to have ill usage in an inn, and to go to a kingdom ? All our discomforts and afflictions are but by the way here ; and crosses are necessary for travellers, and here we are but in a travelling estate. It should, I say, encourage us not to take offence at anything that God exerciseth us with in this world, nor to take scandal at the afflictions of the church.

Use 2. And then *it should strike terror to those that will not endure so much as a scratch, a scoff, a word, a chip of the cross, that will endure nothing.* Do they know that this is God's order ? Do they avoid crosses in any degree ? and do they think to have comfort ? No ! God will not change his order for them. He hath established this order, and heaven and earth shall fail, rather than God's order shall not be sure. If we will have comfort, we must suffer. If we will avoid suffering, and think to go to heaven another way than God hath ordained, we may take our own way, but we must give him leave to take his way in comforting and advancing whom he will, and that will not be us, because we will not frame ourselves to his order. We must not look for his dignity. ' If we will not suffer with him, we shall not reign with him,' Rom. viii. 17.

The next thing observable in the order is this, that

Doct. Those that suffer as they should are sure of comfort.

There is a threefold conformity with Christ, in *suffering, grace, glory.*

Those that are not conformable to him in suffering, they cannot be conformable to him in grace ; and if they be not in grace, they shall not in glory. He took upon him our nature abased first; and our nature purified, and our nature glorious, he hath now in heaven. So our nature in us must keep this order. First, it must be abased, as our flesh was in him, and then filled with grace, by little and little, and then glorious, as our nature is in him. If we will not suffer our flesh to be abased and exercised with afflictions, and let God work his own good work as he pleaseth this way, we are not conformable to Christ, who was first abased, and then advanced. What was wrought in his blessed flesh, must be wrought in his mystical body, in all his members, by little and little. Therefore those that are tender and wayward to endure anything, when God calls them to it, they are enemies to their own comfort. God hath set down this order, if they do not partake of the sufferings of the church, they shall not partake of the comfort.

Oh, it is a cursed estate to be out of the condition of God's people, and it is a comfortable thing to have part with those that are good, yea, even if it be in suffering with them. It is better to have communion with God's people in suffering, than to have communion with the wicked in the world, in reigning and triumphing.

And that is the reason that the Spirit of God in the prophet made him desire, ' Deal with me, Lord, as thou usest to deal with those that fear thy name,' Ps. cxix. 124. He knew he deals well enough with them. ' Visit me with the salvation of thy children,' Ps. cvi. 4. He knew that was a special salvation. So to have God deal with us, as he deals with his, and to visit us in mercy and love, as he visits his own, it is a special favour. It is better to bear the cross with them, that we may partake with them in the comfort, than to have all the comforts that the wicked have, and to share with them in the misery afterward. Therefore let us be content to share with God's people in their suffering. When we hear of any that suffer for a just cause, though we have no sufferings of our own, let us bear a part with them, and with the bond of the communion of saints, help what we may.

And it is as true on the contrary, if we partake with the wicked in their sins, we shall partake with them in their punishment. Therefore the Scripture saith, ' Come out of Babylon, my people, lest if you partake of her sins, so you partake of her punishments,' Rev. xviii. 4. Now, atheistical people think it nothing to enter into league, and amity, and society with profane people, that are professedly so, not only by weakness, but those that are stigmatized. But what saith the Scripture?—and the Holy Ghost doth not trifle with us.—' Come out of Babylon, my people, lest you partake of her plagues ;' which is not meant so much locally to come out of the place, as in disposition to come out in respect of liking, and converse, and secret intimate communion. Lot's sons-in-law, they thought it was but trifling. They gibed as atheists do now, when they hear the ministers encourage people to make much of religion, and to set against those that are opposite. They think they are enforced to it, and it is upon mistake, &c., though it be as palpable as the light of the sun. They deal as Lot's sons-in-law, when he warned them to come out of Sodom, and he was pulled out. They would believe nothing till fire came down from heaven, and destroyed them all. It was too late then. Therefore let us hearken to the counsel of the angel, let us not make this a matter of scorn, a light matter; but as we desire to have no part in their confusion, so avoid their courses. The Scripture is terrible to those that, after the breaking out of the light, will be such. There is not more direct Scriptures against any kind of men, than those that wilfully cleave to antichrist. Therefore we should not esteem it a light matter, but think of it seriously indeed.

And not only in respect of them, but all wicked society. Were it not pity that men should be severed from them hereafter, whose company they will not be severed from now? If thou see an adulterer, a blasphemer, a wicked, licentious, atheistical person, and thou runnest into the same excess of riot with him, thou wilt not be drawn by any persuasions, ministerial or friendly, or by thine own light, which knows his course to be naught, to retire from his society,—dost thou not think to share with him afterward in his judgment? As you are all tares, so you shall be bound in a bundle, and cast into hell together, Mat. xiii. 30. As the wheat shall be gathered into heaven, so the tares, a cursed company, that will cleave together though they be damned for it. As they clave together as burs and tares here, so they shall be cast into hell together. That is the end of dissolute, unruly creatures, that nothing will sever them from those who in their own consciences they know their courses to be naught.

'*Our hope of you is stedfast.*' There is a double certainty, a certainty of the truth of the thing, and a certainty of the estate of the person. The certainty of the truth is this, *those that suffer with Christ and his church, shall be glorified with Christ and his church.* The certainty of the truth is more certain than heaven and earth. Now, besides the certainty of the truth, or thing, there is interposed a certainty of the persons, that as they were interested in the sufferings, so they should be in the comforts. And this is true as well as the former. For God's promises are not mere ideas wanting truths, that have no performance in the persons; but if the thing be true, it is true in the person to whom the truth belongs. Suffering goes before glory. Therefore if we suffer we shall be glorified. But this is the condition, if they suffer with Christ. Then St Paul takes it for certain that they shall be glorified with Christ. There is not the same certainty of the persons as of the truth itself. The truth is certain by a certainty of faith, but the certainty of the persons is the certainty of a charitable persuasion. I am persuaded that you will suffer with me in sympathy, and therefore I am persuaded in the certainty of charity that you shall of a certain have the comfort.

'Our hope of you is stedfast.' St Paul, you see, hath a good conceit of them, that he might encourage them to sympathise and take to heart his crosses, and to take good by them. A good hope of others hath a double efficacy.

1. It hath one efficacy in the party that hath the good hope of another. It stirs him up to be diligent to take all courses that may be for the good of another. As the speech is, Hope stirs up to work; it stirs up endeavour; so it doth in the husbandman, and in every kind of trade. Hope quickens endeavour. A man will never sow upon the sands. He

loseth his cost. A man will never bestow his pains upon those that he thinks are desperate. And what is it that dulls and deads endeavour? I despair of ever doing such a man good. When those despairing thoughts enter into the soul, there is a stop of all endeavour. And surely Christians are much to blame that way. When they might have ground, if charity were in them, at least of hope of others; upon some hard, despairing conceits they cast off hope, and so neglect all endeavours of doing good to others. The Spirit of God is witty* in the hearts of his children to observe all advantages of doing good. Therefore it is willing to entertain all offers of good in others. If they be but willing to hear reproof, if they be willing to hear comfort, and to hear good discourse, it will make a good construction of their errors, if it may be, except it be those that are maliciously obstinate. It will impute it to passion, or to ill company, to one thing or other. As far as possible it will admit of a good construction. Love in God's children will admit of it; and love stirs up to hope, and hope stirs up to deal with them for their good.

I know that charity is not sottish; but yet it is willing to think the best. Where there is probability of good for the present, or where there is a tractableness, where there is a willingness to entertain communion, where there is any propension,† we must be of our blessed Saviour's disposition, 'who will not quench the smoking flax, nor break the bruised reed,' Mat. xii. 20. We must draw all, and drive none away. This is one special fruit and effect that hope hath in the party that doth hope toward another.

Now, as it is good for the speaker to be well conceited; so it is a good preparative in the hearer. It hath a winning power in the party hoped of. It is a great attractive; for we willingly hear those that conceit good of us. St Paul here works upon the natural disposition in all, which is, that they love to be well thought of; and natural dispositions are strong. It is the natural disposition for every man to love where he is well thought of; and it is not sinful, unless it be in vainglory, to desire to have good place in the esteem of others. And there a man will labour to carry himself answerable to the good conceit had in him.

There is a conflict in the worst man. Where he is well conceited of, he labours to maintain it, except it be those that are mightily enthralled, as some wretches are, to blasphemy, and to a cursed life, that they care not. But else if they be well thought of, it will stir them up to maintain it. He is a dissolute man, he is not a man, so far as he is careless of this, he is brutish and senseless. St Paul, in saying 'our hope is stedfast concerning you,' he wins himself into their good opinion; and so by that means he hoped to prevail with them for greater matters. So hope, it stirs up men to do good, and it makes the other willing to receive good. For it makes them willing to content them that hope well of them. St Paul was led with this heavenly wisdom, and that which made him so industrious, was hope of prevailing; and that which made him prevail with others, was the good conceit he had of them. He would gather upon every one. When he saw Agrippa come on a little, 'Agrippa, believest thou the Scriptures?' Acts xxvi. 27. I know thou believest. 'Almost thou persuadest me to be a Christian,' saith he, ver. 28·; and so he comes in a little. It is good, as much as may be, to have hope of others.

But what is his degree of hope? 'Our hope of you'—is stedfast.

He had a stedfast hope, that if they were sufferers, they should be partakers of the comfort.

* That is, 'wise.'—G.　　　　　　　† That is, 'inclination.'—G.

The observation may be this, that

Doct. Divine truths are such as we may build a stedfast hope on the performance of them.

Divine truths, divine comforts, they are of that nature, that though we do not yet enjoy them, yet we may build certainly upon them. I hope stedfastly, that if you be partakers of the sufferings, you shall be partakers of the comforts. A man cannot say so of any thing else but divine truths. A man cannot say of any other, or of himself, I hope stedfastly to be rich, I hope stedfastly to be great, or I hope stedfastly to live long. The nature of the thing is uncertain. The state of the world is vanity; and life itself, and all things here, will not admit of a certain apprehension. For the certainty in a man's understanding, it follows the certainty of the thing, or else there is no adequation.* When there is an evenness in the apprehension to the thing, then it is true; but if we apprehend anything that is here, that either riches or life, or favour will be thus, or thus long, it is no true apprehension. We cannot build a certain hope upon an uncertain ground. But of divine truths, we can say, if we see the one, undoubtedly the other will follow; if we see the signs of grace in any man, that he is strong to endure any disgrace for religion, any discomfort, then we may say, certainly, as you partake of the afflictions of Christ, and of the afflictions and sufferings of his people, his body mystical; so undoubtedly you shall be partakers of the comfort of God's people: heaven and earth shall fail, but this shall never fail.

Is not this a comfort to a Christian, that when he is in the state of grace, he hath something that he may build on, when all things else fail? In all the changes and alterations of this life, he hath somewhat unalterable,—the certainty of divine comforts, the certainty of his estate in grace, though he be in an afflicted estate. As verily as he is afflicted, so verily he shall be comforted. ' If we suffer with Christ, we shall be glorified with him,' Rom. viii. 17.

Upon what ground is this certainty built, that if we suffer we shall be glorified?

It is built upon our union with Christ. It is built upon the communion we have with the church of God. We are all of one body. And it is built upon his own experience. As verily as I have been afflicted, and have comfort, so shall you that suffer be comforted: what I feel, you shall feel.

Because in things necessary there is the like reason from one to all; if one be justified by faith, all are justified by faith; if one suffer and receive comfort, all that suffer shall receive comfort. Divine comforts are from one to all, from the head to the body, from the body to every member. If Christ suffered, I shall suffer, if I be of his body; if Christ was comforted, I shall be comforted. Divine truths they agree in the head and the members. If it be true in one, it is true in all. St Paul felt it in his own person; and, saith he, as I have felt afflictions increase, and comforts increase, so it shall be with you; you shall be partakers of the comforts now, or hereafter. And it is built likewise upon God's promise, which is surer than heaven and earth. ' If we suffer with him, we shall be glorified with him,' as the apostle saith, Rom. viii. 17. All these are grounds to found this stedfast hope on. And then the nature of God: he is a just God, a holy God, and when we have taken the ill, we shall find the sweet, as in

* That is, ' proportion.' This is a superior example of the use of the word to that given by Richardson, *sub voce* from Fuller—G.

2 Thess. i. 6. ' It is just with God, to render to them that afflict you
trouble, and to you comfort.' God hath pawned his justice upon it, and
he will observe this order. Where he begins in trouble, he will end in
comfort. It is just with God, and therefore I may be persuaded.

It should be a special comfort to all that are in any sanctified cross, whether it be for a good cause or no. If a man find that he stands out for a
good cause, then there is more matter of joy. It is matter of triumph then.
But if they be crosses common to nature, if a man find them sanctified, (as
they are only to God's children, they learn humility by them, they learn
heavenly-mindedness, they learn patience, they learn more carefulness by
their afflictions, if it be thus sanctified), then a man may say to such a one,
' As you partake of the sufferings, so you shall partake of the comfort,'
though you feel it not for the present.

Is it not a comfort for a patient to have his physician come to him,
whom he knows to be wise, and speaks by his book, to say to him, Be of
good comfort, you shall never die of this disease ; this that I give you will
do you good : there was never any that took this potion but they recovered.
Would not this revive the patient ? Now when the physicians of our souls
shall come and tell a man, by discerning his state to be good, by discerning signs of grace in his abasement, Be of good comfort, there is good
intended to you ; your sufferings shall end in comfort, undoubtedly ;
we may well be persuaded of this, God will never vary his order.
Therefore, when we are in any trouble, and find God blessing it to us, to
abate our pride, to sharpen our desire, to exercise our graces, when we find
it sanctified, let it comfort us, it shall turn to our further comfort. We find
a present good that it is a pledge of a further good. It will make a bitter
potion to go down, when the physician saith, it will do you good. How
many distasteful things do poor creatures endure and take down to cure
this carcase ! It were offensive to name what distasteful things they will
take to do them good (r*).

Let us take this cup from God's hand, let us endure the cross patiently,
whatsoever it be. It is a bitter cup, but it is out of a Father's hand, it is
out of a sweet hand. There may be a miscarrying in other physic, but
God's physic shall certainly do us good. God hath said it, ' All things
shall work for the best to those that love him,' Rom. viii. 28. He hath
said it beforehand. We may presume, and build our persuasion upon this
issue, that all things shall work for our good. What a comfort is this in all
the intercourses and changes of this life, when we know before, that whatsoever we meet with, it hath a command from God to do us good, it is me-
dicinable, though it seem never so ill, to do us good, to work ill out of us,
by the blessing of God. But to proceed.

VERSES 8, 9.

' *For we would not, brethren, have you ignorant of our trouble which
came to us in Asia, that we were pressed out of measure, above strength,
insomuch that we despaired even of life : But we had the sentence of death in
ourselves, that we should not trust in ourselves, but in God which raiseth the dead.*'

Here St Paul comes to the particular explication of what he had generally spoken before. He had generally said before, that he had both comfort and affliction ; but now he specifies what afflictions they were. ' I would
not have you ignorant of the troubles which came to us in Asia,' &c.

'*I would not have you ignorant of!*' He knew it was behoveful for them to know: therefore, to insinuate into their respect the more, he tells them of it. Indeed, to know both together is very sweet and comfortable, to know both the afflictions of God's people and their comforts, as here, he tells them what ill he endured in Asia, and how God delivered him: to see how these are linked together in God's people, is very comfortable. Therefore ' I would not have you ignorant.'

Now, that they might not be ignorant, he sets before their eyes the particular grievance that he suffered in Asia. And see how he doth raise himself by degrees, and represent it to them most lively.

First of all, saith he, ' We were pressed out of measure.' There is one degree, ' we were pressed.' It is a metaphor. ' We were pressed,' as a cart is pressed under sheaves, as a man is pressed under a burden ; as a ship that is over laden is pressed deep down with too much burden. So it was with us, we were pressed with afflictions. Afflictions are of a depressing nature, they draw down the soul as comfort raiseth it up.

' Out of measure.' There is the second degree ; they were not only pressed, but pressed ' out of measure.'

' Above strength.' Above my strength, above ordinary strength. And he riseth higher still. The waters rise higher, ' insomuch that we despaired of life.' We despaired of any escaping out of trouble at the present encounter, nay, we did not see how we should escape for the time to come.

Nay, it was so great, in the first place, that we passed ' the sentence of death upon ourselves.' It is a speech taken from malefactors that are condemned ; for even as they, having the sentence pronounced upon them; we account them dead men, they esteem themselves so, and so do others esteem them, the sentence being passed upon them ; so I even passed the sentence on myself, seeing no evasion or escape out of the troubles I was in, the sentence of death passed upon me. ' We had the sentence of death in ourselves.' It was not passed by God, nor by the world ; for they had not decreed to kill him, but he passed it upon himself when he saw no way to escape. He was deceived, though, as ofttimes God's children are, for he died not at that time.

And then afterwards he sets down the end why all this was, a sweet end, a double end, ' That we should not trust in ourselves.' What should we trust in then ? ' But in God that raiseth the dead.'

First to speak of his' grievance, and then of the reason why God did thus follow him.

' *We would not have you ignorant.*' He prevents all scandal by this. ' I would not have you ignorant.' I am so far from caring, or fearing, or being ashamed, that you should know of my affliction that I suffer, that ' I would not have you ignorant of it.' For know this, that when you know my afflictions you shall know my deliverance also. St Paul was wondrous scrupulous at this, lest they should take any offence at his sufferings. Indeed it is the state of God's children ; their worst cross. Sometimes are censures upon them for the cross, the harsh censures of others in their troubles. It was the last, and the greatest of Job's troubles, that, and his wife together. When his house was overthrown, his children killed, his goods taken away, himself stricken with boils, then for his indiscreet friends to become ' miserable comforters,' those that should have comforted him, to become censurers and judges of him, as if he had been a man deserted and forsaken of God, as if all had been from God as a punishment for his sins, this was his greatest cross, as it was his last, when his wife in his bosom, she that should have comforted him most, should solicit him to ill, and his friends by their rash and vile censures to make his cross heavier. So it is with God's children in the world. They cannot endure hardness in the world, they cannot be used otherwise than their cause deserves. But they must also undergo hard censures ; that grieves them more than the cross itself. It was the case of this blessed apostle. The Spirit of God in him therefore sets him to mention his affliction with boldness and confidence, yea, with comfort and joy. ' I would not have you ignorant,' I am not of the mind of carnal men, that would* have it concealed, nay, I would not have you ignorant, I pray understand it. He lays it open to their view, that they might be affected with it, as he was ; for those things that we are affected with, we are large in the discourse of them. He shews that the misery, though it were past, and were off, yet he was affected with it. ' We were pressed out of measure above strength.'

Obj. This seems to thwart another place of Scripture in 1 Cor. x. 13, ' God is faithful, and will lay no more upon you than you shall be able to bear ; ' and yet here he saith, ' we were afflicted above strength.' How can these hang together ?

I answer, God will not suffer his children to endure anything above strength, above that they are able to bear, especially in spiritual evils, but for sickness and persecution or such, sometimes he may lay more upon them than they have present strength to bear.

But, put the case that St Paul speaks of, inward grievance, and outward afflictions too, as both usually accompany one another. St Paul's meaning is here undoubtedly, ' We were pressed above strength,' that is, above ordinary natural strength, that unless God had made a supply by a new supernatural strength, we had never been able to endure it. Therefore take it so, above ordinary natural strength ; for extraordinary crosses must have extraordinary strength, and crosses with grievance of spirit must have more than natural strength to bear them.

Obj. Again, where it is said, ' Insomuch that we despaired of life,' as if he had cared much for his life,—this seemeth to cross another place, Phil. i. 23, ' I desire to be dissolved, and to be with Christ ; ' and here he seems to be very careful, in a strait, lest he should die.

Ans. I answer, we must take St Paul in diverse considerations and respects. As St Paul hath finished his course, and done his work, so ' Henceforth is laid up for me the crown of righteousness,' 2 Tim. iv. 8 ; so he thinks of nothing but life and glory ; he cares not for his life. But take St Paul in the midst of his course, and so he had a care to his charge. Take St Paul as he looked to glory, so he desired to be dissolved ; take him as he was affected to edify the church, so he laboured to live by all means, and so he saith he despaired of life, as desiring to live to do good to the church.

Obj. Again, it may be objected against the last, ' We received the sentence of death in ourselves.' St Paul died not now, and he had the Spirit of God in him, to know what he spake ; how doth this agree then that he had the sentence of death passed ?

Ans. I answer, St Paul spake according to the probability of second causes, according to the appearance of things ; and so he might pronounce of himself without danger, as being no sinful error, that indeed I am a dead man, I see no hope of escaping. If I look to the probability of second causes, all my enemies are about me, I am in the lion's mouth, there is but

* ' Not ' inserted here by a self-correcting misprint.—G.

a step between me and death. He doth not look here to the decree of God, but he looks to the disposing of present causes. So God's children are often deceived in themselves in that respect. It is no great error; for it is true what they speak in regard of second causes, though it be not true in regard of God's decree.

The objections being satisfied, we may observe some points of doctrine.

And out of the first part of St Paul's trial, which some take it to be that in Acts xix., [when] at Ephesus, Demetrius the smith raised up a trouble against him, when they cried out, ' Great is Diana of the Ephesians.' But those are but conjectures. It may be it was some great sickness; it may be some other affliction. The Scripture is silent in the particular what it was. To come then to the points themselves. In the first part, this is considerable in the first place, that

God suffers his children to fall into extreme perils and dangers.

And then secondly, that *they are sensible of it.*

For the first,

God suffers his children to fall into great extremities. This is clear here, we see how he riseth by degrees. ' We were pressed above measure, above strength, that we even despaired of life, we received the sentence of death in ourselves.' He riseth by five steps, to shew the extremity that he was in. This is no new thing, that God should suffer his children thus to be exercised.

It is true in the head, it is true in the body, and it is true of every particular member of the body.

It is true of our head, Christ Jesus himself. We see to what exigencies he was brought, in what danger of his life ofttimes he was, as when they would have cast him down from the mount, Luke iv. 29, and when, in apprehension of his Father's wrath, he sweat ' water and blood ' in the garden, Luke xxii. 44 ; and on the cross cried out, ' My God, my God, why hast thou forsaken me ?' Mark xv. 34. None was ever so abased as he was. He ' humbled himself to the death of the cross,' Philip. ii. 8, nay, lower than the cross ; he was in captivity in the grave three days. They thought they had had their will on him there, they thought they might have trampled on Christ ; and no doubt but the devil triumphed over the grave, and thought he had had him where he would. But we see afterward God raised him again gloriously.

Now, as the head was abased, even unto extremity; so it is true of the whole body of the church from the beginning of the world. The church in Egypt was in extremity before Moses came ; therefore, a learned Hebrician Capne (s), that brought Hebrew into these western parts, was wont to say, When the tale of brick was doubled, then comes Moses, that is, in extremity. When there was no remedy, then God sent them deliverance. In what a pitiful case was the poor church and people of God in Esther's time. There was but a hair's-breadth between them and destruction. It was decreed by Haman, and they had gotten the king's decree too. They were, as it were, between the hammer and the anvil, ready to be crushed in pieces presently, had not God come between. And so in Babylon the church was in extremity, insomuch as that when deliverance was told them, ' they were as men that dream,' Ps. cxxvi. 1, as if there had been no such matter ; they wondered at it. And so in the times of persecution, God hath suffered his church to fall into extreme danger, as now at this time the church is in other parts. I might draw this truth along through all ages. It is true of the whole body of the church. It is true likewise of the particular members. Take the principal members of it. You see Abraham, before God made good his promise, he was brought to a dry body, and Sarah to a dead womb, that they despaired of all second causes. And David, though God promised him a kingdom, yet he was so straitened that he thought many times he should have died. 'I said in my haste, All men are liars,' Ps. cxvi. 11. They tell me this and that, but there is nothing so. He was hunted as a 'partridge in the wilderness,' 1 Sam. xxvi. 20.

It was true of St Paul. We see what extremity he was brought unto, as the psalmist saith, Ps. cxviii. 18, 'I was afflicted sore, but I was not delivered to death,' even as we say, only not killed. It is and hath been so with all the members of the church from Abel to this day. Sometime or other, if they live any long time, they shall be like Moses at the Red Sea. We see in what a strait he and his company was there. There was the Egyptians behind them, the mountains on each side of them, the Red Sea before them. What escaping was here for Moses? So it is with the poor church and children of God ofttimes. There are dangers behind them, and perils before them, and troubles on all sides. God brings them so low as death's door, sometimes by sickness, as there is an instance in Ps. cvii. 18, of those that go down to the sea in ships. 'He brings them to death's door,' saith the psalmist.

What is the reason that, by persecution and afflictions, by one grievance or another, God brings his children to such a low ebb?

The reasons are many.

Reason 1. The first may be, *he will thus try what mettle they are made of.* Light afflictions, light crosses, will not try them thoroughly; great ones will. Jonah, that slept in the ship, he falls a-praying in the whale's belly. He that was pettish out of trouble, and falls a-quarrelling with God himself in trouble, he falls to praying when he was in the bottom of hell, as he saith himself. Little afflictions may stand with murmuring and repining, but great ones try indeed what we are. What we are in great afflictions, we are indeed.

Reason 2. Again, *to try the sincerity of our estate,* to make us to know ourselves, to make us known to the world and known to ourselves, what good we have and what ill we have. A man knows not what a deal of looseness he hath in his heart, and what a deal of falseness, till we come to the cross and to extremity. Whereas before I thought I had had a great deal of patience, a great deal of faith, and a great deal of heavenly-mindedness; now I see I have not that store laid up as I thought I had. And sometime a man is deceived on the contrary. I thought I had had no goodness in me; and yet in extremity such a one goes to prayer, he goes to the word of God, to the communion of saints, he delights in good things, and only in those. Extremity makes him discern and know himself for ill and for good, and makes others to know him too. That is another end.

Reason 3. Again, God suffers us to fall into extremity, *to set an edge upon our desires and our prayers,* to make us cry to him. 'Out of the deep I have cried unto thee, O Lord,' Ps. cxxx. 1. When a man is in the deep, it is not an ordinary prayer will serve, but he must cry. God loves to hear his children speak to him. He loves the voice of his children. It is the best music that he delights in. Therefore, he will take a course that he will be sure to hear from them; and rather than they shall neglect prayer, he will suffer them to fall into some rousing sin, into such a state and condition, that they may dart up prayers, that they may force prayers out of the anguish of spirit, that their prayers may be violent, that will take no denial, that they may be strivings with God, that they may wrestle with

God, as we see in Jacob and the woman of Canaan, that they may be importunate, and never leave him, nor take any denial.

Reason 4. Again, God suffers his children to fall into this extreme peril and danger, not only to try them, what good they have in them, but when he hath tried it to exercise it, *to exercise their faith and their patience.* St Paul had a great deal of grace in him, and God would be sure to have a great deal of trial and exercise of it; and therefore he suffered him to fall into extreme dangers, that so all the patience and all the faith he had might be set on work. And so it was in Job. God had furnished his champion with a great measure of patience, and then he singles him out to the combat ; he brings him into the lists to encounter with Satan, and to triumph over Satan and all the evils he suffered whatsoever.

Reason 5. Again, *it is to perfect the work of mortification*, to let patience have her perfect work, and faith and prayer to have their perfect work, to perfect all graces, and so to perfect the work of mortification. For in extreme dangers he weans us perfectly from the world as much as may be ; nothing will do it if these will not. St Paul came to many cities, and there he thought ofttimes to have great matter of entertainment; and instead of that, he was whipped and misused. God used the matter so to mortify pride and self-confidence in St Paul. He scoured him so from pride, that he should not go out of the city but he should be well scoured first by misusage. So, rather than God will suffer his children to go to hell, and rather than he will suffer them to live in the world here without glory to their profession, without manifesting of grace, to mortify and subdue their base, earthly affections, he will scour them, to subdue their pride and to subdue their earthly-mindedness. We might prevent the bitterness of the cross if we would. We might prevent his mortifying of us by afflictions, by the mortification of the spirit ; but because we are negligent in that work, to perfect the work of mortification he is forced to lay here many crosses and extreme dangers upon us.

Reason 6. Lastly, God doth this for another end, *that he might be sure by this means to prepare us for greater blessings ;* for in what deep measure we are humbled by any deep affliction, in that measure we are prepared for some blessing. Humility doth empty the soul, and crosses do breed humility. The emptiness of the soul fits it for receipt. God therefore doth empty us by crosses, that we may be fit vessels to receive some larger measure of grace and comfort. For, as it is said before, ' As our tribulations increase, so our comforts increase.' Therefore, it is a good sign that God intends much spiritual good to any man, when he lays some heavy load upon him in this world. All is to prepare for some greater comfort and some greater measure of grace.

Why doth the husbandman fall upon his ground, and tear and rend it up with the plough, and the better the ground is, the more he labours to kill weeds ? Is it because he hath an ill mind to the ground ? No. He means to sow good seed there, and he will not plough a whit longer than may serve to prepare the ground. It is the Holy Ghost's comparison, Isa. xxviii. 24. So likewise the goldsmith, the best metal that he hath, he tempers it, he labours to consume the dross of it, and the longer it is in the fire, the more pure it comes forth. So God keeps his children under crosses, and doth plough them. They neglect to plough themselves, and he is fain to set ploughers that will do it indeed,—some ill-minded men, or some cross. If they would plough themselves and examine themselves, they might spare God the labour. But when they are negligent, God takes the labour into his own hand, and sets others on work that will do it to purpose. But all is to prepare them for heavenly seed, for grace and comfort, that in what measure we have been depressed, as he saith here, ' we were pressed above measure,' in that measure he means to lift us up by heavenly comfort.

And, which is a clause of that, *that we might set a price upon the comforts when they come;* for when he hath so prepared us for it, and then we receive it, then comfort is comfort indeed. Comfort in itself is all one, and glory in itself is all one, first and last; but it is not all one to the person. Comfort is endeared to a person that hath been kept under and been dieted before. Then when it comes he sets a great value upon it, when he hath been without it so long.

Our nature is so, that we value things by the want of them rather than by the present enjoying of them. After we have wanted it, and have been long time prepared for it, then when it comes it is welcome indeed. For these and many such like ends we must be willing to approve of God's holy and wise dispensation in this, in ordering matters so with his children, in bringing them to great dangers of body, in danger of life, sometimes to spiritual desertions, leaving them to themselves, as if he had no care of them. But St Paul speaks especially here of outward crosses. You see the reasons of it.

Use 1. The use of it, is first, *that we should not pass a harsh, unadvised, rigid censure upon ourselves, or others, for these respects,* for any great affliction or abasement in this world. The world is ready to pass their verdict presently upon a man. Oh, such a one, you see what a kind of man he was, you see how God follows him with crosses. So uncharitable men judge amiss of ' the generation of the righteous.' Whereas they should set the court in their own hearts, and begin to censure there, and to examine themselves, they go out and keep their court abroad. But I say, pass not a harsh censure upon others, or on thyself, no, not for extreme dangers. For God now is making way for great comfort. Let God go on his way, without thy censuring of him.

Use 2. Again, this should teach us, *that we should not build overmuch confidence on earthly things, on the things of this world,* neither on health of body, or on friends, or on continuance of life. Alas! it is God's ordinary course, to strip us of all in this world. We think of great reputation; but, saith God, I will take that from you; you shall learn to trust in me. You think you have strong and vigorous bodies, and you shall live long, and therefore you will venture upon such and such courses. Aye, but God suffers his children to come to extreme dangers and hazards, that they think the sentence of death is passed upon them.

And since this is God's course with the body, and with the members, and with our head Christ himself, shall we think to have immunity, and to escape, and not look to God's order?

The church is in great misery, and we are negligent in prayer; we think there are many good people, and there is strong munition, &c., as if when God's people are in security, and forget him and his blessings, it were not his course to strip them of all, to suffer them to fall into extreme dangers. Have we not the church before our eyes to teach us? Let us trust, therefore, in nothing in this world.

So much for that point.

The second thing in the first part is this, that

Doct. As God's children are brought to this estate, so they are sensible of it.

They are flesh and not steel, ' they have not the strength of steel,' as
Job saith, Job vi. 12. They are men, they are not stones. They are
Christians, they are not Stoics. Therefore St Paul, as he was in extremity,
so he apprehended his extremity ; and with all his heart he would have
escaped if he could. He looked about to all evasions how he might escape
death. God's children are sensible of their crosses ; especially they are
sensible of death, as he speaks here of himself, ' We despaired even
of life itself.' The word is very significant in the original. We were in
such a strait that we knew not how to escape with life, so that ' we despaired
of life' (t). We would have escaped with our lives, but we saw no way
to escape. To make this clear, there are three things in God's children.
There is *grace*, *nature*, corrupt nature, nature with the tang * of corruption.

Grace, that looks upward, to glory and comfort. Nature looks to the
present grievance, nature looks not to things to come, to matters revealed
in the word, to supernatural comforts : nature looks to the present cross,
even nature without sin. Corrupt nature feels, and feels with a secret
murmuring and repining, and heaviness and dulness ; as indeed corrupt
nature will alway have a bout † in crosses ; it will alway play its part, first
or last. There are alway these three works in the children of God, in all
extremities. Grace works, and that carries up, up still. ' Trust in God.'
It looks to heaven, it looks to the end and issue, that all is for good.
Nature it fills full of sense and pain, and makes a man desire remedy and
ease. Corrupt nature stirs a man up to fret, and say, what doth God
mean to do thus ? It stirs a man ofttimes to use ill means, indirect
courses.

St Paul was sensible, from a right principle of nature ; and, no doubt,
here was some tang* of corruption with it. He was sensible of the fear of
death. Adam in innocency would have been affected, and exquisitely sensible, no doubt, if his body had been wronged ; for the more pure the complexion,‡ the more sensible of solution. As physicians say, when that which
should be knit together, if anything be loosed by sickness, or by wounds,
that should by nature not be hurt, but continue together, it breeds exquisite pain, as to cut that which should not be cut, to disjoin that which
should be together. This is in nature.

The schoolmen say (*u*), and the reason is good, that Christ's pains were the
greatest pains, because his senses were not dulled and stupified with sensuality, or indirect courses. He had a body of an excellent temper, and he
was in the perfection of his years when he died. Therefore he received such
an impression of grief in his whipping, and when he was crowned with
thorns. That was it that made him so sensible of grief, that when he
sweat, he sweat drops of blood, and upon the cross it made him cry out,
' My God, my God, why hast thou forsaken me ?' Mark xv. 34.

God's children, out of a principle of nature, are sensible of any grievance
to this outward man of theirs, to the body, especially in death, as we see
here St Paul. And there is most patience where there is most sense. It
is stupidity and blockishness else.

Quest. Why are God's children so sensible in grief, especially in death ?

Ans. Oh, there is a great cause. Indeed, in some regards, they are not
afraid of it ; for death is an enemy to nature, it is none to grace. But
when I speak not of grace and glory, but of nature,

* That is, = ' taint,' or ' touch.'—G.　　　† That is, ' turn,' ' part.'—G.
‡ That is, = ' conjunction,' or ' union.'—G.

Reason 1. *Hath not nature great cause to tremble at death, when it is an enemy to nature, even to right nature?* It is the king of fears, as Job saith, Job xviii. 14. It is that tyrant that makes all the kings of the earth to tremble at him. When death comes, it is terrible. Why? because it strips us of all the contentments of this life, of all comforts whatsoever we have here. Nature without sin is sensible of earthly comforts that God hath appointed for nature; and when nature sees an end of them, nature begins to give in, and to grieve.

Reason 2. Again, *death parts the best friends we have in this world, the body and the soul*, two old friends; and they cannot be parted without exquisite grief. If two friends that take contentment in each other, common friends, cannot part without grief, how shall these bosom friends, these united friends, body and soul, part without grief? This marriage between the soul and the body cannot be disunited without exquisite pain, being old acquaintance.

Reason 3. Again, nature abhors death, [because] *it hinders us of all employment*. It hinders of all service of God in church and commonwealth. And so grace, which is beyond nature, doth a little desire the continuance of life.

But nature, even out of no sinful principle, it sees that now I can serve God no longer, I can do God no more service, I can do good no longer in this world. And therefore it takes it to heart. Our Saviour saith, ' While you have light, walk: the night cometh, when no man is able to work,' John ix. 4, the night of sickness and death. So it breeds discomfort, and is terrible that way.

Reason 4. Again, in death *we leave those that cast their care upon us*, we leave ofttimes wives and children, without husband or father; those that had dependence upon us. And this must needs work upon nature, upon a right principle of nature. Indeed the excess of it is with corruption alway.

Reason 5. Again, in death, *there is great pain*. They say, births are with great pangs, and so they are. Now death is a birth, the birth of immortality. No wonder then if it have great pangs. Therefore nature fears it even for the pangs, the concomitants that are joined with it.

Reason 6. And then in death, nature considers *the state of the body presently after death*, that that goodly body, that strength and vigour I enjoyed before, must now be worms'-meat. I must say ' to the worm, Thou art my brother, and to corruption, Thou art my mother,' and the like, as it is in Job, Job xvii. 14. That head, that perhaps hath ruled the commonwealth, the place where I lived, it must lie level with others; and that body that others were enamoured with, it must now be so forlorn, that the sight of it will not be endured of our best friends. Nature considers what the estate will be there, that it shall turn to rottenness ere long; that the goodliest persons shall be turned to dust, and lie rotting there till the day of the resurrection.

Faith and grace looks higher; but because we have nature as long as we are men, these and such like respects work upon nature, and make death grievous.

Reason 7. But besides the glass of nature, and these things here in the world, look upon it *in the law of God*, in that glass; and so nature trembles, and quarrels at death. Death! what is it? It is the ' wages of sin,' Rom. vi. 23, it is the end of all comfort; and nature cannot see any comfort after that. It is beyond nature. Nature teacheth us not that there will be a resurrection of the body, nature teacheth us not that the soul goes to God. Here must be a great deal of grace, and a great deal of faith, to convince the soul of this. Nature teacheth it not.

Now, when besides this, the law of God comes and saith, death came in by sin, 'and sin is the sting of death,' 1 Cor. xv. 56, death is armed with sin, and sin comes in with the evidences of God's anger. Here, unless there be faith and grace, a man is either as Nabal, a stone and a sot in death, or as Judas and Cain, swallowed up with despair. It is impossible for a man that is not a true Christian, that is not a good man, but that either he should be as a stone, or desperate in sickness and death, without grace. He must be one of them. If he be a wise man, he cannot but despair in the hour of death. For is it a matter to be dallied with, or to be carried bravely out, as your Roman spirits and atheists think? They account it a glory to die bravely, in a stout manner. Is the terrible of terribles so to be put off? When all the comforts in this world shall end, and all employments cease, when there is eternity before a man; and, after death, hell, and eternal damnation of body and soul, are these matters to be slighted? It would make a man look about him. If a man have not faith and grace, he must either despair or die like a stone. None but a good Christian can carry himself well in the hour of death. Nay, a good Christian is sensible of death; and till he see God's time is come, he labours to avoid it by all means, as St Paul doth here.

Reason 8. But St Paul had another ground beyond nature to avoid death. *He knew himself ordained for the service of the church;* therefore he desired to escape, that he might serve God a longer time for the good of his church.

Use 1. Are God's children sensible of death, and the danger of it, and out of a principle of nature and grace too? *How then should carnal, wretched men look about them,* that have not made their accounts even with God? The report of death to them should be like the handwriting upon the wall to Belshazzar, Dan. v. 24. It should make their knees beat together, and make their countenance pale. It should strike them with terror; and, like Nabal, make their hearts to die as a stone within them.

Use 2. But it is a use of comfort to *poor, deluded Christians.* They think, alas! can my estate be good? I am afraid of death, I tremble and quake at the name of death, I cannot endure to hear of it, but it most of all affects me to see it. Therefore I fear I have no grace in me, I fear I have no faith in me.

Be not discomforted, whosoever thou art, that sayest so, if thou labour to strengthen thy faith, and to keep a good conscience; for thou mayest do thus out of a principle of nature. Nature trembles at death.

A man may do two things from diverse principle, from diverse repects, and both without sin. For example, in fasting, nature without sin desireth meat, or else fasting were not an afflicting of a man's body; but grace, that hath another principle, and that desires to hold out without sustenance, to be afflicted. So here is both a desire, and not a desire, and both good in their kind. So a man in the time of sickness and death, he may by all means desire to escape it, and tremble at it out of a principle of nature; but out of a higher principle he may triumph. ' O death, where is thy sting? O grave, where is thy victory?' 1 Cor. xv. 55; and 'they that believe in Christ shall never die,' John xi. 26. ' We are in heavenly places together with Christ,' Eph. i. 3. We are as sure of heaven as if we were there. So out of such kind of principles we may triumph over death, by faith and grace.

So let none be discouraged. Nature goes one way, and faith and grace another. A man may know when it is nature, and when it is grace. When grace subdues nature, and subordinates it to a higher principle, a man need not be much troubled.

Christ himself our head, he was afraid of death when he looked on death as death; but when he looked upon death as a service, as a redemption, as a sweet sacrifice to God, so ' with a thirsting I have thirsted,' saith he, Luke xxii. 15. He thirsted after death in that respect. Looking to his human nature, to the truth of his manhood, then saith he, ' O that this cup might pass from me,' Mat. xxvi. 39 ; but in another consideration, he willingly gave his soul a sacrifice for sin to God.

The desire is as the objects are presented. Let heaven and happiness be presented, so death is a passage to it, so death is the end of misery, and the beginning of happiness, so God's children ' desire to be dissolved, and to be with Christ,' as St Paul did, Philip. i. 23. But look upon death otherwise, as it is an enemy to nature, as it is a stop of all employment in this world, and of all service to the church, that we can do God no longer service ; and so a man may desire to live still, and be afraid of death, if he look upon death in the glass of nature, and in the glass of the law, likewise that it comes in as a punishment of sin, so indeed it is terrible, it is the king of fears. But look upon it in another glass, in the glass of the gospel, as it is sweetened and as it is disarmed by Christ, and so it is comfortable. ' Better is the day of death than the day of birth,' Eccles. vii. 1 ; for in our birth we come into misery, in death we go from it. So upon diverse considerations we may be diversely affected, and have diverse respects to things ; for the soul of man is framed so to be carried to the present objects, and therefore in a good man in some respects, at some time, death is terrible ; he trembles at it, which upon higher considerations and respects, he embraceth willingly.

Indeed, it is a sign of a wise man to value life. It is the opportunity and advantage to honour God. After death we are receivers, and not doers. Then we receive our wages. But while we are here, we should desire even for the glory that is reserved for us, to do all the good we can, because the time of life is that blessed advantage of doing good and of taking good. It is to be in heaven before our time to do others good, and to get evidence of heaven for ourselves. This is the second thing, that as God's children are suffered to fall into extreme dangers, so they are very sensible of them, especially in matter of death, which is the last enemy. There the devil sets upon them indeed. He knows that that is the last enemy, and that there he must get all or lose all ; and he labours to make death more terrible than it is or should be.

The way not to fear death, and not to let nature have overmuch scope, is to disarm death beforehand, to pluck out the sting of it by repentance ; weaken it beforehand, that it may not get the better, even as we do with our enemies. The way to overcome them is to weaken them, to weaken their forces, to starve them if we can, to intercept all their provision. What makes death terrible and strong ? We put stings into it, our sins, our sins against conscience. The time will come when conscience will awaken, and it will be then, if ever, to our comfort ; and then our former sins will stare in our faces, the sins of our youth, the sins that we have before neglected soundly to repent for. Therefore let us labour this way to make death less terrible.

Again, that we may not fear it overmuch, let us look upon it in the glass of the gospel, as it is now in Christ, as it is turned clean another way. Now, it hath sweet names. It is called a dissolution, a departure, a sleeping, a going to our Father's, and such like. God doth sweeten a bitter thing, that it may enter into us with less terror. So it must be our wisdom to sweeten the meditation of it, by evangelical considerations, what it is now by Christ.

And withal to meditate the two terms, from whence and whither. What a blessed change it is if we be in Christ! It is a change for the better, better company, better employment, a better place, all better. Who would be grieved at, and afraid of, death? Let us recall the promise of the presence of God. He will be with us to death, and in death. 'Blessed are those that die in the Lord,' Rex. xiv. 13. And especially faith in Christ will make us, that we shall not fear death, when we shall see him our head in heaven before us, ready to receive us when we come there; and to see ourselves in heaven, already in him; as verily in faith and in the promise, as if we were there. 'We are set in heavenly places' with Christ already. Let us have these and such like considerations to sweeten the thought of death.

But to touch this, which is an appendix to that formerly mentioned, that

Obs. God's children are deceived concerning their death ofttimes.

The time of death is uncertain. St Paul thought he should have died when he did not; he was deceived. There is a double error about death. Sometimes we think we shall not die, when indeed we are dead men. Sometimes we receive the sentence of death, we pass a censure upon ourselves, that we cannot live, when God intends our escape. So it is uncertain to us the hour of death. Sometime we are uncertain when it is certain; sometime we think it certain when it falls not out so. Both ways we are deceived, because God will have us, while we live here, to be at an uncertainty for the very moment of death. 'Our times are in his hand.' Our time of life is in his hand. We came into the world when he thought good. Our time of living here is in his hands. We live just as long as he will have us. Our time of death is in his hand. The prophet saith not only, my time is in thy hands, but ' my times,' my time of coming into the world, my time of living in the world, and my time of going out of the world shall be when thou shalt appoint me. Therefore he will have us uncertain of it ourselves, till the moment of death come. St Paul was deceived, ' He received the sentence of death in himself,' but he died not at that time.

So that the manner and circumstances of death are uncertain, whether it shall be violent or fair death, [whether] it shall be by diseases or by casualties, whether at home or abroad. All the circumstances of death are hidden from us, as well as death itself and the time of it.

And this is out of heavenly wisdom, and love of God to us, that we should at all times be provided, and prepared for our dissolution and change. It is left at this uncertainty, that we might make our estate certain, to be fitted to die at all times. Let us make that use of it to provide every day. Oh, it were a happy thing if we could make every day, as it were, another life, a several life; and pass sentence upon ourselves, a possible and probable sentence; it may be this day may be the last day. And let us end every day as we would end our lives. How would we end our lives? We would end them with repentance for our sins past, with commending our souls into the hands of God, with resolution and purpose to please God in all things, with disposing all things wisely in this world. Let us end our days, every day so, as much as possible may be ; let us set everything right ; let us set the state of our souls in order, set all in order as much as may be every day. It were a blessed course if we could do so.

And this is one part, one main branch of our corruption, wherein it shews itself strongly, that we live in an estate that we are ashamed to die in. Come to some men, and ask them, how it is with you ? have you repented of your sins past? have you renewed your purposes for the time to come? Yes ; we do it solemnly at the communion. But we should renew our repentance, and renew our covenants every day, to please God that day. Do you do so now? If God should seize upon you now, are you in the exercise of faith ? in the exercise of repentance ? in the exercise of holy purposes, to please God ? are you in God's ways ? do you live as you would be content to die ? But Satan and our own corruption bewitcheth us with a vain hope of long life, we promise ourselves that, that God doth not promise us ; we make that certain that God doth not make certain. Indeed we are certain of death, but for the time, and manner, and circumstances we know them not. Sometimes we think we shall die when we do not, and sometimes we die when we think we shall not.

Oh, will some say, if I knew when I should die, I would be a prepared man, I would be exact in my preparation. Wouldst thou so ? thou art deceived. Saul knew exactly he should die. He took it for exact when the witch in the shape of Samuel told him that he should die by to-morrow this time, and yet he died desperately upon the sword's point for all that. He did not prepare himself. It must be the Spirit of God that must prepare us for this. If we knew never so much, that we should die never so soon, we cannot prepare ourselves. Our preparation must be by the Spirit of God. Let us labour continually to be prepared for it.

And let no man resolve to take liberty a moment, a minute of an hour to sin. God hath left it uncertain the day of death. What if that moment and minute wherein thou resolvest to sin should be the moment of thy death and departure hence ? for it is but a minute's work to end thy days. What if God should end thy days in that minute ? Let no man take liberty and time to sin, when God gives him no liberty in sin. If God should strike thee, thou goest to hell quick, thou must sink from sin to hell. It is a pitiful case, whenas eternity depends upon our watchfulness in this world. But to come to the end and issue, why he was thus dealt with by God, carrying him through these extremities.

'*That we might not trust in ourselves, but in God that raiseth the dead.*' Here is the end specified that God intended, in suffering him to be brought so low, even to death's door, that there was but a step between him and death. The end is double, 'That we should not trust in ourselves, but in God that raiseth the dead.' It is set down negatively and positively. First, 'That we should not trust in ourselves,' and then that we should 'trust in God.' And the method is excellent. For we can never trust in God till we distrust ourselves, till our hearts be taken off from all confidence in ourselves and in the creature ; and then when our hearts are taken off from false confidence, they must have somewhat to rely on, and that is God or nothing; for else we shall fall into despair. The end of all this was, that 'we might not trust in ourselves, but in God that raiseth the dead.'

The wisdom of heaven doth nothing without an end proportionable to that heavenly wisdom ; so all this sore affliction of the blessed apostle, what aimed it at ? To pull down, and to build up ; to pull down self-confidence, ' That we might not trust in ourselves ; ' and to build up confidence and affiance in God, ' but in God that raiseth the dead.'

We being in a contrary state to grace and communion with God, this order is necessary, that God must use some way that we shall not trust in ourselves ; and then to bring us to trust in him. So these two are subordinate ends one to another. ' We received the sentence of death, that we might not trust in ourselves.'

From the dependence this may be observed, that

Doct. The certain account of death, is a means to wean us from ourselves, and to make us trust in God.

The sentence of death, the assured knowledge that we must die, the certain expectation and looking for death, is the way to wean us from the world, and to fit us for God, to prepare us for a better life. You see it follows of necessity, ' We received the sentence of death, that we should not trust in ourselves,' &c.

The looking-for of death therefore, takes away confidence in ourselves and the creature. Alas ! in death, what can all the creatures help ? What can friends, or physic, or money help ? Then honours, and pleasures, and all leave us then.

This the rather to note a corrupt atheistical course in those that are to deal with sick folk, that are extreme sick, that conceal their estate from them, and feed them with false hopes of long life. They deserve ill of persons in extremity to put them in hope of recovery. Physicians that are not divines in some measure, what do they ? against their conscience, and against their experience, and against sense, Oh, I hope you shall do well, &c. Alas ! what do they ? they hurt their souls, they breed a false confidence. It is a dangerous thing to trust upon long life, when perhaps they are snatched suddenly away, before they have made their accounts even with God, before they have set their souls in that state they should do.

Therefore the best way is to do as good Isaiah did with Hezekiah, ' set thy house in order, for thou must die,' 2 Kings xx. 1, that is, in the disposition of second causes, thou shalt have a disease that will bring thee to death, and God had said so. God had a reservation, but it was more than Isaiah knew at that time. ' Set thy house in order, for thou must die.' So they should begin with God, to tell them, as we say, the worst first. It is a pitiful thing that death should be accounted the worst, but so it is, by reason of our fearfulness. Deal plainly with them, let them ' receive the sentence of death,' that so they may be driven out of themselves and the creature altogether, and be driven to trust in ' God that raiseth the dead.' Put thy soul in order. You are no man of this world ; lest they betray their souls for a little self-respect perhaps, because they would not displease them.

It may be in some cases discreet to yield, to make the means to work the better; but where there is nothing but evident signs of death, they ought to deal directly with them, that they may receive the sentence of death. It wrought with St Paul this good effect, ' I received the sentence of death, that we might not trust in ourselves, but in God that raiseth the dead.'

It is God's just judgment upon hypocrites, and upon many carnal wretched persons, that are led with a false confidence all their life, that trust in the creature, trust in friends and riches, that will not trust in God, and will not be taught to number their days in their lifetime. It is just with God [toward those who], to their very death [are filled] with false confidence, when they come to death, to suffer them to perish in their false confidence, and so to sink into hell. It is just with God to suffer them to have atheists about them, or weak persons that shall say, Oh, you shall do well enough, and then even out of a very desire to live, they are willing to believe all, and so they die without all show of change; and as they live, so they die, and are wretched in both. The life of a wicked man is ill, his death worse, his estate after death worst of all; and this is one way whereby God suffers men to fall into the snare of the devil, when he suffers not those that are about them to deal faithfully. St Paul received the sentence of death, that it might force him not to trust in himself, but in God that raiseth the dead.

The second thing that is observable hence out of this first part, which is the negative part, is this, that,

Doct. God's children are prone to trust in themselves.

The hearts even of God's dear children are prone in themselves, if they be left to their own bent and weight, to self-confidence, and will not hold up in faith and affiance in God further than they are lifted and kept up by a spirit of faith, which God puts into them. It was not in vain that God used this course with blessed St Paul. Here is an end set down, that he 'might not trust in himself.' What, was he in peril to trust in himself? Alas! St Paul, though he were an holy excellent man, yet he was a man; and in the best man there is a double principle, a principle of nature, of corrupt nature, and a principle of grace; and he works according to both principles. There is an intermixture of both in all his actions, and in all his passions too, in his sufferings. Corruption shews itself in his best deeds, and his best sufferings, in everything. ' That we should not trust in ourselves,' that is, in anything in ourselves, or out of ourselves, in the creature; it is all one. We see by the example of St Paul that the best are prone to trust in themselves. All this hard usage of St Paul, that he received the sentence of death, it was that 'he should not trust in himself.' What, was there danger in St Paul to trust in himself? a man that had been so exercised with crosses and afflictions as he had been, no man more, one would think that he had been scoured enough of pride, and self-confidence! the whippings and misusings, the stocks, the dungeons, &c., would not all this work pride, and self-confidence out of the apostle? No! So deeply it is invested into our base nature, our trusting to present things, that we cannot live the life of faith, we cannot depend upon God, whom we cannot see but with other eyes than nature hath. It is so deeply rooted in our nature, that the blessed apostle himself must have this great help, to be taught to go out of himself, and to depend upon God. We see in what danger he was, in another place, to be lifted up with the revelations. He was fain to have a ' prick in the flesh, a messenger of Satan to buffet him,' 2 Cor. xii. 7.

Hezekiah, his heart was lifted up, as the Scripture speaks, in his treasures, that he shewed to the King of Babylon's ambassadors, as if he were such a rich prince. And so holy David, in numbering the people, to shew what a mighty prince he was. It was his vain confidence. Therefore God put him to a strange cure. He punished him in that that he gloried in. He took away so many of his people. And so Hezekiah was punished in that he sinned in. He was fain to have a purge for it. His treasure was taken away and carried to Babylon. ' I said in my prosperity,' saith holy David, ' I shall never be moved,' Ps. xxx. 6. The best are subject to false confidence to trust in themselves.

One reason partly, because there is a mixture of corruption in us while we live here, and corruption looks to this false principle in us, that will never be wrought out with all the afflictions in the world. Till death make an end of corruption, there will be a false trust in ourselves and in the creature. We cannot trust God perfectly as we should do.

Reason 1. Again, the reason is, *because the things of this life are useful and commodious unto us, and we are nouzelled* up in the use of them,* and when Satan doth amplify them in our fancy to be greater in goodness than they are ; and opinion sets a greater worth on them, if there were no devil. But he presenting these things in all the lustre he can, he helps the imagination, which he hath more to do with than with all the parts of the soul. And the soul looks in the glass of opinion upon these things, and thinks they are goodly, great matters, learning and wisdom, honour and riches. Looking upon them as they are amplified by the false fancy of others and the competition of the world wherein we live, every man is greedy and hasty of these things. All men have not faith for better things. Therefore, they are mad of these. So the competition of others and the enlarging our conceits upon them above their worth, these make us put greater confidence in them, and then we come to trust in ourselves and in them, and not in God.

Reason 2. *Naturally we cannot see the nothingness of the creature,* that as it came out of nothing, so it will turn to nothing. But because it is sensible, these good things are sensible, and present, and necessary, and useful ; and naturally we live by our senses. Therefore, we place our delight in them, that when they are taken away all the soul goes with them. As he that leans upon a crutch, or anything, when that is taken away, down he falls, so it is with a man by nature ; he trusts to these things, and when they go, his soul sinks together with the things. Even as it is with those that are in a stream, when they are in a running stream they are carried with the stream, so all these things go away, they are of a fleeting condition. We see them not in their passage. When they are gone, we see them past. We see not ourselves vanish by little and little out of this life. We see not the creatures present, we see not death, and other things beyond death, as we should by the eye of faith. So things pass, and we pass with them ; the stream and we run together. It must be a great measure of faith that must help this. We are prone to trust to sensible things naturally. We know what it is to live by sense ; but to live by faith it is a remote thing, to lead our lives by reasons drawn from things that are not seen, to live by promises, it is a hard thing, when things that are sensible cannot work upon us. When we see men die, and see the vanity of things sensible, it will not work upon us ; how then do we think that things that are supernatural, which are remote† far above sense, should work on us ? It is a hard thing not to trust to ourselves, we are so addicted to live by sense ; and there is some corruption in St Paul, in the best men, to trust to present things.

Who doth not think but he shall live one day longer, and so trusts to life ? As the heathen man could say, ' There is not the oldest man but he thinks he may live a little longer, one day longer ' (*v*). Who makes that use of mortality and the uncertain, fading condition of this life as he should ? And all because of a false trust ; as in other things, so in the continuance of life. We see we are prone to trust, to put base, false confidence in somewhat or other while we live in this world.

Reason 3. Again, *our nature being prone to outward things, and sunk deeply into them, it can hardly be recovered ;* it cannot be sober without much ado

* That is, 'nourished.'—G.   † That is, 'removed.'—ED.

and brought from trusting of present things. You have some men that have things at will in this world. They never know what faith means. All their life they live by sense. Their conscience is not awaked, and outward afflictions seize not on them and supply of earthly things they have. What religion means, and what God and heaven means, they have heard of them perhaps, but throughly and inwardly what it means they never come to know in this world, without there be some alteration and changes. They must have some changes. ' The wicked have no changes,' saith the prophet, Ps. lv. 19. But while they be as they are, they know not God, nor themselves, nor the vanity of earthly things. We speak the truth of God to a company ofttimes that are besotted with sensuality, and that have perpetual supply of earthly things. Speak to them of faith, and of things that are remote from sense, &c., they hear them as if they were in a dream. Nature is prone to trust in present things, even in the best, in St Paul himself.

Use 1. Now, our proneness to it *doth justify God's dealings in many things, as* (1.) *Why doth God humble great ones with great afflictions?* Why doth he humble great men, great and excellent Christians, with great falls? That they might not trust in themselves ; no, not in their own present graces. God will not bring a man to salvation now by grace in himself to give him title to heaven. His graces must only be to help his evidence that he is not an hypocrite, and to give evidence to others, that others ' may see his good works,' &c., Mat. v. 16. But if he come to trust in them once, to set them in Christ's stead, God will abase his pride by suffering him to fall, that he may go out of himself, to be saved by Christ, and to seek for mercy in Christ.

(2.) And this is the reason why God in his providence *doth great things by small means, without means, and against means sometimes.* When he crosses and curses great means, it is that we might not ' trust in ourselves.' We are prone to self-confidence ; and because God will cure it, for we must not carry it to heaven with us, therefore he is forced to take this kind of dispensation.

Proud flesh will always devise something but that which it should do, to uphold itself withal. It will not be driven from all its holds ; God hath much ado to work it out from all its holds. If it have not wealth, it will have wit and policy ; or if it have not that, it will have civil life, and outward works to trust to, and to swell it with. But to come and give God the glory of salvation only by mercy, and to depend only on God, and to see an insufficiency in any thing we do, it can hardly be brought to pass. Insomuch that that article of justification by the obedience of Christ only, it is merely a spiritual thing, altogether transcending nature.

No marvel if we find such opposition from the Church of Rome, and all, unless it be the true church; they understand not the main article, of salvation only by mercy, because nature is so desperately prone to self-confidence.

Use 2. Let us *take heed of false confidence in the things of this life,* of confidence in any thing but God.

But to come to some trials. You will say, how shall we know whether we put over much confidence in them or no?

(1.) It is an easy matter to know it. We trust them too much when we grow proud upon any thing, when our spirits are lifted up. ' Charge rich men that they be not high-minded,' 1 Tim. vi. 17, insinuating that they are in danger to be high-minded. ' If riches increase, set not your hearts upon them,' saith the Psalmist, Ps. lxii. 10. There is great danger when the heart is set on them, and lifted up, when men think themselves so much the better as they are greater. Indeed, if they weigh themselves in a civil balance it is so, but the corrupt nature of man goes further, and thinks a man intrinsically better, and more beloved of God for these things. It is a dangerous sign that we trust too much to them.

(2.) Again, *overmuch grief, if they be taken away any of them, or if we be crossed in them.* The grief in wanting betrays the love in enjoying. It is a sign that Job had gotten a great measure of self-denial, not to trust in himself or his riches, though he were a rich man, because when they were taken away, ' Blessed be God,' saith he, ' thou gavest them, and thou hast taken them away,' Job i. 21. He that can stand when his stay is taken from him, it is a sign he trusts not too much to his stay. He that is so weak that when his stay is taken away, down he falls, it is a sign he leans hard. Those that when these things are taken from them, when their friends are taken away, or their honours, or riches are taken away, yet they can support themselves out of diviner grounds, it is a sign they did not overmuch trust these things. Nature will work something, but overmuch grief betrays overmuch love always.

Again, which is but a branch of the other, we may know that we overmuch set by them, *by fretting to be crossed in any of these things.* A man may know Ahithophel trusted too much to his policy and wit : when he was crossed he could not endure it. We see he made away himself for very shame, 2 Sam. xvii. 23. When a man is crossed in his wit and policy, when he is crossed in those projects he hath laid ; when he is crossed in his preferment, or riches, or friends, then he is all amort,* he frets, which is more than grieving ; when he not only grieves, but with Ahithophel he goes to ill courses. It is a sign he trusted too much, and too basely to them before.

(3.) Again, when the enjoying of these things *is joined with contempt and base esteem of others,* it is a sign that we rest too much in them. There is more trust put to them than they should bear. We should not, in the enjoying of honour, or riches, or pleasures, or any thing, think the meaner of others.

(4.) Especially, *security shews that we trust too much in them,* when we bless ourselves, I shall do well. ' Soul, soul, thou hast goods laid up for many years,' Luke xii. 19, saith the fool, and he was but a fool for it, to promise certainty for uncertainty. A man cannot stand in that which cannot stand itself. To promise life in a dying condition, to promise any thing in this world, when the very nature of them is uncertain, ' Thou fool,' saith the Scripture. If his soul had been so full of faith as his barns were of corn, he would never have said, ' Soul, soul, take thy rest,' for these things ; but he would have trusted in God. It is a sign we trust too much to these things, when we secure ourselves all will be well, and bless ourselves, as the Scripture speaks.

(5.) Again, it is a sign we trust too much to these things, *when upon confidence of these things we go to ill and unwarrantable courses, and think to be borne out by these things.* As when the younger sort shall pour forth themselves to vanity, and are careless of swearing and licentiousness, that they care not what to do, they shall live long enough to repent, &c. This is a diabolical trust, that God will give them no security in. So when men

---

* That is, 'spiritless,' 'inanimate.' This from Sibbes supplements excellently Richardson, *sub voce.*—G.

that have riches will venture on bad causes, and think to carry it out with
their purse, they trust in matter of oppression, and think to bear out the
matter with their friends, or with their place, or with their wits ; this is
false trust. ' Thy wisdom hath caused thee to rebel,' as the prophet saith
concerning Babylon, Isa. xlvii. 10. They thought they had reaching heads,
and so ventured upon rebellious courses. When any of these outward
things draw us to unwarrantable, unjustifiable courses, it is a sign we plant
too much confidence in them : and it is a sign, if we belong to God, that he
intends to cross us in them. The very confidence in these things hath
drawn many to ill courses, to do that that they should not do, as good
Josiah, Hezekiah, David, and the rest.

Thus we see how we should examine ourselves, whether we trust too
much in these things or no.

Now, since we are thus prone to this false confidence, and since we may
thus discern it ; if we discern it in ourselves, how shall we cure it ? That
in the next doctrine:—*That we might not trust in ourselves.* From whence
observe,

Doct. It is a dangerous state to trust in ourselves.

This ill disposition, to trust in ourselves, or anything out of ourselves,
but only in God, in whom we should trust, it is dangerous. For a man
may reason thus from the text : That which God is forced to take such desperate courses for, as to bring such an excellent man as St Paul to such
extremity, and all that he should not trust in himself, that he was not only
prone to, but it was a dangerous estate for him. But God brings him to
death's door, that he ' received the sentence of death, that he might not
trust in himself,' that he might see the nothingness of all things else. Therefore it was a dangerous estate for him to trust in himself.

It is ill in respect of I. *God* ; II. *ourselves.*

I. *In respect of God.* To trust to ourselves, or the creature, is

1. *To idolize ourselves, or the creature.* We make an idol of the thing we
trust in. We put God out of his place, and set up that we trust in, in
God's room ; and so provoke God to jealousy. When men shall trust
their wits in matters of religion, as in popery they do (they serve God after
their own inventions), what a dishonour is it to God ? as if he were not wise
enough to prescribe how he will be worshipped. ' Go after me, Satan,'
saith Christ to Peter, Mat. xvi. 23. He calls him devil. Why ? what
hurt was it ? He came with a good intention ? That which papists[*] think
they please God most in, they are devils in ; and these things that they
teach are ' the doctrines of devils,' 1 Tim. iv. 1. ' But the wisdom of the
flesh is death ; it is not subject to the law of God, nor can be subject,'
saith the apostle, Rom. viii. 7. So it is dangerous, because it is offensive
to God. ' There is a way that seemeth right in a man's own eyes : the
issues whereof are the issues of death,' Prov. xiv. 12. It is idolatry in
regard of God.

2. And it is *spiritual adultery.* For what should take up our affections ?
Should we not place our joy, our delight, which follows our trust alway;
for trust carries the whole soul with it : what should take up our joy and
delight ? Should not God, and heaven, and heavenly things ? should not
these things have place in our hearts, as they have in their own worth ?
When we take these affections from God, and place them upon the creature,
they are adulterous affections. When we love riches or pleasures better
than God that gave us all, it is an adulterous, whorish love. ' Oh ye

* Misprinted ' popery.'—G.

adulterers and adulteresses,' saith blessed St James, ' know ye not that the love of this world is enmity with God ?' James iv. 4.

3. It is likewise *falsehood*. For it makes the creature to be that that it is not, and it makes God that which he is not. We despise him, and set up the creature in his room. There is a false witness alway in false confidence. Indeed there are many sins in it.

4. There is *ignorance;* not knowing the creature to be so vain as it is. There is ignorance of God, not knowing him to be ' all in all,' Col. iii. 11, as he is.

5. And there is *rebellion*, to trust in the creature, when God will not have it trusted in.

6. And there is *impatience*. When these supports are taken away, then men grow to murmuring. There is almost all sins hidden in self-confidence and self-sufficiency. You see the danger of it to God.

II. Besides that, it is dangerous *to ourselves*. It brings us *under a curse*. ' Cursed is the man that maketh flesh his arms,' Jer. xvii. 5, that trusts in anything but God. It brings us under a curse, as I said, because it is idolatry and spiritual adultery. And then again, because leaning to a false prop, that being taken away that shored us up before, down we fall, with that we leaned on.

Now all things but God being vanity, we, relying upon that which is vain, our trust is vain, as the thing is vain. We can hope for no better condition than the things we trust to. They are vain, and we are vain; so there is a curse upon them.

Therefore we have great cause to hate that upstart religion, that hath been devised for their own ends, for their own profit, because it would bring us under a curse. They would have us to trust to our own works in matter of salvation, to trust to our own satisfaction to be freed from purgatory, &c. They would have us to trust to creatures, to something besides God ; to trust in the mediation of saints, to be our intercessors, &c. And what doth this false trust ? It breeds despair at length.

What is the reason that a well-advised papist, that knows what he doth, cannot but despair, or else renounce popery ? Because popery carries the soul to false props in matter of justification. They renounce their own religion at the hour of death, as Bellarmine did (*w*). They live by one religion, and die by another, which would not be if their religion were good. For their hearts tell them that they have not done so many works that they may trust in them, and they have not been so well done that they may trust in them. It is a dangerous thing. ' Cursed is he that trusts in man,' or in anything in man.

Nay, we must not trust our own graces, as they are in ourselves, not by way of merit; no, not by way of strength. We must not trust our present graces to carry us out, without new supply to further us. It was Peter's fault. ' Though all men deny thee, yet will not I,' Mat. xxvi. 35. He trusted to his present strength ; he forgot that if he had not a new supply from the spring of grace, that he should miserably miscarry, and so he died.* All our righteousness to trust to, it is a ' broken reed,' Isa. xxxvi. 6. It is somewhat, if we place it in the due place, to give us evidence that we are true Christians ; but to trust in it by way of merit, the devil will pick so many holes in that kind of title, and conscience will see so many flaws in it, if we bring no better title, than either the holiness in us, or the works from us, the devil and our own conscience will spy so many flaws and

* That is, spiritually, and for the moment of his backsliding.—G.   Qu. ' did ?'—ED.

cracks in it at the time of death, that we shall not dare to trust in it, but we must run out of ourselves to Christ, or else we die in desperation. Let us know these things. All things but God, the more we know them, the less we trust in them. But it is clean contrary of God, the more we know him, the more we shall trust in him. The more we meditate, and enlarge our hearts in the consideration of his divine essence every way, the more we shall trust in him. 'They that know thy name, will trust in thee,' Ps. ix. 10. Let us trust in no outward thing.

No! not in the humanity of Christ. I add that further. We are very prone to trust in things sensible; and the apostles, because Christ was present with them, and comfortable among them (as indeed he was sweet and loving, bearing with their infirmities, and encouraging them upon all occasions); O they were loath to part with him. He tells them that he must leave them, but they should not fare the worse, he would 'send them the Comforter.' 'The flesh itself profits nothing,' John vi. 63, without the Godhead, saith he.

Trust not in the sacraments above their place. It is a dangerous thing to put too much in any creature (God is extremely offended at it), as not only our adversaries the papists, but proud persons among us, that are weary of the doctrine of the church, and will not submit, in their pride, to riper judgments. They attribute too much to the sacraments, as some others do too little. They attribute a presence there. They make it an idol. They give it such reverence as they will not do to God himself, and from a false conceit. Oh, there is I know not what presence. Therefore the Lutherans must needs in a great degree be idolaters, by their consubstantiation; and the papists by their transubstantiation, by their real presence. Coster saith, and saith truly, if Christ be not there, we are the greatest idolaters in the world (x).

But there is a more subtle kind of attributing to the sacraments, that alway God gives grace with the sacraments, the sacraments convey grace alway. As a plaster it hath a kind of power to eat out the dead flesh, and as physic hath a power to carry away the ill humours, so the conveying of grace is included in the sacraments. So they tie God's grace to these things.

Indeed, there is grace *by* them, though not *in* them. God gives grace to the humble receiver; but otherwise, to him that comes not with an humble, believing heart. They are seals to a blank. There is no validity in them. All the good use they have is to strengthen faith; and if there be not something before to be strengthened, and confirmed, and assured, they are but seals to a blank. It is in these things according to our faith, and according to our preparation; and then God in the holy, and humble, and faithful use of them blesseth his own ordinance, for the increase, and confirming of our faith, and for the increase and strengthening of all grace.

So that there is not anything in the church, but the proud, naughty heart of man will take hurt by it, rather than submit to the pure, and powerful truth of God. It will have by-ways to have 'confidence in the flesh,' Philip. iii. 4, one way or other.

And many men, rather than they will trust to sound repentance and humiliation for sin, they will trust to the words of absolution without it, and when they are said, go to hell with a pardon about their necks. The false heart will trust to outward things though it be damned for it. In their place they are good, if they be used only as helps in their kind. We lay more weight upon outward things, upon the sacraments, and upon the words of the minister than they will bear, and never care for the inward powerful work of grace. Everything of God is excellent in their order and kind, but our corrupt hearts bring an ill report upon the things.

You see then, it is a dangerous disposition to trust any too much. It is to idolise them, and to wrong God, to take the honour from God. It is to hurt ourselves, and bring ourselves under a curse; and to wrong the things themselves, to bring an evil report upon the things. It is universally true. You shall never see a false, bitter heart, that will not stoop to God's plain truth (they will have by-ways of their own), but in some measure or other they are barren of great matters, and given up to some sensible bitterness, to self-conceitedness, and self-confidence. They are alway punished in that kind with a spiritual kind of punishment.

We must take heed therefore of trusting too much to anything but God himself. God is jealous of our trust. He will have us trust in nothing but himself in matters of salvation. No; not in matters of common life, not in matters politic and civil. We must not build our trust in any creature so much as to think ourselves happy by them, or to think they cannot deceive us. They are creatures of nothing. Therefore they are prone to deceive. They are prone to turn to nothing. Therefore we must not build upon them overmuch, no not in civil matters.

Indeed, if we see the image of God in any man, we may trust him: if we see him faithful, and loving, and good. Yet trust him as a man alway, that is, as such a one as may deceive, and yet he may be a man and a good man. So in other creatures, in the use of physic, and wars, and arms, &c. In danger we may in some subordinate consideration trust to them; but we must use them as means, that is, as such as God hath free liberty to use to good to help us, and free liberty not to use. We must use them, but not trust to them. 'Some trust in chariots, and some in horses; but our trust is in the Lord,' Ps. xx. 7. And, 'Trust not in princes,' Ps. cxlvi. 3, as the psalmist saith. Trust not in anything.

If we trust in anything, it must be subordinate to our trust in God. It must not be co-ordinate, as we say, that is, not in the same rank, much less above God. As worldlings trust in their wealth, they trust in their friends above God; they trust not so much in heaven and happiness there, they think not themselves so happy for that as they do for earthly things. Nay, they trust against God in confidence of their friends and of their purse. A carnal man makes riches 'his stronghold;' he trusts them above God, and against God. We must neither trust them with God, in a co-ordinate proportion with him, nor above God, much less against God. What makes base flesh and blood devilish in that respect, to attempt cursed means, against the truth, and against good causes?

They bear themselves out with these things; perhaps the truth crosses them in their designs, and shames them, and frets them. What makes them undermine good causes, and go desperately to kick against the pricks, to dash themselves against wrath which is stronger than they? They think to bear themselves out with their greatness, with their friends, with some carnal support or other. This is to trust against God, which is worst of all.

And this makes that harlot of Rome so confident against the church of God. 'I sit as a queen,' saith Babylon, Rev. xviii. 7; not only outward Babylon, that was the type, but spiritual Babylon, 'I sit as a queen.' I shall be hereafter as I am now. Therefore saith God, 'Thy destruction shall come in one day,' Rev. xviii. 8. Thy destruction shall come unrecoverably and suddenly, because she blest herself in an ill course ; as now at this day they think all is sure.

If we trust anything but God, we must trust them as instruments, as helps in their rank and place which God hath set them ; so much and no more. ' Let a man esteem of us as ministers of Christ,' saith St Paul, 2 Cor. vi. 4. If they esteem of us more, it is too much ; if less, it is too little, just so much ; as ministers, but ' as ministers of Christ.' So there is a due to everything. No more; for then you wrong God ; no less; for then you wrong the thing and God too. Just so much as God would have it, and then we shall have just the grace that God intends.

Seeing there is such a danger in false confidence, let us take heed of it by all means.

' *That we may not trust in ourselves.*' That is, in any earthly thing in ourselves, or out of ourselves, wit, honour, riches, learning, or whatsoever, but God and his truth and promises. Let us labour to have a sanctified judgment in everything ; to judge of things in their nature and order and rank as we should do, and be not carried with opinion of things. Judge of them as the Creator of things judgeth of them, as God judgeth, and the Scripture judgeth.

Now, of all outward things that we are prone to trust in, how doth the Scripture judge of them ? How doth God judge of them ? They are uncertain riches. ' Riches they have wings,' Prov. xxiii. 5. They are nothing, as the prophet saith. ' Wilt thou set thy heart upon that which is nothing?' Job vii. 17. They are vanity ; they are of nothing, and they tend to nothing.

When the hour of death comes, what, will all these do good ? They are uncertain, and weak, and inefficacious for that for which we trust them. They will not make us happy. They commend us not a whit to God. He hates us no more if we want them. He loves us no more if we have them. They make us not the better in ourselves, but the worse. They make us more indisposed to good things.

We say of those that are intoxicate with any kind of frenzy or lunacy, twice as much physic will not serve their turn as will serve another, because of the distemper of their brain, and the inflammation of their blood and spirits. Certainly it is true of those that are spiritually drunk with the conceit of the creature, with honour, with riches, &c. Three times, many times so much means, will not serve the turn, to bring them to goodness, as will serve meaner men.

What is the reason the poor receive the gospel ?

Because there is a lesser distance between them and the blessed truths of God than in others, though perhaps they belong to God too ; for the things of this life will work a little.

We say of weak brains, that strong drink doth much weaken them ; and so weak stomachs, hard meat will not digest in them, it will overcome them. And weak brains, though strong water overcome them not, yet it will weaken them. So in these things, great parts and great place set a man further off from the gospel. A great deal of corruption cannot be overcome and digested without a great measure of grace. The proportion of grace it must be great, it must be treble to men that have great matters in this world ; it must be greater than to poorer men, who [are] in a less distance from heaven.

Hence we may see the reasons of God's dispensation, why God doth seldom work by great means. I say seldom, sometimes he doth, to shew that they are good means. As it is said and observed by an ancient father, that seldom he saw any good come by General Councils. Why? They are good in themselves, but men trust too much upon them, and therefore God disappoints them of that they trust to. Because the naughty nature of man puts too much trust in these things, therefore God will not give that issue that we look for, but, on the contrary, a curse.

Why doth not God bless great preparations, many times, to war? &c. Because we put too much trust in them. Here are too many, saith God to Gideon, Judges vii., *et alibi*. Take away some, here are too many to go to war. What is the reason that God, where the greatest excellencies are, adds some imperfection to balance them? Because they should not trust in themselves.

What is the reason that in the church God chooseth men of meaner parts and sufficiencies, the disciples fishermen? If they had been great men, men would have said place had carried it; if they had been scholars, men would have said that their learning had carried it; if they had been witty* men, they would have said their wit had carried it. It had been no marvel if they should win the world. But when they saw they were mean men, fishermen, sitters at the receipt of custom (and perhaps their parts were not great), then they might attribute it to the divineness of the gospel, to the divineness of God's truth, and to God's blessing upon it.

What is the reason that God suffers excellent men to fall foully sometimes, St Peter himself, and David? &c. Because they should not trust in themselves, not trust in their grace, not trust in anything, no, not in the best things in themselves.

What is the reason that God goes by contraries in all the carriage of our salvation? 'That we should not trust in ourselves.' In our calling he calls men out of nothing. 'He calls things that are not as if they were,' Rom. iv. 17. In justification, he justifies a sinner, he that despairs of his own righteousness. That no man should trust in anything he hath, or despair if he want any perfection, God justifies a sinner that despairs of himself. In sanctification, God sanctifies a man when he sees no goodness in himself. Most of all, then, he is a vessel fit to receive grace. And he doth sanctify him sometimes by his falls. He makes him good by his slips, which is a strange course to make a man better by. Saith St Austin, 'I dare say, and stand to it, that it is profitable for some men to fall; they grow more holy by their slips' (*y*). As Peter, he grew stronger by his infirmity. This strange course God takes. Why so? That we should not trust in ourselves. In our calling, in our justification from our sins, 'that we should not trust in ourselves,' nor despair.

In sanctification. Nay, he takes a course that we shall grow better by our falls, that we may be ashamed of them, and be more cautelous† and humble, and more watchful for the time to come. In glorification he will glorify us, but it shall be when we have been rotten in our graves before; we must come to nothing. So in every passage of salvation he goes by contraries, and all to beat down confidence in ourselves, and that we should not distrust him in any extremity; for then is the time for God to work his work most of all.

'That we might not trust in ourselves.' To help us further against this self-confidence, let us labour to know ourselves well, what we are, distinct from the new creature, distinct from grace and glory. Indeed, in that respect we are something in God. If we go out of ourselves and see what

---

* That is, 'wise.'—G.   † That is, 'cautious.'—G.

we are in Christ, we are somebody. For we are heirs of heaven, we are kings and rulers over all, all things are subject to us, hell, and sin, and death. We are somebody there. But in that wherein our nature is prone to put over much confidence, what are we? What are we as we are strong, as we are rich, as we are noble, as we are in favour with great ones? Alas! all is nothing, because ere long it will be nothing. What will all be in the hour of death, when we must receive ' the sentence of death?' What will all favours do us good? They will be gone. What will all relations, that we are styled by this and that title, what good will it do? Alas! these end in death; all earthly relations shall be laid in the dust. All the honours in the earth, all riches and contentments, all the friends that we have, what can they do? Nothing! All shall leave us there. And for us to trust in that which will fail us ere long, and which being taken away, we receive a great foil* (for he that leans to a thing, if that be taken away, down he falls), what a shame will it be?

As the heathen man said, that great emperor, ' I have been all things, and nothing doth me good now,' when he was to die (z). Indeed, nothing could do him good. ' Let not the rich man glory in his riches, nor the wise man glory in his wisdom, nor the strong man in his strength,' saith the prophet; ' but let him that glorieth, glory in the Lord,' Jer. ix. 22.

Consider what the best thing is that we have of inward things, our wisdom. Wisdom, if it be not spiritual, it is only a thing for the things of this life, and we are ofttimes deceived in it. It makes God to disappoint us ofttimes to make us go out of ourselves. An excellent place for this we have in Isa. l. the last verse, ' Behold, all ye that kindle a fire, and compass yourselves about with sparks, walk in the light of your own fire,' &c. (it is a kind of *ironia*†), ' and the sparks that you have kindled; this you shall have of my hand, ye shall lie down in sorrow.' Walk in the light of your own fire, walk according to your own devices and projects; this ye shall have at my hand, ye shall lie down in sorrow. God catcheth the wise in the imagination of their own hearts; he disappoints the counsel and the projects of Ahithophel. God takes a glory in it, to shame the policies and projects of those that will be witty in a distinct way against God. The best policy is to serve God and to walk uprightly.

' *That we should not trust in ourselves, but in God who raiseth the dead.*' This is the other branch, what we should trust in, in God. All this humbling of the blessed apostle, even to death's door, that ' he received the sentence of death,' it was first to subdue carnal confidence in himself. He was prone to think himself stronger than he was, or that he should be upheld, that something or other should keep him from death. That he might subdue this carnal confidence, and then that he might trust in God, it was all for these two ends, ' that we might not trust in ourselves (or in any means), but in God that raiseth the dead.'

Was St Paul to learn to trust in God, that had been so long a scholar in Christ's school, nay, a master in Israel? Was he to learn to trust in God?

Yes; doubtless, he was. It is a lesson that is hardly learned, and it is a lesson that we shall be learning all our life, to go out of ourselves and out of the creature, and to go further into God, to rely more and more upon him. It is a lesson that we can never learn as we ought. Therefore, weak Christians ought not to be discouraged when they find defects and weakness

* That is, ' fall.'—G.   † That is, ' irony.'—G.

in their trust. Our hearts are false, and prone to trust outward things; but do they groan under their corruptions? Do they complain of themselves? Do they go out of themselves? Their estate is good. The estate of a Christian, it is a growing, it is a conflicting estate. He comes not to full trust and confidence in God till he have gathered many experiments,* till God have exercised him to the proof throughly; therefore, let them not be discouraged. A Christian is not alway like himself; he is in a growing estate. There is a weak faith and a strong faith. ' O, ye of little faith,' Mat. vi. 30. The disciples had a little faith as well as Abraham, ' that was *strong* in faith. As long as we are on the complaining hand, and on the striving hand, and growing hand, all is hopeful. St Paul himself still strived against self-confidence, and still learned to trust in God more and more.

But mark the order. First, God doth all this, ' that we should not trust in ourselves.' But that is not the thing he doth mainly aim at, but another thing, that we should trust in God who raiseth the dead.' Whence we may observe, that

Doct. God, to make us trust in himself, is fain to cast us out of ourselves.

His proper work is not to drive us out of ourselves, that is a work subordinate to a higher. But the furthest and last work is, that we should ' trust in him,' as the prophet saith. ' God doth a strange work,' Isa. xxviii. 21. He doth a work strange to himself, that he may do his own work. He doth a work that doth not concern him so properly, that he may do his own work, as he is God, that is, to confirm and settle us upon himself. But that he may do this, he must set us out of ourselves by crosses and afflictions. That is not his own proper work, to afflict us, and to bring us low; for he is the ' Father of mercies.' But that he may do his own work, to bring us to him, and then do good to us, he must take this in his way, and do this first. To make it clear. A carpenter, he pulls down a house, he takes it in pieces. His art is not to pull down houses, but to build them up. But he doth that which doth not belong to him properly, that he may do that which doth belong to him; for he will not build upon a rotten foundation. So neither ' will God build upon a rotten foundation.' He will not build upon carnal confidence, upon carnal trust, upon pride, and covetousness; but he will demolish that rotten foundation with afflictions and crosses. He will use such means that we shall have small joy to trust in sin. He will by crosses and afflictions force us to go from our sins. He will demolish that rotten foundation, that he may raise up an excellent edifice and frame of the new creature, that shall endure to everlasting. The work of a physician is to cure nature, and not to weaken it. It is not his work to make people sick, but to make them sound. If the body be distempered, it must be weakened. He must carry the burden of ill and noisome humours before it be strengthened. To make people sound he must give them strong purgations, that shall afflict them and affect them as much as the disease for a while. But all is to make them lighter and stronger after, when they are eased of the burden of noisome humours: and so it is in every other trade. So God shews his skill in this great matter in bringing us to heaven this way. He doth that work which doth not properly concern him, to work at last his own blessed good work. He afflicts us to drive us out of ourselves, that we may come at last to trust in him, in whom is all our happiness and good.

The reason of it is clear. For in a succession of contraries there must

* That is, ' experiences.'—G.

be a removing of one contrary before another can be brought in. If a vessel be to be filled with a contrary liquor, the first must have a vent; it must be emptied of the worse, that the better may come. So it is with us. We are full of self-confidence, as a vessel of naughty liquor. Out must that go, that better things may come in. So it is in ploughing, and in everything else. This is taken as a principle in nature. The order generally is this, that we should not trust in ourselves, that we might be brought to trust in God. He brings us low, to 'receive the sentence of death,' to drive us out of ourselves, that he may bring us to rely on him.

Use 1. The use we should make of it, among many others, is this, *that we should not take offence at God when he is about this strange work*, as we think. When he is making us sick with physic, with afflictions, and troubles, let us not think that he hates us. Doth the physician hate the patient when he makes him sick? Perhaps he stays a good while from him till his physic have wrought throughly, but he doth not hate him, but gives it time, and suffers it to have its work, that so he may recover himself. Doth the goldsmith hate his precious metal when he puts it into the fire, and suffers the fire to work upon it? What is lost? Nothing but the dross. What is lost in the body by sickness? The ill humours that load the body and distemper the actions and functions of it, that it cannot work as it should. There is nothing lost but that that may well be spared. So when God goes about his work, he afflicts thee and follows thee with losses and crosses. He takes away friends and credit, this outward thing and that. All this is to give thee a purge. He works a strange work, that he may work his own work, that he may bring thee to himself.

Therefore let us be far from murmuring at this blessed work of God: let us rather bless God for his care this way, that he will not suffer us to perish with the world. God might have suffered us to rot upon our dregs, that we should have no changes, as the world hath not. But he hath more care of us than so. The husbandman will not plough in the wilderness. The heathy ground shall go unploughed long enough. He loves it not so well as to sow good seed there. So when God takes pains, and is at cost with any man; when he purgeth him, and ploughs him, and hammers him; all this is to consume that which is naught, to plough up the weeds, to fit him for the blessed seed of grace, to fit him for comfort here and glory in another world. Why then should we murmur against God? Let us rather be thankful, especially when we see the blessed issue of this, when we see our earthly-mindedness abated, when we see ourselves more heavenly-minded, when we see ourselves weaned from the world, when we see ourselves take more delight in communion with God. Then, blessed be God for crosses and afflictions, that he hath taken the pains, and would be at the cost with us to exercise us. It is a ground not only of patience, but of thankfulness, when God humbles us. Be not discontent, man! Grudge not! murmur not! God doth a work that seems strange to thee, and which is not his own proper work, that he may do his own work, that he may bring thee nearer to himself. Why dost thou murmur at thy own good?

The patient cries out of the physician that he torments him. He hears him well enough, but he will not be advised by his patient. He means to advise *him*, and to rule *him*. He would fain have comfort. He is in pain, and cries for ease. But his time is not yet come. So let us wait, and not murmur under crosses. God is doing one work to bring to pass another. He brings us out of ourselves, that he may bring us nearer to himself.

Use 2. And another use that we may make of it, let us examine ourselves *whether our afflictions and crosses have had this effect in us, to bring us to trust in him more.* If they have, all is well. But if they make us worse, that we fret and murmur, and feel no good by them, it is an ill sign; for God doth bring us low, that we may not trust in ourselves, but in him. *Quem præsentia mala non corrigunt,* &c. Whom the presence of ill and grievance amends not, they bring to eternal grievance. 'This is Ahaz,' saith the Scripture, 2 Chron. xxviii. 22: a strange man, a wicked king, that notwithstanding God followed him with judgments, yet he grew worse and worse. This is Ahaz! He might well be branded. When a man belongs to God, everything brings him nearer to God. When a man is brought to be more humble, and more careful, and more watchful every way, to be more zealous, more heavenly minded; it is a blessed sign that God then is working a blessed work, to force him out of himself, and to bring him nearer himself, to trust in him. This we cannot too much consider of.

Use 3. It should teach us likewise this, *that we judge not amiss of the generation of the righteous, when we see God much humbling them.* When we see him follow them with sickness, with troubles and disgraces in the world, perhaps with terror of conscience, with desertions, be not discouraged. If he be thy friend, censure him not; add not affliction to his affliction. Is not his affliction enough? Thou needest not add to* thy unjust censure, as Job said to his friends. The more we are afflicted of God, the more good he intends to work to us. The end is to bring us from ourselves to trust in him.

It is a wicked disposition in men that know not the ways of God. They are ignorant of the ways that he takes with his children. When they see men that are Christians, that they are humbled and cast down and troubled, they think they are men forsaken of God, &c. Alas! they do not know God's manner of dealing: He casts them down that he may raise them up. They 'receive the sentence of death' against themselves, that he may comfort them after, that he may do them good in their latter end. Let this therefore keep us from censuring of other men in our thoughts for this hard course which God seems to take with them.

Use 4. And let us make this use of it, when we are in any grievance, and God follows us still, *let us mourn and lament the stubbornness of our hearts, that will not yield.* God intends to draw us near to him, to trust in him. If we would do this, the affliction would cease, except it be for trial, and for the exercise of grace, and for witness to the truth. When God afflicts, sometime for trial and for witness, there is a spirit of glory in such a case, that a man is never afflicted in mind. But, I say, when God follows us with sickness, with crosses, with loss of friends, and we are not wrought upon, let us censure our hard hearts, that force God to take this course.

And 'justify God in all this,' Job i. 22, *et alibi.* Lord, thou knowest I could not be good without this, thou knowest I would not be drawn without this; bring me near to thyself, that thou mayest take away this heavy hand from me. The intemperate man that is sick makes the physician seem cruel. It is because I set my affections too much on earthly things, that thou followest me with these troubles. We force God to do this. A physician is forced to bring his patient even to skin and bone. An intemperate patient sometimes, that hath surfeited upon a long distemper, he must bring him to death's door, even almost to death, because his distemper is so settled upon him, that he cannot otherwise cure him. So it is with God, the physician of our souls. He must bring us wondrous low. We are so prone,

* Qu. 'to it?'—ED.

so desperately addicted to present things, to trust to them, and to be proud of them, and confident in them, that God must deal as a sharp physician. He must bring us so low, or else we should never be recovered of our perfect health again, and all is that we might trust in God.

Observe we from hence another point, that

Doctrine. God in all outward things that are ill, intends the good of the soul.

He takes liberty to take away health, and liberty, and friends, to take away comforts. But whatsoever he takes away, he intends the good of the soul in the first place. And all the ills that he inflicts upon us, they are to cure a worse ill, the ill of the soul; to cure an unbelieving heart, a worldly, proud, carnal heart, which is too much addicted to earthly things. We see here how God dealt with St Paul. All was to build up his soul in trust and confidence in God, all was for the soul.

The reason is; other things are vanishing, the soul is the better part, the eternal part. If all be well with the soul, all shall be well otherwise at last. If it be well with the soul, the body shall do well. Though God take liberty to humble us with sickness, and with death itself, yet God will raise the body and make it glorious. A good soul will draw it after it at last, and move God to make the body glorious. But if the soul be naught, let us cherish and do what we will with the body; both will be naught at last.

This life is not a life to regard the body. We are dead in that while we live. 'The sentence of death' is passed. We must die. We are dying every day. 'The body is dead because of sin,' Rom. viii. 10. We are going to our grave. Every day takes away a part of our life.

This is not a life for this body of ours. It is a respite to get assurance of an eternal estate in heaven. God takes our wealth, and liberty, and strength, &c., that he may help our souls, that he may work his own blessed work in our souls, that he may lay a foundation of eternal happiness in our souls.

Therefore, hence we should learn to resign our bodies and estates to God. Lord, do with me what thou wilt! only cure my soul, only strengthen my faith. I give thee liberty with all my heart to take what thou wilt, so thou save my soul. Give me not up to an unbelieving heart, to an hypocritical, false heart, to false confidence, to trust in false grounds, and to perish eternally; for my estate and body, do what thou wilt. We should be brought to this. Why? Because indeed the state of the soul is the true state either in good or ill. If all be naught with that, all will be naught at last. We shall try it to our cost.

And therefore let us even rather thank God, and desire God to go on with his work. Lord, rather than thou shouldst give me up to a hard heart, to a stubborn heart, and perish and have no sound change, rather than suffer me to perish thus, use me as thou wilt.

And thank him when we find any degree of goodness or faith. Lord, thou mightst have followed me with outward blessings, and so have given me up in my soul to hypocrisy, and to pride, that I should never have felt the power of grace, that I should never have known thee, or myself throughly, or the vanity of outward things. But this thou hast not done, thou hast not given me liberty in outward things, that thou mightest do good to my soul, blessed be thy name. Let us not only take it well, but thankfully at God's hands. To proceed,

'That we might trust in God that raiseth the dead.'

Obs. The soul must have somewhat to trust to. The foundation must be laid;

for the soul is a creature, and a dependent creature. Somewhat it must have to rely on ; as all weak dependent things have somewhat to depend on. The vine is a weak plant. It must have the elm or somewhat to rely on. It will sink else, it will become unfruitful and unprofitable. All things that are weak, are supported by somewhat that is stronger. It is an inclination and instinct in things that are weak, to look for supply from things that are stronger than themselves to support them ; and it is their happiness to be so. The creatures that are unreasonable* are guided by those that have reason, by men ; and the creatures that are reasonable are guided by superiors, by God, and by angels that are above them, and have the care and charge over them. It is the happiness of weaker things to be under the supportation of that which is stronger. And some support it will have, good or bad.

The soul, if it have not God, it will have pleasures, it will have profit. The worst of men, that think there is little for them in heaven, by reason of their blasphemy, and filthy courses, they will have base pleasures to go to, that they will trust to, and carnal acquaintance to solace themselves withal. The worst of men will have some dirty thing or other, to give their souls to, to support themselves withal ; something the soul will have.

God loves the soul, and hath made it for himself ; and as he hath made it for himself, to join with himself, to solace himself in it (' My son, give me thy heart,' Prov. xxiii. 26) so when he takes it from outward things, he will not have it empty, to rely upon nothing, but he takes it to himself. All this is to take our hearts from ourselves, and from self-confidence, that we may trust in him. God is for the heart, and that is for him ; as I said, he calls for it, ' My son, give me thy heart,' give me thy affection of trust, of joy, of delight. All the affections, they are made for God, and for heaven, and heavenly things. Our affections that we have, they are not made for riches. Our souls are not made for them. The soul is larger than they. They will not content the soul. The soul is a spiritual substance, and they are outward things. The soul is large, they are scanty in their extent. They are uncertain, and momentary ; the soul is an eternal thing. It outlives those things. And thereupon the soul is not made for them, and they are not made for the soul.

They are to give contentment to the outward man for a while here. They are made for our pilgrimage, to comfort us in the way to heaven ; but the soul is not for them.

The soul is the chamber, and the bed, and, as it were, the cabinet for God himself, and Christ to rest in only.

All outward things must be kept out of the heart. We may use them ; but we must keep them out of the heart. It is not for them. We must not joy in them, and solace ourselves, and delight in them over much, further than we seek God in them, and enjoy God in them. But as they are sensible * things, the heart is not for them. Therefore God takes the heart from self-confidence, and from other things. He suffers it not to wander ; but he takes it to himself, that we may trust in him.

The next thing, then, that we may observe is, that when we go out of ourselves, we must have somewhat to rely on, which is better than all things else. We lose not by the change ; but when we are stripped of ourselves, and of all earthly things, we have God to go to.

Doctrine. God is the object of trust.

God is the proper object of trust of the Christian soul. He is the object of trust, as well as the author of it. He is the cause and worker of it by

* That is, ' without reason.'—G.   † That is, ' outward.'—G.

his Spirit, and he is the object of it. If we trust to other things, it must be as they are God's instruments, as they are God's means. But if we trust anything, either wealth, or friends, or anything, to neglect the worship of God, or to please ourselves in it, to put our hands to ill courses, in confidence of the creature, in confidence of men, or anything else, to take any false cause in hand, this is to trust them above their respect. We must trust to them as instruments, as voluntary instruments, which God may use when he pleaseth, or not use when he pleaseth. When we use them otherwise, we forget their nature. Then we use them not as instruments, but as the chief. We forget the order.

God is the object of trust. We must rest on him for grace and glory ; for the best things, and for the things of this life, as far as they are good.

So far as we trust to anything else to move us to security, to rest in them, or to sin for them, it is a sinful trust. Other things we may trust ; but in the nature of vain instruments, changeable instruments, that God may alter and change. He that is rich to-day, may be poor to-morrow. He that hath a friend to-day, may have him taken away to-morrow. And so all outward things, they are changeable and mutable. But we may trust God all times alike. He is eternal. He is infinitely able, and infinitely wise, to know all our grievances. We may trust him with our souls, with our hearts. He is faithful, and loving, and eternal, as our souls are. He gives eternity to the soul. Therefore at all times we may trust in him, in all places, everywhere. He knows our hearts, he knows our grievance everywhere. He hath all grounds of one that may be trusted to. He hath power and goodness, and mercy and wisdom. He is the object of trust.

But how considered, is he the object of trust, God out of Christ, Mediator ?

Oh, no! God in covenant with us in Christ,—he is the object of our trust, or else there is such a distance and contrariety between man's nature and God, that he is a ' consuming fire,' Heb. xii. 29. Since the fall from the covenant of works, we cannot be saved by that ; but he hath vouchsafed to be ours in a better covenant in Christ, in whom ' all the promises are yea and amen,' 2 Cor. i. 20. This good comes from God to us by Christ. Christ first receives it, and he derives* it to us, as our elder Brother, and as our head. All the promises are made in him, and through him. He receives it for us. We receive it at the second hand. God hath filled him first. ' And of his fulness we receive grace for grace,' John i. 16.

' Without him we can do nothing,' John xv. 5. With him we can do all things. So we trust in God reconciled ; God made ours in the covenant of grace in Jesus Christ, who hath made our peace. Else God is a ' sealed fountain.' He is a fountain of good, but a sealed fountain. Christ hath opened this fountain. His love is open to Christ, and derived to Christ, in whom our flesh is. He is ' bone of our bone, and flesh of our flesh,' Eph. v. 30, that we might be bone of his bone, and flesh of his flesh by being united with him. So now we trust in him, as God, the Father of Christ, reconciled. '.I believe in God the Father Almighty,' as it is in the creed. God thus considered is the object of trust. There are two ojects of trust : God the Father, Son, and Holy Ghost ; and Christ Mediator.

Use. If this be so, that God reconciled now is the object of trust, for all things that are good, not only for salvation, but for grace, and for all com-

* That is, ' transmits.'—G.

forts, to bring us to heaven, then *we see the vanity of all other confidence whatsoever*, as I touched before.

And is it not a blessed thing that God will be trusted, that he hath made himself such a one as we may trust him? Now blessed be God for Christ, that he having received satisfaction to his justice by him, he may be trusted, and desires that we should trust him; that now in Christ he hath made himself a Father, that we should not fear him, nor run away from him. It is a great favour that God will be trusted of us, that he will honour us so much.

He accounts it an honour when we trust him, but indeed it is an honour to us that we have a throne of grace through Christ to go to; that he hath devised a way that we might trust him, and not run from him; that we may go to him in Christ, who sits at his right hand, who is our intercessor, who hath redeemed us with his precious blood. It is our happiness that he hath made himself a gracious and loving Father, that he calls us to him, and thinks himself honoured by our trusting in him.

Again, we see here that,

Doct. Trust in God is a main duty.

He is the object of trust, and it is a main duty. It is a spring of duty out of which all contes; for we see here all doth aim at this. Afflictions they come to mortify our self-confidence. Self-confidence is subdued that we may trust in God. Our trust must be carried to him. He is the object of it. And this trust in God is a main duty, which in this world we ought to labour for. It is that that God doth aim at, and it is that that we should aim at. God doth aim at it in exercising of us; and we should aim at it on our part, in our hearing, in our receiving the sacrament, in everything, that our trust and affiance and confidence may be in God, and that we may grow more and more and more in it.

Well, since God is the object of trust, and trust is such a necessary grace, that God doth all to bring us to trust in him, let us come to search ourselves, how shall we know whether we trust in God or no? And then to direct us, how to come to trust in him, to give some means and helps.

1. He trusts in God reconciled in Jesus Christ *that flies to him in extremity*. That a man trusts unto, that when he is pinched he flies unto. How shall a man know that he is a covetous worldling? If he be in extremity, he goes to his purse, he makes a friend of that. How shall a man know that he trusts to the arm of flesh, that he trusts his friend too much? In extremity he runs to him, presently he goes to a friend he hath. What we run to, that our trust is in. A Christian, he runs to his God; and happy is that Christian that is in covenant, that he hath a God to run to in all extremities, in sickness, in death, at all times. He is happy that he hath a God, when all fails, to trust in.

Wilt thou know therefore whether thou trustest in God or no? Whither goest thou? A carnal man, he goes to one earthly prop or other. If God answer him not presently, then he goes with Saul to the witch, to the devil himself perhaps. If God do not send him present help, he goes to one carnal help or other, to fetches* of his wit, to policy, to crack his conscience, to bear out things with impudence. He hath not learned to trust in God, and he runs not to him, but to some wicked course or other.

All that go not to God in the use of good means (for we must put that in, we must go to God in the use of his means, in the use of good means only), they trust not God; for God will not be tempted, but trusted. We

* That is, 'devices.'—G.

must go to him by prayer, and in the use of lawful means, and only of lawful means ; or else, if we trust him and do not use the means, we tempt him. We must serve God's providence in using the means.

2. Therefore, secondly, he that trusts in God *useth his means.* He that trusts God for a harvest must plough, and sow, and do all that belongs to the providence of God.

So a merchant that will increase his estate, he must get a ship and other provision to do it with, for we must serve God's providence as well as trust God's providence. When we neglect good and lawful means, and run into ill courses, and use ill means, we serve not God, nor trust him. Those that grow rich by calling ' evil good, and good evil,' Isa. v. 20, they have not learned to trust in God. Those that think except they leave their posterity great they shall not be happy, and therefore they will neglect the Sabbath, and neglect all, to scrape an estate ;—is this to trust in God ? Have they learned to trust in God, when sacrilegiously they take away the time dedicated for the salvation of their souls and the service of God ? Is this one means that God hath ordained to trust him in ? They that flatter and serve men's humours when they know them to be in a naughty and ill way, is this to trust God, when they go out of his means and way, and make an idol of flesh and blood to serve their own turn'?

Alas ! we need not name these things. If men had learned what it is to trust in God, and depend upon him in the use of lawful means, and would rather be content to want in this world than to have anything with a cracked conscience !

I beseech you, let us examine our own hearts in this. There are many that think they trust in God when they do not. They trust their policy, they trust flesh and blood, and by consequence they trust the devil, if they trust not in God.

3. In the next place, he that trusts in God, *his mind will be quieted in some comfortable measure, when he hath used the means that are lawful, and cast himself upon God.* He will be quiet, and let God work then. When he hath taken pains in his calling lawfully, and desired God's blessing, if God send wealth, so it is ; if not, he is not much troubled. He knows that all shall be for the best to them that trust in God. When he cannot have it in the use of lawful means, he is quiet. He that trusts a physician, when he hath used the direction of the physician, he is quiet. He thinks he is a wise man, an experienced physician, and now he will not trouble his mind any longer. If a man vex himself, and think all will not be well, he doth not trust his physician. And so in other professions we trust to a man's counsel, if we think him wise and honest. We follow his direction, and then we will be quiet.

Now, God is infinitely wise. When we have used lawful means, and commended the means to God ; for as he will be trusted in, so he will be sought unto. ' I will be sought to by the house of Israel for this,' Ezek. xxxvi. 37. For except we pray to him, he is not trusted. But when we have prayed to him, in the use of lawful means, let us be quiet, let us not be distracted with dividing cares about this and that, as if there were not a God in heaven that had care of us, that had a providence over things below. Certainly he hath. Do thou do thy work, and let him alone with his work. The care of duty belongs to thee. When thou hast done thy duty, rest thou quiet, or else thou honourest him not as a God, thou trustest him not, thou dost not make a God of him. It is a great dishonour to God. A man thinks himself dishonoured when he is not trusted ; when we see he hath alway been faithful to us, and is so reputed, and yet we call his credit in question, and will not be quiet. We should do as children do. They follow their books, and let their father take care for all provision for meat and drink, and clothes and such things. They beat not their heads about it. They know they have a father that will take care for that. If we were true children of God, and have the disposition of heavenly children, we will do so. If we trouble ourselves, and beat our heads, it is a sign that we fear that God is not our Father. Therefore I add that to other signs, a resting of ourselves quiet. When we are quiet, God will do more than when we vex ourselves. ' Be still, and see the salvation of the Lord,' saith Moses at the Red Sea, Exod. xiv. 13. So let us be still and quiet, and see the salvation of God. He will work wonders.

4. Again, it is a sign that we trust in God, *when there are no means, yet notwithstanding we will not despair, but hope and trust in God.* When we see nothing in the eye of flesh and blood, no means of recovery, yet we trust in God. He can work his way though we see not how; he can make a passage for us. When God is thus honoured he works wonders. This is to make a God of him, when there is no means, to believe that he can work against means. If my life shall be for his glory and my good, he can recover my life though the physician say I am a dead man. If he have employment for me in this world, he can do it. He can work with means, or against means, or without means. And so in desperate troubles, if God see it good for me, he can deliver me though there be no means. He is the Creator of means. Do not tie him to his own creature. If all be taken away, he can make new.

5. Again, he trusts in God that labours *to make God his friend continually;* for he whom we trust unto we will not provoke. Certainly we will not provoke a man whom we mean to make our friend. Those that live in swearing, in defiled courses, in contempt of God and holy things, of the ordinances of God, of the day appointed to holy and religious uses, those that ' wax stubborn against God,' 1 Tim. v. 11, as the Scripture speaks, do we trust him against whom we walk stubbornly? Will a man trust him that he makes his enemy by wicked courses? Thou makest God thy enemy, and provokest him to his face, to try whether he will pour vengeance upon this* or no. He tells thee thou shalt not be unpunished if thou ' take his name in vain,' Exod. xx. 7 ; yet thou wilt be stubborn, and not make conscience of these things. Dost thou trust him? No! thou provokest him. Thou mayest trust him; but it must be to damn thee, to give thee thy reward with rebels ; thou mayest trust him for that. But for good things thou doest not, thou canst not trust him in wicked courses.

Who will trust his enemy, especially he that hath made his enemy by his ill course of life? A man that goes on in an evil course, he cannot, he doth not trust in God.

6. He that trusts in God's promise *will trust in his threatening.* Where there is an evangelical faith, there is a legal faith alway. He that believes that God will save him if he trust in Christ, he believes that if he do not believe in Christ he will damn him, if he live in his natural course without repentance.

There is a legal faith of the curse, as well as an evangelical of the promise. They are both together. If thou do not believe God's curse in wicked courses, thou wilt never believe him for the other. Therefore, I will add this to make up the evidences of trust in God. True trust looks to

* Qu. ' thee?'—Ed.

God's truth, and promise, and word in one part of it as well as another. Thou trusts God for thy salvation and the promises of that; but thou must trust him for the direction of thy life too. Faith doth not single out some objects; I will believe this, and not that. Faith is carried to all the objects, it believes all God's truths. Therefore, if I believe not the threatenings and directions, to be ruled by them, I believe not the promises. In what measure thou believest the promise of mercy to save thy soul, in that measure thou believest the directions of God's word to guide thy soul. He that receives Christ as a Priest to save him, he must receive him as a King to rule him.

All the directions, and all the threatenings, and all the promises must be received and believed.

A man hath no more faith and trust in God than he hath care to follow God's direction; for faith is carried to all divine truths. All come from the same God. Thousands go to hell, and think, Oh, God is a merciful God, and I will trust in him! But how is thy life? Is it carried by God's directions? Thou art a rebel. Thou livest in sins against conscience. Thou wilt trust in God in one part of his word, and not in another. Thou must not be a chooser.

7. Again, the last that I will name at this time, if thou trust God for one thing, *undoubtedly thou will trust him for all.* If thou trust him with thy soul, certainly thou wilt trust him with thy children. Some men hope to be saved by Christ. Oh, he will be merciful to their souls; and yet even to their death they use corrupt courses to get an estate and to make their children rich; and except they have so much, they will not trust in God. If they have nothing to leave them, they think not that there is a God in heaven who is a better Father than they. Put case thou hast nothing, hast thou not God's blessing? Canst thou trust thy soul with God, and canst thou not trust him with thy family? Is he not the God of thy seed? Hath he not made the promise to thy posterity as well as to thyself? If thou trust him for one thing, thou wilt trust him for all. Wilt thou trust him for heaven, and wilt thou not trust him for provision for daily bread? Wilt thou not trust him for this or that, but thou must use unlawful means? He that trusts God, he trusts him for all truths and for all things needful, with his family, with his body, with his soul, with all. And so much for the trials, whether we trust in God or no.

Let us not deceive ourselves. It is a point of infinite consequence, as much as the salvation of our souls. What brings men to hell in the church? False confidence. They trust to false things, or they think they trust in God, when indeed they do not.

The fault of a ship is seen in a tempest, and the fault of a house is seen when winter comes. Thy trust, that is thy house that thou goest to and restest in, the fault of that will be seen when thou comest to extremity. In the hour of death, then thou hast not a God to go to, then thy conscience upbraids thee; thou hast lived by thy shifts * in carnal confidence and rebellion against God, and how canst thou then willingly trust God, whom thou hast made thine enemy all thy lifetime?

To go, then, to some helps. If upon search we find that we do not so trust in God as we should, let us lament our unbelieving hearts, complain to God of it, desire God, whatsoever he doth, that he would honour us so much as that we may honour him by trusting in him; for it is his glory and our salvation.

* That is, 'expedients.'—G.

But because I will not go out of the text, the best way is that which follows, to know God as he is.

How come we to trust a man? When we know his honesty, his fidelity, his wisdom, and his sufficiency, then we trust him. Therefore, St Paul adds here that we should 'trust in God that raiseth the dead,' that is, 'in God Almighty.' From whence I raise this general, that

The best way to trust in God is to know him as he is.

We know his attributes by his principal works. We know his nature by his works, as here is one of the principal set down, he is God 'that raiseth the dead.' A sound, sanctified trust in God is by knowing of him. 'They that know thy name will trust in thee,' Ps. ix. 10.

There are three ways of the knowledge of God:

His nature, promises, and works—

To know what he hath engaged himself in, in all the promises that concern us; and then to know his strength, how able he is to make good these promises; and then to know his works, how his nature hath enabled him to make good those promises.

1. Especially *his nature;* as to consider his goodness and his wisdom. Every attribute, indeed, doth enforce trust, for he is good freely, he is good to us of his own bowels. We may trust him that hath made himself a Father, out of his own mercy in Christ, when we were enemies. His goodness and wisdom is infinite as himself, and his power and his truth. As the Scripture saith ofttimes, 'Faithful is God that hath promised,' Heb. xi. 11.

St Bernard, a good man in evil times, saith he, 'I consider three things in which I pitch my hope and trust, *charitatem adoptionis,* the love of God in making me his child; and *veritatem promissionis,* the truth of God in performing his promise. His love is such, to make me his child; his truth is such, to perform his promise. Thirdly, I consider his power, that is able to make good that that he hath promised' (*w*).

This threefold cable is a strong one. His love in adoption, his truth in performing his promise, and his power in making good all this. This threefold cable will not easily be broken. Let my sottish flesh murmur against me as long as it will. As the flesh will murmur, who art thou, that thou darest trust in God? What is thy merit, that thou hopest for such great glory? No, no, saith he; 'I know whom I have believed,' 2 Tim. i. 12, as St Paul saith. I answer with great confidence against my sottish, murmuring flesh, 'I know whom I have trusted.' He is able, he is good, he is true. This that holy man had to exercise his faith.

I name it, because it is the temper of all believing souls that are so in truth. The believing heart considers the nature of God, the promise of God, and though the murmuring, rebellious flesh say, What art thou? how darest thou that art flesh and blood look to God? Oh! he is faithful, he is good and gracious in Christ. He hath made himself a father. I know whom I have believed. God is all-sufficient.

Trust and confidence doth grow in the soul, in what measure and proportion the knowledge of him whom we trust in grows, and as his strength grows. The more rich and strong a man grows, in whom I trust, and the more gracious and good he grows, and the more my knowledge of him is increased with it too, that I see he is so able, so true, so loving a man, a man so affected to me, the more he grows, and my knowledge of him, the more my trust is carried to him. So a Christian, the more he considers the infiniteness of God's love, of his wisdom and goodness, the more he is carried in trust, and confidence to it.

Not to trouble you with many places, the 42d Psalm is an excellent psalm for trust and confidence in God. The whole psalm is to that purpose, to stir up himself to trust in God; for that follows knowledge; when upon knowledge we rouse up our hearts. ' God is my rock, and my salvation, and defence.' Is he so? Then, my soul, ' trust in God.' He chargeth it upon his soul, ' Therefore I will trust in God.' And then he blames his soul, Is God so? Why art thou so disquieted, O my soul?'

This is the exercise of a Christian heart, when, upon sound knowledge, he can charge his soul to trust in God, and check his soul, ' Why art thou cast down? Still trust in God.' Why dost thou not trust in him? Is he not true? Is he not wise? He is the ' God of my salvation.' And in ver. 8, ' Trust in God at all times,' in prosperity, in adversity. Why? ' God is my refuge.'

There he sets forth his nature. If our troubles be never so many, there is somewhat in God that is answerable; as in Ps. xxviii. 7, ' He is a rock and a shield.' He hath somewhat in him that is opposite to every ill.

And withal, ' pour out thy heart to God;' for where there is trust there is prayer. ' Trust in God at all times, and pour out thy heart before him, for he is our refuge.'

And so, ' trust not in oppression and robbery. If riches increase, set not your heart upon them; for God hath spoken once, and twice, that power belongs to God,' Ps. lxii. 11. Trust not any other thing but God. Power and mercy belong to him. This is a notable way to trust in God, to know that power and mercy belong to him. If another man love me, hath not God another man's heart in his hand? ' The king's heart is in his hand,' Prov. xxi. 1. Therefore trust in God for the favour of men. Hath he not all the power? That that another man hath that affects me, it is but a derived power from him. He hath inclined him to do good to me. All mercy and love, it is from God; and he turns and disposeth it as it pleaseth him. As it is the Scripture phrase, the language of Canaan, the heart is in God's hands; he inclined the heart of such a man. The knowledge of God, with prayer and stirring up ourselves to trust in God, and checking our souls for the contrary, it is a notable means to trust in God.

And though we feel no present comfort from God, trust him for his word, trust him for his promise, though he seem now to be a God hidden. As a child in the dark he holds his father fast by the hand. He sees not his father, but he knows his father's hand is strong. And though he see him not, yet he believes it is his father, and holds him though it be in the dark.

Men they cast anchor in the dark, at midnight. Though they cannot see, yet they know that the anchor will hold fast. Cast anchor upon God in darkness and temptation. Hold God fast in the dark night, although we see nothing. We shall alway find this, that he is a God able to fulfil his promise, that he is a true and faithful and able God. Cast anchor in him therefore. Though thou feel or see nothing, be sure in all extremities to trust in God.

2. Besides other things, trust in God is properly and primarily wrought *by the promises*. Trust in God so far as he hath discovered himself to be trusted. I can trust a man no farther than I have a writing or a word of mouth from him, or a message from him.

Now, what have we from God to trust him for? We have his word written, and that is sealed by the sacrament. The way to trust in God, therefore, is to know the promises.

(1.) The *general promises* that do concern all Christians and all conditions and estates of men. ' God will be a sun and a shield;' a sun for all good, and a shield to keep away all evil. ' And no good thing shall be wanting to him that lives a godly life,' Ps. lxxxiv. 11. Again, general promises for issue. ' All things shall work for good to them that love God,' Rom. viii. 28. And, ' He will give his Spirit to them that ask him,' Luke xi. 13. It is a general promise to all askers whatsoever, that they shall have the Spirit of God, which is a promise that hath all particular graces in it. For the Spirit is the fountain of all grace. It is the Spirit of love, of faith, of hope. All are in the promise of the Spirit, and God hath promised this. Let us trust in God for these general things.

(2.) And for *particular promises.* He hath made a promise to be ' a husband to the widow, and a father to the fatherless,' Ps. lxviii. 5. He will ' regard the cause of the widow,' Ps. cxlvi. 9 ; and he is a God ' that comforteth the abject,' 2 Cor. vii. 6. He hath made promises to those that are afflicted, to all estates and conditions of men. Trust in God for these.

But how ? He hath made these with conditions in regard of outward things. Let us trust him so far forth as he hath promised, that is, he will either protect us from dangers or give us patience in dangers. He will give us all outward things, or else contentment, which is better. Take him in that latitude. Trust in him as he will be trusted to. For outward things, he will either give the things or give the grace, which is better. He will either remove the grievance, or he will plant the grace, which is better. If he remove not the evil, he will give patience to bear it. And what do I lose if he give me not the good thing, if he give me contentment ? I have grace to supply it, which makes me a better man.

If he give me the thing without the grace, what am I the better ? A carnal reprobate may have that.

So let us trust him, as he will be trusted. For grace and spiritual things, all shall be for our good without fail ; but for the things of this life, either he will give them, or else graces.

Let us trust God, therefore, as he will be trusted in his word and promises.

Now this trusting of God (to speak a little to the present purpose, because St Paul was now in great affliction. When he learned to trust in God, he was in fear of death), let us see how we are to exercise this trust in great crosses, and in the hour of death. St Paul was in these two.

The point is very large, and I will take it only according to the present scope.

How doth a Christian exercise trust in extremity, in extreme crosses ? for then he must go to God ; he hath none else to go to.

1. *He is beaten from the creature;* and, as I said before, the soul will have somewhat to go to. The poor creatures, the silly conies, they have the rocks to go to, as Solomon saith, Prov. xxx. 26. The soul that hath greater understanding, it is necessitated to trust in God in afflictions. Then the soul must say to God, ' Lord, if thou help not, none can,' as Jehoshaphat said in 2 Chron. xx. 12, ' We know not what to do, but our eyes are to thee.' In great afflictions we exercise trust, because we are forced.

2. And because then we are put to this, *we put the promises* in suit, the promises made to us for extremity.

(1.) He hath promised to be with us ' in the fire, and in the water,' Isa. xliii. 2. There is a promise of *God's presence,* and the soul improves that. Lord, thou hast promised to be present in great perils and dangers, as there are two of the greatest specified, fire and water. Thou hast promised thou wilt be present with us in the fire, and in the water. Now, Lord, make good thy promise, be thou present. And when God makes good this promise of presence, then the soul triumphs, as in Ps. xxiii. 4, ' Though I walk in the valley of the shadow of death, I will not fear, because thou art with me, Lord.' So in Ps. xxvii. 1, he begins triumphantly, ' The Lord is my shield, whom shall I fear ? of whom shall I be afraid ? ' Let us exercise our trust this way in extremity. ' God is with us, and who can be against us ? ' saith the apostle, Rom. viii. 31. Thus the Christian soul lives by trusting in God. In all extremity of crosses whatsoever, the soul is forced to God, and claims the promises of presence.

And not only the promise of his presence, but

(2.) The promise *of support and comfort, and of mitigation.* There is a promise in 1 Cor. x. 13, ' God is faithful, and will not suffer us to be tempted above our strength.' Here faith is exercised. Lord, I am in a great cross now, I am in affliction ; thou hast promised that thou wilt not suffer me to be tempted above that I am able to bear.

Now make good this promise of thine, be present, and be present by way of mitigation ; either pull down the cross, and make it less, or raise up my strength, and make that greater. For thou hast promised that thou wilt not suffer us to be tempted above our strength.

3. And then the soul lives *by faith of the issue in great extremities.* I am in great extremity, but I know all shall end well. Thus we trust in God in all extremity of afflictions whatsoever ; in the hour of death, when we receive the sentence of death, how do we then exercise trust in God ! In Ps. xvi. 9, ' My flesh shall rest in hope, because thou wilt not suffer thy Holy One to see corruption.' Because God did not suffer Christ to see corruption, who is our head, therefore my flesh likewise shall rest in hope, when I die. Our Head triumphed over death, and is in heaven, and I die in faith ; I trust in God that raised him from the dead, who was my Surety. I know my debts are paid ; my Surety is out of prison. Christ, who took upon him to discharge my debts, he is out of the prison of the grave, he is in heaven, therefore my flesh shall rest in hope. [We could not thus speak] if it were not for this, that Christ were risen. When we have the sentence of death, we overlook the grave, we see ourselves in heaven, as David saith, ' I should utterly have failed, but that I looked to see the goodness of the Lord in the land of the living,' Ps. xxvii. 13. Then faith looks beyond death, and beyond the grave. It looks up, and with Stephen it sees Christ at the ' right hand of God,' Acts vii. 56. We see Christ ready to receive our souls.

Then we trust in God that raiseth the dead ; nay, we see ourselves, as it were, raised already.

Use. Thus we see *how we should trust in God, in great crosses, and in the sentence of death.* This, in a word, should be another ground of patience, and not only of patience, but of contentment, in extreme crosses, in the hour of death, that all that God doth is for this, that we may exercise trust in him. And if the soul clasp to him, who is the fountain of life, the chief good, it cannot be miserable. But this it doth by trust. Our trust makes us one with him. It is that which brings us to God ; and afflictions, and death itself, force us to exercise faith in the promises, and drive us to him. So God hath overpowered all crosses, extreme crosses, even death itself, that he hath sanctified them to fit us to trust in him ; and who can be miserable that trusts in God ?

What construction should we make of crosses and afflictions? Surely this is to take away false confidence; this is to drive me to God. Shall I be impatient and murmur at that which God hath ordained to bring me nearer to himself, to trust in him, to take away all false confidence in the creature?

No! This should cut the sinews of all carnal confidence, and make us patient and thankful in all crosses; because God now is seeking our good, he is drawing good out of these crosses. He labours by this to bring us nearer to himself. Blessed is that cross, blessed is that sickness, or loss of friends whatsoever, that brings us nearer to God! Why doth God take away our dear friends? That we might cling nearer to him, because he will have us to see that he is all-sufficient.

What doth a man lose when he trusts in God, though he lose all the world? Hath he not him that made the world at the first, and can make another if he please? If a man lose all, and have God, as he hath that trusts in him, and in his word; for God will not deny his word and truth. He that trusts in God hath him, and if he have him, what if he be stripped of all? He can make another world with a word of his mouth. Other things are but a beam to him; what need a man care for a beam, that hath the sun?

All the afflictions of this world are to draw or to drive us to God, whether we will or no. As the messengers in the gospel, to force the guests to the banquet with violence, Luke xiv. 23; so afflictions they are to force us to God. This blessed effect they have in all God's children.

But those that do not belong to God, what do they in the hour of death and in extremity? They are either blocks, as Nabal was, senseless creatures; or raging, as Cain, Ahithophel, and Judas; either sots, or desperate in extremity. Saul in extremity goes to the witch, to ill means. David in all extremity he goes to prayer, he goes to his rock and shield; to God who was his 'all in all.' He knew all this was done to drive him to trust in God. 'Why art thou disquieted, O my soul? why art thou vexed in me? trust in God,' Ps. xlii. 11. All this is to make thee trust in God. He checks and chides his own soul. A child of God doth check himself. When his base heart would have him sink and fall down, and go to false means, then he raiseth himself up, 'Trust in God, O my soul.'

But such as Saul, proud, confident hypocrites, when all outward things are taken away, they go to the witch, to the devil, to one unlawful means or other, and at the last to desperate conclusions, to the sword itself.

As we desire to have evidence of a good estate in grace, that we belong to God, so let us desire God that we may find him drawing us so near to him by all crosses whatsoever, that we may see in him a supply of whatsoever is taken from us; if we lose our friends, that we may trust God the more. As St Paul speaks of the widow, 1 Tim. v. 10, seq., when her husband was alive, she trusted to him; but now she wants her former help to go to, she gives herself to prayer, she goes to God, she trusts in God. So it should be with all. When friends are taken away we should go to God. He will supply that which is wanting. Those that are bereft of any comfort, now they should go to God. What do we lose by that? We had the stream before, now we have the fountain. We shall have it in a more excellent manner in God than we had before.

And that makes a Christian at a point in this world. He is not much discouraged whatsoever he lose. If he lose all, to his life, he knows he shall have a better supply from God than he can lose in the world. Therefore he is never much cast down. He knows that all shall drive him nearer to God, to trust in God. As St Paul saith here, ' We received the sentence of death, that we might not trust in ourselves, but in God that raiseth the dead.'

One means to settle our trust the better in God reconciled to us, in the covenant of grace through Christ, his beloved, and our beloved, is the blessed sacrament. And therefore come to it as to a seal sanctified by God for that very purpose, to strengthen our trust in God. How many ways doth God condescend to strengthen our trust? because it is such an honour to him. For by trusting in him we give him the honour of all his attributes, we make him a God, we set him in his throne, which we do not when we trust not in him. How many ways doth he condescend to strengthen our trust !

(1.) We have *his promise*, 'If we believe in him, we shall not perish, but have everlasting life,' John iii. 15.

(2.) We have *a seal of that promise*, the sacrament ; and is not a broad seal a great confirmation ? If a man have a grant from the king, if he have his broad seal, it is a great confirmation. Though the other were good, yet the seal is stronger. So we have God's promise, and in regard of our weakness there is a seal added to it.

(3.) If that be not enough we have more, we have *his oath*. He hath pawned his life. ' As I live, saith the Lord,' &c., Ezek. xviii. 32. He hath pawned his being. As he is God, he will forgive us if we repent. We have his promise, seal, and oath. Whatsoever among men may strengthen trust and faith, God condescends unto to strengthen our faith, because he would not have us perish in unbelief.

(4.) Besides that, he hath given us *earnest*. A man's trust is strengthened when he hath earnest. Every true Christian hath a blessed earnest, that is, the Comforter. He hath the Spirit in him, the first fruits. Where God gives an earnest, he will make good the bargain at the last. Where he gives the first fruits, he will add the harvest. God never repents of his earnest. Where ' he hath begun a good work, he will finish it to the day of the Lord,' Philip. i. 6. An earnest is not taken away, but the rest is added.

(5.) And the same Spirit that is an earnest is also a *pawn and pledge*. We will trust any runagate, if we have a pawn sufficient. Now God hath given us this pawn of his Spirit. Christ hath given us his Spirit, and hath taken our flesh to heaven. Our flesh is there, and his Spirit is in our hearts, besides many evidences that we have in this life as pawns.

Indeed, in extremity sometimes we must trust God without a pawn, upon his bare word. ' Though he kill me, yet will I trust in him,' saith Job, chap. xiii. 15 ; but God ordinarily gives us many pawns of his love.

The sacrament is not only a seal of the promise, but likewise it hath another relation to strengthen our faith. It is a seizon (*x*), as a piece of earth that is given to assure possession of the whole. As a man saith, Take, here is a piece of earth, here is my land ; here are the keys of my house ; so in the promises sealed by the sacrament, here is life, here is favour, here is forgiveness of sins, here is life everlasting. What can we have more to strengthen our faith ? God hath condescended every way to strengthen us, if we will come in, and honour him so much as to trust him with our souls, and our salvation. Therefore let us come to the sacrament with undoubted confidence. God will keep his credit. He will not deceive his credit. ' He will never forsake those that trust in him.' Ps. ix. 10. But to answer an objection.

Obj. Oh ! all these are confirmations indeed, if I did believe and trust in God, but my heart is full of unbelief.   Indeed all these are made to some that believe already in some measure.   They have this seal, and oath, and earnest, and pawns, and first fruits, and all, if they believe ; but I cannot bring my heart to trust in God.

Ans. What hinders thee ?

I am a wretched creature, a sinful creature.

Dost thou mean to be so still?   It is no matter what thou hast been, but what thou wilt be.   The greater the sickness, the more is the honour of the physician in curing it ; the greater thy sins, the more honour to God in forgiving such sins.   Retort the temptation thus upon Satan.   God works by contraries, and whom he will make righteous he will make them to see their sins ; and before he will raise us up he will make us rotten in our graves ; before he will make us glorious he will make us miserable.   I know that God by this intends that I should despair in myself.   God intends that I should despair indeed, but it is that I should despair in myself, as the text saith here, that ' we should not trust in ourselves,' when we have a sight of the vileness of our sins ; ' but in God that raiseth the dead,' that raiseth the dead soul, the despairing soul, that it should trust in him.   Therefore retort the temptation upon Satan, because I see my sins, and despair in myself, therefore I trust in God,   ' He that is in darkness and sees no light, let him trust in the Lord his God,' Isa. l. 10.

Mark for thy comfort, the gospel calls men who in their own sense and feeling think themselves furthest off ; he that is poor, and sees his want, ' Blessed are the poor in Spirit.' Mat. v. 3.   But I have no grace, Oh that I had grace !   ' Blessed are they that hunger and thirst,' Mat. v. 6.   If thou mourn for thy sins, ' Blessed are they that mourn,' Mat. v. 4.   Thou findest a heavy load of thy sins, ' Come unto me all ye, that are weary, and heavy laden, and I will ease you,' Mat. xi. 28.   The gospel takes away all the objections and misdoubtings of the unbelieving heart, God is so willing to come to him.   Therefore stand not cavilling, interpret all to the best.   God will have us to despair in ourselves, that we may trust in him ; and then we are fittest to trust in God, when we despair in ourselves ; then we make God all in all.   He hath righteousness enough, holiness enough, satisfaction enough, he hath all enough for thee.

And for men that are not yet believers, how wondrously doth God labour to bring such men to a good hope !   If they yield themselves and come in, there is an offer to every one that ' will come in and take the water of life,'

There is a command.   He that hath commanded, ' Thou shalt not murder, Thou shalt not steal,' he lays a charge on thee that thou believe, 1 John iii. 23, ' This is his command, that we believe in the Son of God.'   And think with thyself, thou committest a sin against the gospel, which is worse than a sin against the law ; for if a man sin against the law, he may have help in the gospel.   But if he sin against the gospel there is not another gospel to help him.   God offers thee comfort.   He commands thee to trust in him.   And thou rebellest, thou offendest him, if thou do not believe.

Is not here encouragement, if thou be not more wedded to thy sinful course, than to the good of thy soul ?   If thou wilt still live in thy sins, and wilt not trust in God, then thou shalt be damned.   There is no help for thee if thou believe not, ' the wrath of God hangs over thy head,' John

iii. 36. ' Thou art condemned already,' John iii. 18, by nature. If thou believe not, thou needest no further condemnation, but only the execution of God's justice.

Naturally thou art born the child of wrath, and God threateneth thee, to stir thee up, and to make thee come in. He useth sweet allurements, besides the commands and threatenings, ' Come unto me, all ye that are weary and heavy laden, and I will ease you,' Mat. xi. 28. And ' Why will ye perish, O house of Israel,' Jer. xxvii. 13. And, ' O Jerusalem, Jerusalem, how oft, &c.,' Mat. xxiii. 37 ? God complains of thee, he allures thee, he sends his ambassadors. ' We are ministers in Christ's name to beseech you to be reconciled,' 2 Cor. v. 20, to come in, to cast down your weapons, your sins, to believe in God, and trust in his mercy, and to hope for all good from him. What should keep thee off ? He is willing to have thee believe.

Obj. ' Oh, if I were elected,' &c.

Trouble not thyself with dark scruples of his eternal decree ! Obey the command, obey the threatening, and put that out of doubt. If thou yield to the command, if thou obey the threatening, if thou be drawn by that, undoubtedly thou art the child of God. Put not in these doubts and janglings, things that are too high for thee till thou believe. Indeed, when thou believest, then thou mayest comfort thyself ; I believe, therefore I know I shall be saved. ' Whom he hath chosen, them he calls ; and whom he calls, he justifies,' Rom. viii. 30. I find myself freed from the sentence of condemnation in my heart, therefore I know I am called, I know I am elected. Then with comfort thou mayest go to those disputes. But not before a man obeys. Put those cavils out, and obey the gospel, when salvation is offered, when Satan puts these things to thee, when thou art threatened and commanded.

How shall this justify God at the day of judgment against damned wretches, that have lived in the bosom of the church, and yet would not believe. They will believe after their own fashion ; if God will save them, and let them live in their sinful courses. But they will rather be damned than they will part with them. Are they not worthy to be damned ? judge thyself, that rather than they will alter their course, and receive mercy with it, rather than they will receive Christ, whole Christ, as a king and a priest, to rule them as well as to satisfy for them—they will gild over their wicked courses, and will have none of him at all. They will rather be damned than take another course ; their damnation is just.

If thou take whole Christ, and yield to his government, he useth all means to strengthen thy faith after thou believest, and he useth all means to allure thee to believe. It is a point of much consequence, and all depends upon it. It is the sum of the gospel to trust in God, in Christ. Therefore I have been a little the longer in it. Till we can bring our hearts to this we have nothing.

When we have this, then when all shall be taken from us, as it will ere long, all the friends we have, and all our comforts ; yet our trust shall not be taken from us, nor our God in whom we trust shall be taken from us. We shall have God left, and a heart to trust in God. That will stand us in stead when all other things shall fail. ' That we might not trust in ourselves, but in God which raiseth the dead.'

These words have a double force in this place.

First, St Paul might reason thus, I am brought to death, as low as I can be, even to receive the sentence of death ; but I trust in God, who will raise me when I am dead. Therefore he can raise me out of sickness. Though there be no means, no physic, he can do it himself. Or if it were persecution, he might reason, I am now persecuted ; but God will raise me out of the grave ; therefore he can raise me out of this trouble if it be for my good. It hath the force of a strong argument that way.

And it hath another force, that is, put case the worst, ' I received the sentence of death,' that is, if I die, as I look for no other, yet I trust that God that raiseth the dead, he will raise me ; the confidence of the resurrection makes me die comfortably. As we sleep quietly, because we hope to rise again ; and we put our seed into the ground, with comfort, Why ? we hope to receive it in a more glorious manner in the harvest. So though my body be sown in the earth, it shall rise a glorious body. I trust in God, though ' I receive the sentence of death,' yet I shall sleep in the Lord. As when I go to sleep, I hope to rise again ; so I trust when the resurrection shall come, that my body shall waken and arise. ' I trust in God that raiseth the dead.' Because he raiseth the dead, he can recover me if he will. If not, he will make this body a glorious body afterward. So every way it was a strong argument with St Paul, ' I trust in God that raiseth the dead.'

The apostle draws an argument of comfort from God's power in raising the dead. And it is a true reason, a good argument. He that will raise the dead body out of the grave, he can raise out of misery, out of captivity. The argument is strong. Thus God comforts his people in Ezek. xxxvii., in that parable of the dry bones that he put life in. So the blessed apostle St Paul, he speaks of Abraham, ' He looked to God who quickeneth the dead, who calleth things that are not, as though they were,' Rom. iv. 17. What made Abraham to trust in God, that he would give him Isaac again ? he considered if God can raise Isaac from the dead, if he please he can give me Isaac back again ; and though Isaac were the son of promise, yet he trusted God's word, more than Isaac the son of his love. Why ? He knew that God could raise him from the dead, though he had sacrificed him. He trusted in God, ' who quickeneth the dead.'

Doct. The resurrection, then, is an argument to strengthen our faith in all miseries whatsoever.

It strengthens our faith before death, and in death. I will not enter into the common-place of that point concerning the resurrection ; it would be tedious and unjust, because it is not intended here, but only it is used as a special argument. Therefore I will but touch that point.

Doct. God will raise us from the dead.

Nature is more offended at this, than any other thing. But St Paul makes it clear, that it is not against nature, that God should raise the dead, 1 Cor. xv. 35, *seq.* To speak a little of it, and then to speak of the use the apostle made of it, and of the use that we may make of it. Saith the apostle in that place, speaking to witty atheists, that thought to have cavilled out the resurrection from the dead, Thou fool, thou speakest against nature, if thou think it altogether impossible.

Look to the seed, do we not see that God every spring raiseth things that were dead. We see in the silk-worm, what an alteration there is from a fly to a worm, &c. ? We see what men can do by art. They make glasses, of what ? Of ashes. We see what nature can do, which is the ordinary providence of God. We see what it can do in the bowels of the earth. What is gold, and silver, and pearl ? Is it not water and earth, excellently digested, exquisitely concocted and digested ? That there should be such excellent things of so base a creature ! We see what art and nature can do. If art and nature can do so great things, why do we call in question the power of God ? If God have revealed his will to do so, why do we doubt of this great point of God's raising the dead ?

The ancients had much ado with the pagans about this point. They handled it excellently, as they were excellent in those points which they were forced to by the adversaries, and indeed they were especially sound in those points. I say they were excellent and large in the handling of this : but I will not stand upon that. It is an article of our creed, ' I believe the resurrection of the body.'* Indeed, he that believeth the first article of the creed, he will easily believe the last. He that believes in ' God the Father Almighty, maker of heaven and earth,' he will easily believe the resurrection of the body.

But I will rather come to shew the use of it. God will raise the dead. Therefore, God's manner of working is, when there is no hope, in extremity, as I touched before. He raiseth us, but it is when we are dead. He doth his greatest works when there is least hope. So it is in the resurrection out of troubles, as in the resurrection of the body. When there is no hope at all, no ground in nature, but it must be his power altogether that must do it, then he falls to work to raise the dead.

Use. Therefore *our faith must follow his working.* He raiseth the dead. He justifies a sinner. But it is when he is furthest from grace, a sinner despairing of all mercy. Then he hath the most need of justification. He raiseth the dead, but it is then when they are nothing but dust ; then it is time for him to work to raise the dead. He restores, but it is that which is lost. God never forgets his old work. This was his old manner of working at the first, and still every day he useth it; ' he made all of nothing,' order out of confusion, light out of darkness. This was in the creation ; and the like he doth still. He never forgets his old work. This, St Paul being acquainted with, he fasteneth his hope and trust upon such a God as will raise the dead. Therefore make that use of it that the apostle doth. When the church is in any calamity, which is as it were a death, when it is as in that 37th of Ezekiel, ' dry bones,' comfort yourselves. God comforted the church there, that he would raise the church out of Babylon, as he raised those dead bones. The one is as easy as the other. So in the government of the church continually, he brings order out of confusion, light out of darkness, and life out of death, that is, out of extreme troubles. When men think themselves dead, when they think the church dead, past all hope, then he will quicken and raise it. So that he will never forget this course, till he have raised our dead bodies ; and then he will finish that manner of dispensation. This is God's manner of working.

We must answer it with our faith, that is, in the greatest dejection that can be, to ' trust in God that raiseth the dead.' Faith, if it be true, it will answer the ground of it. But when it is carried to God, it is carried to him that raiseth the dead. Therefore, though it be desperate every way, yet notwithstanding I hope above hope. I hope in him whose course is to raise the dead, who at the last will raise the dead, and still delights in a proportion to raise men from death, out of all troubles and miseries.

Well ! this God doth, and therefore carry it along in all miseries whatsoever, in soul, in body, or estate, or in the church, &c.

God raiseth from the dead, therefore we must feel ourselves dead before we can be raised by his grace. What is the reason that a papist cannot be

* Article XI.—G.

a good Christian? He opposeth his own conversion. What is conversion? It is the first resurrection, the resurrection of the soul. But that which is raised must be dead first. They account not themselves dead, and therefore oppose this resurrection. And so, when we are dead in grace or comfort, let us trust in God that raiseth the dead. And so for outward condition in this life and the estate of the church.

The conversion of the Jews, which seems a thing so strange. When a man thinks how they are dispersed, and thinks of their poverty and disgrace, he thinks, Is this a likely matter? Remember what God hath said, he will raise the dead. And because this is a work that seems as hard as the raising of the dead, therefore their calling and conversion is called a kind of resurrection, Rom. xi. 15. Let us hope for that. He that raiseth the body will raise that people, as despicable as they are, to be a glorious people and church.

And so for the confusion of the 'man of sin.' The revelation of the gospel, when it came out of the grave of darkness, out of the Egyptian darkness of popery, was it not a raising of the dead?

When Luther arose for the defence of the truth, a man might have said to him, What! dost thou set thyself against the whole world? Go to thy cloister, and say, 'Lord, have mercy upon us.' Dost thou hope to reform the world against all the world? Alas!* he trusted in God 'that raiseth the dead,' that raiseth men to conversion when he pleaseth, and that raiseth the church when he pleaseth, even from death. He raised the church out of Babylon, and he will raise the Jews that now are in a dead state. Why should we doubt of these things, when we believe, or profess to believe the main, the resurrection from the dead?

And every day in the church God is raising the dead spiritually. The dead hear the voice of Christ every day. When the ministry is in power, when there is a blessing upon it, conveying it to the heart, then he is raising the dead. So 'wisdom is justified of her children,' Mat. xi. 19. The gospel is justified to be a powerful doctrine, having the Spirit of God clothing it, to raise people from the dead, those that are dead in sin.

There are none that ever are spiritually raised, but those that see themselves dead. And that is the reason why we are to abhor popery, because it teacheth us that we are not dead in ourselves, and then there can be no resurrection to grace; for the resurrection is of the dead. The more we see a contrariety in nature to grace, the more fit objects we are for the divine power of God to raise. 'He raiseth the dead.'

Thus we see how to go along with this. In all troubles God will raise the dead, therefore he will bring me out of this trouble, if he see it good. Therefore in extremity let us thus reason with ourselves. Now I know not which way to turn me; 'there is but a step between me and death,' 1 Sam. xx. 3. If God have any purpose to use my service further, he that raiseth the dead will raise me from the grave; 'to him belong the issues of death,' Ps. lxviii. 20. He can give an evasion and escape if he will; if not, if he will not deliver me, then I die in this faith, that he will raise me from the dead.

This is that that upholds a Christian in extremity. This made the martyrs so confident. This made those three young men so resolute that were cast into the fiery furnace. What was their comfort? Surely this, God can deliver us if he will, say they. He is able to deliver us now; but if he

* 'Alas!' The peculiar use of this interjection by Sibbes has elsewhere been noted. It will be frequently met with thus used in the present volume.—G.

will not do this for us, he will raise our bodies. If he will not deliver them here, there will be a final deliverance at the resurrection.

So in Heb. xi. 16, those blessed men, 'they hoped for a better resurrection,' and this made them confident.

This makes us confident to stand out against all the threatenings and all the crosses of the world, that we may hold our peace with God, notwithstanding all the enticements and allurements to the contrary, because we trust in God that raiseth the dead.

Again, let us learn to extract contrary principles to Satan out of God's proceedings. What doth he reason when we are dead, either in sin or in misery? What hast thou to do with God? God hath forsaken thee. No! saith faith, God is a God raising the dead. The more dead I am in the eye of the world, and in my own sense, the nearer I am to God's help. I am a despairing sinner, a great sinner; but the more, God will magnify his mercy, that 'where sin hath abounded, grace may abound much more,' Rom. v. 20. Retort home the argument, draw contrary principles to him. This is a divine art which faith hath.

Oh, but then you may presume, and do what you list.

Not so, retort the argument again upon him; if I do so, God will bring me to death, he will bring me to despair; and who is it that delights to have that course taken with him, to be brought so low? So every way we may retort temptations from this dealing of God. If I be careless, he will bring me as low as hell. I shall have little joy to try conclusions with him.

And if thou be low, despair not, thou art the fitter object. God raiseth the dead, therefore I will not add to my sins legal. I will not add this evangelical sin, this destroying sin of despair and unbelief; but I will cast myself upon the mercy of God, and believe in him that raiseth the dead; and desire him to speak to my dead soul, which is as rotten as Lazarus's body, which had been so long in the grave, that he would say to it, 'Come forth' of that cursed estate. It is but for him to speak the word, to bless his word, and then it will come out by faith. It is the art of faith to draw contrary arguments to Satan, and those that belong to God do so in all temptations. But those that do not, they sink lower and lower, having nothing to uphold their souls. They have not learned to trust in God that raiseth the dead.

God is the God that raiseth the dead. Therefore let us oft think of this; think what God means to do with us, that we may carry ourselves answerably, 'I trust in God that raiseth the dead.' Therefore let us honour God while we live, with that body that he will raise; let us be fruitful in our place. St Paul draws this conclusion, 1 Cor. xv. 58, from the resurrection, 'Finally, my brethren, be constant, unmoveable, alway abounding in the work of the Lord, knowing that your labour is not in vain in the Lord.' Especially considering that he will raise the dead bodies after a more glorious manner than they are now, he will make a more glorious body. For alway God's second works are better than his first. He raiseth the dead, and will make our bodies like the glorious body of Christ.

But the point of the resurrection is very large, and perhaps I shall have better occasion to speak of it afterward. I only apply it to the present purpose, how it strengthens faith in misery and in the hour of death.

A man is strengthened in his faith when he thinks, now I am going 'the way of all flesh,' Josh. xxiii. 14, I am to yield my soul to God, and death is to close up mine eyes; yet I have trusted in God, and do trust in God that will raise my body from the grave. This comforts the soul against the horror of the grave, against that confusion and darkness that is after death.

Faith seeth things to come as present, it sees the body, after it hath a long time been in the dust, clothed with flesh, and made like the glorious body of Christ. Faith sees this, and so a Christian soul dies in faith, and sows the body as good seed in the ground in hope of a glorious resurrection.

And that comforts a Christian soul, in the loss of children, of wife, of friends, that have been dearest and nearest to me. I trust ' in God that raiseth the dead,' that he will raise them again, and then we shall all be for ever with the Lord. It is a point of singular comfort. For the main articles of our faith they have a wondrous working upon us, in all the passages of our lives. It is good to think often upon the pillars of our faith, as this is one, ' that God will raise us from the dead.'

But I go on to the next verse.

VERSE 10.

' *Who delivered us from so great a death, who doth deliver us; in whom we trust that he will yet deliver us.*' St Paul sets down his troubles to the life, that he might make himself and others more sensible of his comforts, and of God's grace and goodness in his deliverance. These words contain his deliverance out of that trouble, his particular deliverance out of a particular trouble. And this deliverance is set down by a triple distinction of time. As time is either past, present, or to come ; so God, who is the deliverer for all times, ' he hath delivered us' for the time past, ' he doth deliver us' for the present, ' in whom we trust that he will deliver us' for the time to come.

Who delivered us from so great a death.' After St Paul had learned to trust in God, after he had taken forth that lesson, a hard lesson to learn, that must be learned by bringing a man to such extremity, I say, after he had learned ' to trust in God that raiseth the dead,' God gave him this reward of his diligence in the blessed school of afflictions. He delivered him, ' who hath delivered us, and who doth deliver us' continually. He will not take his hand from the work, and for the time to come I hope he will do so still.

St Paul here calls his trouble a death. It was not a death properly. It is but his aggravation of the trouble that calls it a death ; because God's mercy only hindered it from being a death. It was only not a death. It was some desperate trouble, some desperate sickness. The particular is not set down in the Scripture. We know what a tumult there was about Diana of Ephesus, Acts xix, and in 1 Cor. xv. 32, ' He fought with beasts at Ephesus (which is in Asia), after the manner of men.' Whether it were that, or some other, we know not. Whatsoever it was, he calls it a death. He doth not call it an affliction, but a death ; and a great death, to make himself the more sensible.

Wherefore have we souls and understandings, but to exercise them in setting forth our dangers, and the deliverances of God ? to consider of things to affect us deeply ? The apostle here to affect himself deeply, he sets it down here by a death.

And ofttimes in the Psalms, the psalmist in Ps. xviii. 4, and Ps. xi. 6, he calls his afflictions death and hell, and so they had been indeed, except

God had delivered him.   But to come to the points that are considerable hence.   First of all we may observe this, that

> God, till he have wrought his own work, he doth not deliver ; he brings men to a low ebb, to a very low estate, before he will deliver.

Secondly. *After God hath wrought his own work, then he delivers his children.*

Thirdly. *He continues the work still, ' he doth deliver me.'*

Fourthly. *That upon experience of God's former deliverance, God's children have founded a blessed argument for the time to come.*   'He hath, and he will deliver me.'   God is alway like himself.   He is never at a loss.   What he hath done, he doth, and will do, reserving the limitations, as we shall see afterward.

Doct. 1.   *God doth not at the first deliver his children.*

He delivered St Paul, but it was after he had brought him to ' receive the sentence of death,' and after he had learned not to trust in himself, but ' in God that raiseth the dead.'   God defers his deliverance for many reasons.   To name a few.

Reason (1).   God doth defer his deliverance when we are in dangers, partly, as you see here, *to perfect the work of mortification of self-confidence*, to subdue trust in any earthly thing.   St Paul by this learned not to trust in himself.

2.   And then to *strengthen our faith and confidence in God ;* when we are drawn from all creatures to learn to trust in him.

3.   And to *sweeten his deliverance when it comes, to endear his favours ;* for then they are sweet indeed, after God hath beat us out of ourselves. Summer and spring are sweet after winter.   So it is in this vicissitude and intercourse that God useth.   Favour after affliction and crosses, is favour indeed.   That makes heaven so sweet to God's children when they come there, because they go to heaven out of a great deal of misery in this world.

4.   And partly likewise God defers it *for his own glory*, that it may be known for his mere work ; for when we are at a loss, and the soul can reason thus, God must help or none can help, then God hath the glory. Therefore in love to his own glory he defers it so long.

5.   Again, he useth to defer long, that he might *the more shame the enemies at length ;* for if the affliction be from the insolency and pride of the enemies, he defers deliverance, till they be come to the highest pitch, and then he ariseth as ' a giant refreshed with wine, and smites his enemies in the hinder parts,' Ps. lxxviii. 66.   He is as it were refreshed on the sudden.   And as it is his greatest glory to raise his children when they are at the lowest ; so it is his glory to confound the pride of the enemies when it is at the highest.   If he should do it before, his glory would not shine so much in the confusion of them, and their enterprises against his children.   One would think he should not have let Pharaoh alone so long ; but he got him glory the more at the last, in confounding him in the Red Sea.   So Haman came very far, almost to the execution of the decree he had gotten by his policy and malice ; and then God delivered his church and confounded Haman.   These and the like reasons may be given to shew that God in heavenly and deep wisdom doth not presently deliver his children.

Use.   The proper use of it is, that we should learn *not to be hasty and short-spirited in God's dealing*, but learn to practise that which we are often enjoined, to wait on God, to wait his good leisure.

Especially considering that which is the second point, let that satisfy us, that *Doct.* 2. *After God hath done his work, he will deliver.*

Let us wait, for he will deliver at length. Perhaps his time is not yet that he will deliver; but usually when all is desperate, when he may have all the glory, then he delivers. He delivered the three young men, but they were put into the fire first, and the furnace was made seven times hotter, that he might have the glory in consuming their enemies. So he delivered Hezekiah in his time, but it was when the enemy was even ready to seize upon the city, Isa. xxxvii. 14, *seq.* He promised St Paul that not one man should perish in the ship, but yet they suffered shipwreck, they went away only with their lives, Acts xxvii. 24, 44. God doth so deliver his, that he doth not suffer them to perish in the danger.

Use. Therefore let us *stay his time, and wait.* It may be it is not God's time yet.

When shall we know that it is God's time to deliver, that we may wait with comfort ?

(1.) God knows his own time best; but usually it is when *we are brought very low*, and when our spirits are low. When we are brought very low, both in regard of human support, and in regard of our spirits, when we are humble, when our souls ' cleave to the dust,' Ps. cxix. 25. ' Help, Lord,' for we are brought very low. ' Help, Lord, for vain is the help of man,' Ps. lx. 11.

When the church can plead so, it is a good plea. When we are at the lowest, and the malice of the enemy is at the highest, when the waters swell, ' Help, Lord, for the waters are come into my very soul,' Ps. lxix. 1 ; when we are very low, and the enemies very high, as we see in Pharaoh ; and so in Herod, when he was in the height of his pride, when he was in all his glory, God takes him there.

Thus God delivers his, and confounds his enemies. I join them both together, for the one is not commonly without the other. The annoyance of God's children is from their enemies. Therefore when he delivers the one he confounds the other. When the malice of the one is at the highest, and the state of the other is at the lowest, and their spirits are afflicted and cast down with their estate, then is the time when God will deliver.

(2.) Again, *when our hearts are enlarged to pray*, when we can pray from a broken heart. As you see here, he joins them together. God will deliver me, but it must be by your prayers. When we have hearts to pray, and when others have hearts to pray for us, that is the time of deliverance. Usually there goes before deliverance an enlarged heart to pray to God, as we see in Daniel, chap. ix., a little before they came out of Babylon, he had a large heart to pray to God. And when we can plead with God his promise, ' Remember, Lord, thy promise wherein thou hast caused us to trust,' Ps. cxix. 49 ; when we can cast ourselves upon God's mercy with prayer, and plead with God to remember his promise, it is a sign God means to deliver us. When the heart is shut and closed up, that it cannot speak to God, when there is some sin or other that doth stifle the spirit, that it cannot vent itself with that liberty to God, it is a sign that it is not the time yet of God's deliverance.

God will at the length deliver. Therefore from both these, that he doth defer deliverance, and that he will deliver at length, let us infer this lesson of waiting ; let us wait therefore, and wait with comfort. Let us remember these principles.

First, God hath a time, as for all things, so for our deliverance.

Secondly, that God's time is the best time.   He is the best discerner of opportunities.

Thirdly, remember that this shall be when he hath wrought his work upon our souls, specially when he hath made us to trust in him.   As here, when St Paul had learned to trust in God, then he delivered him.   And why should we desire to do our bodies good, or our estates good, till God hath wrought his cure on our souls ? for God intends our souls in the first place.   Our souls, they are the whole man, in a manner.   The welfare of the soul draws the welfare of the body, and the welfare of the estate after it.   The body shall do well, if the soul do well.

Therefore we should desire rather that the Lord would let the affliction stay, than that it should part without the message for which God sends it. Every affliction is God's messenger.   We should desire the Lord to let it stay for the answer for which he hath sent it.

And indeed, it will never part without the answer for which God sends it, till it have humbled us, till it have brought us to trust in God, till we be such as we should be.   And a Christian soul rather desires to be in the furnace, to be under the affliction, to be purged better yet, than to have the cross and affliction removed, and not to be a whit the better for it.   Therefore, considering that there will be a time, and that God's time is the best time, and that this time will be when he hath fitted us, we should learn to wait in any cross, and not to be over hasty.

Again, consider, though the time be long, yet he will deliver at length by death.   Death will end all miseries.

And consider, that how long soever we endure anything, yet what is that that we endure here, to that that we are freed from by Christ ?   We are freed from misery, from all misery, from the wrath of God, from damnation. And what is that that we can suffer here, to the glory and joy that remains for us in heaven ?   What is all that we can suffer here, to that that Christ hath endured for us ?   What is all that we can endure here, to that that we have deserved ?   Considering, then, what we are delivered from, what God hath reserved for us, what Christ hath endured, and what we deserve, it will make us wait, and wait with patience.   Especially considering, as I said before, that God is working his good work for our good.   Though we at the first, perhaps, for a while do not see the meaning of the affliction, the meaning of the cross, we cannot read it perfectly, yet in general we may know it is for our good.   God of his infinite wisdom will not suffer a hair to fall from our heads, without his providence.   ' And all shall work together for the best to those that love him,' Rom. viii. 28.

It is long then, we see, ere God deliver ; and why ? and at the last he will deliver one way or other ; and therefore let us wait quietly.   And this the saints of God have practised in all ages.   ' Yet, my soul, keep silence to the Lord,' Ps. lxii. 5.   He had a shrewd conflict with himself, when he saw how good causes were trampled on, and he saw the insolence of wicked persons, how they lift up their heads, ' Yet, my soul, keep silence to the Lord.'   So he begins, 'Yet God is good to Israel,' Ps. lxxiii. 1, for all this. And God chargeth it upon his people that they should wait, ' If I tarry, wait thou,' Hab. ii. 2.   And the blessing is promised to those that can wait and not murmur, as in Ps. cxlvii. 11.   It is a duty that we are much urged to, and very hardly brought to the practice of.   Therefore we are to hear it pressed the more, ' The Lord taketh pleasure in them that fear him, in those that hope in his mercy,' Ps. cxlvii. 11, in those that trust in his mercy.

The like you have in many places: ' Therefore will the Lord wait, that he may be gracious to you ; therefore he will be exalted, that he may have mercy upon you : he is a God of judgment, blessed are all that wait for him,' Isa. xxx. 18. So in Lam. iii. The church still waits upon God. How oft doth David charge himself, ' Wait, and trust in God, O my soul,' Ps. xlii. 5. Let us learn this upon these grounds, that God is long ere he deliver, but at last he will deliver ; and that is sufficient to force this, to wait still upon God with patience and silence.

Well, thus we see God doth deliver, ' who delivered us,' &c. What will he do for the time present ? He hath delivered, and doth deliver, and he will deliver. From all jointly together, you see that

Doct. God's people in this world stand in need of deliverance alway.

They have always troubles. When one is past, another is present. Deliverance supposeth dangers.

1. *There have been dangers, there are dangers, and there will be dangers.* Our life is a warfare, a temptation. We are absent from God. We are alway exposed to dangers. We live in the midst of devils and of devilish-minded men. We have corruptions in us that expose us to sin, and sin draws on judgments. We are alway in danger one way or other while we live in this world. But our comfort is, that as there have been dangers, and are dangers, and will be dangers ; so there hath been deliverance, there is deliverance, and there will be deliverance. It is a trade that God useth. It is his art. ' God knoweth how to deliver his,' as St Peter saith, 2 Peter ii. 9. He hath alway exercised it, he is excellent at it. He hath delivered his church, he doth deliver his church, and he will deliver his church ; and so every particular member, he hath, and doth, and will deliver them.

Wonderful is the intercourse that God useth with his people and their estate. Even as in nature there is a change and intercourse of day and night, of light and darkness, of morning and evening, of summer and winter, of hot and cold ; so in the life of a Christian there are changes, dangers, and deliverances. There is a ' sowing in tears, and a reaping in joy,' Ps. cxxvi. 5. There is a night of affliction, and a morning of joy and prosperity : ' Heaviness may be in the evening, but joy cometh in the morning,' Ps. xxx. 5.

And thus we go on till we end our days, till we be taken to heaven, where there shall be no change, where ' all tears shall be wiped from our eyes.'

If we had spiritual eyes, eyes to see our danger, to see how full the world is of devils ! And then to consider how many dangers this weak life is subject to, how many casualties ! We cannot go out of doors, we cannot take a journey, but how many dangers are we subject to ! We are en-vironed with perpetual dangers. The snares of death compass us almost everywhere, abroad and at home, in our greatest security.

But our comfort is, that God doth compass us with mercy, as it is, Ps. xxxii. 6, As dangers are round about us, so God is a ' wall of fire about us.' We have dangers about us, devils about us. We have a guard about us, we have God about us, we have angels about us, we have all his crea-tures about us. ' All things are yours,' saith the apostle, 2 Cor. iv. 15, &c.

It is God that hath delivered us, that doth deliver us. Who restrains the devils from having their wills of us ? They are enemies not only to our souls and to our salvation, but to our bodies. They are enemies to our health, as we see in Job. We live in the midst of lions ; ofttimes in the midst of enemies. Who restrains their malice ? We are preserved from dangers day and night. Who shuts in the doors, who watcheth over us, but he that keeps Israel? It is God that delivereth us. Without his deliverance all deliverances were to little purpose. All shutting in were to little purpose, except he shut us in that shut Noah into the ark. He must watch over us. It is God that delivereth us.

But doth he deliver us only outwardly?

2. No! *He hath delivered, and he doth deliver, us spiritually.* He hath delivered us from the power of hell and damnation. He doth deliver us from many sins that we should commit; and when we have sinned, he delivers us from despair. He delivers us from presuming, by touching our hearts with saving grief for sin. If we belong to him, one of the two ways he delivers; either from the sin or from the danger of the sin; either from the committing of the sin, or from despairing for the sin, or presuming in a course of sin.

Who delivereth us from our inbred corruptions? Should we not run every day into the sins that we see others commit? Who cuts short our lusts, and suppresseth them, that we are not swearers, that we are not licentious persons, that we are not godless persons? Are we not hewn out of the same rock? Who keeps us from sin? Is it any inbred goodness? Are we not all alike tainted with original sin, children of wrath? Who puts a difference between us and others? It is God that hath delivered us, and that doth deliver us.

It is his mercy that we do not commit sin, it is his preventing deliverance; and when we have committed sin, it is his mercy to pardon it. There is his preserving deliverance from despair after the committing of sin.

All are beholden to God for deliverance. Those that have committed sin, that he delivers them from the wrath to come, from the damnation that they deserve; and those that have the grace not to commit sin, they are beholden to him, that he delivers them from that which their corruptions else would carry them to, if he should take his government from their hearts.

We have an inward guard as well as an outward, an invisible guard, ' We are kept by the Spirit of God through faith to salvation,' 1 Pet. i. 5. We have a guard that keeps us from despair, from sinking. God delivereth us from ourselves by this inward guard. There is not the vilest atheist that lives, but let God open his conscience, and let loose himself upon himself, to see what he deserves, to see what he is ready to sink into, if he see not God's mercy to deliver him, if he see not an intercessor, a mediator to come between God and him, what would become of him? Therefore saith St Paul in Philip. iv. 7, ' The peace of God which passeth all understanding shall "guard" your hearts and minds;' for so the word is in the original, ' shall guard your hearts and minds.' *

We have not only a guard outward, but we have a peace in us, the Spirit of God, the strengthening power of God, the sight of the love of God. God delivers us, as from all others, so from ourselves. Judas had no enemies. God let him loose to himself. What became of him? Ahithophel had no enemy. God let him loose to himself too; and then we see what a desperate conclusion he came to.

So, whosoever thou art that comtemnest religion, that makest anything of greater moment and respect than that, if thou hadst not an enemy in the world, but all were thy friends, as Judas had all to be his friends. The Pharisees were his friends. He had money of them. But God opened

* See note *k*, vol. i. p. 334.—G.

his conscience, and he could not endure the sight of it. It spake bitter things to him, when God opened an inward hell in his conscience. So God doth deliver us outwardly and inwardly, and the inward is double ; partly from despair, partly from the rage of corruptions, as I said before. Is it not God that ties up our corruptions ? There is such a world of sin in the heart of a man, as often he finds the experience of it, when he meets with a fit temptation to his disposition, that God's children complain of themselves that the sins of their hearts have deceived them. So God delivers men from the rage of lusts. He ties up their corruptions, and delivers them from them. And when we fall, and are ready to despair for them, he delivers us from despair. He doth deliver, he is perpetually delivering. It implies that we alway stand in need of deliverance.

Therefore, we should alway look up to God. He is the breath of our nostrils ; ' In him we live, and move, and have our being,' Acts xvii. 28. In him we stand, and in him we are delivered in the midst of all our enemies. It should stir up our hearts thankfully to depend upon God. He that hath delivered us, he doth deliver us. If he should not continue his deliverance, we should be continually in extreme danger.

' *Who hath delivered us, and doth deliver us,' &c.* A Christian is never in so great perplexity but God is delivering of him, even in trouble. So the church saith, Lam. iii. 22, ' It is God's mercy that we are not all consumed.'

The church was in a pitiful estate then. One would have thought they were as low as almost they might be. Yet, notwithstanding, the Spirit of God in those blessed men that lived in those times, they saw that they might have been worse than they were ; and they saw that there was some danger from which they were delivered, ' It is thy mercy that we are not all consumed.' God delivered them from extremity.

Nay, in troubles God doth deliver so as there may be a distinction, for the most part, between his and others. ' When I gather my jewels, it shall be known who serves me, and who serves me not,' Mal. iii. 17. God continually delivers, more especially at some times.

As we say of providence, providence is nothing but a continued act of creation. And it is true. The same power that created all things of nothing, the same power sustains all things. God upholds all things with his right hand.

For even as it is with a stone which is upheld by a man's hand, let him withdraw his hand, and down it falls. So naturally all things, as they are raised out of nothing, so they will fall to their first principles except they be sustained by that continual act of creation which we call providence, to maintain them in the order wherein they were set at the first. So there is a continual act of deliverance till we be delivered out of all troubles, and set in a place where there shall be no more annoyance at all, either from within us or without us. God doth still deliver.

Use. Oh ! let this move us to a renounce* of the eye and majesty of the great God, of the presence of God. Who will willingly provoke him of whom he stands in need to deliver him ?

Let God withdraw his deliverance, his preventing deliverance, or his rescuing deliverance. For, as I said, there is a double deliverance. He prevents us from trouble, he delivers us that we do not fall into it ; and

---

* That is, ' renunciation.' And yet this can hardly be what Sibbes intended here. Query, does he use it etymologically, as = to report, and by inference, recognise ?—G.

when we are fallen into it he rescues us. If God should not thus deliver us, there is no mischief that any others fall into but we should fall into the like were it not for his preventing deliverance.

As St Austin saith well, A man that is freed from sin ought to thank God as well for the sins that he hath not committed as for the sins that he hath had forgiven; for it is an equal mercy that a man fall not into sin as for his sin to be pardoned. And so for troubles too. It is God's mercy to prevent troubles as well as to deliver out of trouble when we are fallen into it.

Who would not reverence this great God? What miscreant wretches are they that inure their tongue to swearing, to tear that majesty, that if he should withdraw his deliverance and protection from them, what would become of them?

Where there is perpetual dependence upon any man, how doth it enforce reverence and respect even amongst men? It is atheism, therefore, for men to inure their tongues to speak cursed language, to inure their hearts to entertain profane thoughts of God, and to neglect the consideration of his majesty. Holy men in Scripture are said to walk with God, that is, to have God in their eye in all times, in all places, as he had them in his eye to delight in them, to prevent troubles, and to deliver them from troubles when they were in them.

We should take notice of God's special providence in this kind, that God by deliverance often gives us our lives, and it should teach us to consecrate our lives to God, ' who doth deliver us.'

'*In whom we hope*,' or trust, or have affiance, ' *that he will yet deliver us*.' The holy apostle doth take in trust here the time to come. He speaks as if he were assured of that as of anything past; and he doth found his hope for the time to come upon that which was past and present. As he saith in Rom. v. 4, ' Experience breeds hope,' so it doth here in the blessed apostle, ' He hath delivered, and he doth deliver,' and why should I not trust in so good a God for the time to come? I hope he will deliver me. And surely so may we do.

Doct. A Christian may rely on God for the time to come.

Upon what ground, upon what pillars is this confidence built of the holy apostle?

1. *Upon the name of God, the name of his nature,* ' Jehovah,' ' I am,' which signifies a constant being, ' I was, I am, and am to come.'

There was danger, there is danger, and there will come danger. There was a God, there is a God, and there will be a God, Jehovah, I am. If there be a flux, a perpetual succession of ill, there is a perpetual being and living of the living Jehovah. So Christ is proved to be Jehovah, because he calls himself, Rev. i. 8, ' He that was, and is, and is to come,' Jehovah, alway like himself.

Now, if God be Jehovah, alway like himself, then if he have delivered, if he doth deliver, he will deliver. He is I AM in himself.

2. Now, as his name is, *so is his nature and properties*. He is ' I AM ' in his love to his church. He is alway in the present tense. ' Whom he loves, he loves to the end,' John xiii. 1. He is unchangeable. ' I, the Lord your God, change not; therefore, you are not consumed,' Mal. iii. 6. The reason why, notwithstanding our many provocations of him, that we are not consumed, it is because his love to us is unchangeable. Though we are up and down, ' he cannot deny himself,' 2 Tim. ii. 13; and there is

the foundation of our comfort, that though we change oft, yet he never changeth. There is no outward thing can change him; for then that were God, and not he. There is no inward thing can change him; for then he were not perfectly wise. So there is nothing either in himself or in the creatures that can change God. He is alway like himself. Therefore, this is a ground of confidence for the time to come.

3. Likewise *his covenant and promise.* The covenant that he hath made with his children is an everlasting covenant, that he will be their God to death, and for ever; and the gifts and graces of God, his inward love, they are without repentance, and their union with Christ is an everlasting union.

4. And also *experience built upon these grounds,* that God is Jehovah. What he hath done he will do; and his properties are answerable to his name; he is unchangeable, and his promise and covenant are unchangeable. Therefore, experience from the time past comes to be a good argument from these three grounds: because he is Jehovah, ' I AM;' and because he is unchangeable, being Jehovah; and because his covenant is everlasting, because he is unchangeable.

For the foundation of all comfort is the name and being of God, Jehovah. From his being, issue and flow his properties, and they are like him unchangeable and eternal, and from his properties comes that to be unchangeable that comes from him, his word, and promise, and covenant. Considering then that his name and being is such, that his properties are such, that his covenant is such, issuing from his nature and properties, experience then of trust in the love and mercy of God, is an unanswerable argument against all temptations. He hath loved, he doth love, and he will love; he hath delivered, he doth deliver, and he will deliver, and will ' preserve us to his heavenly kingdom,' 2 Tim. iv. 18.

It is a good argument that God that is Jehovah, that God that is unchangeable, that God that is in covenant with me, that is my God, and I his, that God of whom I have had experience for the time past, that he hath been my God. Why should I doubt for the time to come? Unless I will call in question the very being of God, the very properties of God, and the truth of God in his covenant, and overturn all, I may as well trust him for the time to come, as for the time present; ' He hath delivered me, he doth deliver me, and he will deliver me.'

Obj. But it may be objected, God doth not deliver alway, and therefore it seems not to be a current truth. How doth God deliver his children, when we see how they miscarry in troubles and persecutions, both the church in general and particular Christians, as there be many instances. It seems God doth not deliver his. They die martyrs. St. Paul himself died a bloody death. Therefore, how is this true that we may build a certain confidence upon it, ' he hath delivered, he doth deliver, and he will deliver?'

Ans. I answer, we must take it in the latitude, this deliverance.

1. God delivers them so as stands with their desires to be delivered; for there may cases come wherein God's children will not be delivered, as we see the three young men when they were cast into the fire, they would not be delivered *out of* the fire, but they were delivered *in* it. And so in Heb. xi. 35, there is a notable example. ' Tender women receive their dead again raised to life, and others likewise were tortured, and would not accept of deliverance.' They would have none upon ill terms. So sometimes God doth not deliver his children, no, nor they will not be delivered,

because perhaps their deliverance is promised upon ill terms; that they may redeem their lives if they will by denying God and religion; an ill bargain (cc).

2. Again, I answer that howsoever God doth not deliver his from trouble, yet he delivers them in trouble, as in Isaiah xliii. 2, he promiseth to be with them, and to deliver them in ' the fire, and in the water.'

God did not keep the martyrs out of the fire, but God was with them in the fire, and in the water, to support them by the inward fire of his Spirit, that they might not be overcome of the outward fire and flame. So God delivers them in trouble, though not out of trouble.

There is an open deliverance visible to the world, and a secret, inward, invisible deliverance. There is an open glorious deliverance, as we see in the deliverance of the three young men, and many other examples. And there is an invisible deliverance, which is only felt of them, and of God, who delivers them. He delivers them in the inward man. He delivers them from the ill of troubles, from sin and despair; that they put not their hands to sinful courses. He supports them inwardly with comfort, and supports them inwardly in a course of obedience. And that spiritual, inward deliverance is the best, and that which God's people more value than deliverance out of trouble. He doth not deliver them from suffering ill, he delivers them from doing ill, as in that notable place, 2 Tim. iv. 17, 18, ' I was delivered out of the mouth of the lion, and the Lord shall deliver me from every evil work.' He doth not say, God shall deliver me from death, and from suffering evil works of tyrants; no, but he shall deliver me from carrying myself unseemly and unbefitting such a man as I am, that I may not disgrace my profession. ' He shall deliver me from every evil work.' And that is that which the saints and martyrs and all good people desire, that God would deliver them, that they may not sink in their minds, that they despair not, that they carry not themselves uncomely in troubles, but so as is meet for the credit of the truth which they seal with their blood (dd). ' He hath delivered me, and he will deliver me from every evil work.' And what saith he afterwards? ' He shall preserve me to his heavenly kingdom.'

He doth not say, he shall preserve me from death. He knew he should die. But, ' he shall preserve me to his heavenly kingdom.' So put the case that God do not deliver *from* death, yet he delivers *by* death.

There is a partial deliverance, and a total deliverance. There is a deliverance from this and that trouble, and there is a deliverance from all troubles. God delivers us most when we think he delivers least; for we think how doth he deliver his children when we see them taken away by death, and ofttimes are massacred?

That is one way of delivering them. God by death takes them from all miseries. They are out of the reach of their enemies. Death delivers them from all miseries of this life, both inward of sin, and outward of trouble. All are determined in death. Therefore, God when he doth not deliver them from death, he delivers them by death, and takes them to his heavenly kingdom.

God oft-times delivers his by not delivering them out of trouble; for when he sees us in danger of some sin, he delivers us into trouble to deliver us from some corruption. Of all evils God's children desire to avoid the delivering up to themselves, and to their own lusts, to their own base earthly hearts, to a dead heart. He delivers them into trouble therefore to deliver them from themselves.

God will deliver us for the time to come, so that we depend upon him, and humble ourselves, and be like ourselves. When God delivereth us at the first, it may be we are like ourselves, but perhaps afterward we grow prouder, and self-confident, and will not do that we formerly did. Therefore, God sometimes though he put us in hope of deliverance, yet he will not deliver us, because we are not prepared, we are not thoroughly humbled. As we see in Judges xx. There the Israelites were to set on the Benjamites. They go the first time, and had the foil.* They go the second time, and are foiled. The third time they set on them with fasting and prayer, and then they had the victory.

What was the reason they had it not at the first time? They were not humbled enough; they did not flee to God, with fasting and prayer. It may be there is some sin, some affection unmortified, of revenge and anger. When God hath subdued that, and brought it under, and brought us to fasting and prayer, then God will deliver us; as at the third encounter they carried away the victory. When we have not made our peace with God, we may come the first and second time, and not be delivered; but when we are thoroughly humbled, and brought low, then God will deliver us.

And then, we must know that alway these outward promises have a reservation to God's glory, and our eternal good. 'God hath delivered me,' and he doth, and will deliver me, if it may stand with his glory and my good. And therefore the soul saith to God, with that reserved speech of him in the gospel, Lord, 'if thou wilt, thou canst heal me,' Mat. viii. 2. If thou wilt, thou canst deliver me. If it be for thy glory, and my eternal good, or for the church's good, thou wilt do it. And neither the church nor the particular members of the church, desire deliverance upon any other terms. But when it may be for the glory of God, and for the church's good; when they may be instrumental by long life to serve God, and to serve the church; and when it is for their own advantage to gather further assurance of their salvation, then he hath, and doth, and will deliver still. This is enough to build the confidence of God's children upon, for their deliverance for the time to come.

God will deliver his church and children, and he will deliver them out of all. He will 'deliver Israel out of all his troubles,' Ps. xxv. 22. He will not leave a 'horn or a hoof,' as Moses said, Exod. x. 26. He will not leave one trouble. He will deliver us at the last out of all, and advance us to his heavenly kingdom. His bowels will melt over his church and children; he is a father, and he hath the bowels of a mother. This may serve to answer all objections that will arise in our hearts, as indeed we are ready to cavil against divine truths and comforts; especially in the time of trouble and temptation, our hearts are full of complaints and disputes; therefore I thought good to answer this.

But what is the argument of the apostle here? Especially experience; 'He hath delivered, he doth deliver, and he will deliver me.'

Doct. As God will deliver his church for the time to come, so this is one main argument that he will do it, experience of former favours and deliverances.

This St Paul useth familiarly, 'I was delivered out of the mouth of the lion,' and 'the Lord shall deliver me from every evil work, and preserve me to his heavenly kingdom,' 2 Tim. iv. 17, 18—a blessed arguing. So David argues, 'God delivered me from the bear and the lion, and therefore he will deliver me from this uncircumcised Philistine,' 1 Sam. xvii. 37. So Jacob pleads, that God would deliver him from Esau. He had had

* That is, = 'defeat.'—G.

experience of God's mercy till then, and therefore he trusted that God would deliver him from Esau.

It is a good argument, to plead experience to move God to care for us for the time to come.

It was used by the Head of the church, by the body, the church, and by every member of the church.

1. It was used by *the Head*, Ps. xxii., which is a psalm made of Christ, ' I was cast on thee from my mother's womb, therefore be not far from me.'

It was typically true of David, and it was true of the Son of David.

2. So *the church pleads with God* in divers places, in Isa. li. 2, God calls to his people to make use of former experience. ' Look to Abraham your father, and to Sarah that bare you,' &c. Look to former times, ' to the rock whence you were hewn, and to the hole of the pit whence you were digged.' He that was your God then, is your God now. ' Look to Abraham, your father,' and from thence reason till now. So in Isa. lxiii. 7, ' I will mention the lovingkindness of the Lord, and the praise of the Lord, according to the great goodness of the Lord bestowed upon us.' ' In all their afflictions he was afflicted,' &c. He speaks of former experience : 'In love he bare them, and carried them all the days of old.' So in Ps. xliv. 1, ' Our fathers have told us ' this and this. So both the Head of the church and the church itself, plead with God from former experience, and God calls them to former experience : ' Remember the rock whence you where hewn.' And he upbraids them, because they forgat the works done to their fathers, in Ps. cv., and divers others. He objects to them that they did not make use of God's former favours, ' They forgot their Saviour, that had done great things in Egypt,' &c., Ps. cvi. 11, 12. They forgat his former favours. And in the 13th verse of that psalm, ' They soon forgat his works, and waited not for his counsel.'

And so it is with every particular saint of God. They have reasoned from experience of God's favours, from the time past to the time to come. The Psalms are full of it. Among the rest, ' I remembered the days of old, and meditated on all thy works ; I mused on the works of thy hands,' Ps. cxliii. 5. And in Ps. cxvi. 3, ' The sorrows of death,' (as the apostle saith here, ' I was delivered from so great a death,') ' the sorrows of death compassed me, the pains of hell took hold on me. I found sorrow and trouble. I cried unto the Lord : O Lord, I beseech thee, deliver my soul. The Lord preserveth the simple : I was brought low, and he helped me.' What doth he build on that ? ' Return unto thy rest, O my soul ; the Lord hath dealt bountifully with thee. Thou hast delivered my soul from death, mine eyes from tears, and my feet from falling.' What will he do for the time to come ? ' I will walk before the Lord in the land of the living.' Thus we see how we may plead with God, as the psalmist doth excellently in Ps. lxxi. He goes along with God there from the beginning of his days, in verse 5. ' Thou hast been my hope, Lord, and my trust from my youth ; by thee I have been held from the womb ; thou tookest me out of my mother's bowels : my praise shall be continually of thee.' What doth he plead from this now, when he was old ? In verse 9, ' Cast me not off in the time of my old age ; forsake me not when my strength faileth.'

Why ? Thou hast been my God from my youth ; thou hast held me from the womb : therefore cast me not off in my old age, forsake me not when my strength faileth. So he pleads with God, verse 17, ' Lord, thou hast taught me from my youth ; now when I am old and grey-headed, forsake me not, till I have shewed thy strength to this generation, and thy power to every one that is to come.' Thus we see how the Spirit of God in his children makes a blessed use of former experience, to reason with God for the time to come ; and it will afford us arguments in all kinds. We may reason from former spiritual favours to spiritual favours. As for instance, God hath begun a good work in us, therefore ' He will finish it to the day of the Lord,' Phil. i. 6. ' His gifts and graces are without repentance,' Rom. xi. 29. And we may reason from spiritual favours past to all favours to come that are of a lower nature, Rom. viii. 32, ' He that spared not his own Son, but gave him to death for us all, how shall he not with him give us all things ? ' It is a strong reason. He hath done the greater, therefore he may well do the less. We may reason from one favour to another. Thus, from temporal to temporal. He hath delivered me, therefore if it be for his glory and my good he will deliver me. We may reason from once to all of the like, Ps. xxiii. 1, ' God is my shepherd,' &c. ' He hath been with me in the valley of death,' ver. 4. He hath shewed himself to be my shepherd in all my troubles. What doth he build on that, for the time to come ? ' Doubtless the loving-kindness of the Lord shall follow me all the days of my life,' ver. 6.

Use 1. This should teach us then, this holy practice, *to lay up observations of God's dealing*, and to take them as so many pawns and pledges to move God for the time to come to regard us. It is wondrous pleasing to him. It is no argument to prevail if we come to men, to say, you have done this for me, therefore you will ; because man hath a finite power which is soon drawn dry. But God is infinite. He is a spring. He can create new. What he hath done he can do, and more too. He is where he was at the first, and will be to the end of the world. He is never at a loss. Therefore it is a strong argument to go to God, and say, 'Lord, thou art my God from the womb,' thou hast delivered me from such a danger, and such an exigence. When I knew not what to do, thou madest open a way. I see by evident signs it was thy goodness, thou art alway like thyself, to be the same God now. Therefore we should treasure up observations of God's dealing with us.

Use 2. And *consider with them the promises*, and see how God hath made good his promise by experience, and then join both together, and we may wrestle with God. Lord, thou hast promised thus and thus, nay, I have had the performance of this promise in former times. And now I stand in need of the performance of that promise which before I have had experience of.

Use 3. And *desire God by his Spirit to sanctify our memories*, that we may remember fit deliverances, and fit favours, that when the time shall come we may have arguments from experience. What is the reason that we sink in temptation ? that we are to seek when troubles come ? It is from baseness of heart, that though God have manifested his care and love to us by thousands of experiments,* yet we are ready upon every new trouble to call all into question, as if he had never been a good God to us. This is base infidelity of heart ; and our neglecting to treasure up blessed experiments of God's former favour.

It should be the wisdom of every Christian to be well read in the story of his own life, and to return back in his thoughts what God hath done for him, how God hath dealt with him for the time past, what he hath wrought in him by his Holy Spirit. Let us make use of it, both in outward and in inward troubles, in disconsolations of spirit, and in inward desertions ; let

* That is, ' experiences.'—G.

us call to mind what good soever hath been wrought in us, by such a means, by such an ordinance, by such a book, by such an occasion.

Let us call to mind how effectually God hath wrought in us in former times, and make use of this in the midst of the hour of darkness, when God seems to hide his face from us.

I see not the sun in a cloudy day, yet notwithstanding the sun is in the sky still. At midnight we hope for the morning. The morning will undoubtedly come, though it be midnight for the present. So David comforted himself in Ps. lxxvii. 11, ' I will remember the works of the Lord; surely I will remember thy wonders of old, I will meditate of all thy works, and talk of thy doings,' &c. See his infirmity. When he was in trouble of mind, his sins began to upbraid him that God had left him. ' I said in my infirmity, God hath forgotten me, &c., and hath God forgotten to be gracious ? hath he shut up his tender mercies in displeasure ? then saith he, this was my infirmity, but I will remember the years of the right hand of the Most High,' &c. And the same he hath in many other places, as Ps. cxliii. 4, 5.

It argues the great weakness of our nature, which is ready to distrust God upon every temptation of Satan, as if God had never dealt graciously with us, as if God were changeable like ourselves. Let us labour to support ourselves in the time of temptation with the former experience of God's gracious goodness, and his blessed work upon our souls. He that delivered us from the power of Satan, and keeps us from him still, that we sink not into despair, he will keep us for the time to come, so that ' neither things present, nor things to come,' as the apostle saith, ' shall be able to separate us from the love of God in Christ,' Rom. viii. 35. And let us, as it were, make diaries of God's dealing to us. This is to be acquainted with God, as Job speaks, Job xxii. 21 ; this is to walk with God, to observe his steps to us, and ours to him. It is a thing that will wondrously strengthen our faith, especially in old years, in gray hairs. What a comfortable thing is it when an aged man can look back to the former part of his life, and can reckon how God hath given him his life again and again ! how God hath comforted him in distress ! how God hath raised him up in the midst of perplexity, when he knew not which way to turn him, how God comforted him when he was disconsolate ! All these meeting together, in our last conflict, when all comfort will be little enough, what a comfort will it be !

And those that disfurnish themselves by their negligence and carelessness of such blessed helps, what enemies are they to their own comfort !

Therefore consider God's dealing, remember it, observe it, think of it, and desire God's Spirit to help your minds and memories herein, that nothing may be lost. For, I say, all will be little enough, the comforts of others, our own experience, the promises of Scripture, our hearts are so ready to sink, and to call in question God's truth, and Satan will ply us so in the time of temptation.

Especially those that are old and grow into years, they should be rich in these experiments, and able even to have a story of them. We should be able to make a book of experiments from our childhood. God's care to every man in particular, it is as if there were none but he, and there is no man that is a Christian but he observes God's ways to him, that he can say, God cares for me as if he cared for none but me. Let us, therefore, treasure up experiments. We see one notable example in David, how he pleads with God, Ps. lxxi. 3, from his former experience, ' Be thou my

habitation, wherein I may continually rest: thou hast given command to
save me; for thou art my rock and my fortress.' Whatsoever is comfortable in the creature, God hath taken the name of it to himself, that in all
troubles we might fly to him as the grand deliverer; for it is he that delivers, whatsoever the means be, whether it be angels or men. It is he
that sets all on work. Therefore he is called a ' rock' and a ' fortress,' &c.
' Thou hast given command to save me,' Ps. lxxi. 3, that is, God hath the
command of all creatures. He can command the fish to give up Jonah.
He can command the devils to go out. Christ did it when he was on
earth in the days of his flesh. Therefore much more now he is in heaven. He can command winds and storms, and devils and all troubles.
He hath the command of all, as he saith to Elias, ' Behold, I have commanded a widow to feed thee,' 1 Kings xvii. 9. ' The hearts of kings
are in his hand, as the rivers of waters,' Prov. xxi. 1. He that commands the creatures can command deliverance, ' Thou hast commanded
to save me,' for the time past. What doth he say for the time to come?
' Deliver me, O God, from the wicked: thou art my hope and trust from
my youth, &c. Cast me not off in mine old age; when my strength faileth
me, forsake me not.' It is a good argument, ' Thou hast been my God
from my mother's womb, therefore cast me not off in my old age.'

Well! we see here the practice of God's children in all times. Let it be
a pattern for our imitation, that we ' do not forsake our own mercy,' as Jonah
saith, ii. 8.

When God hath provided mercy, and provided promises to help us with
experience, let us not betray all through unbelief, through base despair in
the time of trouble. If we had but only God's promise that he will be our
God, that he will forgive our sins, were not that enough? Is it not the
promise of God, of Jehovah, that is truth itself? But when he hath sweetened his promise by experience, and every experience is a pledge and an
earnest of a benefit to come, what a good God have we, that is content, not
only to reserve the joys of heaven for us, but to give us a taste, to give us
the assurance and earnest of the time to come, and, besides his promise, to
give us comfortable experience, and all to support our weak faith!

But remember withal that this belongs only to God's children, and in a good
cause. For wicked men to reason thus, ' He hath, and therefore he will,'
it is a dangerous argument. They must not trust former experience. We
must hope that God will continue as he hath been, upon this ground, that
we are his, or else the ground of the ruin of wicked men is presumption
that God will bear with them as he hath done. ' The king of Sodom' and
his people were rescued out of trouble by Abraham and the army that he
raised; yet they were pitifully consumed. not long after, by fire from heaven. Pharaoh was delivered by Moses's prayer. God delivered him from
ten plagues. They made not a good use of it, and they perished after
miserably in the Red Sea. Rabshakeh comes and tells of the former prosperity of Sennacherib, ' Where are the Gods of Hamath and Arpad,' &c.
2 Kings xviii. 34. Hath not my lord overcome all? Aye, but it was immediately before his reign.* Herod, he prospered, and had good success in
the beheading of James, and therefore he would set upon Peter. He
thought to trust to his former success. He was flushed in the execution of
James. He thought God hath given me success, and blessed me in this.
He thought God was of his mind, as it is, Ps. l. 21, ' Thou thinkest me to
be like thyself,' thou thinkest I hate those that thou hatest, that are my

* Qu, ' ruin?'—ED.

dear children. Therefore Herod presumed to go on and lay hold on Peter. But the church falls a-praying, and God smites Herod with a fearful death. He was eaten up with lice, with worms bred in his body, Acts xii. 23.

So I say it is no good argument to say, I have prospered in wicked courses, I do prosper, and therefore I shall prosper. I have gotten a great deal of goods by ill means, and I have kept such ill company; and though some mislike my courses, yet I hope to-morrow shall be as to-day, &c. Take heed, bless not thyself. ' God's wrath will smoke,' Deut. xxix. 20, against such. ' Treasure not up wrath unto thyself against the day of wrath,' Rom. ii. 5. Argue not so upon God's patience. It is an argument for God's children. He hath been my God, he is my God, and he will be my God. It is a sophism else for others, and as the prophet Amos saith, ' He that hath escaped the lion shall fall into the hands of the bear,' v. 19. So the wicked that escape one danger shall fall into another at length. It is no good argument for them to hope for the like of that they have had.

Nay, rather it is the worst outward sign in this world of a man in the state of reprobation, of a man hated of God, to prosper and have security in ill courses. God blesseth him, and lets him go on in smooth courses. As the streams of Jordan go on smooth and still, and then enter into the Dead Sea; so many men live and go on in smooth, easy courses, and we see at length they either end in despair, as Judas, or in deadness of heart, as Nabal. So that of all estates it is the most miserable when a man lives in a naughty course, and God interrupts him not in his course with some outward judgment. It is a reason only for the children of God to support themselves with, in a good cause, wherein they walk with a good conscience. Then they may say truly, God, that hath been my God till now, will be my God to the end of my days.

Use. Is God so constant to his children in his love, and in his fatherly care and providence, that whom he hath delivered, he doth deliver and will deliver? *Let us be constant in our service, and love back again.* Let us return the echo back again, and say, I have served God, I do serve God, and I will serve God; because he hath loved me, he doth love me, and he will love me. He hath delivered me, he doth deliver me, and he will deliver me. As he is constant in love to me, so will I be constant in respect, in reverence and obedience to him.

Therefore we see the saints of God, as God loves them from everlasting to everlasting, being Jehovah, as he never alters in his nature, so not in his love to them; so they never alter in their love to him. Therefore it is a clause in Scripture expressed by holy men, ' To whom be praise for ever,' Ps. cxi. 10. As they knew that he was their God for ever and for ever, so they purposed to be his people, and to praise him for ever and for ever. And because they cannot live here alway themselves, they desire that there may be a generation to praise him for ever and for ever, and they lay a plot and ground so much as they can, that God's name may be known, that religion may be propagated for ever. They know God is their God for ever. They know he is constant in love to them, and they are constant in their love to him, and for his glory, ' To whom be glory for ever.'

See here the happiness of a true Christian that is in covenant with God; he can say, I have had my happiness and my portion, I have it, and I shall have it for ever. Take a worldling, can he say so? He cannot. God will confound his insolence if he should say so. I have been rich, I have prospered in my course, I have attained to this and that means, I yet thrive, and I shall thrive, Aye, is it so? No! Thou buildest upon the sands. Howsoever God hath done, and howsoever he doth, thou canst not secure thyself for the time to come. Only the Christian that makes God his rock and his fortress, his shield and strong tower of defence, he may say he hath had that which is certain, he enjoys that which is immutable and constant. God is his portion, his eternal portion. He hath been good, he is good, and he will be good to eternity. No man else, that hath a severed happiness out of God, can say so.

A sound Christian, take him in all references of time, he is a happy man. If he look back, God hath delivered him from Satan, from hell and damnation, and many dangers. If he look to the present, he is compassed about with a guard of angels, and with the providence of God. God doth deliver him. He hath a guard about him that cannot be seen but with the eye of faith. The devil sees it well enough, as we see in Job, 'Thou hast hedged him about,' Job i. 10. How can I come to him? He looked about to see if he could come into Job, to see if the hedge had any breach, but there was none. God's providence compassed him about. God hath and doth deliver. And if he look to the time to come he will deliver, he seeth that 'neither things present, nor things to come, shall be able to separate him from the love of God,' Rom. viii. 38.

And this is not only true of outward dangers, but especially in spiritual. God hath been gracious. He hath given Christ. 'How shall he not with him give us all things?' Rom. viii. 32. A Christian is in the favour of God now, how shall he be* so for ever? He hath eternity, world without end, to comfort himself in, that God, as long as he is God, he hath comfort. As long as he hath a soul, so long Jehovah, the living God, will be his God, both of his body and soul. He is the 'God of Abraham,' therefore he will raise his body. He is the God 'that raiseth the dead,' and he will for ever glorify both body and soul in heaven.

Look which way he will, a Christian hath cause of much comfort. Why should he be dismayed with anything in the world? Why should he not serve God with all the encouragement that may be, when he hath nothing to care for but to serve him? As for matter of deliverance and protection, it belongs not to us, but to him. Let us do that that belongs to us, and he will do that that belongs to him, if 'we commit our souls to him as to a faithful Creator in well-doing; he hath delivered us, he doth deliver us, and he will deliver us, and preserve us to his heavenly kingdom.'

VERSE 11.

'*You also helping together by prayer for us.*' In these words the holy apostle sets down the subordinate means that God hath sanctified to continue deliverance to his children. 'He hath delivered, he doth deliver, and he will deliver us for the time to come.' Was this confidence of St Paul a presumption without the use of means? He will deliver us, 'you also helping together by prayer for us.' The chief cause doth not take away the subordinate, but doth establish it. And though God be the great deliverer, and 'salvation belong to the Lord,' Ps. iii. 8, as the Scripture speaks, salvation and deliverance it is his work; yet notwithstanding he hath, not for defect of power, but for the multiplication and manifestation of his goodness, ordained the subordinate means of deliverance; and as he will deliver, so he will deliver in his own manner and by his own means.

* Qu. 'not be?'—G.

He will deliver, but yet notwithstanding you must pray : ' you also helping together by prayer for us.'

The words have no difficulty in them, ' you helping together,' that is, you together joining in prayer with me. I pray for myself, and you together helping me by prayer, God will deliver me.

The points considerable in these words are these :—

First of all, that in the time of peril, or in the want of any benefit, the means to be delivered from the one, and to convey the other, *it is prayer*. God will do this, ' you praying.'

The second is this, *that God's children can pray for themselves*.

The third is, that notwithstanding, though they can pray for themselves, *yet they require** the joint help of others*, and they need the help of others.

The fourth is, *that our own prayers, and the prayers of others joining all together, is a mighty prevailing means for the conveying of all good, and for the removing of any ill*. God will ' deliver me, you helping by your prayers.'

Doct. Prayer is a means to convey all good, and to deliver from all ill.

Because God hath stablished this order, ' Call upon me in the day of trouble, and I will deliver thee,' Ps. l. 15. He joins deliverance to calling upon him. So in Ps. xci. 15, a notable place; besides others. Indeed, the psalms are wondrous full in this kind. ' He shall call upon me, and I will answer him ; I will be with him in trouble, I will deliver him, and honour him.' Mark it, ' He shall call upon me, and I will deliver him ; ' and more than so, for God's benefits are complete, he doth not only deliver, but he honours, ' I will deliver him, and advance him,' Ps. xci. 15. God doth not only deliver his children by prayer, but he ' delivers them from evil works, and preserves them to his heavenly kingdom.' He delivers them and advanceth them together. He doth not do his work by halves. ' The eyes of the Lord are over the righteous, and his ears are open to their cry,' Ps. xxxiv. 15. His eyes are upon them, to see their miseries and wants. Aye, but though his eyes be open, his ears must be open too, to hear their cry. If his eyes were open to see their wants, if his ears be not open to hear their cry, his children might be miserable still.

Sometimes God delivers wicked men. He preserves them. But the preservation of a wicked man is but a reservation of him for future judgment, to feed him for the slaughter ; and that deliverance is not worth the speaking of. But for his children, his eyes are open on them, and his ears to hear their cry. As they be in misery that he sees them, so they must cry that he may hear them. God hath stablished this order. He will deliver, but prayer is the means.

Now, the reason that he hath established this order,

It is for *his glory* [and] *our own good*.

Reason 1. It is for his own glory; because prayer gives him the glory of all his attributes. For when we go to him, do we not give him the glory of his omniscience, that he knows our hearts and knows our wants ? Do we not give him the glory of his omnipotence, that he can help us ? Do we not give him the glory of his omnipresence, that he is everywhere ? Do we not give him the glory of his truth, that he will make good his promise which we allege to him and press him with ? What a world of glory hath God by prayer.

Reason 2. And then *for our sakes* he hath established this order to convey all by prayer, to

(1.) Shew *our dependence on him.* For we being in such a low distance

* That is, = ' seek.'—G.

under God, it is good that we should know from whom we have all. Therefore, he will have us to pray to him. He commands it. Prayer is an act
of self-denial. It makes us to look out of ourselves higher. Prayer acknowledgeth that we have that which we have, not of ourselves, but from him.
Prayer argueth a necessary dependence upon him to whom we pray ; for if
we had it at home, we would not go abroad.

(2.) And then, again, it doth us good, because, as it gives God all the
glory, so likewise *it exerciseth all the graces in a man.* There is not a grace
but it is put into the fire, it is quickened and kindled by prayer. For it
sets faith on work to believe the promise. It sets hope on work to expect
the things prayed for. It sets love on work, because we pray for others
that are members of the church. It sets obedience on work, because we
do it with respect to God's command. Prayer sets humility on work. We
prostrate ourselves before God, and acknowledge that there is no goodness
or desert in us. There is not a grace in the heart but it is exercised in
prayer.

The devil knows it well enough, and therefore of all exercises he labours
to hinder the exercise of prayer, for he thinks then we fetch help against
him ; and, indeed, so we do. For in one prayer God is honoured, the church
is benefited, grace is exercised, the devil is vanquished. What a world of
good is by prayer ? So that God hath established this order upon great
reasons, fetched from our own comfort and good, and from his glory.

Since God hath established this order, away with idle suggestions, partly
carnal and partly devilish. God knows what we want, and God knew
before all time what we have need of, and he may grant it if he will. Aye,
but that God that decreed, at the same time that he decreed to convey good,
at the same time he decreed to convey it this way by prayer. Therefore,
let us not disjoin that which God hath joined. Christ knew that God decreed all, and yet spent whole nights in prayer. And who knew God's love
more than he ? Yet because as he was man he was a creature, because as
he was man he received good from his Father, to shew his dependence
he continually prayed, he sanctified everything by prayer. And all holy
men of God from the beginning, the more certain they were of anything by
promise, the more eager, and earnest, and fervent they were in prayer. It
was a ground of prayer. They knew that this was God's order. Therefore,
if they had a promise, they turned it into prayer presently.

The means of the execution of God's decree, and the decree itself of the
thing, they fall under the same decree. When God hath decreed to do
anything, he hath decreed to do it by these means. So prayer comes as
well within the decree as the thing prayed for. In Ezek. xxxvi. 37, ' I will
do this, but I will be inquired of by the house of Judah.' I will do it, but
they shall ask me, they shall seek to me first. So there is a notable place,
Phil. i. 19, ' I know that this shall turn to my salvation through your
prayers.' We must not, then, so reason as to make the chief cause to take
away the subordinate means ; but let us serve God's purpose and providence,
let us serve God's order. He hath stablished this order and course, let
us serve it. This is the obedience of faith, the obedience of a Christian.

Doct. 2. The second thing is, that

God's children are enabled to pray for themselves. I observe this the rather
because the vilest men that live, when they are in trouble, as Pharaoh, Oh,
go to Moses, let him pray for me ! He could not pray for himself. He
was such a desperate, wretched creature, he knew that God would not regard him. Therefore he saith, Go to Moses. And so Simon Magus, who

was a wretch, yet when Peter denounced a judgment against him, ' Pray thou that none of these things light upon me,' Acts viii. 24. You are accepted of God ; my conscience is so full of terror and horror, and so full of sin, that I dare not pray. A wicked man may desire others to pray for him ; but, alas ! his conscience is surprised with horror for his sins, and his purposes are so cruel, so earthly, and so base, that he knows he cannot pray with acceptance for himself. God's children, as they desire the prayers of others, so they can pray themselves. They do not desire that others should do all, but that they would ' help together with their prayers.'

Reason. Now, the reason of this, that God's children can pray for themselves, and must pray for themselves, it is because they are children ; and as soon as ever they are new born, they are known by their voice, by crying. A child, as soon as he is born, he cries. A new-born child cries as soon as he is new born. He cries, ' Abba, Father.' He goes to his Father presently. In Acts ix. 11, as soon as Paul was converted, he cries, he goes to God by prayer. Therefore God, when he directs Ananias to him, saith he, Go to such a place, and there thou shalt find Paul, ' he is praying.' As soon as he is converted he is praying.

God's children have the spirit of adoption, the spirit of sons. God is their Father, and they exercise the prerogative and privilege they have. They go to their Father, and cry to him. In Zech. xii. 10, you have there a promise ' that God would pour the Spirit of supplication ' upon his children. They cannot pray of themselves, but God pours a Spirit of supplication into their hearts ; and his Spirit being poured into them, they can pour forth their prayers to him again.

Use. The use of this is, not to content ourselves to turn over this duty of prayer to the minister and to good people, ' Oh, pray you for us.' Aye, we do so ; but pray for thyself. If thou wilt have another man's prayers do thee good, thou must help with thy own prayers, be good thyself.

Men turn it off with slight phrases and speeches, ' You must pray for us,' &c.

Alas ! what will our prayers do thee good if thou be a graceless, blasphemous, carnal, brutish person ? If thy conscience tell thee by the light of nature (for the word of God it may be thou dost not care for) that thou art so, what can our prayers do thee good ? If thou mean to be so, though Noah, Daniel, and Job, saith God, should stand before me for this people, I would regard them for themselves, I would not hear them for this people, Ezek. xiv. 14. Let us be able and willing to help ourselves, and then we shall pray to some purpose.

God loves to hear the cries of his children. The very broken cries of a child are more pleasing than the eloquent speech of a servant. Sometimes the children of God have not the Spirit of prayer as at other times ; and then they must do as Hezekiah did, they must ' mourn as a dove, and chatter as a swallow,' Isa. xxxviii. 14. And as Moses at the Red Sea, he cried, and the Lord heard his prayer, though he spake never a word. So in Rom. viii. 26, ' The Spirit teacheth us to sigh and groan.'

When we cannot pray, we must strive with ourselves against unbelief, and deadness of heart, by all means possible. Sighs and groans are prayers to God, ' My groans and my sighs are not hid from thee,' saith the prophet David, Ps. xxxviii. 9. And so in Lam. iii. 56, the church being in distress, saith she, ' Thou hast heard my voice, hide not thine ear at my breathing.' Sometime the children of God can only sigh, and breathe, and groan to God ; for there is such a confusion in their thoughts, they are so amazed at their troubles, they are so surprised that they cannot utter a distinct prayer; and then they sigh, and breathe, and groan; they help themselves one way or other. If thou be a child of God, though thou be oppressed with grief, yet cry and groan to God, strive against thy grief all thou canst; and though thou canst not cry distinctly, yet mourn as well as thou canst, and God knows the groans of his own Spirit, and those cries are eloquent in his ears, they pierce heaven. But this being but supposed as a ground, the third observation is, as God conveys all blessings by prayer, and God's children have a spirit of prayer; so *God's children desire the prayers of others, and it is the duty of others to pray for them.* 'You also helping by your prayer for us.'

Doctrine 3. *Christians ought to help one another by prayer.*

The holy and blessed apostle was sure of God's love to him, and of his care of him; yet notwithstanding he was as sure that God would use both the prayers of himself and others to continue this his goodness to him; and therefore the greater faith, the greater care of prayer. And where there is no care of prayer, either of our own or of others for us, there is no faith at all.

There is an article of our faith, which, I think, is little believed. Though it be said over much, and heard often, yet it is little practised, ' I believe in the communion of saints.' Is there a communion of saints? wherein doth this communion stand? Among many other things, in this, that one saint prays for another.

This is one branch of the communion of saints, as they communicate in privileges; for they are all the sons of God, they are all heirs of heaven, they are all members of Christ, they are all redeemed by the blood of Christ; and so all other privileges belong to all alike. As there is a communion in privileges, so there is a communion in duties one to another. One prays for another. There is a mutual intercourse of duty. And those that truly believe the communion of saints, do truly practise the duties belonging to that blessed society, that is, they pray for one another. I mean here on earth. Here we have a command, here we have a promise, here we have mutual necessities. I have need of them, and they have need of me. We have need one of another.

In heaven there is no such necessity; yet there may be, as divines grant, a general wish for the church, because the saints want their bodies, and because they want the accomplishment of the elect.

Where there is want of happiness, there will be a general desire that God would accomplish these days of sin; but for any particular necessities of ours, they cannot know them. ' Abraham hath forgotten us, and Israel knows us not,' Is. lxiii. 16. There is a communion of saints, and this blessed communion and society trade this way in praying for one another. God commands that we should ' pray one for another,' James v. 13, 14.

Every Christian is a priest and a prophet. Now the priest's duty was to pray, and the prophet's duty was to pray. Now, as the priest carried the tribes on his breast, only to signify that he had them in his heart, and that he was a type of Christ, who hath us in his heart alway in heaven, to make intercession for us; so in some sense, every true Christian is a priest. He must carry the church and people of God in his heart. He must have a care of others. He must not only pray for himself, but for others, as he himself would have interest in the common prayer, ' Our Father,' as Christ teacheth us. Not that a Christian may not say, ' My Father,' when we have particular ground and occasion to go to God. But Christ being to direct the Church of God, he teacheth us to say, ' Our Father.' There is therefore a regard to be had by every true Christian of the estate of others.

Reason. The reason is, God's children sometimes cannot so well pray. Though they have alway a spirit of prayer, that they can groan to God, yet in some cases they cannot so well pray for themselves, as in sickness. Affliction is a better time to pray in than sickness ; for affliction gathers and unites the spirits together. It makes a man more strong to pray to God. But sickness distempers the powers of the soul. It distempers the instruments that the soul works by. It distempers the animal spirits which the understanding useth. They are inflamed, and distempered, and confused. Now the spirits, that are the instruments of the soul, being troubled with sickness, sickness is not so fit a time for a man to pray for himself. Though God hear the groans of his Spirit, as David saith, ' My sighs are not hid from thee,' Ps. xxxviii. 9 ; yet notwithstanding it is good at this time to send for those that can make a more distinct prayer, though, it may be, they be great Christians. Therefore, saith St James, ' Is any man afflicted ? let him pray ; is any man sick ? let him send for the elders of the church, and let them pray for him,' James v. 13, 14 ; not that he is not able to pray for himself, but let them help by joining together with him to God, ' And the prayer of faith shall save the sick, and the Lord shall raise him up.'

Nay, I add more, for the illustration of the point, it is so true that God regards the prayers of one for another, that he regards the prayer of weak ones, for grand ones. Great Christians are helped by mean ones ; yea, pastors are helped by the people. St Paul, a man eminent in grace and place, a grand Christian, and for place an apostle, yet he was helped by the prayers of the weak Corinthians. So that a weak Christian in grace and place, may help a greater Christian than himself, both in grace and in place. Parents are helped by the prayers of their children. Magistrates by those that are under them. The rich are helped by those that are poor. The ministers by the prayers of the people, ' You helping by your prayers.' The prayers of the people prevail for the ministers ; for though there be a civil difference which shall all end in death, yet notwithstanding in the communion of saints, there is no difference. ' A poor man may be rich in faith,' as St James saith, ii. 5, and one may have as much credit in the court of heaven as another. As St Austin saith well, God hath made the rich for the poor, and the poor for the rich : the rich to relieve the poor, and the poor to pray for the rich ; for herein one is accepted for another.

St Paul stands much upon the virtue and efficacy of the prayers of the Corinthians, for himself a great apostle. And so in Rom. xv. 30, ' I beseech you for the love of Christ, and for the blessed work of the Spirit, strive by prayer together with us.' As ever you felt Christ do good to you, and as ever you felt the efficacy of the Spirit, strive with God, wrestle by prayer for me ; and so in every epistle he begs their prayers.

And ministers need the prayers of people to God, as well as any other, or rather more ; for, as God conveys much good to others by them, so Satan maligns them more than other men. ' Aim not at small nor great, but at the King of Israel,' 1 Kings xxii. 31, pick out him. So the devil aims not at small nor great, but at the guides of God's people, at the leaders of his army. ' I will smite the Shepherd, and the sheep shall be scattered,' Zech. xiii. 7.

Therefore pray for them, that they may have abilities, that they may have parts and gifts, and that they may have a willing mind, a large heart to use them, that they may have success in using them, that they may have strength of the outward man, that they may have protection from unreasonable men, ' Pray for us, that we may be delivered from unreasonable and absurd men,' 2 Thess. iii. 1, 2. ' Absurd men ; ' for none but absurd men will wrong those that God conveys so much good by, as he doth by the ministry. It is their lot to be vexed with such men ofttimes; and, therefore, pray for us.

What is the reason of this, that mean Christians may help great Christians by their prayers ?

God will have it thus. Great Christians have not the spirit of prayer alike at all times. Though it be supposed they have it, yet the more help there is, the more hands are put to the work, the sooner it is despatched. As in the removing of a burden, the more join together, the sooner it is removed ; and so in the drawing of anything, the more hands, the speedier despatch.

So when we would draw blessings from heaven, the more prayers there be that offer violence to God, the more we draw from him. If it be a judgment that hangs over our heads, the more there be that labour to put away the judgment by prayer, and to remove the cloud that hangs over our heads, the sooner it passeth by. Many help much, as many brands make a great fire ; and many little rivers running into a common channel, they make the river swell greater ; so prayer is strong when it is carried by the spirits of many ; yea, those that are not, perhaps, so well experienced.

But, as I said, sometimes men not only great in place, but great in grace, need the help of others. The spirit of prayer is not in a like measure in them. Sometime they are too secure, sometime they are too presumptuous, sometime too negligent and careless, in stirring up the grace of God in them, sometime they are prone to be lifted up too much, sometime to be cast down too much.

If this be so, what a benefit is this then to have the help of others ? when ofttimes a man meaner in gifts may have as great a measure of the spirit of prayer as another.

Prayer, it is not a work of gifts, but of grace. It is a work of a broken heart, of a believing heart.

And in prayer there be divers gifts which are far more eminent in one than in another, yet all excellent good in their kind. Some have the gift to be fluent, to be large in words, in explication of themselves. Some men have not so much in that, but they have a broken heart. Some again have it in zeal and earnestness of affections. So that there is something in the very action of prayer which helps in many. One helps with his ability, with his large gift of speech ; another with his humble and broken spirit ; another with his zeal and ardency to wrestle and strive with God to get a blessing.

Moses was a man of a stammering tongue, and yet Moses was a man for prayer. Aaron and Hur were silent, and were fain to hold up his hands, but Moses must pray ; and yet Moses was no man of eloquence, and he pretends that for his excuse when he was to go to Pharaoh, Exod. iv. 13.

Therefore it is a matter of the heart, a matter of grace, of humility, of strong faith, and not a matter of words, though that be a special gift too.

Reason 1. God will have it thus in his wise dispensation, *because he will have every man esteemed, and because he will have no man to be proud.* He will humble his own to let them know that they stand in need of the prayers of the weakest. Every man in the church of God hath some gifts, that none should be despised; and none have all gifts, that none should presume over-much and be proud. In the church of God, in the body of Christ, there is no idle member. In the communion of saints there is none unprofitable. Every one can do good in his kind.

Reason 2. God will have this, because *he will have none despised.* It was a fault in St James's time, ' The brother of high degree,' James i. 9, did despise the brother of low degree, that is, the rich Christians despised the poor Christians. But saith St James, ' Hath not God chosen the poor in the world, rich in faith ?' James ii. 5. Now faith is the ground of prayer. It is a fault in all times. Men have swelling conceits against the meaner sort, and undervalue them. God will not have it so. He will have us see that we stand in need of the meanest Christians; and by this he will raise up the dejected spirit of weak Christians.

What a comfort is it then, that I should be able to help the greatest man in the world ? That he should be beholden to me for that duty ? So it abaseth the greatest, that they stand in need of the meanest; and it raiseth the meanest, that the greatest are helped by them, and it knits all into a sweet communion. For when a great Christian shall think, yonder poor Christian, he is gracious in the court of heaven ! Howsoever he be neglected in the world, he may do me good by his prayers. It will make him esteem and value him the more, and it will make him value his friendship. He will not disparage him. He will not grieve the spirit of such a one, whose prayer may prevail with God, and draw down a blessing for him. We see here the Corinthians help the apostle by their prayers.

You see the reason of it, that God will knit Christians together; and humble them that think themselves great, and that he might comfort every mean Christian.

Use 1. Therefore *let no Christian slight his own prayers, no, not those that are young ones.* That great divine Paulus Phagius, who was a great Hebrecian in his time, and one that helped to restore the gospel in England (*ee*), it was a good speech of him, he was wont to say, ' I wish the prayers of younger scholars; for their souls are not tainted with sin, and God often hears the poor young ones (that are not tainted, and soiled with the sins of the world, as others are) sooner than others. A weak Christian, that hath not a politic head and a devilish spirit, meaner persons that are but young ones, they have more acquaintance, many times, with God than others.' Despise not the prayer of any. And let none despise his own prayer. Shall I pray to God, will some say ? I pray! do you pray for me. Why dost thou not pray for thyself ? I am unworthy. Unworthy ? Dost thou so basely esteem of it, when God is not only willing that thou shouldst pray for thyself, but requires thee to pray for others ? Hast thou so base an esteem of this incense ? ' Let my prayers be directed in thy sight as incense,' saith David, Ps. cxli. 2. God esteems this as odour, and wilt thou say, I am not worthy ? Abase not that which he hath vouchsafed so to honour. God esteems so highly of it, that he will not only hear thy prayers for thyself, but for others.

Use 2. Again, *there is no pretence for any man to be idle in the profession of religion.* Thou hast not riches, thou canst not give ; thou hast not place, thou canst not shew countenance to others ; but if thou be a child of God, thou hast the Spirit of prayer, the Spirit of adoption, the Spirit of a son in thee, which enables thee to pray for thyself and others. There is no Christian but he may do this, ' You also helping together by your prayers for me.'

The fourth and last observation out of these words is, that

Doct. 4. *Prayer is a prevailing course with God.*

It prevails for the removing of ill, or for the preventing of ill, or for the obtaining of good, 'I shall be delivered,' I shall be continued in the state of deliverance ; but yet you must pray. Your prayers will obtain and beg this of God.

Reason 1. Prayer is a prevailing course, because, as I said, it is obedience to God's order. He bids us call upon him, and he will hear us. Prayer binds him with his own promise. Lord, thou canst not deny thyself, thou canst not deny thy promise, thou hast promised to be near all those that call upon thee in truth ; and though with much weakness, yet we call upon thee in truth ; therefore we cannot but be persuaded of thy goodness that thou wilt be near us. So it is a prevailing course, because it is obedience to God's order.

Reason 2. And *it is a prevailing course,* because likewise it sets God on work. Faith, that is in the heart, and that sets prayer on work, for prayer is nothing but the voice of faith, the flame of faith. The fire is in the heart and spirit, but the voice, the flame, the expression of faith, is prayer. Faith in the heart sets prayer on work. What doth prayer ? That goes into heaven, it pierceth heaven, and that sets God on work ; because it brings him his promise, it brings him his nature. Thy nature is to be Jehovah, good and gracious, and merciful to thine ! thy promise is answerable to thy nature, and thou hast made rich and precious promises. As faith sets prayer on work, so prayer sets God on work ; and when God is set on work by prayer (as prayer must needs bind him, bringing himself to himself, bringing his word to him ; every man is as his word, and his word is as himself), God being set on work, he sets all on work. He sets heaven and earth on work, when he is set on work by prayer. Therefore it is a prevailing course. He sets all his attributes on work for the deliverance and rescue of his church from danger, and for the doing of any good. He sets his mercy and goodness on work, and his love, and whatsoever is in him.

You see then why it is a prevailing course, because it is obedience to God, and because it sets God on work. It overcomes him which overcomes all. It overcomes him that is omnipotent. We see the woman of Canaan, she overcame Christ by the strength that she had from Christ. And Moses he overcame God, ' Let me alone,' Exod. xxxii. 10, why dost thou press me ? ' Let me alone.' It offers violence to God, it prevails with him ; and that which prevails with God, prevails with all things else. The prayer of faith hath the promise. ' The prayer of a righteous man,' in faith, ' it prevails much,' saith St James, v. 16. Consider now, if the prayer of one righteous man prevail much, what shall the prayer of many righteous men do ? As St Paul saith here, my prayers and your prayers being joined together must needs prevail.

For instances, the Scripture is full of them, how God hath vouchsafed deliverance by the help of prayer. I will give but a few instances of former times, and some considerations of later time.

For former times : in Exod. xvii., you see when Amalek set upon the people, Moses did more good by prayer than all the army by fighting. As long as Moses' hands were held up by Aaron and Hur, the people of God prevailed : a notable instance to shew the power of prayer. In 2 Chron xiv., Asa prayed to God, and presseth God with arguments, and the people of God prevail. In 2 Chron. xx., there you have good king Jehoshaphat. He prays to God, and he brings to God his former experience. He presseth God with his covenant, with his nature, and the like arguments spoken of

before ; and then he complains of their necessity, ' Lord we know not what
to do, our eyes are towards thee,' 2 Chron. xx. 12. And God's opportunity
is when we are at the worst, and the lowest. Then he is near to help,
' We know not what to do, but our eyes are towards thee,' saith that blessed
king, and then he prevailed.

So the prophet Isaiah and Hezekiah, they both join together in prayer
to God, and God heard the prophet, and the prayer of the king. They
spread the letter before the Lord, and prayed to God, when Rabshakeh railed
against God, and they prevailed mightily, Isa. xxxvii. 14.

Esther was but a woman, and a good woman she was. The church was
in extremity in her time. She takes this course. She fasted and prayed,
she and her people ; and we see what an excellent issue came of it, the confusion of proud Haman, and the deliverance of the church. In Acts xii.,
Herod having good success in the beheading of James, being flushed with
the blood of James, he would needs set upon Peter too. The church, fearing the loss of so worthy a pillar, falls to praying. See the issue of it, God
struck him presently. Woe be to the birds of prey, when God's turtle
mourns ! When God's turtle, the church, mourns, and prays to God, woe
be to those birds that violently prey on the poor church ! Woe be to Herod,
and all bloody persecuting tyrants ! Woe be to all malignant despisers of
the church, when the church begins to pray ! For though she direct not
her prayers against them in particular, yet it is enough that she prays for
herself, and herself cannot be delivered without the confusion of her enemies.
You see these instances of old.

I will name but some of later times. What hath not prayer done ? Let
us not be discouraged. Prayer can scatter the enemies, and move God to
command the winds, and the waters, and all against his enemies. What
cannot prayer do, when the people of God have their hearts quickened, and
raised to pray ? Prayer can open heaven. Prayer can open the womb.
Prayer can open the prison, and strike off the fetters. It is a pick-lock.
We see in Acts xvi., when St Paul was cast in prison, he prayed to God
at midnight, and God shakes the foundations of the prison, and all flies
open, Acts xvi. 26. So St Peter was in prison, he prays, and the angel
delivers him, Acts v. 19. What cannot prayer do ? It is of an omnipotent power, because it prevails with an omnipotent and almighty God.

Oh that we were persuaded of this ! But our hearts are so full of
atheism naturally, that we think not of it. We think not that there is such
efficacy in prayer ; but we cherish base conceits, God may if he will, &c.,
and put all upon him, and never serve his providence and command, who
commands us to call upon him, and who will do things in his providence,
but he will do them in this order. We must pray, first to acknowledge our
dependence upon him. If we were thoroughly convinced of the prevailing
power of prayer, what good might be done by it, as there hath been in
former times ! Certainly we would beg of God above all things the spirit
of supplication. And if we have the spirit of prayer, we can never be
miserable. If a man have the spirit of prayer, whatsoever he want he
causeth it from heaven. He can beg it by prayer. And if he want* the
thing he can beg contentation,† he can beg patience, he can beg grace, and
beg acquaintance with God ; and acquaintance with God it will put a glory
upon him.

It is such a thing as all the world cannot take from us. They cannot take
God from us, they cannot take prayer from us. If we were convinced of

That is, ' be without' = denied.—G.   * That is, ' contentment.'—G.

this we would be much in prayer, in private prayer, in public prayer, for ourselves, for the church of God.

The church of God now abroad, you see, is in combustion. If the Spirit of God in any measure and degree be in our breasts, we will sympathize with the state of the church. We wish them well, it may be; but wishes are one thing, and prayer is another. Dost thou pray for the church? If we could pray for the church, it would be better. We should do more good with our prayers at home than they shall do by fighting abroad; as Moses did more good in the mount by prayer than they did in the valley by fighting. Undoubtedly it would be so.

We may fear the less success, the spirits of men are so flat and so dead this way. The time hath been not long since that we have been stirred up more to pray, upon the apprehension of some fears, to pray with earnestness and feeling, expressing some desire in wishing their welfare; but now a man can hardly converse with any that have so deep an apprehension as they have had in former times.

Now therefore, as we desire to have interest in the good of the church, so let us remember to present the estate of the church to God. And let us present the church of God to him as his own, as his turtle, as his love.

You know when they would move Christ, they tell him, ' Him whom thou lovest is sick,' Lazarus ' whom thou lovest,' John xi. 3. So, Lord, her whom thou lovest, the church, whom thou gavest thy Son to redeem with his blood; the church to whom thou hast given thy Spirit to dwell in; the church wherein thou hast thy habitation amongst men; the church that only glorifieth thee, and in whom thou wilt be eternally glorified in heaven, that church is sick, it is weak, it is in distress, it is in hazard.

Let us make conscience of this duty, let us help the church with our prayers. St Paul saith, ' I shall be delivered, together with the help of your prayers,' Philem. 22. Without doubt the church should be delivered, if we had the grace to help them with our prayers. And God will so glorify the blessed exercise of calling upon him, that we, I say, shall do more good at home than they shall do abroad. Let us believe this; it is God's manner of dealing.

In the book of Judges, in that story of the Benjamites, concerning the wrong done to the priest's concubine, the rest of the tribes of Israel, when they set on the Benjamites, they asked counsel of God twice, and went against them, and were discomfited; but the third time they come to God, Judges xx. 26, ' Then all the children of Israel came to the house of the Lord, and wept, and sat there before the Lord; and fasted that day till the evening.' They thought because they had a good cause, they might without fasting and prayer, and without seeking to the Lord, prevail, and therefore they went against them twice, and were shamefully foiled, to their great loss. But when at the last they came and humbled themselves before God, and fasted, and inquired of God the cause of that ill, after that they had a glorious victory.

Christ tells his disciples that there were some kind of devils that will not be cast out by fasting and prayer, Mat. xvii. 21. So there are some kind of miseries, some kind of calamities, some kind of sins, that will not be overcome, and which God will not deliver the church from, but by fasting and prayer.

And so for private Christians, they have some sins that are master-sins, personal sins. It is not a slight prayer and a wish that will mortify them. There must be fasting, and prayer, and humiliation; and that way those devils are cast out. I would we were persuaded of it, that it is such a prevailing thing, holy prayer, to help ourselves in sin, and to help us in misery, to help the church of God.

Use. Well, since the prayers even of the meanest Christians are so prevailing, let us learn *to respect them ;* for, as they can pray, so their prayers will prevail. And take heed we grieve not the Spirit of God in any poor saint, that so they may pray for us with willingness and cheerfulness. Do but consider what a blessing it is to have a stock going, to have our part in the common stock. As there is a common stock of prayer in the church, every Christian can pray, and pray prevailingly. What a blessing is it to be a good Christian, to have a portion in the prevailing prayers of others ! That when a man is dead and dull, and unfit himself, this may comfort him, that others have the spirit of zeal, and will supply his want. It is a blessed thing ! Let us consider the excellency of this duty of prayer, from the prevalency of it, to whet us on to the exercise of it. It is a happiness to have a part in it. It is a blessing whereby we can do good to others. We can reach them that are many hundred miles off, those that be at the farthest end of the world. When we cannot reach them other ways, we can reach them by prayer. We cannot speak to them, they are far off, but we can speak to God for them ; and he can convey that good to them that we desire. What a blessed condition is this !

Quest. But some man may say, How shall I know that I can pray, that I am in a state to help the church of God, and to prevail for it by my prayers ?

1. I answer, first of all, thou shalt know it *if thou be as willing to help otherwise, if thou canst, as well as by prayer.* St James speaks in his time of certain men that would feed the poor people of God with good words, James ii. 16. Now good words are good-cheap ; but they will do nothing. They will buy nothing, they will not clothe, nor feed. So St James tells them, that that is but a dead faith.

So there are a company that will only pray for the church when they are able to do other ways, when they have countenance, and estate, and riches, and friends, and place, and many things that they might improve for the good of others, and for the good of the church. Some will be ready to say, I pray for the church, and I will pray. Aye, but art thou not able to do somewhat else ? St Paul when he wishes them to pray for him, he means not only prayer, but that duty implies to do all that they pray for, to help their prayers, or else it is a mocking of God. If thou pray aright for the church, thou art willing to relieve them; if thou pray for thy friend, thou art willing to help him, and succour him ; if thou pray for any, thou art willing to countenance them. That is one trial, which discovers many to be hypocrites. If their prayers were worth anything, and the times stood in need of them, it is likely they should not have them, because they only give good words, and nothing else.

2. Again, he that is in a state of prayer, he must be such a one *as must relinquish in his purpose all wicked, blasphemous, scandalous, unthrifty courses whatsoever.* He that purposeth to please God, and to have his prayer accepted of God, he must leave all. For as the Psalmist saith, ' If I regard iniquity in my heart, the Lord will not hear my prayer.' For a man to come with a petition to God, with a purpose to offend him, is to come to practise treason in the presence-chamber ; to come into the presence of God, and to have a purpose to stab him with his sins. Dost thou purpose to live in thy filthy courses, in thy scandalous evil course of life, to be a

blasphemer, a swearer, and yet dost thou think that God will hear and regard thy prayer ? ' If I regard iniquity in my heart, the Lord will not hear my prayer,' Ps. lxvi. 18. That is another thing that thou mayest know it by, whether thou be in such an estate as that thou mayest pray successfully for thyself, and for others.

3. In Prov. xxviii. 9, there is a third discovery, ' He that turns his ear from hearing the law, even his prayer shall be abominable.' Thou mayest know it by this, if thou be in such an estate as that God will regard thy prayers for thyself or for others, that they may be prevailing prayers ; how standest thou affected to God's truth and word ? how art thou acquainted with the reading of the Scriptures, and with hearing the blessed word of God unfolded and broken open by the blessed ordinance of God ? How doest thou attend upon God ? Wouldst thou have him who is the great God of heaven and earth to hear thee, and to regard thee, when thou wilt not hear and regard him ? Thou wouldst have him to regard thy prayers, and thou regardest not him speaking by the ministry of his word. Thou despisest his ordinance which he hath left with thee. He hath left thee the mysteries of his word, and thou regardest them not, but spendest thy time altogether either about thy calling, or about some trifling studies, and neglectest the main, the soul-saving truth ; will he hear thy prayer ? No, saith the wise man ; ' He that turns his ear from hearing the law, that man's prayer shall be abominable.'

Since prayer is so prevailing a thing, so pleasing to God, so helpful to the church, and so helpful to ourselves, who would be in such a case that he cannot pray, or if he doth pray, that his prayer should be abominable, that God should turn his prayer into sin ? It is a miserable case that a man lives in, that is in league with sin, that allows himself in any wicked course, in rebellion to God's ordinance. Such men are in such a state that God doth not regard their prayers for themselves or for others. Some do so exalt and lift up their pride against God, that they do not regard the very ordinance of God. No, not while they are hearing it, but set themselves to be otherwise disposed at that very time. How can such expect that God will regard them ? This shall be sufficient to press that point. Saith Saint Paul, ' I shall be delivered by your prayers.'

Obs. God will deliver the ministers by the people's prayers.

God will be good to the ministers for the prayers of the people. This concerns us that are ministers. Prayer is prevailing even for us. And as it is our duty to give ourselves to preaching and prayer, so it is the people's duty to pray for us likewise, and for these particulars, as I named.

To pray for ability,—to pray for a willing mind to discharge that ability,—to pray for success of that discharge. For we must be able to preach to the people of God, and we must be willing, and there must be success. It doth much discourage God's people, and those that are ministers, when they find no success of their labours. Isa. xlix. 4, saith the prophet, ' I have laboured in vain.' Elias was much discouraged in his time, Romans xi. 4, 1 Kings xix. 18 ; and Isaiah and Elias were good men, yet they were much discouraged. They saw little fruit of their labour. Therefore let us help the ministers with our prayers in this respect, that God would enable them ; that God would enlarge their hearts with willingness. For there are many that are of ability, but they are so proud, and so idle, that they think themselves too good to preach to them, whom God and the church hath called them to bestow their labours on. They have ability, but they want a large heart. And those that have both ability and a large heart, they want success, they see little fruit; because the people pray not for them; and they perhaps are negligent in the duty themselves; their labours are not steeped in prayers.

Again, a fourth thing that we ought to pray for for them, *is strength and ability of the outward man;* and all that fear God, and have felt the benefit of the ministry, they do this, and God doth answer it.

Likewise to pray *for protection and deliverance from unreasonable men,* to pray for strength of spirit, and likewise for protection. For, as St Paul saith, ' All men have not faith. Pray for us, that we may be delivered from unreasonable, absurd men : all have not faith,' 2 Thess. iii. 2. Men that believe not God's truth, that believe not God's word, that are full of atheism, full of contempt and scorn, they are ' absurd men.' Though they think themselves the witty* men of the world, yet they are unreasonable and absurd men. ' Pray for us, that we may be delivered from unreasonable men.'

Likewise from him that *is the head of wicked men, the Devil.* He sees that the ministers they are the standard-bearers, they are the captains of God's army. They stand not alone, and they fall not alone. Many others fall with them. There is no calling under heaven by which God conveys so much good, as by the dispensation of his ordinance in the ministry ; therefore we should help them by our prayers. There are no men better if they be good, nor none more hurtful if they be bad ; none worse. As Christ saith, ' They are the salt of the earth,' to season the unsavoury world, ' and if the salt have lost the savour, it is good for nothing but to be cast on the dunghill,' Luke xiv. 34, 35. Therefore pray that God would deliver them from the devil, who maligns them. They are the butt† of his malice, by his instruments.

There are many that come to hear the word to carp, and to cavil, and to sit as judges to examine, but how few are there that pray for the ministers ! and surely, because they pray not, they profit not. If we could pray more, we should profit more. I beseech you in the bowels of Christ, put up your petitions to God, that God would teach us (that are inferior to you in other respects, setting aside our calling) that we may teach you, that we may instruct his people. As John Baptist saith, ' The friends of the bride learn of the bridegroom,' John iii. 29, what to speak to the spouse. So we learn from prayer, and from reading, we learn from Christ what to teach you. If you pray to God to teach us that we may teach you, you shall never go away without a blessing.

And therefore, as I said, we see how the apostle desires the Romans to strive and contend with him in prayer. He useth all protestations, and obtestations, ' For the love of Christ and of his Spirit,' &c., Romans xv. 30. And, pray for us, ' that the word may have a free passage, and be glorified,' 2 Thess. iii. 1. In every epistle still he urgeth, ' Pray for us.' The blessed apostle was so heavenly-minded, that he would neglect no help that might further him in the ministry. So if we have Christian hearts, we will neglect no helps, not the help of the meanest Christian that we are acquainted with. When he that was a great apostle saith, ' Pray for us, strive in prayer for us,' he prays for the help of others' prayer. So the more gracious we are, and the nearer to God, the more we understand the things of God, the more careful we shall be of this Christian duty of prayer, for the ministers, and for ourselves, and others. Upon this ground, that it is God's ordinance ; and there is nothing established by God that shall

* That is, ' wise.'—G.   † That is, ' mark.'—G.

want a blessing. Therefore if we have faith, we will pray; the more faith the more prayer; the greater faith the greater prayer. Christ had the greatest faith, and he prayed whole nights together. St Paul was mighty in faith; he was mighty in prayer. Where there is little faith, there will be little prayer; and where there is no faith, there will be no prayer. ' You also helping together by prayer for us.'

Mark the heavenly art of the apostle. He doth here insinuate and en-wrap an exhortation by taking it for granted that they would pray for him. It is the most cunning way to convey an exhortation, by way of taking it for granted, and by way of encouragement. ' The Lord will deliver me.' He doth not say, therefore I pray help me by your prayers; but the Lord will deliver me if you help me, and I know I shall not want your prayers. He takes it for granted that they would pray for him; and granted truths are the strongest truths. It is the best way to encourage any man, if we know any good in him, to take it for granted that he will do so; and so ' I shall be delivered, you helping together by your prayers.'

' *That, for the gift bestowed upon us by the means of many persons, thanks may be given by many on our behalf.*' After he had set down the means that God would convey the blessing by, which was prayer, then he shews the end, why God would deliver him by prayer. For the gift of health and deliverance bestowed upon me, by the means of many prayers of many persons, ' likewise thanks shall be given by many on our behalf;' that is, on my behalf. Yea, as many shall be ready to thank God for my deliver-ance and health, as before many prayed to God for it. So that in this regard, God in love to his own praise and glory will deliver me by your prayers, because he shall gain praise, and praise of many.

' That for the gift bestowed,' &c. And first for the words somewhat. ' For the gift bestowed on us.' Deliverance and health is a gift, *charisma*,* a free gift. If health be a gift, what are greater things? They are much more a free gift. If daily bread be a gift, certainly eternal life is much more a gift. ' The gift of God is eternal life,' Rom. vi. 23.

Away with conceit of merit! If we merit not daily bread, if we merit not outward deliverance, if we merit not health, what can we do for eternal life? It is a doting conceit, a mere foolish conceit then, to think that the beggar merits his alms by begging, prayer being the chief work we do. What doth the beggar merit by begging? Begging, it is a disavowing of merit. Health, you see here, it is a gift bestowed by prayer, that ' for the gift bestowed upon us,' &c.

Things come to be ours either by contract or by gift. If it be by con-tract, then we know what we have to do. If it be by gift, the only way to get a thing by gift is prayer. So that which is gotten here by prayer, it is called a gift, not only a gift for the freeness of it, but because health, and deliverance out of trouble, is a great and special gift. For, as it seems, St Paul here was desperately sick (I rather incline to that than any other deliverance), ' I received the sentence of death,' &c.

Is not health a gift? Is it not the foundation of all the comforts of this life? What would riches comfort us? What would friends comfort us? Bring all to a sick man, alas! he hath no relish in anything, because he wants the ground of all earthly comforts, he wants health. Therefore you know the Grecians accounted that a chief blessing. If they had health, they were contented with any estate (*ff*). A poor man in a mean estate,

* That is, ' χάρισμα.'—G.

with a little competency, is more happy than the greatest monarch in the world that is under sickness and pain of body.

Health! it is comfort itself, and it sweetens all other comforts.

Therefore it is a matter that especially we should bless God for, both for preventing* health (God keeps us out of sickness), and likewise for delivering us out of it, for both are like favours. And they that have a constant enjoyment of their health should as well praise God, as they that are delivered out of sickness. It is God's goodness that they do not fall into sickness. There is the ground of sickness in every man. Though he had no outward enemy in the world, yet God can distemper the humours; and when there is a jar and disproportion in the humours, then follows a hurting of the powers, and a hindering of the actions, &c. We should bless God for the continuance of health. It is a special gift. 'For the gift bestowed.'

'By the means of many persons.' God bestowed health on St Paul, but it was by the means of many prayers of many persons.

Quest. Would not God have bestowed health upon St Paul if he had not had their prayers?

Ans. Yes, doubtless. But yet notwithstanding when there are many prayers, they prevail much more. Many streams make a river run more strongly, and so many prayers prevail strongly. Health is such a blessing as may be begged by others.

Therefore it is a good thing in sickness, and in any trouble, to beg the prayers of others, that they may beg health and deliverance of God for us. The good Corinthians here, they pray St Paul out of his trouble. And God so far honours his children, even the meanest, that they are a means to beg health and deliverance for others, even to pray them out of this or that trouble.

And what a comfort and encouragement is this, that a Christian hath so many factors for him! He hath all the saints in the world that say, 'Our Father,' praying for him. He must needs be rich that hath a world of factors, that hath a stock going in every part of the world. A Christian hath factors all the world over. He is a member of the mystical body, and many prayers are made for him. It is a great comfort.

And it is a great encouragement for us to pray for one another, considering that God will so far honour us. St Paul's health here, it was a gift by the prayers of many.

Obj. But thou wilt object: I am a weak Christian, a sinful creature. What, should God regard my prayers? Alas! my prayers will do you little good.

Solution. Yes, they will do much, not only for thyself, but for others. What are prayers? Are they not incense kindled by the fire of the blessed Spirit of God? Are they not in themselves good motions, stirred up by the Spirit? Themselves in their nature are good, though they be imperfect and stained. The Spirit that stirs them up is good, the good Spirit of God. 'We know not how to pray,' Rom. viii. 26, but the Spirit teacheth us. The Mediator through whom they are offered, who mingles his odour with them, Rev. viii. 3, 'He is the angel that mingleth odours with the prayers of the saints,' and makes them acceptable to God. The person likewise that offers them is good. What is he? Is he not God's child? Do not parents love to hear the voice of their children? If, therefore, the person be good, though weak, and the prayer be good, and the Spirit good,

* That is, = keeping off ill health.—G.

and the Mediator so good, then let no man be discouraged, not only to pray for himself, but to pray for others. God would hear the Corinthians, though they were stained with schism, and many other weaknesses. They were none of the most refined churches that St Paul wrote to, as we may see in the first epistle ; yet saith St Paul, my health and deliverance is a gift, and a gift by the prayers of many, weak and strong joining together.

Obj. It is the subtilty of Satan, and our own hearts join with him in the temptation. What should I pray ? My conscience tells me this and that.

Ans. Dost thou mean to be so still ? Then indeed, as it is, ' If I regard iniquity in my heart, the Lord will not hear my prayer,' Ps. lxvi. 18. But if thou have repented thee of thy sins, and intendest to lead a new life for the time to come, God will hear thy prayers, not only for thyself, but for others. God will bestow gifts upon others, by means of thy prayers.

To go on.

' Thanks may be given by many persons.' God's end in delivering St Paul by prayer, was that he might have many thanks for many prayers, when they were heard once. ' That thanks may be given by many on our behalf,' that is, because we are delivered, and restored to health and strength again, to serve the church as we did before. You see here how

Obs. Praise follows prayer.

Many prayers, and then many praises ; these follow one another. Indeed this is God's order ; and we see in nature, where there is a receiving, there is a giving. We see the earth, it receives fruit, it yields fruit, as Christ saith of the good ground, sixty-fold, many-fold. You see bodies that receive the sun, they reflect their beams back to the sun again.

The streams, as they come from the sea, so by an unwearied motion they return back again to the sea. And men do eat the fruit of their own flocks, they reap the fruit of their own orchards and gardens. In nature, whatsoever receives, it returns back again. The influence and light that those heavenly bodies, the stars, and the planets, &c., have from the sun, who is the chief light of all, they bestow it upon the inferior bodies. You see it in nature, much more is it in grace. What we receive from God by gift, obtained by prayer, he must have the praise for it. Many prayers, many praises. As soon as ever a benefit is received, presently there is an obligation, a natural obligation, and a religious obligation. Upon the receipt of a benefit, there must be some thought of returning something presently.

It teacheth us what a horrible sin ingratitude is. It is the grave of all God's blessings. It receives all, and never returns anything back again. As those lepers, they never came back again to thank Christ, but only the tenth, a poor Samaritan, Luke xvii. 17. Men are eager to sue to God, restless till they have that they would have, but then they are barren and unfruitful, they yield nothing back again. After prayer, there must be praise and thanksgiving. It condemneth our backwardness and untoward-ness in this kind. Like little children, they are ready to beg favours, but when they come to thanksgiving, they look another way, as if it were irksome to them. So it is with our nature. When we go about this heavenly duty, we give God a formal word or two, ' Thanks be to God,' &c. But we never work our hearts to thankfulness. ' That thanks may be given by many.'

As the prayers of many are mighty with God to prevail, so likewise the praises of many are very grateful and acceptable to God, even as it is with instruments. The sweetness of music ariseth from many instruments, and from the concord of all the strings in every instrument. When every instrument hath many strings, and are all in tune, it makes sweet harmony, it makes sweet concord. So, when many give God thanks, and every one hath a good heart set in tune, when they are good Christians all, it is wondrous acceptable music to God, it is sweet incense; more acceptable to God than any sweet savour and odour can be to us. That is one reason why God will have many to pray to him, that he may have many praises.

God doth wondrously honour concord, especially when it is concord in praising of him. It is a comely thing for ' brethren to live in unity,' as it is Ps. cxxxiii. 1. If to praise God be a comely thing, and if concord be a comely thing, then when both meet together, it must needs be wondrous beautiful, and wondrous acceptable to God, when many brethren meet and join to praise God. Therefore it is said, in the church's new conversion, ' They met all together as one man,' Acts ii. 46, they were of one heart and one soul, and they were given to prayer and to praising of God. A blessed estate of that beginning church ! They were all as one man, of one heart, of one spirit, of one soul.

As the blessed angels and blessed spirits in heaven, they all join together, as it is in Rev. xiv. 2, 3. The blessed man heard a voice in heaven as the voice of many waters, and of great thunder ; and he heard the voice of harpers, ' and they sang a new song.' There were many harps, but one song, one thanksgiving, one heart, one spirit in all, wondrous acceptable to God.

This should make us in love with public meetings. Severed thanksgiving is not so acceptable a thanksgiving. God doth bestow all good upon us in the body, as we knit ourselves not only in thanksgiving to him, but in love to the church. As all things are derived from God to us in the body, so let our praise return to God in the body as much as we may.

It shews what a hateful thing schism and division is in the church. Besides many other inconveniences, God wants glory by it. God loves to be praised by many joining together. As the apostle saith here, ' Thanks shall be given by many,' &c. Many ! not as they are many persons, but as they are many godly persons that are led by the Spirit of God.

Use. Therefore, if the praise of many be so acceptable, it should first be an encouragement to union. In John xvii. 21, saith our Saviour Christ there, ' I pray that they may be one, as we are one.' It was the sum of that heavenly prayer, the unity of the church to the end of the world, ' That they may be one, as we are one.' The Trinity should be the pattern of our unity. Because, I say, all good is in union, and all that comes from us that is accepted of God, it must be in peace and union.

God so loves peace, and a quiet disposition inclinable to peace, that he neglects his own service till we have made peace one with another, Mat. v. 24, ' If thou have any offence with thy brother,' if thou have done him any wrong, or he thee, ' go and be reconciled to him, and then come and bring thy offering.' God will stay for his own offering ; he is content to stay for his own service, till we be at peace one with another. Whether it be prayer or praise, if we be not at peace, it is not acceptable. Again, this should teach us to stir up others, when we praise God, and others have cause as well as we, ' that thanks may be given by many.' When we are in trouble, call upon others; and as it is the common and commendable fashion, desire others to pray for us, that prayer may be made by many ; and when we receive any favour, any deliverance from any great danger, acquaint others

with it, that thanks may be given by many.   It was the practice of David,
in Ps. lxvi. 16, ' Come! I will tell you what the Lord hath done for my
soul.'   And in Ps. xxxiv. 4, and in Ps. cxlii. 7, ' Bring my soul out
of trouble, that I may praise thy name,' and what shall others do ?   ' Then
the righteous shall compass me about, for thou hast dealt bountifully with
me : ' shewing that it is the fashion of righteous men, when God hath
dealt graciously with any of his children, they compass him about, to be
acquainted with the passages of divine providence, and God's goodness
towards them, ' The righteous shall compass me about, for thou hast dealt
bountifully with me.'

Holy David, in Ps. ciii. 20–22, he stirs up every creature to praise God,
even the creatures of hail, of storms, and winds, and everything, even the
blessed angels, as we see in the latter end of that psalm, as if thanksgiving
were an employment fit for angels ; and indeed so it is.   And, as if all his
own praise were not enough, except all the creatures in heaven and earth
should join with him in that blessed melody to praise God ; the angels, and
all creatures praise God.   Let us stir up one another to this exercise.

How do the creatures praise God ?   They do praise God by the tongue.
Although they have a kind of secret praise which God hears well enough,
for they do their duty in their place willingly and cheerfully ; but they
praise God in our tongues.   Every creature gives us occasion of praising
God.

' That thanks may be given by many,' &c.

Many give thanks here for one, St Paul, for the minister.   We see here
God's end, that many should praise God, not only for themselves, but for
others, especially for those by whom God conveys and derives good unto
them, whether outward or spiritual good.   The apostle exhorts us ' to pray
for all men,' 1 Tim. ii. 1, 2 ; ' for kings,' yea, though they were persecuting
kings at that time.   And surely if we ought to pray to God for all mankind,
we ought to praise God for all sorts of men, especially for governors and
ministers, &c., because God by them bestows his greatest blessings.   Obey.
the magistrate.   ' Let every soul be subject to the higher powers ; for the
powers that are, are ordained of God, and he is the minister of God for thy
good,' Rom. xiii. 1.   So the governors and ministers of God are for our
good.   We ought therefore, as to pray for them, that they may execute
their office for our good, so to praise God for the good we have by them.
You know David stirred up the people to mourn for Saul, though a tyrant.
' He clothed you and your daughters,' saith he, ' with scarlet,' 2 Sam. i. 24.
If they should praise God for a persecuting king, and mourn for him when
he was gone, much more should we for those that are good.

And so likewise for pastors, we ought to praise God for them, and all
that have good by them will pray to God, and praise God for them.   And
undoubtedly it is a sign of a man that hath no good by them, that prays
not for them, and that praiseth not God by them.   We ought to praise
God in that proportion, as well as to pray to God one for another.

And this should stir us up to be good to many, that many may praise
God, not only for themselves, but for us.   If it be our duty to pray for
those that we derive good by, and to praise God for them, then let us labour
to be such as may communicate to others.   Good is diffusive, and good
men are like the box in the gospel, that when it was opened, all the house
smelled of it, John xii. 3.

The heathen philosopher said that a just man, a good man, is a common
good, like a public stream, like a public conduit, that every man hath a

share in. Therefore, as the wise man saith, ' When good men are exalted, the city rejoiceth,' Prov. xi. 10, many rejoice. Who would not, therefore, labour in this respect to be good, to have a public disposition, to have a large heart, to do all the good we can, that so we may not only have more prayers to God for us, but we may have more praise to God for us, that God may gain by it, ' that thanks may be given by many on our behalf ? '

Let us take notice of our negligence in this kind, and be stirred up to this blessed duty. And, therefore, consider wherein it consists.

1. It consists in our *taking notice of the favours of God to ourselves and others*, and in valuing the good things that we praise God for, to esteem them. The children of Israel, they did not bless God for the manna, they did not value it, ' This manna, this manna,' in scorn, Num. xi. 6. So in Ps. cvi. 7, ' They neglected God's pleasant things, they set light by them.' Hos. viii. 12, ' He gave them the great things of his law, and they accounted them as slight, as strange things,' not worthy to be regarded.

2. Praise consists *in taking notice*, and not only in taking notice, but in *remembering and minding them*, as in Ps. ciii. 2, ' My soul, praise the Lord, and forget not all his benefits.'

3. And likewise *in an estimation of them ;* and likewise,

4. *In expressing* this thankfulness in words, ' Awake, my glory,' Ps. lvii. 8. Our tongues are our glory, especially as they are instruments to praise and glorify God. We cannot use our language better than to speak the language of Canaan in praising of God.

5. Likewise, praise consists in doing good, which is real praise, though we say nothing. Moses cried to God, though he spake not a word. Evil works have a cry, although they say nothing. Abel's blood cried against Cain, Gen. iv. 10. And as evil works, so good works have a cry. Though a man praise not God with his tongue, his works praise God. Job saith, ' The sides of the poor blessed him,' Job xxxi. 20. What! could their sides speak ? No ; but there was a real thanksgiving to God. Their sides blessed God. So our good works may praise God as well as our tongues and hearts. The heavens and the earth, they praise God, though they say nothing, because they stir us up to say something. ' Let men see your good works,' Mat. v. 16, that they may take occasion from thence to bless God, saith Christ. Or else your praising of God is but a mere complimenting with God ; to give him thanks with the tongue, and after to dishonour him with your lives, Ps. l. 16, ' What hast thou to do to take my name into thy mouth, sith thou hatest to be reformed ? ' What hast thou to do to take my name into thy mouth, either in prayer or in praise, when thou hatest to be reformed ? ' High words are unseemly for a fool,' saith the the wise man, Eccles. v. 3, x. 14. And what higher words than praise ? Therefore, praise for a man that lives in a blasphemous course of life, in a filthy course of life, praise is too high a word for a fool. We must praise God in our lives, or else not at all. God will not accept of it. It consists in these things.

Now some directions how to perform it for ourselves and others.

1. If we would praise God for ourselves, or for any, then *let us look about us, let us look above us and beneath us, let us look backward, look to the present, look forward.* Everything puts songs of praise into our mouth. Have we not matter enough of our own to praise God for ? Let us look about us, to the prosperity of others. Let us praise God for the ministry, praise God for the magistracy, praise God for the government wherein we live. There

are many grievances in the best government, but a Christian heart considereth what good he hath by that government, what good he hath by that ordinance, and doth not only delight to feed on the blemishes, as flies do upon sores. It is a sign of a naughty heart to do so. Although a man should not be insensible of the ills of the times (for else how should we pray against them ?), yet he is not so sensible as to forget the good he hath by them. If we would praise God, let us look to the good, and not so much upon the ill.

Look up to heaven, look to the earth, to the sea. David occasions praise from every creature. Every creature ministers matter of praise, from the stars to the dust, from heaven to earth, from the cedar to the hyssop that grows by the wall. Is there not a beam of God's goodness in every creature ? Have we not use of every creature ? We must praise God not only for the majesty and order that shines in them, but for the use of them in respect of us.

And so let us look to the works of providence, as well as to the works of creation. Look to God's work in his church, his confounding of his enemies, his deliverance of his church, the churches abroad, our own church, our own persons, our friends. Thus we should feed ourselves, that we may have matter of praising God. God gives us matter every day. He renews his favours upon the place wherein we live and upon us, as it is Lam. iii. 22, ' It is his mercy that we are not all consumed.' Let us look back to the favours that we have enjoyed ; let us look for the present. What doth he do for us ? The apostle saith here, ' God doth deliver us.' Doth he not give deliverance, and favour, and grace, inward grace for the time to come ? Hath he not reserved an inheritance, immortal and undefiled, in the heavens for us ? Wherefore doth he bestow things present, and wherefore doth he reveal things laid up for us for the time to come, but that we should praise him, but that we should praise him for that which he means to do afterwards ? ' Blessed be God the Father, who hath begotten us to an inheritance, immortal, and undefiled,' &c., saith St Peter, 1 Pet. i. 4. God reveals good things that are to come, that we are heirs-apparent to the crown of glory. This is revealed that we might praise him now, that we might begin the employment of heaven upon earth. Let us look upward and downward, let us look about us, look inward, look backward, look to the present, look forward. Everything ministereth matter of praise to God.

Yea, our very crosses. Happy is he whom God vouchsafeth to be angry with, that he doth not give him over to a reprobate sense to fill up his sins, but that he will correct him, to pull him from ill courses. Happy is he that God vouchsafeth to be angry with in evil courses. There is a blessing hid in ill, in the cross. ' *In all things* give thanks,' saith the apostle, Eph. v. 20. What! in afflictions ? Aye, not for the affliction itself, but for the issue of it. There is an effect in afflictions to draw us from the world, to draw us to God, to make us more heavenly-minded, to make us see better into these earthly things, to make us in love with heavenly things. ' In all things give thanks.' When we want matter in ourselves, let us look abroad, and give thanks to God for the prosperity of others.

2. And withal, in the second place, when we look about us, *let us dwell in the meditation of the usefulness of these things, of the goodness of God in them, till our hearts be warmed.* It is not a slight ' God be thanked' that will serve, but we must dwell upon it. Let our hearts dwell so long on the favours and blessings of God till there be a blessed fire kindled in us. The

best bone-fire * of all is to have our hearts kindled with love to God in the consideration of his mercy. Let us dwell so long upon it till a flame be kindled in us. A slight praise is neither acceptable to God nor man.

3. And then let us consider *our own unworthiness, let us dwell upon that.* ' I am less than the least of all thy favours,' saith good Jacob, Gen. xxxii. 10. If we be less than the least, then we must be thankful for the least. Humility is alway thankful. A humble man thinks himself unworthy of anything, and therefore he is thankful for anything.

A proud man praiseth himself above the common rate. He overvalues and overprizeth himself, and therefore he thinks he never hath enough. When he hath a great deal, he thinks he hath less than he deserves, and therefore he is an unthankful person ; and that makes a proud man so intolerable to God. He is alway an unthankful person, a murmuring person. A humble man, because he undervalues himself, he thinks he hath more than he deserves, and he is thankful for everything. He knows he deserves nothing of himself. It is the mere goodness of God whatsoever he hath.

The best direction to thanksgiving is to have a humble and low heart. Therefore David, 1 Chron. xxix. 14, when he would exercise his heart to thankfulness, when the people had given liberally, saith he, ' Who am I, or what is this people, that we should be able to offer willingly after this sort ? All comes of thee, and all is thine own that we give.' What am I, or what is this people, that we should have hearts to give liberally to the temple ? See how he abaseth himself. And Abraham, ' I am dust and ashes, shall I speak to my Lord ?' Gen. xviii. 27. And Job, ' I abhor myself in dust and ashes,' xlii. 6, when he considered God's excellency and his own baseness. A humble heart is alway thankful, and the way to thankfulness is to consider our humility. ' What am I ?' saith David. He had a heart to be thankful. ' Of thine own I give thee.' Not only the matter to be thankful for, but of thine own I give thee ; when I give thee thanks, thou givest me a thankful heart.

As the sacrifice that Abraham offered was found by God, so God must find the sacrifice that we offer, even a thankful heart. Of thine own, Lord, I give thee, even when I give thee thanks.

Therefore you may make that a means to have a thankful heart, to pray for a thankful heart. And when we have it, bless God for it, that we may be more thankful. God must vouchsafe the portion of a thankful heart with other blessngs. He that gives matter to be thankful, must give a heart to be thankful.

4. Again, to make us more thankful, do but consider *the misery of ourselves if we wanted the blessings we are thankful for, and the misery of others that have them not.* Thou that hast health, if thou wouldst be thankful for it, look abroad, look into hospitals, look on thy sick friends that cannot come abroad. Thou that wouldst be thankful for the liberty of the gospel, look beyond the seas, look into the Palatinate, and other countries, and certainly this will make thee thankful, if anything will. If we would be thankful for spiritual blessings, consider the misery of those that are under the bondage of Satan, how there is but a little step between them and hell, that they are ready to sink into it. There is but the short thread of this life to be cut, and they are for ever miserable. If we would be thankful for any blessing, let us consider the misery to be without it. If we would be

* That is, ' bon-fire,' = boon-fire, or fire of joy, voluntarily kindled. Cf. Richardson, *sub voce.*—G.

thankful for our wits, let us consider distracted persons. What an excellent engine to all things in this life, and the life to come, is this spark of reason! If we want reason, what can we do in civil things? What can we do in matters of grace? Grace presupposeth nature. If we would be thankful for health, for strength, and for reason, if we would be thankful for common favours, consider the misery of those that want these things.

Would we be thankful for the blessed ordinance, consider but the misery of those that sit in darkness, and in the shadow of death, how they are led by Satan and want the means of salvation. Those that would be thankful for the government we have, let them consider those that live in anarchy, where every man lives as he lists, where a man cannot enjoy his own. The consideration of these things it should quicken us to thankfulness, the consideration of our own misery if we should want them, and the misery of those that do want them.

5. And let us *keep a catalogue of God's blessings.* It will serve us, as in regard of God to bless him the more, so in regard of ourselves, to establish our faith the more; for God is Jehovah, alway like himself. Whom he hath done good unto, he will do good to. He is constant in his love. ' Whom he loves, he loves to the end,' John xiii. 1. God shall have more thanks, and we shall have more comfort.

Again, to add some encouragements and motives to thankfulness, which may be a forcible means to make us thankful, do but consider.

(1.) *It is God's tribute, it is God's custom.* Do but deny the king his custom, and what will come of it? Deny him tribute, and you forfeit all. So you forfeit all for want of thankfulness.

What is the reason that God hath taken away the gospel from countries abroad, and may do from us if we be not more thankful? Because they were not thankful. It is all the tribute, all the impost he sets upon his blessings. ' I will give you this,' but you shall glorify me with thanksgiving. It is all the honour he looks for. ' He that praiseth me honoureth me,' Ps. l. 23. And ' now, O Israel, what doth the Lord require of thee,' for all his favours, but ' to serve him with a cheerful and good heart?' Deut. x. 12, to be thankful.

What is the reason that the earth denies her own to us, that sometimes we have unseasonable years? We deny God his own. He stops the due of the creature, because we stop his due.

When we are not thankful he is forced to make the heavens as iron, and the earth as brass. We force him to make the creature otherwise than it is, because we deny him thankfulness.

The running of favours from heaven ceaseth when there is not a recourse back again of thankfulness to him. For unthankfulness is a drying wind. It dries up the fountain of God's favours. It binds God. It will not suffer him to be as good as his word. If ever God give us up to public judgments, it will be because we are not thankful to God for favours and deliverances, as that in '88, by sea,* and from the gunpowder treason by land.† Was it not a sick state after Queen Mary, when Queen Elizabeth received the crown? The church and commonwealth were sick. Now if we be to praise God for our particular persons, when we have recovered our health, much more should we praise God, when the state, when the church is delivered, as it was at the coming in of Queen Elizabeth, and afterward in '88; and of late time, and continually he doth deliver us. And if we look that

* That is, from the Armada, 1588. See note, vol. I. p. 318.—G.
† ' Treason.' See note *e.* vol. I. p. 315.—G.

he should deliver us, not only our persons, but the state wherein we live, let us pray to God that he would do so, and praise God for his former deliverance.

(2.) Again, this is another motive, the praising of God for former deliverances, *it invites him to bestow new blessings.* Upon what ground doth the husbandman bestow more seed? Upon that which hath yielded most in time past. Will any man sow in the barren wilderness where it is lost? No; but where he looks to reap most, and hath done formerly. Where he sees a soil that is fruitful, he will sow it the more; and where the heart is a barren wilderness, that it yields nothing back again, he takes that away that he gave before.

You know there is a debt in giving. There must be a returning of thanksgiving alway; and kindness requires kindness. There is an obligation. And where benefits are taken, and men are thankful, that is the way to get more, to be thankful for that we have. For God minds his own glory above all things, and he will especially be bountiful to those from whom he sees he hath most glory. Therefore alway those that have been richest in grace, and in comfort, they were most in thankfulness, as we see in David, ' a man after God's own heart,' 1 Sam. xiii. 14, Acts xiii. 22, and in divers others. Let this encourage us.

First, if we be not thankful, it stops the current of benefits.

Secondly, if we be thankful God will give us more mercies and deliverances. When we praise him in our hearts, in our lives, in our bounty to others, in real thankfulness, when we are ready to good works, then he is ready to bestow new still.

(3.) Again, to stir us up to this duty of praising God for ourselves and others, consider *it is the beginning of heaven upon earth.* What a happiness is it, that when our persons cannot go to heaven till we die, till our bodies be raised, yet we can send our ambassadors, we can send our prayers and thanksgivings to heaven; and God accepts them, as if we came in our own persons. ' Let your conversation be in heaven,' saith the apostle, Philip. iii. 20. How is that? By praising God much. I pray, what is the employment of heaven, of the angels, and blessed spirits? They praise God continually for the work of creation, and for the work of redemption. That is their especial task in heaven. Our duty is to be much this way, in praising God. Self-love forceth prayer ofttimes; but to praise God comes from a more heavenly affection.

(4.) Again, do but consider, *that no creature in the world is unthankful,* but devils only, and devilish men; and good men, only so far as they are corrupt and hold correspondency with their corruptions. For every .creature praiseth God in his kind, set the devil aside, who is full of envy and pride and malice against God. Therefore, except we will be like the devil, let us be thankful. God hath made all creatures to praise him, and to serve us, that we may praise him; and when they praise him, shall we blaspheme him? May not the swearer think with himself, every creature blesseth God, even the senseless creatures, and shall I dishonour God by my tongue which should be my glory, to glorify him? Shall I blaspheme him, and be like to the devil? Shall I be more base than the senseless creatures? What glory hath God by many men that live in the church, that blaspheme God; and their whole life is a witness against God, as the whole life of a Christian, after he is in the state of grace, is a witness for God, and a praising of him. His whole life is a thanksgiving. So the whole life of wicked and careless creatures, is a dishonour of God, it is a witness against God. There are none but devils, devilish-minded men, but they praise God, even the very dumb creatures. Let us labour to have a part in that blessed music and harmony to praise God. If we do not praise God here, we shall never do it in heaven.

But we must remember, by the way, that this thankfulness it must be a fruitful thanksgiving. As for us to pray to God to bless us, and then to do nothing, it is a barren prayer ; so to thank God, and then to do nothing, it is a barren thanksgiving. Our deeds have words, our deeds have a voice to God. They speak, they pray. There is a kind of prayer, a kind of thanks in our works. Works pray to God. They have a kind of cry to God, both ill works and good works. And if good works have a cry to God in prayer, they will have a voice in thanksgiving. This fruitful, this real thanks, is that which God stands upon.

And therefore it is alway joined with a study how to improve the things that we thank God for to the best advantage. If we thank God for health, and recovery, and deliverance, we will labour to improve it to God's glory. If we be thankful to God for riches, for peace, we will improve that to grow in grace, to do good to others. There is never a thankful heart, but it studies to improve that which it is thankful for really, that God may have the glory, and it the comfort, and benefit by it ; or else it is but a lip-labour, but a lost labour.

Let us shame ourselves, and condemn ourselves for our unthankfulness ; and that will be done by comparing our carriage to men with our carriage to God. If so be that a man do us a little courtesy, how are we confounded if we have not returned some thanks ? And yet, notwithstanding, from God we have all that we have, all that we are, all that we hope to have ; and yet how many benefits do we devour, and do not return God thanks ?

This disproportion will shame the best Christian, that he is not so quick in his devotion to God to be thankful there, as he is sensible of small kindnesses done by men. This is a good way to make us more thankful.

And now when we come to the sacrament, let us bless God. The Eucharist is a thanksgiving. Where there are many, there should be thanksgiving. Where there is a communion there is many ; and thanksgiving should be especially of many met together to thank God for Christ, and for the good we have by him. For if many joined together in praise for St Paul that was but a minister, that was but an instrument to set out the praise and the doctrine of Christ, much more should we be thankful to God for Christ himself, which is the gift of all gifts, and for which he gives us all other gifts. If he give us him, can he deny us anything ? If we be thankful for the health of our bodies, as indeed we should, if we be thankful for the peace of our humours, much more should we be thankful for the peace of our consciences, when our souls are set in tune, when God and we are friends, when the soul by the Spirit of God is set at peace, and is fit for the praise of God, and is fit to do good ; when it is a healthful soul.

As in the body, it is a sign it is sick when the actions are hindered ; so it is likewise with the soul.

We should bless God for ability to do good, for any health in our souls, more than for health of body. Do but consider, if we are to thank God for the instruments of good, much more are we to thank him for the good things themselves. If we should thank God for the ministers (for now I stand upon that, many prayers and praises were given to God for St Paul) much more should we be thankful for that which we have by the ministry, that is, for all the blessings of God, for grace and glory, for life and salvation. It is the ministry of life, 'and the power of God to salvation,' Rom. i. 16. We should be thankful to God for peace, 'we are the messengers of peace,' Eph. vi. 15. We should be thankful to God for grace, and for his Holy Spirit; the Spirit is given with it. We should be thankful especially for spiritual favours. A man cannot be thankful to God for health and liberty, unless first he know God to be his, that he can bless God for spiritual favours. 'Blessed be God, the Father of our Lord Jesus Christ, who hath blessed us with all spiritual blessings in Christ, Eph. i. 3. We should be thankful for Christ, and all the benefits we have by Christ, much more than for any other blessings whatsoever.

Therefore, now seeing we are a communion, let praise be given by many.* We have greater matters than the health of a minister (or any particular person, either ourselves or others) to be thankful for. We have greater cause, being to bless God for the greatest gift that ever he gave, even for Christ. The disposition in a feast is to be joyful, and cheerful, to praise God. Now we are to feast with God, and with Jesus Christ. Christ is not only the food, but he invites us, he is with us. What will we do for Christ if we will not feast with him? What a degree of unthankfulness is it, when we will not so much as feast with him? when we will not willingly receive him? What will he do for Christ that will not feast with him? How unfit will he be to praise God, and praise Christ, that when Christ makes a feast of himself, and gives himself together with the bread and wine, representing the benefit of his body and blood, broken, and shed for us, and all his benefits? If we will not feed upon himself, when he stoops so low as to give himself for us, and to feed us with himself, what will we do? How can we be thankful for other blessings, when we are not thankful for himself? And how can we be thankful for himself, when we will not come and partake of him?

Let us stir up our hearts and think now to take the communion; as for matter of repentance and sorrow, it should be despatched before. It is the Eucharist, a matter of thanksgiving. We should raise our hearts above earthly things. We should consider that we are to deal with Christ, and these are but representations.

When the bread is broken, think of the body of Christ; and when the wine is poured out, think of the blood of Christ. And when our bodies are cheered by these elements, think how our souls are refreshed by the blood of Christ by faith. If we should be thankful to God for bodily deliverance, how much more should we thank him for our souls, being delivered from hell by the blood of Christ, which is the grand deliverance? Let us dispose our hearts to thankfulness. It is a fit disposition for a feast.

And, as I said, take heed of sin. It chokes thankfulness. Therefore examine thy purposes, how thou comest. If thou come with a purpose to live in sin, thou art an unfit receiver. The place we stand in is holy, the business is holy, we have to deal with a holy God; and therefore if we purpose not to relinquish wicked courses, and to enter into covenant with God, to abstain from sin, we come not aright. 'When thou comest into the house of God, take heed to thy feet,' saith the wise man, Eccles. v. 1. Take heed to thy affections; consider with whom thou hast to deal. But if thou hast renewed thy repentance, and thy purposes with God for the time to come, come with cheerfulness, with a thankful disposition. Thankfulness

* Margin-note here, 'It was a sacrament day.'—G.

is a disposition for a feast. If it be a disposition for bodily deliverance, it is much more for the deliverance of the soul; and much more for Christ, and the blessings we have by him, who is ' all in all.' ' That thanks may be given by many on our behalf.'

VERSE 12.

' *For our rejoicing is this, the testimony of our conscience,*' &c.   St Paul in these words doth divers things at once.

1. *He shews a reason why many should pray for him, and give thanks on his behalf.*   You have cause, saith he, ' for our rejoicing is this, the testimony of our conscience,' &c.   Therefore if many of you give thanks to God for me, it is your duty.   My conscience bears me witness that I have carried myself well towards you.   You have cause to pray for us, and to praise God for our deliverance, for you have received much good by us.   God conveys much good by public persons to those that are under them.   Therefore there ought to be many prayers, and many thanks, for them.

2. And again, they ought to pray and give thanks for him, *because they should not lose their labour, they should not lose their prayers, their incense;* because it should be for a man that was gracious with God, that had the testimony of his conscience that he walked in simplicity and godly sincerity, as he saith, ' Pray for us, for we are assured that we have a good conscience,' Heb. xiii. 18.   So they are a reason of the former.

3. Another thing that he aims at is, *the preventing* of some imputations.* He was accused in their thoughts at least, and by the words of some false teachers, that were his worst enemies, as you have no enemy, next to the devil, to a minister, like a minister.   If a man would see the spirit of the devil, let him look to some of them.   St Paul had many enemies, many false brethren, that laid false imputations upon him to disparage him in the thoughts of others, in the thoughts of his hearers.   They accounted him an inconstant man, that he came not to them when he promised ; and that he suffered affliction, and it was like enough for some desert.   They accounted him a despicable man.   He suffered afflictions in the world.   He wanted discretion to keep himself out of the cross.   Nay, saith he, whatsoever you impute to me, and lay upon me, ' our rejoicing is this, the testimony of our conscience,' &c.

4. Again, he aims at this, *to lay the blame upon those false brethren who deserved it.*   They think I am a deceiver, they think I am wily.   No! I do not walk so, I do not walk in fleshly wisdom as they do that seek themselves, and not you.   So I say, St Paul aims at divers things in bringing in these words.

We see here, first of all, that

Doct. The more eminent a man is for place and gifts, the more he should be prayed for, and the more thanks should be given for him.

You have cause, saith St Paul, to do it for me; for our rejoicing is this, that ' we have walked in simplicity and sincerity, &c., and more abundantly to you-ward.'   St Paul was a brother as he was a Christian.   He was a father, in regard he had called them to the faith ; and he was an apostle. In all regards they ought to praise God for him ; because he was a father, because he was the father of them, ' you have not many fathers,' saith he,

* That is, 'anticipating.'—G.

and because he was an apostle, a man eminent, by whose means God conveyed a world of good to the church.

To make way to the main thing, observe this in general, that

Obs. Christians are often driven to their apology.

Especially ministers, the fathers of Christians. Holy men in the church
are driven to their apology and defence; because those that shine in their
own consciences, wicked men labour to darken them in their reputation,
that their own wickedness may be the less seen and observed. It hath
alway been the policy of Satan, and of wicked men, that so all might seem
alike, to lay aspersions upon those that were better men than themselves.
St Paul is forced to make his apology, to retire to the testimony of his
conscience. 'Our rejoicing is this, the testimony of our conscience,' &c.

Use. Therefore make this use of it, *not to think it strange if we be driven
to our apology.*

Quest. But some may say, Is not the life the best apology? as St Peter
saith, 'that you may stop the mouths of gainsayers.'

Ans. Yes, of all apologies life is the best, to oppose to all imputations;
but notwithstanding it is not enough.

A man is cruel if he make not his apology and defence sometimes.
Because his imputations * tend to the hurt of others, being public persons,
especially ministers, who have so much authority in the hearts of people,
as they can gain by their good life and desert. And if any imputation lie
upon them, they are to clear it in words. Their life will not serve the turn,
but they must otherwise make their apology, if it be needful, for themselves,
as St Paul doth here. It is not only lawful, but expedient sometimes, to
speak by way of commendation of ourselves.

In what cases?

1. Not only in case of thankfulness to God, to praise God for his graces
in us.

2. And likewise in case of example to others, a man may speak of God's
work in him, he may tell what God hath done for his soul, and in his soul,
that God may have glory, and others may have benefit.

3. But likewise in the third place, and it was St Paul's case here, a man
may speak of himself, by way of apology and defence, that the truth suffer
not. It is a kind of betraying the cause, for a man to be silent when he is
so accused. Though, as I said, a good life be the best apology, and except
there be a good life the verbal apology is to little purpose, yet the apology
of life ofttimes in public persons is too little. In these cases we must speak
of ourselves, and of the good things of God in us.

Quest. But another query† may be here, May a man glory in that which
is in him, of the grace of God that is in him? Our glorying should
be in Christ, in the obedience and righteousness of Christ, and in God reconciled through Christ. Can a Christian glory in anything that is in him,
which is imperfect?

Ans. I answer briefly, St Paul doth not here glory in the court of justification, but in the court of a Christian conversation. Therein a man may
glory in the work of grace in him, in those inward works, and the works
that flow from them. When a man is to deal with men, he may set forth
his life, nay, when a man is to deal with God, he may set forth his sincerity,
not, I say, in the court of justification, but in the court of sanctification,
and a holy life. There good works are the ornament of the spouse. They
are her jewels. But come to the court of justification, all are dung, as the

* That is, imputations against him.—G.   † Spelled 'quere.'—G.

apostle saith, 'all are dung and dross,' Philip. iii. 8; not worthy to be named. They are not able, they are not strong enough. All that comes from us, and all that is in us, it is not able to bear us out in glorying in the court of justification. 'All are stained as menstruous cloths,' Isa. xxx. 22. But mark, St Paul speaks of glorying before men, of a sanctified life. He glories not in his conversation and sincerity as a title, but he glories in it as an evidence that his title is good. That whereby he hath his title, is only by the righteousness of Christ. That he hath heaven, and is free from hell, that is the title. But what evidence have you that Christ and his righteousness is yours? There must be somewhat wrought in you, and that is sincere walking. So he allegeth it as an evidence of his state in grace, that that was good. So we see in what case he gloried in his sincerity.

To come to the words.

For the words themselves, they contain the blessed temper of St Paul's spirit in the midst of disgraces, in the midst of imputations. The temper of his spirit it was joyful, glorying.

'Our rejoicing is this.' The ground of it is, 'the testimony of our conscience.'

The matter whereof conscience doth witness and testify, it is conversation. That is the thing testified of.

And the manner positively, 'in simplicity and godly sincerity.' 'In simplicity.' You would think this to be a simple commendation, to commend himself for simplicity; but it is a godly simplicity, whereby we are like to God, to be simple without mixture of sin and hypocrisy, without mixture of error and falsehood. That simplicity that is despised by carnal wretches that stain and defile their consciences, and call them what you will, so you account them not simple. They despise the term of an honest, simple man.

Simplicity is not here taken for a defect of knowledge, as the word is commonly used, but for an excellency whereby we resemble God; that is, free from all mixture of sin and ignorance. 'In simplicity and godly sincerity.' And then negatively, 'not in fleshly wisdom.'

And then, because this setting out of himself might seem to be ostentation, to set down his glorying in his conscience, and in his simplicity, here is a qualification of it likewise. Indeed I glory in my simplicity, and sincerity, that is, in my conversation; but it is by the grace of God. By the grace of God my conversation hath been in godly sincerity, and not in fleshly wisdom. For St Paul was wondrous jealous of his heart, for fear of pride; not I, saith he, 'I laboured more than they all; O, not I, but the grace of God that was in me,' 1 Cor. xv. 10. He was afraid of the least insinuation of spiritual pride, and so he saith here 'Our rejoicing is the testimony of our conscience, that in simplicity and sincerity, by the grace of God.'

And then the extent of this conversation, thus in simplicity and sincerity, in regard of the object. It hath been thus, 'In the world, towards all men that I have conversed with. They can say as much, wheresoever I have lived; 'And more abundantly to you-ward.' My care and conscience hath been to carry myself as I should, 'more abundantly to you-ward,' with whom I have lived longest. This is an excellent evidence of a good man, that he is best liked where he is best known. Now St Paul had lived long amongst them, and he was their father in Christ; and therefore, saith he, my conversation is known, especially to you-ward.

Many men are best trusted where they are least known. Their public conversation is good and plausible, but their secret courses are vile and naught, as those know that are acquainted with their retired courses. But you, saith the apostle, with whom I have lived longest, with whom I have been most, you can bear witness of my conversation, that I have lived so and so in the world, and more abundantly to you-ward.

'This is our rejoicing,' &c. We see here the temper and disposition that St Paul was in. He was in a glorying, in a rejoicing estate. We see then that

A Christian, take him at the worst, his estate is a rejoicing estate.

'Our rejoicing is this.' The word in the original is more than joy, for it is καύχησις, a glorying. 'Our glorying' is this, which is a joy manifesting itself in the outward man, when the heart and the spirit seem as it were to go outward, and, as it were, to meet the thing joyed in. A Christian hath his joy, his glorying, and a glorying that is proper to himself. It is a spiritual joy, as it follows after, 'Our rejoicing is the testimony of our conscience.'

So good is God, that in the worst estate he gives his children matter of rejoicing in this world. He gives them a taste of heaven before they come there. He gives them a grape of Canaan, as Israel. They tasted of Canaan, what a good land it was, before they came thither. So God's children, they have their rejoicing. St Paul swears and protests it, 1 Cor. xv. 31, 'By our rejoicing in Christ Jesus I die daily.' As verily as we joy in all our afflictions, so this is true that I say, that I die daily.

Use. Therefore we should labour *to be of such a temper, as that we may glory, and rejoice.* A Christian hath his rejoicing, but it is a spiritual rejoicing, like his estate. Every creature hath his joy, as St Chrysostom speaks. We do all for joy. All that we do is that we may joy at length. It is the centre of the soul. As rest is to motion, so the desire of all is to joy, to rest in joy. So that heaven itself is termed by the name of joy, happiness itself, 'Enter into thy master's joy,' Matt. xxv. 21. Every creature hath his joy proper to him. Every man hath his joy. A carnal man hath a carnal joy, a spiritual man hath a holy joy.

1. First, he joys in his *election*, which was before all worlds, that his name is written in heaven, as it is, Luke x. 20, 'Rejoice in this, that your names are written in heaven, and not that the devils are subject unto you.'

2. And then, he joys in his *justification*, that he is freed from his sins, Rom. v. 1, 'Being justified by faith we have peace with God through Christ, and we rejoice in afflictions.' Being justified first. There is the way how this joy comes in. A Christian being justified by faith, and freed from the guilt of his sin, it worketh joy.

3. And then, there is a joy of *sanctification*, of a good conscience, of a holy life led, as we see here, 'Our rejoicing is this, the testimony of our conscience, '&c.

4. And then, there is a joy *of glory to come.* 'We rejoice under the hope of glory,' saith the apostle, Rom. v. 2. So a Christian's joy is suitable to himself.

There is no other man that can glory, and be wise, because all men but a Christian, 'they glory in their shame,' Philip. iii. 19, or they glory in vanishing things. A Christian is not ashamed of his joy, of his glorying, because he glories not in his shame. Therefore the apostle here justifies his joy. Our rejoicing is this, I care not if all the world know my joy, it is the 'testimony of my conscience.' As if he should say, Let others rejoice in base pleasures which they will not stand to avow; let others rejoice in riches, in honours, in the favour of men ; let them rejoice in what they please, my joy is another kind of joy. ' I rejoice in the testimony of my conscience.' A Christian, as he hath a joy, so he hath a joy that he will stand to, and make it good. There is no other man but he will blush, and have shame in his forehead, that joys in anything that is baser than himself, that joys in outward things. He cannot stand to it, and say, This is my joy. But a Christian hath the warrant of his conscience for that which he joys in, and therefore he is not ashamed of it. Another man dares not reveal his joy.

All the subtilty of the world, is to have the pleasures that sin will afford ; and yet withal they study to cover it, that it may not appear. Where is the joy of the ambitious ?

His study, his thought, and his joy is to have respect, Haman-like ; and yet he studies to conceal this. He dares not have it known. He dares not avow it. ' This is my rejoicing ;' for then all the world would laugh at him for a vain person.

Again, the joy of the base-minded man, is in his pleasure, but he dares not avow this. He dares not say, my rejoicing is this ; for then every man would scorn him as a beast. The rich man, he joys in his riches, but he dares not be known of this, for he would then be accounted a base earthly-minded man. Every man would scorn him. He studies to have all the pleasure, and all the comfort that these things will afford, and yet to cover them. Because he thinks, that there is a higher matter that he should joy in, if he were not an atheist.

A Christian is not ashamed of his joy, and rejoicing. ' I rejoice in this,' saith he. For,

1. *It is well bred.* It is bred from the Spirit of God witnessing that his name is written in the book of life, witnessing that his sins are forgiven, witnessing that he lives as a Christian should do, witnessing that he hath the evidences of his justification, that he hath a holy life, the pledge likewise of future glory. His joy is well bred.

2. Likewise *it is permanent.* Other men's joy and rejoicing is but as a flash of thorns, as the wise man calls it, as it were, a flame in thorns ; as the crackling of thorns, which is sooner gone. And it is an unseemly glorying and rejoicing, for a man to glory in that which is worse than himself, and in that which is out of himself. As all other things are out of a man's self, and worse, and meaner than a man's self ; therefore a man cannot rejoice in them, and be wise. It is a disparagement to the wisdom of a man, to glory in things that are meaner than himself, and that are out of himself. A holy Christian hath that in himself, and that which is more excellent than himself, to glory in. ' This is our rejoicing, the testimony of our conscience.'

All other rejoicing it is vain glory, and vain rejoicing. Therefore in Jer. ix. 23, saith he, ' Let not the wise man glory in his wisdom, let not the strong.man glory in his strength, let not the rich man glory in his riches ;' but if a man will glory, ' let him glory that he knows the Lord to be his,' and that he knows himself to be the Lord's. When he knows the Lord to be his, and himself to be God's by faith, and a good conscience, then there is matter of glorying.

Of all kind of men, God doth hate proud boasters most of all ; for glory is the froth of pride, and God hates pride. He opposeth pride, and sets himself in battle array against it, and who can thrive that hath God for his enemy ? Boasting and pride in any earthly thing it is against all the commandments almost. It is idolatry, it makes that we boast, and glory in, an idol; whereas we should glory in God that gives it.

And it is spiritual adultery, when we cleave in our affections to some outward thing more than to God. It is false witness. Pride is a false glass. It makes the things and the men themselves that enjoy them to seem greater than they are. The devil amplifies earthly things to a carnal man in a false glass, that they seem big to him; whereas if he could see them in their true colours, they are false things, they are snares and hindrances in the way to heaven, and such names they have. The Scripture gives an ill report of them, 'They are vanity and vexation of spirit,' Eccles. i. 14 ; because we should be discouraged from setting our affections on these things, and from glorying in them.

Therefore let us take heed of false glorying. If we will glory, we see here what we are to glory in. ' This is our rejoicing, the testimony of our conscience,' &c. And this we may justify and stand by that. It is good. It is the ' testimony of conscience.'

' This is our rejoicing, the testimony of our conscience.'

The testimony of conscience, it is a matter and ground of joy to a true Christian. Here we are to consider these things.

First, to consider a little *the nature of conscience.*

And then, *that conscience bears witness;* that there is a testimony of conscience.

And that this conscience bearing witness *is a ground of comfort.*

For the first,

Every man feels and knows what conscience means. There be many rigid disputes of it among the schoolmen that had leisure enough; and of all men knew as little, and felt what it was, as any sort of men, living under the darkness of popery and superstition, and being in thraldom to the pope, and to the corruptions of the times they lived in. They have much jangling about the description of it, whether it be the soul itself, or a faculty, or an act.

In a word, conscience is all these in some sort, in divers respects. Therefore I will not wrangle with any particular opinion.

1. *For what is conscience, but the soul itself reflecting upon itself?* It is the property of the reasonable soul and the excellency of it, that it can return upon itself. The beast cannot ; for it runs right forward. It knows it is carried to the object; but it cannot return and recoil upon itself. But the soul of the reasonable creature, of all even from men to God himself, who understands in the highest degree, though he do not discourse as man doth, yet he knows himself, he knows and understands his own excellency. And wheresoever there is understanding, there is a reflect act whereby the soul returns upon itself, and knows what it doth. It knows what it wills, it knows what it affects, it knows what it speaks, it knows all in it, and all out of it. It is the property of the soul. Therefore the original word in the Old Testament that signifies the heart, it is taken for the conscience (*gg*). Conscience and heart are all one. I am persuaded in my soul, that is, in my conscience ; and the Spirit witnesseth to our spirit, that is, to our conscience. Conscience is called the spirit, the heart, the soul ; because it is nothing but the soul reflecting and returning upon itself.

Therefore it is called conscience, that is, one knowing joined with another ; because conscience knows itself, and it knows what it knows. It knows what the heart is. It not only knows itself, but it is a knowledge of the heart with God. It is called conscience, because it knows with God ;

for what conscience knows, God knows, that is above conscience. It is a knowledge with God, and a knowledge of a man's self.

And so it may be the soul itself endued with that excellent faculty of reflecting and returning upon itself. Therefore it judgeth of its own acts, because it can return upon itself.

2. Conscience likewise in some sort may be called *a faculty*. The common stream runs that way, that it is a power. It is not one power, but conscience is in all the powers of the soul; for it is in the understanding, and there it rules. Conscience is it by which it is ruled and guided. Conscience is nothing but an application of it to some particular, to something it knows, to some rules it knows before. Conscience is in the will, in the affections, the joy of conscience, and the peace of conscience, and so it runs through the whole soul. It is not one faculty, or two, but it is placed in all the faculties.

3. And some will needs have it *an act, a particular act,* and not a power. When it doth exercise, conscience, it is an act. When it accuseth, or excuseth, or when it witnesseth, it is an act. At that time it is a faculty in act. So that we need not to wrangle whether it be this or that. Let us comprehend as much in our notions as we can; that it is the soul, the heart, the spirit of a man returning upon itself, and it hath something to do in all the powers; and it is an act itself when it is stirred up to accuse or to excuse; to punish a man with fears and terrors, or to comfort him with joy, and the like.

Now conscience is a most excellent thing, it is above reason and sense; for conscience is under God, and hath an eye to God alway. An atheist can have no conscience therefore, because he takes away the ground of conscience, which is an eye to God. Conscience looks to God. It is placed as God's deputy and vicegerent in man. Now it is above reason in this respect. Reason saith, you ought to do this, it is a comely thing, it is a thing acceptable with men amongst whom you live and converse, it becomes your condition as you are a man to carry yourself thus, it agrees with the rules and principles of nature in you. Thus saith reason, and they are good motives from reason. But conscience goeth higher. There is a God to whom I must answer, there is a judgment, therefore I do this, and therefore I do not this. It is a more divine, a more excellent power in man than anything else, than sense or reason, or whatsoever. As it is planted by God for special use, so it looks to God in all.

Therefore the name for conscience in the Greek and Latin signifies a knowledge with another *(hh)* ; because it is a knowledge with God. God and my own heart knows this. God and my conscience, as we use to say.

There are three things joined with conscience.

1. *It is a knowledge with a rule, with a general rule.* That is alway the foundation of conscience in a man *(ii)*. For there is a general rule.—Whosoever commits murder, whosoever commits adultery, whosoever is a blasphemer, a swearer, a covetous, corrupt person, ' he shall not enter into the kingdom of heaven,' as the apostle saith, 1 Cor. vi. 9, *seq.* Here is the general rule. Now conscience applies it, but I am such a one, therefore I shall not enter into heaven. So here the conscience it practiseth with a rule. It is a knowledge of those particulars with a general rule. And then,

2. *It is a knowledge of me, of my own heart.* I know what I have done, I know what I do, and in what manner, whether in hypocrisy or sincerity; I know what I think. And then,

3. *It is a knowledge with God;* for God knows what conscience knows.

He knows what is thought or done.   Conscience is above me, and God is
above conscience.   Conscience is above me and above all men in the
world ; for it is immediately subjugated to God.   Conscience knows more
than the world, and God knows a thousand times more than conscience or
the world.   It is a knowledge with a general rule ; for where there is no
general rule there is no conscience.   To make this a little clearer.   All
have a rule.   Those that have not the word, which is the best rule of all,
yet they have the word written in their hearts ; they have a natural judi-
cature in their souls, their conscience excusing, or accusing one another.
They have a general rule.   You must do no wrong, you must do that which
is right.

In the soul there is a treasure of rules by nature.   The word doth
add more rules, the law and the gospel.   And that part of the soul that
preserves rules is called intellectual, because it preserves rules.   All men
by nature have these graven in the soul.   And therefore the heathen were
exact in the rules of justice, in the principles which they had by nature,
grafted and planted in them.

Now because the copy of the image of God, the law of God written in
nature, was much blurred since the fall, God gave a new copy of his law,
which was more exact.   Therefore the Jews, which had the word of God,
should have had more conscience than the heathen, because they had a
better general rule.   And now we having the gospel too, which is a more
evangelical rule, we should be more exact in our lives than they.

But every man in the world hath a rule.   If men ' sin without the law,
they shall be judged without the law,' Rom. ii. 12, by the principles of
nature.   If they sin under the gospel, they shall be judged by the word
and gospel.   So that conscience, it is a knowledge with a rule, and with
the particular actions that I have done, and a knowledge with God.

In a word, to clear this further concerning the nature of conscience, know
that God hath set up in man a court, and there is in man all that are in a
court.

1. There is a *register* to take notice of what we have done.   Besides the
general rule (for that is the ground and foundation of all), there is conscience, which is a register to set down whatsoever we have done exactly.
The conscience keeps diaries.   It sets down everything.   It is not forgotten, though we think it is, when conscience is once awaked.   As in Jer.
xvii. 1, ' The sins of Judah are written with a pen of iron, and with the point
of a diamond ' upon their souls.   All their wit and craft will not rase it
out.   It may be forgotten a while, by the rage of lusts, or one thing or
other ; but there is a register that writes it down.   Conscience is the
register.

2. And then there are *witnesses*.   ' The testimony of conscience.'   Conscience doth witness, this I have done, this I have not done.

3. There is an *accuser with the witness*.   The conscience, it accuseth, or
excuseth.

4. And then there is *the judge*.   Conscience is the judge.   There it doth
judge, this is well done, this is ill done.

5. Then there is *an executioner*, and conscience is that too.   Upon
accusation and judgment, there is punishment.   The first punishment is
within a man alway before he come to hell.   The punishment of conscience,
it is a prejudice* of future judgment.   There is a flash of hell presently
after an ill act.   The heathen could observe, that God hath framed the

* That is, 'pre-judgment.'—G.

heart and the brain so as there is a sympathy between them, that whatsoever is in the understanding that is well and comfortable, the understanding in the brain sends it to the heart, and raiseth some comfort. If the understanding apprehend dolorous things, ill matters, then the heart smites, as David's ' heart smote him,' 1 Sam. xxiv. 5. The heart smites with grief for the present, and with fear for the time to come.

In good things, it brings joy presently, and hope for the time to come, that follows a good excusing conscience.

God hath set and planted in man this court of conscience, and it is God's hall, as it were, wherein he keeps his first judgment, wherein he keeps his assizes. And conscience doth all the parts. It registereth, it witnesseth, it accuseth, it judgeth, it executes, it doth all.

Now you see in general, what the nature of conscience is, and why it is planted in us by God.

One main end among the rest, besides his love to us to keep us from sin, and then by smiting us to drive us to conversion and repentance, to turn from our sins to God, another main end, is to be a prejudice,* to make way to God's eternal judgment ; for therein things are judged before. When God lays open the book of conscience, when it is written there by this register, we shall have much to do to excuse ourselves, or to plead that we need many witnesses ; for our conscience will accuse us. We shall be self-accusers, self-condemners, as the apostle saith. Conscience will take God's part, and God will take part with conscience. And God hath planted it for this main end, that he might be justified in the damnation of wicked men at the day of judgment.

Now I come to the second particular, that conscience gives evidence or witness. ' This is the evidence or testimony of our conscience.' The witness of conscience it comes in this order. Upon some general rules, that the conscience hath laid up in the soul, out of nature, and out of the book of God, the conscience doth apply those generals to the particulars.

First, *in directing.* This is such a truth in general, you ought to carry yourself thus and thus, to do this, saith conscience.† So it directeth, and is a monitor before it be a witness. Well, if the monitions of conscience be regarded and heard, from thence comes conscience to witness, that the general rule that directs in particulars hath been obeyed ; and so after it hath done its duty in directing, it comes to judge and to witness, this I have done, or this I have not done. So the witness of conscience comes in that manner.

Now if you would know what manner of witness conscience is. It is, 1. A witness that *there is no exception against.* It is a witness that will say all the truth, and will say nothing but the truth. It is a witness that will not be bribed, it will not be corrupted long. For a time we may silence it, but it will not be so long, nor in all things. Some sins may be slubbered over, but there are some sins that by the general light in nature are so known to be naught‡ that conscience will accuse. Therefore it is a faithful judge and witness ; especially in great sins, it is an uncorrupt witness. It is a true register. It is alway writing and setting down, though we know not what it writes for the present, being carried away with vanities and lusts. Yet we shall know afterward, when the book of conscience shall be laid open.

It is a witness that we cannot impeach. No man can say, I had nobody

---

* That is, ' pre-judgment.'—G.   † Margin-note here, ' Joseph's brethren.'—G.
‡ That is, ' naughty, wicked.'—G.

to tell me. Alas! a man's own conscience will tell him well enough at
the day of judgment, and say to him when he is in hell, as Reuben said to
his brethren, when they were in Egypt in prison, 'Did not I tell you, hurt
not the boy?' Gen. xxxvii. 22, *seq*, meddle not with him. So conscience
will say, Did not I witness? did not I give you warning? Yes, I did,
but you regarded it not. It is a faithful witness. There is no exception
against it.

2. And then it is *an inward witness*, it is a domestic witness; a chaplain
in ordinary, a domestical divine. It is alway telling us, and alway ready
to put good things into us. It is an eye-witness, and an ear-witness; for
it is as deep in man as any sin can be. If it be but in thought, conscience
tells me what I think; and conscience tells me what I desire, as well as
what I speak, and what I do. It is an inward and an eye-witness of
everything. As God sees all, and knows all, who is all eye; so conscience
is all eye. It sees everything, it hears everything. It is privy to our
thoughts.

As we cannot escape God's eye, so we cannot escape the eye of conscience. 'Whither shall I flee from thy presence?' saith David. 'If I
go to heaven, thou art there; if I go down into hell, thou art there,' Ps.
cxxxix. 7. So a man may say of conscience, Whither shall I flee from
conscience? If a man could flee from himself, it were somewhat. Conscience is such a thing as that a man cannot flee from it, nor he cannot
bid it begone. It is as inward as his soul. Nay, the soul will leave the
body, but conscience will not leave the soul. What it writes, it writes for
eternity, except it be wiped out by repentance. As St Chrysostom saith,
whatsoever is written there may be wiped out by daily repentance.

You see, then, it is a witness, and how and what manner of witness conscience is.

Use. Therefore, we should not sin in hope of concealment. What if thou conceal it from all others, canst thou conceal [it from] thy own conscience? As
one saith well, What good is it for thee that none knows what is done, when
thou knowest it thyself? What profit is it for him that hath a conscience
that will accuse him, that he hath no man to accuse him but himself? He
is a thousand witnesses to himself. Conscience is not a private witness.
It is a thousand witnesses. Therefore, never sin in hope to have it concealed. It were better that all men should know it than that thyself should
know it. All will be one day written in thy forehead. Conscience will be
a blab. If it cannot speak the truth now, though it be bribed in this life,
it will have power and efficacy in the life to come. Never sin, therefore, in
hope of concealment. Conscience is a witness. We have the witness in
us; and, as Isaiah saith, 'Our sins witness against us.' It is in vain to
look for secrecy. Conscience will discover all.

Use. Again, considering that conscience doth witness, and will witness,
let us labour *that it may witness well*, let us labour *to furnish it with a good
testimony*. Let us carry ourselves so in all our demeanour to God and men
that conscience may give a good testimony, a good witness. It will witness
either for us or against us.

1. Therefore, first of all, labour *to have good rules to guide it*, and then
labour to obey those rules. Knowledge and obedience are necessary, that
conscience may give a good witness. Now, a good witness of conscience
is twofold: a true and honest witness, and then a peaceable witness follows on it; that it may witness truth, and then that it may witness peace
for us.

That conscience may witness truly and excuse us, conscience must be rightly instructed; for naturally conscience can tell us many things. The heathen men, philosophers, we may read it to our shame, they made conscience of things which Christians, that are instructed by a further rule than conscience, that have the book of God to rectify the inward book of conscience, yet they make no conscience of. How many cases did they make scruple of, to discover faults to the buyer in their selling, and to deal truly and honestly, for the second table especially! It should make Christians ashamed.

But besides that rule, we have the rule of the Scriptures, because men are ready to trample upon and to rase out the writing of conscience, but the book of God they cannot; therefore, that is added to help conscience. And God adds his Spirit to his word to convince conscience, and to make the witness of the word more effectual; for although the word say thus and thus, yet till the Spirit convince the soul, and set it down that it is thus, till it convince it with a heavenly light, conscience will not be fully convict. That conscience, therefore, may be able to witness well, let us regard the notions of nature, preserve them. If we do not, God will give us up to gross sins. Let us labour to have right principles and grounds, to cherish principles of nature common with the heathens, and to lay up principles out of the word of God, to preserve the admonitions, and directions, and rules of the word.

And especially the sweet motions of God's blessed Spirit. For conscience alway supposeth a rule, the rule of nature, the rule of the word, and the suggestions of the blessed Spirit with the word.

Therefore, to note by the way, an ignorant man can never have a good conscience, especially a man that affects ignorance, because he hath no rule. He labours to have none. It is not merely ignorance, but likewise obstinacy with ignorance.

He will not know what he should, lest conscience will force him to do what he knows. What a sottish thing is this! It will be the heaviest sin that can be laid to our charge at the day of judgment, not that we were ignorant, but that we refused to know, we refused to have our conscience rectified and instructed.

And those that avoid knowledge because they will not do what they know, they shall know one day that their wilful ignorance will be laid to their charge as a heavy sin.

Labour to have right principles and grounds. What is the reason that commonly men have such bad consciences? They have false principles. They conclude, May I not do what I list? may I not make of my own what I will? and every man for himself, and God for us all. Diabolical principles! And so, commonly if a man examine men that live in wickedness, they have false principles, God sees not, God regards not, and it is time enough to repent. The cause that men live wickedly is false principles. Therefore they have so vile consciences as they have. Their hearts deceive them, and they deceive their hearts. They have false principles put into them by others. They are deceived, and they deceive their hearts. They force false principles upon themselves. Many study for false grounds to live by for their advantage.

There are many that are atheistical, that live even under the gospel, and what rule have they? The example of them by whom they hope to rise. They study their manners. They square their lives by them. This is all the rule they have.

And again, the multitude. They do as the most do, and custom, and other false rules. These rules will not comfort us. To say, I did it by such an example, I did as others among whom I live did, or I did it because it was the custom of the times ; these things being alleged will comfort nothing. For who gave you these rules ? Doth God say anywhere in his word, You shall be judged by the example of others, you shall be judged by the custom of the times you live in ?

No ; you shall be judged by my word. The word that Moses spake, ' and the word that I speak, shall judge you ' at the last day, John xii. 48. They that have not the word shall be judged by the word written in their hearts. ' Those that have sinned without the law ' shall be judged by that, ' without the law of Moses,' Rom. ii. 12.

God hath acquainted us with other rules. We must take heed of this, therefore, that we get good rules. Take heed that they be not false rules. For the want of these directions men come to have ill consciences. Where there is no good rule, there is a blind conscience ; where there is no application of the rule, there is a profane conscience ; and where there is a false rule, there is an erroneous, a scrupulous, a wicked conscience.

A papist, because he hath a false rule, he cannot have a good conscience. The abomination of popery is, that they sin against conscience ; and conscience, indeed, is even with them, for it overthrows the most of their principles. They sin against conscience many ways, I mean not against their own conscience, but they sin against the conscience of others. For what do they ? That they may rule in the consciences of men (for that is the end of their great prelate, the tyrant of souls), they have false rules, that the pope cannot err. Their rule is the authority and judgment of him that cannot err ; and he, for the most part, is an unlearned man in divinity, that never read over the Scriptures in all his life, and he must judge all controversies. Where this is granted, that the pope cannot err, he sits in the conscience to do what he list. And he makes divine laws ; and cursed is he, saith the Council of Trent, that doth not equalise those traditions with the word of God (*jj*).

From this false rule comes all, even rebellion itself. If he give dispensation from the oath of allegiance because he cannot err, therefore they ought to obey him, and rebel against their governors. All rebellion is from that rebellious rebellion that comes from false principles. These men talk of conscience, and they come not to church for conscience sake. What conscience can they have when they have false rules ? To equivocate and lie,— sins against nature. And other rules, that give liberty against the word; that children may disobey their parents, and get into a cloister, &c.

The most of popery, though there were no word of God, it is against nature, against conscience, which God hath planted in man as his deputy, his tenant.

And as they sin against conscience, so, as I said, conscience is even with them. For let a man trust to his conscience, and he can never be a sound papist : except he leave that, and go upon base false grounds, because other great men do it, and because his predecessors have done it, &c. I appeal to their own consciences, if any man at the day of death think to be saved by his merits, doth not Bellarmine (after long dispute of salvation by merits) disclaim it ?* doth he not put away merits, for the uncertainty of his own righteousness ? So their own consciences do wring away the testimony of trusting to merits.

* See Note *g*, vol. I. p. 313.—G.

Again, that original sin is no great sin. It is but the cause of sin, and it is less than any venial sin. Oh, but when conscience is awaked to know what a corrupt estate it is, it will draw from them that which it drew from St Paul, ' O wretched man that I am, who shall deliver me from this body of death ?' Rom. vii. 24. Conscience, when it is awaked, will tell them that it is another manner of sin, and that it is the fountain of all sin.

And so for justification by works. Conscience itself, if there were no book of God, would say it is a false point. And then they plead for ignorance. They have blind consciences. Their clergy being a subtle generation, that have abused the world a long time, because they would sit in the conscience where God should sit, they ' sit in the temple of God,' 2 Thess. ii. 4, and would be respected above that which is due to them— they would be accounted as petty gods in the world. Therefore they keep the people from the knowledge of the true rule, and make what they speak equal with God's word. Now if the people did discern this, they would not be papists long ; for no man would willingly be cozened. Let us labour therefore for a true rule.

2. And when we have gotten rules, *apply them ;* for what are rules without application ? Rules are instrumental things ; and instruments without use are nothing. If a carpenter have a rule, and hang it up by him, and work by conceit, what is it good for ? So to get a company of rules by the word of God (to refine natural knowledge as much as we can), and then to make no use of it in our lives, it is to no purpose ; therefore when we have rules, let us apply them.

In this, those that have the true rule, and apply it not, are better than they that refuse to have the rule, because, as hath been said, an ignorant man that hath not the rule, he cannot be good. But a man that hath the rule, and yet squares not his life by it, yet he can bring the rule to his life. There is a near converse between the heart and the brain. Such a man, he hath the rule in his memory, he hath it in his understanding ; and therefore there is a thousand times more hope of him that cares to know, that cares to hear the word of God, and cares for the means, than of sottish persons that care not to hear, because they would not do that they know, and because they would not have their sleepy, dull, and drowsy conscience awaked. There is no hope of such a one. It should be our care to have right rules, and in the application of them to make much of conscience, that it may apply aright in directing, and then in comfort. If we obey it in directing, it will witness and excuse ; and upon witness and excuse, there will come a sweet paradise to the soul, of joy and peace unspeakable and glorious.

The last thing I observe from these words is this, that

Doct. The testimony and witness of conscience is a ground of comfort and joy.

The reason of the joining these two, the witness of a good conscience, and joy, it is that which I said before in the description of conscience ; for

1. *Conscience first admonisheth, and then witnesseth, and then it excuseth, or accuseth, and then it judgeth, and executeth.** Now the inward execution of conscience is joy, if it be good ; for God hath so planted it in the heart and soul, that where conscience doth accuse, or excuse, there is alway execution. There is alway joy or fear. The affections of joy or fear alway follow. If a man's conscience excuse him, that he hath done well, then conscience comes to be enlarged, to be a paradise to the soul, to be a jubilee,

* In the margin, ' From the office of conscience.'—G.

a refreshing, to speak peace and comfort to a man. For rewards are not kept altogether for the life to come. Hell is begun in an ill conscience, and heaven is begun in a good conscience. An ill conscience is a hell upon earth, a good conscience is a heaven upon earth. Therefore the testimony of a good conscience breeds glorying and rejoicing.

2. Again, conscience when it witnesseth, *it comforts, because when it witnesseth, it witnesseth with God;* and where God is, there is his Spirit, and where the Holy Spirit is, there is joy. For even as heat follows the fire, so joy and glorying accompany the Spirit of God, ' the Spirit of glory,' 1 Pet. i. 14. Now when conscience witnesseth aright, it witnesseth with God; and God is alway clothed with joy. He brings joy and glory into the heart. Conscience witnesseth with God that I am his.

3. And *it witnesseth with myself that I have led my life thus,* ' Our rejoicing is the witness of *our* conscience.' It is not the witness of another man's conscience, but my own. Other men may witness, and say I am thus and thus, but all is to no purpose, if my own conscience tell me I am another man than they take me to be. But when a man's own conscience witnesseth for him, there follows rejoicing. A man cannot rejoice with the testimony of another man's conscience, because another man saith, I am a good man, &c., unless there be the testimony of my own conscience.

Now it is a sweet benefit, an excusing conscience, when it witnesseth well. Let us see it in all the passages of life, that a good conscience in excusing breeds glorying and joy.

It doth breed joy *in life, in death, at the day of judgment.*

1. *In life,* in all the passages of life, in all estates, both good and ill.

(1.) *In good,* the testimony of conscience breeds joy, for it enjoys the pleasures of this life, and the comforts of it with the favour of God. Conscience tells the man that he hath gotten the things well that he enjoys, that he hath gotten the place, and advancement that he hath, well: that he enjoys the comforts of this life with a good conscience, and ' all things are pure to the pure,' Titus i. 15. If he have gotten them ill, conscience upbraids him alway, and therefore he cannot joy in the good estate he hath. If a man had all the contentments in the world, if he had not the testimony of a good conscience, what were all? What contentment had Adam in paradise, after once by sin he had fallen from the peace of conscience? None at all. ' A little that the righteous hath, is better than great riches of the ungodly,' Prov. xvi. 8, because they have not peace of conscience.

(2.) And so for *ill estate,* when conscience witnesseth well, it breeds rejoicing.

[1.] In false imputations, and slanders, and disgraces, as here, it was insinuated into the Corinthians by false teachers, and those that followed them, that St Paul was so and so. Saith St Paul, You may say what you will of me, ' my rejoicing is this, the testimony of my conscience,' that I am not the man which they make me to be in your hearts by their false reports. The witness of conscience is a good and sufficient ground of rejoicing in this case. Therefore holy men have retired to their conscience in all times, as St Paul you see doth here.

So Job, his conscience bare him out in all the false imputations of his comfortless friends that were ' miserable comforters,' Job xvi. 2. They laboured to take away his sincerity from him, the chief cause of his joy. ' You shall not take away my sincerity,' saith he, Job xxvii. 6. You would make me an hypocrite, and thus and thus, but my conscience tells me I am

otherwise, therefore 'you shall not take away my innocency from me.'
And in Job xxxi. 35, 'Behold, it is my desire, that the Almighty would
answer me, and that my adversaries would write a book against me, I would
take it upon my shoulder, I would take it as a crown unto me.' Here was
the force of a good conscience in Job's troubles, that if his adversaries should
write a book against him, yet he would bind it as a crown about him,
xxxi. 36. And so David, in all imputations this was his joy, when they
laid things to his charge that he had never done : he takes this for his joy,
the comfort of his conscience. So St Paul, he retires to his conscience,
and being raised up with the worthiness of a good conscience, he despiseth
all imputations whatsoever. He sets conscience up as a flag of defiance to
all false slanders and imputations that were laid against him, as we see in
the story of the Acts, and in this place and others. Saith he in one place,
' I pass not for man's sentence,' 1 Cor. iv. 3, I pass not for man's day.
Man hath his day, man will have his judgment-seat, and will get upon the
bench, and judge me that I am such and such. I care not for man's day.
There is another judgment-seat that I look unto, and to the testimony of
my conscience, ' My rejoicing is the witness of my conscience.'

Holy men have cause to retire to their own consciences, when they
would rejoice against false imputations. So holy St Austin, what saith he
to a Donatist that wronged him in his reputation ? ' Think of Austin what
you please, as long as my conscience accuseth me not with God, I will give
you leave to think what you will ' (*kk*).

If so be that man's conscience clears him, he cares not a whit for reports ;
because a good man looks more to conscience than to fame. Therefore if
conscience tell him truth, though fame lie he cares not much ; for he
squares not his life by report, but by conscience. Indeed he looks to a
good name, but that is in the last place.

For a good man looks first to God, who is above conscience ; and then
he looks to conscience, which is under God ; and then, in the third place,
he looks to report amongst men. And if God and his conscience excuse
him, though men accuse him, and lay imputations upon him, this or that,
he passeth little for man's judgment. So the witness of conscience, it
comforts in all imputations whatsoever.

[2.] Again, *it comforts in sickness.* Hezekiah was sick. What doth he
retire unto ? ' Remember, Lord, how I have walked uprightly before thee,'
Isa. xxxviii. 3. He goes to his conscience.

In sickness, when a man can eat nothing, a good ' conscience is a continual feast,' Prov. xv. 15. In sorrow it is a musician. A good conscience
doth not only counsel and advise, but it is a musician to delight. It is a
physician to heal. It is the best cordial, the best physic. All other are
physicians of no value, comforts of no value. If a man's conscience be
wounded, if it be not quieted by faith in the blood of Christ ; if he have
not the Spirit to witness the forgiveness of his sins, and to sanctify and
enable him to lead a good life, all is to no purpose, if there be an evil conscience. The unsound body while it is sick, it is in a kind of hell already.

[3.] Again, *take a man in any cross whatsoever, a good conscience doth bear
out the cross, it bears a man up alway.* Because a good conscience, being a
witness with God, it raiseth a man above all earthly things whatsoever.
There is no earthly discouragement that can dismay a good conscience,
because there is a kind of divinity in conscience, put in by God, and it
witnesseth together with God. So that in all crosses it comforts.

So likewise in losses, in want, in want of friends, in want of comforts, in want of liberty; what doth the witness of a good conscience in all these? In want of friends, it is a friend indeed; it is an inward friend, a near friend to us. Put the case that a man have never a friend in the world, yet he hath God and his own conscience. Where there is a good conscience, there is God and his Holy Spirit alway. In want of liberty, in want of outward comforts, he hath the comfort of a good conscience.

A man on his death-bed, he sees he wants all outward comforts, but he hath a good conscience. And so in want of liberty, when a man is restrained, his heart is at liberty.

A wicked man that hath a bad conscience, is imprisoned in his own heart. Though he have never such liberty, though he be a monarch, a bad conscience imprisons him at home, he is in fetters, his thoughts make him afraid of thunder, afraid of everything, afraid of himself; and though there be nobody else to awe him, yet his conscience awes him. Where there is a conscience under the guilt of sin unrepented, [though] there is the greatest liberty in the world, there is restraint; for conscience is the worst prison. Where there is a good conscience, there is an inward enlargement. A good man in the greatest restraint hath liberty. Paul and Silas, Acts xvi., in the dungeon, in the hell of the dungeon, in the worst place of the dungeon, in the stocks, and at the worst time of the day, of the natural day, I mean, at midnight, and in the worst usage, when they were misused, and whipped withal, they had all the discouragements that could be; and yet they sang at midnight, these blessed men, Paul and Silas. Because their hearts were enlarged, there was a paradise in the very dungeon.

As where the king is, there is his court, so it is where God is. God in the prison, in the noisome dungeon, by his Spirit so enlarged their hearts, that they sang at midnight. Whereas if conscience be ill, if it were in paradise, conscience would fear, as we see in Adam, Gen. iii. 8. St Paul in prison was better than Adam in paradise, when he had offended God. Adam had outward comforts enough; but when he had sinned, his conscience made him afraid of him from whom he should have all comfort; it made him afraid of God, and hide himself among the leaves. Alas, a poor shift! We see then, conscience doth witness, and the witness of it when it is good doth cause the soul to glory and rejoice, not only in positive ills, in slanders and crosses, but in losses, in want of friends, in want of comforts, in want of liberty.

And so for the time to come, in evils threatened, a good conscience is bold: 'It fears no ill tidings,' Ps. cxii. 8. 'My heart is fixed, my heart is fixed,' saith David. 'Wicked men are like the trees of the forest.' Wicked Ahaz,' his heart 'did tremble and shake as the leaves with the wind,' Isa. vii. 2. The noise of fear is alway in their ears. An ill conscience, when it is mingled with ill news, when there are two fears together, it must needs be a great fear.

2. And a good conscience, when it hath laid up grounds of joy in life, in the worst estate and condition of life, *then it makes use of joy in death;* for when all comforts are taken from a man, when his friends cannot comfort him, and all earthly things leave him, then that conscience that hath gone along with him, that hath been a monitor, and a witness all his lifetime, now it comes to speak good things to him, now it comforts him, now conscience is somebody. At the hour of death, when nothing else will be regarded, when nothing will comfort, then conscience doth. 'The righteous hath hope in his death,' as the wise man saith, Prov. xiv. 32. Death is

called the king of fears, because it makes all afraid. It is the terrible of terribles, saith the philosopher ; but here is a king above the king of fears. A good conscience is above the king of fears, death. A good conscience is so far from being discouraged by this king of fears, that it is joyful even in death ; because it knows that then it is near to the place where conscience shall be fully enlarged, where there shall be no annoyance, nor no grievance whatsoever.

Death is the end of misery, and the beginning of happiness. Therefore a good conscience is joyful in death.

3. And after death, *at the day of judgment*. There the witness of conscience is a wondrous cause of joy ; for there a man that hath a good conscience, he looks upon the Judge, his brother : he looks on him with whom he has made his peace in his lifetime before, and now he receives that which he had the beginnings of before, then he lifts up his head with joy and comfort. So you see how the witness of conscience causeth glory and joy in all estates whatsoever, in life, in death, after death. It speaks for a man there. It never leaves him till it have brought him to heaven itself, where all things else leave a man.

Therefore, how much should we prize and value the testimony and witness of a good conscience ! And what madness is it for a man to humour men, and displease conscience, his best friend ! Of all persons and all things in the world, we should reverence our own conscience most of all. Wretched men despise the inward witness of this inward friend, this inward divine, this inward physician, this inward comforter, this inward counsellor. It is no better than madness that men should regard that everything else be good and clean, and yet notwithstanding in the midst of all to have foul consciences.

Obj. But to answer an objection, and to unloose some knots. It may be said, that when the hearts of people are good, yet there a good conscience concludes not alway for comfort. Where there is faith in Christ, and an honest life, conscience should conclude comfort. Here is the rule, this I have obeyed, therefore I should have comfort.

Now this we see crossed ofttimes, that Christians that live exact lives are often troubled in conscience. How can trouble of conscience stand with joy upon the witness of conscience ?

Ans. I answer, the witness of conscience, when it is a good conscience, it doth not alway breed joy.

1. *It is because our estate is imperfect here*, and conscience doth not alway witness out of the goodness of it. Sometime conscience is misled, and so sometimes good Christians take the error of conscience for the witness of conscience.

These things should be distinguished. Conscience sometime in the best errs, as well as gives a true witness.

If we take the error of conscience for the witness of conscience, there will come trouble of conscience, and that deservedly, through our own folly

Now conscience doth err in good men, sometimes when they regard rules which they should not, or when they mistake the matter and do not argue aright. As for instance, when they gather thus, I have not grace in such a measure, and therefore I have none, I am not the child of God.

What a rule is this ? This is the error of conscience ; and therefore it must needs breed perplexity of conscience. A good conscience, when it is right, cannot witness thus, because the word doth not say thus. Is a nullity and an imperfection all one ? No ; there is much difference in the whole kind. A nullity is nothing. An imperfection, though it be but a little degree, yet it is something. This is the error of conscience, and from thence comes trouble of conscience, which makes men reason ill many ways. As for instance, I have not so much grace as such a one hath, and therefore I have no grace. Now that is a false reasoning; for every one hath his due measure. If thou be not so great a rich man as the richest in the town, yet thou mayest be rich in thy kind.

2. Again, when conscience *looks to the humour.* You are to live by faith, and not by the humour of melancholy. When the instrument of reason that should judge is distempered by melancholy, it reasons from thence falsely. Because melancholy persuades me that I am so, therefore conscience being led by the humour of the body, saith I am so. Who bade thee live by humour? thou must live by rule. Melancholy may tell thee sometime when it is in strength, that thou art made of glass, as it hath done some. It will deceive thee in bodily things, wherein sense can confute melancholy, much more will it if we yield to it in matters of the soul. It will persuade us that we are not the children of God, that we have not grace and goodness when we have.

3. Again, hence it is that conscience doth not conclude comfort in God's children, *because it looks to the ill,* and not to the good that is in them; for there are those two things in God's children. There is good and ill. Now in the time of temptation they look to the ill, and think they have no good, because they will not see anything but ill. They fix their eyes on the remainders of their rebellious lusts, which are not fully subdued in them, and they look wholly on them. Whereas they should have two eyes, one to look on that which is good, that God may have glory and they comfort.

Now they, fixing their eyes altogether on that which is naught, and because they do not, or will not, see that which is good, therefore they have no comfort; because they suffer conscience to be ill led that it doth not its duty.

And conscience in good men, it looks sometimes to that that it should not in others, in regard of others. It looks to the flourishing of wicked men, and therefore it concludes, ' Certainly I have washed my hands in vain,' since such men thrive and prosper in the world, Ps. xxxvii. 35, *seq.,* and Ps. lxxiii. 13. Who bade thee look to this, and to be uncomfortable from thence, that thy estate is not good, because it is not such an estate? ' So foolish, and as a beast was I before thee,' saith David, because I regarded such things, Ps. lxxiii. 22. No marvel if men be uncomfortable that are led away by scandals. Look to faith, go to the word, to the sanctuary. ' I went to the sanctuary,' saith he, ' and there I saw the end of these men,' ver. 17. So conscience must be suffered to have its work, to be led by a true rule.

4. Again, conscience sometimes concludes not comfort, when there is ground of comfort, *from the remainders of corruptions and infirmities;* whereas we should be driven by our infirmities to Christ. And conscience sometimes in good men doth not exercise its work. It is drawn away with vain delights, even in the best of men.

And conscience, of its own unworthiness, and of the greatness of the things it looks for, being joined together, it makes a man that he joys not when he hath cause. As for instance, when the soul sees that God in Christ hath pardoned all my sins, and hath vouchsafed his Spirit to me, and will give me heaven in the world to come, to such a wretch as I am; here being a conflict between the conscience and sense of its own unworthiness, and the greatness of the good promised, the heart begins to stagger, and to doubt for want of sound faith.

Indeed, if we look on our own unworthiness, and the greatness of the good things promised, we may wonder ; but alas !* God is infinite in goodness, he transcends our unworthiness ; and in the gospel, the glory of God's mercy, it triumphs over our unworthiness, and over our sins. Whatsoever our sin and unworthiness is, his goodness in the gospel triumphs over all.

In innocency God should have advanced an innocent man ; but the gospel is more glorious. For he comes to sinners, to condemned persons by nature, and yet God triumphs over their sins and unworthiness. He regards not what we deserve, but what may stand with the glory of his mercy. Therefore we should banish those thoughts, and enjoy our own privilege, the promises of heaven, and happiness, and all comforts whatsoever. So much for the answer of that objection.

Now if we would joy in the witness of a good conscience, we must especially in the time of temptation live by faith, and not by feeling, not by what we feel for the present. But as we see Christ in his greatest horror, ' My God, my God, why hast thou forsaken me ? ' Mark xvii. 34, he goes to *my God* still, we must ' live by faith and not by sense,' 2 Cor. v. 7.

And then if we would rejoice in extremities, remember that God works by contraries. God will bring us to heaven, but it must be by hell. God will bring us to comfort, but it must be by sense of our own unworthiness. He will forgive our sins, but it must be by sight and sense of our sins. He will bring us to life, but it must be by death. He will bring us to glory, but it must be by shame. God works by contraries ; therefore in contraries believe contraries. When we are in a state that hath no comfort, yet we may joy in it if we believe in Christ. He works by contraries.

As in the creation he made all out of nothing, order out of confusion; so in the work of the new creation, in the new creature, he doth so likewise ; therefore be not dismayed.

Remember this rule likewise, that in the covenant of grace God requires truth, and not measure. Thou art not under the law, but under the covenant of grace. A little fire is true fire as well as the whole element of fire. A drop of water is water as well as the whole ocean. So if it be true faith, true grief for sins, true hatred of them, true desire of the favour of God, and to grow better; truth is respected in the covenant of grace, and not any set measure.

What saith the covenant of grace ? ' He that believes and repents shall be saved,' Mark xvi. 16, not he that hath a strong faith, or he that hath perfect repentance. So St Paul saith, as we shall see after, ' This is our rejoicing, that in simplicity and sincerity we have had our conversation among you,' 2 Cor. i. 12. He doth not say, that our conversation hath been perfect. So if we would have joy in the testimony of conscience, we must not abridge ourselves of joy, because we have not a perfect measure of grace ; but rejoice that God hath wrought any measure of grace in such unclean and polluted hearts as ours are. For the least measure of grace is a pledge of perfection in the world to come.

' *This is our rejoicing, the testimony of our conscience,*' &c. Hence we may gather clearly, that

Obs. *A man may know his own estate in grace.*

* See note, p. 169.—G.

I gather it from the place thus, ' Our rejoicing is this, the testimony of our conscience, that in simplicity,' &c.

Where there is joy, and the ground of joy, there is a knowledge of the estate ; but a Christian hath glorying, and a ground of glorying in himself, and he knows it. He hath that in him that witnesseth that estate. He hath the witness of conscience ; therefore he may know and be assured of it. If this testimony were not a true testimony, it were something. But all men naturally have a conscience ; and a Christian hath a sanctified conscience. And where that is, there is a true testimony, and true joy from that testimony. Therefore he may be assured of his salvation, and have true joy and comfort, a heaven upon earth before he come to heaven itself.

If conscience testify of itself, and from witnessing give cause of joy, much more the Spirit of God coming into the conscience, ' The Spirit bears witness with our spirits.' If our spirit and conscience bear witness to us of our conversation in simplicity and sincerity, and from thence of our estate in grace, much more by the witness of two. ' By the witness of two or three everything shall be confirmed,' Matt. xviii. 16 ; but our spirits, and conscience, and the Spirit of God, which every child of God hath, witnesseth that we are the children of God, Rom. viii. 14, *et alibi*. ' The Spirit witnesseth with our spirits that we are the sons of God.' Therefore a Christian may know his estate in grace.

The spirit of a man knows himself, and the Spirit of God knows him likewise, and it knows what is in the heart of God ; and when these two meet, the Spirit of God that knows the secrets of God, and that knows our secrets, and our spirit that knows our heart likewise, what should hinder but that we may know our own estate ? It is the nature of conscience, as I told you, to reflect upon itself and upon the person in whom it is, to know what is known by it, and to judge, and condemn, and execute itself, by inward fear and terror, in ill ; and in good, by comfort and joy in a man's self. It is the property that the soul hath above all creatures, to return and recoil upon itself. If this be natural to man, much more to the spirit of a man. For if a man know what is in himself naturally, his own wit, and understanding, which is alway with him, bred up with him, much more he knows by his spirit the things that are adventitious, that come from without him, that is the work of grace.

If a man, by a reflect knowledge, know what naturally is in him, in what part he hath it, and how he exerciseth it ; if he know and remember what he hath done, and the manner of it, whether well or ill ; then he may know the work of the Spirit that comes from without him, that works a change in him.

We say of light, that it discovers itself and all other things ; so the soul it is lightsome, and therefore knows itself and knows other things.

The Spirit of God is much more lightsome. Where it is it discovers itself, and lighteneth the soul. It discovereth the party in whom it is. As the apostle saith, 1 Cor. ii. 12. ' We have the Spirit, whereby we know the things that we receive of God.' It not only worketh in us, but it teacheth us what it hath wrought. Therefore a Christian knows that he is in the state of grace, he knows his virtues, and his disposition ; except it be in the time of temptation, and upon those grounds named before.

Therefore we should labour to know our estate, to ' examine ourselves whether we be in the faith or no, except we be reprobates and castaways,' as the apostle speaks, 2 Cor. xiii. 5. A Christian should aim at this, to understand his own estate in grace upon good grounds.

Obj. But it may be objected ; how can we know our estate in grace, our virtues are so imperfect, our abilities are so weak and feeble.

Ans. I answer, the ground of judging aright of our estate, it is not worthiness or perfection, but sincerity. We must not look for perfection. For that makes the papists to teach that there may be doubting, because they look to false grounds ; but we must look to the ground in the covenant of grace, to grace itself, and not to the measure. Where there is truth and sincerity, there is the condition of the covenant of grace, and there is a ground for a man to build his estate in grace on.

The perfect righteousness of Christ is that that gives us title to heaven ; but to know that we have right in that title, is the simplicity and sincerity in our walking, in our conversation, as the apostle saith here, ' This is our rejoicing,' &c. Therefore Christians, when they are set upon by temptations of their own misdoubting hearts, and by Satan, they must not go to the great measure of grace that is in others, that they have not so much as others, and therefore they have none ; nor to the great measure of grace that they want themselves, but to the truth of their grace, the truth of their desires and endeavours, the truth of their affections. ' Hereby we know that we are translated from death to life, because we love the brethren,'

Use. This should stir us up *to have a good conscience, that we may rejoice.* Why should we labour that we may rejoice ? Why ? what is our life without joy ? and what is joy without a good conscience ?

What is our life without joy ? Without joy we can do nothing. We are like an instrument out of tune. An instrument out of tune it yields but harsh music. Without joy we are as a member out of joint. We can do nothing well without joy, and a good conscience, which is the ground of joy. A man without joy is a palsy-member that moves itself unfitly, and uncomely. He goes not about things as he should. A good conscience breeds joy and comfort. It enables a man to do all things comely in the sight of God, and comfortably to himself. It makes him go cheerfully through his business. A good ' conscience is a continual feast,' Prov. xv. 15. Without joy we cannot suffer afflictions. We cannot die well without it. Simeon died comfortably, because he died in peace, when he had embraced Christ in his heart, and in his arms, Mat. ix. 36. Without joy and the ground of joy we can neither do nor suffer anything. Therefore in Psalm li. 12, David, when he had lost the peace and comfort of a good conscience, he prays for the free Spirit of God. Alas ! till God had enlarged his heart with the sense of a good conscience in the pardon of his sins, and given him the power of his Spirit to lead a better life for the time to come, his spirit was not free before. He could not praise God with a large spirit. He wanted freedom of spirit. His conscience was bound. His lips were sealed up. ' Open my lips, and my mouth shall shew forth thy praise,' Ps. li. 15. His heart was bound, and therefore he prays to have it enlarged. ' Restore to me thy joy and salvation,' Ps. li. 12 ; intimating that we cannot have a free spirit without joy, and we cannot have joy without a good conscience sprinkled with the blood of Christ, in the pardon of our sins.

If it be so, that we cannot do anything nor suffer anything as we should, that we cannot praise God, that we cannot live nor die without joy, and the ground of it, the testimony of a good conscience ; let us labour, then, that conscience may witness well unto us.

Especially considering that an ill conscience, it is the worst thing in the world. There is no friend so good as a good conscience. There is no foe so ill as a bad conscience. It makes us either kings or slaves. A man that hath a good conscience, that witnesseth well for him, it raiseth his heart in a princely manner above all things in the world. A man that hath a bad conscience, though he be a monarch, it makes him a slave. A bad conscience embitters all things in the world to him, though they be never so comfortable in themselves. What is so comfortable as the presence of God? What is so comfortable as the light? Yet a bad conscience, that will not be ruled, it hates the light, and hates the presence of God, as we see Adam, when he had sinned, he fled from God, Gen. iii. 8.

A bad conscience cannot joy in the midst of joy. It is like a gouty foot or a gouty toe covered with a velvet shoe. Alas! what doth it ease it? What doth glorious apparel ease the diseased body? Nothing at all. The ill is within. There the arrow sticks.

And so in the comforts of the word, if the conscience be bad, we that are the messengers of comfort, we may apply comfort to you; but if there be one within that saith thus, It is true, but I regarded not the word before, I regarded not the checks of conscience, conscience will speak more terror than we can speak peace. And after long and wilful rebellion, conscience will admit of no comfort for the most part. Regard it, therefore, in time; labour in time that it may witness well. An ill conscience, when it should be most comforted, then it is most terrible. At the hour of death we should have most comfort, if we had any wisdom. When earthly comforts shall be taken from us, and at the day of judgment, then an ill conscience, look where it will, it hath matter of terror. If it look up, there is the Judge armed with vengeance; if it look beneath, there is hell ready to swallow it; if it look on the one side, there is the devil accusing and helping conscience; if it look round about, there is heaven and earth, and all on fire, and within there is a hell. Where shall the sinner and ungodly appear? ' If the righteous scarcely be saved, where shall the sinner and ungodly appear,' 1 Pet. iv. 18, at that time?

O let us labour to have a good conscience, and to exercise the reflect * power of conscience in this world; that is, let us examine ourselves, admonish ourselves, judge ourselves, condemn ourselves, do all in ourselves. Let us keep court at home first, let us keep the assizes there, and then we shall have comfort at the great assizes.

Therefore, God out of his love hath put conscience into the soul, that we might keep a court at home. Let conscience, therefore, do its worst now, let it accuse, let it judge; and when it hath judged, let it smite us and do execution upon us, that, ' having judged ourselves, we may not be condemned with the world,' 1 Cor. xi. 32.

If we suffer not conscience to have its full work now, it will have it one day. A sleepy conscience will not alway sleep. If we do not suffer conscience to awake here, it will awaken in hell, where there is no remedy.

Therefore, give conscience leave to speak what it will. Perhaps it will tell thee a tale in thine ear which thou wouldst be loath to hear, it will pursue thee with terrors like a bloodhound, and will not suffer thee to rest; therefore, as a bankrupt, thou art loath to look in thy books, because there is nothing but matter of terror. This is but a folly, for at the last conscience will do its duty. It will awaken either here or in hell. Therefore, we are to hope the best of them that have their consciences opened here. There

* That is, ' reflex.'—G.

is hope that they will make their peace with God, that ' they will agree with their adversary while they are in the way,' Mat. v. 25. If thou suffer conscience to be sleepy and drowsy till it be awaked in hell, woe unto thee! for then thy estate is determined of; it will be a barren repentance. Now thy repentance may be fruitful, it may force thee to make thy peace with God. Dost thou think it will alway be thus with thee? Thou besottest thy conscience with sensuality, and sayest, ' Go thy way, and come another time,' as he said to St Paul, Acts xxiv. 25. I will tell thee, this peace will prove a tempest in the end.

Conscience of all things in the world deserves the greatest reverence, more than any monarch in the world; for it is above all men, it is next unto God. And yet what do many men? Regard the honour of their friends more than conscience, that inward friend that shall accompany them to heaven, that will go with them to death and to judgment, and make them lift up their heads with joy when other friends cannot help them, but must needs leave them in death. Now, for a man to follow the humours of men, to follow the multitude, and to stain conscience, what a foolish wretch is he! Though such men think themselves never so wise, it is the greatest folly in the world to stain conscience to please any man, because conscience is above all men.

Again, those that follow their own humours, their own dispositions, and are carried away with their own lusts, it is a folly and madness; for the time will come that that which their covetous, base lust hath carried them to, that shall be taken away, as honours, riches, pleasures, which is the fuel of that lust which makes them now neglect conscience; all shall be taken away in sickness or in the time of despair, when conscience shall be awaked. Now, what folly is it to please thy own lust, which thou shouldst mortify and subdue, and to displease conscience, thy best friend! And then when thy lust is fully satisfied, all that hath been fuel to it, that hath fed it, shall be taken away at the hour of death, or some special judgment, and conscience shall be awaked, and shall torment thee for giving liberty to thy base lusts and to thyself. And those eyes of thy soul that thy offence delighted to shut up, there shall some punishment come, either in this life or in that to come, that shall open those eyes, as Adam's eyes were opened after his sin. Why? Were they not open before? He had such a strong desire to the apple, he did not regard them; but his punishment afterward opened those eyes, which his inordinate desire shut. So it shall be with every sinner. Therefore, regard no man in the world more than thy conscience. Regard nothing, no pleasure, no profit, more than conscience; reverence it more than anything in the world. Happy is that man that carries with him a good conscience, that can witness that he hath said, nor done nothing that may vex or grieve conscience. If it be otherwise, whatsoever a man gains he loseth in conscience, and there is no comparison between those two. One crack, one flaw in conscience, will prove more disadvantageous than the rest will be profitable. Thou must cast up the rest again. ' They are sweet bits downward, but they shall be gravel in the belly,' Prov. xx. 17.

We think when we have gained anything, when we have done anything, we shall hear no more of it, as David said to Joab, when he set him to make away Uriah, ' Let not this trouble thee,' 2 Sam. xi. 25. So, let not this ill gain, let not this ill speech or this ill carriage, trouble thee, thou shalt hear no more of this. We take order to stop and silence conscience, thinking never to hear more of it. Oh, but remember, conscience will have its work; and the longer we defer the witness and work of conscience, the more it will terrify and accuse us afterward.

Therefore, of all men, be they never so great, they are most miserable that follow their wills and their lusts most; that never have any outward check or inward check of conscience, but drown it with sensual pleasures. As Charles the IXth, who at night, when conscience hath the fittest time to work, a man being retired, then he would have his singing boys, after he had betrayed them in that horrible massacre,* after which he never had peace and quiet; and as Saul sent for David's harp when the evil spirit was upon him, 1 Sam. xvi. 23, so wicked men, they look for foreign helps. But it will not be; for the greatest men with their foreign helps are most miserable.

The reason is, because the more they sink in rebellion and sin against conscience, the more they sink in terrors. It shall be the greatest torment to those that have had their wills most in the world. The more their conscience is silenced and violenced in this world, the more vocal it shall be at the hour of death, and the day of judgment. Therefore judge who are the most miserable men in the world (although they have never so much regard in the world besides), those that have consciences, but will not suffer them to work, but with sensuality within them, and by pleasing, flattering speech of those without them, they keep it down, and take order that neither conscience within, nor none other without, shall disturb them; if they do, they shall be served as Ahab dealt with Micaiah, 2 Kings xxii. 24. These men that are thus at peace in sinful courses, of all men they are most miserable. They enjoy their pleasure here for a little time, but their conscience shall torment them for ever; and shall say to them, as Reuben said to his brethren, ' I told you this before, but you would not hearken to me, and now you shall be tormented.'

Conscience is an evil beast. It makes a man rise against himself. Therefore of all men, those that be disordered in their courses, that neglect conscience, and neglect the means of salvation, that should awaken conscience, they are the most miserable. For the longer they go on, the more they sink in sin; and the more they sink in sin, the more they sink in terror of conscience; if not now, yet they shall hereafter.

If we desire therefore to have joy and comfort at all times, let us labour to have a good conscience that may witness well. And therefore let us every day keep an audit within doors, every day cast up our accounts, every day draw the blood of Christ over our accounts, every day beg forgiveness of sins, and the Spirit of Christ to lead us, that so we may keep account every day, that we may make our reckonings even every day, that we may have the less to do in the time of sickness, in the time of temptation, and in the time of death, when we have discharged our consciences before by keeping session at home in our own hearts.

This should be the daily practice of a Christian, and then he may lay himself down in peace.

He that sleeps with a conscience defiled, is as he that sleeps among wild beasts, among adders and toads, that if his eyes were open to see them, he would be out of his wits. He that sleeps without a good conscience, he is an unadvised man. God may make his bed his grave, he may smite him suddenly. Therefore let us every day labour to have a good conscience, that so we may have matter of perpetual joy.

A good conscience especially, is an evangelical conscience; for a legal

* That is, of Bartholomew. The after-dread of Charles IX. is recorded by all his historians and biographers. See footnote, vol. i. p. 149.—G.

good conscience none have; that is, such a conscience as acquits a man that he hath obeyed the law in all things exactly. A legal complete good conscience none have, except in some particular fact; there is a good conscience in fact. As the heathen could excuse themselves, they were thus and thus, Rom. ii. 15; and God ministereth much joy in that. But an evangelical good conscience is that we must trust to; that is, such a conscience that though it knows itself guilty of sin, yet it knows that Christ hath shed his blood for sinners; and such a conscience as by means of faith is sprinkled with the blood of Christ, and is cleared from the accusations of sin.

There is an evangelical conscience when, by faith wrought by the Spirit of God, in the hearing of the gospel, we lay hold upon the obedience and righteousness of Christ. And such is the obedience and righteousness of Christ, that it pacifieth the conscience, which nothing else in the world will do. The conscience, without a full obedience, it will alway stagger.

And that is the reason that conscience confounds and confutes the popish way of salvation by works, &c. Because the conscience alway staggers, and fears, I have not done works enough, I have not done them well enough; those that I have done they have been corrupt and mixed, and therefore I dare not bring them to the judgment-seat of God, to plead them meritorious. Therefore they do well to hold uncertainty of salvation; because, holding merit, they must needs be uncertain of their salvation. A true Christian is certain of his salvation, because his conscience lays hold on the blood of Christ, because the obedience whereby he claims heaven is a superabundant obedience, it is the satisfaction of Christ, as the apostle saith in that excellent place, Heb. ix. 14, 'The blood of Christ, which offered himself by the eternal Spirit (that is, by the Godhead), shall cleanse your consciences from dead works to serve the living God.' The blood of Christ that offered himself, his human nature by his divine, to God as a sacrifice, it shall purge your consciences from dead works. The blood of Christ, that is, the sacrifice, the obedience of Christ, in offering himself, fully pacified God, and answered the punishment which we should have endured; for he was our Surety. 'The blood of Christ speaks better than the blood of Abel,' Heb. xii. 24. It speaks better than our sins. Our sins cry vengeance, but the blood of Christ cries mercy.

The blood of Christ out-cries our sins. The guilty conscience for sin cries, Guilty, guilty, hell, damnation, wrath, and anguish; but the blood of Christ cries, I say, mercy, because it was shed by our surety in our behalf. His obedience is a full satisfaction to God.

Now, the way to have a good conscience is, upon the accusations of an evil conscience by the law, to come to Christ our surety, and to get our consciences sprinkled by faith in his blood, to get a persuasion that he shed his blood for us, and upon that to labour to be purged by the Spirit. There are two purgers, the blood of Christ from the guilt of sin, and the Spirit of Christ from the stain of sin; and upon that comes a complete good conscience, being justified by the blood of Christ, and sanctified by the Spirit of Christ. Therefore Christ came not by blood alone, or by water alone, but by water *and* blood; by blood in justification, by water in sanctification and holiness of life.

Quest. Why do we allege this now for the sacrament?

Ans. We speak of a good conscience, 'which is a continual feast,' Prov. xv. 15. How comes a good conscience to be such a continual feast?

An evangelical conscience is a feast indeed; because it feeds on a higher feast: it feeds on Christ. He is the Passover lamb, as the apostle applies it, 1 Cor. v. 7. He is the 'Passover, slain for us;' and there is represented in the sacrament, his body broken and his blood poured out for our sins. He came to feast us, and we shall feast with him.

Hereupon, if we bring repentance for our sins past, and faith whereby we are incorporate into Christ, then our consciences speak peace; and as it is in 1 Pet. iii. 21, the conscience makes a good demand. 'It is not baptism, but the demand of a good conscience.' When the conscience hath fed on Christ, it demands boldly, as it is Rom. viii. 33, of Satan and all enemies, 'Who shall lay anything to our charge? It is God that justifieth. It is Christ that died, or rather that is risen again.' It boldly demands of God, who hath given his Son. The bold demand of conscience prevails with God, and this comes by faith in Christ. Now, this is strengthened by the sacrament. Here are the visible representations and seals that we are incorporate more and more into Christ; and so feeding upon Christ once, our conscience is pacified and purged from all dead works, and we come to have a continual feast.

Christ is first the Prince of righteousness, the righteous King, and then 'Prince of peace;' first he gives righteousness, and then he speaks peace to the conscience. 'The kingdom of God is righteousness, peace, and joy in the Holy Ghost,' Rom. xiv. 17.

So that all our feast and joy and comfort that we have in our consciences, it must be from righteousness. A double righteousness: the righteousness of Christ which hath satisfied and appeased the wrath of God fully; and then we must have the righteousness of a good conscience sanctified by the Spirit of Christ. We must put them together alway. We can never have communion with Christ, and have forgiveness of sins; but we must have a spirit of sanctification. 'There is mercy with thee, that thou mayest be feared,' Ps. cxxx. 4. Where there is mercy in the forgiveness of sin, there is a disposition to fear it ever after. Therefore if for the present you would have a good conscience, desire God to strengthen your faith in the blood of Christ poured out for you; desire God to strengthen your faith in the crucified body of Christ broken for you; that so feeding on Christ, who is your surety, who himself is yours, and all is yours, you may ever have the feast of a good conscience, that will comfort you in false imputations, that will comfort you in life and in death, and at the day of judgment. 'This is our rejoicing in all things, the testimony of our conscience;' first purged by 'the blood of Christ,' and then purged and sanctified by the Spirit of Christ, that we have had our 'conversation in simplicity and sincerity,' &c.

'*Our rejoicing is this, that in simplicity and sincerity.*' This is the matter of this testimony of conscience, that is simplicity and sincerity. St Paul glories in his simplicity and sincerity. And mark that by the way, it is no vain glorying, but lawful upon such cautions as I named before. But to add a little,—a man in some cases may glory in the graces of God that are in him; but with these cautions.

First, if so be that he look on them *as the gifts of God.*

Secondly, if he look on them *as stained with his own defects*, and so in that respect be humbled.

Thirdly, if he look upon them *as fruits of his justification*, and as fruits *of his assurance of his salvation*, and not as causes.

And then, if it *be before men that he glories: not when he is to deal with*

God. When men lay this and that imputation upon a man, he may rejoice, as St Paul doth here, in the testimony of his conscience, ' in simplicity and sincerity.'

The matter of the testimony of conscience wherein he glories is ' simplicity and godly sincerity,' or, as the words may well be read, ' in the simplicity and sincerity of God,' such as proceeds from God, and such as aims at and looks to God, and resembles God. For both simplicity and sincerity come from God. They are wrought by God; and therein we resemble God. And both of them have an eye to God, a respect to God. So it is in the original, ' in the simplicity and sincerity of God ' (*ll*).

There is not much difference between simplicity and sincerity. The one expresseth the other. If you will have the difference, simplicity especially respects men, our conversation amongst men. Simplicity hath an eye to God in all things in religion, opposite to hypocrisy in religion. ' Simplicity,' that is opposed to doubleness. Where doubleness is, there is alway hypocrisy, opposed to sincerity; and where simplicity is, there is alway sincerity, truth to God. But it is not good to be very exact and punctual in the distinction of these things. They may one express the other very well.

' Simplicity.' St Paul's rejoicing was, that his conscience witnessed to him his simplicity in his whole conversation in the world, his whole course of life, which the Scripture calls in other places a ' walking,' Acts ix. 31. St Paul means this first of himself; and then he propounds himself an example to us.

Quest. How was St Paul's conversation in simplicity ?

Ans. Not only if we consider St Paul as a Christian, but consider him as an apostle, his conversation was in simplicity. It was without guile, without seeking himself, without seeking his own ; for rather than he would be grievous to the Corinthians, the man of God he wrought himself. Because he would not give any the least scandal to them, being a rich people, he had rather live by his own labour than to open his* mouth. He did not see't himself. In a word, he did not serve himself of the gospel. He served Christ. He did not serve himself of Christ.

There are many that serve themselves of the gospel, that serve themselves of religion. They care no more for religion than will serve their own turn. St Paul's conversation was in simplicity. He had no such aim. He did not preach of envy, or of malice, or for gain, as he taxeth some of the Philippian teachers, ' Some preach Christ,' not of simplicity and sincerity, ' but of envy,' &c., Philip. i. 18.

Then again, as an apostle and a teacher, his conversation was in simplicity ; because he mingled nothing with the word of God in teaching. His doctrine is pure. ' What should the chaff do with the wheat ?' Jer. xxiii. 28. What should the dross do with the gold ? He did not mingle his own conceits and devices with the word : for he taught the pure word of God, the simple word of God, simple without any mixture of any by-aims. So the blessed apostle was simple both in his doctrine and in his intentions ; propounding himself herein exemplary to all us, that, as we look to hold up our heads with comfort, and to glory in all estates whatsoever, so our consciences must bear us witness that we carry ourselves in the simplicity and sincerity of God.

Now simplicity is, when there is a conformity of pretension and intention, when there is nothing double, when there is not a contradiction in the spirit of a man, and in his words and carriage outwardly. That is simplicity,

* Qu. ' their ? '—G.

when there is an exact conformity and correspondence in a man's judgment and speech, in his affections and actions. When a man judgeth simply as the truth of the thing is, and when he affects as he judgeth, when he loves and hates as he judgeth, and he speaks as he affects and judgeth, and he doth as he speaks, then a man is a simple man.

Simple, that is properly, that hath no mixture of the contrary. As we say, light is a simple thing; it cannot endure darkness : fire is a simple body ; it cannot endure the contrary with it : so the pure majesty of God cannot endure the least stain whatsoever. So it is with the holy disposition of a Christian. When he is once a new creature, there is a simplicity in him. Though there be a mixture, yet he studies simplicity ; he studies to have nothing opposite to the Spirit of God ; he studies not to have any contradiction in him ; he labours that his heart may not go one way, and his carriage another ; that his pretensions be not one, and his intentions another. He bears the image of Christ. You know Christ is compared to a lamb, a simple creature, fruitful to men, innocent in himself. So the Holy Ghost appeared in the shape of a dove, a simple creature, that hath no way to avoid danger but by flight ; a harmless creature.*

The devil takes on him the shape of a serpent, a subtle, wild creature. The Holy Ghost appeared in the shape of a dove. You see then what simplicity is. It is a frame of soul without mixture of the contrary.

1. We must not take simplicity *for a defect;* when a man is simple because he knows not how to be witty. Simplicity is sometimes taken in that sense for a defect of nature, when a man is easily deluded ; but here it is taken for a grace. A man that knows how to double with the world, how to run counterfeit, how to be false in all kinds ; but he will not. He knows the world, but he will not use the fashions of the world. So simplicity here is a strength of grace.

2. Likewise, simplicity and plainness, it must not be taken *for rudeness* and unnecessary opening of ourselves; for that is simplicity in an evil sense, profane rudeness.

You shall have some that will lay about them, they care not what they speak, they care not whom they smite ; but, as Solomon's fool, they throw ' firebrands,' Prov. xxvi. 18. They speak what they list, of whom they list, against whom they list. Here simplicity and plainness is no grace. This is no virtue. This is but an easing of their rotten, corrupt, and vile heart.

We know there are two kinds of sepulchres, open and shut sepulchres. They are both naught.† But yet, notwithstanding, your hidden sepulchre is less offensive. That which is open stinks that none can come nigh. That is very offensive. An hypocrite, that is a hidden sepulchre, a ' painted sepulchre ' without, and nothing but bones within, he hath a naughty, rotten heart : yet, notwithstanding, he is not so offensive as the open sepulchre, which offends all that come near it. So these men that say they cannot dissemble, and they have a plain heart, though they will swear, and dissemble, and detract, and throw firebrands against any man ; is this a plain heart ? It is an open sepulchre, that sends a stench to all that are near.

3. Again, let us take heed, that we do not for simplicity *take credulity.* ' The simple man,' saith Solomon, ' will believe everything,' Prov. xiv. 15. This is simple credulity. A man must not believe everything, for there is much danger comes by credulity. Jeremiah, and Gedaliah, and others,

---

* Cf. ' Bowels Opened,' vol. II., pp. 76–79.—G.
† That is, ' naughty ' = filthy.—G.

they were much harmed by credulity. It is a good fence not to be too hasty to believe ; for incredulity and hardness to believe is a good preservative ; and he is a wise man that will not believe everything. So you see there are some things that come near this simplicity, as defect, rudeness, and credulity; which yet are not that simplicity that St Paul saith he walked in.

And this simplicity may well be called the simplicity of God ; because God is simple. ' He is light, and in him there is no darkness at all,' 1 John i. 5. There is no mixture of fraud, or contrariety. He is pure, simple, and sincere. And as he is in his nature, so he is in his carriage to men every way. There is a simplicity that he doth in his word testify. And indeed he hath shewed that he loves us. Would we have a better evidence of it than his own Son ? There is no doubling in God's dealing to men. And therefore as it comes from God, so this simplicity it resembleth God.

For alas ! if God had had by-respects, what would the creature yield him ? Doth he stand in need of us, or doth he need anything we have ? All counterfeiting, and insincerity, and doubling, is for hope of gain, or for fear of danger. Now what can God have of the creature ? What cause hath he in us of his dealing toward us ? In his giving, in his forgiving, in all his dealing, he is simple.

So every one that is the child of God, he hath the virtue of simplicity. Simplicity is such a grace as extends to all the parts of our conversation. As the apostle saith here, ' My conversation in the world hath been in simplicity.'

By nature man is contrary to this simplicity, since the fall. God made him right and straight, and simple, but as the wise man saith, ' he sought out many inventions,' Eccles. vii. 29. So that a man without grace is double in his carriage. And that from self-love, from self-ends, and aims.

And hereupon he must be double ; for there must be something that is good in him. For else evil is destructive of itself. If there were not some thing good, men could never continue, nor the place could never continue. And if all were good, and all were plain, and honest, that would destroy the ill which men labour to nourish. Men have carnal projects to raise themselves, to get riches, and this must be by ill means. There is an idol in their hearts which they serve, which they sacrifice to. Their self-love, either in honour, or in riches, or in pleasure, they set up something. Therefore a man without grace, he studies to be strongly ill ; and because he cannot be ill except he be good, for then all the world would see it ; hereupon comes doubling. Good there must be to carry the ill he intends the more close ; ill there must be, or else he cannot have his aim. And hence comes dissimulation and simulation, the vices of these times, both opposite to simplicity, and such vices as proceed from want of worth and want of strength.

For when men have no worth to trust to, and yet would have the profit of sin, and the pleasure of sin, and would have reputation, then they carry all dissemblingly. Where there is strength of worth, and of parts, and reputation, there is less dissembling alway. It is a vice usually of those that have little or no virtue in them. A man of strength carries things open and fair.

This dissimulation it comes from the want of this grace of simplicity, both

Before, in, [and] *after* the project.

1. *Before*, as you see in Herod. He intends mischief, when he pretends he would be a worshipper of Christ, Mat. ii. 8. And so Absalom, he pretends he had a vow to make, when he intends murder, 2 Sam. xv. 7 ; a dissimulation, pretending good when there is an intention of ill before.

2. So there is a dissimulation *in* the project for the present, which comes from this doubling ; when men carry things fairly outwardly to those with whom they live, and yet notwithstanding have false and treacherous hearts ; as Judas had all the while he conversed with Christ. He covered his ill with good pretexts, a care for the poor, &c.

3. So *after*. When the ill is done, what a world of doubling is there to cover ill, to extenuate it, and excuses, and translations ! This is the simplicity that reigns among men where there is no strength of grace. Where there is want of simplicity there is this dissembling.

And with dissimulation there is simulation, that is, when we make ourselves sometimes worse than we are ; when we are better than we seem to be. Sometimes that wins on us too. Then we carry not ourselves simply.

For if we were good, we would be good everywhere. But a man that useth simulation, if he be in evil company he fashioneth himself to the company, he speaks that which his conscience checks him for, he carries himself vainly and lightly, he holds correspondence with the company. So that by dissimulation and simulation, there is a fault committed against simplicity, which yields the testimony of a good conscience.

It is a base fault this simulation, which we think to be a lesser fault than the other, which is dissimulation. For whom do we serve ? Are we not the sons of God ? Are we not the sons of our heavenly Father, the sons of the great King ? and for us to carry ourselves not to be such as we are in the midst of the wicked world, it is a great want of discretion. St Paul would discover who he was, even before the bar ; David 'would speak of God's righteous testimonies even before princes, and not be ashamed,' Ps. cxix. 46.

And this is that which Christ saith, ' He that is ashamed of me before men, of him will I be ashamed before my heavenly Father,' Mark viii. 38. Let us take heed of dissimulation and simulation, which are opposite to this simplicity.

Again, this simplicity is opposite to curiosity, and fineness. And thus the apostle ! Both in his calling and conversation, St Paul conversed in simplicity, as a Christian, and as an apostle.

As an apostle, he was not overcurious in words. He reproveth those foolish, vainglorious spirits, that were so among the Corinthians. He delive ed the word plainly, and plainness is best in handling the word of God ; for who will enamel a precious stone ? We use to enamel that that hath not a native excellency in itself, but that which hath an excellency from something without. True religion hath this with it alway, that it is simple ; because it hath state enough of its own.

The whore of Babylon hath need of a gilded cup, and pictures, and what not, to set her out ; but the true religion is in simplicity.

Christ himself when he was born, he was laid in a cratch.* He was simple in his carriage, and his speeches. It was a common speech in ancient time, when the chalices were gold, the priests were wood. In religion, fineness and curiosity carry suspicion of falsehood with them.

Those that overmuch affect fineness of speech, they are either deceived

* That is, ' crib or manger.'—G.

or will deceive. That which is not native, and comes not from within, it will deceive. Some falsehoods carry a better colour than some truths; because men set their wits on work to set some colour upon falsehood alway. And here take notice of the duty of ministers, that they should utter divine truth in the native simplicity of it. St Paul as a minister, delivered the plain word plainly.

And as a Christian in our common course of life, as we should take heed of doubling, so of too much curiosity. For too much curiosity in diet or apparel, it implies too much care of these things, which hinders our care of better things, as our Saviour Christ saith to Martha, ' Martha, thou art troubled about many things,' Luke x. 41.

The soul is finite, and cannot be set about many things at once. Therefore, when there is overmuch curiosity in smaller things, it implies little or no care in the main. What is more than for decency of place, it argues carelessness in the main. Therefore the apostle, labouring to take off that, he bids women that they should not be ' decked with gold and broidered hair,' &c. ; but to look to the ' hidden man of the heart,' 1 Tim. ii. 9. And therefore Christ took off Martha from outward things, because he knew it could not be without the neglect of better things. Seriousness in heavenly things, it carries a carelessness in other things. And a Christian cannot choose but discover a mind that is not earthly and vain. When he is a true believer, he regards other things as poor petty things, that are not worthy estimation.

A Christian when he hath fixed his end, to be like to God, to be simple as God is, he still draws toward his end; and therefore he moderates his carriage in all things. What is unnecessary he leaves out. His end is to be like God, and like Christ, with whom he shall live hereafter. Now the best things are the most simple, as the heavens, the sun, and the stars, &c. There is diversity, but no contrariety. There is diversity in the magnitude of the stars, but they are of the same nature. So in a Christian there are many graces, but they are not contrary one to another. So that a Christian hath his main care for better things ; he cares not for the world, nor the things thereof. And therefore he accounts them, in comparison of better things, as nothing ; and that is the reason that he is careless and negligent of those things that he did formerly regard, as having better things to take up his thoughts.

We see then that simplicity, as it is opposed to doubling, so it is opposed to fineness and curiosity.

And usually where there is a fineness and curiosity, there is hypocrisy ; for it is not for nought when men affect anything. Affectation usually is a strain above nature. When a man will do that which he is not disposed to by nature, but for some forced end, it is hypocrisy. So the Corinthian teachers argued* the falseness of their hearts by the fineness of their teaching. They had another aim than to please God and convert souls. Usually affectation to the world is joined with hypocrisy towards God.

Again, this simplicity is contrary to that corruption in popery, namely, equivocation. What simplicity is that, when they speak one thing, and mean another ? when there is a mental reservation, and such a reservation, that if that were set down that is reserved, it were absurd.

Or else there may be a reservation: a man may reserve his meaning. A man may not speak all the truth at all times, except he be called to it, in judgment, &c. Otherwise truth, as all good actions, it is never good but

* That is, ' proved.'—G.

when it is seasonable; and then it is seasonable when there is convenient furniture of circumstances, when a man is called to it. For there may be a reservation. A man is not bound to speak all things at all times, but to wait for a fit time. One word in a fit time is worth a thousand out of time. But mental reservation, to speak one thing, and to reserve another, it is absurd and inconsequent, and so is dissimulation. There is a lie, in fact. A man's life is a lie, that is a dissembler. Dissimulation is naught.*

A man may sometimes make some show to do something that he intends not. Christ made as though he would have gone further when he did not mean it, Luke xxiv. 28 (*mm*). But dissimulation is that which is intrinsically naught.*

Obj. But some man will say, Except I dissemble, I shall run into danger.

Ans. Well! it is not necessary for thee to live, but it is necessary for thee to live like an honest man, and keep a good conscience. That is necessary.† For come what will upon true dealing, we ought to deal truly, and not dissemble. Those that pretend a necessity, they must do it, they cannot live else, they cannot avoid danger else, unless they dissemble: saith Tertullian very well, There is no necessity of sin to them, upon whom there lies no other necessity but not to sin (*nn*). Christians, they are men that have no necessity lies upon them but not to sin. It is not necessary they should be rich, it is not necessary they should be poor, it is not necessary they should have their freedom and liberty. There is no necessity lies upon them, but that they be good, that they do not sin. Can he pretend I must sin upon necessity, who hath no necessity imposed upon him by God, but to avoid all sin?

As for lying, which is against this simplicity that should be in speech, all kinds of lies, officious‡ lies, or pernicious lies. Officious lies, to do a good turn to help ourselves or others with a lie, it is a gross sin. It is condemned by St Austin in a whole book, which he wrote against lying.§ Therefore I pass it. I shall have occasion to speak somewhat of it afterward. It is intrinsically ill every lie, because it is contrary to the hint|| of speech. God hath made our reason and understanding to frame speech, and speech to be the messenger and interpreter of reason, and of the conceit.¶ Now when speech shall be a false messenger, it is contrary to the gift of speech. Speech should be the stream of understanding and reason. Now when the fountain is one, and the spring is another, there is a contradiction. It is against nature, so it is intrinsically ill. It is not only against the will of God, but it is against the image of God, which is in truth. It is ill, not by inconvenience or by inconsequence, but a pernicious lie is inwardly ill. Jesting lies, pernicious lies, officious lies, all lies, let them be what they will, they come from the father of lies, the devil, and are hated of God, who is truth itself.

Besides that, it is a sin opposite to society, and therefore by God's just judgment it is punished by society. All men hate a liar, a false dissembler, as an enemy to society, as a man that offends against that bond whereby God hath knit men together.

Now, to move us the better to this simplicity, this direct course of life, that there may be a conformity and harmony between the outward and inward man, in the thoughts, speeches, and actions, that they may be one.

1. Consider, first of all, that this simplicity, *it is a comely thing.* Come-

---

* That is, 'naughty ' = bad.—G.
† See note *l*, vol. I. p. 210.—G.
‡ That is, ' o fficial.'—G.
§ That is, his ' *De Mendacio*.'—G.
|| That is, ' end.'—Ed.
¶ That is, ' conception.'—G.

liness and seemliness, it is a thing that is delightful to the eyes of God, and to a man's own conscience ; and it stands in oneness and proportion. For you know where there is a comely proportion, there all things suit in one ; as in a comely body, the head and all the rest of the members are suitable. There is not a young green head upon an old body, or a fair face on a deformed body, for then there is two ; the body is one, and the complexion another. Beauty and comeliness is in one, when there is a correspondency, a proportion, a harmony in the parts.

In Rev. xiii. 11, *seq.*, you have a cruel beast there with the horns of a lamb. There is two, there is a goodly pretension and show, but there is a beast that is hid within. Dissimulation is double, and where there is singleness and doubleness, there is deformity alway. It is an ugly thing in the eyes of God, it is a misshapen thing, it is a monster : Jacob's voice, and Esau's hands : words ' as smooth as oil, and war in the heart.' Prov. v. 3, Ps. lv. 21. It is a monstrous thing. Even as there be monsters in nature, so there be in disposition. Where there is such a gross mixture, the devil and an angel of light, outwardly an angel of light and inwardly a devil ; to hide a devil in the shape of an angel of light, there is a horrible deformity.

It is a comely thing, therefore, when all things hold conformity and correspondence in our lives, when they are even amongst men, when we labour to have sanctified judgments of things, and speak what is our judgment, and have outward expressions answerable to the inward impressions wrought by the Spirit of God every way, then a man is like himself, he is one. There is not a heart and a heart. Adam at the first was every way like himself, but after falling from God to the creature, the changeable, corruptible creature, to have his corruptible end, he fell to this doubleness.

2. And as St James saith, ' A double-minded man is *unconstant in all his ways.*' That is another reason to move us to simplicity of disposition ; for where doubling is, a man is unconstant in all his ways. What doth St James mean by this, where he saith, ' A double-minded man is unsettled ?' Because a double-minded man, he looks with one eye to religion, and to those things that are good, and with another part of his heart to the world ; and hereupon he can never be settled any way. Why ? Because having unsettled intentions, having false aims, double aims, he will be crossed continually. Please God he would, he would be religious. That is one intention. But now comes the world and religion to dash one against another, and then he must be inconstant, because he hath not simplicity, he hath not a ' single eye,' as Christ saith, ' If the eye be single, then the body is light.' He hath not a right intention, a right judgment of things ; he judgeth too high of the world, and not high enough of grace and goodness. And hereupon it comes, that when the world comes to cross his good intentions, having his mind on earthly things, because it is cross to religion, his mind is unsettled.

Again, by terrors of conscience, a double-minded man, that will please God, and yet be a worldling, is inconstant in all his ways. If his eye were single, then all his body would be light ; that is, if a man had a single judgment to know what is right, to what in life, and in death to stick to, all would be single. The judgment and intentions go together. When a man's judgment is convinced of the goodness of spiritual things, upon judgment follows intention. When a man desires and resolves to serve God, and to please him in all things, then all the body and his affections are lightsome. His affections and his outward man goes with a single eye. A man that hath a false, weak judgment, and thereupon a false, weak, double intention, his body is dark, he hath a darksome conversation. A double-minded man is inconstant in all his ways. Therefore we should labour for this simplicity in all our conversation.

3. Again, we should the rather labour for this simplicity, because *it is part of the image of God.* Therein we resemble God, in whom is no mixture at all of contraries : but all is alike.

4. And as it resembles God, so it bears us out in the presence of God, and our own conscience ; as he saith here, ' Our rejoicing is this, the testimony of our conscience, that in simplicity,' &c. Now God is greater than conscience. A man that carries himself in simplicity, and in an uniform, even manner to God, and to men, that man hath comfort in his conscience, and comfort before God.

And of all other sins, the time will come that none will lie heavier on us than doubling, both with men and with God, when it will appear that we have not been the men that we carried ourselves to be.

The reason is, the more will there is in a sin, and the more advisedness, the greater is the sin ; and the greater the sin is, the greater the terror of conscience ; and the greater that is, the more fear and trembling before God, that knows conscience better than we do.

Now where there is doubling, where a man is not one in his outward and inward man, in his conversation to men, when there is a covering of hatred, and of ill affections with contrary pretences, there is advisement, there is much will and little passion to bear a man out, to excuse him ; but he doth it, as we say, in cool blood, and that makes dissimulation so gross, because it is in cool blood. The more will and advisement is in any sin, the greater it is, so the aggravation of sin is to be considered ; and where temptations are strong, and the less a man is himself, so there is a diminution, and a less aggravation ; as when a man is carried with passion, with infirmity, or the like. But usually when men double they plot.

David he plotted before and after his sin. He doubled before and after his sin. That was laid to his charge more than all that ever he did in his life. He was a man ' after God's own heart, except in the matter of Uriah,' 1 Kings xv. 5. Why ? Because in that he plotted. We see before what many shifts, and windings, and turnings he had to accomplish it. He sends Uriah to Joab, and gives him a letter to place him in the fore front, and useth many projects.

And after it was committed, how did he cover it ? And when it was hid from men, he would have hid it from God a great while, till God pulled him from his hiding-place, and him* confess roundly, Ps. xxxii. 3, till he dealt directly with God, ' My bones were consumed, and my moisture was turned into the drought of summer.' He hid it from men, and would have hid it from God. Therefore, because there was much plotting in that sin, that is set down as the only blemish in all his life. He ' was a man after God's own heart, except in the matter of Uriah.' Many other faults are recorded in the Book of God of David ; but because there might be some excuse, they were from infirmity, or out of passion, or oversight, &c., they are not so charged on him. But this was with plotting. It was in cold blood. There was much will and advice in it ; therefore this is doted† for a great sin.

And if it be in our dealing amongst men, we should consider who it is we deceive, who it is we go beyond in doubling, who it is that we circum-

* Qu. ' made him ? '—Ed.   † Qu. ' noted ? '—G.

vent, and who it is that doth it. Are we not all Christians? We are or should be all new creatures. And who do we do it to? To our fellow-members and to our brethren. Therefore, in Eph. iv. 25,* when the apostle dissuades the Ephesians from this, from double dealing, and double carriage to men, saith he, ' You are members one of another.' Let us consider who we are and whom we deal with.

Now there be some persons, and some courses, that are likelier and more prone to this doubling than others, for want of this grace of simplicity.

Where there is strength of parts, there is ofttimes a turning of them against God, and against our brethren. Where grace hath not subdued strong imaginations, strong thoughts, and brought all under it, there is a turning of those parts against God, and against our brethren. And as it is in particular persons, so some callings are more prone to double-dealing, to this carriage that is not fair and commendable before God, nor comfortable to the conscience. As we see now a-days it reigns everywhere, in every street.

We see amongst men of trade, merchants and the like, there is not that direct dealing. They know one thing, and pretend another.

So likewise in the laws there are many imputations, I would they were false, that men set false colours upon ill causes ; to gild a rotten post, as we say, to call white black and black white. There is a woe in Isaiah pronounced against such as justify hard causes, such ' as call evil good, and good evil,' Isa. v. 20. It is a greater sin than it is usually taken for.

So, go to any rank of men. They have learned the art of dissimulation in their course ; they have learned to sell wind, to sell words, to sell nothing, to sell pretexts, to overthrow a man by way of commendations and flattery. Such tricks there are, which are contrary to this simplicity. To cover hatred with fair words, to kill with kindness, as we say, to overthrow a man with commendations ; to commend a man before another who is jealous of the virtues he commends him for ; to commend a man for valour before a coward ; to commend a man, and thereby to take occasion to send him out of the way ; to commend a man, and then to come in with an exception, to mar all ; to cover revenge and hatred with fair carriage, thereby to get opportunity to revenge—such tricks there are abroad, which ofttimes discover themselves at length. For God is just. He will discover all these hidden windings and turnings ; for plotting makes it more odious. Of all men doublers are most hateful.

How shall we come to attain this grace, to converse in the world in simplicity ?

First of all, take it for a rule, though many think it no great matter to be a dissembler, *our nature is full of dissimulation since the fall* The heart of man is unsearchable. There is a deep deceit in man. Take a child, and see what dissimulation he learns. It is one of the first things he learns, to dissemble, to double, to be false. We see the weakest creatures, what shifts, what windings and turnings they have to save themselves ?

It is a virtue to be downright ; for therein a man must cross himself. It is no thanks for a man to shuffle, and to shift in the world. Nature teacheth this, to dissemble, to turn and wind, &c. A man need not to plough to have weeds. The ground itself is a mother to them, though it be a stepmother to good seed. So we need not teach men to dissemble. Every man hath it by nature. But it must be strength of grace that makes a man downright. Take that for a ground.

* Misprinted ' 1 Thess. iv.'—G.

There are a company of sottish men, that take it for a great commendation to dissemble; and rather than they will be known not to dissemble in business, they will puzzle clear business. When a thing is fair and clear, they will have projects beyond the moon, and so carry themselves in it as if they desired to be accounted cozeners and dissemblers. Alas! poor souls. Nature teacheth men to be naught in this kind well enough. Know therefore, whosoever thou art that studiest this art of dissembling and doubling, thy own nature is prone enough to this, and the devil is apt to lead thee into it. This being laid for a ground, how may we carry ourselves in the world in holy simplicity, that may yield comfort to our conscience in life and in death?

1. First consider, that the time will come *that we shall deal with that that will not dissemble with us.* Let the cunningest dissembler hold out as long as he can, he shall meet with sickness, or with terror of conscience, he shall meet with death itself, and with the judgment of God, and hell torment. Although now he carry himself smoothly, and dance in a net, as we say, and double with the world, though he make a fair show, yet ere long thou shalt meet with that that will deal simply with thee, that will deal plain enough with thee. Thou shalt be uncased, and laid open to the world ere long (*oo*). Let us consider this.

We see a snake or serpent, it doubles, and winds, and turns when it is alive, till it be killed, and then it is stretched forth at length. As one said, seeing a snake dead, and stretched out, so, saith he, it behoved you to have lived. So the devil, that great serpent, that ancient 'old serpent,' Rev. xii. 9, he gets into the snake, into the wily wit, and makes it wind and turn, and shift and shuffle in the world. But then some great cross comes, or death comes, and then a man is stretched out at length to the view of the world, and then he confesseth all, and perhaps that confession is sincere when it is wrung out by terror of conscience, then he confesseth that he hath deceived the world, and deceived himself, and laboured to deceive God also.

If we would have comfort in the hour of death, labour we to deal plainly and directly; and of all other sins, as I said before, remember this is that which will lie the heaviest on us, as coming nearest the sin against the Holy Ghost. For what is the sin against the Holy Ghost? When men rush against their knowledge in malice to the truth known. Where there is most knowledge, and most will, there is the greatest sin. Now in lying and dissembling, and double-dealing, a man comes near to the sin against the Holy Ghost; for he knows that he doth ill, he plots the ill that he knows; and when there is plotting, there is time to deliberate; a man is not carried away by passion.

Consider, the time will come when you will be uncased, when you will be laid open and naked; and then at that time, of all sins, this will lie heavy on thee, thy dissembling in the world. Therefore every one in his calling, take heed of the sins of his calling, among the rest, of this one of double-dealing.

2. And therefore that we may avoid it the better, *labour for faith, to live by faith.* What is the reason that men live by shifts, and by doubling in the world? They have not faith to depend upon God, in good and plain downright courses. Men are ready to say, If I should not dissemble and double, and carry things after that manner, how should I live? Why, where is thy faith? The righteous man lives by his faith, and not by his shifts, not by his wits. God will provide for us. Are we not in covenant

with God ? Do we not profess to be God's children ? Do children use to shift ? No ; a child goes about to do his father's will and pleasure, and he knows that he will maintain him. It is against the nature of the child of God, as far as he knows himself to be a child of God, to use any indirect course, any windings and turnings in his calling. Let us depend upon God as a child depends on his father ; and of all others God will provide most for them that in simple honesty, in plain downright dealing, depend on him in doing good.

For God accounts it a prerogative to defend and maintain them that cast themselves on him. He will be their wisdom that can deny their own wisdom, and their own shifts by nature, and in conscience labour to deal directly. He will be wise for them and provide for them. It is his prerogative to do so, and not to suffer his children to be deserted. A little faith therefore would help all this, and would make us walk in simplicity. If we could make God our all-sufficiency once, then we should walk uprightly before God and men.

For what makes men to double ?

This certainly makes men to double. They think they shall be undone if they be direct ; for if they deal directly, they shall lose their liberty, or their lives, or their opportunity of gaining, &c. Well ; come what will, deal thou directly, and know this for a rule, thou shalt have more good in God's favour, if thou be a Christian, than thou canst lose in the world, if upon grounds of conscience thou deal directly in what estate soever thou art.

If thou be a judge, if thou be a witness, deal directly, speak the truth. If thou be a divine, speak directly in God's cause, deal out the word of God as in God's presence, come what will, whatsoever thou losest in thy wealth, or liberty, &c., thou shalt gain in God. Is not all good in him ? What is all the good we have, is it not from him ? And the nearer you come to him, the more your happiness is increased ; the more you are stripped of earthly things, the more you have in God. Hath not he men's hearts in his hands ? When you think you shall endanger yourselves thus and thus by plain direct dealing without doubling, if you be called to the profession of the truth, &c. ; hath not he the hearts of men in his hands to make them favour you when he pleaseth ? In Prov. x. 9, ' He that walketh uprightly, walketh boldly.' He that walketh uprightly, not doubling in his courses, he walketh safely. God will procure his safety. God that hath ' the hearts of men in his hand as the rivers of water,' Prov. xxi. 1, he can turn them to favour such a man.

A man's nature is inclined to favour downright-dealing men, and to hate the contrary. You see the three young men, when they were threatened with fire, come what will, ' O king, we will not worship the image of gold which thou hast set up,' Dan. iii. 14, seq. They would be burned first. What lost they by it ?

Howsoever, if we should lose, as it is not to be granted that we can lose anything by direct dealing, ' For the earth is the Lord's, and the fulness thereof,' Ps. xxiv. 1, and the hearts of men are his. But suppose they do, yet they gain in better things, in comfort of conscience, and expectation and hope of better things. Faith is the ground of courage, and the ground of all other graces that carry a man's courage in a course of simplicity in this world.

Therefore, if we would walk simply, and have our conversation in the world in this grace, let us labour especially for faith to depend upon God's promises, to approve ourselves to him, to make him our last and chief end, and our communion with him, and to direct all our courses to that end. This is indeed to set him up a throne in our hearts, and to make him a God, when rather than we will displease him or his vicegerent, his vicar in us, which is conscience (that he hath placed in us as a monitor and as a witness), we will venture the loss of the creature, of anything in the world, rather than we will displease that vicar which he hath set in our hearts. This, I say, is to make him a God; and he will take the care and protection of such a man. St Paul here, in all the imputations, in all crosses in the world, he retires home, to himself, to his own house, to conscience; and that did bear him out, that 'in simplicity he had his conversation in the world.' The next particular is,

'In sincerity.' The apostle adds to simplicity, this 'godly sincerity.' And he may well join these two together, for plainness and truth go together. A plain heart is usually a true heart. Doubleness and hypocrisy, which are contrary, they always go together. He that is not plain to men will not be sincere to God. Simplicity respects our whole course with men. Sincerity hath an eye to God, though, perhaps, in matters and actions towards men. Sincerity is alway with a respect to God; and so it is opposed to hypocrisy, a vice in religion opposite to God.

Now this sincerity that the apostle speaks of, it is *a blessed frame of the soul, wrought by the Spirit of God, whereby the soul is set straight and right in a purpose to please God in all things (and in endeavours answerable to that purpose), and to offend him in nothing.*

I make a plain description, because I intend practice. There may be some nicer descriptions.

But, I say, it is a blessed frame of the soul, wrought by the sincere Spirit of God, whereby the soul is set straight and right to purpose, and to endeavour all that is pleasing in God's sight; and that with an intention to please God, with an eye to God, or else it is not sincerity. It is such a disposition and frame of soul that doth all good, that hates all ill, with a purpose to please God in all, with an eye to God.

And therefore it is called 'sincerity of God,' or 'godly sincerity;' and it is called so fitly: because God is not only the author of it, but God is the aim of it, and the pattern of it; for he is the first thing that is sincere, that is simple and unmixed. God is the pattern of it. It makes us like to God, and he is the aim of it. A man that is sincere aims at God in all his courses: wherein he aims not at God he is not sincere. It comes from God, and it looks to God. For naturally we are all hypocrites. We look to shows. Therefore sincerity is from God.

And it is the sincerity of God especially, because, where this sincerity is, it makes us aim at God in all things, it makes us have respect to him in all things, as the creature should have respect to the Creator, the servant to the master, the son to the father, the subject to the prince. The relations we stand in to God should make us aim at him in all things.

The observation from hence is this,

Doct. A Christian that hopes for joy, must have his conscience witness to him, that his conversation is in the sincerity of God.

As the apostle saith here, ' This is the testimony of our conscience, that in simplicity and godly sincerity we have had our conversation,' &c.

Now to go on with this sincerity, and lay it open a little. Sincerity, it is not so much a distinct thing, as that which goes with every good thing. Truth and sincerity, it is not so much a distinct virtue, and grace, as a truth joined to all graces ; as sincere hope, sincere faith, sincere love, sincere repentance, sincere confession.   It is a grace annexed to every grace. It is the life and soul of every grace, and all is nothing without it.

Therefore it behoves us to consider of it, I say, not so much a distinct thing from other graces, as that which makes other graces to be graces, without which they are nothing at all.   So much sincerity, so much reality. So much as we have not in sincerity, we have nothing to God.   It is but an empty show, and will be so accounted.

In philosophy, you know, that which is true, only hath a being and consistence.   All truth hath a being, all falsehood is nothing.   It is a counterfeit thing.   It is nothing to that it is pretended to be.   An image is something, but St Paul calls it nothing, because it is not that which it should be, and which the idolater would have it to be.   He would have it to be a god, but it is nothing less.   All is nothing without sincerity. Therefore let us consider of it.   And that we may the better consider of it, let us look upon it in every action.

All actions are either good, ill, indifferent.

How is sincerity discovered in good actions ?

1. Sincerity is tried in good actions many ways.

(1.) First of all, a man that is sincere in the doing that which is good, *he will have a mind prepared to know all that is good;* to know the good he stands disposed to, to know good, and to learn by all good means.   Therefore he hath a heart prepared with diligence to be informed in the use of means.   So far as a man is careless and negligent in coming to the means of knowledge, and to be put in mind of good duties, so far a man is an hypocrite and insincere.

(2.) Again, in regard of good duties, a true, sincere Christian *hath an universal respect to all that is good.*   He desires to know all, and, when anything is manifested to him, he intends to practise all.   'We are here in the presence of God,' saith Cornelius, 'to practise all things that shall be taught us by God,' Acts x. 33.   'I will have respect to all thy commandments,' Ps. cxix. 6, one and another.

The ground of it is this, sincerity looks at God.   Now God, he commands one thing as well as another ; and therefore, if a man do anything that is good, in conscience to God, he must do one as well as another.   As St James saith excellently to this purpose, 'He that offends in one is guilty of all,' ii. 10.   Because, abstaining from one sin, and doing one good for conscience, he will do all for conscience if he be sincere.

Therefore it is true in divinity,—a man that repents of one sin, he repents of all, if he repent of any sin as it is a sin, because all sins are of one nature. We must not single out what pleaseth us, and leave what doth not please us.   This is to make ourselves gods.   The servant must not choose his work, but take that work that his master commands him ; therefore sincerity is tried in universal obedience.

Partial obedience is insincere obedience.   When a man saith, This sin I must keep still, herein 'God be merciful to me,' this stands with my profit, I must not leave this ; this sin I am affected to, as we see in Saul,— this is insincerity.   It is as good as nothing to God-ward.   It may keep a man from shame in the world, &c., but to God it is nothing.   A man must have respect to all God's commandments.   It is not done to God else.

(3.) More particularly, he that is sincere, *he will have regard of the main duties, and he will have regard likewise of the lesser duties, and especially of the lesser*, such as are not liable to the censure of men, or to the censure and punishment of the law; for there a man's sincerity is most tried. In great duties, there are great rewards, great encouragements; but for lesser duties, there are lesser encouragements. But if a man do them, he must do them for conscience sake.

Therefore this is sincerity, to practise good duties though they be lesser duties, and though they be less esteemed in the world, and less countenanced; to practise them though they be discountenanced by the devil, and by great ones; yet to practise them, because they be good; and to love good things that the world cares not for, because they be good.

The practice of private prayer morning and evening, it is a thing we are not expressly bound to, but as conscience binds us. Therefore if a man be sincere he will make conscience of that, as well as any other duty, because God bids us ' pray alway,' 1 Thess. v. 17. So, to fear an oath for conscience sake, not to swear common or lighter oaths,—for I count him not worthy the name of a Christian, that is an ordinary swearer; but—lighter oaths a Christian makes conscience of, because he looks to God. Now God looks to little sins as well as to great; and there is no sin little indeed that toucheth the majesty of God.

The practice of all duties, therefore, is a notable evidence of sincerity. Herod did many things, but he had a Herodias, that spoiled all. And so if thou obey in many things, and not in all, thou hast a Herodias, a main sin. Alas! all is to no purpose! thou art an hypocrite.

(4.) Again, for good things, one that is sincere in respect to God, he is *uniform in his obedience*, that is, he doth all that is good, and he doth it in one place as well as another, and at one time as well as another. He doth it not by starts.

Therefore there is constancy required in sincerity. Where sincerity is, there is constancy to do it in all times, in all places. Or else it is but a humour. It is not sincerity when a man doth it but in good moods, as we say. Therefore a man that is sincere, he makes conscience of private duties as well as of public; of personal duties between God and his own soul, as well as of the duties that the world takes notice of; in one place as well as another. He is holy not only in the church, but in his closet; not only in his calling as he is a Christian, but when he is about his particular business. He considers he is in the presence of God in every place, at all times.

St Paul everywhere laboured to have a good conversation. When he was at the bar, he remembered where he was, and he laboured to convert others. In the prison he converted Onesimus, Philem. 10. When he had his liberty, he spread the gospel everywhere.

So in all places he was uniform like himself, which shewed that he had a good conscience. And therefore he doth not say, I do now and then a good action, but my course of life, ' my conversation, is in sincerity.' So there must be sincerity in our walking, our whole conversation. Thus we see in good actions how to try our sincerity.

(5.) A sincere man in the very performance of good duties, *he is humble;* because he doth all things in the eye of God. He doth it in sincerity with humility. He doth all good with reverence, because he doth it to God.

Humility, and reverence, it is a qualification of sincerity; because whatsoever we do, we do it in the eye of God. Therefore we are reverent in our very secret devotions in our closets. We carry ourselves reverently;

because when no eye seeth us, the eye of heaven seeth us, in one place as well as another. A sincere christian, is a reverent, and humble Christian, and this reverence accompanies all his good actions.

(6.) And when he hath done all, a sincere Christian that doth them to God, he is humble, *and then he is thankful;* for he knows that he hath not done it by his own strength, but by God, and therefore God hath the glory.

He is humble, because *they are mixed with some infirmities of his.* A sincere Christian is alway humble, having an eye to God. Though to the eye of the world he hath done excellent well, yet he knows that God seeth* as he seeth. He seeth some defects, God seeth more, and that humbleth him. As we see David, 1 Chron. xxix. 14. Saith he, ' Who am I ? or who is this people, that we should be able to offer willingly after this sort ? All things come of thee ; of thine own I have given thee.' So he humbled himself in thankfulness to God.

2. For ill actions, (1.) a true sincere Christian beforehand *he intends none.* He regards none in his heart. Ps. lxvi. 18, ' If I regard iniquity in my heart, the Lord will not hear my prayers.' His disposition is to regard none. He is in league with none. If he were, his heart were false, his conscience would tell him he were an hypocrite. He is subject to infirmities, but he doth not respect them, he doth not regard them. He intends not in his heart to live in them.

(2.) Again, if he fall into any sin, *he is sincerely grieved for them.* His heart is tender, and he sincerely confesseth them, without guile, Ps. xxxii. 2. ' Blessed is the man in whose spirit there is no guile,' who when he sees he hath sinned, he doth not guilefully cloak and extenuate his sin. As we see Saul, he had many evasions, and excuses for himself, 1 Samuel xiii. 12. A true Christian will lay open his sin with all the aggravations that his conscience tells him of. As David saith, what a fool, ' and what a beast was I,' Ps. lxxiii. 22 ; what an unthankful creature was I to sin against so many benefits and favours ! He will be ashamed and confounded in himself.

(3.) And of all sins, a sincere Christian is most careful *to avoid his personal sins.* You may know sincerity by that. He that takes not heed to that which he is most inclined unto, he shall be tripped in it.

An hypocrite and false-hearted man, he doth good, but it is with a purpose to be favoured in some sin wherein he strengtheneth himself. He will do something, that God may be favourable to him in other things.

But a true sincere Christian, though he be inclined by temper of body, or by his calling, or by the former custom of his unregenerate life, to some sin more than another, and he hath not shaken some sin wholly off, he hath not purged himself wholly of the dregs of it, but he finds still a propenseness in his nature to it; yet as far as he is sincere, he gets strength, especially against that. A false-hearted man favours himself, especially in those sins ; and will swell if he be found out in them. He will not bear a reproof. But a Christian that is sincere, that intends amendment, that intends to be better, he would reform his heart if it be amiss, and is willing to be discovered in his most particular and personal sins that he is prone to.

We may try ourselves by this, not only by hating sin in general and at large, but how we stand affected, especially to those particular sins we are most prone to. Sincerity, as it hates all wicked ways, so it hates those sins

* Qu. ' seeth not ? '—G.

that are most sweet, that we are most prone to, as well as any other, nay, more than any other ; because those especially endanger the soul. A child of God will abstain from all evil. He will be careful, not only that others abstain from sin, but he will abstain from sin himself most of all. Noisome things we hate them always, but we hate them most when they are nearest us. As a toad, we hate it afar off, much more when it is near. So a sincere Christian hates sin most in his own breast.

(4.) Now because sincerity hath an eye to God, *I must hate all sin as well as any*, or else I am not sincere.

A man that hath the point of his soul to God-ward, he will hate all manner of ill, little ills as well as great ; because all sin agrees in this,—all sin is against God. It is contrary to the mind of God ; and all sin is pernicious to the soul. All sin is against the pure word of God, and considering it is so, therefore I must hate all sin, if I hate any ; because God hates all, and all sin is contrary to the image of God ; and not only contrary to the image of God, but contrary to the revealed will of God, contrary to my soul's comfort, contrary to communion with God, and contrary to the peace of my conscience. Those regards come in every sin. Every sin hinders that.

(5.) Again, where the soul and conscience is sincere, there will be *a special care for the time to come of the sins we have been overtaken withal.* So we see how this sincerity may be tried, in abstaining from evil, as well as in the good we do.

3. For actions that are of a more common nature, *that in themselves are neither good nor ill, but as the doer is, and as the doer stands affected,* a true Christian may be tried by them thus—

(1.) For the actions *of his calling*, though they be good in their kind, yet they be not religious, thus he stands affected if he be sincere,—he doth them as God's work. Common actions are as the doer is affected. A sincere man considers what he doth as God's work. He is commanded to serve God in his calling as well as in the church ; and, therefore, he will not do it negligently. 'For cursed is he that doth the work of the Lord negligently,' Jer. xlviii. 10.

He will not do it falsely. He will not profane his calling. I will not prostitute my calling to serve my lust, or to serve my gain. Doth not God see it ? is not he the author of my calling ? is it not his work, saith conscience ? Yes ! and therefore he doth common actions with an eye to God, and so he makes them good and religious actions. For the grace of God is a blessed alchymist ! Where it toucheth, it makes good and religious. Though the actions be not so in their own nature, it raiseth the actions, it elevates them higher than themselves.

It makes the actions of our calling, that are ordinary actions, to be holy, when they are done with an eye of sincerity to God. As St Paul saith, the very servant serves God in serving his master.

(2.) And so for actions that we account most indifferent, *as recreations and liberty to refresh ourselves.* A sincere man considers of them as a liberty bought to him by the blood of Christ, and considers himself in the presence of God. And, therefore, whatsoever he doth, ' whether he eat or drink.' &c., 1 Cor. x. 31, he still useth his refreshings as in the presence of God, and doth all as in the sight of God. His conversation, that is, his whole course, whatsoever he doth, is sincere with an eye to God. He knows his corruption is such that it most watcheth him in his liberties ; for the more lawful a thing is, the more we are in danger to be entangled in it.

In excess, in open ills, there is not so much danger as in things that seem indifferent, lawful recreations, &c. Recreations, and such things, are lawful ; but to spend whole nights unthriftily, basely, scandalously this way, it is not only against religion, but against civility. In a civil man's judgment, it is a scandal to the place and person. Therefore he that hath any truth of grace in him, he will look to himself, and look to God in the most free actions of all. You see then how we may judge of our sincerity whatsoever we do. A sincere Christian stands thus affected in some measure, in some degree, in the good he doth, in the ill he abstains from. Whatsoever it be, he thinks he hath to deal with God.

Use 1. Now to stir us up to this blessed state, to labour for this frame of soul, to be sincere, to have our conversation in sincerity, what needs be added more than this, that without it all is nothing.

1. *All our glorious performances are mere abominations, without sincerity.* God will say, you did it not to me, you did it for vainglory, you did it for custom or out of education, for vain and by-respects, and not to me, and do you look for a reward of me ? You did it not for conscience ; for conscience alway looks to God. And what we do not in conscience and obedience to God, in our general or particular calling, it stands not on our reckoning with God. It is as good as if it were not done, in regard of God, and of the life to come. ' You have your reward,' saith Christ, Mat. vi. 2. It is no matter what your respects be here. If you carry yourselves carefully in your place, to have the credit of men, to gain the favour of men, you have your reward. Will you look for a reward from God, when what you did, you did it to the world ?

What a pitiful thing is this, that a man should do many things, many years together, and yet do nothing that may further his day of account, because it was not done out of conscience of his duty ? His conversation was not in sincerity to God. Now, if we have not truth we have nothing in religion. St Paul saith, as I said before, ' Of an idol, it is nothing,' Why ! it is a piece of wood, or a piece of gold, the materials of it is something, but it is nothing to that which it should be. If a man be not true in religion, he is nothing in that. He is a true hypocrite, but a false Christian. He is nothing in Christianity. He is something in hypocrisy, but that something is nothing.

All the shows in the world, and all the flourishes, they are nothing. What is the reason that excellent clerks,* men of excellent parts, die comfortless many times ? Why ! God is not beholden to them for all that they did. They sought their own praise. As the prophet Isaiah saith, ' When you fasted, did you fast to me ?' Zech. vii. 5. When you did good works, did you do them to me ? may God say. There was no truth in it. So much simplicity, so much comfort. Sincerity is all that we can come to in this world. Perfection we cannot attain to. Christ is perfection for us. Truth is all that we can reach to, and without that all is nothing. Therefore we ought to regard it especially.

2. Again, on the other side, this is a great encouragement to be sincere, to be true-hearted in all our courses and actions ; *because it gives acceptance to whatsoever we do ;* and it is that by which God values us. God values us not by perfection, not by glorious shows, but by what we have in truth. So much truth, so much worth. A little pearl is worth a great deal of rubbish.

A little sincerity, because it is God's own creature, it is ' the sincerity of God,' it is wrought by him, it is his stuff. There is an almighty power to

* That is, = ' ministers of the gospel.'—G.

work truth in us; for by nature we are all false. God gives to some men to carry themselves more civilly than others; but it is nothing worth except God change a man by grace; because God accepts us according to sincerity. God values us by truth. So much truth, so much esteem of the God of truth.

And where this sincerity is, God bears with many infirmities. As in marriage, the husband that is discreet, that knows what belongs to marriage, if the heart of the wife be true, though she have many woman-like infirmities, he passeth by them as long as the conjugal knot is kept unviolate. So a Christian, if his heart be true, that he looks to God in all things, though he have many infirmities, God passeth by them. As we see in Asa; how many faults had he committed? He trusted in the physicians, he used the prophet hardly, and many other faults, and yet it is said that his heart was upright all his days, because he had truth in him. It was in passion that he did this or that otherwise. So Hezekiah, although he had many infirmities, yet he could say that he 'had walked uprightly before God,' Isa. xxxviii. 3; and God did well esteem him for it. And when he speaks of those that were to come to the passover, 'Be merciful to those that prepare their hearts,' 2 Chron. xxx. 19, those that have true hearts, though they have many weaknesses.

Now, if the heart be false, though a woman have many virtues, yet if she want the main, if she have a false heart to her husband, what is all the rest? So the soul that is married to God, that hath sweet communion with God, if the heart and soul be naught, what are all the shows in the world? They are nothing. Let us take it to heart, therefore, and labour to approve our hearts and souls to God in all that we do, more than our lives and outward conversations to the world. Let them think what they will, so God approve of our hearts, and intentions, and purposes; we are not to 'pass what the world judgeth,' as St Paul saith of himself, 1 Cor. iv. 3.

3. Again, this should encourage us to labour for sincerity and truth, because wheresoever that is, *there is a growing to perfection.* 'To him that hath shall be given,' Mat. xiii. 12. 'If we order our conversation aright,' as the psalmist saith, Ps. l. 23, and labour to please God in all things, the more we do, the more we shall have grace to do; and the more we have, the more we shall have. 'To him that hath shall be given;' that is, he that truly hath, and doth not seem to have, but [he that] hath not indeed, that seemeth to have goodness, and hath none indeed, that which he hath shall be taken from him.

A true Christian is alway on the mending hand. It is a blessed prerogative. He is alway mending and bettering by God's blessing. For where God gives in truth, if it be but a little, if it be but a grain of mustard-seed, if it be true, he will cherish it till it come to be a tree. He will add grace to grace, one degree of grace to another. Where there is truth, it is alway honoured with growth. It is not only a sign of truth, but where truth is there will be an endeavour of growth. It is a prerogative. Where God bestows truth, he will always add the grace of growth, though not at all times alike. Yet if Christians sometimes do not grow, their not growing and their failings shame them, and makes them grow more afterward, and recover their former backwardness. A true Christian is alway on the mending hand. An hypocrite grows worse and worse alway, till he be uncased altogether, and turned into hell. These and such like considerations may stir us up to labour to have a conversation in simplicity and godly sincerity.

Use 2. Now, how shall we come to carry ourselves in sincerity, that we may have comfort in all estates ?

That we may carry ourselves in sincerity,

1. First, *we must get a change of heart.* Our nature must be changed. For by nature a man aims at himself in all things, and not at God. A man makes himself his last end. He makes something in the world, either profits, or pleasures, &c., the term that he looks unto. Therefore, there must be a change of heart. A man must be a good man, or else he cannot be a sincere man. Such as we are, such our actions will be. Therefore, we cannot be sincere till we have our hearts changed.

2. No man can aim at God's glory, but he *that hath felt God's love in himself.* Therefore as a particular branch of that, labour to get assurance of the love of God in Jesus Christ ; for how can we endeavour to please him unless we love him ? And how can we love him unless we be persuaded that he loves us in Christ ? Therefore let us stablish our hearts more and more in the evidences of his love to us ; and then knowing that he loves us, we shall love him, and labour to please him in all things. These are grounds that must be laid before we can be sincere ; to get assurance of God's love to us in the pardon of our sins. ' Our conscience must be purged from dead works, to serve the living God,' as the apostle saith, Heb. ix. 14 ; that is, we cannot serve God to our comfort till our consciences are sprinkled with the blood of Christ, which assures us of the pardon of our sins. Therefore saith Zacharias, ' We are redeemed, that we might serve him in righteousness and holiness before him all the days of our life,' Luke i. 75. So that unless a man be redeemed, he cannot serve him in righteousness and holiness ' before him ' all the days of his life ; that is, he cannot serve God in sincerity.

For who will labour to please his enemy ? Therefore the papists maintain hypocrisy when they say we ought not to be persuaded of the love of God, for then we ought to be hypocrites. For how shall we seek him with the loss of favour, and of credit, and of life itself, if we know not that his favour will stand us in stead, if we lose these things for him ?

3. Again, that we may be sincere, let us labour *to mortify all our earthly affections to the world ;* for how can we be sincere when we seek for honours, and pleasures, and riches, and not for better things ? Therefore we must know that there is more good to be had in truth, in a downright Christian profession, than in all worldly good whatsoever. And if we be hypocrites in our profession, there is more ill in that than in anything in the world. This will make us sincere, when we can be persuaded that we shall get better things by being sincere in religion than the world can give us, or take away from us. For why are men insincere and false-hearted ? Because they think not religion to be the true good. They think it is better to have riches than to have a good mind. These things therefore must be mortified ; and a man must know that the life of a Christian is incomparably the best life, though it be with the loss of liberty, yea, with the loss of life itself.

Simon Magus grew to false affections in religion, because he thought to have profit by it. So the Pharisees, they had naughty hearts, and therefore they had no good by religion. No man can profit by religion so long as his heart is naught, so long as there is some idol in his heart. A good Christian had rather have a large heart to serve God, and rather grow in the image of God, to be like him, than to grow in anything in the world, and that makes him sincere out of a good judgment ; because Christian excellency is the best excellency incomparably. For he knows well what all else will be ere long. What! will all do good, riches, honours, friends? What good will they do in the hour of death? There is nothing but grace, and the expression of it in the whole conversation, that will comfort us. Therefore he undervalues all things in the world to sincerity and a good conscience.

4. Again, that we may have our conversation in sincerity, let us labour in everything we do *to approve ourselves to the eye of God.* We see the Scripture everywhere shews, that this hath made God's children conscientious in all their courses; even when they might have sinned not only securely, but with advantage. What kept Joseph from committing folly with his mistress? ' Shall I do this, and sin against God?' Gen. xxxix. 9. And so Job in chap. xxxi., he shews what awed and kept him from ill-doing; in ver. 3, ' Doth not he see my ways, and account all my steps?' This was it that kept him in awe. So the church of God, Ps. xliv., being in great distress, they kept themselves from idolatry, and from the contagion of the times wherein they lived. Upon what ground? You shall see in verse 21, ' If we had done thus and thus, shall not God search it out? for he knows the very secrets of the heart.' So a Christian being persuaded of the eye of God upon him, it makes him sincere. The eye of God being ten thousand times brighter than the sun, he being light itself. He made the heart, and he knows all the turnings of the heart. The consideration of this will make us sincere in our closets, in our very thoughts; for they all lie open and naked to his view.

What is the reason that men practise secret villany, secret wickedness, and give themselves to speculative filthiness? Because they are atheists. They forget that they are in the eye of God, who sees the plots and projects of their hearts, and the nets that they have laid for their brethren. Therefore David brings them in saying, ' Tush! God sees us not,' Isaiah xxix. 15. And that is the reason they are unconscionable in their desires, in their hearts, in their secret thoughts. It is from a hidden atheism. For if we did consider that the eye of God sees us in all our intents and actions, and sees us in what manner we do all, and to what end; that he sees every action, with the circumstances, the aims, and ends; if the heart did well ponder this, it would prevent a great deal of evil.

Conscience is the witness of our conversation, a witness that will keep us from offending. If there were a witness by, and that witness were a great person, a judge, &c., it would keep us in our good behaviour. Now when a man shall consider, I have a witness within me, my conscience; and a witness without, which is God, who is my Judge, who can strike me dead in the committing of a sin, if he please: this would make men, if they were not atheists, to fear to sin.

Let us labour therefore to approve our hearts to God, as well as our conversations to men; set ourselves in the presence of God, who is a discerner of our thoughts as well as of our actions; and that which we should be ashamed to do before men, let us be afraid to think before God. That is another means to come to sincerity.

5. Another direction to help us to walk sincerely is, *especially to look to the heart,* look to the beginning, to the spring of all our desires, thoughts, affections, and actions, that is, the heart. The qualification of that is the qualification of the man. If the heart be naught, the man is naught. If that be sincere, the man is sincere. Therefore look to the heart. See what springs out thence. If there spring out naughty thoughts and desires,

suppress them in the beginning. Let us examine every thought. If we find that we do but think an evil thought, execute it presently; crush it: for all that is naught comes from a thought and desire at the first. Therefore let us look to our thoughts and desires. See if we have not false desires, and intents and thoughts answerable.

God is a Spirit, and he looks to our very spirits: and what we are in our spirits, in our hearts and affections, that we are to him. Therefore, as a branch of this, what ill we shun, let us do it from the heart, by hating it first. A man may avoid an evil action from fear, or out of other respects, but that is not sincerity. Therefore look to thy heart, see that thou hate evil, and let it come from sincere looking to God. ' Ye that love the Lord, hate the thing that is evil,' saith David, Ps. xcvii. 10: not only avoid it, but hate it; and not only hate it, but hate it out of love to God. And that which is good, not only to do it, but to labour to delight and joy in it. For the outward action is not the thing that is regarded, but when there is a resolution, a desire and delight in it, then God accounts it as done. And so it is in evil. If we delight in evil, it is as if it were done already. Therefore in doing good, look to the heart, joy in the good you do, and then do it; and in evil, look to the heart, judge it to be evil, and then abstain from it.

This is the reason of all the errors in our lives. Because we have bad hearts, we look not to God in sincerity. Judas had a naughty heart. He loved not the Lord Jesus Christ, and therefore he had a naughty conclusion. What the heart doth not, is not done in religion. Thus we see how we may come to have our conversation in sincerity, that we may rejoice in the testimony of our conscience.

Use. Therefore now, to make an use of exhortation, *we should labour for sincerity, and esteem highly of it, because God so esteems of it.* Truth is all that we can allege to God. We cannot allege perfection. St Paul himself saith not, I have walked exactly or perfectly: no, but he saith, ' This is our rejoicing, that we have walked in sincerity.' So, if a man's conscience can excuse him of hypocrisy and doubling, though it cannot free him from imperfections, God in the covenant of grace looks not so much at perfection as at truth.

Obj. Here I might answer an objection of some Christians. Oh, but I cannot pray without distraction, I cannot delight so in good things, &c.

Ans. Though a Christian's heart cannot free him from this, yet his heart desires to approve itself to God in all things; and his heart is ready to say to the Lord, as David said, ' Lord, try me, if there be any way of wickedness in me,' Ps. cxxxix. 23. And therefore he will attend upon all means to get this sincerity. He will be diligent in the word of God, for therein the mind of God is manifestly seen. The word of God, it is a begetting word, it makes us immortal, it makes us new creatures. It is truth, and the instrument of truth. Truth will make truth. The true sincere word of God, not mingled with devices, it will make what it is. The word of God, being his word who is Almighty, it hath an almighty transforming power from him. It is accompanied and clothed with his Almighty Spirit. Truth will cause truth. Such as it is in itself it will work in our hearts.

In that mongrel, false religion, popery, they have traditions, and false devices of men, and so they make false Christians. Such as they are they make. Strain them to the quintessence, and they cannot make a true Christian. Truth makes true Christians. Therefore attend upon God's ordinance with all reverence, and it will make thee a sound heart. It is a transforming word. Those that desire to hear the word of God, and to have their consciences to be informed by the hearing of it, they are sincere Christians ; and those that labour to shut up the word of God, that it may not work upon the conscience, they are false-hearted.

A heart that is sincere, it prizeth the word of God that makes us sincere. The word of God hath this effect, especially being unfolded in the ministry of it, that a man may say, as Jacob did, ' Doubtless God is in this place,' Gen. xxviii. 17. It is all that is ours. Nothing runs upon our reckoning but sincerity. For what I have not done truly, conscience saith I have not done to God, and therefore I can expect no comfort for it ; but what I have done to God, I look to have with comfort: for I know that God regards not perfection, but sincerity. He requires not so much a great faith, as a true faith ; not so much perfect love, as true love, and that I have in truth, as St Peter said, ' Lord, thou knowest that I love thee,' John xvi. 30.

This will make us look God, who is the Judge, in the face. It gives us not title to heaven, for that is only by Christ ; but it is a qualification required of us in the gospel. Nothing is ours but what we do in truth.

And again, consider that it will comfort us against Satan at the hour of death. When Satan shall tempt us to despair for our sins, as that he will do, we may comfort ourselves with this, that we have been sincere. We may send him to Christ, for that must be the way, who hath fulfilled God's will, and satisfied his Father's wrath. Satan will say, This is true ; it is the gospel, and therefore it cannot be denied ; but it is for them that have walked according to the Spirit, and not according to the flesh ; for those that have obeyed God in all things. Now when our conscience shall join with Satan, and say, we did nothing to God, we have not obeyed him, how can we answer him ? we must needs yield to the tempter. But when we can say with Peter, ' Lord, thou knowest that I love thee,' thou knowest I have laboured to approve my heart to thee, and that I have prosecuted this desire with endeavours ; this will comfort a man in the time of temptation. Therefore let us labour to have our conversation in sincerity.

It will afford us much comfort in this life, as it did St Paul. St Paul here was in some grievous sickness, even to death, and he was disgraced as a person that regarded not his promise of coming to them. Now what doth he do in all this sickness and disgrace ? what doth he answer to them ? He comforts himself in this, ' My rejoicing is, that my conscience doth testify my sincerity.' He runs to God, and to his sincerity, as his stronghold. He approves himself to God. Something we shall have in this life first or last; afflictions, or disgraces, and troubles will come. What is then the stronghold of a Christian ? Then he runs to his sincerity. What would Hezekiah have done when he received the ' sentence of death,' [if it had not been] that he had walked before God in uprightness and sincerity ? Sincerity then is worth more than the world. And he that will not labour for that which is worth more than all the world, it is a sign he is ignorant of the worth of it. A man at the hour of death he would lose all the world if he had it, for sincerity.

Therefore let us not part with our sincerity. Let us not offend against sincerity and truth by falsehood in our carriage, and in our tongues, or conversations any manner of way, since it will yield us so much comfort in temptations, and afflictions, and at the tribunal and judgment-seat of Christ.

Let us not have false aims and ends, and do things in a false manner.

It is not action only that God requires, but the manner.   If we regard not the manner, God will not regard the matter.   The matter of the Pharisees' performances was very good for stuff, but their hearts being naught, God regarded it not.   Let us look to the manner of doing all that we do, that we do them to God, that we do them in sincerity, in a holy manner.   The Scripture requires this, receive the sacrament, but thus, ' Examine yourselves,' 1 Cor. xi. 28.   ' Take heed how you hear,' Mark iv. 24.   Let your conversation be in the world, but thus, ' in simplicity and godly sincerity.' St Paul doth not say that he rejoiced in miracles, or in the great works that he had done, in converting of nations, &c., which yet were matters of joy ; but when he comes to joy indeed, here is his joy, that his conversation had been in ' simplicity and godly sincerity.'

And Christians must take heed that they reason not against sincerity another way, that is, to conclude they have no goodness, because they see a great deal of corruption and imperfections ; for imperfections may stand with truth.   Asa, as I said, had many infirmities in his life, yet notwithstanding it is said, that he walked in sincerity.   So Hezekiah, it is said he ' walked before God uprightly,' yet he had many infirmities and imperfections.   Nay, a man may well retort this upon such poor souls, that are witnesses with Satan against themseves, in the sight of their sins, that their sins being known by them, especially with hatred of them, it is a sign of sincerity.

Again, others are ready to say, I am not sincere, because God follows me with afflictions and distresses.   Reason not so, for he therefore follows thee with afflictions, because he would have nothing but sincerity in thee. He would make thee wholly sincere, and purge thee as metal is purged in the fire from the dross.   Therefore take heed thus of sinning against sincerity.   Do nothing in hypocrisy.   And when we are once sincere, let us not sin against it by yielding to the devil.   This comforted Job, when his friends alleged his corruptions.   ' Well,' saith he, ' you shall not take away my sincerity from me,' Job xxvii. 6.   He looked to the eye of God, that saw him, to whom he approved his heart ; and that consideration made him sincere, and thence he comforted himself.   So let us comfort ourselves in our sincerity against Satan's allegations ; as a condition of the covenant of grace, which respects not perfection but truth.

To add one thing more.   As there is an order of other graces ; so there is an order in this sincerity which we should labour for.   There is this order to be kept.

1. *We must dig deep.*   We must lay a sincere foundation.   What is that ? A deep search into our own hearts and ways by sound humiliation.   We say of digestions, if the first be naught, all are naught ; if the first concoction in the body be naught, there can never be good assimilation, there can never be good blood.   So if there be not a good, a sincere foundation, there can never be a sincere fabric.   Therefore many mistake, and build castles in the air, comb-downes, as we say (*pp*).   They build a frame of profession that comes to nothing in the end ; because it is not sincere in this order.   They were never truly humbled.   They had a guileful heart, in the confession of their sins.   They never knew what sin was throughly, and feelingly.   ' Blessed is the man in whose spirit there is no guile,' Ps. xxxii.

2. The psalmist especially means and intends there, in regard of downright dealing with God in the confession of sins.   For he himself when he did not deal roundly and uprightly with God in the confession of his sins, with detestation, and with resolution never to commit the same again, he

was in a pitiful plight both of soul and body ; his moisture was turned into
' the drought of summer,' Ps. xxxii. 4.

2. But when without guile he laid open his soul to God, then he came
from sincere humiliation, and sincere confession, *to sincere faith*. Therefore,
for the order, let us first labour to be sincere in the sight of that which is
ill in us, in the confession of our sins, and then we shall be sincere, the
better to depend upon God's mercy in Christ by faith.

3. And from thence we shall come to *sincere love*. When we believe that
God is reconciled in Christ, we shall love him. Our love is but a reflection
of his love to us. When once we know that he loves us, we shall love him
again.

The spring of all duty is sincere love, coming from sincere faith ; as
sincere faith is forced out of the sincere sight of our sins, of the ill and
miserable estate we are in. A man will not go out of himself, so long as he
sees any hope in himself ; and therefore sound knowledge of the evil condition we are in, it forceth the grace of faith, which forceth a man to go out
of himself. And then when he is persuaded of God's love in Christ, he
loves him again.

Love is that which animates, and quickens, and enlivens all duties. What
are all duties, but love ? Christ reduceth all to love. It is a sweet affection
that stirs up and quickeneth to all duties. It carries us along to all duties.
All are love. What need I stand on sincere patience, sincere temperance,
sincere sobriety, &c. ? If a man have sincere love to God, it will carry him
to all duties. Remember this order.

Especially every day, enter into your own souls, and search impartially,
what sin there is there unconfessed, and unrepented of, and make your peace
with God by confession. And then go to sincere dependence on God by
faith in the promises. And then stir up your hearts to love him ; and
from the love of him to love one another in sincerity, not in hypocrisy.
Thus we have the manner of the blessed apostle's carriage in the world,
whereupon his rejoicing was founded. ' Our rejoicing is this, the testimony of our conscience, that in simplicity and godly sincerity,'

' *We have had our conversation in the world.*' I will speak a little of
those words, before I come to the negative part, ' Not in fleshly wisdom.'

' Our conversation.' By ' conversation,' *anastrophe*,* he means the
several turnings of his life, in what relation soever he stood to God, to men,
as a minister, as a Christian, as a friend, as a neighbour, at home or
abroad, in all estates, in all places, and at all times. His conversation was
' in simplicity and sincerity.'

' In the world,' that is, wheresoever he had lived. And mark how he joins
them together. His conversation in the world amongst men, it was with
sincerity to God. It was that that did rule his conversation in the world.
And so it should be with us wheresoever we are, or whatsoever we do in
the world, our carriage here must be directed by a higher aspect. The ship
while it is tossed in the sea, it is ruled by the pole-star. That must guide
it. So in our conversation in the world. The stuff of our conversation
may be the business we have in the world, but the rule, the regiment† of all
must be from heaven, with an eye to God. I touch that from the knitting
of these together.

Now where he saith, that his conversation was in simplicity and sin-

* That is, ἀναστροφή, turning about, = manner of life.—G.
† That is, ' government.'—G.

cerity, you may see here then that all the frame, all the passages of his life were good. This makes good that which I touched before, which hath its proper place here, that

Sincerity extends itself to all the frame of a man's life.

He that is sincere, is sincere in all places, and at all times; in all the turnings and windings and passages of his life; or else he is not sincere at all. His conversation must be sincere, wheresoever he lives, or whatsoever he doth, in prosperity or adversity, at home or abroad.

The veriest hypocrite in the world, hath he not pangs sometimes? Take an oppressor, he thinks that he should not die so, he thinks, I must be called to an account if I do thus. Doth not Ahab lie upon his sick-bed sometimes? Is not Herod sometimes troubled in conscience? Hath not a wicked man sometimes twitches of conscience which the world sees not, secret checks of conscience? Oh, yes! There is not the vilest man living, but he hath his good fits, he hath pangs of goodness. But what is this to a conversation? Our conversation must be in sincerity in all the turnings and passages of it.

God judgeth us by the tenor of our life, and not by single particular acts. A good man may be ill in a particular act; and an evil man may be good in a particular act. But I say, God doth not judge us by a distinct severed passage, but by the tenor of our life. Uniformity, equability, and evenness of life, it is an undoubted evidence of a good man.

Because he is a new creature, and being a new creature, he hath a new nature; and nature works uniformly. Art works differently, and enforcedly. Teach a creature somewhat that is against nature, it will do something, but a lion will have a lion's trick, and a wolf will have a wolf's trick. Teach them never so much, a lion will be a lion in all places; a wolf will be a wolf, and an eagle will be an eagle. Every creature will observe its own nature, and be like itself.

A Christian, as far as he is good, as far as he is a Christian, is uniform. His conversation is good, he is like himself, in all places, in all times, upon all occasions, in prosperity, in adversity. The very word shews that the universality of a man's course must be in sincerity, wheresoever he is. God is everywhere, and sincerity hath an eye to God. It makes a man good everywhere; or else it doth nothing to God. Doth not God see everywhere, abroad, and at home in our closets? If we plot villany, there sees he it as well as abroad. Therefore if I do it anywhere, I regard not the eye of God.

Again, where he saith, ' our conversation,' it implies constancy, as well as uniformity. He was so in all places and in all times. But that I noted before, therefore I pass it. ' Our conversation *in the world.*'

That is, amongst other men, wheresoever I was, and have lived. Whence we see, that

Obs. Christianity may stand with conversing abroad in the world.

Men need not be mued*up in a cloister, as the foolish monks in former times. They thought that religion was a thing confined to solitariness; whereas ofttimes it requires greater strength of grace to be alone than to be in company. We know the proverb, ' Woe to him that is alone,' Eccles. iv. 10. A good Christian converses in the world, and that in simplicity and sincerity. We need not, I say, cloister ourselves up to be good men, to be sincere Christians. We may converse in the world in sincerity if we have St Paul's spirit.

* That is, ' mured,'= immured.—G.

But that which I will press more, is this, that

Obs. True religion, where it is in strength, doth carry a man in the world, and yet he is not tainted with the world.

St Paul conversed in the world in sincerity. The world is an hypocrite, as he said of old. The whole world acts a part. It is an hypocrite, and a cruel opposer of sincerity and truth. St Paul lived abroad in the world, amongst men that had aims of their own, and abused themselves in the world, and yet he walked in ' simplicity and sincerity.' He was a good man for all that. A man that is not of the world, but begotten to be a member of a higher world, he may carry himself in the world without the corruptions of the world, he may carry himself so in the world that he may not be carried away of the world. We see St Paul did so.

Noah was a good man in evil times, ' a good man in his generation,' Gen. vi. 9. Enoch, in evil times ' walked with God,' Gen. v. 22. In Acts xiii. 22, ' David in his generation served the purpose of God ;' and his generation was none of the best. For you know there was Ahithophel, and Doeg, which were bad companions, yet in his generation he served the purpose of God. So every man in his time may live and converse in the world, and yet not be carried away with the corruptions of the times.

What is the reason ?

Reason. The reason is, that a true Christian hath a spirit in him above the world. As St John saith, ' The Spirit that is in you is stronger than he that is in the world,' 1 John iv. 4. The child of God hath a spirit in him, a new nature, that sets him in a rank above the world. Christians are an order of men that are above the world. They are men of another world. And therefore having a principle of grace that raiseth them above the base condition of the world, they can live in the world, without the blemishes and corruptions of the world. They are men of a higher disposition.

Even as sickness in the body hurts not the reasonable life, so anything that a Christian meets with in the world, it hurts not his Christian life, which is his best life, because it is a life of a higher respect, of a higher nature. St Paul's ' conversation was in heaven,' Philip. iii. 20, it was above the snares here below. He was ' crucified to the world,' Gal. vi. 14. He was a dead man to all that was evil in the world, and to that which was good and indifferent in the world. For pleasures, for honours, for meat and drink, and such necessaries ; the counsel that he gave to others, he practised in himself, for worldly callings, and refreshings, and the like, 1 Cor. vii. 29. ' The time is short, let us use the world as though we used it not.' He used indifferent things in the world, which are good or evil as they be used, as if he had not used them. He lived in the world, as a traveller or passenger. He knew he was not at home. He knew he had another home to go to. ' Here we have no continuing city,' Heb. xiii. 14, and therefore he used the world as though he used it not. As a traveller useth things in his way as far as they may further him ; but let his very staff trouble him, he throws it away. So a Christian useth indifferent things in the world, which are good or evil according as himself is, he useth them well ; because ' all things are pure to the pure,' Titus i. 15. He useth them so as that he doth not delight in them, because he hath better things to solace himself in. He doth not drown himself in these as worldlings do.

And for the ills of the world, a Christian in a good measure is crucified to the world, and the world to him. And he hath his conversation in heaven, ' But our conversation is in heaven,' Philip. iii. 20. Many serve their bellies, ' whose end is damnation, but our conversation is in heaven.'

Now his conversation being heavenly, that is the reason that he can converse in the world in sincerity, though the world be of another strain.

So you see then that a Christian is of a higher nature, of a higher condition than the world ; and he is crucified to the world ; and he knows himself to be a passenger and a traveller in the world, and therefore he useth the world as though he used it not. And withal he hath his employment above the world. The birds that have the air, as long as they are there, they are not catched with snares below ; and Christians that have their conversation above, they are not ensnared with the things of the world as other men are. We see St Paul conversed in the world in sincerity.

I observe it the rather, because it is the common exception of weak, and false spirits.—We must do as the world doth, or else we cannot live. He that knows not how to dissemble, knows not how to live. And the times are naught ; so that which is naught and grounded in themselves, they lay all the blame of it upon the times.

Indeed the times are naught, like themselves. As he said, There is a circle of human things. The times are but even as they were. Things come again upon the stage. The same things are acted. The persons indeed are changed, but the same things are acted in the world to the end of the world. The times were naught before, they are naught, and they will be so. Villany is acted upon the stage of the world continually. The former actors are gone, but others are instructed with the same devices, with the same plots. The corruption of nature shews itself in all. Only now we have the advantage for the acting of wickedness in the end of the world ; because, besides the old wickedness in former times, we have the new wickednesses of these times. All the streams running into one, make the channel greater.

Men say, Alas ! alas ! the times are ill. Were they not so in Noah's time ? Were they not so in David's time ? Were they not so in St Paul's time ? Men pretend conformity to the world upon a kind of necessity. They must do as others do.

If they were true Christians it would not be so ; for Noah was good in evil times. Nehemiah was good in the court of the king of Babel.* Joseph was good, even in Egypt, in Pharaoh's court. This can be no plea. For a Christian hath a spirit to raise him above the corruption of the times he lives in ; he hath such a spirit likewise as is above prosperity or adversity, which will teach him to manage both, and to govern himself in all occasions and occurrents† of the world. ' I can do all things,' saith St Paul, ' through Christ that strengtheneth me ! '

As we say, the planets have one course whereby they are carried with the first mover every twenty-four hours, from east to west, as the sun is, whereby he makes the day. But the sun hath a course of his own back again. And so by creeping back again he makes the year in his own course. So the moon hath one course of her own ; but yet she is carried every day another course by the first mover.

So, a good Christian that lives in the world, he is carried with the world in common things ; he companies, and traffics, and trades, and deals with the world. But hath he not a motion of his own contrary to all this at the same time ? Yes ; though he converse in the world, yet notwithstanding he is thinking of heaven, he is framing his course another way than the world doth. He goes a contrary course, he swims against the stream of the world.

* That is, ' Babylon.'—G.   † That is, ' occurrences.'—G.

There are some kind of rivers, they say, that pass through the sea, and yet notwithstanding they retain their freshness. It seems as an emblem to shew the condition of a Christian. He passeth through the salt waters, and yet keeps his freshness, he preserves himself. Therefore, I say, it is no plea to say that times are naught, and company is naught, &c. A man is not to fashion himself to the times. An hypocrite, chameleon-like, can turn himself into all colours but white ; and as the water, which we say hath no figure of its own, but it is figured by the vessel that it is in (if the vessel be round, the water is round ; if the vessel be four-cornered, the water is so), it being a thin, airy, moist body. It hath no compass of its own, but is confined by the body it is kept in.

So some men they have no religion, they have no consistence, no standing, no strength or goodness of their own ; but such as their company is, such they are, and they think this will serve for all. I must do as others do ; it is the fashion of the world. If they be among swearers, they will swear ; if they be among those that are unclean, they will pollute themselves. They frame themselves to all companies. They will be all, but that which they should be. This will not serve the turn.

A Christian may pray for the assistance of God to keep him in the world ; and he may know that God will. What ground hath he ? Our Saviour Christ, saith he, ' Father, I pray not that thou shouldest take them out of the world, but that thou keep them in the world,' John xvii. 15. He prays for his apostles and disciples, that God would keep them in the world from the contagion of sin, and from the destruction of the world. St Paul, you see, lived and conversed in the world, wheresoever he was, in sincerity and simplicity. He was not carried away with the stream, and errors of the times wherein he lived.

Nay, to add more, it doth unite the power of grace together, and make a man the better, the worse the company or the place is where he lives. We know in nature, the environing of contraries increaseth the contrary ; and holy men have been better ofttimes in the midst of temptation, and have gathered their forces and strength of grace together, more than when they have been more secure. The envy and malice of the world is quick-sighted, and the more they live amongst those that are observers of them, the more cautelous * they are of their carriage. You know it is the apostle's reason, ' Redeem the time, because the days are evil,' Eph. v. 16. Be you the better, because the days are evil. Witness for God in an ' evil generation,' in evil times. He doth not say, Do you sin, because the days are evil. God's people do always witness for him.

Let me add this likewise, to give farther light, that we must not take occasion hence, to conform and fashion ourselves to any company, to cast ourselves into evil company when we need not. We must not tempt God ; for then it is just with God to suffer us to be soiled with the company. And by our carelessness in this kind, we offend the godly, that easily hereupon take us to be worse than we are. And as we grieve the Spirit of God in them, so in ourselves ; and we build up and strengthen wicked persons. And, therefore, this living in the world ' in simplicity and sincerity,' it must be when our calling is such, that we live in the world, that we need not any local separation to sever ourselves. But when in the world, we are cast on men without grace, by our callings, and occasions, we may presume that God will keep us by his Spirit.

Let us not be weary of hearing of this point. For ere long we must all

* That is, ' cautious.'—G.

appear before God, and then what an honour will it be for us, that **we** have witnessed for God in this world! that we have stood for God **and** good causes in the midst of the world, and ' shined as lights in the midst **of** a crooked generation' ! Philip. ii. 15. That we have managed the **cause** of God, and stood for religion, and held our own in the midst of papists and atheists, and profane persons, and witnessed for the best things in spite of all, when we have been called to it. We are not to thrust ourselves into unnecessary troubles, no, not for the best things, unless we **be** called to it ; but when we are called, and can witness for the best **things,** what an honour will it be for us !

And on the contrary, saith Christ, ' He that denies me, and is ashamed of me before men, of him will I be ashamed before my heavenly Father,' Mark viii. 38. What a fearful thing is this ! Let us look to God in simplicity and sincerity, and God will keep us that the world shall not hurt us.

Obj. What will become of us ? will some say, this trouble we shall **come** into, and that persecution will befall us.

Ans. It is not so. Christ was opposed when he was here upon earth ; but till his hour was come they could not do anything. Every man hath his hour, every man hath his time allotted to serve God in here. God hath measured out his life ; and till his hour be come, that God will take **him** out of the world, God will bind up the endeavours of men. Their **plots** shall be to no purpose. God will keep them, and watch over **them** that are downright. ' Because thou hast kept my word, I will keep thee,' Rev. iii. 8–10, saith God. Let us keep the word of God in evil times, **and** God will keep us ; let us stand for God, and he will stand for us.

It is no plea to say, I shall run into this danger, and that danger. ' God will be thy buckler and thy shield,' Ps. xci. 4, if thou stand for him. And that which brings danger is too much correspondence with the world. When men forsake their sincerity in the world, when men will be on both sides, they carry things unhappily, and unsuccessfully. A downright atheist will carry things with better success than a halting Christian. **For** his policy and subtlety will carry him to actions inconvenient ; but then comes his conscience after, when he is in the midst of them, **and** damps him that he cannot go forward nor backward. Therefore **the** only way is to resolve to live in the world in simplicity and sincerity. If we do so, we may carry holy businesses strongly. God will assist **us** therein. He will increase our light, and make our way plain and clear to us.

But if a man be not sincere, but double, and carnal, and pretend love of religion, and yet take courses and do actions that are not suitable to religion, it will not succeed well. God will curse it. He will strike him with amazement. He will strike his brain with errors in judgment, &c. There is no pretence therefore to make us live falsely, and doubly in **the** world ; but we ought to live as St Paul did, let the world be as bad as it will, or as it can be, ' in simplicity and sincerity.' God will shew himself strong for those that walk uprightly. He will be wisdom to such. But if we walk doubly, and falsely, and make religion our pretence, God will shew himself our enemy.

Where be your neuters then ? Where be your politicians in religion, **that** will keep their religion to themselves ? St Paul conversed in the world, wheresoever he was, in sincerity. He made show what he was. He walked not according to carnal wisdom, as he saith afterwards. Where be your *Nullifidians**** then, that are of all beliefs, and yet are of no belief? that fashion themselves to all religions? And if they be of the true religion, yet it is their wisdom to conceal it. St Paul did not so. But I shall have occasion to touch that in the negative part afterward, 'not in fleshly wisdom,' &c.

Again, where he saith, 'My conversation hath been thus in the world,' he means, in this life my conversation here hath been sincere. I will give you a touch on that. Though it be not the main aim here, yet notwithstanding it may well be touched, that,

Obs. We must, while we live here in this world, converse in simplicity and sincerity.

We must not turn it off to live as we list, subtlely, politicly, and carnally, and then think to die well. No ; we must live ' soberly, righteously, and justly in this present world,' Tit. ii. 12. Do you think to begin to live well when you are gone hence? No ; that is a time of reward, and not a time of work. This world is God's workhouse ; here you must work. This is God's field ; here you must labour. This is God's sea ; here we must sail. Here we must take pains. We must sweat at it. Here we must plough and sow, if ever we will reap.

Dost thou think to carry thyself subtlely, to have thy own ends in everything here, and then when death comes, a ' Lord, have mercy upon me' shall serve for all? No ; thou must converse as a Christian while thou livest here in this world, ' in simplicity and sincerity.' God must have honour here by thee. Thou must have a care of thy salvation here. Dost thou think to have that in another world which thou dost not care for here? Dost thou think to have glory in another world, which thou didst not think of here? Dost thou think to reap in another world that which thou didst not sow here? Let us in this world stand for the glory of God, openly and boldly, and for the example of others, for the exercise of our own graces. A true Christian hath his conversation in ' sincerity in this world;' the more blame to the world then to deprave their dealing! Why? Because they are lights in the world, and they serve the world to good purpose, if the world would take benefit by them. They shine in the world to lead them the way to heaven. But the world is willing to let them go to heaven alone if they will.

But if the carriage of God's children be like St Paul's, as it is true, for they are all of one disposition, they ' converse in simplicity and sincerity wheresoever they are,' wicked, slanderous, malicious, depraving persons are to blame, that lay to their charge hypocrisy, and this and that, when it is nothing so. They deserve well of the wicked unthankful world, and God upholds the world for their sakes. ' When the righteous are exalted, the city rejoiceth,' saith Solomon, Prov. xi. 10. Because wheresoever they live, they live not only in simplicity and sincerity, but they live fruitfully. The city, the whole community, all the people are the better. They make the times and the places the better wherein they live, because a good man is a public good. The Spirit of God, when it makes a good man, it puts him out of himself, and gives him a public affection. It teacheth him to deny himself. It teacheth him to love others. It teacheth him to employ and improve all that is in him, that is good, for the service of God and of men ; to serve God in serving men in the place he lives in. Therefore malicious and devilish is the world to deprave such kind of men as live in the world in simplicity and sincerity, that serve God and the world by all the means

* That is, ' no-faith's.'—G.

they can. ' Our conversation hath been in simplicity and sincerity in the world.'

' *But more abundantly to you-ward.*' Why? Was it in hypocrisy to others, and in sincerity to them only? No; that is not the meaning. But thus, that wheresoever he had lived in the world, in what estate soever he was, he carried himself in ' simplicity and sincerity ;' but to you I have made it more evident than to any other. Why? Because he had lived longer with them ; and they were such as he was a Father unto in Christ. Therefore, saith he, I have evidenced my ' simplicity and sincerity more abundantly to you than to any other.' Whence we may observe, that

Obs. *A sincere Christian is best where he is best known.*

It is a note of a truly good and sincere man to be best where he is best known, as I touched when I opened the words. It is otherwise with many. Their carriage abroad is very plausible ; but follow them home : what are they in their familes? They are lions in their houses. What are they in their retired courses and carriage? They do not answer the expectation that is raised of them abroad. They never pray to God, &c. Those that know them best will trust them least. It is not so with a Christian. My conversation in the world hath been good wheresoever it hath been. But among you, with whom I have conversed more familiarly, who have seen my daily carriage and course of life, among you my conversation was best of all. It is a note of a man that is sincere, that the more he is seen into, the more he shines. The godly are substantially good, and therefore where they are best known, they are best approved.

For Christians they are not painted creatures, that a little discovery will search them to the bottom, and then shame them. They are not gilded, but gold ; and therefore the more you enter into them, the more metal you shall find still. They have a hidden treasury. The more you search them, the more stuff you shall have still. Their tongues are as ' fined silver,' and their heart is a rich treasury within them. A Christian he labours for a broken heart still. He labours to get new grace, and new knowledge of the word of God still ; and the more you converse with him, the more you see him, the more you shall approve and love him, if you be good as he is. Therefore saith the apostle, I have carried myself well to all, but especially to you with whom I have lived longer.

Use. Therefore, as we would have an evidence of our sincerity, which is the best evidence that we can have in this world, that we may be able to say that we are sincere and true Christians, which is better than if a man could say he were a monarch, that he were the greatest man in the world, let us labour *to carry ourselves in our courses to those that know us best, and in our most retired courses, like to Christians.* And not to put on the fashion of religion, as men put on their garments : their best garments, when they go abroad, and so to make good things serviceable to our purpose. But to be so indeed at home amongst our friends, among those that know us, when we are not awed, as there is a great deal of liberty amongst friends. Wheresoever we are, let us remember we are alway in the eye of God ; and labour to approve ourselves most to them that know our courses most.

God knows more than men, therefore let us chiefly labour to approve ourselves to him. And next to God, let us approve ourselves to conscience. Fear conscience more than all the monarchs in the world ; because that knows most, and will be most against us.

And then again, for others that know our conversations, good men that converse with us, let us approve ourselves to them most that have the best and the sharpest judgments.

A true Christian, as he loves goodness, so he loves it most that it should be in his own heart. He lives more to God and to conscience, than to fame and report. He had rather be than seem to be. And as he hates all ill, so he hates even secret ill. The nearer corruption is, the more he hates it, as a man hates toads and venomous creatures ; and the nearer they are, the more he hates them. The most retired carriage of a Christian is most holy, and best of all.

Again, where he saith, ' My conversation hath been in simplicity, &c., to you-ward,' here is a good note for preachers, that if they look to convert any by their doctrine, they must win them by their conversation likewise in simplicity and sincerity. St Paul being to gain the Philippians to Christ, he doth it not by words only, by arguments of logic, and by persuasions only, to convince the understanding of the truth of that which he taught ; but he demonstrates to them how they should live. ' Walk as you have me for an ensample,' Philip. iii. 17. I shew you that that which I teach is possible, by my practice. I shew to high and low, how I carry myself. ' My conversation hath been in simplicity and sincerity.' Those that I would convert by my doctrine, I labour by my conversation to gain them. So I say, ministers have here a special direction how to carry themselves.

And others likewise that have a gaining disposition, as indeed we should not stand upon terms of this and that, but every one labour to gain others. Would you work upon others, and gain them from popery, &c. ? Then not only shew them arguments to convince their judgments, which must be done, that is certain ; but likewise let them see that the things that you speak are possible things, things that you are persuaded of. And if you be not good, and press them to goodness, you cannot persuade them of the truth of that you speak. They will think it is not possible ; for then you would act it yourselves. But when they see one go before them, and demonstrate it to their eyes, how they should carry themselves, this is the way to teach them to be sound Christians indeed. But I hasten to the negative part.

' *Not in fleshly wisdom*,' &c. Here is a secret wipe, a secret taxing of the false apostles and teachers. ' My conversation hath been in simplicity and sincerity,' whatsoever you think of me. ' Not in fleshly wisdom,' as theirs is.

' Not in fleshly wisdom.' To distinguish it a little.

1. There is a *natural wisdom* planted in the soul of man, even as there is a natural light in the eye, to see both things that are hurtful, and that are good, for the outward man. So in the soul of man, which is his eye, there is an inbred light of natural wisdom, a common light to discern of things and of creatures ; a natural kind of wisdom, which may be polished and advanced to a higher degree by experience and art. As the eye of the body, it sees better when it is helped with an outward, with a foreign light. This is natural wisdom.

2. There is likewise a *politic or civil wisdom*, gotten by observation, and increased by observation ; and withal, it is a gift of God, though it be a common gift, as Ahithophel's. It was not merely carnal wisdom that was in him, but he had a gift of policy. So some men, though they be not

truly religious, yet God gives them a gift of politic wisdom, to be able to discern the difference of things, to lay states and commonwealths together, to be able to judge, and resolve, and to execute wisely, and politically, and prudently. It is an especial gift of God. This the apostle doth not aim at ; neither natural nor civil wisdom, though it be a gift of God, I say, which is increased by observation and by other means.

3. Besides this, there is *a spiritual, a heavenly wisdom*, whereby the soul having a right end and aim set and prefixed to it, it directs all its courses to that end ; whereby the soul is able to deliberate, to consult, and to resolve on heavenly things, and what hinders heavenly comfort ; and to resolve upon good duties, and to resolve against that which is ill, to resolve upon all advantages of doing good to the church, and of all hindrances of ourselves, and of the church, and of the places we live in. It is a heavenly kind of prudence to guide our own ways, yea, and to guide others too.

4. But besides all these, there is another wisdom which is here the ' *wisdom of the flesh ;*' which because the flesh hath correspondency with Satan, it is also a devilish wisdom, for the most part. For the devil ploughs with our heifer. The most mischief that he hath done in the world, it is by the correspondency that he hath with our flesh, our enemy within. The flesh and Satan do join together, and work all strongly with the mischievous policy of the world : and therefore it is called likewise ' worldly wisdom.'

And hereupon Christians that are mere professors, and not Christians soundly, some are called flesh, because they are ruled of the flesh. And they are called the world, because they frame themselves to the wisdom and to the courses of the world. And if you would anatomize them, there is nothing but the world in them, worldly pride and worldly ends. And they are called devils too, as Judas was called a devil, John vi. 70. They plot with Satan by carnal wisdom. They yield to Satan. They savour not the things of God.

Men have their name and denomination in the Scripture, by that which they are ruled by. When they are ruled by the flesh, they are called flesh ; when they are ruled by the world and the evil examples thereof, they are called the world. And when they are ruled by Satan, so far as they are ruled by him, they are called Satan. ' One of you is a devil,' saith Christ.

' Not in fleshly wisdom.' What is meant here by ' fleshly wisdom ? ' If it be fleshly, why is it wisdom ? Wisdom is but one. There is but one wisdom. Wisdom we know, in itself, it is a knowledge of principles and grounds, and deductions and conclusions from principles. A wise man knows both the grounds and principles, and he knows what may be raised from thence ; and likewise a man that is truly wise, he not only knows them, but he knows how to act them, how to work and act his principles and conclusions to an end. He hath principles, and conclusions, and workings out of his brain ; and when he hath done all in the brain, when he hath framed the aim of his principles, and the manner how to act them, then he goes about to work ; and a wise man can work answerable to his end and rules.

Now there is a carnal wisdom that initiated this ; for carnal wisdom hath aims, and ends, and principles, and it hath conclusions from those principles, and it acts to an end. A true Christian he hath his ends. His aim is supernatural : to please God in all things, to be happy in another world, to enjoy God, to have nearer acquaintance with him while he lives here. Many such subordinate ends, besides the main end, he hath. And some principles likewise he hath out of the word of God concerning this end ; and then he hath directions out of the word of God suitable to those principles. And then he sets on working, and all that he works is in order to his end, and in virtue of the end he propounds. As a man that travels, every step that he goes in his journey, every step is in virtue and strength of his first intention, and the end that he propounds, though he think not of his end in every step, and he consults and asks about the way, and all to that end.

So it is with a carnal man too, he that walks after carnal wisdom. Carnal wisdom hath its end, and that is a man's self; for a carnal man himself is the idol, and the idolater. His end is himself, either in his honours, or in his pleasures, or riches, &c. Himself is the centre into which all the lines of his life fall. And he hath rules. Seek thyself in all things. Love thyself above all. And what then ? If thou love others, love them for thyself, as far as they may serve thy turn. Care for no man further than thou canst make use of him for thyself. Respect him so far, and no further.

But it may be there are many that stand in the way. Then again he hath principles. Undermine them, ruin them, make way to thine own ends by the ruin of as many as thou canst. And if another man's light over-shine thine, that thou art nobody to him, carnal wisdom bids thee deprave him, slander him, backbite him. The more he seems to be vile, the less thy nakedness shall appear. Here is carnal wisdom.

There is no envy in goodness, in strength and ability. They would have all to be so ; but baseness is joined with much envy. When it sees another overshadow it, it labours to eclipse him with slanders and base reports. This is a principle of carnal wisdom. And hence comes all that working and undermining, secret conveyances, and laying nets for others, as the prophet speaks.

All carnal wisdom hath carnal ends, and carnal rules, and carnal courses answerable. It consults upon the attaining of its end. It deliberates and consults, and shrewdly too ; for it is whetted by Satan. And then it goes with the stream of the world, and therefore it is carried very strongly towards its end. And then it resolves strongly ; because fleshly wisdom usually is with the times. And then it executes. God suffers it oft-times to come to execution, and to enjoy its plots and projects. And therefore in regard that it hath the same passages, though in a contrary kind, with other wisdom, it is called wisdom, though indeed it be not wisdom. And thereupon it hath a diminishing term here, it is 'fleshly wisdom.'

Now this wisdom is called 'fleshly,' because it is led with reasons from the flesh, and it tends to the maintenance of the flesh. It comes from it, and it tends to it.

I take not 'flesh' here, for one part of a man, his body; but for the unregenerate part, which is carried to changeable things, to the creature, and sets up some creature to be an idol, instead of the Creator, 'blessed for evermore.'

And that from this reason, because the creature, the things below are near to us, and pleasant to us ; and because we are brought up in these delights of the creature that are sensible ; and therefore the flesh, the baser part, is ready to draw away the soul to the delights of it ; because the delights of it are pleasant, and we are trained up in them from the beginning of our life to the end of it. Now these things below, the profits, and pleasures, and honours, they work first upon the senses, upon the outward man; and from the senses they ascend to the fancy, and imagination, and that being carnal by nature esteems more highly of them than there is cause, and esteems of the contrary to these as the greatest ills. Oh! poverty is worse than hell to a carnal man! and he had rather be dead than be disgraced. He had rather damn his soul, than to be denied of his pleasure. Imagination makes them such great things, and the devil helps imagination. He hath much affinity with that part, with the imagination; and imagination, when men have strong conceits of these things, that labours to draw the will and affections to itself, to sway that part, So that the will, the commanding part of the soul, for the most part it yields to these imaginations of base things. It conceives of them highly, and the contrary to be vile and base. And hereupon the will comes to approve of these things, and to choose these things; yea, and the understanding part itself, that blessed spark of wisdom that is left in us, capable of better things, and fit for the image of God. Yet that, by our corruption, being stripped of the grace it had in the creation, and now being under original corruption, being under the law of sin, it is led by a carnal will and imagination, and by sense, and is ruled by them. So that that which should rule all, is ruled by base, earthly things.

The soul of man, while we live here, is between things better than itself, and worse than itself, meaner than itself. Now by corruption it cleaves to things meaner than itself. It is witty to devise them. It is willing to choose them. It delights in them. It bathes itself in them. So that whereas it should rule the body, the body and the lower parts rule the soul. When it yields to that which is better than itself, to the sanctifying Spirit of God, and to the word of God, and is clothed with the image of God, when it yields to better things, then they raise it to a degree of excellency even above itself when it was at the best. For a man that is in Christ, that hath the image of Christ upon him, in some sort, is better than Adam was in innocency. His estate is more sure ; and the dignity he is advanced to by Christ is greater than he should have had if he had stood still in Adam. This is the condition of the soul. An excellent creature, it is capable of the image and likeness of Christ, and of God, capable of all grace.

Again, if it submit itself to base creatures, it becomes even as them ; and therefore men are called ' the world.' They are called ' flesh.' They are called after that which leads them. The very soul itself, as it were, is flesh, For, as the very body of a holy man in some sort is spirit; and everything in him is spirit ; as it shall be at the day of judgment, as St Paul saith, ' it shall be raised a spiritual body,' 1 Cor. xv. 44 ; because it shall be subject to the motions of the Spirit of God in all things ; and it shall not be supported by bodily means. Now the very soul is bodily and carnal. Such a degeneration is wrought in man since the fall. He makes his soul that was given to guide him in this world, and which is made apprehensive of better things, of the things of another world. This soul he makes it the bawd to serve his base lusts and pleasures.

' Not in fleshly wisdom.' Now wisdom is a middle word. It may be either spiritual or carnal, as the man is in whom it is. If a man have moral honesty in him, and good things in him that way, it makes him a good politician, a wise man, useful in his place. Though he be not a sound Christian, yet he may be a wise man in his place ; and God useth such kind of men in the world, and they have their reward here, they are advanced, &c.

But if it is light in a devilish nature, in a crooked, oblique nature, then it is malicious, devilish wisdom.

And, note this by the way. All men that have flesh in them, have not fleshly wisdom ; for some are carried with the flesh, with the rage of fleshly lusts. As the swine in the gospel were carried headlong into the sea, they are carried by their lusts to hell, as your common swaggerers and roarers ; so that they may escape the danger of the laws, they care not for God nor man—irregular, wild persons. These have flesh, they are ruled by the flesh, but they have not so much as ' fleshly wisdom ;' for they take courses to overthrow themselves in the world, to overthrow their names, and their bodies and all. They have not so much as policy in them, their lusts so reign in them. Such wretches we have ofttimes amongst us, that think themselves somebody, but they have not so much as carnal wisdom in them to carry themselves better than a devil.

Now, in other men the flesh hath a wisdom that carries them not after this fashion ; but it whets their wits, and they are as bad in another kind. As, take the same man, when he is young he is carried by his brutish lusts, without any wisdom at all, even as the hurry of his lusts carry him, and transport him : when he grows old he is carried subtlely with the wisdom of the world. He is alway under lusts, alway under the flesh. When he is young he is carried with base lusts ; and when he is old he is under the flesh, and fleshly wisdom still. He is carried with slavish covetousness to the world, as formerly he was subject to base lusts in his youth. All this is naught.

Where these differ in the subject, in the person, usually the base lust serves the witty. Those that are carried with base lusts, they are subject, and enthralled, and overruled by those that are carried with the wisdom of the flesh. As your subtle men, your usurers, and subtle oppressors, great witty men, they make other men serviceable to their turn. Other men are slaves to them.

But to come nearer that that I mean to stand on.

' My conversation hath not been in fleshly wisdom.' You may see by the coherence, which I will not dwell on, what to judge of ' fleshly wisdom.'

Observ. Fleshly wisdom is, where there is no simplicity nor sincerity : because he opposeth them here. Where ' fleshly wisdom' is, there is neither ' simplicity' nor ' sincerity.' For take a subtle wise man, he is all outside, and there is no simplicity in him. He that is not wise to God, but to the world, he wraps himself in ceremonies in matters of religion, and studies the outside of things to approve himself to the world, and to attain his own ends ; but there is no simplicity or sincerity. He that is wise to the world hath no respect to God.

Sincerity hath an eye to God ; and a sincere man, as far as he is sincere, hath an eye to God, and he doth this and that because God seeth him, and because God is pleased with it ; but he that works according to fleshly wisdom, he hath aims contrary and distinct to that. Therefore the apostle saith, ' We walk in the sincerity of God' (as it is in the original*), ' and not according to fleshly wisdom.'

So you may know from the opposition, that fleshly wisdom is where there is no sincerity. Where there is no love to God or to men, there is

* That is, ' εἰλικρινείᾳ Θεοῦ.'—G.

no simplicity, all is for show; and where there is all for show, there is double carriage, not in simplicity aiming at God's glory. There is ' fleshly wisdom.' That for the connection.

But the point of doctrine proper to the place is this, that

Doctrine. God's children have another manner of rule to live by than the world: the rule that a godly wise man goeth by, is not fleshly wisdom.

A man that looks for any joy, that looks to be in the blessed estate that St Paul here was in, he must not be ruled by fleshly wisdom. ' Our conversation,' saith he, ' in the world hath not been in fleshly wisdom.' St Paul, no question but he had flesh in him, and likewise he had ' fleshly wisdom :' because flesh is in all parts, and it mingles itself with all graces. In the understanding there is light and darkness; in the will there is rebellion and pliableness to God. So St Paul had the stirrings of fleshly wisdom in him. When he was in danger, no doubt but the flesh would stir in him, you may avoid it by shifts if you will. And when he was before great ones, you may flatter and betray the truth if you will.

No doubt but St Paul, as he expressed himself, Rom. viii., as he had a conflict in himself in other regards : so there was a conflict between wisdom and wisdom. The wisdom of the flesh did stir against the wisdom of the spirit. Aye, but it is one thing to have fleshly wisdom in us, and it is another thing to make it our rule. It is one thing to have flesh in us, and another thing to ' be in the flesh,' as the Scripture phrase is.* This conflict wondrously afflicted St Paul. No doubt but it was one sharp conflict.

No question but carnal wisdom set St Paul to shift for himself many times; but by the power of the Spirit he checked it and kept it under. It was not his rule.

Now, the reasons of this doctrine, that the godly guide not themselves by fleshly wisdom, which hath worldly aims, and carnal means to bring those aims to pass, they are,

Reason 1. First, because God's children *will not cherish that in them, and make that their rule, which is contrary to God, which is enmity to God.* But this carnal wisdom, which prowls for the world, and looks for ease, and profit, and pleasure, it is ' enmity to God,' Rom. viii. 6–8. The apostle proves it at large. They being subject to God, children of God, being under him in all kind of subjection, as servants, as children, as spouses, they will not cherish that which is rebellion to God, which is not subject to God, neither can be. As we may say, a papist that is jesuited, he is neither a good subject, nor can be ; so the wisdom of the flesh, neither is it subject to God, nor can be subject. In the nature of it, it is rebellion. It is God's enemy; it withstands all the articles that he hath given us to believe. Fleshly wisdom hath some opposition against all truth. It opposeth every command that God gives us to obey. There is something in flesh and blood to withstand every command. It is the greatest enemy that God hath.

2. And as it is an enemy to God, so it is to us. It is contrary to our good. It is death, ' the wisdom of the flesh,' Rom. viii. 4. Saith the apostle, Rom. vii. 8, ' The flesh deceived me and slew me.' There is no wise man will cherish that which is death, and which is God's enemy, and his own too. The wisdom of the flesh, as it is opposite to God's Spirit, a rebel and an enemy to him, so it is death to a Christian, and therefore he will not frame his course of life by it.

* Cf. 2 Cor. xii. 7 ; Gal. ii. 20 ; Philip. i. 22.—G.

It brings us to eternal death, it betrays us to Satan. Sampson could have had no harm had not Delilah betrayed him; so the devil could not hurt us unless it were for fleshly wisdom. The devil is not such an enemy to a man as his own fleshly wisdom.

Reason 2. Again, a Christian knows, that as it is contrary to God and contrary to his good, *so it is base and unworthy, as well as dangerous.* It is base and unworthy for a Christian, that is an heir of heaven, that is raised to be a child of God, to abase his wits, to prowl for the world. How base and unworthy is it for him to seek the things below, that is born again ' to an inheritance, immortal and undefiled, that is reserved for him in heaven?' 1 Pet. i. 4.

How unworthy is it for him that hath his understanding and all his inward parts and powers dedicated and consecrated to God, to make his understanding a bawd for the base purposes of the flesh! The high indignity of the thing makes the child of God ashamed to be ruled by the flesh, to prostitute the strength of his soul to the flesh; to make his soul, that should carry the image of God, to carry the image of the devil; to make his wit and understanding 'a bawd to accomplish earthly things, which God hath sanctified to attain grace and comfort in this world, and to live as a Christian should do, that he may die with comfort, and enjoy heaven.

Reason 3. Again, God's children will not be ruled by that which they should *mortify and subdue.* But this wisdom of the flesh is the object of mortification. They are redeemed from it.

A Christian, as he is redeemed from hell and damnation, so he is redeemed from himself. He is redeemed and set at liberty from the slavery of his soul to Satan, to the world, and worldly projects. He is redeemed from the base conversation he was in before. What hath he to do to be ruled by him from whom he is redeemed? These things might be amplified at large; but you see the truth evident, what ground a Christian hath not to be ruled by fleshly wisdom.

Reason 4. But to make it a little clearer. A Christian hath no reason to be ruled by earthly wisdom, for the yielding to it *doth all the mischief in the world.* It is the cause of all the misery in the world, unto Christians especially. God catcheth ' the wise in their own craftiness,' Job v. 13, though they be politic and wise. Especially if a Christian give way to carnal politic wisdom, God will universally shame him. I never knew a Christian thrive in politic courses. When he hath secret conveyances for the world, God crosseth him every way, in his reputation, in his projects, and purposes.

But consider, to amplify that which I gave in a branch before, what reason hath a Christian to be ruled by ' fleshly wisdom,' when it hinders him from all that is good, if he yield unto it, and keeps him in imperfect good?

I speak especially now to those that are not in the state of grace. What reason hath any one of you to be ruled by fleshly wisdom, when it keeps you in the state of unregeneracy? It keeps you perhaps in some good, but it is imperfect good. You think you are good enough, and that all is sure, and God will be merciful, &c., whenas a reprobate may go beyond you.

It hinders from good actions with pretences, for fleshly wisdom will tell us there will be danger, you shall be reproached if you do this and that, you shall be accounted thus and thus, and run into obloquy.

It hinders from doing good. ' There is a lion in the way,' Prov. xxvi. 13.

It forecasts this and that danger. It keeps us in imperfect good that will never save us. It objects dangers. The sluggard that will not set on his spirit to labour, he thinks himself wondrous wise in forecasting dangers. Oh, I shall want myself, &c.

It dulls and distracts us in good. He that hath a carnal protecting head, it eats up his soul, that when he comes to pray, or to hear, or to meddle with spiritual matters, the marrow and strength of his soul is eaten up with carnal projects, and he doth things by halves.

Nay, carnal wisdom, as far as it is in us unmortified, it sets itself against good by depraving good, that we may seem to be mischievous, and ill, and wicked with reason. Men are loath to go to hell without reason. There was none that ever went to hell yet without wisdom, a great deal of wisdom. And how doth their wisdom bring them to hell? As in other respects, which I named before, so in this; it whets the poisonfulness of their nature to invent and to raise scandals, or to be willing to take scandals when they are offered.

A carnal wise man, when he knows that such a degree of religion is contrary to his carnal projects, he fasteneth all the disgrace on it that he can, that he may be the less observed. Religious he would be, but with a limitation, with a reservation and restraint, as far as may stand with his carnal projects and purposes; and so much religion as goes beyond that, and discovers him to be false and halting, so much he opposeth. The wisdom of the flesh is bitter and sharp against all the opposers of it, and stirs the cursed nature of man to the opposing of that which is contrary to it.

Take a carnal man, either in magistracy or ministry, if he be not humbled with pains in his calling and with the word that he teacheth, what doth he most hate in the world? What doth he oppose? Is there anything but saving grace? Is there anything but that which God loves most, and which is best for his soul, that is the object of his spite and of his poison and malice?

To be led by this is even as if a man should be led by a pirate, by a thief, by an enemy. And what can become of that man, to be led ' as the fool to the stocks,' as Solomon saith, Prov. vii. 22. He is in the way of death. ' There is a way that seemeth good to a man in his own eyes, but the issues of it are death,' saith Solomon, Prov. xiv. 12; and that is the way that carnal wisdom dictates to men.

It hinders also from the reforming of ill. Policy overthrows policy, as we say. Policy overthrows commonwealths. Tell a man that is in place, You ought to reform this abuse and that abuse. He is ready to think, Oh, if I be not wary, others will inquire into my life too, and find me out.

So this cursed policy, this carnal wisdom, it makes men unfruitful in their places, by forecasting dangers; and so it hinders from doing good, and from reforming gross abominations and abuses.

So it hinders from suffering when God calls to it. It forecasts: if you be religious, you must suffer, it will bring your good name in question, it will bring your life in question, it will hazard your estate. Whereas, indeed, all the world is not worth the truth of God; and a man loves not his life that will not hate it in such a case; if it come to case of confession, and standing for the truth in a good quarrel.

But here fleshly wisdom objects this and that danger; as we see in Spira and others. And thus man, yielding to fleshly wisdom, he grows desperate at length (*qq*).

There are two men in a man, as it were. There is the flesh and the spirit. The flesh saith as Job's wife said, ' Curse God and die,' or ' Bless God and die,' read it whether you will (*rr*). There is the murmuring part in the cross that bids us curse God; and as Peter said unto Christ, ' Oh ! save yourselves, this shall not befal you,' Mat. xvi. 22 ; pity yourself, have regard of yourself.* The flesh when we are to suffer saith as Eve to Adam, as Job's wife to him, or as Peter to Christ, Oh spare yourself, be wise, be wise. And to colour the matter the more, there must be a pretence of wisdom ; whenas it is the greatest folly in the world to redeem any earthly commodity, even life itself, with the cracking of conscience, with the breach of that ' peace which passeth understanding,' Philip. iv. 7, and perhaps with the loss of our souls. It is the greatest folly in the world ; it is to be penny wise and pound foolish. So we see whensoever we are about to suffer, carnal wisdom hinders us. As it hinders us from good, and in good, and hinders us from reforming evil; and in suffering when we are called to it. So it provokes us to evil. And that we may swallow down the evil with the greater pleasure, and more deeply, it colours ill with good. We may thank this politic carnal wisdom, that truth and goodness ever goes with a scratched face, that it goes under disgrace, that it goes in a contrary habit; and that hypocrisy goes in its ruff, in its colours. I say we may thank carnal wisdom; for if truth were presented in its own view, it would stir up approbation from all. And if men could see vice and wickedness uncased, if they could see it in its own hue, they would all detest it. Carnal wisdom sees that this is not for the advancing of the projects it hath, and therefore it disgraceth that which is good, and sets false colours on that which is ill.

I say, it stirs up to ill, and it keeps us in ill. Carnal wisdom saith, You may do this, you may continue thus long. It deceives us with vain hopes of long life.

I might enlarge the point. You see then what reason God's children have, not to be ruled by fleshly carnal wisdom.

By the way, let me give this caution, *that oftentimes that is accounted carnal wisdom that is not.* The weaker sort, they are to blame ofttimes to lay imputations upon those that God hath given greater gifts to ; and they account that carnal wisdom that is not so, but is spiritual prudence. I must needs add that caution by the way. As for a man to keep his mind, and not to speak against evil in all places. ' The prudent man shall keep silent,' saith the prophet, Prov. xii. 23. The times and the place may be such, that the prudent man may keep silence. It is best to do so.

And likewise to be cautelous to prevent danger so far as it may be without breach of a good conscience. St Paul, you know, when he was called before the Sadducees and the Pharisees, he escaped by a shift.* It was not a sinful shift. He said he was a Pharisee, and so he set them together, and they falling into contention, St Paul in the mean time escaped, Acts xxiii. 7. Many things might be done, if we would take heed of carnal wisdom, and that with a great deal of wisdom and approbation too.

Jeroboam might have settled his kingdom, and yet he need not have set up the two calves in that cursed policy. It was foretold that he should have those tribes, but he would be wiser than God, and he would devise a way of his own, 2 Chron. xiii. 8, *et alibi.*

David might have escaped from Achish the king of Gath. He need not have made himself a fool. Ahithophel might have provided well for himself under David his old master. He need not have proved a rebel.

* See Note *g*, vol. II., p. 194.—G.   † That is, ' expedient.'—G.

There is nothing that carnal wisdom doth, but heavenly wisdom will do it better if men could light on it ; and God would give them better success in their carriage. But there is a way for heavenly prudence, I say, and that must not be accounted carnal wisdom.

It is for want of this that people are too credulous. Gedaliah, he trusted too much, he was too credulous to trust. Considering that men are subject to infirmities, and subject to falseness, it is good to be doubtful, to be suspicious sometimes ; and it is no carnal wisdom neither. The very loadstone of a lie is credulity. What emboldens people to deal falsely with men ? They know them to be credulous and weak. They will believe anything.

But for the most part the error is on the contrary, over-much jealousy. Your carnal politicians are over-jealous. Jealousy is good, suspicion is good, considering that we live in a false world ; but not to be over-jealous. We see Herod, he thought, Oh ! Christ is born ; and out of jealousy he kills a number of poor infants, and his own among the rest. Alas ! * Christ came not to take away his kingdom, but to give a heavenly kingdom. So the Jews they were very jealous that if Christ were not condemned, the Romans would come and take away their kingdom, John xi. 48 ; but that which wicked men fear, out of such jealousy, shall come upon them. And so the subtlest and most devilish men in late times, that grounded the persecution of the poor Protestants, upon jealousy, absurd jealousy; for they, by the rules of their religion, walk in sincerity. It ties them from plotting. And yet out of fear and jealousy, they exercised a world of cruelty against them.

And if any man shall but consider and read Stephen Gardiner's letters (a man of a devilish jealousy), to see out of his wit he projected what hurt would come by suffering the gospel to remain, it will seem strange (*ss*). Alas, poor man ! the commonwealths beyond the seas and our own nation never prospered better than by entertaining the gospel. Yet this devilish-witted man, whose wit was set and sharpened by the devil, was in fear and jealousy of the gospel. And God usually punisheth it this way, that those subtle heads that are jealous of those that mean them no harm, but all the good that may be, usually, they are over-credulous in another kind. They trust those that deceive their trust, they trust those that the weakest, the very dregs of the people, will not trust, they trust those that are notoriously false. God strikes their brains and besots them, that they trust men that all the world know to be underminers ; notwithstanding where they should trust, and cast themselves into the bosom of their true-hearted friends, there they are all full of fear and jealousy. But this caution by the way.

You see the thing proved, that godly men when they give their names to God, they ought to be ruled by God, and not by carnal policy or fleshly wisdom. You see the reasons of it.

Use 1. The use that we will make of it *shall be to stir us up to imitation of the blessed apostle St Paul.* I speak to them that their breeding and parts have raised many of them I hope from base filthy lusts ; so that the danger is now of ' fleshly wisdom.' The devil is more in the brain than in the heart, as he said of a cursed politician. Many men have the devil in their head. He is not altogether in the heart and affections, but in the brain ; and there he works his engines. And politic subtle men, they are the great engineers of Satan ; and that which he cannot do by himself, he doth it by them.

Therefore, I beseech you, let us not be instrumental to Satan, who was the first author of this carnal wisdom; for by his temptation we offended God, and then came all shifts upon it. You see what shifts came presently upon Satan's temptation.

Man did naturally affect wisdom; to know good and evil. What wisdom did he get after he had fallen? He had wisdom to flee from God. There was his wisdom, to run from God. So all the wisdom of a man that hath not grace, it is to shift, to run away from God, and to have helps and supports against God. A foolish thing it is, as if he could do it! And then, another shift of Adam was, to cover himself with fig-leaves, a silly shift. And then to translate his fault upon another. So, this shifting of carnal wit it came presently upon the fall. Take heed, therefore, of carnal wisdom; it is devilish: presently upon yielding to the temptation of the devil it came in.

And that you may not make it your rule, and live by carnal wisdom, consider seriously what I said before, how it hinders you from all that is good; how it hinders you from reforming that which is ill in your places and callings; how it stirs up to all that is ill; how it stirs you up to cover ill. It teaches you wit to do ill, and to cover ill when it is done. As we see in David's adultery, what a deal of wit there was to practise it. And then what a many windings and turnings there were to cover it. But God laid him open, and brought him to shame in this world, being a good man.

And as I said, who will be ruled by his enemy? If a man be on the land, and be ruled by a thief that will lead him out of his way, it is extremity of sottishness. Or if he be on the sea, and be guided by a pirate, what good can come to that man that is ruled by those that seek his ruin? Now if a man be ruled by carnal wisdom, he is ruled by his enemy; and if all the enemies in the world should plot to do a man that mischief that his own head and carnal wit doth him, he would cry out of them. In Isa. xlvii. 10,* 'Thy wisdom hath made thee to rebel.' It is wisdom that makes men to rebel against God. Too much trusting to tricks and shifts of carnal wisdom, it makes men take contrary courses to God, and so provoke him. 'Are we wiser than he? are we stronger than he?' 1 Kings xx. 23, 25. Doth he not daily and continually make those the butts† of his displeasure and wrath, that adventure their wisdom and policy against his wisdom? Yes, surely! God delights to catch the wise in their own craftiness; he delights to overturn the builders of Babel. It is but a building of Babel to rear anything by politic wisdom, contrary to the rules of religion, and contrary to the practice of piety. To do anything against conscience and honesty; to do anything against the truth by politic shifts, it is to build a Babel that will fall upon our own heads. It is like the foolish fire that leads a man out of his way.‡ This foolish fire of carnal wisdom, it leads men to hellish strength: it makes them forsake God's light, and the light of his Spirit and word, and follow a false light of their own imagination and invention. And therefore you see what the prophet Isaiah saith of the people that were in those times, Isa. l. 11, that did much plod in tricks of policy, 'Behold, all ye that kindle a fire, that compass yourselves about with sparks: walk in the light of your fire, and in the sparks that ye have kindled: this ye shall have of my hand, ye shall lie down in sorrow.' So, consider this, it falls out ofttimes, that God suffers a man to walk in the light of his own fire that he hath kindled, and in his own comforts. He will have comforts, and a distinct way from God's ways; and he will

---

* Misprinted 'Jeremiah.'—G.   ‡ That is, the *Ignis fatuus.*—G.
† That is, 'marks.'—G.

have distinct rules from God's rule. Well, well! you have kindled a fire; walk in the light of your own fire, but be sure you shall lie down in sorrow.

It is the greatest judgment that God can shew in this world, to give us up to our own wits, to our own devices; for we shall wind, and turn, and work our own ruin. And that is the hell of hell in hell, when the soul there shall think with itself, I brought myself hither. God will be exceedingly justified when men by their own wit shall damn themselves; when God hath revealed to man, and taught them, this is the way, 'O man, I have shewed thee what is good, and what doth the Lord require of thee,' Deut. x. 12. He hath revealed it in his word, do this and do that, and he hath given conscience to help; and yet out of policy to contrive thy own pleasures, and profits, and advantages in the world, thou hast done the contrary. When a man's soul shall reason thus, My own wit brought me hither; I am damned by wit, I am damned by policy. A poor policy it is that brings a man to damnation!

Therefore we should beg of God above all things, that he would not deliver us up to ourselves. As St Austin hath a good speech, 'Lord, free me from myself, from my own devices and policy' (tt). The devil himself is not such an enemy, as I said, as our own carnal wit; for it is that that betrays us to Satan. Satan could do us no harm unless he had a friend within us. Therefore beg of God above all things, Lord, give me not up to my own brain, to my own devices (for man is a beast by his own knowledge); but let thy wisdom and thy will be my rule.

Use 2. Again, if so be that we ought not to make this carnal, fleshly wisdom the rule of our life, then let us have *a negative voice ready presently for it.* Whensoever we find any carnal suggestion in our hearts, say nay to it presently, deny it presently, have a jealousy presently. When any plot ariseth that is not warrantable by the word of God, and that is contrary to conscience and to simplicity and sincerity, presently deny it; consult not with flesh and blood, as St Paul saith of himself, 'I consulted not with flesh and blood,' Gal. i. 16.

And when you have anything to do, considering that this is not the rule you are to live by, or when you have anything to resist, when you have anything to suffer, consider what God requires; consider what is for the peace of conscience; consider what is for the good of yourselves, and for the good of the church; consult with these advisers, with these intelligencers, and not with flesh and blood. Consider not what is for your profit, for your pleasure, for your ease; but resolve against them. Get the truth of God so planted in your hearts that it may carry you through all these impediments, and all these suggestions whatsoever.

Use 3. And because we cannot do this without a change, we cannot have a disposition contrary to carnal wisdom without a change (for except a man be born anew, except he be a new creature, he cannot have holy aims), you must labour therefore more and more *to have the spirit of your mind renewed, and to grow in assurance of a better estate.* For what makes men carnally to project for this world? They are not sure of a better. They reason thus with themselves: It may be I may have heaven, it may be not. I am sure of the pleasures present, of the profits present, although, alas! it be but for a short time. Whereas, if thy soul were enlightened with heavenly light, and thou wert convinced of the excellent estate of God's children in this world in the state of grace, that a Christian is incomparably above all men in the first-fruits of heaven, in the peace of conscience, and 'joy in the Holy Ghost,' Rom. xiv. 17, which is above all prosperity, and all profit whatsoever; and that in heaven, which is above our capacity and reach, every way they shall be happy. If men were convinced of this, certainly they would not prostitute their pates to work so worldlily. If they were sure of heaven, they would not so plod for the earth.

Let us therefore labour to grow daily in the assurance of salvation; beg of God his Spirit to have your minds enlightened.

Use 4. And withal, to join both together, *to see the vanity of all earthly things, which set carnal wisdom on work.* For, first, outward things they work upon the sense, upon the outward man. Profits and pleasures are outward things, and therefore they work upon sense, they work upon opinion. In opinion they be so, as indeed worldly things are more in opinion than in truth. A carnal wordly man, he thinks poverty a hell, he thinks it is such a misery. It is not so.

Labour to have a right judgment of the things of the earth, that set carnal wisdom on work, to avoid poverty, to avoid suffering for a good cause. The devil inflames fancy. Fancy thinks it is a great hurt to be in poverty; fancy thinks it is a great good to be in honour, to be in credit, to have great place, that other men may be beholden to us. Alas! get a sanctified judgment to see what these things be that set our wits on work. What are all these things? ' Vanity, and vexation of spirit,'

Let our meditations walk between these two. Often think of the excellent estate of a Christian in this world, and in the world to come; and that will set heavenly wisdom on work. It will make you plot, and be politic for heaven. And then withal see the vanity of all other things, of pleasures, and honours, and profits, and whatsoever, that we may not prostitute our souls to them which are worse than ourselves; that our souls may not set themselves on work to project and prowl for these things that are worse than themselves.

Let this be your daily practice. The meditation of these two things is worthy to take up your cogitations every day. To consider the vanity, the vexation, and uncertainty that accompanies all these things, when you have got them; as we see in Ahab, when he had gotten the vineyard. Besides the vanity of them, consider how you have gotten them, and how miserable will you judge yourselves presently! How doth God meet the carnal wits of men in the attaining of things! ' The wicked man shall not roast that which he took in hunting,' Prov. xii, 27. He hunted after preferment, he hunted after riches, to scrape a great deal for his posterity; how doth God deal with such? He overthrows them utterly; and his posterity, perhaps they spoil all. Himself roasted not that which he took in hunting. Ahab got much by yielding to the carnal wisdom of Jezebel, ' Hast thou gotten, and also taken possession,' 1 Kings xxi. 19. What became of Ahab with all his plots and devices?

Ahithophel and others, God may give them success for a while, but afterward he gives them the overthrow. Herod, he had success a while in killing of James, and, therefore, he thought to work wisely and get Peter too; God struck him with worms, Acts xii. 23. Pharaoh, in the overthrow of God's people, saith he, ' Let us work wisely,' Exod. i. 10. How wisely? They were overthrown and drowned themselves. Their wisdom brought them into the midst of the sea. Consider the vanity of earthly things. And then consider how just it is with God to cross them either in their own time; as the rich fool in the gospel, when he had riches for many years, ' This night shall they take away thy soul!' Luke xii. 20. That we may not walk according to the false rules of fleshly wisdom, let us oft think of these things.

And to add another thing out of the text. You see here that St Paul rejoiced in this, that his conscience could witness that he had not walked in ' fleshly wisdom ; ' so if you do not walk according to the rules of fleshly wisdom, you shall have this benefit, *your conscience shall glory in it.*

To make it clear to you,—take in your thoughts a politician upon his deathbed, that hath striven so much for riches, that hath striven to root himself by policy, to attain to such and such places, to obtain his pleasure and delights in the world; what glory, what comfort hath he in this ? There is nothing more opposite to comfort than plotting ; for, as I said before when I spake of simplicity, the more will there is, the more deliberation and plotting there is in sin, the more is the sin ; because it is done coolly, as we say. So of all persons usually, if their wits be their own, the greatest plotters die most desperately. For then their conscience tells them, that they have set their wits on the rack, to do this mischief and that mischief ; and here his comfort is cooled, his peace of conscience is broken. What comfort can there be, when that which he sinned for, that which he broke the peace of his conscience for, that is gone, and he must be taken and hurried away from that. But the wound of conscience, the crack of conscience, that remains for ever ; when he shall think, that for which I sinned is vanished, but my terror abides for ever.

A man therefore that walks after the rules of fleshly wisdom, he can never say with St Paul, ' I rejoice.' But on the contrary, let a man be able to witness to himself, as St Paul could ; at such a time my fleshly, subtle wisdom would have discouraged me from doing good ; and the wisdom of flesh and blood in others would have discouraged me from reforming such and such abuses ; but I knew it was my duty, and I did it. Here now is comfort. At such a time I was moved to such evil by flesh and blood in myself, or perhaps in others (as a man shall never want the devil in his friends. The devil comes to us in our nearest friends). But I had the grace to withstand it. I was not led by such and such rules, by my acquaintance, or by my own devices ; but I had grace to resist such motions. What a wondrous comfort is this ?

There is nothing so sharp in conflict as this. To resist carnal wisdom, it is the shrewdest temptation that is from carnal wisdom ; and as the temptation is the strongest, so the comfort is answerable. When Jezebel shall be offered with her enticements, with her colours, with her paint ; and a man can dash her in pieces, and cast her out of the window, when a man can maintain sincerity and honesty, what a comfort is this ! The greater and stronger the temptation is that is resisted, the more is the comfort, when we come to yield our souls to God, when we come to our account. Therefore, be not discouraged when you are set upon by carnal wisdom, by strong reasons of others, or subtle reasons of your own. Is it against the rule ? Is it against conscience ? Is it against the word ? withstand it ! That which is sharpest in the conflict, will be sweetest in the comfort.

Use 5. Again, if so be that carnal, fleshly, worldly wisdom (for it is all one, for the flesh is led by the world, and both conspire together, and hold correspondence to betray the soul, if it) be such an enemy, that it hinders our joy and comfort, and that if ever we will joy, we must not be led by carnal wisdom ; then we ought in our daily courses *to repent, not only of gross sins, but to repent even of carnal devices,* and carnal designs. Why ? It is the motion and the counsel of God's enemy, and of our enemy.

Therefore, as David, Ps. xxxvii. and Ps. lxxiii., when fleshly wisdom did suggest to him carnal motions of doubting of the providence of God, that he began to think well of the ways of the wicked, that they prospered that were led altogether by fleshly wisdom, he censures himself (it is the drift of both Psalms), ' So foolish was I, and as a beast before thee,' Ps. lxxiii. 22 ; as indeed, ' Man is a beast by his own knowledge,' as Jeremiah saith, x. 14. For all carnal men sympathise either with beasts in base lusts, or else with devils in politic lusts ; either they are like devils, subtle, or like. beasts, brutish in all their courses.

Therefore, when any base thought, opposite to the majesty of God and his truth, and to the Spirit of God moving our hearts, ariseth in our hearts, think, this is the motion of mine enemy, of an enemy that lurks in my bosom, of God's enemy, of a traitor ; let us renounce it, and be abased, and censure ourselves for it, as holy David did, ' So foolish was I,' &c. Crush all thoughts and devices of carnal wisdom in the beginning.

We see that the godly, they ought not, nor do not lead their lives by fleshly wisdom ; nay, take it in the best sense, take it for the rules of reason, they do not lead their lives altogether by the light of nature, but only in those things wherein the light of nature and reason may be a judge. For the light of reason, the principle of reason, is given us as a candle in the dark night of this world, to lead us in civil and in common actions, and it hath its use. But yet natural reason, it becomes carnal reason in a man that is carnal. ' All things are impure to him that is impure, even his very light is darkness,' Tit. i. 15 ; Mat. vi. 23. Not that the light of nature, and that reason, which is a part of the image of God, is in itself evil. It is good in itself, but the vessel taints it. Those that have great parts of learning, that have great wits, and helps of learning as much as may be, what do they ? They trust in them, and so they stain them. Therefore, Luther was wont to say, ' Good works are good, but to trust in good works is damnable ' (*uu*). So nature, and reason, and learning, they are good in themselves ; but trusting in them they become carnal, when a man neglects better rules for them. When men scorn religion, as your politicians usually do, then natural reason, in regard of this tainture, it becomes carnal. ' Not with fleshly wisdom,' or not with natural wisdom, as it is a higher rule of life.

What then shall become of a Christian, when he hath renounced that which is in him by nature ? when he hath denied his wit and his will ? when he hath renounced a bad guide, shall he have no guide at all ? Yes! For a man is never lawless. He is always under some guide or other. A man is alway under one kingdom or other. When he ceaseth to be under the kingdom of Satan, he comes under the kingdom of Christ; and when he is not led by the flesh, he is led by the Spirit. God's children, when they have renounced natural, carnal wisdom, they have not renounced all wisdom. They are wise still ; but they are wise by a supernatural light, they are wise in supernatural things. Yea, and in natural things after a supernatural manner. They are new creatures, advanced to a higher rank and order of creatures. So their wisdom is a gracious wisdom, when they are Christians.

When a Christian hath renounced carnal wisdom, God leaves him not in the storm in the world as a ship without a stern.* He leaves him not as having no pole-star to guide his course by, but he gives him better direction. He hath the word of God, he hath the Spirit of God, he hath

* That is, ' helm.'—G.

the grace of God to guide him. Therefore, after the negative here, ' Not in fleshly wisdom,' the holy apostle tells us how the child of God is led in his own person, but

' *By the grace of God.*' It is good for inferiors alway to be under the government of superiors, and so God hath framed the world. For beasts, because they have no wisdom of their own, they are led and guided by men: and man, because he is, as I said before, ' a beast by his own knowledge,' and hath but a finite, a limited understanding, he is guided by a larger understanding, he is guided by God if he be good. And it is the happiness of the creature to be under the guidance of a better wisdom. All things in the world are guided to their end. Things without life are guided to their end without their privity. We see there is an end in everything. There is nothing in nature but it hath its end ; whereupon comes that saying of the philosophers, which is good, that the work of nature is a work of deep understanding. Not so much as the leaves, but they serve to shelter, and cover the fruit from the sun, and the storms, that it may thrive the better. There is nothing in nature but it is of great use. The work of nature is a work of deep understanding. Now man, because he hath a principle of understanding in himself, he is so guided by the wisdom of God to his end, as that he understands his own end himself. He is so led by the wisdom of God, as that God hath created a work of wisdom in himself, that he together with God is carried to his end. Now, as I said, when we are out of the regiment and government of the flesh, we come under the gracious government of God. Therefore the apostle saith here, ' Not in fleshly wisdom, but by the grace of God.'

The holy apostle means here especially, the particular grace opposite to fleshly wisdom, that is, spiritual wisdom.

Quest. But why should the apostle here not say thus, ' Not with fleshly wisdom, but with spiritual wisdom ?' Why should he not say so, rather than thus, ' Not with fleshly wisdom, but by the grace of God ?' Why should he put grace instead of wisdom ?

Ans. I answer, he doth it for heavenly ends.

1. First, to shew that that wisdom whereby we are governed, it is not from ourselves, *but it is a grace.* He considers wisdom, not so much as it is in ourselves, in the conduit ; but as it is in the spring, in the free love of God. It is a divine consideration, to consider all habitual graces in us, not as they are streams derived to us, and resting in us, but as they are knit to a spring which is never drawn dry; which besides is a free spring. Therefore they are graces.

And that is the reason of the comfort of a Christian. He knows he shall never be destitute of necessary strength, of necessary comfort, of necessary direction and grace to lead him to heaven ; because those things that are necessary in him, he considers them as graces, not as habits, as it was the proud term of the philosophers to call them (*vv*).

We must consider them not as things in us invested in our nature, but as things that have their original from the free, constant, and eternal love of God ; as, what is so free as grace ? So a Christian looks on his disposition wrought by grace, and on every particular grace he hath ; as love, wisdom, patience, he looks to all as graces, as they come from the free love of God that is constant ; for ' whom he loves, he loves to the end,' John xiii 1. And his joy is more in the spring than in the stream ; it is more in the sun, in Christ himself, than in grace from him. Therefore the apostle, instead of the abstracted distinct grace of wisdom, or any such thing, he saith, 'grace.' There is a savour in the very terms of Scripture, a sweet taste in the very language of the Holy Ghost.

2. And then to shew that we are not only governed by wisdom, but by other graces, *to shew the connection of it with other graces* ; therefore he saith, ' We have had our conversation, not in fleshly wisdom, but by the grace of God.'

3. To shew likewise, *that where wisdom fails in us, it is supplied by grace ;* for the wisdom of God *for* us, is larger than the wisdom of God *in* us. The wisdom that God works in us by his Spirit, it teacheth us to avoid dangers, and teacheth us how to lead our lives ; but we are led by a higher wisdom. The grace of God for us, it is higher than that which is in us.

The wisdom of God for us, it watcheth over us, it keeps us from more evil, and doth more for us, than that which is in us, although that be spiritual and heavenly. Therefore the apostle here, he names not distinctly ' gracious wisdom,' which he mainly intends, as we see by the opposition, ' Not by fleshly wisdom, but by gracious wisdom ;' why doth he not say so, but ' by grace ?' Because our Christian conversation it is not only by wisdom in us, but by grace and love, partly in us and partly for us.

For indeed there is a watchful providence, there is a waking love about the guiding of a Christian in his course to heaven, that keeps him in, more than any grace that is in him. And a Christian at the hour of death, and at the day of judgment, will be able to say with experience, that the wisdom of God for me hath been more than any wisdom he wrought in me : though by the wisdom in me, he enabled me to discover many discouragements, to see many wants, and to take many good courses that he blessed for me.

But his wisdom for me was greater in preventing occasions above my strength, in offering means that I never dreamed of, in fitting occasions and opportunities to me.

The wisdom of God about and toward a Christian is more than any wisdom that is in him. For, alas ! having to do with the devil and with malicious spirits, and with the world, the stream whereof is against grace, it is hard for that beam of wisdom in us, that little wisdom we have, though it be an excellent, spiritual, divine thing. Yet notwithstanding there is a heavenly wisdom that watcheth for us, and gives issue and success to all the good we do, and turns away all evil that is above the proportion of grace and strength in us. Therefore, saith he, our conversation is in the grace and favour of God, not only *in* me, but *for* me. I find experience of grace ; not only the grace that is in me, but of grace every way for me in all my courses.

And that is the reason why weaker Christians are sometimes the safer Christians. Another Christian that is wiser, he meets with troubles perhaps.

Aye, but God knows that he hath but a little proportion in him, and therefore God's wisdom is more for him without him. God doth wondrously for infants and weak persons. The lack in them is supplied by his heavenly wisdom.

And that makes Christians confident, not to take thought what they shall speak, or how to carry themselves, more than is meet ; not to have distracted thoughts, I mean, to be discouraged in a good cause. He thinks I have not only a promise of grace to direct and guide me, but likewise the wisdom of heaven for me, to discourage others, to take away occasions of discouragement from me, to offer me encouragements, and to lift up my spirit when occasion serves.

This is the comfort of a Christian, that God is his strength. ' He hath wrought all our works for us,' saith the prophet, Isa. xxvi. 12. He not only works gracious works in us, but he works all our works for us.

In that the apostle mentions grace, when his meaning is of the particular grace of wisdom, as the opposition shews, the first thing that I will observe from it is this, that

Obs. A Christian stands in need of wisdom.

When he is out of the fleshly government of fleshly wisdom, he stands in need of another wisdom, and that is grace, the wisdom of God.

We stand in need of wisdom ; for, alas ! what can we do in this world without wisdom ? what can we do without light ? For bodily inconveniences we have a bodily light, an outward light to shew us what is noisome ; for reasonable inconveniences that our common wits apprehend, we have the light of reason.

1. But there be many inconveniences, *many dangers to the soul.* Now there must be a light of wisdom answerable. We need a heavenly wisdom to avoid devilish inconveniences and dangers to the soul, which without wisdom we cannot avoid.

2. Again, there is a necessity of wisdom that is heavenly, when we have renounced carnal wisdom, *there is such a likeness between that which is good, and that which is evil, between truth and falsehood.* ' Likeness is the mother of error.' * Falsehood is wondrous like truth. Evil is wondrous like good ofttimes, in show, when a sophister hath the handling and the propounding of it. Though there be as much distance between them as between light and darkness ; yet to the appearance of man, to his shallow judgment, they are wondrous like one another. Here is need of wisdom to discern, and distinguish between these.

3. Again, there is wondrous need of wisdom, because *there are a great many hindrances from the doing of that which is good.* It is good to have wisdom to see how to remove those hindrances. There are a great many advantages to help us to do good. There is much wisdom requisite to take all the helps and advantages to do that which is good ; and unless we have wisdom we cannot take the advantages to do good, as we should.

4. Again, *good is not good without wisdom.* Virtue is not virtue without discretion, when to speak, and when not to speak. ' A fool speaks all his mind at all times,' saith the wise man, Prov. xxix. 11. Now to do things in season, to be trees of righteousness to ' bring forth fruit in season,' Ps. i. 3. ' To speak a word in season it is like apples of gold with pictures of silver,' Prov. xxv. 11. One word in season is worth ten thousand out of season. Good is such a thing, that it is never good indeed except it be clothed with all convenient circumstances. One inconvenience in the circumstance mars the good things. And a world of wisdom there needs to see the things that are about good actions to help them, or to hinder them ; and if there be helps and advantages, to know how to use them, there needs a great deal of heavenly light. So we stand in need of wisdom. As we stand in need of our eyes to walk in our common ways, so much we need a heavenly eye in our souls, a heavenly light of wisdom.

5. Again we see, by the policy of Satan, that that which is good, the best good, *it is hid under evil.* The best wisdom goes under the name of folly, and unnecessary niceness ; and the vilest courses go under policy and wis-

* See Note *y*, vol. II. page 435.—G.

dom. Now there is need of much wisdom to discover things, and to see them in their right colours, when things are thus carried. In a word, such difference there is of things, that there needs a great deal of discerning and heavenly wisdom, and a greater light than a man hath by nature, to guide him to heaven. I need not stand to multiply reasons ; you see a man hath need of a great deal of wisdom. And, which is the second branch, as he needs it,

So *he may have wisdom.*

He may have this heavenly wisdom. As St Paul saith here, ' I walk not according to fleshly wisdom, but by the grace of God.' The grace of wisdom he means, according to heavenly wisdom. As he needed it, so he had it. St James tells you how you may have it, ' If any man lack wisdom,' to guide his life either in prosperity or adversity, how to abound without pride, and how to bear afflictions ; how to make his prosperity that it be not a snare to him, ' If any man lack wisdom, let him ask it of God,' James i. 5, who is the fountain of wisdom ; let him light his candle at God's light. Carnal wisdom lights its candle at hell-fire. A carnal man, rather than he will miss of his ends, he will go to hell, he, and his riches, and policy, and all. It is otherwise with heavenly wisdom. We have need of wisdom, and wisdom we may have.

The vessel that we must fetch it in is faith, and the vent of faith is prayer. Faith sends its ambassador prayer to God. ' If any man lack wisdom, let him go to God.'

And surely thus Solomon did. He is an example of that. He saw he lacked wisdom to govern so great a people as was committed to his charge. God was so well pleased with his petition, that he gave him wisdom, and wealth, and honour too.

Use. Make this use of it. Let us consider what relation we stand in, in what rank God hath set us ; let us consider what good we are advantaged to do by the place we are in, what helps we have to do it, and what mischiefs, and inconveniences may come ; and let every man in his place and standing consider what good he may do, and what evil he may avoid, *and let us go to God for wisdom.*

He that is a magistrate, let him do as Solomon did, desire God above all things to give him wisdom to rule as he should, 2 Chron. i. 10, that God would give him a public heart for a public place, and he will do it. And those that in their families would have wisdom to go in and out before them, let them go to God for wisdom, that they may avoid the snares that are incident to family-government, distrustfulness, worldliness, unfaithfulness in their particular calling. And so for personal wisdom, to guide and manage our own persons, let us desire wisdom of God, to know the hidden abominations of our own hearts, the deceits and subtleties of our own hearts, which is out of measure deceitful. To know our particular sins, to know what hurts us, and to know how to avoid it, and how to carry ourselves in our particular ways, to order ' our conversation aright ' every way. We see here St Paul led his life and conversation by that wisdom. As it was needful for him, so he had it ; and we must go all to the same spring for it : we must go to God.

And we must know that God will not only make us ' wise to salvation,' 2 Tim. iii. 15, that he will not only give us wisdom in things that merely concern heaven ; but the same love, the same care that gives us wisdom that way, will give us wisdom in our particular callings, to take every step to heaven ; the same Spirit of God doth all. He gives us grace necessary to salvation, and he gives us grace likewise for the leading of a Christian life.

Therefore it is an abominable conceit to distinguish religion from policy and government, as if the reasons of religion were one and the reasons of state were another ; and as if these were distinguished one against another. It is an abominable atheistical conceit ; for the same heavenly Spirit of God that reveals the mysteries of salvation, reveals likewise to men the mysteries of state.

Christ hath the keys of heaven, of the mysteries of God; and he hath the keys of all earthly policy whatsoever. He hath the greater ; hath he not the less ? Doth he guide us by his Spirit in heavenly mysteries ; and then for matters of policy, and government of states and commonwealths, are we to be guided by the devil, by devilish, carnal wisdom ? No ! He gives all wisdom in its due place, even wisdom for common things.

Therefore consider, when men will not be ruled by God, by wisdom from above, in the regiment and government of their lives, how fearfully and shamefully they miscarry ! Partly by reason of the accidents of this life, and the variety of business. You know wisdom, as it governs our life about the things of this world, it deals with things unstable, uncertain, and vain. As Solomon saith, they continue not long in the same state. Therefore, if a man have not a better wisdom than his own, he shall be mightily to seek. Partly because of the imperfection of his wisdom. The things are imperfect ; and the wisdom, without it be guided from heaven, is much to seek ofttimes.

Take the wisest man, when he leaves heavenly wisdom once. As we see in Solomon, he thinks to strengthen himself by combination with idolaters that were near to him. Did he not miscarry foully ? And hath not God made the wisest men that ever were in the world exemplary for gross miscarriages, because they had too much confidence in their parts, and neglected the guidance of God in the course of their lives ? Who was more fool than Ahithophel ? Who was a greater fool than Saul, and than Herod ?

The emperors had great conceits. Constantine the Great, a good Christian emperor, he had a conceit, if he could stablish a new seat at Byzantium (Constantinople it was called afterwards), he would seat the empire there ; he would rule Rome by a viceroy, by another, and he would be there himself and rule all the eastern parts of the world. A goodly conceit he had of it ; but this proved the ruin both of east and west. For hereupon, when he was absent from Rome, the pope of Rome he came up and grew by little and little. The emperors they thought they did a great matter to advance the pope, who was Christ's vicar, a spiritual man. They consulted with carnal wisdom, and he came and over-topped them, and ate them out, and out-grew them, as the ivy doth the tree that nourisheth it. The pope never left growing till he had over-topped them. So men, when they go to carnal wisdom, and neglect prayer, and neglect the counsel of God and the wisdom of God, to guide them in the matters of this life as well as for the life to come, they come to miscarry grossly.

Therefore let us take St James his counsel. We all lack wisdom, let us every day beg it of God ; desire God every day that he would ' make our way plain before us,' Prov. xv. 19, in our particular goings in and out ; that he would discover to us what is best.

Use. And here I might take occasion *to reprove sharply the atheism of many* that would be accounted great statesmen, that bring all religion to reasons of state. They bring heaven under earth, and clean subvert and overthrow the order of things ; and therefore no wonder if they miscarry. They care not what religion it be, so it may stand with peace. Whether it be false or true, if it may stand with the peace of the state, all is well. Give me leave to touch it but in a word. It is a most abominable conceit. Religion is not a thing so alterable. Religion is a commanding thing. It is to command all other things, and all other things serve that. And it is not a matter of fancy and opinion, as they think out of their atheism, to keep men in awe. It is stablished upon the same ground as that there is a God : that upon the same ground that we say God is, upon the same ground we may say religion is. It teacheth us that, that God is to be observed ; and that Christ is equal to him as God, and inferior to him in regard of his humanity, &c. So that there is the same ground that there is a God, and that there is a religion.

And so again, by the same reason that there is one God, by the same reason there is but one religion. And it is not any religion that will serve the turn. For that one God will be worshipped his own way. ' There is one God, one truth.' And that one religion must needs be that in which that one God discovers and reveals himself, and not that which man deviseth. For will any master be served with the device of his servant ? And will God suffer his creature to devise a religion to serve him ? Therefore there is of necessity, as one God, so one religion ; and that one religion must be that which that God hath left in his word.

Therefore those that are to govern states, as they will answer to that one God, they are to establish that religion that he hath left to the world in his word, and not any religion : not that which men have devised. To go a little further.

In that one religion that is left by him, there must be a care had, that the people live by the rules of that one. For this is a rule in nature. Nothing in religion will help him that will not live according to the rules of it. Therefore it concerns all that are not atheists to labour to stablish one religion, and obedience to that one.

And every particular man, as he looks for good by his religion, is not to live by the rules of fleshly wisdom, but by the rules of religion.

And here a man might deplore the misery of poor religion above all other things, above all other arts and trades. In other arts and trades he is accounted nobody that works not according to his trade, and that hath not, besides some speculative skill and rules in his head, that hath not skill to work. He is accounted nobody but a talker, except he *doth*. But in religion men think it is enough to know. Practice it goes under base names. Any common conscience, any common care, and obedience to the rules we must be saved by, is reproached and rejected. Religion will not do a man good, except he be ruled by it. Wherefore serves the rule, but to bring things to it ? But I will not stand on this point longer.

There is a necessity of wisdom, And this wisdom may be had. And this wisdom it leads not only to salvation, but it reacheth to the state. And it leads every man in his calling. Well ! we may see, to touch that by the way, in the third place,

Obs. True wisdom toucheth conversation.

' My conversation hath been by the grace of God,' that is, in wisdom. He puts the general for the particular. There were other graces besides ; but together with them there was this wisdom. So wisdom tends to conversation.

Mark what I said, wisdom is not in word, but in work. A man that will be master of his trade must work. When a man can work well, he is master of his trade, and not till then. Religion tends to practice. You know what Christ saith, ' If you know these things, happy are ye if ye do them,' John xiii. 17. He entails happiness to doing, ' If you know these things,' he saith not, you are happy if you know them : no ! ' If you know these things, happy are you if you do them.' For indeed true wisdom is not only speculative. This wisdom, understanding, and knowledge, when it is true and spiritual, it alway tends to practice ; and practice is never sound but when it springs from wisdom, from things known. Every article in the creed it tends to practice in a Christian's life, and quickens practice [of] every article.* So wisdom tends to conversation.

Now, besides that main wisdom which properly concerns salvation, there is another wisdom which is more particular, that tends to conversation, which is called spiritual prudence, for particular actions. This comes from the Spirit of God, ' I wisdom dwell with prudence,' Prov. viii. 12. Wheresoever there is wisdom to salvation, there is prudence to the guidance of a Christian's life.

Use. But in a word, if so be that wisdom tend to conversation, and is joined with it, *you may see that all naughty livers are nobodies in religion;* they are fools in religion. Wherefore serves knowledge ? wherefore serves light, but to walk by ? wherefore serves an instrument, but to work by ? wherefore serves wisdom, but to guide our lives by ? Is it to be matter of discourse and talk ? Therefore this doth demonstrate clearly to any man that thinks there is any religion, or any heaven, who be the best Christians, even those that by the Spirit know the wisdom that God hath revealed in his word, and apply it in their lives and conversations to be ruled by it, to work to that end. Wisdom prefixeth an end alway, and those that work to that end, they are wise men. He is a wise man that works to attain his end. Now there is no man that can attain his end by mere knowledge. He attains his end by working, by doing. Therefore the wisest Christian, he sets himself to converse wisely and holily ; and he shews his religion in his particular calling, in everything. ' If any man be religious, let him shew it in holy conversation, let him be unspotted of the world,' James i. 26, 27. So much for that.

' But by the grace of God.' To give a little further light to the words. Grace is either—

1. *The free favour of God in himself,* issuing from his goodness, whereupon we have forgiveness of sins, and acceptation through Jesus Christ to life everlasting. This is grace resting in the breast of God, but is only entertained of us, and works no change in us of itself. Or else,

2. Grace is *something from that favour,* from that free grace of God wrought in us. And that grace wrought in us is—

(1.) First, *the grace of a whole, universal change ;* for whomsoever God accepts graciously to life everlasting, he gives them the gifts of grace, with his favour ; he changeth their nature, that they may be fit to entertain fellowship with him. For when by grace he accepts us to favour, if he should not alter our natures, alas ! what a case were we in ! were we fit for communion with God ? No ! Therefore, that we may have communion with God, he alters our dispositions, that we may be holy as he is holy. This change is the first change in Christianity.

(2.) Now in this gracious change, which is a work of the gracious Spirit,

* Qu. ' practice quickens every article ?'—ED.

derived to us by Christ, in whom our nature is filled with all grace, and in whom we receive ' grace for grace,' there are *graces wrought:* as—

[1.] *A heavenly light* to see a further end than ever we saw before ; a heavenly convincing light to see the love of God, to see life everlasting, to see glorious things.

[2.] And withal comes the *grace of love* to carry the whole inward man to the things that we see.

[3.] Then there is the *grace of hope* to expect, and *patience* to endure all till we be possessed of that which our understandings are enlightened to see.

[4.] And *faith* persuades the soul where to have it, and relies on the promise. So particular graces are wrought. Therefore that is one reason why the apostle names not wisdom in particular, when he saith, ' We have not led our conversation according to carnal, fleshly wisdom, but by grace.' His meaning is that a Christian, when he hath heavenly wisdom, he hath all graces and wisdom together. There is a connection, a combination of graces, as I said. So he leads his life by all graces ; for all graces are necessary to a Christian life. Therefore instead of wisdom, he puts the word grace.

(3.) Now besides these, besides the favour of God accepting us in Christ ; and besides the working of these graces in us, in and after our conversion, there is another degree of grace requisite, *which is a particular exciting, applying, strengthening grace*, which is required to every good act, to act every good work, and resist every evil, and to enjoy good things as we ought to enjoy them. I say, there is a grace necessary to withstand temptations in all evil, besides graces habitual that are wrought in us, of faith, and love, and hope, &c. These, except they be actuated and enlivened by the continual work of the Spirit, except they be brought to act, and a new strength put into them, they are not sufficient for a Christian life. Therefore St Paul here by grace, means not only the graces of the Spirit, habitual graces ; but the power of the Spirit acting, enlivening, quickening, and strengthening him against every evil in particular, and to every good work in particular.

' But by the grace of God.' In that the apostle here, though he principally mean wisdom, yet he means grace, the next point I will observe is this, that

Doctrine. All the wisdom that we have it comes from grace.

All the wisdom we have comes from grace, merely from grace. And this grace is not wanting to us when we have renounced our fleshly wisdom. Heavenly wisdom comes altogether from grace. To make this a little clear. Whatsoever is spiritual it comes from Christ. Since the fall we have nothing but by especial grace. God being reconciled by Jesus Christ, he hath placed all fulness of grace in him : he hath enriched our nature in him with wisdom, and all graces whatsoever. ' All the treasures of wisdom are in him,' Col. ii. 3, and all other graces. God the Father, and our Saviour Christ, they send the Spirit, they communicate the Spirit, which takes of Christ, and doth enlighten, and quicken, and guide all those that are members of Christ. All in particular, all inward things come from grace. Grace comes from the Spirit, the Spirit from Christ, and this is the descent of grace and wisdom.

Thereupon they are taken indefinitely in Scripture, sometimes to ' walk wisely,' Eph. v. 15, to walk graciously, sometimes to ' walk in the Spirit,' Rom. viii. 1, sometimes to ' walk in Christ,' Col. ii. 6. It is all one. Sometimes to be in Christ. ' Whosoever is in Christ,' &c., 2 Cor. v. 17.

And to walk in the Spirit, and by the Spirit, to pray in the Spirit, and in wisdom, and in faith, or to live by faith, or to live by grace, or in grace, they are all one, because they are subordinate. For Christ is the treasure of the church. All that is good for the church is laid up in him, 'wisdom,' and whatsoever. 'Of his fulness we receive grace for grace,' John i. 16. Grace, answerable to the grace that is in him. He vouchsafes us his Spirit.

Now the Spirit guides us not immediately, but it works a habit in us, as we call it, it works somewhat in us to dispose us to that which is good. And when that is wrought, the Spirit guides us to every particular action. These things that the Spirit works in us are called graces: because they come from out of ourselves by the Spirit. So wisdom is called grace, because it comes from the Spirit. The Spirit comes from Christ, and Christ hath grace, not only grace in himself, but he infuseth grace into us. He hath not only abundance, but redundance; not only grace flowing in himself, but redundant, overflowing to all his members. This St Paul means, when he saith, 'We have had our conversation by the grace of God,' that is, by such blessed habits of wisdom, faith, love, &c., as are wrought by the Spirit of God; which Spirit is given us by Jesus Christ our head.

Hence we learn, that everything that is necessary to bring us to heaven, it is a grace, that is, it comes from without us. Adam had it within him. He was trusted with his riches himself. But now in Jesus Christ we have all of grace: we have all out of ourselves. Christ is the Sun. We have all our beams from him, all our light, all our life from him. He is the head. All our motion is from him. And this is not only true of habits, as we call them, that is, a constant work, or disposition wrought in God's children, which for the most part they carry about with them; but likewise in all the particular passages of their life. They have need of grace for every particular action. And herein the soul is like to the air. The air stands in need of light, and if it be not enlightened by the sun, it is presently dark. So a man is no wiser in particular actions than God will make him on the sudden. Put case he be a man of a wise spirit for the most part, that he passeth for an understanding man, and is so: yet except he have the grace of God's Spirit, except he have wisdom to guide him in particular, he is no wiser than God at that time will make him to be. You see all motion in the body it comes from the head. Let the spirits in the head be obstructed never so little, and there follows an apoplexy, there will be no motion. So all our wisdom, all the direction that we have to lead our lives as becomes Christians, it comes from Christ, it comes from grace; not only the disposition, but likewise every particular action. For we need grace continually to assist us, to excite and stir up our powers, and to strengthen them against oppositions; and if the opposition be strong, we have need of a stronger grace.

There is never a good work that we do, but it is opposed from within us, from without us. From within us, by carnal wisdom, as I said before, and by carnal passions and affections. From without us, by Satan, by the world, and by men that are led by the spirit of the devil. Therefore there is need of a strength above our own. Besides the grace that is in us ordinarily, there needs a new particular strength and light, to particular actions.

Use. Doth all come from God and from his grace? Let us take heed when we have anything, of sacrilegious affections, of attributing anything to ourselves, to our own wisdom, and let us give all presently to grace. Mark the phrase of St Paul here, ' Not by fleshly wisdom, but by the grace of God.' Ho doth not say, by any habit in myself. He doth not say, by any wisdom that is in me. But he chooseth that which is in God, grace and favour; because he would not rob God of any honour. It was a proud term the philosophers had, as I said, sometimes they called their moral virtues habits (*ww*); and if we consider them merely as they are in the person, they are habits; but indeed they are graces. The Scripture gives them a more heavenly term, ' grace,' those things that we guide our lives by, as wisdom, love, temperance, sobriety. Grace is a fitter word than habit, because then we consider them as they come from God freely. They are graces. They come from grace and favour. And when men differ one from another in wisdom, they differ in grace and favour. He gives more light, he opens the understanding of one more than another. Therefore St Paul was wise, and careful this way, when he speaks of that he had done himself, lest he should rob God. ' Not I, Oh not I,' 1 Cor. xv. 10, ' but the grace of God that was in me; that was all in all.' For indeed we are what we are, and we do what we do, by grace. Even as by ourselves we are men, we are what we are, and we do what we do, by our souls, by our reason and understanding. So it is with spiritual grace. We are what we are out of ourselves by spiritual grace, and we do what we do by spiritual grace. And when that ceaseth, when God suspends the blessed motions of his Spirit to humble us, alas! we are dark. A man is a confused creature, he is at a loss, he is in darkness for the particular managing of his life. He knows not what to do, he knows not what to speak, he is puzzled in every particular action. And therefore when he hath spoken, or done that which is fit, he should consider it as a grace.

' My conversation hath been in the grace of God,' saith the apostle. Therefore let us sanctify God in our hearts this way. And when we stand in need of any direction, desire God of his grace to give us wisdom, and to give us the grace that we stand in need of. This is for the phrase. The point as I told you was this, that

All wisdom comes from grace, and God is ready to give us his grace.

For saith St Paul, ' My conversation' hath been in grace, which God did minister to me, and hath ministered to me to lead my life by.

The reason is this—*Christ hath undertaken to give us grace if we be his.* Men under grace shall never want grace to lead a Christian life. For Christ hath undertaken to be our head, to be our husband, to be our guide in our way to heaven. As our head, he is to give us motion, to move us as his members. As he is our shepherd, as he saith, ' I am the good shepherd,' John x. 11, so he is to lead us in our ways and passages, in his paths, to conduct us to happiness. And as he is our husband, so he is to be the head of his wife. To guide us, it is his office. And he works according to his own office. He is a king to subdue in us whatsoever is contrary to his good Spirit, to subdue our rebellions, and to bring all our imaginations under his Spirit; as well as to be a priest to make peace between God and us. He is a king to rule us, and to overrule in us whatsoever is ill. And he is a prophet to teach us and to guide us. He is the angel of the covenant, the great counsellor, that hath the spirit of counsel in him, Isa. ix. 6, not for himself only, but for his church.

Therefore as all things that we need come from grace, and from the favour of God; so we need not doubt of the grace of God in Christ. Being reconciled, he is willing to give us grace.

This I observe, to cut off all cavils of flesh and blood, and to arm us against all discouragements.

There are two things that greatly hinder us from a Christian course,—presumption and despair.

Presumption, to set upon things, without asking grace of God, without depending upon his direction, by the strength of natural parts, of natural wit. And then *despair*, when a man saith, What should I go about these things? I shall never bring them to pass. No. First, consider thy standing, thy place and calling; and then consider the abilities that God hath given thee. Consider thy parts, consider thy duty that thou art to do. And beg of God assistance and strength; and if it be a thing that belong to thee, go on, set on all the duties that belong to thy place, in this confidence that thou shalt have grace.

Go to the fountain, to Christ, for grace for the direction of thy life. He is the light of life, he is the way, he is ' all in all' to bring us to heaven.

Wherefore serves all the promises, not only of life everlasting, but even of grace ? but to encourage us to set on holy duties in confidence, that if we have a will to be out of Satan's kingdom, and if we have a will to be out of ' fleshly wisdom,' God will take us into his kingdom, and into his government. ' He will give the Spirit to them that ask him,' Luke xi. 13. Now the Spirit is a Spirit of direction, a Spirit of assistance, a Spirit of strength and comfort. It serves all turns. How many promises are wrapped in that promise of the Spirit ? In want of direction he shall be our counsellor; in want of strength, to assist us. In perplexities, when we know not which way to turn us, to advise us. In extremities, when we are ready to sink, to comfort us. He will give us his Holy Spirit to supply all our defects in a fit time if we ask him ; if we find our need, and if we will renounce our carnal wisdom. Therefore set on those duties that God calls you to.

And withal, do as St Paul doth here (he sets the negative before the affirmative), renounce carnal wisdom, be not guided by that; trust perfectly to the word of grace, and to the Spirit of grace. For the word of grace and the Spirit of grace go together. And then you shall find that God will do ' abundantly above all that you are able to ask or think,' Eph. iii. 20. Luther when he set on the work of reformation, those that saw him at the first might have said, ' Get thee into thy cloister,' and say, ' Lord, have mercy upon thee,' for thou settest on a work impossible. But he saw the parts that God had given him, that he had wit to understand the abuses of the times, and he had given him courage. He saw by his profession he was called to be a divine. His conscience was awakened to see the abominations of the times, and he set on to discover these things. Did Christ leave him? No! He did not, but gave success to him to be admired* of all. When all the world was set against one man, yet he prevailed against them all; even because he walked as St Paul did here, ' in sincerity and simplicity,' that is, he looked to the truth of the cause, and not to his own honour, or profit, or pleasure. He was content to be no wiser than the book of God would have him to be ; to be no richer or greater in the world than God would have him; but committed himself to God ' in simplicity and sincerity.' How did God maintain him? Wondrously, to admiration ! I instance in him to shew how base distrust causeth things to be no better carried than they are.

Now to encourage you to go to the grace of God, to go to the fountain, and not to be held under carnal wisdom, under these pretexts, Oh ! if I do not

* That is, ' wondered at.'—G.

hearken to carnal wisdom, I shall be a beggar, I shall never rise, I shall never do this or that in the world, I shall never escape this and that danger. Fie upon those base conceits. St Paul here renounceth the regiment of carnal wisdom. What became of him ? Did he want a guide ? Grace took him up. 'Not by carnal wisdom, but by the grace of God.' When we come under the government of God, we come under the government of grace. And we shall want nothing either for heaven or earth that is for our good.

Whatsoever we had that was good before we were gracious, that we keep still, and it is under a better guide. Were we learned before ? were we wise before ? had we authority before ? were we noble before ? We lose none of these when we come under Christ; but he advanceth and elevates these, he makes them better. If we were wise, he makes us graciously wise ; if we were learned, if we were noble, he makes us doubly noble. We lose nothing, but we are under a sweeter government, the government of grace, which is a mild government ; a government that tends to the advancing of us above ourselves, that advanceth us to be the spouse of Christ and the heirs of heaven.

Those that are in Christ Jesus, and are led by his Spirit, they are his. In Rom. viii. 1, *seq.*, there is excellently set down the prerogatives that they have. Those that lead their conversation ' in simplicity and sincerity,' those that are in Christ, and in the Spirit, and in grace, there is ' no damnation to them.' And then again, if they suffer anything, saith he, ' The afflictions of this world are not worthy of the glory that shall be revealed,' Rom. viii. 18. If they have any infirmities, saith he, ' the Spirit helps our infirmities,' ver. 26. The ' Spirit teacheth us how to pray,' ver. 26, when we know not how to pray. If we suffer any evil, God ' turns all to good.' ' All things shall work together for the best to them that fear God,' ver. 28. For infirmities in other things we have Christ, and he makes intercession in heaven. ' Who shall lay anything to the charge of God's people ' that are in Christ, ver. 33, that are in grace, that are in the Spirit, such as St Paul was here ? ' It is Christ that is dead, or rather that is risen again, and makes intercession for us,' ver. 34. And ' if he have given us Christ, shall he not with him give us all things else ? ' ver. 32. If he have given us Christ, he will give us grace to bring us to heaven. See the excellent estate of a Christian that is under the regiment of Christ, that is led by the Spirit. That chapter may serve instead of all.

And see the sweet combination here, how he knits these things together. ' My rejoicing is this, that I have not had my conversation in fleshly wisdom, but by the grace of God.' Here is a knitting together of divers things that seem to differ, as here is ' wisdom ' *and* ' simplicity.' I have had my conversation by the grace of God, by wisdom, and yet in simplicity. For it is wisdom to be simple. When a man hath strength of parts, it is wisdom to bring them parts of simplicity.

It is wisdom to be simple concerning that which is evil ; for a man to be simple there is his best way. There is ' wisdom ' joined with his ' simplicity.' Then, again, besides wisdom and simplicity, here is ' our conversation ' and ' God's grace,' both joined together. St Paul by grace guided his conversation. So God stirs us to do all that we do. We see, but he opens our eyes to see ; we hear, but he opens our ears ; we believe, but he opens our hearts to believe.

This I speak to reconcile some seeming difference. Doth God's Spirit do all, and we do nothing ? We do all subordinately ; we move as we are moved ; we see as we are enlightened; we hear as we are made to hear; we are wise as far as he makes us wise. We do, but it is he that makes us do.

St Paul here led his conversation, but it was grace that moved him to lead it graciously. Well, then, he that joins simplicity and wisdom together, the wisdom of the serpent and the simplicity of the dove ; he that trusts in God and grace, and yet in trusting to grace doth all that he can, and goes on in a Christian course, he shall rejoice. ' Our rejoicing is this, that we have had our conversation in simplicity, and according to the rule of grace, not by fleshly wisdom.'

Consider seriously of it, what a joy will this be, that we have led our lives by a rule different from the world, that we have led our lives and courses according to the motion of God's blessed Spirit ! This must needs bring joy and rejoicing with it in what estate soever.

The world join these together, simplicity and sincerity of life, where they see them, that they may slander them, that they may lay imputations upon them. They see they are courses opposite to theirs, and they lay loads on them. But what doth God ? Where there is simplicity and wisdom and a holy conversation, he adds his Spirit, he joins the Spirit of grace, which is a Spirit of joy always. As light and comfort go with the sun, so the Spirit of joy and comfort go alway with the Spirit of grace. St Paul here, in regard of the world, was afflicted, ' he received the sentence of death,' he was slandered and misused ; yet to God-ward, saith he, ' Our rejoicing is this, that we have led our conversation according to grace,' according to the motion of God's blessed Spirit, and ' not with fleshly wisdom.'

If this be so, that the joy of God's Spirit goes with the grace of God's Spirit, and that those that lead their conversation by grace have a rejoicing above all imputations and slanders whatsoever, let this be an encouragement to us to lead a godly life. We all seek for joy. Every creature seeks for joy. If we would have joy within us, if we would have a spring of joy, let us labour to lead a conversation by this rule, by grace, by the motion of God's Spirit, which is ready to guide us if we commit ourselves to his guidance.

' But by the grace of God.' To come then to make an use of trial, whether we lead our lives by this gracious wisdom or no, and not by carnal wisdom. And then to come to direct us how to lead our lives by the grace of God, which is the ground of all joy and comfort, as St Paul saith here.

Quest. How shall a man know whether he lead his life by this spiritual, gracious wisdom, or no ?

Ans. I answer, mark the opposition here, ' Not with fleshly wisdom, *but by the grace of God.*' He then doth lead his life by the ' grace of God,' that doth renounce carnal and fleshly wisdom. Carnal wisdom is a false rule, and it cannot stand together with grace ; they one expel another. ' A double-minded man,' saith St James, ' is inconstant in all his ways,' James i. 8, that is, he that hath two strings to his bow ; he that will be content to be led by the grace of God, and by the word of God, which is the ' Word of his grace,' and yet notwithstanding he will have carnal policies, he will have shifts too, he is a double-minded man ; he is now under the government of grace, he halteth, as the prophet tells the Israelites, ' Why do you halt ?' 1 Kings xviii. 21. So he halteth between carnal and heavenly wisdom. He is loath to renounce carnal wisdom. No, he thinks if he do, he shall be a fool, he shall lose this way of getting, and that way of rising.

But he that is under the Spirit of God ; that is under grace, and is guided by it, he will renounce the motions and stirrings of carnal wisdom. When carnal wisdom, like to Eve, or like Job's wife, or like Peter, shall suggest, Oh, spare yourself, why will you do this ? why will you go on in these courses ? yet notwithstanding he is able to renounce it.

The most of God's judgments in this world, on his children, it is for this halting. They have much carnal wisdom in them ; and God, to work it out of them, is forced to cross them sharply in their projects and courses ; and all to bring them to rely on grace, to rely on his government in the use of good means ; for we must serve God's providence in the use of good means.

A man may know by God's afflicting of his children, that they deal too much in carnal wisdom ; for if it were not for carnal wisdom, if we would submit ourselves to his sweet and easy guidance, and use the lawful means that he hath discovered in a lawful calling ; if we would observe lawful courses ; alas ! we should see a clear light, and an easy passage. We need not to use these shifts. But because we cannot do so, we are loath to trust him. But we are double-minded. We will be ruled by him a little, but we will be politic and subtle. Therefore he sends crosses upon crosses upon our carnal ends and projects ; especially those that are his children, he will not suffer them to prosper in ill courses.

Sign 1. That is one sign, those that are led by the grace of God, *they will not be led by God's enemy, and the enemy of their own souls.* Now God and our own souls have not a worse enemy than carnal, fleshly wisdom. That is evident from the opposition.

Those that deny carnal wisdom, that deny themselves, and put themselves upon God, it is a good evidence. And as it is a sign, so it is a cause. You see in holy Abraham, when he had put himself on God, and left his country, and his father's house, God guided him, God took him into his government. ' I am God all-sufficient, walk before me, and be perfect,' Gen. xvii. 1. God means this, that by leaving all other things, and cleaving to me, thou shalt lose nothing, thou shalt have all in me, I will be ' all-sufficient ; ' therefore ' walk before me, and be perfect,' be sincere. A man shall never know what God will do for him till he put himself upon him, and cease to try him, and begin to trust him ; trust him once, honour him of his word ; have not a double eye, partly to carnal means, and partly to him, but have a single eye to his wisdom, and know that he will reward thee and keep promise. It is an excellent thing to deny carnal wisdom.

How many cavils might blessed Noah have had, before he built the ark ? The world would scorn him as an old doating man, that would go about to be wiser than all the world besides. But he denies all carnal reason, and rejects the scorns of sinful persons, and obeys God ; and we see how God protected him, and went on with him. And so in David, and St Paul.

And to add a little to that I touched before, God usually strangely crosses carnal wisdom, because men will not deny their carnal will, and their carnal wit. There was never any politician in the world that ever was, but complained of it, if he lived any time in the world, that God went beyond him. Saith the heathen man Tully, ' I thought myself wise, but I never was so ; ' (*xx*) and so they may all take up the same complaint. God dashes the imaginations of the proud. They build a Babel, a confusion to themselves and others, that are led by carnal wisdom, that will not trust to the grace of God.

Let no man flatter himself, but trust in God, and not rely upon carnal wisdom, and such courses. Those that will bring religion to reasons of state, and policy ; and subject the highest thing in the world to the basest thing, which is carnal wit, as I said before, we see what they do. The nature of man infinitely desireth the accomplishment of their will. We see that where corruption may have the greatest advantage in greatness, let them have their will, they will overthrow a world to have it ; their wit is bent to serve their will.

All witty men, that account it a heaven upon earth to have their will, instead of law, and conscience, and all, they set their wits on the strain to serve their will, and so set themselves against God. Is it not God's honour to set himself against them ? ' Was there ever any fierce against God and prospered ?' saith Job, ix. 4. Denial of fleshly wit, and will, and wisdom, it is both a sign and evidence of grace ; and it is a means likewise why * God's grace will lead us. When we deny that which is strong in us, God will make a supply by his grace. We are no losers by it.

Sign 2. Again, you see here in the text, where the life is led by the grace of God, by the Spirit of God stirring us, acting us, leading, moving, and strengthening of us, there *a man's courses are in simplicity and sincerity.* The soul that is under grace will put itself simply upon God. That soul will be no wiser than the word of God makes it to be. It will be no happier, no richer than God makes it. It will use no other means than what God allows. This is plainness, and singleness, and simplicity of heart.

Again, it will be in sincerity. Where a man leads his life graciously, his actions are sincere. This grace, as it comes from God, so it tends to God. Sincerity looks to God : it doth things as to God. So that where grace is, it carries a man above himself, to seek the glory of God, and life everlasting, to have spiritual and heavenly ends, to seek God in all things. The grace of God in St Paul guided him to lead his life in the simplicity and sincerity of God, that is, sincerity that looks to, and aims at, God in all things.

And indeed, a gracious man, and only a gracious man, can look out of himself to an end above himself ; only a gracious man can aim at God's glory, at the pleasing of God. Why ? Because only a gracious man knows that he hath better things in God than in the world. A worldly man makes himself his term,† he makes himself his last end ; because he knows not better out of himself than in himself. He dares not venture upon God's favour, to put all upon that. He knows not whether he be his friend or no. He thinks he is his enemy, as he may well enough, by his ill courses. Only the gracious man can put himself upon God. He knows he is redeemed out of a miserable condition into a glorious estate ; and if he should be denied of all the world, yet he knows he hath more happiness in him than he can look for here. He knows he would be all-sufficient for him. He is assured of his salvation. Therefore he hath higher ends, he is sincere in all things.

God when he is honoured by trusting of him, when in sincerity we make him our wisdom, and make his word our rule, and the happiness that he hath promised our chief happiness that we aim at, and rest in him ; when we honour him so far, then he makes a supply of all other things. But I spake of sincerity to the full before, only I bring it now, to shew how it is a note of a man that makes the grace of God his guide—he walks sincerely, he seeks the glory of God.

Sign 3. Thirdly, He that walks by the grace of God, and in the grace of God ; by it as a rule, and in it as a principle : he that walks in it, and by

---

* Qu. ' whereby ?'—ED.   † That is, = ' termination, end.'—G.

it, and through it : you shall see it *by the ability that is in him above nature, by the things that he doth, that other men cannot do, that walk not by grace.* Therefore you have a trial of a man that converseth by grace, from hence. He can cross the common corruptions of the place, and of the time he lives in. He is not a slave, he is not enthralled to common fears, to common hopes, to the common joys and delights that the world is carried withal. But as grace is a thing that is mighty, and strong, and powerful of itself, it is a Spirit (the Spirit is like the wind, as Christ tells Nicodemus, John iii. 8) ; it is a mighty, powerful, strong thing : so it makes him strong, it enables a man's spirit to do above himself, above that which he could do, if he had not grace. It makes him deny himself in matter of pleasure, in matter of profit ; it will make him cross himself in matter of revenge, as David spared Saul, when he had him in his power, 1 Sam. xxiv. 4. It will make him triumph over all estates. He can abound, and he can want, as St Paul saith, Philip. iv. 12.

Other men are changeable with their condition ; they are cast down in adversity, they are puffed up in prosperity, they can deny themselves in nothing ; they are always enthralled to their base pleasures, and profits, and honours ; they are always swayed with some carnal end or other. Grace, it raiseth a man above nature. He can do that which another cannot do ; he can endure that which another man cannot endure. He can die, he can endure shame, he can resist that which another man cannot resist.

Sign 4. In a word, you may know grace in a man *that hath great parts of nature.* How shall we distinguish grace from nature in him ? Thus, you shall have him *subdue his parts unto grace, and to the rules of religion.* If he have a strong wit, he will not make show of the strength of it, as though he would break through business with his wit ; but he will consult with conscience. You may know a man that is led by grace, especially where there are great parts ; he can deny not only his corruptions, but other things, if they stand not at that time with the will of God ; he forbears ostentation of learning when he sees it is hurtful, when it is rather to shew himself, than to get glory to God, or to win souls. When a man sees that such and such courses might crush another, and advance himself ; yet if it touch upon conscience, he will not do [it]. Here is a conflict between parts, and the grace of God, and goodness. Now when a man in this can deny himself, it is a sign that a man makes grace his guide.

It is not so easy in weaker dispositions ; for men seem sometimes to be good, when it is defect of parts ; but in men of ability, it proceeds not from defect, or want of parts, but it is the power of grace only whereby they are swayed. Such a man dares not do it. He wants not ability or skill ; but he dares not offend God, he dares not seek himself, he dares not give scope to his wit, and to his vain mind ; he knows what spirit in him moves such things, and he suppresseth them presently, and yields to the motions of God's blessed Spirit.

But yet in weaker men a man may know when such a one is ruled by grace. Thus, when a man sees something in him that strengthens nature, as, grace takes not away nature, but betters it. When you see a man that otherwise is simple, yet he is wondrous skilful in resisting a temptation, skilful in giving advice, skilful in keeping the peace of his conscience, skilful in giving reproof, even above himself : a man may know that he hath a better schoolmaster : that the Spirit of God, the Spirit of grace, is his schoolmaster.

So that whether a man have strong or weak parts, a man may know whether he be led by grace or no. In the weaker, it raiseth him above himself; in the stronger, when the exercise of his parts of nature and grace cannot stand together, it makes him deny himself. That he may be led by the one, he denies the other altogether. This is gracious wisdom.

Sign 5. Again, a man may know that he leads his life in gracious wisdom, or by gracious wisdom, *when he fetcheth reasons for his actions, not from things below, but from religion, from conscience, from spiritual things.* He doth not fetch the reason of his actions from this, that this will profit me, or I shall advantage myself thus and thus; but he fetcheth the reasons and ground of his actions higher: this is pleasing to God, this is according to the peace of my conscience, this is for the good of the church, for the good of the state I live in, this is for the good of my Christian brethren. The strongest reason of a Christian is that that makes for religion, and for conscience. If he may gain in his own particular one way, and gain to the state or religion another, he considers not, what will it advantage me? but, what is it for religion? It is the chief prevailing reason, how he may gain to religion, and the glory of God. He will not redeem his life to impeach the glory of God and religion. This is a man that leads his life by grace.

Sign 6. Again, where grace is, *there graces are together.* There is a sweet linking of them. Therefore St Paul, instead of wisdom, names ' grace of God,' all grace. A man, therefore, may know that he is led by grace, when there is no solitary grace; for where grace is solitary, it is not at all, it is but a shadow.

For there is not one grace, but it is of special use in the managing of a Christian's life and conversation; therefore St Paul, instead of wisdom, puts grace here. For instance, there is a great necessity of seeing by a light above nature, things above nature. If a man lead a life above nature, there is a necessity of heavenly illumination, and conviction that there is a better happiness than the world affords. And then there is a need of love to carry the soul to that happiness that is discovered. But then there are a world of impediments between us and heaven and happiness, that is discovered to us in the gospel by Christ Jesus. There must be heavenly wisdom, therefore, to discover the impediments, and to remove them. And there are many advantages how to attain our end. We must use this and this means, these and these helps that God hath ordained. Here must be heavenly wisdom to use the advantages, and to avoid the hindrances. But there is a world of troubles between our end and us, between heaven that is discovered, and us. Therefore saith the apostle, ' Ye have need of patience.' And patience, that is sustained by hope. Hope casts anchor in heaven, and assures us of happiness there; and then patience sustains us in whatsoever befalls us in this world. Therefore the apostle saith not, I lead my life by wisdom, but by grace; by wisdom, as it hath a connection with all other graces.

Therefore a man that, out of hearing of the word, or reading, &c., hath it discovered, that there is a better way than he takes, and yet notwithstanding hath not love to carry him to it, nor wisdom to remove the impediments, he works not towards his end; there is no grace at all. There is illumination, but it is not sanctified illumination, but a mere common work of the Spirit; because where true wisdom is, there is love, and patience, and hope, and all other graces, to carry the whole soul to that happiness that is discovered.

Therefore by this you may know a gracious wise man, he works to his end always. Another man hears and wishes, Oh! it were well if I could attain heaven. But carnal policy and base affections hold him in a beastly course of life, that he works not to that end. Only he hears such things, and thinks God will be merciful, and Christ hath died; and when he cannot enjoy the world longer, he will have good words that way. But that will not serve the turn. A man must lead a life in grace, that will die, and be saved by grace. He must work, and carry the whole man with it; and not only have knowledge, but faith, and love, and all. A man must work with it.

Who is a wise man in outward matters? Is he a wise man that only talks of state matters, out of books he hath read? No! but he that, when he comes to a business to negotiate in the world, can remove hindrances, and attain his end, and overthrow the plots of his enemies, when it comes to particular actions. Here is a wise man, that can attain his end by working; that doth work to his end, till he have attained it. So he proves graciously wise in religion, that works to his end; or else he is a foolish man, a foolish builder. As Christ saith, ' If ye know these things, and do them not,' Mat. vii. 26, you are as a man that builds on the sands; your profession will come to nothing.

Sign 7. Again, a man may know that he is guided by grace, that he doth everything by gracious wisdom, *when he doth provide for himself best in the best things, out of a sanctified judgment*, when he doth judge aright of differences; when he considers that there is a difference between the soul and the body, between this life and eternal life. There is a main difference between the glorious eternal life in the world to come, and this fading life which the soul communicates to the body in this world. When a man judgeth the difference between true riches and these things that we are so set upon, that are but lent us for a little while; when he judgeth between the true honour to be the child of God, and the fading honours of this world that shall lie down in the dust with us, and shall all depart and be gone, it appears then he hath a sanctified judgment; he ' discerns of things that differ,' Heb. v. 14.

And according to this, if he lead his life in gracious wisdom, he makes his provision. He makes his provision as his judgment leads him. His judgment leads him to the best things, therefore he provides for the best things. As Christ saith of the children of this world, ' they are wise' in their courses, ' in their generation.' They provide against beggary, they make friends beforehand, as we see in that unjust steward, Luke xvi. 8. So a Christian provides for his soul, he looks to that, he ' makes him friends of his unrighteous mammon,' xvi. 9; he makes him friends of his earthly things, that is, he doth deserve well of men that they pray for him, and so help him to heaven. He daily makes his account ready, he cuts off impediments that he meets with in the way, he troubles not himself with impertinences, he spends not more time than needs about worldly things; he useth them as they may help his work to be better and better in grace, to be fitter and fitter for glory. As he discerneth differences, so he makes his provision answerable; he provides for the best in the first place. Or else he were a foolish merchant, a foolish builder, a foolish man every way. The Scripture saith he is no better that cannot discern the difference, and provide well for himself when other things fail.

The Scripture doth well call wicked men fools. They have no judgment, they do not provide for themselves; they prefer these things, say what they will, before better things; they are fools in their provision. Ahithophel, he made provision, he set his house in order, and what became of him after? He hanged himself. He made much provision for the world, and at last he knew not how to forecast and provide for his soul. The Scripture calls the rich man in the gospel, ' a fool,' Luke xii. 20. He was wise enough to contrive for himself, yet he was but a rich fool. 'The fool,' as the wise man saith, 'knows not the way to the city,' Eccles. x. 15; so a wicked man he knows not the way to heaven, he discerns not the difference, he provides not, he knows not the way thither. He cannot do one thing that is gracious, not one action that may further his account.

I might be very large in the point. It is profitable, because we do infinitely deceive ourselves in that point, which is of more consequence than the whole world; for the man is, as the rule that he is led by is. Carnal men are led by carnal rules; gracious and holy men guide their lives by heavenly wisdom, by a gracious rule.

Now if you find yourselves defective, for a good Christian may be defective in this; but if he have hearkened to carnal wisdom, if he have forgotten himself, if he have troubled himself too much about the world, he will come to his centre again, he will come to his old way again, he will not be long out of it; his way and course is by grace. Sometimes he may have a policy that is not good, as David had, yet his way is gracious. I say, if you find yourselves defective, I will shew some helps how we may guide ourselves, ' not by fleshly wisdom, but by the grace of God,' that is, by gracious wisdom, by the Spirit.

Now the Spirit leads us not immediately, but works graces in us, and stirs up those graces in us. The Spirit guides a godly man, by working grace in him, by making him better, by using those graces in him. Sometimes the Spirit of God moves a wicked man, but it makes him not better. He puts conceits into his head, and makes him do that which otherwise he would not; but he is not bettered. The Spirit guides a good man by making him better, he works a gracious disposition, a gracious bent in him, that his judgment concurs with God's, his affections concur with the Holy Spirit, and make him holy and pure. There is a disposition wrought in a good man like to the Spirit that sanctifies him, and like to the disposition of Christ to whose image he is renewed.

Now that we may guide our lives by the Spirit working in us spiritual and gracious wisdom,

First of all, *consider what I said before of fleshly wisdom.* There are none but they have one of these two guides, either the flesh, and by consequent the devil; for the devil dwells in our carnal reason: that is his fort, that is his tower, his castle. Carnal, fleshly imaginations is the devil's forge: there he works all his tools, all his instruments. For the devil works not so much immediately, as by carnal men that are led with him.

Our wit and policy, and carnal wisdom, it is the shop, the forge of the devil, wherein he works all his mischief to overthrow us. It is the devil's workhouse, where he engines with all his tools and instruments.

Then considering that there are but two guides, the flesh, the world, and Satan, which alway go together in one, or God's Spirit and grace, 1. Let us be willing *to submit our thoughts and desires, to submit our projects and our aims, and all to the Spirit of grace;* submit to the word of grace, and to the motions of the word; the word of God having the Spirit of God accompanying of it. The word of grace accompanied by the Spirit of grace, is forcible, as the apostle saith, 1 Cor. x. 4. It beats down strongholds,

' strong imaginations.' Satan fortifies himself in strongholds, as the Scripture calls them, in high thoughts, working discoursive thoughts. Now when we come to hear the word, which teacheth the simple, sincere truth of God, that teacheth us how we should be saved, and how we should guide our lives ; if we will be guided by grace, if we will yield to God's simple truth, let him erect a throne in us, let us lay down all. When we come to hear the word, let us think, I come to hear the wisdom of heaven itself, I come to hear that word that shall make me wise to salvation ; I will not entertain projects, I will not entertain a wisdom that is contrary to it; when they rise in my soul contrary to the direction of the Spirit, and of the word, down they shall, I will not own them. This is the wisdom of a man that intends to make grace his rule.

Now a carnal hearer, a carnal reader, a common Christian, he brings his naughty, proud heart, he brings his high conceits to the hearing and reading of the word, he comes as a censurer, as a judge, he comes to talk of what was said in this passage and in that passage, he comes not as to hear God speak in his ordinance, he comes not as a humble man; he comes not to hear it as the ordinance of God with reverence ; and that makes him come and go out again as a beast. As the beasts that went out of Noah's ark, they went out as they came in; so many come into the church and go out again as beasts. They go out worse than they came in, because they bring not hearts to submit themselves to God and to his word. O ! a spirit of subjection, it is a blessed thing.

Self-denial is some help to this. Be content in the guiding of your common life, and in the guiding your way to salvation, to be no wiser than God's Spirit, and God's word will make you, to have no will nor no wisdom contrary to his will and wisdom. But you will live as men that have nothing of their own, nothing different from God, no distinct will, no contrary will and wit to God, but you will let God take the guidance of you himself ; and whom he guides must needs come to a happy end, as the psalmist saith excellent well, ' Thou wilt guide me by thy counsel, and after bring me to glory,' Ps. lxxiii. 24. Those that submit themselves to be guided by God's counsel, he will bring them to glory.

2. Serviceable to this is that which is pressed everywhere in the Scripture, humility. God gives grace to the humble, that is, he gives them not only forgiveness of sins, and acceptation to life, but he gives them grace for the regiment of their lives ; ' He gives grace to the humble.' Those that humble their wits to God (for there is a humiliation of the wit as well as of the affections), that they care not for the 'depths of Satan,' Rev. ii. 24, they care not for school tricks ; they care to know nothing but ' Christ and him crucified,' as St Paul saith, 1 Cor. ii. 2. God's word is of power and majesty enough to save me, I need not bring my wit for my acceptance to God. It is truth that is accepted, not a strong brain to cavil. ' God gives grace to the humble.' Those that bring their understandings to be led and taught by God, he gives grace to them.

3. Again, in the third place, if we would have our thoughts guided by counsel, *let us have a high esteem of wisdom*, above all precious stones and pearls. Solomon presseth it, Prov. iv. 7, *et alibi ;* have a high estimation of wisdom, of the government of God's Spirit as the best government. And be out of love with carnal reason, with carnal affections and their guidance; account them as base things, not worthy to come into the esteem of a Christian heart. Those that highly prize wisdom, God will lead them by it ; those that sell all for the pearl shall have it, Mat. xiii. 46. There must be a

high price set on the guidance of God's Spirit, and on grace, as indeed it is worthy of it, and then we shall have it.

4. Again, if we would lead our lives according to spiritual and heavenly wisdom, according to grace, and gracious wisdom; let us learn, as it is, Job xxii. 21, *to be more and more acquainted with God by prayer;* for grace comes not from within us.   Grace is in Christ as in the root, as in the spring, as in the sun ; we have it but as the beam, as the stream.   Therefore let us learn to be acquainted with God, and with Christ by prayer and meditation, and search into his word by reading, and by hearing him speak to us, and let us often speak to him.

Let us acquaint ourselves with him by prayer, and by hearing his word, and then we shall have his grace to guide us.   For grace is a fruit of his peculiar love.   He gives grace to his own peculiar people.   How do you think, shall he have a peculiar delight in us, if we labour not to be more and more acquainted with him ?   by often speaking to him, by often hearing of him, by coming into his presence, and attending as much as we can upon his holy ordinances, by conversing as much as we can in the holy things of God.   Those that will be warm, they come under the beams of the sun ; those that would have the Spirit work effectually, they must come where the Spirit is effectual, where the Spirit works.   Now the Spirit is effectual in the word preached.   The Spirit fell upon Cornelius and the rest when they were hearing of St Peter, Acts x. 44.   And the Spirit is where there is conversing in good company.   ' Where two or three are met together, I will be in the midst of them,' saith Christ, Mat. xviii. 20.   ' If we walk with the wise, we shall be wiser,' Prov. ix. 9.

It must be the heavenly wisdom of a Christian, if he would lead his life by grace, to attend upon all the means of grace.   Because the Spirit of God is effectual by his own means, he works by his own means ; therefore use the means that the Spirit hath sanctified for the working of grace.   I do wonder at a company of vain sottish creatures, that carry themselves according to their vain conceits, according to the whirling of their own brain, in toys* and baubles that come into their heads !   They care not for the hearing of God's blessed truth.   Either they abstain altogether, or else they hear it carelessly, as if it were a thing that concerned them not.   Oh, but those that will lead their lives by grace, they come to it by the Spirit, and the Spirit is only effectual in holy ordinances.   It must be our wisdom therefore, to bring ourselves under some means or other, that the Spirit may be effectual.

The wisest and the best men in the world are no longer gracious than they are wise this way.   If they neglect good company, good acquaintance, if they neglect the hearing of the word, if they neglect prayer, they will grow dead, and dull, and carnal-minded ; they will be possessed with base thoughts.   How do men differ one from another ?   Not so much by any habitual grace that is in them, as by avoiding all that might prejudice them in a Christian course, and by using all means whereby the Spirit of God may be effectual.

5. Again, the way to be under the grace of God's Spirit *is often to meditate of the grace of God, the free love of God in Jesus Christ:* for so it comes first.   The first grace of all is God's free love in the forgiving of our sins, and accepting us to life everlasting ; and then he doth alter and change our natures more and more, he transforms us more and more.   When we find therefore any defect of grace in our hearts, when we find coldness, and

* That is, trifles.—G.

deadness, and dulness, go to the first fire, to the first Sun, to the free grace of God in Christ, pardoning all our sins, and accepting us to life everlasting, and promising us grace to lead our lives in the mean time. If you have fallen into any sin by the temptation of Satan, or your own weakness, beg not first grace to alter your course, to sanctify your life ; but renew every day your interest in the first grace, in the forgiveness of sins, and your acceptation to everlasting life. For till God have pardoned your sins, and have witnessed to your souls that you stand reconciled, he will not give the best fruit of reconciliation, which is grace.

Therefore every day examine your lives, if you have offended God, in what terms you stand with God, and if you stand in ill terms, that there is any sin against conscience, the best way is not presently to amend that ; for that will not be, except the heart be warmed with God's love and favour in the pardon of your sins first, and in the acceptation of you in Christ, notwithstanding your sins ; as he justifieth us every day, not only in the first act of conversion, but daily. He acquits our consciences daily from our sins. And therefore in the Lord's prayer Christ teacheth us every day to say, ' Forgive us our sins,' Mat. vi. 12. And then, after forgiveness of sins, to beg the particular graces for our lives that we want. I would this were better thought on.

6. *Challenge likewise the covenant of grace.* We have a promise of all grace, and the spring of all grace. We have a promise of love. God will teach us to ' love one another,' John xiii. 34. We have a promise of fear. He hath promised that ' he will put his fear into our hearts, that we shall never depart from him,' Jer. xxxii. 40. We have a promise of the Holy Spirit. Let us challenge these promises every day. So much for the directions how to lead our lives by grace.

' But by the grace of God.' St Paul here makes it the ground of his rejoicing, that he led not his life by ' fleshly wisdom, but in simplicity and sincerity,' and ' by the grace of God ;' and all that are led by St Paul's spirit live thus.

There is a religion in the world that bears itself very big, on high terms of universality, succession, antiquity, &c., and they will have it thought to be a spiritual and holy religion. Well ! if a man be a carnal man that is led with fleshly wisdom, and not by the grace of God, that religion must needs be a naughty religion that hath only the support and the foundation of it in fleshly wisdom, which is an enemy, and opposite to the grace of God, and to simplicity and sincerity.

But popery is this. Take it in the regiment and government of it, take it in the worship, take it in the opinions : you may draw all to one of those three heads.

1. *For the government of it.* There is a wisdom, a wondrous wisdom, a fine subordination to one head, the pope, to hear all controversies ; and under him the cardinals, and under them the generals, and all at Rome ; and they have their provincials under them. Here is a wondrous fine subordination ; but all this is by ' fleshly wisdom.' For this ' beast ' riseth out of the earth, and out of the sea, out of the tumult of the people, out of base earthly respects. Therefore it is said in the Revelation, when the bishop of Rome became pope, and was at the highest, that a star fell, Rev. ix. 1. He fell when he rose. When he was at the highest, he was at the lowest. Why ? Because his rising was carnal and earthly ; or lower if you will, it was hellish and devilish.

Their government is opposite to Christ's government, and being so, it

must needs be mightily opposed by him again ; and therefore it must needs
down, the fabric of it being opposite to the frame of Christ's government,
though it be wondrous witty. Therefore in the Revelation, 666 is the
'number of a man.' If you mark the frame of the Romish policy, it is
wondrous accurate, it goes smoothly, by tens and by hundreds, 666. This
Babylon is the number of a man ; a fine policy ! But it is but the number
of a man. It is the device of carnal wisdom itself. Therefore it is devilish
wisdom. Thus it is in the government of it.

2. *And their worship* is according to the wisdom of the flesh. Some
wisdom there is in not going to God immediately, but by saints and angels.
What ! is it not wisdom in the prince's court, first to go to the favourite,
and by him to the prince ? So, is it not wisdom not to go directly to God ?
It is bold rashness to come immediately to God, but by saints and angels.
This is the wisdom of a man, this is the wisdom of the flesh, Col. ii. 8, *seq.*,
this is carnal wisdom. It is opposite against the truth.

Doth not Christ bid us come all to him ? Do angels love us better than
he ? Is not he the great Favourite of heaven ? I will not enter into controversy, but only shew how they work by 'fleshly wisdom.' Here is
wisdom, when we cannot raise ourselves up to God, to bring him down to
us. As in the sacrament, they shew carnal wisdom. Oh ! it is a fine thing
that Christ's body and ours should be joined together ! It seems to be a fine
point, that Christ should be hid in the bread, &c. But here is no spiritual
wisdom.

The union that the Scripture speaks of is by faith, ascending into heaven, laying hold on Christ there ; and going back to the cross, and seeing
Christ crucified there, and so ' he is meat indeed, and drink indeed,' John
vi. 55, as we see him crucified, and satisfying God's wrath for us, for our
sins.

And so again, is it not a pretty wisdom to draw men by pictures, and
likenesses ? Are not men delighted with the images of their friends and
of their parents ? And therefore is it not a good religious policy to have
pictures of Christ, and pictures of God the father ? Here is wisdom correspondent to the dealing and affairs of men, but all this is fleshly wisdom. The Scripture speaks mightily against making of images, the word
of God is directly against it. This is fleshly wisdom. Grace doth not rule
here.

So, that the souls when they go out of this world being very unclean,
that they should be purged, that there should be some satisfaction, some
purgatory, &c., here seems to be wisdom. But wherefore serves the blood
of Christ then ? That is the only purgatory, that purgeth from all sins, mortal sins, venial sins, all sins.

Again, is it not a seeming wisdom to come to heaven by our own works,
by our own merits, that so we may set the people on to good works ? or
else we dull their spirits and endeavours. Aye, but this is ' fleshly wisdom,'
this is devilish wit, and so it will prove in the end ; for the Scripture goes
only to Christ, only Christ. ' We are saved by faith,' Eph. ii. 8, only by
Christ. I will not enter into the point, I only shew you what a seeming
wisdom they have ; but it is not heavenly, but merely carnal.

3. And that their religion is carnal, do but consider *that all the points
wherein they differ from us, may be resolved either to belly-policy, or to state-
policy ; either to ambition, and riches, or the belly.* Wherefore is their
monarchy, all their great preferments, but to increase their ambition ?
Wherefore are their pardons, and indulgences, but to get money basely, **as**

some of their own writers confess ? And their purgatory, &c. ? These
things be for carnal ends. It is a religion fitted for their own ends. They
make what they list to serve them. Religion, nature, reason, conscience,
whatsoever is good, they make all stoop to interest their own cause in.
Their orders, that is, their spiritual good, must be their advancement.
It is but a colour put upon carnal ends. The spiritual good is their
own advancement. They aim at their own peculiar interest in all their
villanies ; as if God stood in need of our lie, as if God's glory were advanced by the devil.

As well their government as their religion is lies. It is defended by lies,
by equivocation, and rebellion, by withdrawing the allegiance of subjects,
and murdering of princes. Laws, and religion, and all must stoop to their
wisdom, under pretence of *bonum spirituale*. These things are known. I
do but touch them, to breed a deeper hatred of this religion, which is altogether fleshly and carnal. And so far as they are led by carnal wisdom,
they are not led by the grace of God. Wherefore is their lying for advantage ? their dispensations, and horrible allowing of anything ? Is it not
merely carnal wisdom ?

In a word, their religion is merely policy, if it be not too good a word
for it. It is merely carnal policy. It came not from heaven, but from the
' bottomless pit,' Rev. ix. 2.

Then they fell from heaven when they grew to their highest, when they
were in their top. This I thought good to touch collaterally from the text,
which doth characterise a true Christian indeed in his temper, that he is
joyful when he is as he should be ; and the ground of it is from a good conscience, and that good conscience ariseth out of a course of life and conversation led in simplicity and sincerity to God. For religion hath majesty
enough in itself, without far fetches and devices. And the principle from
whence, ' By the grace of God,' in the evidence of the Spirit, and not according to fleshly and carnal wisdom.

In a word therefore, labour that from the evidence of the Spirit, having
your souls sanctified by the Spirit, you may reflect on yourselves, and
look into your lives, and say truly, as St Paul doth here. My care in my
course of life and conversation hath been in simplicity, I have cast myself
upon God and his government, and not looked to the world ; and in sincerity I have aimed at God in all things, I have had no false and by-aims,
I have not spared even my life by any carnal end : I have not served myself either in religion, or in my course of life, but I have laboured to serve
God in serving my brethren, and have led my life by the grace of God, and
by the word of grace, which I laboured to know that I might follow. Let
us be able, in some measure, in truth to say thus. And then we may say
further with St Paul, that ' this is our rejoicing, the testimony of our conscience.' We shall never want joy. And then let the world judge of us as
it will, there is such a strength and power, such a prerogative, and majesty
in Christian comfort, when a man can, as I said, reflect thus on himself,
that though in a weak measure, yet in truth, his conversation and course of
life hath been, though his tidings* have been something, ' in simplicity and sincerity,' that nothing can daunt it in this world.

It is above all discouragement, above all eclipse of good name, the testimony of conscience, which hath God's testimony with it.

The witness of two is a strong witness. The witness of God, and conscience, it will so settle our souls, that neither ill reports nor any usage in

* Qu. ' failings ? '—ED.

the world shall daunt us; we shall have comfort in all the passages of our lives, be they what they will. Whereas other men that lead not their lives in a constant course of holy simplicity and sincerity, they are as the prophet saith, ' like the leaves of the forest,' Isa. vii. 2, shaken with every alteration, with every rumour of ill news. But a sound Christian in the worst alteration, there may be combustions, there may be alteration of state, yet his ' heart is fixed,' Ps. lvii. 7, he is not moved.

Likewise, in the hour of death he can say with Hezekiah, ' Thou knowest, Lord, I have led my life in simplicity,' Isa. xxxviii. 2, that I have served thee ' with a perfect heart,' that is, in sincerity. I have desired, and endeavoured to grow better, which is all the perfection we have in this world. Sincerity witnessed by growth, and strength against the contrary, this will comfort us in all the alterations and changes in this world, which is as a sea full of trouble, and at the hour of death likewise, and at the day of judgment. This is that only that will make us able to look Christ in the face.

Truth hath a divinity in it, this simplicity and sincerity, more than any earthly thing. It hath that in it that is real and spiritual.

A man that hath the grace of God in the truth of it, there is a great deal of majesty in it. There is the greatest majesty in heavenly things when they appear most simple, because of their excellency. There is something of God's in sincerity. So much as a man hath in truth, so much of God's. He partakes of the divine nature, as St Peter saith, 2 Peter i. 4, so much as he hath in truth, though it be never so little. And being a branch of God, it will make him look upon God in the day of judgment. Why? Because he knows he is in the covenant of grace, that he hath title to heaven by Christ.

When a man's conscience can tell him that he hath led his life, not by carnal wisdom, but in the truth of grace, it will make him out-look Satan, and all the troubles of the world, and look unto Christ with comfort. Who would not be in such a state ? Thus we see a Christian leads his life, ' Not in fleshly wisdom, but by the grace of God.' I will add one thing more, and so finish the verse.

We may see hence, *that the most religious men are the best statesmen.*

I know proud, carnal Machiavellian dispositions make a scorn at these positions. They think them to be austere and poor principles, till they come to death; as that wretch said himself, when he came to die, ' That he had provided for all things but for death ' (*yy*). But while they are in their ruff, they think they can manage states, and do all, when, indeed, they bring the vengeance of God upon their own persons, and upon the state they live in; for God is neither in them, nor with them. He is not *in* them; for they want grace, they are led by carnal wisdom altogether. And he is not *with* them. God will not give them good success, unless it be to increase their judgment. He will not give good success to those projects that they take up contrary to his rule.

Therefore, those that will be guided by reasons of religion, and submit themselves to the guidance of God's blessed Spirit, they are best for the state of their own souls, and best for the public estate. For doth not God know the mysteries of state better than any man ? Is not he a better politician than any Ahithophel in the world ? If they have any state policy that is worth the naming, is it not from him ? Is it not a beam from that sun ? Yes ! why then, who is the better ? the difference of parts excepted. But take them alike, a gracious man, and another that is not so ; let the

one fetch his counsel from hell, from darkness, and the other be ruled by
reasons of conscience and religion, there is no comparison.

God will cross and curse their projects that are for their own ends, both
in themselves, and in the state too.

As for the other that are under grace, and the government of grace, God
will be wise in them by his Spirit, and he will be wise for them. ' Whatsoever a good man doth, it shall prosper,' Ps. i. 3. It is a large promise.
How wondrous happy and wise were the children of Israel, when they kept
the covenant of God. ' This is your wisdom, to keep the commandments
of God,' Deut. iv. 6 ; and their wisdom made them happy. How happy
were they in David's time, who made the statutes of God, ' the man of his
counsel,' Ps. lxxiii. 24. How happy was the state in Solomon's time, till
Solomon did warp and bend to carnal counsel to strengthen himself. How
happy was his government till that time, but never after that. They were
environed with enemies round about. But, alas ! who could hurt the people
of God, so long as they submitted themselves to the government of grace !
they were alway happy.

Therefore it is an idle thing to suppose that there will be any good success by carnal projects ; no, the only good statesman is the religious man.
And it was never better with the church of God, before or since the time
of Christ, than when those were in the stern.* Do but think of this oft,
as St Jude saith, ' God only wise,' ver. 25. We must all of us light our
candle at that fire.

All wisdom, even this poor spark of reason that God enlighteneth ' every
man that comes into the world' withal, it comes from Christ Jesus. ' In
him are all the treasures of wisdom, God, and God-man, only wise,' Col.
ii. 3. There is no wisdom without him, therefore let us submit ourselves
to his government ; let us pray to him, and seek for wisdom of him in all
things. But I go on to the next verse.

VERSE 13.

' *For we write none other things unto you than what you read or acknowledge, and I trust you shall acknowledge even to the end.*' Here St Paul
strengthens himself by another course. First, he retires to his own heart
and conscience, ' My rejoicing is this, the testimony of my conscience,' &c. ;
and he sets this as a bulwark against all the slanders and detractions of his
opposers whatsoever. He sets it as a flag of defiance, the testimony of his
own conscience.

But to set himself the more upright in their hearts, whom he was to deal
withal, knowing what a great advantage it was to have the good opinion of
them, and to wipe away all imputation, he passeth from his conscience to
their conscience. For my own conscience my rejoicing is this, that you
cannot accuse me that I have led my life by carnal false principles, but by
reasons of religion, and by the blessed motions of God's Spirit. Nay, I
can go further than so. For what I say of mine own conscience, I dare
say you can say too ; for ' I write no other things than what you read or
acknowledge.'

' What you read.' Some take it, ' what you know or acknowledge,' because these are distinct things. The word *anaginoskein*,† signifies to know
or to read ; but usually, to read. We may well, therefore, take it so as

* That is, = ' helm.'—G. † That is, from ἀναγινώσκω. Cf. Robinson, *sub voce.*—G.

most translate it here, 'I write no other thing,' concerning my simplicity, 'but what you read or acknowledge.' I write of my simplicity simply. I speak not of my sincerity insincerely, but what I write, you read or acknowledge ; because St Paul knew he had a place in their conscience, they could not but acknowledge what a man he was ; for the Spirit was wondrous effectual by his ministry in their hearts ; and they were his epistle, as he saith in another place, 2 Cor. iii. 2. And, therefore, he appeals to their acknowledgment, to their conscience, ' We write no other thing,' &c. And for the time to come, ' I trust you shall acknowledge to the end.'

So he doth appeal to their conscience for the present, and he doth take in trust the time to come, what their thoughts shall be of him, and what his estate shall be. You shall have grace to think well of me to the end, because you shall have ground to think well of me for my constancy. ' I hope you shall acknowledge to the end ;' and you shall have wisdom, and experience of my goodness to acknowledge to the end.

I will give a touch on these things, because they be useful ; and but a touch, because I stood somewhat on them before, and shall have fit occasion for them severally after.

Obs. ' We write no other things than what you read.'

This seemeth strange. Why, how could they read other things than what he wrote ? Yes ! If he had written falsely, if he had not expressed his thoughts in his writings, then they had read one thing and he had been another. As a woman that is painted, there is *prosopon* and *prosopeia ;* * there is the visage and the true natural countenance. She is not the woman she appears to be, her face is one and herself is another ; but I am as I express myself. His meaning is, I speak of my simplicity and sincerity, simply and sincerely. I speak not of my virtues to go beyond you, but I speak sincerely ; what I speak you read. For I think not that he means his former epistle, but what he wrote concerning himself and the leading of his life. That which I speak concerning myself, that you read ; and what you read that I speak (*zz*). It yields me this observation, which though I had occasion to speak of when I handled simplicity, yet I shall now touch it, that

A Christian man is one man, he doth act one man's part.

He hath not a heart and a heart, he is not a man and a man. There is a harmony between his thoughts and resolutions, between his speeches and his actions. They all sweetly accord together. What he thinks and resolves on, that he speaks ; what he speaks, that he writes ; what he writes and speaks, that he doth ; he is one man in all, he doth not deal doubly.

It is the easiest thing in the world to be politic, to be naught, to double. The nature of man teacheth a man to be false. Man's heart is full of naughtiness. It is a hard thing for a man to be one ; and till a man be a gracious man, he shall be a double man.

Therefore you must take heed of a fault, which is called the abuse of signs, of such signs as serve to express what a man is inwardly. Let your inward disposition and the signs that express it accord. The signs of expression that come from one man to another are speech, writing, countenance, and the like.

A man should not be one thing within, and his speech another. He should not be one thing, and his writing another. He should not be one thing, and any other expression another.

* That is, πρόσωπον, = a face, visage ; and προσωπεῖον, = a personification.—G.

This abuse of signs and expressions, when they are one way, and the heart another, besides the odiousness of it to God (as being contrary both to his nature and to his word, it is contrary to his nature; for he is simple and sincere, he is one in all, ' there is no shadow of change in him,' James i. 17, there is no mixture. As it is contrary to his nature, so it is contrary to his word, that bids us not ' dissemble nor lie one to another,' Col. iii. 9), it makes a man most like the devil, who never appears in his own shape, but always in another. He comes in our friends as ' an angel of light,' 2 Cor. xi. 14. He never discovers himself in his own colours. Besides all these and such like respects, it is the overthrow, it cuts the sinews, of human society ; for what is the band of human society but the intercourse by speech, and writing, and the like ? Now, if there be abuse of these signs, that they are one thing and we another, that we do not express what is the true thought and impression of our hearts, all society is dissolved.

Therefore we cannot too much hate popish principles, of not keeping fidelity with heretics, as they call them. It is the custom of them to deal so. As you know in a war of theirs with the Turks—the story is well known—when the cardinals had broken their promise, after they had in a manner gotten the victory, the Turks even cried to Christ that he would revenge their treachery ; and the Turks came again upon them, and overcame them, and gave them a mighty overthrow (aaa). Their gross principle of equivocation, and the like, which stands in the abuse of expressions and signs ! Yea, their abuse of the blessed sign and seal, an oath, which is the sign of all truth between man and man. Their abuse of the sacrament too ! They have abused all God's signs, and all to ill purposes, to swear with private reservations ; whereas the old principle of Isidore is constantly and everlastingly true (bbb), ' Conceive the oath as you will, it must be understood as he to whom it is sworn understands it, and not as he that swears.' Therefore undoubtedly popery must fall every day ;* and judicious men, though they be not gracious, they see it must fall. It should make us hate them deeply, because the courses they take are the overthrow of society. This abuse of expressions, of that excellent gift that God hath given, namely, the tongue, whereby what is in my heart another man may understand ; and also writing, whereby a man may convey his mind many hundred miles. Now, these excellent gifts that God hath given for society, for men to turn them against God, and against society, it must needs provoke the majesty of God.

And as it is a sin against society, so it is a sin that is punished by society. All men must needs hate them that do so. Those that have no other argument against popery, they have argument enough from their equivocation. Those that are not subtle-headed to see other things, when they look to the gunpowder treason and to their equivocation, there is argument enough for any plain, simple man to hate popery.

Therefore let us be like ourselves in all that we do to God or to men. I had occasion to press the point when I spake of simplicity, therefore I will not dwell further on it.

' *I write no other thing than what you read or acknowledge.*' He means, they acknowledged it in their heart and conscience. What I write of my conversation, that which you have heard, it is no other than that you read, and you acknowledge it too ; for they had felt the power of his ministry. Whence first of all observe, that

Qu. ' way ?'—ED.

Obs. Where the minister converseth by the grace of God, and not by carnal wisdom, God is not only wise in him, but for him.

He is gracious and good for him, he gives him success in the hearts of others. When a man is led by the Spirit of God, the same Spirit that guides him in speaking, guides his auditors in hearing, and gives a sweet and a strong report in their hearts of what he saith, What I write of myself you acknowledge, that my conversation hath been in sincerity; and not only my conversation, but my doctrine; every way you have acknowledged me. The same Spirit that guided me to do so, wrought in you an acknowledgment of it in your conscience.

Therefore, if you would have the speeches of the ministers to take effect, you should desire God not only to guide them in what they are to say, but likewise with the same Spirit to work in the hearers; and when the same Spirit works in both, what a glorious success is there! As we see here, St Paul carried himself in his own person, and in his ministry graciously, in simplicity, and sincerity; for it is meant of both. He taught simple doctrine without any glossing, without any far-fetched beauty from wit, or eloquence, or the like; and he looked to God in his life and conversation; and as God guided him, so he stirred them up to pray for him: as the word and prayer they are alway joined together. The word had a report in their hearts, as it had in his own, ' What I speak, you acknowledge,' &c.

It is not for us to deliver our minds, and there an end; but when we are to speak, we ought beforehand to look up to God, and desire his Spirit to be effectual in us, that we may speak in the wisdom and grace of the Spirit; and likewise that it may be effectual to them, that they may acknowledge it, that they may feel in their souls and consciences the power of what we speak and feel in ourselves. So you see the truth of what I said before, that God was not only wise in St Paul, but he was gracious and good for him in those that he was to deal with.

And there is the glory of a good minister that is a humble man, and denies carnal wisdom : that God will delight to honour himself by using him as an instrument to do good to others. God usually will give report of what he saith to the hearts of others.

Proud men, that speak what they speak by carnal projects, and carnal wisdom, and seek themselves, usually the hearts and consciences of other men give no report to them. For man naturally is proud, and when he sees that the most excellent man in the world hath by-aims, he will not be gone beyond by him, say what he will. If a man set up sails for himself, he doth not win upon others. But he that discovers himself, that he seeks the glory of God, and the good of the souls that he deals with, and denies himself in that which otherwise he could do, that useth not the strength of parts which he hath, because he would discover the simple word, which is most majestical in simplicity, God seeing this simple and sincere desire, he honours and crowns the ministry of such a man with success in the hearts of the people. Therefore saith St Paul here, ' I write no other thing' concerning myself, but God hath honoured me with the issue of it in your hearts likewise, that you ' acknowledge' what I say.

' You acknowledge.' *Acknowledge* is a deep word. It is more than to ' know.' It is more than a conviction of the judgment. It is when the heart and affections yield, when the inward Spirit upon experience yields, I feel and acknowledge this is true. It is more, I say, than knowledge. The next point then that I observe is this, that

Obs. *God doth give his children that love him in simplicity and sincerity, a place in the conscience of men.*

He gives them place in the consciences of those that have conscience : for there are some that have no science,* and therefore they have no conscience : as popish superstitious persons, &c. But those that deal faithfully, that live in the church, and see the glory of God, God gives them a place in the conscience of those that they live amongst and deal with. And they seek more to have place in their conscience, than in their fancy, than in their opinion, and imagination, and humour. A carnal man, so he may have the humour, the fancy, and imagination of his hearers delighted, he regards not what inwardly they may feel from him : he regards not how he warms their hearts, and conscience, and how they acknowledge him within ; and therefore, perhaps, if he have a good word for the present, Oh, a glorious man, &c., it is all he cares for ; but he hath no place in their conscience, because they feel him not working there, and he hath no aim to be there. A good man seeks to edify, and build up the conscience in sound principles, in good courses, in the faith of Christ, in holy obedience : things that will hold out in life and death. If I were to speak to ministers, I would enlarge the point further.

Use. Let us all in our conversations labour rather *to approve ourselves to the consciences of men*, that they may acknowledge us to be honest, downright, faithful men, rather than to please their humours and fancies ; for, as Solomon saith, ' he that tells a man the truth, shall have more favour at the last, than he that dissembleth,' Prov. ix. 8, xxiv. 25, *et alibi :* for his conscience will witness that he hath dealt rightly, and faithfully with him, that he is an honest man, and goes on in the same principles still.

Let us therefore first look to our own conscience, and then to the conscience of others ; and if we cannot approve ourselves to our own conscience, and to the conscience of others, alas ! what will become of us ? how shall we approve ourselves to God and to Jesus Christ at the day of judgment ? There is no man but a sound Christian that approves himself to the conscience of another man. For any other man, it is just with God in his judgment to find him out first or last. He may wind himself into the conscience for a time, as the superstitious papists do, but first or last he is found out to be a dissembler, and to bring false wares.

And so for civil conversation, there is none that will have place in the conscience of other men, to think them and their courses good, but those that are sound Christians. For the most, those that are not led by the grace of God's Spirit, all mens' consciences condemn them. They are smitten, and censured there, and judged there. Besides, their own conscience, which perhaps they will not give leave to tell them somewhat in their ear that they would be loath to hear, this you are, this you did, and this you spake amiss : they will not suffer conscience to speak, but drown it in sensuality, and stifle it. They take this course, they think they are well enough, and they would never be themselves. A carnal man will hardly give conscience leave to speak, till it will, whether he will or no, at the hour of death, and the day of judgment, when God lets it loose upon him. But let them take this course as long as they will, yet in the conscience of other men they have no place : for they live not, as St Paul saith here, ' in simplicity and sincerity, not by carnal wisdom, but by the grace of God.'

This is the benefit that a good man hath in this life, that howsoever he

* That is = ' knowledge'.—G.

have the ill words of carnal men sometimes, and their humour is against him : yet notwithstanding if they be in the church, and have any illumination, any judgment, he hath their conscience for him. Nay, I say more, they cannot but think reverently of a man of God, of a good Christian (I speak not of ministers only), they cannot but think reverently of them, and reverence them in their consciences, do what they can. For it is not in men's power to frame what conceits they will, to frame what opinions they will of men ; but as there is a necessity of reason, as the principles we say are so strong, that a man cannot say they are false, do what he can, because the light is visible to the understanding ; as a man cannot say the sun shines when it is night, when it is dark, because it is a sensible falsehood ; so a man cannot deny the principles of any art, if they be principles ; because there is such a light of truth that overpowers him, and as it were compels the inward man. So it is here : there is such a majesty in grace, and good courses of a Christian, that another man that lives a wicked life he cannot think of him what he would. He may force himself to speak what he list, and force odd* opinions of him, but when he is sober himself, he must needs if he have any relics of conscience in him, if he be not altogether a sot, he must needs think well in his conscience of such a man's courses. This is the majesty and honour of good things, that however they may have the humour, and passion, and fancy of men against them, yet they have their conscience for them ; yea, of wicked men when they are themselves.

Take the wickedest man at the hour of death, if he have himself at command, that his spirits be not disturbed, and ask him whether he justify the courses of such and such men ? he will answer, Oh yes ! I would I had led them myself. What is that that besots them ? Sensuality, and such courses ; for men that are not led by the grace of God, are led with outward things which besot the judgment for a time ; but when that dulness is past, when a wicked man is stripped of all, and is best able to judge, then he likes such courses.

If the worst men shall in their conscience acknowledge the best persons, and the best things one day, nay, they do now, if they will suffer themselves to be themselves, then let us take such courses as our own consciences may justify, as St Paul saith here, ' This is my glorying, the testimony of my conscience ;' and likewise the conscience of those I live with, ' I write no other thing,' but what you acknowledge in your consciences yourselves.

' *And I trust you shall acknowledge to the end.*' This word, ' Trust,' doth not imply, as usually it doth in common speech, an uncertainty of a thing, a moral conjecture, I trust, or hope it may be so ; it may be otherwise, but I hope well. It is not an uncertain conceit with the fear of the contrary ; but the word implies a gracious, dependent disposition upon God, ' I trust in God,' as it is so expressed in some other places.†

Now you acknowledge me, and ' I trust in God you shall acknowledge me to the end.' So here St Paul sets down what he resolved to be by the grace of God, and what in the issue he should be ; because holy resolutions are seconded with gracious assistance.

And likewise he sets down what they should judge of him to the end ; I trust as you acknowledge me now, so to the end you shall have grace so to

---

* That is 'singular, extraordinary.'—G.

† Cf. Philip. ii. 24 ; Philem. 22 ; Heb. xiii. 18 ; 2 John 12.—G.

do, and I shall have grace so to be; I shall be as I am, and have been; I have led my life 'in simplicity, and sincerity;' and as you have acknowledged me to be such a one, so you shall have grace still to acknowledge me, 'I hope, or trust.' I will not enter into any common place, only I will speak that which the text puts to me.

'I trust you shall acknowledge to the end.' Here he begins with his hope of their judging of him, to continue so to the end.

Saint Paul here takes a good conceit, a good opinion of his children whom he had begotten to the faith in Corinth. I hope as you are, and as you do judge of me, so you will judge of me to the end.

Why hath St Paul such a trust of them as of himself?

Reason 1. Among many reasons this is one, *He knew that where God had begun a good work, he would finish it.* He saw that he had begun a good work in them, and therefore he knew that he would go on with it.

Reason 2. And then again, God planted in him a good hope and trust of them; *because hope and trust stir up endeavour to the thing hoped for.* Desperation doth quell all courage, and cool all endeavour. Now God, because he would have us constant in our carriage, and in the expressions of our love to other men, he stirs up in us a trust that all shall be well with them.

Reason 3. Likewise St Paul sets down his hope that God had put into his heart of them, *for his own comfort;* for it is a great comfort to a minister, or to a Christian, when he is to deal with such as he trusts are good, and will be good. It is a heaven upon earth, and therefore God doth plant good conceits of other men in us for this end; partly, to stir up our endeavour to do all good to them, and partly to comfort us. For if the final estate of any man were discovered to us, that God had no delight in them concerning their salvation, who would do any service of love for them? or who would have comfort in conversing with them? But when God stirs up in our hearts a good opinion of them, partly it is good for them, to stir up our endeavour to do all good for them; and it is good for us, it is a great comfort.

And again, it was an encouragement to them when they heard of Saint Paul's trust of them to the end, that they should continue as they were. For to have a good conceit and opinion of another man, especially the good conceit of a pastor, it is a great encouragement. And the best Christians in the world have need of it ofttimes. Besides the judgment of themselves, which is sometimes shaken by Satan, that they give a false witness of their own estate. Oh! it is comfortable that a man have the judgment of a man that looks without passion, and temptation on him; you have been thus, and my trust and confidence is in God, and the promise of God, looking to your former course, that you will be so to the end; he gives not a false witness.

Saint Paul speaks thus to stir up his own endeavour to do good to them; and to comfort them, that so great an apostle should have so good an opinion of them.

Therefore let us labour, I say, to entertain as good a conceit of them among whom we live, as their carriage will bear. Two things usually are the object of our hope and trust. While men are here, before their estate be determined of in hell, God may have mercy on them, and deliver them out of the snares of Satan. That hope should stir up some endeavour to pray for them; seeing their estates are not desperate, they are not yet sunk into hell (*ccc*). Or else if we see them in the state of grace, we should express our love in the services and offices of love, because God hath already set his stamp on them.

There is no man living but we may trust, and hope of him one way or other. Those that we see no grace in, as the apostle saith, 2 Tim. ii. 24, we may have ' patience towards them,' seeing if at any time God will have mercy on them to deliver them out of the ' snare of the devil.'

It is not good to cast off all conceit, and all hope of any man living. The worst sign is, when we see men malicious, and oppose known truths, because it comes near the sin against the Holy Ghost ; but because we may err in that, it is good to take the safest way. But where we see evidences of grace, though in never so little a measure, let us entertain and cherish a good hope ; because it will cherish that which we are all bound to, to love one another. We are bound to love one another, and to shew all the offices of love. Now that which stirs up love and all the offices of love, is hope. Faith works by hope, as well as by love. Faith works by love in all duties ; and it works by hope in this duty. If we hope that God will have mercy on them, that will stir up our endeavour ; but we are not much in this error : we are rather ready to conceit over-well, than too ill of men.

' I trust you shall acknowledge to the end.' Saint Paul here, besides his good conceit of them to the end, doth imply his own resolution and purpose to hold on in good courses to the end. My trust in God's grace is, that you shall acknowledge to the end what I have written to you of mine own courses. As if he had said, I am Paul now, and you shall find me Paul hereafter ; you shall find me always an honest man like myself ; for as he whom I have trusted ' is yesterday, to-day,' to-morrow, ' and the same for ever,' so likewise by God's grace I hope to be the same that I have been, I hope I shall be like myself.

The grounds of St Paul's trust that he should be so, is partly the act itself, together with the endeavour, ' I trust' I shall be so ' to the end ;' because I trust in God to the end, and God is good to them that trust in him. How often is it repeated in the Psalms ! ' He is the God of them that trust in him,' Ps. xxxvii. 3 ; ' he is a sun and a shield,' Ps. lxxxiv. 11 ; he is all that is good, and he keeps away all evil. All the promises are entailed to trusting in God. Now because I have confidence in it that God will do so, I stir up my endeavour to shew that it is not a presumptuous trust. I trust in him that will perform the conditions of the covenant which is made to them that honour him by trusting in him.

St Paul knew what God had done. He knew that he that had bestowed the first fruits, he would make up the harvest ; he knew that he that had laid the first stone, he would set up the roof ; he knew that God had begun a good work in him by experience, and that he would finish his own work. That he knew by former experience.

And then he knew the promises of God, the promises of the covenant. Many such grounds St Paul had to bear him up that he should continue to the end in a course of simplicity and sincerity, and in the grace of God.

But withal St Paul did add a holy and heavenly course to come to this end, together with his trust. What course did St Paul take ?

St Paul, that he might hold out constantly in holy resolutions to the end, *First, he did judiciously consider what might hinder him, between that and the end of his race and course.* He balanced all things that he possibly could suffer ; and he laid in the other balance the things that he had in hope and promise ; and he resolves, all that I can suffer that should shake me off from my course, it is not 'worthy of the glory that shall be revealed,' Rom. viii. 18. Saith he, if you balance both, you will conclude this.

There are many things that may shake us in our Christian course. St Paul thought of all Satan's snares, 'I am not ignorant of his enterprises,' 2 Cor. ii. 11, saith he. And then for the world, that might cast trumpery in his way, saith he, 'I am crucified to the world, and the world is crucified to me,' Gal. vi. 14. And for anything that might happen to him, he knew that the issue of all things should work for the best to them that love God. He includes himself, Rom. viii. 28. Saith he, we know it beforehand, we believe, before troubles or evils come ; come what will, the issue of all things is in the regiment and power of God, and as he pleaseth all shall work for the best to those that love God ; and therefore as I am, so I will be. What should hinder ? if all things help me, nothing can hinder me.

And then St Paul took this course, he looked forward still, ' I press forward to the prize of the high calling,' Philip. iii. 14. He forgat that which was behind, and he resolved to go forward. He had a mind to grow better and better alway, and this comforted him that he should hold out to the end. For it is the reward of a growing Christian to have a sweet sense of his present state of grace in God's favour, and to hold out to the end. Such a man is like the sun that grows* up still, till he come to high noonday, as Solomon saith, Prov. iv. 18. St Paul took this course. He strove for perfection, he had a crown in his eye, a crown of righteousness and glory, and that will not suffer a man to be idle and cold that hath such a thing in his eye. St Paul, to whet his endeavour, not only looked forward, but to glory ; for as Christ looked to ' the glory, and despised the shame,' Heb. xii. 2 ; so St Paul looked to the crown, and despised all his sufferings.

Then besides, St Paul was conscious of his own sincerity ; for grace carries its own witness with itself, as he saith here, I know my conversation. ' This is the testimony of my conscience, that in simplicity and sincerity I have walked before you.' He knew that sincerity is accompanied with constancy and perseverance. It is a rule that alway constancy and perseverance are companions with simplicity and sincerity. I have begun in sincerity hitherto, now I am sincere, and have expressed to you the truth of my heart, and of my courses ; and as I am, so I mean to be ; therefore, having begun in sincerity, I know I shall end in perseverance and constancy.

Truth of grace is accompanied with constancy. All other things are but grass, they are but shows, they will vanish ; but sincerity, the truth of grace, is a divine thing. ' The word of the Lord,' that is, grace wrought by ' the word of the Lord, that endures for ever,' 1 Pet. i. 25. Where there is truth of grace, though it be but as a grain of mustard-seed, there is perseverance to the end. St Paul knew this well, and therefore he builds his trust on these things, on these courses that he took.

We should all take the like course, look to St Paul's grounds, and take his courses. Those be they that will hold out to the end. Judicious consideration of all the difficulties, to put into the balance what impediments we shall have from the world, and what will be great to us when it is balanced with the glory to come ! And withal, to aim forward still, as St Paul did. And take another course that he took likewise, to depend upon grace continually. He knew there was a throne of grace open to him alway for the time to come, as well as for the time past, and present. He knew that Christ in heaven was alway full of grace ; he knew he should not want in any exigent when he should go to him ; he knew that God would not des-

* Qu. ' goes ?'—ED.

titute or forsake any of his children, them that he hath called to see the necessity of wisdom, and of courage, and comfort. Let us do therefore as St Paul was answered from heaven, say, 'His grace is sufficient for us,' 2 Cor. xii. 9 ; if not to keep us from all sin, yet to keep us in comfortable courses, to keep us in sincerity and simplicity. The grace of God is sufficient to bring us to heaven.

Let us persuade ourselves, that if we go on in Christian courses, in that confidence, God will give us grace to bring us to heaven. This was St Paul's confidence, therefore he saith, 'I trust you shall acknowledge to the end,' because I know that I shall continue in simplicity and sincerity to the end. God will keep me, I shall have grace to beg, and he will give me grace ; for his gifts in this kind can never be repented of.

Let us take from St Paul this course, and this comfort : this course to trust in God for the time to come ; to have constant resolutions for the time to come, to cleave to God, and to good courses.

Let us every day renew our covenants in this kind, and our resolutions to do nothing against conscience, to go on in Christian courses ; let it be our constant course. For as God's children know they shall continue to the end, so it is wrought from resolution so to do ; and this resolution stirs them up to depend upon God by prayer, that he would ' knit their hearts to him, that they may fear his name,' Jer. xxxii. 40 ; that he would give them grace sufficient, &c., that he would establish their hearts, as David prays.

This resolution, it drives them to prayer, and to all good courses, that God would stablish them in every good work, in every good thought and desire, and that he would knit their hearts nearer to him. Resolve, therefore, every day, in dependence upon God, to take good courses, that so whensoever any judgment of God shall come, or when the hour of death shall light on us, it may not come as a snare, that it may take us in good resolutions. It is no matter how we die in outward respects, if we die in good resolutions.

As we resolve, so we are ; for our resolutions are full of will. Wishes and resolutions : they carry the whole man with them ; and God esteems a man by his will. For if there be impediments that are not impossible to man, resolution will break through all. God judgeth men by their resolutions : ' Teach me, O Lord, thy statutes, and I will keep them even to the end. I have sworn, and I will perform it, that I will keep thy righteous judgments,' Ps. cxix. 106. Every day take we these promises to ourselves, and bind ourselves with them to God.

In vows, be chary. I do not speak of them now, I speak of purposes and resolutions, alway take in God with them. I trust in God, depend upon God in good courses (that God do not punish us, and give us into desertion for our presumption), and then we may know that our state is good. Look to St Paul, and see the property of a good conscience. It looks back, it looks to the present, and to the time to come. ' Our rejoicing is this,' that we have had our conversation hitherto well. Is that enough for a good conscience ? No ! you have acknowledged me to be as I have written, to have a good conscience in my ministerial course, and in my conversation ; and you shall acknowledge me still.

This is the glory of a good life, that whether a man look above him, he hath God to witness for him. Or whether he look to the world, to right judging persons, he hath them to judge for him. He dares appeal to their conscience. Or whether he look within him, he hath a good witness from his own conscience. Which way soever he looks he hath comfort. ' You have acknowledged me,' and you shall acknowledge : I know God will not leave me for the time to come. So that which makes up a complete good conscience, is the looking to the time to come, as well as to the time past and present. A good conscience that is purged by the blood of Christ from the guilt of former sins, shall alway have grace to stablish the heart in good resolutions. For where there is a cleansing from the guilt, where there is pardon of sin, there is alway given a power against sin for the time to come.

We usually say in divinity, that the grace of God, and a purpose to live in any sin, cannot dwell in one heart ; and it is true, if there be not a purpose to obey God in all things, to ' leave every wicked way,' Isa. lv. 7, if there be an inclination to any iniquity, the heart and conscience is not good. A good conscience gives testimony of the time past, present, and to come.

And always, as I said, remember to take God in all your resolutions, or else you are liable to St James his exception in a higher degree. ' Go to now, ye that say, We will do this, to-day and to-morrow,' James iv. 13, and that in strength and confidence of your own, not remembering the uncertainty of human events, how many things may fall out that God may cross it. If it be a presumptuous speech in matters of this life, how much more in matters of grace for the time to come, which God only hath in his keeping, and ' gives the will and the deed according to his good pleasure,' Phil. ii. 13. Therefore we should ' make an end of our salvation with fear and trembling,' Eph. vi. 5.

Let us do as St Paul did, trust in God. My trust and dependence on God is this, that I shall do so ; because I have a constant resolution to be so to my life's end.

Therefore join them both together. Every day renew our dependence on God, and his promises. The life of a Christian is a life dependent. Salvation is wrought out of us by Christ, procured by him : and our carriage to salvation is wrought out of us by grace coming from Christ. He keeps the fountain, and he lets out the streams more or less as we humbly depend on him. So that both salvation is out of us, and the carriage to salvation is of grace ; all is out of us. How should this make us carry ourselves humbly, in a dependence on Christ for salvation, and the carriage of it ! And therefore resolve not to offend God in anything, but to trust in God, and to look to his word. To trust in God and his word is all one, Ps. cxxx. 5. Thus we should take St Paul's course, to trust in God, and renew our purposes every day.

And then take St Paul's comfort to yourselves, persuade yourselves, that ' neither things present, nor things to come,' as St Paul saith, Rom. viii. 38, nothing shall intercept your crown. For what he said here beforehand, that he experimentally saith of himself, 2 Tim. iv. 7, *seq.*, a little before he died (which was the last epistle that ever he wrote), he saith here, they should acknowledge him to the end ; and there, when his end was come, what saith he of himself? ' I have fought a good fight, I have kept the faith, I have run my race ; now henceforth is laid up for me a crown of righteousness,' &c. Before this time, I depended upon God, that he would carry me to my end, as he hath done ; and now I am to close up my days, and my sun is to set : all this I have done ; God, that was with me from the beginning, is with me to the end : I have done all this, and what remains now but a crown of righteousness ?

Therefore, I beseech you, take in trust the time to come, as well as any time past ; resolve well, and trust with your resolution ; live by faith and obedience—join them both together, the one to be the evidence of the truth of the other : then, take in trust for the time to come all the good that you can promise yourselves from God. You cannot honour him more.

'I trust you shall acknowledge to the end.' St Paul saith of himself, that the grace of God should lead him to his end, and that they should acknowledge it. You shall not acknowledge me to the end to be rich, or to be in favour, &c., but this you shall acknowledge, that I shall be the like man. It is uncertain for anything in the world. We cannot promise ourselves, nor others cannot promise for us ; but you shall acknowledge this, that I will be as I have been to the end. 'You have acknowledged, and you shall acknowledge,' &c.

Seeing acknowledging is repeated twice as an evidence of a good Christian, to approve of the image of God in another, and to acknowledge it, therefore often examine your hearts what you acknowledge. Do you acknowledge that the abstaining from evil courses, from fraud and cunning in your callings, that the abstaining from sensual living, from carnal policy, is good ? Why then, take that course, resolve upon it. Are the courses of God's children good ? Why will you oppose them ? St Paul gives an excellent rule, Rom. xiv. 22, 'We should not condemn ourselves in that which we allow.' Do you allow in your judgment and in your conscience the best courses ? as, indeed, you will do one day. Then do not condemn yourselves in the present for them. 'Happy is the man that condemneth not himself in that which he alloweth,' saith the apostle, Rom. xiv. 22.

Examine ofttimes seriously, how your judgment stands in the ways of God ; how it is built, whether upon human fancy, to please any man, or upon divine directions, the word of God. If it be so, take heed that you do not condemn yourselves in those courses, and those persons that you allow. Do you in your soul justify such persons ? Why do you not join with them ? Why do you not walk their ways ? Are such courses good ? Why do you not take them ? Your justifying them in the end will be little to your comfort, if you condemn them all your life against your conscience ; for afterwards it is not so much a work of grace for you to justify good courses, and to acknowledge good things. In most men it is not so much a work of grace as it is the evidence of the thing. And when the cloud of sensuality, and the fume that riseth out of worldly pomp is taken away, then the natural conscience comes to see clearly better things, not from the love of them, not that it is changed and transformed with the love of them ; but God so discovers it to them, to make them justify his sentence of damnation the more. He discovered to them better courses than they took : it shall justify their damnation.

We are deceived ofttimes in men's ends. They acknowledge good ways and good courses ; and on the other side some of God's good children they pronounce the contrary. But let none trust to that. Good courses are so evident and clear, that if men be not atheists, they must acknowledge them, especially when the impediment that hindered them before is taken away. You must acknowledge, therefore 'acknowledge' now ; not in your hearts only, but acknowledge them in laying aside your opposition, in casting away your weapons, and by joining with them in good courses. Set not your hands against good courses and good persons ; set your tongues to speak for their good. Take God's part; stand on God's side. It is the best side. If you allow it only hereafter, it will be a barren allowance, it will be no comfort to you; it often falls out to be so.

O beloved! whatsoever courses else you take, they will sink and fall. They will sink first in your own souls, and none will be readier to condemn you than your own conscience. When God shall make you wiser, you will censure yourselves, What folly was it! How was I deluded with this ill company and with that! As wicked company is wondrous powerful to infuse ill conceits : as the spies they infused discouragement by the oration they made of the giants in the land, &c., they altered the mind of the whole people, Numb. xiii. 33. It is a dangerous thing to converse with naughty persons. The devil slides together into the soul with their carnal reasoning, and alters the judgment for the time, that they are not so wise as conscience would make them, and as they might be, if they did not hearken to the hissing of the serpent.

First, if you take any course but good, *your own conscience is by, and will be the first that will find you out.* For sin is a base thing, a work of darkness. It must be discovered. It is a madness. It must be manifest to all men. Popery and all their sleights must be discovered, and the whore must lie naked and stink. Nothing shall be so abominable as popery and popish persons ere long.

Truth will get the victory in the consciences of people ; and good courses will get approbation. Therefore, if you approve them not, first you shall be unhappy in this life, and everlastingly hereafter. This shall be the principal torment in hell, that you saw better courses than you lived in, and you would not give your judgments leave to lead you. There was something better, conscience told you, but you gave way to your lusts, and to the insinuations of wicked men, instruments of the devil, rather than to the motions of conscience, and of God's Spirit, that awakened conscience.

This I say will more ease * your torment of hell that you might have done otherwise if you had had grace. But you willingly betrayed yourselves, you silenced conscience, you willingly condemned yourselves in the things that you acknowledged were naught, you did that which you condemned, and you did not practise that which your judgment did allow.

God will have little to do at the day of judgment with most men in the church, to condemn them ; for, alas ! their own consciences will condemn them, the consciences of all will condemn them that their courses were naught.

And that makes wicked men so cruel, especially if they get into place of authority. They know they are not allowed, they are not acknowledged in the consciences of those that are judicious, they know they are condemned there, and they fret and fume, and think to force another opinion of themselves upon others, but it will not be ; and that makes them that they cannot endure the sight of them that are of a contrary judgment; they think themselves condemned in the hearts of such men, and that makes them cruel. Especially those that have some illumination. They cannot abide their own conscience to take its course, they cannot abide to see themselves. They think themselves condemned in the judgment of others ; and those that think they have the prejudice† of others that their courses are naught, they carry an implacable hatred. It is a desperate case. Hast thou knowledge that they think thy courses naught, and on good

* Qu. ' increase?'—ED.   † That is, = pre-judgment.—G.

ground, and dost thou hate them? And hate to be reformed thyself? Will this alway hold out? No! As I said before, truth is eternal! That which thou acknowledgest must continue. It will be acknowledged. It will get the victory at the day of judgment by men and angels. Truth will have the victory. It is eternal. Take that course for the present, that thou mayest be good for the present, and hold out to the end, as we see the Corinthians here, ' You do acknowledge me, and you shall acknowledge me to the end,' and testify to the world that you acknowledge the best things, and the best persons, that you may be one with them by love here, and in heaven for ever hereafter.

' I trust you shall acknowledge to the end.' To shut up this point. Let me seal it up with this, make this *query* * to yourselves, What estate you are in when you come to the communion, whether it be well with you or no? If not, why will you live any whit at all, in the uncertainty of our lives, and the shortness of them, and the danger of the wrath of God, when there is so little between you and eternal damnation, in a doubtful, in a dangerous, estate? Are you resolved to be naught then? No! If you be not atheists you will not say so. Do you intend to be good, and come and make your covenant with God? Yes! Why, then, resolve to be so.

A good conscience looks not only back to sins past, to repent of them; but for the time to come it resolves to please God in all things, and to hold out to the end.

Some make a mockery of the holy things of God. One part of the year they will be holy; a rotten, foolish affection of people that are popish. In Lent they will use a little austerity, oh! they will please God wondrously! but before and after they are devils incarnate. So they make that part of the year as a good parenthesis, in an unlearned and unwitty speech. A good parenthesis is unseemly in a wicked speech, and a good piece is unseemly in a ragged garment; so their lives that make a good show then (and there are few that do so, they are scarce among us; men are such atheists that there is not outward reformation, but if there be), if they give themselves leave to be civil, and to respect holy things a little time, afterward they return to their looseness again. Doth this patching out of a holy life please God? No, no! ' I have sworn, and I will perform it, that I will keep thy righteous statutes,' saith David, Ps. cxix. 106. And St Paul, ' I have resolved to be so to the end ;' I will be myself still. So where grace is, there is a resolution against all sin for the time to come. If you entertain not this resolution, to walk ' in holiness and righteousness all the days of your life,' Luke i. 75, acknowledge no benefit by Christ's redemption, and come not near the holy things of God.

This is the honest heart that the Scripture speaks of, that receives the seed deep into it; that hates sin above all miseries and ills, and that loves grace above all other good things. Therefore if any infirmity come, he can say it is against his resolution. I purposed not this, I plotted it not, I do not allow myself in it. Here is an honest heart. The word is fixed deeply in such a heart. It comes with an honest resolution. If you come to the sacrament, and purpose to live in sin, you profane the holy things of God. The word of God will do you no good. It will never take deep root to save you. So much for St Paul's resolution for the time to come, ' I trust you shall acknowledge to the end.'

* Spelled ' quære.'—G.

VERSE 14.

'*As also you have acknowledged us in part, that we are your rejoicing, even as ye are ours in the day of the Lord Jesus.*' You have acknowledged us in part, now since you have repented; for when he wrote the former epistle to them, they had many corruptions among them in doctrine and in conversation about the sacrament, many corrupt opinions they had; and in ' conversation ' they endured the incestuous man among them, without casting of him out; and many of them doubted of the resurrection. Now, when he wrote the first epistle, it took a blessed effect in their hearts; they repented, and began to acknowledge St Paul, notwithstanding they were distasted of him by reason of the bad information of some presumptuous teachers. Saith he now again, ' You have acknowledged us in part that now we are your rejoicing,' &c. Observe this, which I touch by way of coherence,

Obs. It is a sign of a repentant man, of a man that hath repented of his sins, and is in a good estate, to acknowledge him that hath told him of his sins, to acknowledge his pastor.

For a false heart swells against the reproof. If the Corinthians had not been sound-hearted, they would never have endured St Paul's sharp epistles. But now he tells them their own plainly (as indeed it is a very sharp epistle in many passages), yet now they acknowledge him to be a good and gracious man, a faithful teacher.

Use. Let it be a trial of your estate, can you endure a plain, a powerful, an effectual ministry? More particularly, can you endure a plain, effectual friend, that brings that which is spoken by the minister more particularly home to your hearts? It is a sign of a good heart, of a repentant heart, that would be better. But if not, it is a sign you have a reserved love to some special sin that will be your bane; it is a sign your souls have not repented. As you see after in another chapter of this epistle, where he sets down the fruits of repentance, vii. 9, 10. And here is one sign, ' You have acknowledged us in part,' &c.

In the words,

First, *there is the thing itself*—' acknowledgment.'

Secondly, *the object-matter of it*, ' that we are your rejoicing, and you are ours.' There is a mutual intercourse of rejoicing.

And then *the time is set down*, ' the day of the Lord Jesus,' the second coming of Christ.

To speak a little of ' acknowledgment.'

' Acknowledgment ' is more than knowledge; for knowledge is a bare, naked apprehension, and acknowledgment is when the will and affections yield to the entertaining and the owning of the thing known. As a father not only knows his son, but acknowledgeth him; a king acknowledgeth his subjects, and the subjects their prince. It is not only a knowledge of such men, but an acknowledging of them, acknowledging a relation to them. So you acknowledge us; that is, in the relation we stand to you, to be faithful and good ministers, and good men too.

What doth St Paul mean by saying, ' You have acknowledged us ? Doth he mean himself ?

No ; not altogether ; but you have acknowledged me in my faithful preaching of Christ to you. Wheresoever the minister is acknowledged as a minister, Christ is acknowledged. For what are we ? We are but the ministers of Christ, no more, nor no less.   Saith St Paul, ' Let a man esteem of us as of the ministers of Christ,' 1 Cor. iv. 1.   If they think of us more than ministers, that we can make and coin things of our own, they think too much of us; if they think meanly and basely of us, they think too little of us.   ' Let a man think of us as of the ministers of Christ,' no more, nor no less.   It is enough that they acknowledge us so as the ministers of Christ.   So they are never acknowledged, but Christ is acknowledged by them; for they have a relative office, they are the ministers *of Christ.*

How shall we know then whether we acknowledge the minister or no ?   If we acknowledge Christ first by him.

How shall we know that we acknowledge Christ ?

1. *To acknowledge Christ, God-man in his natures, that we have a great deal of love to him, that he would be born for us ; and a great deal of reverence, in that he is God.*   We must not think of him but with a great deal of reverence, and meddle with nothing of him but with much love ; he is God-man, God incarnate.   He acknowledgeth Christ in his priestly office, that doth not despair, that doth believe his full satisfaction to God ; and doth not mingle other things, popish satisfaction, and purgatory for venial sins.   He acknowledgeth Christ's priestly office, that goes boldly to God through Christ's intercession in heaven, and boldly trusts in the satisfaction of Christ in the clamours of conscience, and the accusations of Satan.   This is to acknowledge Christ a priest in our boldness and liberty to God, and confidence in our conscience of the forgiveness of sins.   To acknowledge Christ as a King, is to yield subjection to his word, and to suffer him to rule us.   To acknowledge him as a prophet, to be instructed, and guided by him.

But now such as are ruled by their own lusts, and by the examples of others, and care not for the spiritual leading of Christ, they do not acknowledge him.   ' Let not this man reign over us,' Luke xix. 14.   They shake off his bands, they are ' sons of Belial,' Judg. xix. 22, without yoke.   And they shall be reckoned at the day of judgment among them that know not Christ; because to know him, and not to acknowledge him, is to no purpose.   As God knoweth us well enough ; but if he know us not, and acknowledge us to be his, what will become of us at the day of judgment ?   ' I know you not,' Mat. xxv. 12, saith he, that is, he acknowledgeth them not to be his.   So, if our knowledge be to know Christ generally, so as not to give up ourselves to be ruled by him, to be directed by him, this is not to acknowledge him ; and to know him, and not to acknowledge him, will be no comfort for us ; as it will be no comfort to us for him to know us, and not to acknowledge us.   They that acknowledge Paul, or any minister, they are brought to acknowledge Christ by him.

2. And then, to give you a familiar taste of these things, they do acknowledge the minister, *that acknowledge the word to be the word of God, to be from him.*   What is that ?   When they are cast into the form and mould of the word, and are willing to be framed, to be such as the word would have them, to be pliable to it; if it threaten, to be terrified; if it comfort, to be raised up ; to be fashioned every way to the word.   Then they acknowledge the word, then they feel it to be God's word.   Why ?   For they feel it leavening the soul, making all the powers holy and comfortable.   As leaven changeth the whole lump, so the word of God, when we are cast into it, and embrace it, it frames and fashions the whole man to be holy, as the word is holy.

This is to acknowledge the word of God, to hear it as the word of God, to hear it with reverence, as we would hear something from a great potentate, from a judge, from a man that hath to do with us. We know the word of God, and acknowledge him in the minister, when we tremble at it, and hear it with obedience. As Cornelius saith, ' We are all here in the presence of God, to hear whatsoever shall be commanded us of God,' Acts x. 33, ' whatsoever,' without distinction, and turning over, and declining the word, and shifting. When there is a willing yielding to everything that is told us, and a meaning to obey it, this is to acknowledge the word of God, or else we do not.

St Paul saith comfortably to the Thessalonians, ' That they received the word of God, as the word of God,' that is, they acknowledged the word of God, because they heard it with such reverence, and obedience, and respect.

So you may know that you acknowledge the minister, if you acknowledge Christ, if you acknowledge the preacher, and the word that he preacheth ; and you acknowledge him when you will be directed by him ; when he speaks in the name of Christ, to esteem highly of the ' consolations of the Almighty,' Job xv. 11, in his mouth, to suffer the strongholds of sin to be beaten down by his ministry. This is to acknowledge the minister. There is no good taken by God's ordinance, where * it is not only known, but acknowledged.

Christ comes to us in his ministers as well as by the poor, and it shall be known one day that we have rejected, not poor men like ourselves, but Jesus Christ. For we are joined with Christ in acceptation, or in neglect and contempt. What we do in our ministry faithfully, we are joined with Christ in our acceptance. We accept Christ, when we accept and esteem of the minister ; or we reject Christ, when we reject, and refuse, and set light by the ministers of Christ.

The hypocrisy of man's heart is not discerned almost so much in anything as in this. Let any command come from great men that have power of our bodies or estates to advance us, or debase us, Oh! there is much astonishment, and much heed taken. Wondrous heed of penal laws and statutes, that we run not into the dint of them! Now God by his ministers threatens hell, and damnation, hardness of heart, and to throw us from one sin to another ; we hear these things as judges, forsooth, as if they concerned us not. It shall one day be known that they are God's ministers, and that it is God's word, if we have grace to acknowledge them as speaking from God. This is to acknowledge the minister, to be directed by him, and to hear that that he speaks in the name of God. ' We are ambassadors of God,' saith St Paul, ' and entreat you, as if Christ himself were on earth he would entreat you, to be reconciled to God,' 2 Cor. v. 20. Therefore when you refuse our entreaty, you refuse Christ that comes with us. Those that will not hear him here shall hear that sentence hereafter. They must not think to be regarded of him then. But of that I shall speak hereafter.

' As ye have acknowledged us in part.' You acknowledge us ministers, you acknowledge our doctrine, you acknowledge Christ by us.

How do these Corinthians acknowledge St Paul in part ?

' *That we are your rejoicing, even as ye are ours, in the day of the Lord Jesus.*' ' You have acknowledged us, that we are your rejoicing.' What

* Qu. ' but where ?'—ED.

is the meaning of that ? You have acknowledged us, that you have cause to rejoice much, to the day of judgment, and then you shall rejoice to purpose, that ever I was your apostle, that ever you had grace to hearken to me ; that ever you had such a sincere downright apostle, that would tell you the truth, and gain you to Christ.

'That we are your rejoicing.' Whence we may observe, that—

Doct. A faithful minister is the rejoicing of the people.

Those people that are good, and have any grace in them, and not only here, but they will be so at the day of judgment.

Why ?

Reason. Because a faithful minister brings to them him that is the cause of all joy ; him that is Isaac, ' laughter,' Christ Jesus, at whose very birth there was a message of joy from heaven.

For all joy and all glory is originally and fundamentally in God reconciled. That is certain. There is our joy in God reconciled. For naturally, before God be reconciled, our hearts are full of confusion ; they are so far from joy and glory, that they are full of horror. Now God is reconciled by Christ's satisfaction and obedience, his full satisfaction witnessed by his resurrection ; and thereupon comes our glorying, to be in Christ, who hath brought us to be at one with God, with the God of glory. ' Blessed be God, the Father of our Lord Jesus Christ,' saith St Peter, ' that hath begotten us to a lively hope through the resurrection of Jesus Christ,' &c., 1 Pet. i. 3. Now we have a lively hope, we have a glorious hope, we may glory in it, in the resurrection of Christ ; considering that his resurrection is an evidence that the debt is paid, our Surety being out of prison, he being risen again.

But all this must be opened to us, and offered to us, and applied to us, by the ministry. What Christ hath done, and what he will do, it must be opened to us, and offered to us ; to receive Christ thus graciously bringing us to God. And faith must be wrought in us, to join us to Christ ; and this is by the ministry.

Now in the next place, when the ministry doth this, *it doth teach us that God is reconciled by the satisfaction of Christ, and teacheth the nature and offices of Christ, and the benefits we have by Christ.* It unfolds ' the unsearchable riches of Christ,' Eph. iii. 8. The ministry offers Christ ; and God by his Spirit works grace in the ministry, to believe, and to walk worthy of Christ. Hereupon comes glorying in the ministry ; in the preaching of Christ faithfully, crucified and risen, and teaching us to walk worthy of Christ.

So it is not that any man should glory in the minister for himself ; but in that he brings us to Christ, which Christ brings us to God, in whom is all our glory. So we see the ground of it, how St Paul was the rejoicing of the Corinthians, because he brought them to Christ.

The office of the minister is to be wooers, to make up the marriage between Christ and Christians' souls. Now herein is the rejoicing in a good minister, when we are brought to Christ ; and then see the riches of our husband unfolded by the ministry. Here is matter of joy, especially at the day of judgment. Then we shall joy indeed that ever we knew such a minister, that ever we knew such a holy man, that was a means to bring us to Christ, and to God.

Hereupon it is that the ministers are said to be a special gift of God, Eph. iv. 11. ' Christ when he ascended on high, he led captivity captive, and gave gifts to men.' What gifts ? ' Some apostles, some prophets, some pastors, some teachers, to the end of the world, for the building of his church.' Christ when he went in triumph, after his resurrection, when in his ascension he went triumphantly to heaven (as the great emperors, on the day of their triumph, they scattered money, so), he scattered gifts ; and they were not mean gifts, money, and such trifling things ; but when he went in his triumphant chariot to heaven, he had no better gifts to leave to the world, than to give such kind of gifts as these—he left ministers, apostles, to found a church ; he left pastors and teachers to the end of the world. These were the gifts that Christ gave when he went in triumph to heaven ; therefore well may they joy in the ministers as a special gift of God.

So there is a notable place, Jer. iii. 14, 15. There is a promise, if they would turn to God, and be a gracious people, what he would do. ' I will give you pastors according to my own heart, and feed you with knowledge and understanding,' insinuating that it is a special blessing ; it is a blessing above all blessings in this world, indeed, none comparable. To live in a place where all solaces are, where all worldly contentments ; yet to be there where the sound of the gospel is not, where the best things are not, it is but a dead place. What is it to be fatted to destruction ? what life to the life of grace ? and how is the life of grace begun and strengthened, but by the means of salvation ? When God gives pastors according to his own heart, to feed his people with understanding and judgment, it is a great blessing, and so it is matter of rejoicing and glorying. For may not the soul reason thus ?—Who am I ? that when thousands sit in darkness, and in the shadow of death, God should send his ambassadors to me, to offer Christ Jesus with all his riches to me ; and by his Holy Spirit effect it, by such and such a ministry working grace in me, to give me the first fruits of glory, the pledge of salvation, the beginning of grace here, when millions of other people sit in darkness ? Thus a Christian rejoiceth in God first, and then rejoiceth in the minister. He rejoiceth in everything that is an occasion to bring him to heaven.

What is the reason God brings us to heaven by the ministry of men, and doth not send angels, or do all by his Spirit without help ?

Amongst the rest, this is one, he would have one to glory in another, he would tie one to another. Therefore, it ties one man to another, this relation to see the need of God's ordinance, and that people might rejoice one in another as the gift of God. Therefore, he calls man by man, to knit man to man, and that they may see God's love to them in men. They saw Christ's love to them in St Paul. St Paul saw Christ's love to him in them, in their obedience. This is the reason that God useth men to call men.

Therefore, those that neglect the ordinance of God, let them never think of glory by Christ, that glory not in the minister that brings them to Christ. Therefore, 2 Cor. v. 19, they are excellently joined together, ' God was in Christ reconciling the world to himself.' What then ? What need the ministry if God be reconciled to the world in Christ ? God is merciful, and Christ died, and there is an end. No ; he hath put to us apostles, and after us to pastors and teachers, ' the word of reconciliation,' and we, ' as ambassadors, entreat you in Christ's stead to be reconciled to God.' So there is no word of reconciliation effectual to any but we must have the efficacy of it by embassage, it must be offered by the ministry.

This ministry, contemned by the world, must be the means to bring us to Christ. We have no benefit brought to us from God unless it be by the word of reconciliation. Neglect the word, neglect reconciliation itself. Therefore it is called, ' the word of the kingdom,' ' the word of grace,' ' the word of life,' insinuating that if we neglect the word unfolded by God's ordinance in the church, we neglect grace, we neglect life, we neglect [the] kingdom, and all; because we see they are joined together. I will not be long in this point in this place.

Use. Only this, when God doth vouchsafe any abroad wheresoever, or to any of us, to partake of his ordinance in an effectual, holy manner, *to joy in it.* As Solomon saith, Prov. xix. 14, ' Inheritance comes by parents, but a good wife is the gift of God.' So a good minister, or a true Christian friend, is the gift of God that he bestows on men, a special gift; because it is in order to eternal happiness. It is such a gift as Christ gave when he ascended into heaven. So much for that point, ' We are your rejoicing.'

' As also ye are ours.' There is an intercourse of joy. We are your rejoicing, ' and ye are ours,' in the day of the Lord.

How were they St Paul's rejoicing?

They were St Paul's rejoicing as they were gained to God and to Christ by his ministry. When he looked on them, he looked on them as people given him by God. As God said to him of them in the ship when they suffered shipwreck, ' I have given thee all their lives,' Act xxvii. 23, *seq.*

It was a great honour to St Paul that God should give him the lives of all that were in the ship, but more honour that God gave him so many souls. Thou shalt have the honour of saving so many souls. Therefore, they were his rejoicing, in the day of the Lord especially, but now they were his rejoicing, because by faith he apprehended that they should be his special rejoicing when he and they should stand together before the judgment seat of Christ. For faith makes things to come present. ' Ye are our rejoicing, because you shall be our rejoicing then more especially. This is the nature of faith, to present things absent. For blessed St Paul, now in heaven, when at the day of judgment he shall stand before Christ with all the rank about him of Corinthians, Ephesians, Philippians, &c., and all the churches he converted,—when he shall be environed with them as so many brought in triumph under the kingdom of Christ, and pulled from the bondage of Satan (as what a world of people did he bring to God, what triumph did he make over Satan and the corruption of men, bringing men into captivity to Christ!)—when all these shall be set before him, what a glory will this be for holy St Paul, when he shall look on all these blessed people as conquered and brought under Christ's government by him! And so for all the apostles, St Peter and the rest; and so for every minister, when he shall say, ' Here I am, and the souls that thou hast given me,' John xvii. 12. Thou hast honoured me so much as to be an instrument to gain them to Christ, to bring them to heaven, a special glory. The point of doctrine or truth I observe hence is this, that

Doct. The people's proficiency in grace is the minister's joy.

The people's good estate in grace is the minister's joy, and will be, especially after the day of judgment. ' Ye are our rejoicing.' As he saith, Philip. iv. 1, ' Ye are our crown and our glory.' And so, 1 Thess. ii. 19, ' What is our crown and rejoicing? Is it not you?'

In every epistle almost, those good and gracious people, he makes them his hope, and joy, and crown, and rejoicing.

In what sense?

1. Because they were the *objective matter of his joy.* When he looked

on them, he looked on such as yielded him comfort. He could not present them to his thoughts, but he thought of them as matter of joy. Here be the people that God hath honoured me to do much good unto. He could not think of them but as the object of his rejoicing. The word is *Cauchema*,* ' our rejoicing,' that God had given them to him to bring to heaven.

Love descends, we know, and the workman looks upon his work with a kind of complacency. St Paul could not look upon those that he was used as a blessed instrument to do good upon, without a special kind of delight. They were the object matter of his joy.

2. Then, again, they were not only the matter of his joy and rejoicing, presenting to his soul comfortable considerations, but also they *were some means to increase his joy in heaven ;* for ' those that convert souls shall shine as the stars in the firmament,' Dan. xii. 3. Those that are honoured of God so far as to bring souls to God, ' they shall shine as the stars in the firmament,' especially those that convert souls shall have a degree of honour above others, though the substantial glory be by Christ. It is not to be denied that the accidental increased glory comes by the increase of the fruit of the ministry ; and so Christians, those that are fruitful Christians, that do much good, they shall have much glory. St Paul shall have more rejoicing than others that did not so much good as he. ' Ye are our rejoicing,' because you shall be a means of my greater rejoicing. They were the object of his joy and the means of his joy.

3. Then in the third place, they were his rejoicing, because they were the *seal of his ministry, that he was a sound minister.* How was it known whether St Paul were a good minister or no ? Behold his works ! see how he wrought on such and such people ! how many he gained to God ! When he looked on them, he looked on them as a seal of his ministry, that he was a good minister, and in that regard they were his rejoicing.

4. And in some regard likewise in the fourth place, that their gaining *was an evidence to his soul that he was a good man.* Ordinarily (though God convert men by ill men, as Judas no question might convert some, yet) for the most part God honours his servants ; and he that is heat himself, can kindle another. Those that are not heat with grace, they cannot speak of the efficacy and power of the things they feel not in their own hearts, as others do. Therefore no question but it comforted him in the state of Christianity, that God honoured him to be a means to bring others in to Christ. So in many respects the people's goodness is the minister's joy.

Use. If this be so, let those that are under the ministry not deny themselves that comfort, or the ministers that joy to be good. There are many poisonful, spiteful spirits that are in love with damnation, that will cherish the corruptions of their naughty nature, in spite of God and all. Rather than they will acknowledge to be wrought on by such and such, to be their children, they will be as they are ; they will be broken in a thousand pieces before they will bend to any minister, upon such weak resolutions to yield to a poor ordinance of man. Here is the devilish pride and poison of man's corrupt nature. Can we set light by that, but that at the same time we must set light by our own comfort and salvation ?

How were the Corinthians St Paul's joy ? Were they not their own joy first ? They were matter of joy to St Paul, because he saw he had gained them to Christ. The good was especially theirs. It reflected on him only by consideration. When he looked on them he was comforted ; but

* That is, καύχημα.—G.

they were more comforted a great deal. They had more comfort in his rejoicing than he. His was but by reflection of their goodness, a comfort that came by consideration. They had the main comfort of their goodness.

It is little comfort for any to carry themselves so, as that those that are over them in Christ Jesus, when they think of them, can but sigh, when they hear their blasphemies ; when they cannot so much as gain of them to leave courses that the very light of nature condemns. The filthy discoveries of a rotten heart, their vile words, and their offensive carriage, can this be a grief to the minister, and not for the damnation of their souls together ? And they shall find it a heavy and bitter thing to grieve the Spirit of God in others, as well as they wound their own conscience. Both are joined together.

What a happiness is this, that the more a man is interested in the good of another man, the more glory, if he be a means of any good in him ! He shall have good, and you shall have glory.

The best things in nature are communicative and diffusive. The sun gives light to the whole world. So the best man is most fruitful, and communicative. He labours to gain all men by his acquaintance. He knows this, that he is not for himself. He is redeemed for the honour of Christ. And then he knows that another's good will be my glory. It will increase my glory, and be the object of my glory.

On the contrary, we see a company of wretched, despicable creatures, (let their outward estate be as glorious as it will ; but I speak of them as Christian eyes judge and esteem of them), that draw others on to the same course with them. If they be blasphemers themselves, they glory to make others so ; if they be given to sensuality, they labour to make others sottish as themselves ; if they be given to filthiness, they draw others to communion with themselves. Well ! will these people be much for their rejoicing in the day of the Lord, think you ? What will they do when they think of others, such as they have neglected altogether, that God gave them charge of ? The very thought of them, instead of making them rejoice, it will make them astonished. I betrayed his soul,—he was my friend,—or my servant,— I let him live in such sins. Good neglected will torment us hereafter. But then ill infused, by example, and by word, I poisoned him ; suppose I have repented myself, but perhaps the person that I have drawn to communion in my sin, hath not repented ; what a torment will this consideration be ! Good neglected will be matter of torment, much more evil infused, poison infused. When we shall see at the day of judgment, instead of a company that we have gained to God, and been a means to further their salvation, we shall see a company that we have infected with our ill example, and our evil persuasions, this will be in hell an increase of torment.

One will curse another, and say, You brought me hither. The father will curse the son. To get riches for you I cracked my conscience, and lost my soul. And the son shall curse the father. By your riches that you left me, I lived a base and sensual life, whereas perhaps I might have trusted to my good endeavours otherwise. So here shall be cursing. The friend shall curse his friend. You might have told me of this, you strengthened me in evil courses.

As it will be our glory when we shall see such and such, as God hath used as instruments to do good unto ; so it will be a torment indeed to think, such and such I neglected and betrayed, such and such I corrupted. I beseech you, therefore, take heed of it.

And would you have matter of joy in this world, that should joy you when nothing else will joy you ? (as St Paul was in affliction oft) what comforted St Paul ? First, his own conscience, that he was a good Christian, an heir of heaven, a good apostle. But when he wanted joy, what would he do ? when he had no liberty, but was imprisoned, when he had nothing, then he considered, how hath Christ dignified me to do good to others ? This honouring of him to do this, it comforted him more than all his imprisonment, and abasement, and reproaches could discourage him ; the conceit that God did use him as an honourable instrument for his honour and service, to do good to others.

So the testimony of our conscience, that God hath used us to do good to others, not only to make me to gain heaven, but to be an instrument to gain others, this will comfort us in the world, come what will.

Use. This should stir up those that have to deal with the souls of others, (not only ministers, but all others), that have any committed to them, that they should labour to make them good, to work upon them for the good of their souls, that they may have them as matter, and objects, of their joy at that day. If they do not, as I said, when they are presented to them as persons whom they have neglected and betrayed negligently for want of instruction, and reformation of their lives, and as persons whom they have infected with their ill example, which is worse, alas ! what matter of horror will they be. They will not say of them as St Paul saith here, ' You are my joy, and my crown, and my glory,' but they will be matter of horror. These be they that I have betrayed, and neglected, and infected, and brought to hell, to this cursed condition with myself. It will be an increase of the torments of hell at that day, all those whom we have hurt any kind of way.

But what shall it be then of those that have opposed goodness ? that have not only betrayed others by neglect, but have maligned good where they have seen it ? What will become of them, that are so far from making others good, that they have despited the image of God in others, and have exercised their bitterness upon Christ in his members and ministers?

To add one thing more.

What ! these Corinthians, that had so many abuses, and such weaknesses, were they the matter of St Paul's joy ?

Yes ! why, therefore people must take heed how they leave churches that have corruptions in them. Schism ofttimes is a greater fault than the fault upon which they pretend separation. The things for which they pretend a rent, are not so great a fault in the church, as the want of charity in them to do so. If St Paul would have taken occasion to leave them, what good occasion had he ? Alas ! how many corruptions had they in doctrine, and in manners too. But yet, notwithstanding, as ill as they were, he saw what good was in them, and looked not to the evil : he knew that God would perfect the good things that were in them ; and, saith he, notwithstanding all their infirmities, I see you were ready to reform when I wrote an epistle to you, therefore I doubt not but you will be ' our rejoicing.'

' *In the day of the Lord Jesus.*' This is the time. It must be taken inclusively, ' I am your rejoicing, and you are mine, to the day of the Lord Jesus, and in the day of the Lord.' So he means here. It is laid as a ground here, that

Obs. Jesus Christ hath a day.

It is his day by way of eminency and excellency. Jesus Christ hath many days, two especially ; the day of his first coming, and the day of his second coming. The first coming of Christ was the day of the gospel, when he came to work our salvation. His second coming is to accomplish our salvation. In his first day he came to be humbled, and to be judged, to be a sacrifice for us. In his second, he is to come gloriously to judge the quick and the dead. In the first, he came to gain a church to himself ; by his second he shall come to accomplish the marriage. Now is the contract ; there is the Sabbath. After the six days of this life the day of the Lord shall appear, the Sabbath day, the day of jubilee, the solemnisation of the marriage, the solemn triumph over all enemies. The first day was to save our souls, especially from the thraldom of sin and Satan. The second day, this that we speak of here, shall be to save our bodies from the rottenness and corruption in which they have lain rotting in the grave till that day of Christ. As he raised his own body, so at that day he shall raise our bodies, and make them ' like his glorious body,' Phil. iii. 21. That is the main day, the day of all days, for then he will come to accomplish all. That day shall never have a night, it shall be day for ever.

As the cloud that went before the Israelites to Canaan, that side toward the Egyptians was dark, but the other side was lightsome toward the Israelites ; so this day, it shall be a dark day, it shall be both a day of vengeance and a day of glory.

St Paul saith here, ' You shall be my rejoicing,' and I yours at that day. But those that do not believe the gospel, and obey the ministry of it, it shall not be a day of rejoicing to them. It shall be a glorious day when all other glory shall vanish. All other glory in the world shall be eclipsed, even as the stars are not seen when the sun appears in the firmament. All the glory at that day shall be the glory of Christ, and of his church. To omit other things that may be spoken out of other places of Scripture, the point I will observe hence is this, that,

Doct. The measure of a Christian's rejoicing in this world in anything, it is the consideration of what it will be at the great day of judgment.

I say, the rule whereby a Christian judgeth things, and that measure whereby a Christian measures things, to be thus or thus in their excellency and worth, it is as they will be esteemed at that day of the Lord Jesus Christ. Here St Paul saith, ' I am your rejoicing, and you are ours at the day of the Lord Jesus.' What ! is this a vain glorying to commend him ? Oh ! he is a worthy learned rabbi, a great learned apostle ; and then that they were such and such people ! No, no ! They had grace wrought in them ; and St Paul saw such evidences of grace in them, that at that day they should look upon Christ with boldness, because they were sincerely gained to the gospel. So then this must be the rule of the worth of anything, to esteem it as it will be then at that day ; which is a day when all our estates will be determined of, for eternal happiness or eternal misery.

To explain it a little.

We do not value things of short continuance, because they are short, as flowers that are fresh in the morning, and cast away at night ; but we esteem things that will hold out. So our rejoicing, and glory, and comfort, we should consider of it how it will hold out, ' Riches avail not in the day of wrath,' Prov. xi. 4. Things have that degree of goodness or evil in them, they have that degree of vanity, or seriousness, as they will stand out at that day. What are riches in the day of wrath, even in this world ? What will

riches be then at the day of the Lord Jesus ?   Therefore a Christian values
them not ; they are not the good of a Christian ; he esteems not the applause
of men.   And pleasures are nothing, they are momentary, they avail not
when conscience is awaked.   They leave a man, and not only so, but they
leave a sting behind them.

If all the good things in the world will stand us in no stead then, then
what will the sins do that thou hast made so much of ?   What will the sins
do that thou hast betrayed and damned thy soul for ?   Thy filthiness, and
thy betraying of goodness, what will that do ?   How wilt thou look the
Judge in the face, whenas nothing in the world that is excellent will hold
out and avail at that day ?

But what then will avail at that day when Christ shall come to judge
both the quick and the dead ?

Why, this ; that thou hast submitted thyself to acknowledge Christ as
thy king, and thy priest, and thy prophet ; and by means of the ministry
thou hast been wrought on, and the work of the new creature is begun in
thee, true and sincere grace that thou darest look on Christ, that thou art
in the state of grace, this will comfort thee in the day of judgment.

By this you may discern who take the wisest course : he that measures
his life by a right measure and rule.   Who judgeth aright of persons and
things ?   He judgeth aright of things, that values and labours to interest
himself in those things that will comfort him in this world, and stand
by him in the world to come ; he hath a right judgment and esteem of
things.

What be those things ?

Grace, a holy, humble, gracious, believing carriage and disposition.
When a man gives himself to Christ, and renounceth the world, and sees
the vanity of all things but the estate of Christianity, he hath those things
in some little measure that shall be perfected at that day.   Who take the
wisest course ?   Those that seek to please the humour of men, those that
seek to feed their own corruptions and the corruptions of others, those that
will have some present glory in the flesh ?   Aye, but what will they have at
the day of the Lord Jesus ?   Surely, those that labour to approve themselves in sincerity and truth to Christ Jesus in all things.   And so that
they may approve their hearts to him, they care not what the world judgeth
of them, as St Paul saith, ' I pass not what ye judge of me,' 1 Cor. iv. 3.
If there be a day of the Lord, when he shall be judge, then those are the
wisest and the best courses that will hold out at that day.   And those that
will not, we shall be ashamed of them all.

And that is the reason that many men of excellent parts and endowments
are comfortless in the time of temptation.   They did not think to do things
with reference to Christ, in sincerity to please him ; for then they might
hold up their heads at that day.

There is a great deal of atheism in our hearts.   We frame our courses
to present contentments, by reason that we have little belief for the time to
come.

I beseech you, let us often have in our thoughts the second coming of
Christ.   The best things are behind.   Our chief rejoicing is behind.   Our
rejoicing now is our hope that we shall rejoice then.   The Corinthians were
St Paul's joy now, because he knew they should be his main rejoicing then.
If we rejoice in anything now, let it be that our names are written in heaven,
in the testimony of our conscience that we are God's, that our hearts are
rought on, that we have something that Christ will acknowledge when he

sees his stamp and image on us. When he shall look on us, and see his own image upon our hearts, there will be matter of joy in that day.

There will be joy in ourselves, and joy in all the blessed instruments that are under Christ. The ministers, they shall rejoice likewise in us, and all of us shall join in joying in Christ, all shall meet there. For their joying in St Paul, and he in them, it was that Christ was theirs. And 'Christ shall come,' as it is in 2 Thess. i. 10, 'to be glorified in his saints;' not only in himself, but in his believing members; for his glory shall reflect upon them as the sun reflects upon light bodies. All light bodies are made light by the sun. So the 'Sun of righteousness' shall come, and all them that have glory it shall be by reflection from him; they shall be glorious in him. So he is both the minister's joy and the people's. They shall all glory in Christ, whose glory is their glory. He shall come 'to be glorious in his saints.' Therefore frame your courses that way to have glory then, to have comfort in the hour of death, and at the day of judgment. And to end the point,

Let us labour to be acquainted with him now before that day. We shall never have comfort in the day of the Lord Jesus, except we be acquainted with him, and acknowledge him in the ministry now, and in the sacraments; for none shall ever be acquainted with him there, that have not been acquainted with him, and known him in this world.

How do we come to be acquainted with Christ?

To be present where he is present; and he is present where two or three are met together in his name. He is present now in our meetings, he is present when we hear the word. He is present in the sacrament more especially; we have his very body and blood. As verily as we take the outward signs, so verily Christ is present to our hearts; at the same time from heaven, he reacheth us himself with all the benefits of his passion. When the minister reacheth the bread, he reacheth his body. As our outward man is refreshed with the elements, so our souls are refreshed with the spiritual presence of Christ. Now he is excellently present in heaven, he is present to our senses in the sacrament, and by his Spirit in the word.

Would you have him then at his appearing come and own you, and say then, 'Come, ye blessed?' Mat. xxv. 34 ; be acquainted with him now upon all occasions, hear the word, receive the sacrament, and come to the sacrament as acknowledging him there.

How is that?

Why, then, you acknowledge the bread and wine to be seals of him, and of all the blessings by him, when you come prepared, when you come to them as his. Or else you do not acknowledge them. You know them to be such and such things, but you acknowledge them not to be set apart for such a holy use, except you come with prepared hearts.

Will anybody acknowledge him to go to a great person, when he goes deformed and in rags ? Do you know whither you go ? would some say to him. He considers not whither he goes, that comes to the sacrament in his old sins. Come acquainted therefore with Christ, to acknowledge him that shall be your judge at the latter day ; therefore come prepared.

And then, because the sacrament is a means to seal to us all the benefits we have by Christ, and to incorporate us more nearly into Christ, he that comes to the sacrament as he should, must come with joy. Is it not a joyful thing to be united to Christ, and to have further assurance of all the good things by him ? Yes ! it is a matter of great joy. Therefore, when you have repented of your sins, come with joy.

And come with holiness. The things are holy, as our liturgy hath it; let us give holy things to holy persons. Here is presented holy bread and wine, and here you are to deal with Christ. Therefore come with holy reverence in the whole carriage of the business.

And come with faith and assurance, and then you shall acknowledge Christ in this ordinance, in the sacrament. You shall acknowledge that he deals not complimentally with you, to feed you with empty signs; but you shall have himself with his signs; you shall have the Lord himself in the word, and in the sacraments. With the field you shall have the treasure in the field, as the wise merchant had, Mat. xiii. 44. With the word you shall have Christ wrapped in the word. And in the sacrament you shall have Christ and all his benefits. Trust to it, make it your weapon against Satan, he will tempt you to doubt of your interest in Christ. Think with yourselves, Had I grace to receive Christ? to be incorporate nearer into him? why should I doubt to renew my covenant? And though I have fallen by weakness, yet I have a gracious intercessor in heaven that makes my peace continually. Come in faith. Know that God in good earnest here offers Christ with all his benefits.

And come with a purpose and resolution to be led by him. You come to renew your covenant. Here is the covenant, when Christ is given to you, and you give yourselves to Christ. Therefore, as I said, if you come with a purpose to live in sin, come not at all. Christ will not live in a heart where there is a purpose to sin. Therefore resolve to leave all sin, or else you cannot receive him.

To move you to come, and to come thus, do but consider that it will be your joy in this world, and in the world to come, before Christ, that you have been thus acquainted with him here on earth, acquainted with him in the ministry, acquainted with him in the sacrament, in private prayer, and meditation, in all the blessed means that he hath appointed: and then he will look on you as upon his old friends.

But now he that is a rebel, that goes away, or else comes, not acknowledging with whom he hath to deal; him that shall be his judge ere long, the great God of heaven and earth, that shall come in glory and majesty with thousands of his angels. Then he shall be 'wonderful' indeed, as his name is, Isa. ix. 6; and as the apostle saith, 2 Thess. i. 10, where he useth the word, 'he shall be wonderful in his saints.' Then all the world shall wonder at the glory of a poor Christian, when he shall put down the sun, and all the creatures in glory. Consider with whom you have to deal, him that ere long shall be wonderful in his saints. Therefore come prepared, come joyfully, come faithfully, come reverently and holily, and you shall find a blessing answerable. This I thought good to touch concerning the occasion of the sacrament. 'Ye are our rejoicing.'

'At the day of the Lord Jesus.' St Paul esteemed of nothing but that which would comfort him at that day. Therefore let us oft think of the day of the Lord Jesus. Why? What will make us digest labour, and pains, in dealing with the souls of others, in doing good, and being fruitful in our places? The consideration of that day. There is a day will come that will make amends for all, and that is the day of the Lord Jesus.

And considering that there is such a day, let us make much of the day of the Lord that is now left us. What is that? This day. 'The Lord's day.' It is called 'The Lord's day,' Rev. i. 10. And as I said, labour to be acquainted with that Lord that must be judge of quick and dead then.

The Lord hath a day now wherein we may be acquainted with him ; by hearing his word, by yielding obedience to his truth unfolded to us ; therefore let us make much of this day, if we would have comfort at that day. ' Ye are our rejoicing in the day of the Lord.'

VERSE 15.

' *And in this confidence I was minded to come unto you before, that you might have a second benefit, or grace.*' ' In this confidence.' In this assurance, in this persuasion, ' I was minded to come to you.'

' That you might have a second benefit,' saith the last translation (*ddd*). It doth diminish the strength of the word. Therefore go from the text to the margin. You have ofttimes a fitter word in the margin.

Charis.* The word is pregnant in the original. It signifieth grace. If it signify a benefit at all, it signifies a benefit that issues from grace and favour. ' Benefit' is a weaker word. Grace, though it be not so common, is a fit word, and reaches to the strength of the word in the original, to the meaning of the apostle. So it is better to read it so, ' That you might have a second grace.'

St Paul in this verse sets down *what intention he had to come to them.*

And likewise, *the end of his intention.*

In the next verse he sets down, *the manner how he would come to them.*

Fourthly, he shews *why he came not to them ;* it was ' to spare them,' as he saith afterward.

Here in this verse he shews what his intention was. ' My intention was to come to you.' ' In this confidence I was minded to come to you.'

To what end ? ' That you might have a second benefit.'

His intention is set down by the inward moving cause, his ' confidence.' ' In this confidence I was minded to come to you.'

I will speak of his intention and purpose of coming ; and of the end of it. And in his purpose of coming, of the moving cause, his ' confidence.'

' *In this confidence.*' What is that ? ' In this confidence,' because I am assured that you are my rejoicing, and I yours in the day of the Lord Jesus ; in this confidence that you will be so to me, and I to you. ' In this confidence.'

St Paul had a good opinion of them. The inward moving cause of St Paul to come, it was a good conceit of them.

Obs. It is good, as far as possibly we can, to cherish a good judgment, and conceit of others.

Let others have as good place in our affections as possibly may be. Why ?

Reason 1. *If they be good, we wrong them else even in our conceit.* We do not only wrong men in our speeches and actions, but in our sinister judgments, in the censures of our minds. Therefore we should have as good conceit of men as possibly we can in that regard.

Reason 2. And likewise, *because confidence and assurance that they have something in them that is good, and it will be better with them after in the day of the Lord, this will be a means to stir us up to deserve well of them.* Hope stirs up will. We have no mind to a thing that we have not hope of. And likewise hope stirs up endeavour, and hope keeps in endeavour. What

* That is, ' χάρις.' —G.

makes a man so long in endeavouring the good of others? He hath some hope. They are good, and will be better. So it stirs up our will. The bent of it, it stirs. It stirs up endeavour upon will; and it keeps us in endeavour when we hope for good at men's hands.

And therefore we ought not to cast off men, especially those that are young, for imperfections. The Corinthians were weak, and carnal, as you may see in the former epistle, yet in this confidence that they had repented of their ill usage of St Paul, he was minded to come to them. Persons that are the subjects of hope are not free from infirmities. Novices cannot have that perfection that grown Christians have, at the first. Consider further what is of passion, and what is of the poison of nature; consider what is of infirmity, and what is of malice; consider what sins they have been longer accustomed to, and how hardly such sins are suddenly broken off. These considerations would mitigate something where we see any degree of goodness.

Oh! this pleaseth now some vicious disposed persons. They think this makes for them.

Not at all; what I speak is, where there is any ground to hope well of. St Paul had some ground, for he wrote a sharp epistle to them, and he saw they were amended on it. He saw they yielded, they acknowledged, that is, they reformed by his ministry, and by his epistle. So where we discern reformation, that there is a willingness of amendment, we must hope of such, though they be sometimes overtaken. And if they be overtaken, we must construe it to the best. The temptation perhaps was great, and they were not watchful at that time. The subtlety of the opposition and the malice of men was great, and their caution was not so great. Thus we may construe to bear with them, if upon the discovery of their fault they become pliable. But otherwise, if they arm themselves with malice and bitter poison, and resolve to be so still, there is no hope, no confidence of such. St Paul's confidence here was with evidence from their carriage. They gave him some cause to be so confident.

Therefore it is in vain to think that we are too censorious when we tell you of your faults. That very conceit that you think bitterly, and arm yourselves with resolutions, rather to vex those that inform you than to amend that which is amiss, that is as ill a disposition, as ill a state as can be. We can hope for no good of such. Yet notwithstanding we ought so far to hope of them, as not to give them over, as St Paul saith, 2 Tim. ii. 25, 26, 'To prove if at any time God will shew mercy to them, to deliver them out of the snare of the devil.' They are in the devil's snare; yet we ought still to take pains with them. For we know not whether it will please God at that time, or at any time, to have mercy on them, and deliver them out of the snare of Satan.

If God bear with them, we ought to bear with them as well as teach them; but to have a good conceit of them, when we see them maliciously bent against those that tell them of their faults, we cannot.

Use. If this be so, it should be an encouragement for all those that are under others that inform and instruct them, to give them some good occasion and ground to hope well of them. You would have us hope well of you. What ground do you give? What is your company? Shall we think you are good because you converse with those that are swearers? with vicious and carnal company? Would you have us blind? Charity indeed interprets the best, but it is not blind. What shall we judge of you by your outward demeanour and carriage, that is ofttimes scandalous and offensive? when your speeches are filthy and corrupt, joined with blasphemies and oaths, daring God, as it were, whether he will suffer you to carry it away unrevenged and unpunished or not. Where this abominable corruption of heart discovers itself outwardly in the tongue, how can we entertain good conceits of you? You think wo wrong you by not conceiving thus and thus of you. What ground have we? what hold have we from anything that is in you or from you so to conceit? Resolve on this, there cannot be grievance offered to the minister, but you must reward ill to your own souls. If you be not his joy, it will be your sorrow. You will have the worst of it. And therefore study as much as may be to have the good hope and confidence of others. This will stir up willingness, and stir up endeavour, as it did in St Paul. The good hope he had of them by their repentance, and reformation, and pliableness, it stirred up his diligence. They gained by it. But I mean not to stand on that.

'In this confidence,' that you will be my joy, and I yours, in the day of Lord.

'*I was minded to come unto you.*' St Paul was minded to come unto them. You see then that

Obs. Personal presence hath a special power and efficacy.

Personal presence hath more efficacy than writing. For there the holy things that are delivered, they are, as it were, acted to the life. Men are wondrously affected when they see gracious things delivered with life and feeling: it hath a wondrous lively working. Therefore St Paul tells the Romans, Rom. i. 15, that besides his learned and worthy epistle he wrote to them, he was desirous also to preach the gospel to them.

But some object: reading is preaching, say they, some kind of preaching. But not that which the apostle meant; for then St Paul's epistle was preaching, some kind of preaching. But I speak not to sophisters. But, saith St Paul, I desire to preach the word to you by vocal teaching: it hath a special efficacy. It is wondrous good praying for others, and writing to others; but presence, when the minister is the mouth of God with them and to them, their mouth to God, to pray together with them, and God's mouth, to speak to them, this presence is of a wondrous efficacy; therefore St Paul saith, 'I purposed to come to you.'

Use. It should stir up in our hearts an esteem of the ordinance of God of preaching; or else we slight it with the prejudice of our own souls. For doth God appoint it for anything but for our own good? There is a common objection, which (because it is raised out of this epistle, and may be answered out of this epistle) I will answer.

Obj. Oh! say some, a lively voice hath not alway that energy, that operation, that writing and reading have; for we see St Paul's epistle was more terrible than his presence. It is the objection of men that content themselves in their own idleness, wresting off such places as this. Among the rest, 2 Cor. x. 10, say they, 'His bodily presence is weak, and his speech contemptible,' but his letters seem terrible. Therefore this is not alway true, that bodily presence hath more efficacy than writing.

Ans. I answer briefly,—St Paul compares not here his bodily presence with his letters, as if his letters were more efficacious than his bodily presence; but he compares his mild dealing, being present, with his sharp dealing, being absent; his letters, indeed, were sharper than his presence. But to take away such cavils, he tells them after that they shall know, if they reform not, that his presence shall be as sharp as his writings. Let

such a one think this, ' such as we are in word being absent, such will we
be when we are present.' We will be as sharp, if you reform not, in our
presence, as we were absent. So he compares the sharpness of his letter
with the sweetness of his presence. It is not to be taken in that sense,
that his letters were more effectual of themselves than his presence ; for he
saith the contrary, You shall know that my presence shall be as sharp as
my letter was. Therefore, it is but a cavil to think there is more efficacy
in reading, than in preaching.

' *That you might have a second grace.*' I come now to St Paul's end.
His intention and purpose was ' to come.' The end of his coming was
' to bestow a grace on them ' by his presence. In general observe here,
that

Obs. Holy men are set on work from holy moving causes, and holy aims.

Holy aims are the winds that carry them to their business, and they are
the water that drive their mill. I come with a holy confidence that you
will be my joy ; here is my moving cause. What is my aim in coming ?
It is this, to bestow a grace on you. Holy men have holy aims for holy
actions ; they have holy grounds, and holy moving causes.

When two men do the same thing, yet it is not the same thing ; perhaps
their aims differ, their moving causes differ. St Paul comes here to do a
good thing from a good end, from a good moving cause. ' In this confidence I was minded to come,' to bestow a grace on you.

Use. Let us look in all our actions, therefore, to our moving cause, and
to our aims. And especially ministers, their aim it should not be for the
fleece, it should not be to gain respect, or any advantage to themselves,
but to bestow some spiritual good thing. As the apostle saith, ' To bestow some good thing upon you,' Rom. i. 11, some grace, as he calls it.
This should be their aim, not to receive good from them, so much as to do
them good. Ministers are fathers, they should have that tender disposition. Parents do not think of receiving much (they look to that in the
second place, that must be maintained) ; but, especially, they look to their
children's good. ' I come to bestow a grace on you.' How this is observed,
I list not to speak, therefore I leave it, and come to that which concerns us
all. ' I was minded to come to you.'

' To bestow a grace on you.' We see then, that

Doct. The preaching of the gospel is a special grace.

It is a free and bountiful benefit of God. Grace implies freedom, and
mercy, and bounty. It is a free mercy of God to have the gospel.

Why ?

Reason. Because this is the means to work all that is savingly good in
us. This is a means to open to us God's love in Christ, and to work in us
a disposition answerable to his love. Therefore it must needs be a grace.
Heaven is a grace, life is a grace, reconciliation a grace, and such like.
Therefore the word must needs be a grace, by which all these are communicated. Therefore the word hath the name of these things. It is the
word of the kingdom of heaven. It is called the kingdom of heaven, the
preaching of the gospel, because it puts us into the state of the kingdom
of heaven. And the word of reconciliation, because by it we know our
reconciliation with God. It is offered, and wrought in our hearts, and
faith to apply it by this word. ' It is the word of life,' Acts xx. 32 ; the
life of grace, and the life of glory, all come by this word. ' I commend
you to God, and the word of his grace,' saith the apostle. All grace and

spiritual life is wrought in us by the word ; therefore the word preached, it is a special grace and favour of God.

St Paul here calls his coming to them to strengthen and confirm them, ' a grace.' For all means come under the same decree of God's eternal love with the decree itself. When God out of grace resolves and sets down that he will bring such a one to heaven, of his free love, he doth out of the same grace fit him with opportunities of persons and means ; he accommodates him with all means ; for he intends in such a way to bring him to heaven.

And therefore St Austin doth well define predestination ; it is an ordaining to salvation, and a preparing of all means tending thereto (*eee*). Therefore all fall in the compass of grace, both the free favour of God, setting a man down to make him happy ; and likewise by sending men that have an outward calling, and inwardly furnishing them with gifts, and whatsoever,— all is of grace. The preaching of the word is a grace.

Use. It concerns us therefore so to esteem it. Do not many sit in darkness, and in the shadow of death ? Is it not a grace therefore that we partake of the means of salvation ? What is in us by nature better than in Turks and Pagans ? or than many other people under Satan, and under popish teachers, and so rot away in their ignorance ? Nothing. We differ only by the grace of God. Therefore let us esteem it as a grace.

How shall we esteem it as a grace ?

Receive it thankfully, as a largess and bounty, and free grace of God ; receive it as a bounty with thankful hearts. Grace begets grace, it begets thankfulness. So to receive it as a grace, is to receive it with thankful minds, to be more thankful for the means of salvation, than for any outward thing.

How shall we come to be thankful ?

Never, unless we find some grace wrought by the word of grace. Therefore to receive it as a grace, is to receive it as a free, loving gift of God, and to yield to it ; when by it holy motions are stirred in our hearts, not to suppress and quench holy motions, but to yield to them ; not to quench and resist the Spirit, but to yield ourselves pliable to the word. This is to acknowledge it a grace, to be thankful for it, because you find your hearts wrought to holy obedience by it. Give it way in your souls, that it may be an ingraffed word ; that all the inward and outward man may be seasoned with it, and relish of it ; that the word may season your thoughts, and speeches, and desires, and season your course of life ; that what you think may be in the relish and strength of the word, in the strength of some divine truth, and the guide of your actions may be divine truth, or some motives from it. Then you will give thanks for what is wrought on you, when it is an ingraffed word in your souls, and all relish of it, your speeches and actions, and your whole course ; when a man may know by your carriage that there is something invested and ingraffed in your souls, that gives a blessed relish to all the expressions of the outward man. Such a one indeed will account the word a special grace, by a sweet experience wrought in his heart. I will not press that point any further.

Again, whereas St Paul saith, he would come to bestow a second grace on them, we see here that—

Doct. *Those that are in the state of grace already, they need a second grace.*

Those that have initial grace to be set in a good course, they need confirming and strengthening grace. St Paul had planted them before. Aye, but he must come to water them. There is alway somewhat left for the

minister to do, till he see their souls safe in heaven. He hath alway somewhat to do to the Christian souls under him. For he must not only get
them out of Satan's kingdom into a good estate, but he must labour to
build them up. He must water them, and fence them, and strengthen
them against all discouragements.

A man is never safe till he be in heaven. Therefore he saith, ' I will
come to you,' but I will come ' to bestow a second grace on you;' you
have need of it, and my love is such to you, that you shall have it. To
enforce this a little : because we set terms to our growth, and go on plod-
ding in a course, and many years after we are no better than we were at
the first ; and some out of a profane fulness, out of a Laodicean temper,
they think they have enough, they are rich, when indeed they are empty,
and miserable, and wretched, and poor ; and if temptations set upon them,
they have nothing in them, Rev. iii. 17.

To let you see that we stand in need of a second grace, and of a third
grace, and of a fourth grace, that we need continual building up.

Reason 1. First, *look within, what opposition there is to saving goodness
within !* what rebellion of lusts ! what ignorance, and blindness, and darkness, and indisposition ! what head the flesh makes in us against the word
of God. Let a man a little continue out of the means, and he shall see
what growth of corruptions there will be ; a distasting of all means, that a
man shall be ready to begin anew with them almost. Having a double
principle in them, of grace and corruption, there needs continually strengthening and stablishing grace.

Reason 2. Consider *outwardly what discouragements from the ill examples,
and allurements, and seducing of others, from the disgrace that is put on good
things ; what discouragements and scandals from without !*

Reason 3. Again, *are there not ofttimes new and great temptations*, that a
man must have a new measure of grace to resist ? There is continual
occasion of new spiritual strength to oppose new temptations, and new
spiritual strength to endure new crosses, and to enjoy new benefits. In all
the passages of our life, there is a necessity of more grace, of further
supply of grace. A man with that proportion of strength which he had
before, he cannot encounter with new temptations ; and therefore there
must be new grace, and fresh attending upon the means while we live here.

Reason 4. Again, *unavoidable times will come*, when there must be
strength of grace : sickness will come, temptations to despair will come,
conflicts with Satan will come. We need not say, put the case such and
such ; but it is an unavoidable case. They will come, wherein a great
strength of grace will be necessary. Therefore we cannot be too much
careful in attending upon the means of salvation, to be confirmed and
strengthened.

Reason 5. Again, do we not need a great measure of strengthening grace
continually ? *Doth not the devil envy goodness and good actions ?* When
we go about to pray, when the best men are about the best actions, what
a deal of distraction is there ! how doth Satan confound them with distrac-
tions ! What a deal of confirming grace need we to every good work !
When a Christian is taken out of the kingdom of Satan, he is the butt,
the object of his malice, and the malice of those that are his instruments.
We must pull every good work, as it were, out of the fire. We must use
violence to nature, to temptations in every good duty, to perform them
strongly. We need a second and a third grace, many degrees of grace.

Reason 6. Then again, *we are capable of more grace ;* for our under-

standing is such that we may know more still, and our will is such that it
affects * more still, and the more holy truths are made known to us, the
more the will is enlarged to cleave to them; the more we know, the
more we may know.   Our understandings are wondrous large.   There
is a great capacity in them, and our adhesion and cleaving to truths is more
and more.   The more we know, the more the will cleaves to it; as it is,
Acts xi. 23, ' They exhorted them, that with full purpose they would cleave
fast to God.'   We must cleave and adhere fast to the truth and to God;
every day go deeper, get nearer and closer to God, and labour to be
established in good things.   St Paul prays that they might be established
more and more; and David prays that he might be established in good
thoughts, and desires, and resolutions in good purposes, to be stablished
in everything that is good.   Grace is a state that we may grow in, and our
souls are fit to be enlarged; for there is a great capacity in the soul.   Till
we come to heaven, it is not full.   We may grow in every grace stronger
and stronger.   As in the examples of holy men in Scripture, it was
never well with them but when they were growing.   There is a necessity of
growing.

   Use 1.   If this be true, *let us set no pitch to ourselves, and abhor, abhor
even as the temptation of the devil, the conceit of fulness and of self-sufficiency;*
to think, I know enough, what should I know more for? or, perhaps, I could
read at home, as I said before.   It is God's ordinance, and cursed is all
private study when it is done in contempt of the ordinance of God.   Take
heed of such suggestions of fulness and standing at a stay.   No; we need
a second, we need many degrees of confirmation and strength, and all little
enough.   There was never any that repented of the careful use of the
means.   Strengthening, and proficiency, and growth in this kind is a pledge
of perfection, that God will perfect more and more that that he hath
graciously begun.   I beseech you, take it to heart, that we may alway need
a further degree of strengthening grace while we live in this world.

   The strongest Christians are most desirous of strength.   Who have you
that doth most hunger after the means of salvation?   Surely those that
have the greatest measure of grace, because with grace the capacity of the
soul is enlarged to receive more.   The soul is so framed by God that the
more it hath, the more it hungers after; and ' blessed are those that
hunger, they shall be satisfied.'   Who care least for the means?   Debauched, shallow creatures, those that are popishly conceited, such as are
ill bred, such as take scandal at all things in the communion of saints, at
holy exercises, the frequenting of public and private duties, the making
conscience of calling upon God.   A Christian that knows what it is, he
thinks all the means little enough, he will not omit one of them that may
be a means of his growth and strength; he thinks if he neglect one means,
he decays in all.   Therefore, he joins to all means, private duties, and then
public, of hearing the word; and he hears out of season when he finds
himself indisposed.   As the ministers are to ' preach in season and out of
season,' 2 Tim. iv. 2, so he hears in season and out of season.   And therefore, of all men, he that is the most careful of his growth is the great, the
strong Christian.   The better he is, the more he hungers after it.

   Use 2.   *Take this as a trial, if you do not desire to be strengthened in good
things more and more, you have no goodness at all.*   I will press the point
no further at this time, but go on.   Saith St Paul, ' I was minded to come
to you, that you might have a second benefit, a second grace,' that is, a

   * That is, = seeks.—G.

confirming, strengthening grace. We all need, then, a second grace, a confirming grace. Here I might make some use to ministers; I will but touch it, to shew what their duty is to those that are under them. Every man is, as it were, a minister in his place to strengthen another, and to exhort one another, and to bestow grace upon one another. But ministers should do it especially. They are like those that repair the sea banks. The sea gets over ofttimes, and eats out the banks; they must be repaired continually, they will impair else. The minister's pains, it is like the labour of the husbandman. When he hath sown, he must weed; and when he hath weeded, he must fence, to keep it from the birds of prey and the violence of beasts, &c., and he must live by faith till the grain be ready. So the minister, after he hath planted, he must water, and weed, and fence, and all little enough; he must look to the banks, and many times that which he getteth in one day he loseth in another; nay, ofttimes the pitiful condition of a minister is this, that at the week's end he hath all to do again. Another man sees an end of his work, but in this the devil and corruption hath undone all again. We enforce good things on people on the Lord's day; but within one day, ill company and employment in worldly business overthrows all. The sea banks are down; they must be new repaired. Therefore, there is a necessity laid on us of the ordinances to our lives' end, till our souls be in heaven; there is a necessity of repairing them. We cannot be too diligent in our places. And those that have the oversight of others, let them make conscience of it; it is needful. And mark here, in the next point,

Doct. The language of Canaan, the language of the Spirit of God, that he puts the name of grace upon every benefit, especially those that concern a better life. Grace usually we take to be nothing but a gracious frame of heart, the new creature, as we call it; but indeed, in the language of the Holy Ghost, every free gift of God that concerns our souls any way is a grace. The very ministry is a grace. It is the grace and free love of God to give us the ministry. The very heart to embrace it, and to hear it, is a grace. The very heart to give alms is a grace. Saith St Paul, ' Thanks be to God for this unspeakable gift,' 2 Cor. ix. 15, for this unspeakable grace that you had a heart to give; so that everything that is good, it is a grace, a gift of God.

St Paul conceived of his coming to them as a grace. Indeed the grace of God moved and directed St Paul to come to them. It is grace that God directs the preacher to speak to the people. It is a grace that the minister speaks gracious things. It is a greater grace when you close with and entertain that which is spoken,—all is of grace. Your ready minds to do good, it comes of God, it is a grace; your acceptance of God, as well as eternal life, all is of free grace.

The ground of it is this, as Austin, as I said, defines predestination well, it is a destinating and ordaining to a supernatural end, to everlasting salvation in the world to come, and a preparing of all means to that end.* Why, now as it is a grace that God pulls out some men to an eternal estate of salvation in heaven, to a supernatural estate, that they could never attain without his especial grace; so the preparing of all means to that end, it falls within the compass of predestination, within the grace.

So when we have any means prepared to bring us to that end, the offer of the word, and the Spirit of God disposing us to embrace the word, this preparing of the means to that end, it falls within the compass of predes-

* Cf. note *eee.*—G.

tination, we may gather our election by it. When we see the word sent in favour, and have gracious hearts to receive it, this is a preparation wrought to bring us to heaven, a man may know his election by it. All is of grace that falls within the decree of grace. When God decrees to bring a man to heaven, all that helps to the main must needs be grace. The minister is a grace, the word a grace, opportunities to do good a grace, the communion of saints a grace, all that helps a man forward is a grace. A gracious heart sees God in everything, it sees God's love in everything; it considers of everything that befalls it as a grace. Why? From this disposition especially, because with the grace there is grace to make a blessed use of, and to improve everything.

Use. If this be so, *let us look upon every benefit that concerns salvation, though it be remote, even the very direction of good speeches to us, account it a grace.* It is the grace of God that I have this opportunity, especially the public ministry. St Paul calls it ' a grace ;' let us think of it as a grace. And as we do in clocks, we go from the hammer that strikes, to the wheels, and from one wheel to another, and so to the weights that make it strike : we go to the first weight, the first wheel that moves all, and leads all. So when we see good done, look not to the good done only, but go to the wheels, to the weights, that move it, and make it strike. What sets all agoing? The grace and free love of God. When good things are spoken, when any good is done, go higher to the first wheel that sets all agoing, to the grace and free love of God. This is the language of the Scripture and of the Spirit of God. Thus we must speak and think, to the end that God may have the glory of his grace in whatsoever good is done or offered.

When Abigail met David, and diverted him from his bloody intention to kill Nabal, and gave him counsel another way, ' O blessed be God, and blessed be thou, and blessed be thy counsel,' 1 Sam. xxv. 32–34. So when opportunities are offered to do good, and to hinder us from evil intentions, ' O blessed be thou, and blessed be thy counsel.' When a benefit is done, if it be a benefit of this life, take it as a grace coming freely from God. So a poor man, his alms is a grace. ' Thanks be unto God for this unspeakable gift,' saith St Paul, 2 Cor. ix. 15. It is grace in him that hath it, that God should respect him so much as to relieve him. It is grace in the party that gives it, that he hath a heart enlarged to do it. So when anything outward or spiritual is done that is good, look on it as a grace, put that respect on it, and that will make you holy-minded to give God his own.

Our life should be a praising and blessing of God. We should begin the employment of heaven while we are on earth. How should we do that ? ' In all things give thanks,' Eph. v. 20. Every good thing from God, take it as a grace, as a largess ; not as due, not as coming by chance, but as a grace. And this will make us improve it as a grace for the best. It will make us to give God the glory, and improve it to our own good, when we are thankful for grace, that we may have cause to account it a grace. Our hearts would not be so full of atheism, and our tongues so full of blasphemies, if we had learned this lesson; our lives would be a praising of God.

And that we may not want matter to feed a thankful spirit, alway consider, what good things we have are of grace. We deserve not so much as a crumb of bread ; therefore we pray, ' Give us this day our daily bread,' Mat. vi. 11. Everything is a grace, especially the things of a better life. How shall I know that the minister is a grace, or a good speech from a minister to be a grace, as St Paul saith here, I intended you a 'second grace,' that is, to speak gracious things to you?

I shall know it, if by that gracious means, by those gracious speeches, God distil into me a spirit to improve them to gracious purposes. As indeed, God turns all to a gracious end to his children: he gives them a principle of grace to work good out of everything; they see grace in everything: in affliction they see the love of God. In the worst things, grace will pick out somewhat, and make use of it. As God by his providence intends all to good, so his Spirit, by a provident eye to the word, works good out of everything. But those that have not grace, they are not grace to them, but tend to their further hardening.

To end this point; when you come to the communion, come to it as a grace. It is the grace of God that he hath ordained us to salvation. It is the grace of God that he hath sent his word. It is the grace of God that he hath sent his sacrament to seal that word, and all little enough. He knows us better than we know ourselves. He knows we have need of all, to confirm and help us, the word and the sacraments, even to the end of our days. As the apostle saith, Eph. ii. 22, 'To build us up.' The means of grace are not only necessary for the planting, but for the building up of the church. And therefore come with this purpose, to have grace confirmed, and receive it as a grace of God with thankfulness, that God will condescend to our infirmity, to give us helps, to support our weak faith. It is a true proverb, grace begets grace. It begets thankfulness, where it is apprehended as a grace. Therefore come with a thankful disposition to the sacrament; embrace every ordinance of God with thankfulness. Alas! do not thousands 'sit in darkness, and in the shadow of death?' They do; and therefore those that find the benefit of God's ordinances, they are disposed by the same Spirit that works any good in them, to return thankfulness to God again.

'That you might have a second grace.' Saint Paul's purpose was to come to them, to bestow 'a grace,' not to take from them; to bestow good and gracious speeches on them, which he knew the Spirit of God would make effectual to work some good in them.

Obs. A gracious man is a vessel of grace, and he should take all occasions to vent that which is good.

When St Paul saith, he intended to bestow a second grace, his meaning is, that he would utter things that were gracious, that the Spirit of God should seal to the souls of them that heard him, and make them effectual.

Therefore every Christian should have this disposition. St Paul did it as a holy man, as well as a minister. Do we think ourselves vessels of grace, as the Scripture calls the elect, children of God, or no? Yes! God forbid else. Now God's children, God hath appointed some to be vessels of gold, some of silver, as the apostle saith to Timothy, some for this use, and some for that: all for good use, 2 Tim. ii. 20. A vessel is to be filled with something, and to be used for something; therefore set abroach* some good thing when you have the advantage of it, when you are called to it; not unnecessarily to thrust forward yourselves. Let the desire of your hearts be to do good upon all occasions. A vessel of grace must not be an empty vessel. A Christian he is a member of Christ, and he hath a part in the communion of saints, and he hath gifts for that end. There is no Christian, but he can comfort, or instruct, or dissuade from ill when it is moved. There is no Christian, but he is furnished as a member ought to

* That is, 'cause to flow.'—G.

be, in some competent measure. There is no man that hath benefit by the communion of saints, but he hath grace to fit him for that blessed communion. He is fitted to comfort, upon occasion ; and he hath some grace, some knowledge to correct. He that hath not is a dead member, not fit for that communion. Therefore we should bestow grace where we come ; and not leave an ill scent behind us, to infect others with filthy speeches, and blasphemous oaths, to open the rottenness of our own hearts in their presence, and so be conscious of that which is ill in them, because we strengthen it by our example, and by our words. St Paul was a good man. ' I come to bestow a second grace,' that is, to speak that which is gracious, that God's gracious providence shall direct to do you special good. For God's word is inspired by the Spirit ; and the same Spirit that breathed the word of God into the penmen of it, the same Spirit is with the word in the uttering of it. When it is done by a gracious heart, to a gracious man, it works graciously, it hath a blessed operation with it.

Therefore we should upon all good occasions speak gracious things. Divine truths, they will have a wondrous efficacy. If men would set on it, and be more fruitful in this kind, they should have occasion to bless God. But, alas ! the life of a Christian is little known in the world. We have but naked, shallow conceits of the glory of heaven, and of the state of a Christian, and how he lives in this world ; and that makes men live such stained, such base lives, that will not stand with comfort in this world, or glory in the world to come. But a Christian should be such a one as frames his disposition to do good wheresoever he comes ; and he hath ability if he be a sound Christian. How graciously did God bless Abigail's word to David ? yet she was a mean woman. How dost thou know, but that by uttering gracious words in company, in season (as discretion must guide all our actions, all our words), how dost thou know but that thou mayest divert another man from sin, by a word in season ?

I beseech you carry this disposition about you, as you desire to be thought vessels of grace here, and of glory hereafter, to be thought vessels of gold and silver, for the use of God, labour to be employed by the Spirit of God to good purposes, that you may leave a good savour where you come ; that others that are acquainted with you in the ' time of their visitation,' 1 Pet. ii. 12, they may bless God, that ever they were acquainted with such a friend. Blessed be God that I knew him. As it will be our joy at that day, so it will be one another's joy here ; for God blesseth the exhortations and comforts of friends one to another, as well as the ministerial ofttimes. So I come to the 16th verse, how he meant to come to them to Corinth. Saith he, ' I was minded to come to you.'

VERSE 16.

' *And to pass by you into Macedonia, and to come again out of Macedonia unto you, and of you to be brought on my way to Judea.*' See what a circuit the blessed apostle fetched. Indeed, he was industrious after his conversion. He made amends for his harsh* conversion by his speedy labours. For he spread the gospel like lightning, through all the world almost. His course was like the course of the sun ; he went every where spreading the gospel. We see his circuit here, ' to pass by you into Macedonia, and to come again from Macedonia to you, and by you to be brought on my way to Judea.'

* Qu. ' hard ? ' = long delayed.—G.

There is little to be observed here. Because it is a passage to other things, and circumstantial, I will not dwell on it. Only this by the way : we see here, that

Obs. It is a commendable custom among the people of God to bring one another on their way, by way of honour and respect.

Partly it was for his security and safety ; but especially for the honour of his person. And they knew that it would not be a barren courtesy ; for they knew that he was a man of a blessed spirit, so thankful, that he would deceive* all the tediousness of the journey by his heavenly discourse. And he intended their good as well as his own. You may see, therefore, religion establisheth courtesy. Saith the apostle to the Philippians, chap. iv. 8, ' Whatsoever things are of good report, whatsoever things are lovely (he goes over many instances), think of these things.' The same command of God that urgeth, and presseth love, it commands all the expressions of love, and all the means to kindle love.

Now this, their carrying of him, and going on the way with him, which was for honour and respect of so excellent a person, that he deserved so well of them, it was an expression of their love, and a means to preserve it. I shall not need to prove it, it is taken for granted. Those compliments that express and maintain love, they are good, when the outward expression and the inward affection go together.

I speak this by the way, to shew that religion doth not countenance incivility. Therefore those that affect unnecessary sternness, and unnecessary retiredness, it is not out of religion. Religion stablisheth whatsoever is good, ' whatsoever is of good report,' whatsoever may maintain love. So much as a man is defective in this, he is defective in religion ; unless his affections and intentions at that time be deeply taken up by serious things. For then lesser things must give way to the greater, or else there is no excuse. For religion is a thing of a large extent, even duties of civility and courtesy, and whatsoever may express and maintain love, is established by religion. We see in Gen. xviii. 16, when Abraham entertained the angels, he led them on their way. And so in Acts xx. 4, 36, *seq.*, ' The company sent them on their way.' And we see in Scripture many common courtesies.

But I do but touch it by the way : because this whole verse is but a passage to another thing. Therefore I come to the seventeenth verse.

VERSE 17.

' *When I therefore was thus minded (to come unto you), did I use lightness ? or the things that I purpose, do I purpose according to the flesh, that with me there should be yea, yea, and nay, nay ?*' The apostle still goes on to prevent scandal.† ' Woe to the world because of offences,' Mat. xviii. 7, saith our blessed Saviour, especially offences taken. Because our nature is so corrupt, that it is subject to take offence where none is given, it will pick quarrels enough to go to hell. Proud men that have only nature in them, they will not be damned without reason. Tush ! I had been good, say they, but for such and such. Now St Paul was a man much exercised with the cross. He wipes away scandal from that, as we heard in the first part of the chapter. He saith, ' As his crosses' for Christ abounded, so his comforts in Christ abounded. He lost nothing by it.

That is, = 'make them be inobservant of.'—G.   † That is, 'offence.'—G.

Again, they took offence that he promised to come to them, and did not; especially some that were not well-willers to him: therefore he labours to satisfy that.

And *first*, that he might the better satisfy them that he was no inconstant man, no unsettled man, he premiseth a description of his own disposition and course of life, he appeals to his own conscience, ' This is our rejoicing, the testimony of our conscience,' &c.

And *then he appeals to their conscience.* A manifest note of a man confident, that dares appeal to his own conscience, and to the conscience of another. Obnoxious men are always afraid, not only of their own conscience, lest it should tell them that which they would be loath to hear, but they are afraid of the consciences of others likewise. St Paul appeals to their conscience, ' I write no other things than what you read and acknowledge,' &c.

And so he comes more directly to satisfy their suspicion of him for his not coming to them. In this verse he labours to remove their false imputation, ' When I was thus minded to come unto you, did I use lightness ? Wherein you have St Paul's purgation of himself. Here is a prevention of an objection of suspicion, that the flesh will move in them that have doubtful suspicious minds. Why ! if you intended to come, why did you not ? Saith he, ' When I was thus minded, did I use lightness ?' First, Observe hence in general, that

Obs. Men are wondrous prone to jealousy and suspicion.

It is the state of God's children here in this world to have suspicions raised of them. They are obnoxious to slanders and imputations, and they are forced to their apologies. Men are prone to suspicion, yea, and good men too: as here, they took his not coming in the worst part, by the wrong handle.

That is suspicion, when there are two handles of a thing, two apprehensions of a thing, and there is a proneness in the mind to the worst part; to take things in an ill sense. They might have construed it many ways better than thus; but they thought the worst of him: he is light in his promises; he will say, and unsay again: he is off and on. This is in natural men, yea, in Christians: as far as they have old Adam in them, they are prone to suspicion.

Whence is this ?

1. Partly out *of the poison and malice of man's nature in many*, esteeming others by themselves; for the worst natures are alway most suspicious, out of a privity of their own indisposition in themselves. Usually those that deserve worst are most jealous, because there is most cause. Conscience of a man's own imperfections and weakness makes him think others to be as he himself is.

2. And again, *there is envy in man's nature toward excellent persons especially.* The malice of man's nature cannot abide eminency in others. The false teachers among the Corinthians they saw that Paul stood in their light, therefore they labour to eclipse and obscure him all they could. Hence it is, that men are willing to entertain willingly any suspicion. For not being willing out of baseness to rise to their greatness and excellency, they labour to bring them down by their suspicion to their baseness and meanness, that all may be ill alike. Therefore baseness is subject to suspicion, and the fruit of suspicion, that is, slander; to take every thing in suspicion, and to utter it in words; because they would have men of eminency brought down to their meanness; and if they cannot do it indeed,

they will bring them by reports as low as they can, that they speak, and unspeak, and are inconstant as other men. There are many causes of this ; and therefore St Paul seeing the baseness of it, he stands the more upon it.

Quest. How shall we arm ourselves against this suspicion, and the fruit of it ? How shall we carry ourselves against this disposition of men among whom we live ?

Ans. I answer briefly, first, *labour for innocency*, that if they will speak maliciously, yet they may speak falsely. Saith St Ambrose, '*Et nobis malus*,' &c. (*fff*). Our care must be that no man speak ill of us without a lie. Let us live so that no man may believe them; labour for innocency therefore. But that will not do.

2. Therefore *patience* in the next place. For innocency could not fence Christ himself, who was innocency clothed with our flesh. If innocency will not prevail to make men hold their tongue from speaking their suspicious minds, then labour for patience.

3. But that will not do neither, but men go on still ; then *prayer*. That was David's course : that God would defend our innocency, and take our cause into his hands, and bring forth our innocency as the light, to judge for us.

4. And when nothing else will serve the turn, neither innocency nor patience, &c., then *just apology and defence*, as we see the apostle doth here defend himself. For it is not for public persons to dissemble* slanders ; and especially for them not to suffer ill suspicions to rest in the hearts of those that are under them. Therefore the apostle is enforced through Christian prudence to his apology, to wipe away the imputation. ' When I was thus minded, did I use lightness ? ' saith he. This I observe in general.

Quest. Now, because suspicion is a doubtful thing, it is either good or evil, how shall we know when suspicion is naught and evil ?

Ans. 1. First of all, *when it is out of misconstruction.* When it is from weak grounds, or doubtful grounds, then it is ill for the ground.

2. Or it is ill likewise *when it ill affects, and sways, and disposeth the mind;* if it dispose the affections to malice, to the suppression of love ; if it discover itself to come to slander. As here in this place, they thought presently it was lightness in him. Here was a misconstruction, here was a false ground. What did this incline them to do ? From inconstancy presently they fly to his disposition, from suspicion to slander his disposition. They enter into God's throne : his purposes and projects, certainly they were naught. Carnal, proud man will enter into God's throne, and judge a man's thoughts, and purposes, and intentions. Then a man may know his suspicion is not right when it enters too deep, when it riseth from false grounds, from suspicious grounds, and brings men from actions, to go to the disposition. ' Did I use lightness ? or the things that I purpose, do I purpose according to the flesh ? ' that is, carnally, as they thought : this entered to his disposition.

3. Then again, *when it stirs us up to speak in slander, when we speak without cause or ground.* Then when it inclines a man from an error in one thing, to go to the habitual disposition in all things. As here now, because in one thing the apostle was inconstant, and did not come to them, they went to his habitual disposition in all things. Nay, you may see what he is, you see what we are like to have from him in other things, he doth but

* That is, = ' conceal.'—G.

purpose things according to the flesh ; he hath his own aims, I warrant you. So when from one thing we presently judge that he purposeth other things according to the flesh, that is a bad suspicion : when a man goes from one thing to the habitual disposition.

'*When I was thus minded, did I use lightness?*' The more to convince them of their suspicion and hard surmises, he cites them, and propounds as it were interrogatories to them.   I pray answer me, saith he, 'When I was thus minded, did I use lightness,' as you imagine ? ' or the things that I purpose, do I purpose according to the flesh ?' &c.   After he had cleared his purpose before, and cleared his conscience, now he comes to propound it to their conscience ; because he would have them to think, that if he were such a man as he shewed himself before, that he had a good conscience in all things, and a good affection to them, that they should not have had a misconstruction of that particular failing, that he came not to them when he purposed ; for particular actions must be construed according to a man's habitual carriage and affection.   You see how I have laboured in all things to have a good conscience ; and for you, you acknowledge that I purposed to come to you ; therefore you should construe my actions according to that intention.   Now, having cleared my disposition and intention to you, you see your error in misconstruing my not coming to you.   So he comes to it in good season, after he had freed himself to them.

'When I was thus minded, did I use lightness ?' &c.   These things he declines :

1. *Lightness or inconstancy.*

2. *Purposing or deliberating according to the flesh.*

3. And then *inconstancy in his speeches*, that they should be 'Yea, yea, Nay nay.

The point that I observe from the first concerning lightness is, that

Doct. Every Christian, especially ministers and public men, should labour by all means to avoid the just imputation of lightness and inconstancy.

The imputation of lightness is especially to be avoided of those that are in place.   Lightness and inconstancy ! what is that ?   When a man hath not pitched his resolutions and purposes to one thing, when a man doth not stand in his purposes.

Now, a man must avoid imputations of lightness, especially persons of quality.

Why ?

Reason. Not to speak all that might be said in the point, especially for this end, *to preserve authority.*   Authority is that that furnisheth a man in place, in magistracy or ministry, wondrously to prevail, to do good.   I take not authority here for that which the king puts on them, or the chief magistrate ; but authority is that high respect that the people have of the eminency of their parts and honesty, an impression of somewhat more than ordinary in them.   This is that authority, a beam of excellency that God doth infuse, for the strengthening and fortifying of his own ordinance. What reason is there else that a thousand should be subject to one man, but that God doth put a majesty upon his own ordinance, and upon the persons in it ?   And this respect to it must be maintained by a uniform, constant carriage.   Now, when people shall see that they are, as in their place, so in their disposition, great, and serious, and weighty, and firm in their resolutions ; that they may build on them, and know where to have them as we say, it breeds authority, and maintains authority. For then what they say is regarded. And how their affections stand: if it be love, it is much sought after; if displeasure, it is much feared. For they are men of a fixed disposition, it gains wondrous respect.

Let men be never so great, if they be such as St Paul here declines from himself, that they use lightness, they lose their authority. Authority is the special help that governors have to rule, and that ministers have to prevail. Now, nothing weakens esteem and authority more than when men are tossed between the waves of contrary affections; when men are such as we know not where to have them; as we say, off and on, fast and loose, one while sitting, another standing: no man will build on them, or much regard their love or hatred.

Now you know authority is a beam of majesty, and God hath put it upon magistrates above others ; and imprinted likewise the respect of it in the people's hearts, to maintain the world. ' The pillars of the earth will shake else,' as the psalmist saith, Ps. lxxv. 3. What would become of the pillars of government, if it were not for authority in them that are above, and respect of that authority, an impression of it in them that are under.

Now there are many grounds of authority, as success, when God blesseth them with it wonderfully to admiration, and good parts, &c.; but one main ground of authority is constancy and firmness. This raiseth a high respect in the hearts of the people.

I will not multiply reasons why those that are in place should avoid the imputation of lightness. Ministers especially should take heed of it, because they are ministers of God's truth ; and if they take not heed of it, people will be ready to go from their moral civil carriage to their doctrine, and think there is an uncertainty in that they speak, because they do not regard what they say.

But let me add this by the way, *Mater erroris similitudo*, Likeness is the mother of error. So there is somewhat like constancy in governors, and others, when they are nothing less, but merely refractory and obstinate; to maintain the reputation of constancy, they will run into the fault of wilfulness. Such as are subject that way, had need of strong wits to rule their strong wills, to guide them, or else woe be to those that have to deal with them. That I thought good to add, lest we mistake.

We should all labour to avoid inconstancy and lightness in our resolutions, in our purposes, and affections.

If we ought to avoid it, how shall we come to know it ? What is the ground of lightness ? The grounds are many.

1. Sometimes *from the temper of the body*. Some are of a moveable temper, of a moveable, quick spirit, that they cannot out of their constitution fix long, except they set weights upon nature. I am by disposition thus ; but my resolution shall be otherwise : as where grace and wisdom is, it will fix the temper, and fix the resolution, and the thoughts. This I could not do, if I should yield to my own disposition ; but this I will do, and I should do. There are many resolutions, as in the younger sort, and some out of their very temper are more fixed and resolved.

2. But now consider it as it is in religion, lightness comes out of the disposition of the mind.

(1.) *Inconsideration ofttimes is the ground*, when we do not see the circumstances of a thing that we promise or purpose. You know there is nothing comes to action, but it is beset with circumstances. There are

advantages of it, and there are stops and hindrances of it : somewhat may
fall out. Everything that comes to action is besieged with circumstances.
Circumstances, you know, have their name of standing about a business,
about a thing. Now when the things that are about, the impediments, and
the hindrances, and lets are not weighed, a rash man sees not the things, he
considers not the things that he enters upon ; he resolves without considering the circumstances that beset the thing ; he never considers what oppositions he may meet with, or what advantages there be which perhaps he
neglects ; but he thinks of the thing, it is good, and suitable to his purpose ;
he resolves, and never considers the circumstances about a thing, but runs
on in confidence of his own wit and parts, and thinks to rule all by the
strength of his wit, not foreseeing, not casting in his mind, to prevent
beforehand what may fall out. It is just with God to shame such men.
Frustration of their purposes, it is a just reward of their folly. Therefore
we should take heed of inconsideration, and have our eyes in our heads, to
set the soul to foresee what possibility there is of the business, and what
may fall out. This is the right way, if we would avoid imputation of
lightness.

(2.) Again, another ground of lightness, and of that decay in authority
and respect that comes from it, *is the passion of men*. Therefore they are
light. They are carried with the hurry and wind of their passion. And
Satan joins with passion. A passionate man is subject to Satan more than
a man that is led by reason, or with grace. For that is a beam of God.
Even reason itself, judgment, it is an excellent thing, and it prevents many
temptations.

Give not way to passion, for those are unreasonable things. As we see
Saul in his passion, Satan, the evil spirit, mingled with his passion of anger.
So let men be in any passion, over joy, or be over angry ; let them give the
reins to unruly passion, and they give advantage to Satan, that we cannot
settle our souls in any good resolution.

(3.) Again, *in the things themselves there is cause of lightness and inconstancy, from the nature of things ;* and then it is not so great a fault to
change. Then it is not properly inconstancy. But it is inconstancy
when the things are mutable and variable, and we do not think of it as we
should.

Now the things of this life are variable and uncertain ; the event of
things in this life is wondrous variable. Grace and glory, they are certain
things, and the way that God directs us to heaven, they are certain promises,
and certain grounds ; but the things of this life are subject to much change.
God takes a great deal of liberty in altering things in this world, they fall
out divers ways.

(4.) But now therefore we must take heed that we take not inconstancy
for that which is not. Every change of opinion and purpose is not lightness. It is not inconstancy for a man to change his mind and purpose,
when it is from the things. Men are men, and the things that we deal
with in the world are subject to variety and inconstancy ; and for a man to
alter according to the variety of things, it argues no inconstancy, if the aim
be good.

As for example, a mariner, a seaman, he is not inconstant, when one
time he strikes sail, and another time he hoisteth up sail. When he makes
indentures,* and goes with a side wind, he goes on his way, and his aim is
still to come to the haven. He is not inconstant, because he changeth not

* That is = circuits.—G.

his star. He alway aims at the right star, and to his compass and card that he sails by. He varies not from his rule. He varies from the things, because the winds and the seas vary, because he deals with variable objects. The things vary, but he doth not vary. He comes to his project, to the haven, and hath his direction from the North Pole, &c.

So the husbandman, sometimes he sows, sometimes he harrows, sometimes he reaps. Is he inconstant and varies? No! the matter about which he is varies. So in governors, sometimes they do this, and sometimes that. They are about variable matters, yet here is no variableness nor lightness of disposition, because they deal with mutable, with variable objects.

So God in managing his church's affairs, in his dispensation in that point; you see he used one dispensation before Christ, and another since Christ. God changeth not, but the times are changed. In the infancy of the church one dispensation was requisite, and now another. Therefore it is not inconstancy for a man to change on good ground, or when the things themselves change.

Therefore this should have made them thought well of St Paul. His affection was not changed to them, but the business was changed, as we shall see after. Other things let* him. So a good man, his honest resolution should not change. His aim to serve God and his country, and to deserve well of mankind, this should be constant; but the manner how, the circumstance of time and place, and ordering of these things, they are variable. They do not change, but maintain their constancy and resolution, in the variety of occasions that fall out; for we cannot frame our life otherwise than it is, to be unvariable. When a man is guided by a certain principle, though the things of this life be uncertain, and he vary sometimes according to his principle, and aim, and end, yet it is no inconstancy. And it will excuse a man's conscience exceedingly, when his aim is good, and the rules and principles he goes by are good and honest, if things fall out otherwise than he aims at, though there be a change of his course, because his heart tells him his rules and his purposes were good.

3. One other main cause of lightness and sinful inconstancy, *it is irreligion;* casting ourselves upon future things, without a dependence on divine providence. An atheistical independence, when we project things to come, and never call upon God to assist us, and never have divine reservations as we should have, but boast, This I will do; and sometimes negatively, This I will not do, I have time enough to do it; as if we had future times at our command. St James excellently taxeth such people, James iv. 13, 'Go to now, you that say, To-day and to-morrow we will go to such a city, and buy, and sell, and get gain.' 'Go to now:' see here how he shames them by a kind of ironical permission. 'Go to now.' You will do great matters! 'whereas,' saith he, 'you know not what shall be to-morrow.' God that hath given us the time present to repent in, and to do good, the time to come he hath reserved in his own power. We know not what shall be to-morrow. Where he shews the ground of this atheism, and rushing upon business without dependence; they forget the condition of this life, that it is a vapour. 'What is your life? it is even a vapour that appeareth for a little while, and then vanisheth away.' Your life is inconstant. God is the Lord of your purposes. He is the Lord of your life, and of all opportunities and circumstances. 'Your life is but a vapour.' Here all things fall under his providence and guidance. You consider not this, and there-

* That is, 'hindered.'—G.

fore you project so for the time to come. 'What is your life ? it is even a vapour,' &c.

Then he comes to direct them how they should entertain resolutions for the time to come, 'Ye ought to say, If the Lord will;' or if we live, we will do this and that. 'If the Lord will,' in whose power are our intentions, and resolutions, and affections. He guides the inward man, and all the things in the world, to the falling of a hair from our head, to the falling of a sparrow to the ground, even the least things, Luke xii. 7. You should say thus.

And he calls it 'vain boasting.' What makes God confound insolent attempts ? as indeed he triumphs over insolent attempts of kings and captains, or whatsoever, that set up great business in high conceits, they will do this and that. Saith St James, 'You rejoice in your boasting,' James iv. 16. They boast they will do this and that. That makes God confound them so, because they will be gods to themselves. Man is a dependent creature. Everything is God's, and we are dependent. 'In him we live, and move, and have our being,' Acts xvii. 28.

Man being a dependent creature, yet he resolves to do this and that, as if he had the guidance of his own thoughts and purposes. This provokes God to jealousy, when he makes himself a god, and sets not God before him in his actions. He sets upon things without dependence, without prayer, or reservation, if God permit this. Because God rejoiceth to confound these bold attempts, therefore they never thrive in such attempts.

Therefore a true Christian joins modesty for the time to come. He will attempt nothing but what he may expect to have God's protection in. He that thinks God may cross him will do nothing ill that he fears God will cross him in ; he will be modest. The best Christians are the modestest. They consider the uncertainty of the things of this life, and the weakness of man in foreseeing things. They see a dependence of all things on the majesty of God, even to the least things ; that he guides things that are most casual ; and that 'he rules even the hearts of princes,' as Solomon saith, 'as the rivers of water,' Prov. xxi. 1. They are guided by him ; they are in his hand. Hereupon a wise Christian becomes modest for the time to come in his resolutions : he undertakes all with a holy dependence on God, if God will, and if God permit. He will undertake nothing for the time to come, but with warrant, that he may without tempting of God look for his assistance. For to go to God to bless us in ill projects, is to make God the patron of that which is bad, which is contrary to his nature. Therefore he learns to depend upon God for the time to come, and will entertain or enter upon no business but such as he may safely, without tempting of God, depend upon him for his assistance. This is the disposition of a modest Christian.

You see in Ps. ii. how the Psalmist there insults over those that threaten to do this and that. 'Why do the heathen rage, and the people imagine a vain thing, &c., against the Lord, and against his Anointed ?' As if they would swallow up the church, and Christ the anointed : why do they do this and that ? God that sits in heaven, he laughs them to scorn. You see the grounds of lightness, so far forth as is needful. I will name no more.

The way to prevent it may be in observing these grounds of constancy, especially this :—

1. *Stablish your thoughts with counsel for the time to come* ; consult, go not rashly and headlong about matters. It is not with our common life

as with those that run in a race ; for their swiftness gets all. But in matters of government in commonwealth, there the most staid get all ; those that weigh things, and then execute upon mature deliberation ; that ripen things first, and go not rawly, and indeliberately about it. This every man takes for granted, but it is not thought on.

2. Then again, *labour to suppress passion in anything that comes from us.* Speak nothing in passion ; for one of these things will follow. If we execute it, we are in danger for the things in passion, and inconsiderately spoken ; if not, we shall have the shame of being frustrate. We undergo the shame of lightness, that we speak that in our passion and heat that we retract after. One of these inconveniences will follow : either you will do it, and then it will be dangerous ; or you will not do it, and then you will be ashamed, a fit reward of rashness.

God gives us passions to be guided and ruled, and not to rule us. They are good servants and only servants, that should be raised up, and stirred up, only when reason and judgment raiseth them, and not otherwise. But to go on.

3. Another cure of this rashness *is holy dependence on God by prayer, and by faith, to commit our ways to him, our thoughts to him for the time to come.* Leave all to him, entertain nothing wherein we cannot expect his gracious assistance. The best Christian is the most dependent Christian. That is the first thing the apostle declines.

What is the second thing ?

' *Or the things that I purpose, do I purpose according to the flesh ?*' They thought he was a politician ; as this is the lot of God's children sometimes. If so be that God hath given them parts, either of nature or breeding, carnal, devilish men that are led altogether by plots themselves, esteem them by themselves. ' The things that I purpose, do I purpose according to the flesh ?' He propounds this interrogatory to their conscience, not idly ; but he knew that they had a prejudice in them, by his co-rivals, false apostles. There he labours to wipe away that imputation likewise, that he did not purpose and consult of things according to the flesh.

What is flesh here ?

' Flesh' is the unregenerate part of man, whereof fleshly wisdom is the chief; for that guides the ' old man,' that is the eye of old Adam. Carnal wisdom, it is the flesh's counsellor in all things ; therefore especially he means that.

But why is it called flesh ?

For many reasons. Among many this is one, that the soul, so far as it is sinful, it is led with things that are fleshly, that are outward ; and thereupon a man is called flesh. And the soul itself is called flesh, because it cleaves in its affections and desires to earthly things ; and because the poor understanding now, which ruled all, and should rule all, is become an underling to the carnal will and carnal lusts. Therefore itself is called flesh likewise, ' The wisdom of the flesh is enmity with God.' For now it is swayed even which way carnal fancy, and opinion, and the flesh, lead it.

The reason is, it is betwixt God and heavenly things, and betwixt earthly things. And if it were in its right original as it came out of God's hands, being a Spirit, it should be led by God, and by God's Spirit, and God's truth, by better things than itself (as every infirm thing is guided by that which is better than itself; as brute creatures are guided by men, and weaker persons by magistrates, that are, or should be, better); but now since the fall, without grace renew a man, the understanding part of man's soul, instead of lighting its candle from heaven, it often lights it from hell, and is ruled by Satan himself, and takes advices even from things meaner than itself, and plots, and projects altogether for things worse than itself. It was not given for that end, God knows that gave it, this soul of ours, to prowl for earthly things ; for the ease, and honour, and profits, and pleasures of the world. That excellent jewel that all the world is not worth, it was not given for that end. No ! it was given to attain a higher end than this world, to attain communion with God. But now since the fall it is thus with it, that it is a slave. Carnal wit is a slave to carnal will, and that carnal will is drawn by carnal affections. Affections draw the will, and the will draws the wit, and makes it plot and devise for that which it stands for ; for carnal lusts and affections which whet the wit that way. Therefore the whole soul is called flesh, even reason itself.

And hereupon wicked men are called ' the world.' Why the world ? Because they are led with the things of the world, with the guise and fashion of the world.

A man, in the language of the Scripture, is termed by that which he cleaves to ; therefore if the heart and soul cleave to the flesh, and the things of the flesh, it is flesh ; if it be led with the world, and the things of the world, it is called the world. Wicked men are the world, because the best thing in them is the love of worldly things, and their wit is for worldly things. All the inward parts of their soul are spent upon worldly things; therefore they are called flesh, and the world. And sometimes ' Satan' himself. A man, as far as he is carnal, is called Satan, yea, good men ; ' Go after me, Satan,' saith Christ to Peter, Mat. xvi. 23.

A man as far as he yields to anything, he is named from that which he yields to. When fleshly things rule a man, he is called ' flesh;' when worldly things rule him, profits and pleasures, a man is the ' world;' when a man yields to Satan, he is ' Satan.'

Use. This should make us *take heed by whom we are led,* under whose government we come. Saith St Paul, ' Do I purpose according to the flesh ?' That is, according to the profits, and pleasures, and honours which the flesh looks after. Are those my advisers, my intelligencers, my counsellors in the things I take in hand ? what may make for my honour, my pleasure, my estate, my worldly ease here ? No ! saith he, ' I purpose not according to the flesh.' The rule from hence is this, that,

Obs. A Christian man ought by all means to avoid the imputation of carnal policy.

Every Christian, much more a Christian man in authority and place, a minister, or magistrate, ought by all means to avoid it ? St Paul here declines it, ' Did I purpose things according to the flesh ?' Was I politic ? I had just occasion to speak largely of it in the former verse concerning fleshly wisdom, therefore I will speak the less of it now. We ought by all means to decline the imputation of it, and much more the conscience of it, than the report of it ; to be holily wise, and to be accounted so too.

Reason. The reason is, *it is God's enemy, and our enemy.* Should a Christian consult and deliberate with his enemy ? to take his enemy to be his judge, and his friend, and counsellor ? A man that hath his enemy to guide him to a place, that hath a pirate to guide him in a ship, how can he come to good ? He that is led by the flesh he consults with his enemy, when he looks what is for his profit, or his pleasure, &c. These things we should renounce as we promised in baptism, when we gave our names to

Christ. If we live and deliberate ' according to the flesh, we shall die,' saith the apostle peremptorily. It is a dangerous enemy ; death is the issue of all the counsel of the flesh, Rom. viii. 2, *seq.*

Again, it is *a secret enemy, a domestic enemy.* It is in all the powers of the soul. We cannot be too jealous against it. It is a perpetual enemy that accompanies us continually, in all our consultations, in all places ; in prosperity, in adversity. It hinders us from all good, it keeps us from the reformation of anything that is ill.

If a magistrate be suggested by any other, or by a good motion of his own, do this, reform this, Oh ! I shall run myself into danger, I shall incur censure ! So ill is done, and is unreformed, only by consulting with the flesh ; and good is neglected,—I shall be accounted an hypocrite, if I do this.

So there is flesh and blood to hinder in every good thing. The flesh will be foisting bad ends, or bad moving causes, and the flesh will be ready to keep us from reforming ill from fear of danger. And if we do ill, and be in ill, it will be ready to keep us in ill. Oh ! it is time enough to repent, &c. A thousand such policies the flesh hath to keep us in ill till we be in hell itself. Who would be advised, and take counsel by such an enemy ?

Use. Therefore, let us take heed. We have it in us, *but let it live in us only, and not rule in us.* Although it will be in us as long as we live, yet let us not be ruled by it ; let us not admit it to counsel, but suppress it, and keep it under. Especially those that are magistrates, that are called to public business, let them not bring private respects to public business, but bring public hearts to intend the good of religion, and of their country, before any private interest whatsoever. And not consult according to the flesh : If I do this, I shall displease such and such. That is no matter. If it were not for religion, if a man have a public mind, such as the very heathens had, he would lay aside base respects in public business. Therefore, I humbly desire such to examine deeply their intentions and purposes, what they aim at ; whether to serve God, and the church, and their country, or to serve themselves ; that if so be they may be safe, they care not what befall their country, or religion, or whatsoever. That is it that moves God to indignation, to cross their intentions ; for when God sees they set earth above heaven, the world present before the world to come ; and the dirt of the world, base respects before those that are greater, that they invert the order of things, he crosseth them in that they aim at, because they cross him in neglecting their duty. Therefore, as we would have things succeed well, let us labour to consult, not according to the flesh, for our private advantage ; but for what may make most first for religion, and then for the public good.

Again, we may learn from hence, that

Obs. A ground of lightness is to purpose things according to the flesh.

To purpose according to carnal reason, and affection, it is a ground of lightness. For mark the reason of it, when a man is carried in his deliberations by carnal respects, this will be for my profit, this will incline such a man to me, by this I shall get such a place, &c., when he is led by low and base respects, it makes him light with God, though he be never so good otherwise. Because carnal respects build on outward things that are uncertain ; therefore all resolutions built on outward things, and carnal respects, are uncertain. He that takes fleshly wisdom for his counsellor, and adviser, and intelligencer, what doth he ? He is led with by-respects, with one of the three idols of the world, some honour, or pleasure, or base profit, now when the rule of deliberation is the flesh, and the flesh carries to outward things that are variable. A man is alway light and inconstant, that propounds the deliberation of things according to the flesh.

What is the reason that a wicked man (though he be not notoriously, outwardly wicked; but a shrewd man, that is for himself, that makes himself the end of all his projects), what is the reason that such a man can never be a sound friend? He is never a sound friend; he is only a friend, so long as it makes for himself; so long as he gets to his own in all things. As the Jesuits use to say, so it is true of every natural man, they do all they do, and consult in an order to spiritual things; they do this, and that, and overrule kings and states, and this is for the good of society, and in an order of spiritual things. A man that hath not grace in him above nature, and above respects of nature, he can never be a sound friend; for when fleshly advantages come, of pleasures, and profits, and honours, when these rise one way or other, there he leaves the bonds of friendship; because there is a nearer bond between him and the things of this life; he is led with the flesh, and deliberates according to the flesh.

And that is the reason likewise why such a man can never be a good Christian. He can never go through the variety of times. Why? Because he consults of things according to the flesh, and as long as religion stands with his aims, that he may enjoy his riches, and his greatness, and the contentments of this life with religion, so long he is content to be religious; if religion cross him in these, he hath not learned to deny himself, and therefore he is not constant.

Or if times do not fall out so cross, he is not constant in his disposition; and God looks on him as he is in his disposition, and so he will judge him at that day. Now being led with the flesh, his disposition alters, and varies.

How shall I know whether I consult according to the flesh or no?

In a word, examine two things: (1.) the ground, and (2.) the aim of our actions, whence they rise, and what they aim at. Spring they from self-love? Aim they at our self-contentment and private interest? Then a man is led with the flesh.

To use a familiar instance. In marriage, when a man looks more to wealth than to religion, he adviseth according to the flesh. And so for a minister to respect his living more than anything that might weigh with his conscience otherwise, if he were good; he is led with respects according to the flesh. Those that leave their former good acquaintance, and choose such as they only hope to gain by, and forsake those acquaintance that they cannot gain by, though they be never so good otherwise, they are led according to the flesh.

How shall we know that we do not things, and consult not of things according to the flesh?

1. Some men may know it easily; as when men are of pregnant parts, when the strength of their wit leads them one way, *and religion leads them another way*, yet in the awe of God they do not go that way that politic respects would carry them. They could be as errant politicians as the best, but they dare not. Here now is a man that is 'led by the Spirit,' when it is not for want of parts, but out of conscience, he doth not so miscarry by his enemy. Many times an honest man could be rich by ill means as well as another. He knows the way. It is not for want of wit, but because he dares not. The awe of conscience and the awe of God lead him to better rules and aims. So it is easily discerned in eminency of parts.

2. And likewise *in fitness of opportunities*, if there be not parts, when a man hath all outward advantages to satisfy the flesh, to yield to it, to have

his aims, and yet he will not. If a man have power, and yet doth not revenge himself, he consults not with flesh and blood ; for he might be revenged if he would. So I say, when there is something that might sway us another way, and yet notwithstanding out of mere conscience, and better rules, we will not, it is a sign we purpose not, we advise not things according to the flesh, but according to the Spirit ; we are led with better rules than the world is.

In strong suggestions, a Joseph can say, ' How shall I do this and offend against God ?' Gen. xxxix. 9. 'Doth not God see it?' saith Job, xxxi. 4. So a Christian in the strength of temptations, and solicitations, and opportunities to do ill, he considers, ' Doth not God see ? How shall I do this, and offend against God ?' Shall I break the peace of my conscience for the gaining of this, and this ? Why no. Then a man is not led with carnal wisdom.

3. Again, we may know this, that we are not led by the flesh, and advised by the flesh, *when we are humble in all our consultations*. It is a perpetual concomitant of carnal wisdom to be proud. Knowledge mingled with corruption puffeth up.

Quest. But how shall we labour to overcome this, because we have the flesh ready by us, in all our consultations ? We have this counsellor alway ready at hand, as St Paul complains, Rom. vii. 19, ' that when we would do well, evil is present.' It is present at our elbow ; nay, it is nearer, the flesh is mingled in all the powers of our souls ; and with heavenly wisdom there is a mixture of carnal wisdom ; how shall we do that we may not be tainted with it ?

I will give a direction or two.

Ans. First of all, have a prejudice of it, *Cave, time*, &c., saith the holy man St Austin. ' Take heed of the evil man thyself' (*ggg*) ; take heed of carnal reason ; be jealous of it. It is an enemy, and the issues of the ways it adviseth to are death. ' There is a way that seems good to a man in his own eyes, the issues whereof are death,' Prov. xiv. 12, not temporal only, but eternal death. It is a deadly enemy ; have a prejudice of it, and conceit of it to be as it is ; have a jealousy of it, and of our own selves, especially in things that concern ourselves. What is the reason that a man is an incompetent judge in his own cause ? This, because there is natural self-love and flesh that draws all to itself. Consult not with it therefore ; consult with higher rules, and principles, what may make most for the chief end, for the glory of God, for the assurance of our comfort while we live here, and a better estate hereafter, that which may make most for the common good ; let us labour to live by right rules and principles : God will value us by that.

Put the case a man by passion be led another way, what is his rule ? what is his aim ? His aim is not carnal. He may fall by passion, &c. God judgeth not by passion, but by the tenor of our life. God esteems us not by a single particular exorbitant act that by passion or incogitancy a man falls into, but by the tenor of our life. Therefore let us labour to have our rules and aims good, though we fail in particular, yet that our way may be good ; though we step awry, yet our way may be good ; that when judgment shall come, when death shall come, it may not find us in an ill way, in an ill course. Therefore let us consult with God, consult with his word, consult with those that are led by the Spirit of God ; labour to be under the government of God's blessed Spirit, to be guided by the Spirit of God, and by the word of God. This should be our care, to labour that God would guide us by his good Spirit in those ways that may lead to our comfort, that of all other enemies in the world, he would not give us up to our own flesh to guide us, but that he would take the guidance of us to himself, that as he hath right to us by his covenant, so he would take us into his government. And desire Christ that as he is our priest to die for us, so likewise he would be our prophet to instruct us, to subdue all in us. And let divine truth be our counsellor, to bring our inner man into subjection, as it is, 2 Cor. x. 4, ' The weapons of our warfare are mighty,' to bring all into captivity, to subject all high devices and reasonings.

How shall I do this ? I shall miss of my ends, I shall miss of my projects. O ! but religion when it comes and brings down all, it makes not a man to cast away reason, but brings reason under, and brings the soul under God. A man may keep his wisdom and understanding safe still, so he keep it under, and let divine truth sway and bring all in us into captivity to itself.

But, alas ! the scope of the world is contrary ! Instead of bringing the soul into captivity to God's truth, to be led by him, to have no thoughts, no aims contrary to God's will, they make God's truth a captive and prisoner to their own base affections ; as St Paul saith, Rom. i. 18, ' They hold the truth,' they withhold it as a prisoner under base affections. And whereas all should serve the main end, and intend better things, they make a counterfeit loving of good things to serve their carnal ends, they make heaven serve earth, they make God serve man, the Spirit serve the flesh : they invert the order of things clean, which is as contrary to nature as if they had wisdom to consider it, as that the heaven should be under the earth, and the water above the air. It overturns all in religion, when we suffer carnal wisdom to rule all, to imprison that light that God hath put into the heart and conscience, and the light of his word to base affections, and not to bring all into captivity to the Spirit and the word.

When we come to hear God's word, we should consider that we come not for recreation ; but we come to a counsellor, to that that should sway and direct all our ways and words, to that that is not only our comfort in the time of affliction, but our counsellor. As David saith, ' it was the man of his counsel,' Ps. lxxiii. 24, et alibi. So we come here to be counselled, to hear that which must direct us in the way to heaven. We must come with a purpose to be guided by that, to be taught. As Cornelius saith, ' We are here in the presence of God, to hear what shall be said to us from God,' Acts x. 33. St Paul gives this direction, 1 Cor. iii. 18. If a man will ' be wise in heavenly things, let him be a fool first.' It is a strange thing, ' Let him be a fool,' that is, let him be content to be esteemed so, let him be content to lose his reputation of wisdom, ' that he may be wise.' When he knows others to be fools, let him take a substantial course, that the vain world may think him wise.

It is hard counsel ; for of all imputations in the world, many and the most had rather be accounted wicked, than be accounted fools. Account them the veriest fools which are unfit to speak ; think of them in the highest degree of ill you can, Oh ! they have wit enough for that, they have learning, and parts for that ; take not away their learning, and parts, account them not fools, account them what you will. Religion masters this base opinion. Saint Paul saith, ' Let a man be a fool, if he will be wise.' Let no man deceive himself, and think, let poor men be so, and so ; religion is the private man's good, and let them make conscience of such things ; but for us that are in place and authority, we must rule by policy, and he knows not how to rule that is not a politician. Let no man deceive himself; there is no man, great or small, but if he will be wise for heaven, ' let him be a fool,' let him take courses that are conscionable, though he be accounted a fool for his pains.

Let us be jealous of our own hearts in private and public, let us take heed to our own hearts that the flesh come not in. Let us labour to be acquainted with Christ, that he may be our counsellor and our guide in all things.

Specially now when we come to the communion. We now renew our covenant with God, and our acquaintance with Christ Jesus; we come to feast with him. Do we think to have any good by him, any benefit by his death, except we make him our king and prophet, to rule and guide us, except we make him our counsellor? Therefore let us think before-hand, we cannot come as we ought to receive the communion, unless we intend beforehand to renounce the flesh, Christ's enemy. Can you be welcome guests, and resolve after to be led and ruled by his enemy? If you will have good by Christ's death, as a priest to reconcile you to God: (as this sacrament seals the benefits of his death, the breaking of the bread, and the pouring out of the wine,) come with a purpose to be ruled, and guided by this counsellor in all things. He is the great Counsellor, Isa. ix. 7, that is willing to advise us by his word and Spirit in all the particular passages of our lives; and the more we enter into acquaintance with him by the sacrament, and maintain it by private prayer, and by all sacred means, the more ready he will be to do the office of a friend, and counsellor, in all the passages of our lives to advise us what is best. I had occasion in verse 12th to speak at large of fleshly wisdom, therefore I pass it.

' *That with me there should be yea, yea, and nay, nay.*' This sets down the manner of inconstancy, the form of it, ' yea, yea,' to be on the affirmative part once; and then ' nay, nay,' the negative; to be of one mind, and peremptory in it, and then to be of another mind, and peremptory in that. This is the issue of carnal wisdom, and follows on it, ' The things that I purpose, do I purpose according to the flesh, that with me there should be yea, yea, and nay, nay?' insinuating, that those that purpose things according to the flesh, they are ' yea, yea, and nay, nay.' Whence first we may observe, (which I touched before a little, but it issues more properly hence from the dependence) that

Obs. Carnal men are alway inconstant men.

For a fleshly man, led with the flesh, being led with the things of the world, and they being inconstant, he must needs be as that which he is ruled by. A man cannot stand safe upon the ice, because itself is not safe. A man cannot stand in a thing that stands not, that hath no consistence. Now a carnal man he hath no prop to hold him but the things below. He cleaves to them, and they are inconstant, and variable, and uncertain. He that purposeth according to the flesh is ' yea, yea, nay, nay.' Therefore his love is ' yea, yea, nay, nay.' If he may have good by you, he is ' yea, yea,' he is for you; but can you do him no good, he is ' nay, nay,' he will not own you then.

Therefore one way to be constant, is not to be ruled according to the flesh, which I spake of before, for they that are, are ' yea, yea, nay, nay.'

Therefore take heed how you trust carnal men, in near intimate society, as in marriage. Or in near friendship, never take a man that hath his own aims and ends. For he will respect you no more than he can advance his own ends by you. ' Trust not the wife of thy bosom,' saith the prophet, Deut. xiii. 6 ; if she be carnal, she will have her own ends. So a friend that is carnal, he will have his own ends. The idol that he respects more than thee, or than anything in the earth, is his own fleshly wisdom, and his own ends. Every carnal man makes himself his god. He reduceth all to himself. His own ends is his idol ; therefore have no intimate society with such.

' That with me there should be yea, yea ; nay, nay.' Observe again in this place, that

Obs. Carnal men are vehement.

They are vehement in either part. If they be ' yea,' they are ' yea, yea,' and yet they will be ' nay, nay,' naught at the same time. The soul of man will admit of contraries, and yet be still the same in the general ; ' yea, yea,' at one time, and ' nay, nay,' at another time. And usually they that are vehement in business one way, are vehement another, if they be carnal. A carnal man is vehement one way in the pursuit of things, and he is vehement on the contrary if he be crossed.

What is the reason that men that are carnal, some stand against religion and some for religion with like eagerness? The one is ' nay, nay,' as much as the other is ' yea, yea.' Both are flesh, and if those that are ' yea, yea,' were where the other are, they would be ' nay, nay.' For instance, a man is religious only for carnal respects, he is ' yea, yea.' O ! he will have the religion of the times. Why ? He could not be safe else, he cannot have his ends else, he was bred up in it, &c. Another, on the contrary, is as much for the opposite religion. What is the reason ? He was bred in it, it stands for his ends. If a man be religious not for religious respects, he is peremptory, and contrary to him of the opposite religion ; and yet they are equally naught.

A common protestant hath no better ground for his religion than a papist hath for his. The same reason that a papist hath, the same such a protestant hath ; he was bred in it, and the king is of that religion, and he shall attain his ends by it. Hath a papist other reasons ? Except a man be truly changed and altered, he shall be ' yea, yea,' and ' nay, nay,' sometime one, sometime another, peremptory in one and peremptory in another, and all naught.

As, for instance, the sea, sometimes it ebbs, sometimes it flows, sometimes it flows one way, and then flows back another way ; yet it is alway salt and brinish, the nature of it is not changed. So some men are peremptory, ' yea, yea,' they run one way amain, and then they ebb again, yet they alway keep their nature brinish. They are peremptory for good sometimes, and when it stands for their ends they are peremptory against it. Such a cause is so ; it is ' yea ' if it help their advantage, and it is not so if it help not that, as if truth itself in their judgment were flexible and alterable. Thus a carnal man, he alters, and yet he is never good in his judgment. St Paul declines this ; he was not ' yea, yea, nay, nay,' because he did not purpose things according to the flesh.

To come to the point itself. This declining of inconstancy, of ' yea, yea,' ' nay, nay,' it came in St Paul from hatred of inconstancy and falsehood. For ' yea ' and ' nay,' when a man is of one mind and another, it comes from one of these two grounds in a carnal man :

Either because *he is inconstant,* that he is now of one mind and now of another;

Or because *he is false and means to dissemble.*

Now, both are dispositions that are contrary to a Christian man; he should neither be light, nor be false and untrue.

Now, St Paul doth much more decline the imputation of falsehood and dissembling, that he should be ' yea,' when he meant not ' yea,' but ' nay,' when he had declined the imputation of lightness; for a man may truly say he will, and yet change his mind after. But for a man to say he will, and yet mean it not, that is falsehood and dissembling, which is worse. St Paul intends much more to decline the suspicion of that.

Dissemblers are ' yea, yea,' ' nay nay,' not at divers times, but at the same time; they make yea and nay all at once. We say contradictions cannot be true, for a thing to be and not to be at the same time; but dissemblers would have contradictions true. They make as if they loved when indeed they hate.

God is the God of truth, the word is the word of truth, and Christ is the truth, and the devil is ' the father of lies,' John viii. 44. Therefore, as we would be like to God, and as we would be unlike Satan, let us labour for truth in all things. St Paul here labours to avoid the opinion of dissembling.

How would he think, then, of equivocation, when there is yea and nay at a breath? They are not at divers times inconstant, but yea and nay at once, to speak one thing and mean the contrary, to have reservations of the contrary. It is so odious that I will not spend time to speak of it,— only this.

1. If it were allowable, as the best of their writers allow it and practise it (however, if they do not allow it, their practice is so, but they do allow it), *by this means the devil himself should never be a liar*, there would be no lie at all. And it were in vain for God to make prohibitions against lying if there might be equivocation, for there is no lie in the world but it may be salved up with reservations. Therefore, that course that brings the devil from being a liar, that frustrates God's course, and that makes men that they shall not lie, whatsoever they do, it is abominable such a conceit, and odious to God. But to maintain equivocation, is to do all this; for with absurd reservations, what in the world may not be justified?

2. Then, again, we are exhorted to suffer martyrdom, to stand for God's cause. Now, to allow equivocation *is to avoid suffering*. Where is the honour of martyrdom and suffering for God's cause, when men shall speak untruths and justify themselves by a lie? It is contrary, I say, to the whole tenor and stream of Scripture.

3. Then again, *they may call it equivocation to mince it, but it is a lie to speak one thing and reserve another.* For what is a lie? To speak falsehood with a purpose and intention to deceive another. Now, they speak false and with a purpose to deceive. A lie must be esteemed as it is esteemed by another that hears it, not him that speaks it, as it is with an oath. Isidore saith (*hhh*), ' An oath is to be esteemed as he that I speak to esteems it, not as I in my sense esteem it; as God esteems it, and he to whom I speak.' So a lie is to be judged as he judgeth it that I speak to, because God forbids lying as a breach of charity to others, because he would not have others deceived. If I salve it up in my own thoughts and deceive others, it is a breach of charity and a lie, because it is a speech of untruth which another thinks to be a truth; it is an untruth, and to deceive him. But these men will have yea and nay at a breath; they will say, ' Yea,' and yet have a reservation of nay, at once. St Paul would much more decline and abhor this, if he were alive now, when he so declined the imputation of inconstancy, of ' yea, yea,' and ' nay, nay,' at

divers times. Indeed, St Paul reserved this. He promised to come to them if God did permit, with a divine reservation. We may say in all the business we are to do, This I will do, if God permit, and if God will. And, indeed, God hindered his journey. But I say for equivocation, the matter is so odious and palpable, that if it were not that *nondum satis odimus*, &c., we hate not these men enough, I would not have spoken of it. Their religion is so abominable and odious, we do not yet hate it enough ; and, therefore, it is good on all occasions to uncase them, and all little enough. But I go on.

VERSE 18.

' *As God is true, our word to you was not yea and nay.*' The apostle in the former verse having laboured to clear himself from the imputation of lightness and inconstancy, that he did not come to them as he had promised ; and from an imputation likewise of policy for himself, that he did purpose things according to the flesh, which is the cause of inconstancy, ' of yea, yea, and nay, nay,' he comes now to that which he more intended than those particulars. For he was content to be thought to have disappointed them in the matter of his journey ; but that which he aims at was to stablish them in this, that his doctrine was sound, ' As God is true, our word to you was not yea and nay.' Perhaps I promised to come, and did not. It is true. But my preaching was not ' yea and nay.' All that I taught was sound and certain. You may build your souls on it. It was ' yea.' He labours to draw them to be persuaded of the certainty of his ministry, as being very unwilling that a defect in his promise about a business of the world should weaken their faith in the truth that he delivered as a minister.

' *As God is true, our word to you was not yea and nay.*' He seems to make a difference between yea and nay in civil things and in divine. There is a difference when a holy man speaks of the things of this life and when he speaks of divine truths. St Paul promised to come to them ; he meant it honestly, and did intend it, but it was subject to alteration, because God stops our purposes in this life, yea, our good purposes, many times. Good things may have variety. One good thing may be more convenient than another. And the cause why he came not to them was not his inconstancy, but their unfitness. It was from their corruption in manners and in doctrine. They were not ready. As he saith after, ' he came not, *to spare them.*' They were unfit till they were humbled with his former epistle, and then, when they were humbled, he purposed to come. But now in divine truths, what things he spake to them concerning grace and glory, that was certain. ' Our word to you was not yea and nay.'

Quest. A question may be moved briefly, how St Paul could be deceived in his journey and not in his doctrine. Being so good a man, led by the Spirit of God, how could he promise to come, and yet did not ?

Ans. I answer, the difference is much between these two. St Paul had three persons * on him.

He was a *man*, a *Christian man*, an *apostle*.

As a man, he was subject to all things that men are subject unto, that is,

* In the sense of the Latin *persona*, a character which one represents, or part which he acts.—ED.

he desired in truth of heart to come and visit his friends; he purposed a journey, with a reservation that God might hinder him; and so as a man he might have a 'Yea,' that is, a purpose to do a thing; and afterward a 'Nay,' upon the uncertain event of the things of this life. So, as a man he purposed to come. Nay, as a *holy man* he purposed a journey to a good purpose, to stablish them; but with a reservation, if God permit; God might stop his journey. But as *an apostle*, he taught other things, than speaking of journeys. That he spake of only as a man, and as a holy man, alway supposing the condition of human things, and under permission, if God permit. But as an apostle he was not yea and nay. There he was certain. As an apostle he spake divine truths, and was guided infallibly by the Spirit of God; he delivered truths without all conditions and exceptions. As an apostle, he did not admit of any such uncertainty. There is an eminency and excellency in divine truth. It is stable, and firm, and not subject to variety and inconstancy. So his doctrine as an apostle was always 'Yea.'

For his journey, and coming to them, he promised his journey *in veritate propositi*, in the truth of a good purpose of a friend; but as he spake of divine truths, he spake of them in the certainty of the divine Spirit. In the one, he spake in the certainty of truth; in the other, in the truth of affection. As a man, he spake in the truth of a good affection he bare to them; but as an apostle, he spake in the certainty of divine truth.

And you must know this, that God, as he used the apostles and excellent men to write his book, to write the word of God, to be his penmen, yet he hindered them not to be men. As he hinders not godly men to be men, but at once they may be saints and men; so St Paul as a good man, desired to see them, with a reservation; but as an apostle, he was guided by a certain infallible assistance of divine truth.

Nathan, as he was a man, gave David liberty to build the temple. He was overshot in it something. But then he goes to God, and consults with him, whether he should or no; and then Nathan gives David another advice.*

So the prophets and apostles, as men, they might be alterable without sin. For God will allow men to be men, and subject to mistakes. For *nescience*, not knowing the possibility of things to come, is no sin in man; because it is an unavoidable infirmity. So that St Paul, as his usual manner is, in promising things to come, things of that nature, he promiseth them under reservation and permission, if God permit, if God will; and he doth not sin, though he be frustrate of his intention.

It is not the only part of a wise man to divine what will be. St Paul had not providence to see whether his journey should be crossed or no; but out of a Christian intention, he resolved to come, if God did not cross him; that was as a man, and a good man. But as an apostle, his doctrine was without ifs and ands, without exception, as we say, 'if God permit,' &c. 'No,' saith he; 'as God is true, our word to you was not yea and nay.' So in the apostles, we must consider a difference of divine truths that they delivered as apostles, from those things that they purposed as men, and as holy men. Those were subject to be crossed, and without sin too. For God will have men to be men, that is, variable creatures, and such as cannot promise themselves for the time to come any certain thing.

It is God's prerogative to know things to come. We may know them by their causes; we may know when there will be an eclipse a hundred

* Cf. 2 Sam. vii. 3, with 4–11.—G.

years hence ; but to know what weather there shall be, as we may know the eclipse, we cannot ; because there is nothing in the cause. I say, God will have men to be men. St Paul may promise holily, with a reservation to God, as a man, and as a holy man, and without sin too ; but as an apostle, in his doctrine he was not so ; but ' as God is true, our word to you was not yea and nay,' but constant as God himself. That shall suffice to satisfy that. Therefore St Paul makes the difference, I promised to come, but I did not ; but ' as God is true, our word to you was not yea and nay.'

Our voyage to heaven, and the reference we have to a better life, stands not on uncertainties, as the things here in this world. St Paul's journey to Corinth might be frustrate ; but St Paul had another course to heaven ; his religious course stood not on uncertainties. Whatsoever he taught in a religious course, it was ' yea ; ' as he saith in the next verse, ' Christ the Son of God whom we preach, was not yea and nay, but yea ; ' that is, infallibly true, perpetually true, necessarily, eternally true.

' As God is true, our word to you was not yea and nay.' St Paul labours to establish them therefore in a good conceit of his ministry ; and that made him indeed so much decline the suspicion of inconstancy in other things : because carnal men are prone to think a man in his calling, even a preacher in his doctrine, to be inconstant, if he be so in his common course.

St Paul knew their corruption was such, that from a suspicion of lightness in his carriage and common course, they would rise to a suspicion of his doctrine ; therefore he was so curious to avoid the imputation of lightness in his journey, because he would avoid any imputation of lightness in his doctrine. That is it which he more aims at. He stands not on the imputation of lightness in his journey, or such matters ; but he knew the corruption of men is such, that if a man fail in common things, presently they think he is so in his calling. Full of false surmises and suspicions is the nature of man ; and as a man is once, they gather him to be so alway. Therefore he deceiving them in not coming, they might think he would do so at other times too. That makes the apostle labour to clear himself, but especially his doctrine, from all suspicion.

' As God is true, our word to you was not yea and nay.' Here is a truth ; and the seal of it.

His averring the truth is this, ' Our word, our preaching,' as it is in the margin (iii). ' Our word,' as it was unfolded, it was not ' yea and nay,' it was not uncertain.

And the proof and seal of it, ' God is true,' as it is in the original, which is made up in the English tongue, ' As God is true,' it is in our translation ; but in the original it is, ' God is true ; ' and as he is true, and constant, and faithful, so our word is constant and faithful ; you may build on it (jjj). ' As God is true,' as God is to be credited and believed, so my word to you is to be credited as ' yea,' as a certain doctrine that is not ' yea and nay.' It is a kind of an oath.

' As God is true.' The apostle here seals it with an oath.

What is an oath ?

An oath is a religious calling of God to witness, or to be a judge in doubtful things.

It is in doubtful things a calling of God to be a witness of the truth we speak, and to be a revenger if we speak not true. It is to call God to witness and to judge, to make him *testis et vindex*. St Paul here calls God to witness, ' God is true,' and as verily as he is true, ' our word to you was not yea and nay.'

You know oaths are either, as we say, *assertory*, to aver a thing ; or *promissory*, for the time to come to do this or that ; and they are either imposed or voluntary. Now this is an *assertory* oath, not a *promissory*. He avers and avoucheth peremptorily, that as God is true, his word to them was not ' yea and nay, but yea.' And it was a voluntary oath ; for nobody exacted it of him. But he saw there was a necessity to stablish them in the certainty of the doctrine he taught, to seal it with an oath, that they should as well doubt of the truth of God, as of his doctrine. ' As God is true, my word is true.'

Jeremiah the prophet hath three conditions of an oath, ' It must be in truth, in righteousness, and in judgment,' Jer. iv. 2.

In truth. We must speak and swear true things.

And *in judgment;* necessary things, with discretion.

And *in righteousness.*

Now St Paul observed the conditions wondrous well here. For St Paul doth it in a true matter, and in judgment ; for he was forced to it.

An oath is never good but when it is necessary ; not to seal up every idle discourse, as if men would make everything they say to be as true as an oath. Indeed, the life of a man should be an oath. The life of an honest man is an oath, as true ; but we must not call God to question for every idle impertinent thing. St Paul saw it necessary to call God to witness ; it was true and necessary.

I will not enter into a large discourse of an oath, because afterward I shall have better occasion to speak of it. Only thus much at this time : St Paul here useth it. He thinks it to be necessary, to establish their minds the better in his ministry, and a good conceit of it that it was constant. ' God is true, our word to you was not yea and nay.'

Therefore, in such a case we may not make scruple of an oath, if it be

In *charity, piety, necessity.*

In charity ; in matters of controversy of civil life.

In piety ; to establish matters of religion.

And in *matters of necessity*, that cannot be determined otherwise, there is no scruple to be made of it.

And where we are bid ' not to swear at all,' Mat. v. 34, that is, not in ordinary course ; or not to swear by creatures ; but if we do swear, it is a part of God's service, we must swear by him. And, indeed, it is a service of God, and to good purpose, when Christians swear to stablish and determine truths that otherwise are doubtful.

They were doubtful of St Paul's doctrine and his person. Saith he, To put you out of doubt of the truth I speak to you, I dare call God to witness it is true and sound. The apostle doth so once after in this chapter. Therefore I reserve the further handling of an oath to verse 23d, because the word there is more infallible,* ' I call God to record upon my soul,' &c.

The next thing I observe hence is this, that

Obs. The believing that God's word is God's word, and is certain, it is a matter of great consequence.

It is of great consequence, for God's people that look to be saved, to be stablished in their opinion and judgment of divine truth, that it is certain, and not flexible and mutable, according to our wills, and conceits, and dispositions, but is ' yea,' alway the same, as God himself, the author of it.

* That is, ' explicit, unmistakeable.'—G.

For laying this for a ground, that I said before, that St Paul takes God to witness, he would not interpose an oath, but in a matter of great consequence ; therefore, it is a matter of great consequence to be settled in this, that the Scripture is divine truth, unalterable and unchangeable.

An oath is never good, as I said, but when it is necessary. It must not only be in truth, but there must be a necessity. It must not only be taken in righteousness, but in judgment ; a man must do it in discretion, when the thing is not determinable any other way, Therefore it is a matter of great consequence, that men take the word of truth not to be as the oracles of Apollo and of the devil, true one way, and false another (*kkk*). The devil would escape the imputation of a lie, though he be a liar ; but God's oracles be divine, they be ' yea.' And it is good that we think them to be so, to be constant, undoubted, certain, and unmovable. Therefore the apostle seals it with an oath. He would not seal a slight truth by an oath, but saith he, ' As God is true, our word to you was not yea and nay,' &c.

And St Paul saw a disposition in them to suspect the truth of God, as indeed, we are proner to believe the lies of our own hearts, and the suggestions of Satan, and the counsel of politicians, of carnal friends, than to believe God himself. Therefore, partly for the indisposition in us ; and partly for the great exigence and necessity of the thing, to believe that God's word is his word, that it is truth, he seals it with an oath, ' God is true.' It is a point of great consequence.

Reason. The reason is, God can have no service else, and we can have no comfort.

If we do not believe the word of God to be undoubtedly true, in great temptations and assaults, what armour of proof shall we have ? We can have no comfort nor grace. For sometimes subtle and strong temptations to evil come, if the word of God be not more undoubted to me, than the present profit, or pleasure, or whatsoever ; if the temptation be ready, and I be not built on, and settled on some grounded truth that I know to be true as God is true. When the temptation is strong, and our faith weak, where are we ? A man presently yields to base lusts and temptations.

And so in matter of danger and despair. When a man is tempted to despair, if he cannot build on this, ' God is true,' and his word is as true as himself, ' He wills not the death of a sinner,' &c., Ezek. xviii. 32, here a man is swallowed up.

It is no matter how strong the foundation be, if the building on that foundation be weak. If a strong man stand in a slippery place, down he falls ; if a man stand slippery, and have a weak standing on a strong place, on a strong foundation ; if he have a weak building on a strong foundation, he shall soon be cast off. So, the word of God is true in itself : but if we be not persuaded so, that it is infallibly true, that it is alway ' yea,' we shall be shaken with temptations. When we are tempted to sin, the temptation is present, we are sure of the temptation. If we be not more sure of somewhat against the temptation, somewhat out of the word to beat back the darts of Satan, when we are tempted to sin, and to despair for sin, down we go ; and, therefore, it is a matter of infinite consequence to be persuaded of divine truth.

What makes many as they are, in courses that are corrupt in their callings ? Nothing but this : they stagger, whether it be true or no that there shall be a judgment; they stagger, whether it be true or no that the Scripture saith. If they were persuaded that it were ' yea,' as true as God is in heaven, as true as they have souls, so their souls must be called to judg-

ment for that they speak and do, would they do as they do ? Therefore
St Paul stablisheth them by an oath, ' God is true, and as God is true, our
word to you was not yea and nay.'

Use. Therefore take in good part with thankfulness the means that God
hath ordained to strengthen our faith and assurance of the word of God,
and the promises of God. Therefore he hath appointed the sacrament for
that purpose. I say there is nothing in the world so strengthened as the
soul of a Christian, if he give himself to God's truth to be ruled by it.
For if we will believe God, we have his promise, that ' whosoever believes
in Christ shall not perish, but have everlasting life,' 2 Pet. iii. 9; rich promises, ' precious promises,' 2 Pet. i. 4, as the Scripture calls them. We
have not only promises, but they are sealed with an oath. Now an oath
is an unchangeable thing, Heb. vi. 16. We have promises and oath, that
we might have ' strong consolation.' Whatsoever might secure man we
have. Besides his oath we have his seal, his sacrament. It was his love
to condescend to make any covenant with sinful creatures, that upon any
terms he would give them life everlasting. It was a higher degree of love
to set Christ to be the foundation of this peace, and of this covenant, that
now God and we may be at peace with satisfaction to divine justice, that
he is the foundation of the peace between God and us. Now God may be
merciful without wrong, without impeachment to his justice; that is a higher
degree of mercy, to enter into covenant, and to give Christ to be the foundation of all. And then it is a higher degree than that to secure us of the
covenant, that Christ is ours, to seal the word with an oath, and with the
sacrament which is the seal of the covenant; what could God do more ?

What a horrible sin therefore is unbelief, that we should tremble at, to
call God's love and truth in question ! But yet we are prone to it ; or
else why did Christ ordain the sacrament to strengthen and stablish our
faith, and to confirm us, but that he knew our propenseness to unbelief?

In the time of ease and prosperity, it is easy to think, God is merciful,
and Christ died ; but in the time of temptation, all is little enough to shore
and prop up the faith of a drooping Christian. Therefore God, out of
heavenly wisdom, and love to us, hath appointed these ordinances for the
strengthening of our faith. And all is to no purpose, unless our faith
be strong in the promises, as St Paul takes an oath, to build them on the
promises he taught them. And so all is little enough, oath, and promises,
and seal, &c. Therefore we should with all reverence attend upon God's
ordinances for the strengthening of our faith. But to come to the words
themselves.

' As God is true, our word to you was not yea and nay.' Take the
words out of the form of an oath, and the proposition is, that

Doct. God is true and faithful.

In this link of the sentence, ' God is true'—First, it is true that *God* is.
He is truly God. His nature is true ; his properties true. Likewise God
is true and faithful, not only in his nature and properties, but in his free
decrees, in the things that freely come from him. It was free for him to
make promises of salvation or no, as it was free for him to make a world
or no, and whether he would redeem mankind or no ; but when he had
promised, except he should deny himself and his truth, he must send Christ.
So in all the free promises of forgiveness of sins, and life everlasting by
Christ, if we believe in him, we say they are certainly true, because God
that is true hath promised. God is true in his nature, and true in his free
promises, and threatenings ; he is true in his works, true in his word, every

way true. He is true in his nature, all is true within him, and without him. If anything could change him from within, he were not himself, he were not God. And from without there is nothing can change him; for there is nothing stronger than God. God is true in all his purposes, true in his free and voluntary decrees. It was free for him to decree, but having decreed, there is a necessity of performing. It is of the necessity of his nature as he is God. He is true in his free decrees. They are not free in regard of the event, but in regard of the original, as I said. He might have made a world at the first or no, and have redeemed mankind or no; but having made these decrees, of necessity as he is God he must be true in his free decrees.

There is a subordination of truths, whereof one is the cause of all the rest. Now all depends upon this grand truth, *God is*. It is the first truth that ever was of all truths in the world, in heaven and earth, that there is a God, that there is such a thing, such an excellency as God, the Author of all things in nature, the Author of all things in grace and glory. I shall not need to prove this fundamental truth, this truth of truths, that God is. It infers all other truths. For grant this, that God is, and a man must needs grant that that follows upon it, that God is as a God should be, that is, unchangeable, eternal, immutable, almighty, all-sufficient, and all the blessed attributes, that he is the Author of all good in the creature. That must needs follow. God is the first truth; and then God is so and so, as becomes a God. And then this must follow in the next place, that he is a God immutable and unchangeable. He must be so in all the manifestations that come from him, in his free decrees, and in the outward manifestations by promises, and threatenings, and whatsoever; and therefore God is true, immutably and unchangeably true, or else he were not God. He cannot be otherwise, and be God. A man may say of a man, he is a liar, and yet he may be a man. A man may be a man, and a good man, and yet be inconstant and changeable, because he is a creature. But to say a God, and not to be true, is to say a God, and not a God. Of the necessity of his nature he must be true. It is not of the necessity of the nature of man to be true. He may be a man, and be a liar ('Every man is a liar,' Ps. cxvi. 11), because it is not of the essence of man to be true. But God is true out of the necessity of nature. He cannot be God if he be not true, because God cannot deny himself. Man is changeable, because he is a creature, as Damascene's speech is (*lll*), 'All things created are mutable, and man as a creature is changeable.' A man therefore may be alterable, and false, and be a man; but God cannot be so, and be God.

Obj. It will be objected, that God hath threatened oft, and hath not performed; as we see in the Ninevites, and Hezekiah in his sickness, and so in many others.

Ans. But the answer is easy. God is true in all these; for God's promises that come from his truth, they are either absolute or conditional. The absolute are those that have nothing annexed to them, but shall certainly be. As God would have sent Christ without all conditions, Christ should have come without all peradventure, as we say. But now some promises have conditions annexed to them: if a nation repent of their sins, God will repent of the evil he hath threatened, as it is in Jer. xviii. 8. Now those threatenings that are on condition of repentance, if the condition be performed, the sentence is reversed. All the promises are made with exception of the cross; all must suffer before they come to heaven and be glorified. Now all the promises, with the exception of the cross, are conditional. So God is true, both in his absolute promises that are made without condition, and he is true in his conditional promises; because where he performs the condition, he will perform likewise that that is tied to the condition. He changeth his sentence sometimes, and his threatening, but not his decree; for his purpose and decree is to forgive and reverse the sentence, if we repent. I say, it is a clear truth that God is true, unchangeably and immutably true.

And it is the prime truth of all truths, that God is, and God is true. As we say of the heavens, unless the heavens were moved, there would be no motion in the earth. For if the sun had not a motion in the zodiac up and down, where were summer and winter? If he had not his course, where were night and day? the vicissitude and intercourse of all earthly things? If the heavenly motion were not, *nisi moverentur, &c.*, if those did not move, we could not move, because we depend upon that. So, unless it were true that God were, there is a God, and God is unchangeably true, there would be nothing true in the world; for all truth is therefore true, because it is answerable to that exemplar truth that is true in God, answerable to God's conceit and decree of things.

This I observe the rather, because it is a fundamental thing. It doth wondrously stablish our faith in divine truths, when we know it comes from God that is true. If we would seek for evidences of our faith, then we must go within us, and see what love, and what hope, what combat between the flesh and spirit there is; but if we look for anything to stablish our faith, go out of us, consider the unchangeable truth of God, whose truth it is.

God as God creating a reasonable creature, he must give him some revealed truth, he could not be worshipped else. How must we know this revealed truth whereby he will be worshipped by the reasonable creature (for no man will be served by his servant as he pleaseth)? How shall we know these certain truths? Because they come from his nature. God is true; and as God is true, ' so our word to you was not yea and nay,' that is, it was true. There is the same ground of the certainty of evangelical truth as there is of God himself to be true.

To add a little further in the point, consider the truth of God every way, the faithfulness of God, as it signifies in the original, ' as God is faithful.' Consider what relations God hath put upon him in his divine truth, how he will be thought on. And then bring those relations to his nature; for there we must pitch at last. What is he to us? and how hath he revealed himself to us? Thus and thus. What is he in his nature? So and so; and there we must rest.

For instance, the Lord hath made many promises. Who is it that hath made them? He that is true and unchangeably true. There the soul rests in the nature of God. But what relations hath he put upon him? He is a God, and a Lord, and a Judge, and a Father, &c.

Now, as he is God, he is true: therefore he will do all things that a true God should do. He will uphold his creature, while he will have his creature continue; he will give it life, and being, and motion.

And as a Lord he will do with his own what he list, and it is not for us to contend with him why he will do this or that, why he makes one rich and another poor. He is Lord of all, and a true Lord. Therefore we must give authority to this true Lord.

And then, as he is a Judge, he corrects men for sin, and rewards them for the good they do. As a Judge, sometime he punisheth them inwardly in conscience, sometimes outwardly. All the good we have is from this, that he is a faithful and true God; therefore there we must rest. He is a true Judge, he ' rewards every man according to his works, whether they be good or evil,' Mat. xvi. 27.

And so in the relation of a Father, he is a true Father, he corrects when time serves, he rewards and encourageth when time serves, he gives an inheritance to his children, and hath pity and compassion on his children when time serves. He is a true Father. Other fathers do this and that out of passion, not out of truth and goodness; but he doth. So when we consider God in his relations, consider of the attribute of his truth.

All truth, in his word, comes from this, God is true. This truth is sealed by this, that our truth to you, our word to you, was not ' yea and nay,' uncertain. God's truth is not uncertain and variable. There is no ' shadow of change in him,' James i. 17, and his word is like himself. We say usually, in the word of an honest man, and that is something. *In verbum Sacerdotis*, in the word of a priest, it was accounted in former times a great matter. It should be so indeed. In the word of a king is a great matter. But when God saith in the word of a God, ' The word of the Lord hath spoken so,' Jer. x. 1, it is not yea and nay, it was not flexible, and doubtful, because it is the word of him that hath the command of all that he saith. It is his word that is Lord of heaven and earth. Now when he that saith a thing is the Lord of heaven and earth, he is Lord of his own word, therefore what he saith is not ' yea and nay,' uncertain; for he can make good what he saith. There is the same ground of evangelical truth, as there is of God himself to be true. I will speak no more in the unfolding of the point. It is plain that God is true.

Is this true, that God is true, that he is truth itself? Then many things issue from hence. It is a ground of many other truths. It was the ground of all the uses that St Paul makes of the word of God. It is profitable every way. I will name some principal, to avoid multiplicity in a plain point.

Use 1. God is true, and his word is true. *Hereupon the threatenings of God must needs be true,* even as true as God himself. If this be so, then unless we will make another Scripture, another word, this word is ' yea.' That word that threatens sin, that idolaters, and covetous, and wantons shall never enter into the kingdom of heaven, (' Be not deceived,' saith the apostle, 1 Cor. vi. 9,) that word is ' yea.' It is true. God is true. This must follow, therefore, that whatsoever he saith is true; therefore his threatenings are true. It is a truth that hath influence into all other truths whatsoever. That which is prefixed here by St Paul, not only as an oath, ' as God is true,' so his word is not yea and nay, but certain. But I say it hath influence into all other truths whatsoever; threatenings, promises, directions, all are therefore true, because God is true.

Therefore those that shuffle off the threatenings, and think they shall do well, and bless themselves, God's wrath shall ' smoke against them,' Deut. xxix. 20; for God must alter his nature, and his word must be altered, or else his judgments must stick on them death and damnation without repentance. If God should not be avenged on ordinary swearers and blasphemers; if adulterers should live in such sins, and ever come to heaven, they must have another God, and another word of God. This hath said, they shall not enter into heaven that live in these sins. If it be true as God is true, what horrible atheism is in the hearts of men, to think that God will change his nature, though they do not change their course, and that the word of God shall alter, though they will not alter? What hope

can profane, blasphemous persons have, that make but a trifle of swearing,
when God hath said they shall not go unpunished ? and those that live in
a filthy course, when God hath said, ' Whoremongers and adulterers God
will judge ' ? without horrible atheism how can these men hope for favour
from God, when he hath sealed his word with this, that as he is true, and
truth itself, his word is true, they shall never enter into heaven ?

Use 2. So again, if this be true, that God is true, and his word thereupon is not yea and nay, *it serves to comfort us many ways.*

When we are oppressed in the sense of sin, ' If we confess our sins, he
is merciful to forgive our sins,' 1 John i. 9. He that is true hath said it,
whose word is not yea and nay, but yea. Trust to it. If we doubt of
perseverance for the time to come, he that hath ' begun a good work will
perfect it to the day of the Lord,' Philip. i. 6. He is yea, and his word is
yea ; he is true, and his word is true.

Use 3. Again, hence for our judgment we learn this truth, that the word
of God hath the same ground of truth as God himself. Therefore it is
the judge of all controversies. Of all things questionable in religion, the
word of God is judge ; because it is not ' yea and nay, but yea,' and ' it is
true, as God is true.' And it is judge of this controversy too, whether it
be the word of God ?

The question between the papists and us is, whether the epistles and the
prophets be the word of God, or no ? whether is it or no ?

I answer, from apostolical testimony, St Paul saith, ' As God is true,' his
word is true, the true word of God ; and ' All Scripture is given by inspira-
tion,' 2 Tim. iii. 16. The word of God therefore is the judge of all divine
truths, because it is most certain, even as certain as God himself.

What are the properties of a chief judge ?

He must be true, without error ; authentical, without appeal, such as can
from himself without a higher determine. He must be infallible, without
peril of error. All these belong to God's truth.

It is yea, it is true without error, it is alway yea. And then it is authentical. There is nothing higher but God himself, whose word it is, and it
hath the same authority that himself hath, ' As God is true,' so it is true.
It is authentical without all appeal. We cannot go higher than God himself in his word. We cannot call God or Christ from heaven. He hath
left us his word, and therefore it is to be credited of itself.

And it is infallibly true, without danger of error. One depends upon another, ' As God is true, so our word is true.' If God be true infallibly, this
issues by consequence, that the Scripture is the judge, and infallibly true
without danger of error.

Hence we may know what to judge of that Romish assertion. There are
no other judges in the world can be said to be ' yea' alway.

Councils are not alway yea : they are ' yea and nay.' What one council
hath set down, another hath reversed. In the council of Basle, the pope
was above the council. In another council, that is above the pope.

So one pope's decrees thwart another. The popes are ' yea and nay,'
and not yea ; for many hundred years they laboured to cross and thwart
one another. So councils and popes are ' yea and nay,' and not alway
' yea.'

Traditions of the fathers are ' yea and nay,' and not alway ' yea.' They
thwart themselves. St Austin, the best of the fathers, to whom the church
is most chiefly beholden of all the rest, he was ' yea and nay.' Doth he
not retract ? He wrote a book of retractations of his former opinions (*mmm*).

Then he was 'yea, and nay,' and yet a holy man. That which is the judge of controversies must be yea, that is, infallibly true, authentically true, that there be not a higher. From all others, from fathers and councils, there may be appeal to Scripture, but from Scripture to none ; because it is the voice and word of God. All things else are yea and nay, they are changeable, and they may be so without prejudice to the being of them. A council may be a good council, and inconstant in many things. Fathers may be holy fathers, and uncertain. It is only the prerogative of God to be infallible like himself, unchangeable in his nature ; and his word is like himself.

Use 4. Hence likewise issues this, that *whatsoever agrees not with the word of God, which is not yea and nay, is false and naught.* Therefore those opinions of the Church of Rome, that say they cannot err, if they be not yea with this yea, then they are not yea ; for only the word of God is not ' yea and nay, but only yea,' that is, only certain and true. All other religions that are not divine, are yea and nay. Popery is not grounded upon the word of God, because it is ' yea and nay,' that is, it is uncertain. See how they cross many ways this word of God, that is always yea, and true as God himself is true.

Is it ' yea,' that they saw no image of God, and therefore they must make and worship no image ? ' Nay,' saith the Church of Rome. They have a nay for this yea ; they will make images and worship them, the image of Mary, and other saints. ' Yea,' saith the Scripture, ' drink ye all of this.' ' Nay,' saith the Church of Rome. They have a ' nay' for this ' yea ;' only the priest must drink the wine. ' Let the word dwell plenteously in you,' is the ' yea' of Scripture. The Church of Rome hath a ' nay' for this ' yea.' It is dangerous for the people to read the Scripture, and therefore they are forbidden it. We must pray with the understanding as well as with a good affection, 1 Cor. xiv. 15, that is, we must know how we pray. It is proved at large excellently. Nay, understand, or not understand, so the intention be good, saith Rome ; pray in Latin, or howsoever. There is their nay to this yea. ' Let every soul be subject to the higher powers, is the ' yea' of God's book. Therefore the souls of the clergy, and whosoever. The Church of Rome hath a ' nay' for this ' yea.' Therefore their doctrine is bad ; for only God is true, and his word is only ' not yea and nay, but alway yea,' infallible. Therefore that which is contrary to it must needs be false. If only yea be true, then that which is contrary to it must needs be false (*nnn*).

And likewise again, if God's word be not ' yea and nay,' that is, not inconstant, then whatsoever is inconstant, and thwarts itself in contradictions, is not God's word. Popery is full of inconstancy, full of contradictions to itself.

1. First, besides inconstancy, and uncertainty, *it is full of contradictions ;* it is ' yea *and* nay.' For a body to be in many places at once, and yet a true body ; to be in a hundred, in a million of places at once, as they would have Christ's body to be in the sacrament, here is to be, and not to be ; a body and no body, for it hath not the properties and quantity of a body ; for a body can be but in one place at one time. Here is yea and nay.

For Christ to be a perfect Redeemer, and yet notwithstanding to need the help of other mediators and intercessors, here is yea and nay. It is a contradiction.

That the church of Rome is the catholic church ; if it be Roman, it is not catholic. The universal catholic Roman church, it is as much as the

' universal particular church.' It is a contradiction. One thing overturns another.

The sacrifice of the mass, an unbloody sacrifice; a sacrifice is the killing of a thing that was alive; a sacrifice is with blood. The offering of Christ in the bread, is an unbloody sacrifice; a sacrifice, and not a sacrifice. Here is yea and nay, a contradiction. So that besides their thwarting of Scripture, they thwart and contradict themselves in their fundamental points, they are ' yea and nay.'

2. And then *they are full of uncertainties*, they are not undoubtedly ' yea.' There is no papist in the world would end his days so, if he be not drunk, if he be advised, if he be not surprised with passion, if he do not forget himself. Come to a papist, and ask him, what are the main points of popery that you believe always yea? Can you say when you confess your sins, that you confess all? No. Can you then say then you have a perfect absolution, that depends upon your confession? No! it is an uncertain thing. What an absurd thing is popish religion? It wrecks* the conscience of people.

Can you say that the priest intends consecration in these words, ' This is my body?' No! and if the priest's intention be not there, then Christ is not there, and then you are idolaters. Can you tell certainly that transubstantiation depends upon his consecration? No! How full of uncertainties and contradictions is popery! You cannot say the points of popery are always yea. Perhaps they are yea in life, but are they yea in death? It is yea in life, that they merit salvation by works, but is it yea in death? No! Bellarmine disclaims it.† It is safe not to trust in our own merits for danger of vainglory, &c., but to trust only in the mercy of God in Christ. So their doctrine it is yea in life, to sin by, to live riotously by, but then it is nay in death. They reverse it if they belong to God. They disclaim their works, and other things, and cleave only to Christ, and there is hope of them that have grace truly to do so. So their doctrine is not yea, that in life and death they can stick to.

To go on a little further, to lay open the grossness of their tenets,‡ and the danger of their religion. We are better bottomed than they are, which make the word of God our rule and ground, that is not yea and nay, but yea. The canonisation of saints. The pope, he makes Garnet, a traitor, and Thomas of Becket, saints (*ooo*). How can he know that these were saints that he canoniseth? He that makes a saint must know the hearts of men, and search the heart; for the truth of grace is there. Now, it is the privilege of God to know the heart. So that popery is full of uncertainties and pitiful perplexities.

Indeed, they maintain the doctrine of doubting, that we must doubt; as if our nature were not sufficiently prone to doubt, but we must get arguments to make us doubt; as if it were needful to have infirmities to stablish grace in us. Alas! we are too prone to doubt, and the devil is ready to make us stagger in the time of temptation.

Again, the invocation of saints it is a point wondrous full of uncertainties. Can they know and say certainly that the saints hear them? They cannot know that one saint, having a finite power, should hear a hundred petitions at once. A finite creature hath but a finite power to hear one thing at one time distinctly. How can they be persuaded that a finite saint

* Qu. ' racks?' See page 367, line 19 from top —G.   † Cf. note *w*.—G.
‡ Spelled ' tenent,' as in the ' Bloody *Tenent* [*i. e.*, Tenet] Washed ' of John Cotton, 4to, 1647.

in heaven at one time distinctly should hear many thousands that put up their petitions at once ? Can a man that is but a capable creature, though glorified, as Peter or Mary, &c., distinctly consider a thousand petitions that are made ? They cannot. How then can they think that a certain truth, the invocation of saints ?

The main ground of all their religion is ‘ yea and nay.’ The pillar of it, what is that ? The infallible judgment of the pope. But how can they tell when he speaks *ex cathedra ?* For nine or ten exceptions and tricks they have, when he speaks, to be built on, and when not. How can poor souls know when he speaks so, that the people may infallibly build on his judgment ? Because many times he is an illiterate man, that knows nothing in divine things wherein he is to judge. So the very foundation of popery is yea and nay ; that is, a most uncertain thing.

And then the ground of that, that he is the successor of Peter, there is no place of Scripture for it, neither dare they bring any. It is but a tradition. It is somewhat uncertain whether ever Peter were at Rome (*ppp*). That he was bishop there, is more uncertain. But that the pope should be his successor, is most uncertain and impossible of all.

So indeed the religion of popery is a rack to conscience, especially to conscience that is awaked, and knows what religion means at all. Why is it a rack to them ? There is no certainty in it, in the main tenets of it.

It is not only contrary to God’s ‘ yea,’ but it is ‘ yea and nay,’ uncertain in itself. Now, here the apostle, he frees his preaching from this imputation, ‘ our word to you was not yea and nay ;’ and he calls God to record, ‘ God is true,’ and as he is true, ‘ my word to you was not yea and nay,’ but was certainly ‘ yea.’ Thus you see what use we are to make of it for confutation and conviction of our own judgments.

Quest. It may be moved by some perhaps, How doth it appear, how shall we know, by what argument, that it is yea, and not yea and nay ? I answer,

Ans. 1. The testimony of St Paul here is, that it is so ; and his appeal to God, with an asseveration, ‘ as God is true.’

2. But our own experience doth tell us that the word of God is certain and true, if we belong to God ; for we stand convict in judgment by many arguments, which I will not now repeat.

Quest. But how shall any man certainly know * it is yea ? [that] the word is the undoubted word of God, unchangeable wheresoever it is ? In a word, you may know† it is so.

Ans. 1. He thinks it is so, *if he yield obedience to it,* as to such a word, absolute obedience to God’s truth without questioning. When once a thing is clear to be agreeable to God’s truth, [and] he yields obedience to it, then it is ‘ yea.’ If it be a duty, he must do it ; if it be a threatening, he must avoid it by repentance ; if it be a promise, he must believe it. This is absolute obedience.

2. Likewise *reverence in hearing it,* as Cornelius did, Acts x. 33. To hear it as the word of God. ‘ To tremble at the word of God,’ as it is Isa. lxvi. 2. To tremble at it as men do at thunder. The thunder is said to be ‘ the voice of God.’ ‘ The voice of God shakes the cedars of Lebanon,’ Ps. xxix. 8. So it is with the voice of God’s word. ‘ Shall the lion roar, and the beasts of the forest not tremble ?’ Isa. vii. 2. Shall

---

* This seems to be a misprint for ‘shew ;’ at least the answers direct in regard to *shewing* rather than *knowing.*—G.

† If this should not also read ‘ shew,’ then the meaning is, = he knows it is so who yields obedience.—G.

God threaten for sins that we are obnoxious to, and shall we not tremble at his threatenings ? Therefore howsoever we hear it as if it were yea and nay, yet it is yea; therefore let us not think to go on in sin, and escape, and do well enough. No! it will not be so. He that thinks it is the word of God, he trembles at his word, and hath answerable affections to all the parts of God's word. If God direct, he follows; if God threaten, he trembles; if he promise, he believes; if he command, he obeys. He hath a pliable disposition to every passage of divine truth, or else we do not believe it.

What shall we say then of those that come not so far as the heathen man did ? We know Felix, 'when he heard of justice, and temperance, and judgment to come, he trembled,' Acts xxiv. 25. When he heard of things that he was loath to hear, that he should be called to a reckoning for the course of his life, he trembled and quaked. If we hear these things, and live in a course perhaps worse than he, and do not tremble, where is our faith that the word of God is yea, that it is undoubtedly true ?

Let us therefore examine ourselves what power and efficacy the word hath. It is a word that changeth and altereth the whole man. It trans- forms the whole man. It is a word of life. If we find it hath so altered and changed us, we can from experience say it is ' yea.'

And likewise from particular promises. If we observe God's promises made good to us, if we find peace of conscience upon the confession of our sins, we can say God's word is 'yea.' If upon committing of sin we find God punishing and correcting us, we can say God's word is yea; and it is a bitter thing to offend God.

I find carefulness is the best course to please God. He finds me out in my sins, and it is a bitter thing to offend God. This is the best way to say in truth, without hypocrisy, that God's word is ' not yea and nay, but yea.'

Thus we see this truth, that God is true, and what follows thence. His word is true as himself, and not inconstant, yea and nay. Besides all this that I have said, let us make this use of it, *not to think God's word to be too good to be true, but yield obedience to it; yield the obedience of faith to it in the promises.* Here is a foundation for faith. The foundation of faith is without us. The evidences of faith are within us, by love, by purging our hearts, and stirring us up to pray, &c. But the foundation is out of ourselves. Here is a foundation and pillar for faith to lean on. God is true, and his word is true, and not yea and nay. It is eternally true. Therefore apply all the promises in the Old and New Testament to thyself. It was not yea to Abraham, and not to thee. God's promises of forgive- ness of sins were not yea to David, and not to thee. They were not yea to Manasseh, and not to thee. But God's truth is yea, eternally yea. ' What- soever was written heretofore, was written for our comfort,' Rom. xv. 4 ; and we are now the Davids, and the Manassehs, and the Abrahams of God ; we are now the beloved of God. For every one in their age are as they were in theirs ; and as the promises of God were yea to them, and saved their souls, because they trusted on them, so certainly every promise of God is a shield for those that will have recourse to it. ' The name of God is a strong tower,' Prov. xviii. 10 ; and his word is his name whereby he will be known in his promises. Have recourse to it on all occasions, rely on the word, wrestle with him when his dealings seem contrary, though his dealings with us seem to be yea and nay. We have been God's children, he hath assured us that we were in the state of grace ; but now he deals with us as if we were not his children, he afflicts us, he suffers Satan to be let loose on us to tempt us. Here flesh and blood is ready to say, Certainly I am not God's child, can I be ? thus and thus followed as I am. No, no ! God's 'gifts are without repentance,' Rom. xi. 29. Hadst thou ever grace ? God hath said it, who is truth itself, that his 'gifts are without repentance.' Build on it therefore. If thou hadst ever any grace, where he hath begun he will make an end. 'Where he hath begun a good work, he will perfect it to the day of the Lord,' Philip. i. 6.

Therefore wrestle with God in all temptations. When things seem contrary, yet allege God's nature to him; and his word, for both are true ; and one is true, because the other is true.

He is true in his nature and true in his word, and free in his decree, whatsoever his actions seem to be. Yet, Lord, thou canst not deny thyself, thou art unchangeable, thou art truth itself. And thy word that hath promised regard and respect to humble sinners that repent and come to thee, it is unchangeably true as thyself. Therefore, Lord, ' I will not leave thee, though thou kill me,' as Job saith, xiii. 15. Here is a ground of wrestling as Job did. Allege the nature of God and the word of God against his dealing. Let his dealing be what it will, his nature is true, and his word is true. Therefore his promises are true, which is a branch of his word, that if we repent, and confess our sins, he will be merciful to us.

Therefore let us not forsake our own mercy. This will uphold us, as in all temptations, so in divine temptations, when God seems to forsake us : so Christ himself, our blessed head, did. We cannot have a better pattern. When God left him on the cross, and left him to his human nature, to wrestle with the devil's temptations, and the pains of his body, and the sense of his wrath ; ' My God, my God, why hast thou forsaken me ?' Mark xv. 34; yet he upheld himself that God was his God still; and so likewise in the former example of Job. I say it is a special comfort, that God's word is not ' yea and nay.' As I said, it is not doubtful as the oracles of the Gentiles, the oracles of the devil; but God's word is certain. Whatsoever it was to any saint of God heretofore, it is to every believing, to every humble afflicted soul now, and shall be to the end of the world. So much for that.

VERSE 19.

' *For the Son of God, Jesus Christ, who was preached among you by us, by me, and Silvanus, and Timotheus, was not yea and nay, but in him is yea.*' In the words the apostle shews in particular what he preached among them, and we have in them these particulars briefly to be unfolded :

First, That Christ Jesus, in his nature and his offices, is the chief and main object and subject matter of preaching.

Secondly, That to make him profitable to us, he must be preached.

Thirdly, That consent of divines and preachers helps faith.

Fourthly, That Jesus Christ, being preached by the apostles, is an undoubted ' yea,' that is, an undoubted ground and foundation to build on, in all the uncertainties of this life, in all the uncertainty of religion. Jesus Christ preached by St Paul and other holy men of those times, was not ' yea and nay, but yea.'

Doct. 1. *First, Christ Jesus is the main object of preaching.*

It were impertinent here to stand on particulars, to shew you how Christ is the Son of God; for he is brought in here as the object of preaching. Only in a word, we must of necessity believe that Christ Jesus is the Son of God. For how wondrously doth this stablish our faith when we believe in a Saviour that is God; the Son of God, Jesus Christ by eternal generation. In a word, here are these prerogatives of Christ's generation from all other sons whatsoever. Other fathers are before their sons, this Son of God was eternal with his Father. Other fathers have a distinct essence from their sons, the father is one, and the son another; they have distinct existences; but here there is one common essence to the Father and the Son. Other fathers beget a son without them, but this Father begets his Son within him. It was an inward work. So it is a mystical divine generation, which indeed is a subject of admiration rather than of explication, that Jesus Christ is the Son of God and the Son of man. This was typified in the ark. The ark was a type of Christ. The ark had wood, and gold that covered that wood. Christ's human nature was the wood, and his divine nature that contained it, that is the gold. But I should be too large, and besides* the scope of the text, if I should unfold this point. I only touch it by the way. Christ Jesus in his natures as he is God and man, and in his offices as Jesus Christ, that is, anointed as king, priest, and prophet, and in his estates of abasement, and advancement, is the main subject matter of preaching. For what can we say, but it must be reductive, and brought to Christ? If we open men's consciences by the law, and tell them what a terrible estate they are in, what do we but drive them to the physician. What is the law, but as John Baptist was to Christ, to prepare the way, to level the soul, to pull down the high thoughts and imaginations, to make way and passage for Christ? And then in Christ, when we preach Christ, we preach his natures, God and man, and his offices, as king, priest, and prophet, as he is predestinate, and sealed, and anointed by God the Father for that purpose, that we may have a strong Saviour, strong in himself, and authorised by his Father. And we preach his estates of abasement, as he was crucified and suffered for our sins; and his estate of exaltation, as he arose and ascended into glory. These things belong to the preaching of Christ.

And then the benefits we have by him, reconciliation to his Father by his death, and peace of conscience, and joy in the Holy Ghost, and such like wondrous benefits we have by him.

And then our duty to him again, which is faith, and a conversation worthy; to embrace all that is offered by Christ, that it be not lost for want of apprehending. Christ Jesus is the subject matter of our preaching, in his natures, in his offices, in the benefits we have by him, in the duties we owe to him, in the instrument of receiving all,—faith. For in preaching, that faith which we require to lay hold on Christ, is wrought.

For preaching doth not only manifest the benefits we have by Christ, but is a potent instrument of the Spirit of God to work this qualification, to make Christ profitable to us. Now all that we preach of holy duties, is either to humble us if we have them not, to make us fly to Christ by faith; or when we believe, to make us walk answerable to our faith. So whatsoever we preach is reductive to Christ; either to prepare us, or to furnish us to walk worthy of Christ. Indeed, Jesus Christ is all in all in our preaching, and he should be so in your hearing. Of all things you should desire to hear most of Christ. The apprehension of your sinfulness should drive you to Christ. The hearing of duties should be to make you adorn your

* That is, 'beside.'—G.

Christian religion you have taken on you. Naturally men love to hear flashes, witty conceits, and moral points wittily unfolded; but all these in the largest extent do but civilize men. It must be Christ unfolded, and God's love, and mercy, and wisdom in him reconciling mercy and justice together : the wondrous love of God in Christ, and his justice, and mercy; and the love of Christ in undertaking to work our redemption; and the benefits by Christ, his offices, estates, and conditions. These things 'work faith and love. These things do us good.

All other things, take them at the best, they do but fashion our carriage a little; but that which enlivens and quickens the soul is Jesus Christ.

Use. Therefore we should of all other things *be desirous to hear of Jesus Christ.* It is a point that the very angels are students in. For the ark, which I named before, it had the law, and the mercy-seat in it, the mercy-seat to cover the law. Now Christ hath satisfied the law, and reconciled his Father, he hath freed us from the curse of the law, and hath given full satisfaction to the law. He is the mercy-seat, by whom we have access to God the Father.

Now the angels were upon the mercy-seat, interviewing one another, and prying down upon the mercy-seat, insinuating, that the reconciling of God's justice and mercy by that infinite wisdom of God in Christ; that our sins should be punished in him, and yet he be merciful to us ; that he should punish our surety for us ; that he should join these attributes together ; that all the creatures in heaven and earth could not devise it, is a matter for angels to pry into. The very frame of the ark signified this. And shall not we be students in those mysteries, that the angels themselves desire every day more and more to understand ? If Christ be the main thing we are to stand on, let us labour more and more to understand ' Christ, and him crucified ;' let us see our nature in him advanced now in heaven, to make us heavenly-minded; let us see our nature in him punished ; let us see our sinful nature in him cleansed and purged by his death and abasement; let us see our nature in him enriched.

Let us consider him as a public person, and see our interest in his humiliation, and exaltation in glory; because he is the ' second Adam.' These things should raise up our thoughts wondrously to think of his humiliation, and his exaltation, and of the love and mercy of God in him. And then think of what you will, nothing is discouraging; think of death, of hell, of the day of judgment; think of Satan, of the curse of the law; they are terrible things. Aye, but think of the Son of God, of Christ anointed of God the Father to satisfy the law, to satisfy his justice, to overcome Satan, to crush his head, to be our Saviour as well as our Judge at the day of judgment; these things will make all vanish. Things that are most terrible to the nature of man without the consideration of Jesus Christ the Son of God, all are most comfortable when we think of him. Now when we think of Satan, we think of one crushed and trod under foot, as he shall be ere long. When we think of judgment, we think of a Saviour that shall be our Judge. When we think of God, we think of God reconciled in Christ. We have access by Christ to the throne of grace. He is now in heaven, and makes intercession for us. When we think of death, we think of a passage to life where we shall be with him, ' I desire to be dissolved, and to be with Christ,' Philip. i. 23. So the things that are most uncomfortable, yet bring the consideration of them to Christ exalted in heaven, having triumphed over all these in our nature, and sits at God's right hand. The thoughts of these things are comfortable meditations.

Nay, think of that which is the most terrible of all, the justice of God, his anger for sin, it is a matter of comfort above all other. God is just to punish and revenge sin ; what then ? Because he is just he will not punish one thing twice ; but his justice is fully satisfied, and contented in his Son Christ Jesus, whom he hath anointed, and predestinate, and sent himself ; and he must needs acknowledge that satisfaction that is done by him, that he hath sent himself. Hereupon we come to think comfortably of God's justice.

God out of Christ is a ' consuming fire,' Heb. xii. 29. There is nothing more terrible than God without Christ ; but now in Christ we can think of the most terrible thing in God with comfort. Therefore St Paul makes it the main scope of his preaching, and so should we of ours ; and you should make it your main desire in hearing, and the main subject matter of your meditating, something concerning Christ. Let us often think of our nature in him now exalted in heaven, and that we shall follow him ere long. Our head is gone before, and he will not suffer his body always to rot in the earth. Let us think of his natures, and his offices, and all the blessed prerogatives that we have by him, and all the enemies that are conquered by him, that in him we have God reconciled, and the devil vanquished, we have heaven opened, and hell shut ; we have our sins pardoned, and our imperfections by little and little cured ; in him we have all in all.

There are four things that the apostle speaks of, which includes all, 1 Cor. i. 30. ' Of him are ye in Christ Jesus, who of God is made to us wisdom, righteousness, sanctification, and redemption.' Christ Jesus is all in all. If we be ignorant, he is our ' wisdom ;' if we want righteousness and holiness to stand before God, ' he is our righteousness.' We stand righteous, being clothed with his righteousness. If we want grace, ' Of his fulness we receive grace for grace,' John i. 16. He is sanctification to us. If we be miserable, as we shall be to our sense, our bodies shall be turned to rottenness, ' he is our redemption,' not only of the soul, but of the body. He shall make our bodies ' like his glorious body,' Philip. iii. 21. As he makes our souls glorious, by his Spirit conforming them to his own image here, he means here redemption of our bodies from corruption, as well as of our souls from sin. ' He is all in all.' In sin, he is sanctification ; in death, he is life ; in ignorance, he is wisdom. There is nothing ill in us, but there is abundant satisfaction and remedy in Christ. I speak this the rather to shew what reason St Paul had to stand on this, that all his preaching was to bring Christ Jesus among them. I go on.

' *The Son of God, Jesus Christ, preached among you.*'
Doct. 2. *All the good we have by Christ is conveyed by the ministry.*

Despise that, and despise Christ himself. Therefore whatsoever benefits we have by Christ, they are attributed to preaching ; they are attributed to the gospel as it is preached and unfolded ; therefore it is called ' The gospel of the kingdom,' ' The word of reconciliation,' ' The word of life,' ' The word of faith.' All these are by Christ. But it is no matter, whatsoever we have by Christ, we must have it by Jesus Christ unfolded in the ministry of the word. Despise the ministry, that is contemptible to flesh and blood, and despise Christ himself, despise the kingdom, and life, and all ; for Christ preached is that we must rely on, Christ unfolded. The bread of life must be broken, the sacrifice must be anatomized and laid open, Christ Jesus the Son of God must be preached. He profits not but as he is preached. His riches must be unfolded, ' the unsearchable riches of Christ,'

Eph. iii. 8. Therefore God, that hath appointed us to be saved by Christ, hath appointed and ordained preaching, to lay open Jesus Christ among us. But, to come to the third point.

Doct. 3. *Consent of ministers a help to faith.*

Why doth he bring in consent to help ? ' By me, and Silvanus, and Timotheus.' Would not his own authority serve the turn ?

I answer, no ; it would not sometimes. In itself it will, but in regard of the weakness of men, it is necessary to join the consent of others. St Paul was an apostle of Christ, but he knew that they were so weak, that they would regard his testimony the more for the joint testimony of ' Timotheus and Silvanus,' and the rest.

God considers not so much what is true in itself, as how to stablish our faith in it. As in the sacrament, would not God give Christ and his benefits ? is he not true of his word ? Yes ! but he gives the sacrament for us. His promises are sure enough, yet he condescends to our weakness, to add sacrament, and oath, and all the props that may be. So the men of God, that are led by the Spirit of God, though their own authority were sufficient, yet they condescend to the weakness of others. Therefore St Paul allegeth with himself, ' Silvanus and Timotheus,' to strengthen them the better.

Then again, consent is a lovely thing, and proceeds from love. How sweet a thing is it for brethren to dwell together in unity ; therefore we ought to stand much upon consent, if it may persuade us. But as Cyprian saith well, ' it must be consent in the truth' (*qqq*). Consent that is not in the truth, is not properly concord, but conspiracy ; consent in a lie, in falsehood. The builders of Babel they had a consent among themselves when they came for a wicked purpose, as we see ofttimes in Scripture. Consent must be in the truth, in that which is good, or else it is not consent, but conspiracy. By reason of our weakness, consent is useful, and that is the reason why in doubtful cases we may allege antiquity ; not that the word is not sufficient in itself, but to help our weakness, to shew that we do not divert from the truth, but that it is a truth warranted by others before. In doubtful cases this is warrantable. He brings it likewise to enforce obedience the more, when it was a truth brought to them by so many. But that is not a thing I mean to stand on, a touch is enough.

That which I will spend a little more time in, is the next thing, that is, that

Doct. 4. *Evangelical doctrine now is most certain.*

Something I spake of it before in the former verse, but I have reserved something to speak of it now. The Son of God preached by St Paul, with the consent of these blessed men, it was not ' yea and nay,' it was not unconstant. Evangelical truth is not yea and nay ; and the preachers of it, the apostles, were not ' yea and nay' in the delivering of it. As it is true in itself, so it was true in the delivery of it. They were constant in it, they sealed it with their blood some of them.

Quest. How shall we know the doctrine of the gospel concerning Christ to be yea, undoubtedly true ?

Ans. 1. I answer, *how do we know the sun shines ?* I know it by its own light, and by a light that I have in my eye. There is an inward light joined with the outward light. So it is in this business, how do we know divine truth out of the book of God to be divine ? By the light in itself, by the majesty of the Scriptures, by the consent of the Old and New Testament, by the opposition of the enemies, and the confusion of them at the last that have been opposers of it, by the miraculous preservation of it, and the like ; but especially by the powerful work of it on the heart, by the experience of this blessed truth. I know this to be an undoubted truth, I find it quelling my corruptions, changing my nature, pacifying my conscience, raising my heart, casting down high imaginations, turning the stream of nature another way ; to make me do that which I thought I should never have done, only because I have a strong light of divine truth and comfort. There is this experience of Christ, that a man finds in his soul. It sets him down that he can say nothing, but that it is divine truth, because he finds it so (*rrr*).

Ans. 2. Besides this, *the testimony of the Spirit of God, and the work of the Spirit in him.* For as to see, there is an outward light required, and an inward light in the eye ; so to see divine truth there must be a light in itself, a divine sparkle in God's book, in every passage ; but yet I must have an eye to see too. I cannot see it except God witness to my soul, that these things are divine, that they are yea, that they are certainly and infallibly true.

There is a great difference between us and our adversaries. I can but touch it, and I need but touch it. They say we must believe, and we must believe because of the church. I say no. The church, we believe, hath a kind of working here, but that is in the last place. For God himself in his word, he is the chief. The inward arguments from the word itself, and from the Spirit they are the next. The church is the remotest witness, the remotest help of all. For the church is but to propound God's truth, to lay it open ; to be as it were the candlestick. Now the candlestick shines not, but upholds the candle while that shines. So the church is but to propose, to set up divine truth, that of itself being set up will enlighten well enough. The church is to set out the word, and to publish it by the ministry, which word of itself will shine. That work which the church hath therefore is the last, and the inferior ; for the Spirit of God, and the inward majesty of the word, is of more force.

If a messenger come, and bring a relation, or bring a letter from one, and he tells me many things of the man ; aye, but I doubt him, because he may be false for aught I know ; but when I see his hand and seal, and his characters and style, that shews such a spirit to be in him, I know by his own characters certainly this comes from the hand of that man. Now, the messenger brings it and gives it, but I believe it, because I see the characters and hand and seal of such a one, that it is a truth. So the church propounds. It is the messenger that brings the truth of God to us ; but when a Christian soul hears the truth, and sees God's seal upon it, there is a majesty and power that works on the soul. Now, we believe not for the messenger, but for the thing itself. Here is the difference. We believe the Scripture for the seal of divinity that is in itself ; they believe it for the messenger, as if a doubtful messenger should come that is not certain, and a man should believe the things he brought for him, for his sake. We believe and entertain the messenger for the message sake, not the message for the messenger's sake. Our faith is better built than theirs.

Obj. But they say, This all comes to this at the last, God speaks by the church as well as by the Scriptures ; therefore, the church is to be believed more than the Scripture itself.

Ans. I answer, God speaks indeed in his church by his Spirit and by his word ; but his speaking by his word is the cause of his speaking in the church. For what is the church but begotten by the seed of the word? How is the church a church but by the word? Therefore, he speaks first by the Scriptures. There is a majesty and a spirit in the Scriptures. And then he speaks by the church, as cleaving to the Scriptures, in a secondary manner. He speaks by the church mediately, because that goes to the word which speaks immediately. The word was written by men⁺ led immediately by the Spirit of God; and the church relying on that, he speaks by them in the church, but primarily by his word. Having just occasion, I thought to touch this.

Undoubtedly, there are none that are not led with partiality, but incomparably they see our faith is built on a better foundation than theirs. They have a rotten foundation. They talk of a church, and when all comes to all, the church their mother is nothing, but the pope their father. What is their church but the pope himself? For they run from the church essential to the church representative. They run to councils, and when we force them with councils that they may err, then the pope, he is the church virtually. So, I say, the church their mother is nothing but the pope their father; and what manner of men they have been; histories tell us well enough. We see on what ground they build.

Jesus Christ, that is, the gospel by him, is not ' yea and nay, but yea;' that is, it is certainly, and infallibly, and eternally true.

Quest. Hereupon we may answer that curious question that hath been, and now is, everywhere, how we may know that our church was before Luther's time or no,* as they idly say, how we may know that the faith that we profess is the ancient faith.

Ans. I answer hence, Take these grounds:

First. There is but one faith. Men have varied, but faith hath not varied, as St Austin saith well. For there is but one faith, as there is one God, one heaven, and one happiness. There was one faith from Adam. The times vary, but not the faith of the times; the same fundamental truth hath been in all times. Sometimes it hath been more explicated and unfolded, as we have the canon enlarged now in the time of the New Testament in many books. There is not a new faith, but a larger explication of the old faith. Divine truth is alway the same. It was one faith from the beginning of the world, from the first promise to Adam in paradise, till now. Abraham believed as we do now. So they were all saved by faith, Heb. xi.

Even as there is one catholic church, consisting of all the members, the triumphant being the greater part, from the beginning of the world to the end of the world, so there is one faith. Take that for a ground. Indeed, the church varies as a man varies when he is a child and when he is a man. He hath one manner of clothes when he is a child, and another when he is a man. So the church varies in clothes. It was clothed with ceremonies then, which were cast off in Christ; but this is but a variation of garments. The church had one faith.

Second. Hereupon comes a second, *there is one catholic church, that is built on that one faith,* one essential church, one catholic company that believe in Christ, from the beginning of the world to the end of the world, which we believe in the apostles' creed. Well, then, this being so, as it is undeniable that it is so, what church is built upon that one faith that was ' yea ' in the apostles, and was ' yea ' before then, as the apostle saith here, ' Our preaching was yea,' certain and true, you may build on it, what

---

* See note *d,* vol. ii. p. 248; and see *sss.*—G.

church builds on that? That church all the while hath been; for there is but one faith and one truth that runs along in all ages, which is the seed of the church. Therefore, there must be a church in all ages that is a branch of the catholic church. Why? The church must be built upon that one faith; therefore, all particular churches before us, that were branches of the general church, were built upon that preaching of the apostle, which he saith was 'yea.' There is but one faith, and therefore all churches that are true are built upon that one faith. If we can prove that the apostolical doctrine agrees with our times, that ours hath consanguinity with the apostles' doctrine, then our church was before we were, ever since the apostles. It hath been alway yea, for there is but one truth.

The church is built upon the foundation of the prophets and apostles; and Christ saith, Mat. xvi. 18, when Peter said to Christ, 'Thou art the Son of God,' &c., saith he, 'Thou art Peter, and upon this rock,' that is, upon this confession of thine, 'will I build my church.' So the confession of faith is the rock of the church. Now there is alway one rock of the church that is alway yea. If our church be built upon that rock, then it is founded upon apostolical doctrine, upon the prophets and apostles. It was before we were. And if there were any church, then it was ours, which professeth that one faith.

If we conjure the papists, they are silent, they dare say nothing. Dare they say their doctrine is nearer apostolical than ours? They dare not say but ours is nearer. Why, then, our church is built upon the foundation of the apostles. Why so? All the churches since have been built upon one foundation, because there is one faith and one church. Unity of faith makes the unity of the church.

The seed of the church is the gospel, is divine truth. Now, if divine truth hath been alway, there hath been a church alway; and if there hath been a church alway, there hath been divine truth that hath been 'yea' alway. Now, it is an article of our faith in all times to believe a catholic church. Therefore, there is a certain truth that is always yea, to be the seed and foundation of that catholic church. Therefore, we must search out what that 'yea' was, what was the apostolical doctrine, the positive doctrine in those apostolical times, in the virgin-times of the church, before the church was corrupted. The church was not long a virgin, as the Father said. What was the yea of those truths? Some there must be alway that held apostolical truths in all ages. Our church holds that positive truth that the apostles held: for directly in so many words, we defend the apostolical faith out of the apostles. Therefore, we say our church was before Luther, because our doctrine is apostolical, and the church continually hath been apostolical, because it was built upon the apostles' doctrine.

Our church hath no doctrine in the positive fundamental points of it contrary; therefore our church hath continued. Put case we cannot name the men, as idly and ridiculously they urge, what is that to the purpose? Shall we go from ignorance of particular men, to ignorance of the church? We must believe that there is a catholic church; and there must alway be a positive doctrine and truth, the seed of that church.

Obj. The papists cavil with us, and say we possess a negative religion. Ye cut off our opinions, say they, but what have you of your own? what affirmatives have ye?

Ans. It is most certain, that all our affirmatives have been ever since the apostles' time; for we and the papists differ not in affirmatives, only they add patcheries* of their own. Religion stands most in affirmatives, that is the ground first. For we believe negatives, because they agree not to affirmatives : we believe a lie to be a lie, because it is contrary to positive truth, and the truth is before a lie; the affirmation is before the negation; a thing is, before the contrary is not. This laying for a ground, affirmatives being truths, our positive truths that we hold have been held in the apostles' times, before and since, even in the Church of Rome a thousand years after; and even now the affirmatives that we hold.

Do not they believe the Scriptures to be the word of God? Yes! But they add patcheries of their own, the Apocrypha, and their own traditions, to be the word of God too.

Do not they believe that Christ is Mediator? Yes! But he is the only Mediator for redemption, and not for intercession. They join others with him, saints and angels.

We are saved by faith, that is the affirmative, and so say they. But they add of their own, that we are saved by faith and works.

Then again, we say there are two sacraments, baptism and the Lord's supper; and so say they, but they add five of their own. So I might run over all their opinions. Whatsoever we hold, they hold. Therefore in their own confessions, our affirmatives have been ever since the apostles' times. If they had any church, we had a church, because our foundations are included in their religion. All that we say, they say; but then again they say many things that we do not. Therefore they account us heretics, because we make not that that they hold to be our yea too.

Again, the negatives that they believe, and we do not believe, they are but novelties in experience, they are not of the ancient apostolical faith. That the apocrypha should be had in equal authority with the word of God in Scripture, alas! such a conceit was not thought of for six hundred years after the apostles. That the people should not read the Scriptures, it was but since the other day. Transubstantiation, since the Council of Lateran, a thousand years since Christ. That the pope should be supreme, and depose princes, such a thing was not heard of a thousand years after Christ. That he should have authority to canonize saints, it was but since the other day. Equivocation, but of late time. And so their idle babbling of divine service in Latin, and twenty other trumperies. So the things that we deny that are gross and abominable in the judgment of every man that knows anything, they were but since the other day; they were not yea in the apostles' times. Then the apostolical church being not built on them, they must be devised after. As, indeed, a thousand years after Christ the most of these were never heard of. The most of the points of popery wherein they differ from us, nay, not any of them, were never established by a council till the Council of Trent, except transubstantiation, by the Council of Lateran, which was a thousand years after Christ (*ttt*).

The affirmatives that we hold, and they hold too, we say they are constant from the apostles' time; they have been in all ages maintained and affirmed.

Our positive points that we ground out of St Paul, and out of the Scriptures : we seek the 'old way,' and the 'best way,' as Jeremiah adviseth us, Jer. vi. 16. There was none of the popish trash in Abraham's time, in the patriarchs' time, in Christ's and his apostles' time, or in many hundred years after. They came in by little and little, for their own advantage; a

* That is, patches.—G.

mere policy to get money, and to abuse people. I say, they hold all our positive truths; but their error is in addition.

Quest. Now this question may be made, whether their additions may be dangerous or no? Because it may be supposed that some among them will say that heresy is not in addition, but in contrariety to the faith, and detracting; but when one holds more than they should, that is no heresy, because there is somewhat superabounds; now we hold the truth, and more too.

Ans. I say it is gross and false; for if additions did not overthrow the foundation, there should never be any idolatry, nor never any heresy in these times. What was idolatry, especially in the church of God? Among the Jews was there not the worshipping of the true God? Yes! but before an image, their additions, their false manner overthrew the true. There is none of them fundamental points, as we call them, though they make them fundamental. They make their traditions of as much authority as the word of God; and their fooleries as the articles of faith. They overthrow the main foundation. They are such additions as are destructive, to join with the word of God traditions. To worship God under another species and kind, is to be an idolator. Though they worship the true God, if it be after a false manner, it is prohibited. St Paul saith, and with a commination, Gal. i. 8, 'If I or an angel from heaven teach otherwise.' Beside, put case it be not plainly and directly contrary, if he teach other things that are not necessary to be believed, 'let him be accursed.' We ought not to go from the Scriptures in any fundamental point of faith, under pain of a curse. Therefore popery is a cursed religion, in respect of their very additions.

Doth not St Paul tell the Galatians they were 'fallen from Christ,' Gal. v. 4, if they added circumcision to Christ? He doth not say if they did that which was directly contrary to faith: no! but in adding circumcision and works to Christ, they were fallen from Christ. Whole Christ, or no Christ. In some cases additions are heresies, and overthrow the foundation.

Quest. If this be so, we may answer another question easily: the apostolical doctrine you see is only yea: whether then it be safer to be a papist or a protestant, considering that whatsoever we hold they do hold?

Ans. I answer, to be a Protestant is safer in any man's judgment; because all that we say, themselves say: it hath been apostolical. We can prove in all ages of the church our affirmatives, we have a catalogue of witnesses in all ages of them that held what we say. It was founded in the apostles, and then came down to all ages. But what they say distinct, and differing from us, they have not the like testimony for: for indeed they are so beaten that Bellarmine hath this, 'The authority of all councils and fathers, and all depends upon the authority of the present church.' Bring to them councils and fathers! Tush! tush! all authority depends upon the present church. What authority gives the present church, when twenty years after the church varies? What certainty is there, when all authority of former times shall depend upon the present church?

In those things wherein they differ from us, and that we deny, any understanding, reasonable man may see that they are novelties and corruptions. As for the pope to depose princes, if a man have but his naturals,* he may see it abominable. To pray in a 'strange tongue,' to debar the people of the wine, when Christ saith, 'Drink ye all of it,' 1 Cor. xi. 25, who that hath ordinary discretion but will think it absurd? There is nothing that

* That is, = the understanding he has as a man.—G.

we differ from them in, but a man that hath but his naturals will condemn. Therefore ours is safer a great deal by their own confession, the learnedest of them, that it is enough to believe as we do. Do we not believe the articles of the creed? Do we not believe the first four general councils? We do. Who then will not say that these are sufficient, being understood and believed, to make a man that he be no heretic?

Quest. I may answer hence another question, whether a papist may be saved or no? It is a curious question, you will say; but it is so ordinary that somewhat I must say.

Ans. I answer, no doubt but many of them are saved. How comes that to pass? They reverse their false grounds, and stick to those positive truths that they and we hold together; they reject their own works, and help of saints, and go to Christ only; for, as I said, popery is full of contradictions. Now a papist, when he comes to have his conscience awakened, he leaves the pope's indulgences, their five sacraments, justification by works, and then embraceth only Christ, and then he comes to our part. They live by their religion, and die by ours. So the question is, whether living or dying? Luther saith, If they live and die peremptorily in all the points professed in the Tridentine Council, they cannot (*uuu*). But no doubt many of them the Lord hath mercy on, to open their eyes to see the vanity of their works and of all their fooleries, which those that are wise and have their consciences enlightened turn off then, and so may be saved, but it must be with reversing the grounds of their religion, and sticking to ours, which is agreeable to the word.

Nay, to speak a little more of it, I say, we do more safely believe. We are more safe, and on better grounds led into some less errors, than they do believe main truths. It may seem strange, but it is most true.

For if so be a sound protestant maintain an error, it is because he thinks it is in the Scripture, that it is in the word; if it be discovered out of the word of God to be an error, he leaves it. As St Cyprian and other fathers, blessed saints in heaven, they held some errors; but if they saw the Scripture held otherwise, they had prepared minds to believe otherwise. Therefore, holding the main fundamental truths, though they held particular errors, they were saved.

The papists maintain fundamental truths with us. They believe the word of God, they believe in Christ, and to be saved by mercy; but upon what grounds? They believe the truth upon heretical, devilish grounds. As upon what grounds do they believe the articles of the faith to be so, and the Scriptures to be so? Because the church saith so. Who is the church but the pope? And what man is the pope ofttimes? A man, if we believe their own writers, led with a devilish spirit: some of them have been magicians. If they believe the truth, they do it not as divine truth. They believe the truth for matter; but the grounds of believing those truths are human, nay, worse, many times devilish. For you know in the Revelation, the beast is inspired with the spirit of the dragon, with the spirit of the devil, and teacheth the doctrine of devils, 1 Tim. iv. 1. Now, to teach that which is materially true, upon reasons that are diabolical or human (at the best, it is but human), as the testimony of the church is, what an unsafe thing is this!

Nay, I say, it is the most horrible witchery, the most horrible abomination that ever was since the beginning of the world, this principle, that their church cannot err: that is the reason of the believing of all divine truths. Hereupon they come to practise most abominable treacheries, hereupon they defend lies, hereupon they kill princes, and dissolve the bonds of allegiance that subjects owe to princes. And all human and divine things, all the light of nature and Scripture, all becomes a nullity. Why? Because the church cannot err. And this they have from their holy father the pope. He is above all councils and all, and cannot err. We know if principles be false, all other things are false. An error in principles is a dangerous error. An error in the ground is the worst thing in the world. As to maintain treason to be lawful, it is worse than to be a traitor; for his judgment is convinced already; but he that maintains a false principle, he is a dangerous man indeed. So, to have this abominable principle, that the church, that the pope cannot err, hence come all those dangerous practices in this commonwealth ever since the beginning of Queen Elizabeth's time.

Who would have thought, but that God gave up bitter, proud, poisonful spirits, vain spirits that rejected the word of God, that men of parts and understanding should ever be so sotted to believe such a thing, that a wretched ignorant man should get into the chair, and he should judge infallibly of the truths that he never knew in his life, being of another profession, as some are canonists, and not divines? But I leave that point.

To touch one thing more that borders a little upon this, that divine truth is of an inflexible nature, whatsoever men think of it. And that crosseth another rule of theirs, that they will give what sense they will of Scriptures, and the current of the present church must judge of all former councils. Now doth truth vary according to men's judgments, according to the present church? Must we bring the rule to the crooked timber, or the timber and the things to be measured to the rule? Shall the judgment of any man be the rule of truth? shall it be the rule in one time, and not in another? Shall present men interpret it thus, and say it is so now; and others that succeed say, whatsoever it was now, thus it must be believed?

Hereupon likewise, if it be the constant nature of truth alway to be believed; hereupon it comes to cross another thing, their dispensation. No man can dispense with God's law; truth is truth indispensable. Laws divine and natural are indispensable, because they are alike in all things. Reason is reason in Turkey as well as here. The light of nature is the light of nature in any country as well as here. Principles of nature vary not as languages do : they are inbred things.

If the principles of nature be invariable and indispensable, much more divine principles, saith the heathen. Filthiness is filthiness, whether thou think it to be so or no. Opinion is not the rule of things, but the nature of the thing itself.

Therefore whatsoever is against nature none can dispense with. ' God cannot deny himself!' 2 Tim. ii. 13. What was naught in one age is naught in another, and is for ever naught. Whatsoever is divine or natural is indispensable. No monarch in the world can dispense with the law of nature, or the divine law, the word of God ; for the opinion of any man in the world is not the rule of his course, but the undoubted light of God, whether the light of nature or the light of divine truth.

I speak this the rather to cross base parasites, that when God calls them to stand for true causes, what do they make their rule? Not God's constant ' Yea,' but they bend and bow to opinion, as if the opinion of any man in the world were the rule of their faith and obedience. This is to make men, and no men. Is not the written word of God the word of God? Is not the law the law ? (Politic laws I speak not of.) Shall a man yield to men's opinion, especially if the word do not warrant it ? Shall he yield to any man living that is inconstant by his disposition ? There is truth which is certain, that a man must maintain to the death. He is not only a martyr that maintains religion. John Baptist was a martyr that stood out in a matter that was not against heresy, but for the standing out against Herod. He did not yield, as many thousands would have done in such a case. ' Thou must not have thy brother Philip's wife ;' it is unlawful, Mark vi. 18.

Men ought to suffer for the truths of nature, and not deny truth whatsoever, because it is a divine sparkle from God. If it be any truth whatsoever, it must be stood in, because it is constant ; and it is the best thing in the world next to divine and saving truth.

Use. If this be so, that the gospel and divine truth be 'yea,' and that the church at all times hath been built on that, and that whosoever is saved is saved by that yea, let us labour to have a faith answerable to our truth. We say, and distinguish well. There is a certainty of the thing, and a certainty of the mind apprehending the thing. It is certain the sun is bigger than the earth ; but you shall never persuade a simple countryman that it is so. There is a certainty of the object, but not of the subject. He will never believe it, because it is against sense. But now there must be both in a Christian. The apostle's doctrine, the truth he doth believe, the truth in the Scripture is ' Yea,' that is, it is certain and true, and not ' yea and nay,' it is not flexible. It is not as the heathen oracles were, that is, doubtful and wavering. Let our assent be answerable to the truth ; let us build soundly on a sound foundation.

As a ship that is to rest in the midst of the waves, there is a double certainty necessary, that the anchor-hold be good in itself, and that it be fastened upon somewhat that is firm. If it be a weak anchor, or if it be fastened upon ground that will not hold, the ship is tossed about with waves, and so split upon some rock or other. So our souls require a double certainty. We must have an anchor of faith as well as an object of faith; we must have an anchor of hope as well as an object. For the object we may cast anchor there. It is divine truth which will hold. There is no doubt of that. It is yea. But then our anchor must be firm, our faith and affiance. Let us labour to build soundly and strongly upon it. It should be our endeavour continually to stablish our faith, to stablish our hope, that we may know on what terms we live, and on what terms to die.

Do but consider the difference between an understanding, strong Christian and another. A Christian that is judicious and understanding, ask him in what estate he is. Why, comfortable ! What is the ground of his faith ? Why, thus : I live in no known sin, I confess my sins to God, my doctrine is ' yea,' and I labour to bring my life to my doctrine.

Ask another, What do you mean to live so loosely and carelessly ? Why will you stand thus ? Will you be content to die so ? Perhaps he doth not know sound doctrine, or if he do, it is confusedly ; he doth not build on that rock, on that foundation.

Oh ! let us labour to build stronger and stronger on the truth. Our building strongly makes us eternal. God's truth is eternal truth, because it makes us eternal. Is it not a strange thing that man, that is chaff, and vanity, and smoke, whose life passeth as a tale that is told, that yet notwithstanding if he build on this yea, which is certain and infallible, the doctrine of the gospel, it will make him a rock, a living stone, it will make him eternal ? 'All flesh is grass, but the word of God endures for ever,' 1 Pet. i. 25.

What a comfort is this, our life being a vapour, and vanity, and growing to nothing, that the time will shortly come when we shall be no more, no more in this world ; then to have divine truth that will make us eternal ! Ps. xc. Moses, a good man, he saw men drop away. Saith he, 'Thou art our eternal habitation from generation to generation.' What is the meaning of that ? That is, we dwell in thee. Here in our pilgrimage to Canaan we drop away, but 'thou art our habitation from generation to generation.' So when a Christian considers his life is uncertain, all things are vanity that support this life, yet notwithstanding I have a 'yea' to build on, the divine truth. 'The word of the Lord endures for ever,' and it will make me endure for ever. It is a rock itself, it makes me a rock ; it will make me a living stone, built on that foundation, that all the gates of hell shall not prevail against my faith and hope.

What a comfort is this ! We have nothing without this 'yea.' We are 'yea and nay,' and our happiness is 'yea and nay.' We are so happy now, as we may be miserable to-morrow. Let us labour to build on divine truth, which is like itself, that in all the changes of the world we may have somewhat that is unalterable, that is as unchangeable as God himself. As St Paul here brings God himself, 'as God is true, my word to you was not yea and nay, but yea.' So much shall suffice for that verse. I go on to the 20th verse.

VERSE 20.

'For all the promises of God in him are yea, and in him amen.' This comes in after this manner, My preaching to you, saith he, was invariable and constant, because Christ himself is alway 'yea.' If Christ, the matter of my preaching, be always 'yea,' and I preach nothing but Christ, then my preaching is invariable and constant. How doth he prove the *minor ?* How doth he prove that Christ is alway 'yea ?' 'All the promises of God in him are yea, and in him amen.' Christ is invariable, and my preaching of him was not 'yea and nay.' Christ is not 'yea and nay,' because 'all the promises of God in him are yea and amen.'

'The promises of God in him are yea,' that is, they are constant ; 'and in him they are amen.' There is some diversity in reading the words (*vv*). But most constantly the best expositors have it as this translation hath it, 'all the promises of God in him are yea, and in him amen.' The literal meaning is this, 'all the promises of God in Christ are yea,' that is, they are certain, they are made in him ; 'and in him they are amen,' that is, they are accomplished in him. In him they are made, and in him they are accomplished.

I might spend a great deal of time to shew the acception* of the word 'amen,' but it is not pertinent to my purpose.

'Amen' is here certain, undoubtedly certain, as it is here to make way to that which is to be understood.

There are three main senses of 'amen.' It signifies that a thing is positively so, and not no, it is so. 'Yea and amen' signify that such a thing is ; as, 'let your yea be yea,' Mat. v. 37, such a thing is. But now 'amen'

* That is, 'acceptation.'—G.

is more, not only that a thing is, but it is so truly, and so unchangeably; it is 'yea *and amen.*' The promises are 'yea,' they are made in Christ; and then they are true in him, undoubtedly, eternally, unchangeably true.

So take it in the strictest, in the strongest, sense you can; all the promises of God in Christ they are so true, that they are invariably, constantly, eternally true in him, they are made in him, and performed in him; 'they are yea in him, and amen in him.' So the whole carriage of the promises is only in Christ.

The truths we are to deliver out of the words are these:

First of all we must know, that since the fall of man it hath pleased the divine nature, the three persons in Trinity, *to stablish a covenant of grace, and so of salvation in Jesus Christ; and to make him a second principle, a second Adam, by whom mankind is restored to a better estate than ever we had in the first Adam.* God now since the fall takes another course to bring us back again to him. He doth not leave us as he left the angels that fell, in a state of perdition for ever; but as we fell by infidelity and distrust of him, so now we are recovered again by promises, and by faith in them.

There can be no intercourse between God and man but by some promise on his part.

Obs. God deals with man by promises.

Reason 1. The reason is this, *how can man dare to challenge anything of the great majesty of God without a warrant from himself?* How can the conscience be satisfied? The conscience looks to God. It is a knowledge together with God; how can conscience rest but in that it knows comes from God? Therefore for any good that I hope for from God, I must have a promise.

Reason 2. For this *is God's constant dispensation, while we live in this world we are alway under hope.* We are children of hope. ' We are saved by hope,' Rom. viii. 24: ' we rejoice in the hope of glory,' Rom. v. 2: and hope looks to the promises, whereof some part is unperformed. How doth heaven and earth differ? Heaven is all performance. Here is some performance to encourage us, and there is alway some promise still unperformed. We are alway under some promise; and therefore the manner of our apprehending God in this world differs from heaven. Here it is by faith and hope, there by vision. Vision is fit for performance. Faith and hope looks to the promise alway here. Therefore God rules his church by promises; partly, I say, to secure the soul of man. We cannot have any thing from God but by the manifestation of his own good will. How can we look for any thing from God but by promise? Can we look for anything from God by our own conceits? That is a fool's paradise.

Further, God will have his church ruled by promises in all ages, to exercise faith, and hope, and prayer, and dependence upon God. God will try of what credit he is among men, whether they will depend upon his promise or no; so that knowing he is true, by promise, it may be certain to them, they shall have performance in time. He gives men promises to see if they will trust him.

Reason 3. God will have this manner of dispensation to rule his church by promises, *to arm us in this world against fears and discouragements;* therefore we have alway some promise. He might have done us good, and have given us no promise; but now having given us promises, he will try the graces that are in us, and arm us against all discouragements and difficulties, till the thing promised be performed. For we must know that a promise is a divine thing, better than any earthly performance. Let

God give a man never so much in the world, if he have not a promise of better things, all will come to nothing at the last. Therefore God supports the souls and spirits of his children with promises, to arm them against all temptations on the right hand and on the left, that would draw them from trusting in his promise. He will have them live by faith, and that hath alway relation to the promise.

Quest. This is a general ground then, that God now in Christ Jesus hath appointed this way to govern the church with promises. Now what is a promise?

Ans. A promise is nothing but a manifestation of love, an intendment of bestowing some good, and removing some ill. A manifestation of our mind in that kind is a promise of conferring of a future good, or removing of a future ill; therefore it comes from love in the party promising.

There are three degrees of loving steps, whereof a promise is the last. The first is inward love; the second is real performance; and the third is a manifestation of performance intended before it be; and this, I say, is a degree of love. For love concealed, it doth not comfort in the *interim*, in the time that is betwixt. Now God, who is love, doth not only love us, and will not only shew his love in time, but because he will have us rest sweetly in his bosom, and settle ourselves on his gracious promises, in the mean time, he gives us rich and precious promises. He is not only love, and shews it in deed, but he expresseth it in word. And we may well build on his word, as verily as if he had performed it in deed; for whatsoever he saith is 'Yea, and Amen.' This is the nature of a promise. It is not only love, and the expression of love in deed, but the expression of it in word, when he intends to solace, and comfort, and stablish, and stay the mind of man till the good promised be performed.

Therefore, even from this we see how God loves us, that not only he hath an inward love in his breast, and doth good to us, but he manifests it by word. He would have us, as I said, live by faith, and stablish ourselves in hope.

Faith and hope are two graces altogether from promises. If there were no promise there could be no faith nor hope. What is hope? Nothing but the expectation of the things that the word saith. And what is faith, but a building on the word of God? Faith looks on the word that God will give such a thing, and hope looks upon the thing that the word promiseth: as the distinction is good, faith looks to the word of the thing, and hope looks to the thing in the word: faith looks to the word promising; hope looks to the performance of the thing promised. Faith 'is the evidence of things not seen,' Heb. xi. 1, because it sets the things that are absent as if they were present; hope is for the accomplishment of that. If there were no promise to hope, what needed hope? and where were a foundation for faith? Now God being willing to exercise faith and hope, feeds them both, and satisfies both, that we may be heavenly-wise in trusting and believing, and not foolish as men in the world. Therefore God hath given us promises, and sealed them with an oath, as we shall see afterward.

Now all promises coming from love, what love can there be in God to us since the fall, but it must be grounded on a better foundation than ourselves? If God love us, it must be in one that is first beloved: hereupon

Obs. 2. *Comes the ground of the promises to be Jesus Christ, God-man.* For all intercourse between God and us, it must be in him that is able to satisfy God. God will so in the covenant of grace entertain covenant and league with us, as that he will have his justice have full content,* he will be satisfied; and therefore he that will be the foundation of intercourse between God and us, he must be God-man, perfectly able to satisfy divine justice; he must be a friend of God's and a friend to us. Hereupon the promises must come from God's love in Jesus Christ; and he must first receive all good for us, and we must have it at the second hand from him. Hereupon it is said here, that ' all the promises of God *in him* are yea and amen.'

1. It is a rule, the first in any kind is the cause of all the rest. Now *Christ is the first beloved thing;* therefore in Col. i. 3, he is called ' the Son of God's love.' Christ being the only begotten Son of God, he looks on him first, before he looks on anything else; and whatsoever is lovely he looks on it as it is in him in whom his love is first, because he being his only begotten Son, he is the first object of all the respect that God hath. Therefore, whatsoever is beloved, it is as it hath a consistence in Christ. Therefore Christ he must first be loved, and then we in him; consider him as the Son of God.

2. Consider him *as man.* He is the first beloved, being a holy man above all other men; for the nature of man hath a subsistence in the second person in Christ. Therefore, Christ as man is beloved before all others, having a subsistence in his Godhead which is first beloved. He is the prime and most excellent creature as man. God looks first upon Christ as his only begotten Son, and upon Christ as man secondarily: upon the church in the third place as united to Christ; and all other creatures in reference to the church. And, therefore, there was never anything in the world, nor shall be, that ever was or shall be loved, but in the first-beloved Christ Jesus.

3. Again, Christ is first, because Christ *is the mediator between God and man by office.* Consider what relation he hath between God and man, and we may easily see that God first respects him, and us for him. For Christ being *God* and *man,* and *Mediator,* therefore, between God and man, he is loved of both. He is a friend to both, to bring both together. He is first regarded as Mediator, and then we for whose cause he is Mediator.

4. Then again, consider Christ, not as he is between God and us, *but as he is to us,* so he is first beloved. To God, he is his first begotten; to God and us a mediator. *To us a head, to us a husband, to us a brother;* a head from whence there is all influence of life and motion; a husband from whence we have all riches. He is all in all to us in the relations he stands in to us. Therefore he is first in all things, as the apostle saith, ' In all things he must have the pre-eminence,' Col. i. 18; and it is fit it should be so.

Especially since the fall. Leave the consideration of Christ, and this may be a reason. Consider us since the fall, as we are in the mass of corruption, are we fit objects for God's love? Are we not fuel for consuming fire? Is not he a ' consuming fire,' Heb. xii. 29, and we stubble for his wrath? Is not our nature defiled and tainted, and can it otherwise be amiable, than considered as knit to him that is first amiable, that is Christ? It cannot be. So look to Christ as the Son of God's love, whether as God or as man; look to his office as mediator, look on him as in relation to us as our husband and head; look on us without him, you may see that God's love is first founded in Christ, and then in us.

I mean in regard of execution in the passages of our salvation. For at

* That is, ' satisfaction.'—G.

first it was a free love that gave Christ to us, and us to Christ, ' So God loved the world, that he gave his Son,' John iii. 16. That was the first that set all the world in execution ; but in the execution from predestination to glorification, before all worlds he loved us in Christ to everlasting. From the everlasting in election, to everlasting in glory, all is in Christ in regard of execution. We subsist in him, we are sanctified in him, we are justified in him, his righteousness is ours, we are glorified in him, we are loved in him ; God blesseth us with all spiritual blessings in him, ' God hath made us accepted in his beloved,' Eph. i. 5, 6 ; in him who is his beloved Son, in whom he is well pleased ; not only ' with whom,' but ' in whom,' in him and all his, in him as mystical Christ, head and members. God now looks upon our nature as it is united to the person of his only begotten Son ; and thereupon our nature is lovely in the eyes of God, and enriched, and honoured, and advanced in Christ.

Even as a base woman by marriage with a great person is advanced ; so our nature being mean of itself, taking our nature when it was defiled with sin (though that particular mass was sanctified by the Holy Ghost), it was much advanced and ennobled, by having a subsistence in the second person. So God looks on us in Jesus Christ, and loves us in him, and bestows all spiritual blessings in Christ.

Therefore whatsoever we have, Christ must have it first for us ; whatsoever is done to us, must be done first to Christ. Christ is first predestinate, as it is, 1 Peter i. 2. He is the predestinate Lamb of God. He was ordained before all worlds, to be a sacrifice for us, and to be the head of his church. He was ordained before we were ordained. Christ is first beloved, and then we are beloved in his beloved. He is well pleased in him, and then in us. He is first loved, and then we. He is predestinate, and then we. He is the Son of God's love by nature, therefore we are sons of God's love by adoption and grace. What we are by adoption, he is by nature first of all. Therefore we are said to be elected in him, and sanctified in him. He first of all removes all ill, and then we have it removed, because he hath removed it. He is first justified from our sins, he is first quitted and freed from our sins, when he took them upon himself, and on the tree satisfied the wrath of God. ' He bore our iniquities, and by his stripes we are healed,' Isa. liii. 5. If he had not been freed from our sins, we had for ever lain under them. Therefore saith St Paul, ' If Christ be not risen, you are yet in your sins,' 1 Cor. xv. 13, seq. We are free from our sins, because Christ our surety is out of the prison of the grave. He is in heaven.

He must first rise from the dead. ' He is the first fruits of them that sleep ; the first begotten from the dead,' Rev. i. 5 ; 1 Cor. xv. 20. For though some rose before, yet it was in the virtue of Christ, who rose altogether by his own strength. Therefore he hath made a ' living way' to heaven. ' We are born again to a lively hope by the resurrection of Christ from the dead,' 1 Peter i. 3. We have a lively hope, a hope that makes us lively in good works, because our surety is in heaven. Now we hope for an inheritance immortal and undefiled. Because he is risen, we shall rise. He is ascended, therefore we shall ascend. We do ascend in the certainty of faith now, and shall ascend indeed hereafter.

Whatsoever we do, he doth it first ; and whatsoever we have from God, it is at the second hand. He hath it first, and conveys it to us ; the natural Son to the adopted sons. Therefore all the promises come to be made in him, and not directly to us alone abstracted from Christ.

Use. It is a point we should often think of, and seriously consider of ;

for it doth wondrously stablish our hearts. Doth God love me, and doth he do good to me abstracted from Christ, myself alone ? No ; for then, alas ! I should fly from his presence ; but he looks upon me, and considers me as I am in his Son. Therefore in John xvii. 24, in that blessed prayer of Christ, saith he, ' That thou mayest love them with the same love wherewith thou lovest me.' God loves us with the same love that he loves his Son with. ' That the love wherewith thou lovest me, may be in them.' He loves him first, and then he loves us with that love that he loves him. Here is the reason that God looks on us with a forbearing eye, notwithstanding all the matter of anger and wrath in us. He looks on us in his Son, as members of his Son. His love to us is founded on his love to his Son.

Hereupon back again is our boldness to God the Father, that we go to him in his beloved Son, and present his Son to him. Lord, look on thy Son that thou hast given for us, in whom we are members. We are not as in ourselves, but in thy beloved. For as all things descend from God to us, so our souls should ascend to him. All descends from God to us, in his Son. Why! all our comfortable considerations of God must be in his Son Christ. Thereupon we have boldness to God through him, not in ourselves but in and through Christ. Let us bring ' Benjamin,' Gen. xlii. 36, seq., with us, bring Christ, and then we shall be welcome. If we come in the garments of our Elder Brother, then we shall get the blessing.

But of ourselves God cannot endure to look on us ; therefore this is a heathenish conceit in our prayers, to presume to go to God otherwise than he hath clothed himself with the comfortable relation of a Father in Christ. If we consider him as a just God, as a God of vengeance, as a holy God, the more it makes to our terror, if we be not besotted. But go to him as he is now in his Son Christ, and go boldly. The heathens otherwise conceived wavering and doubtingly of a God ; alas ! conceiving him out of Christ, he was nothing but a ' consuming fire ' to them, Heb. xii. 29.

How dares that man that knows himself, and that knows God, how dares he think of God ? He thinks basely of God, that can think of him, and not think of him as he is to him in Christ. Darest thou think of God who is a ' consuming fire,' and not think of him as he is pleased and pacified in thy nature in Christ, that hath taken thy nature to be a foundation of comfort, to be a ' second Adam,' a public person for all that are in him, and members of him ? To see God fully appeased in him who is God-man, thou mayest think of him with comfort then. Never think of the promises of grace or comfort, or anything without Christ.

Therefore St Paul saith, ' Now to Abraham and his seed was the promise made ; he saith not to seeds, as to many, but to thy seed,' Gal. iii. 16 ; as speaking of one, even Christ. All the promises of good to us are made to Christ, and conveyed from Christ to us ; the promises, and likewise the things promised. ' He hath promised to us eternal life, and this life is in his Son,' 1 John v. 11 ; and so grace, and whatsoever, it is in him. The promises and the things promised they are conveyed from God to Christ, and so to us. They are a deed of gift. We have them from and by Christ. Why are the angels attendants upon us ? The angels attend upon Jacob's ladder, that is, Christ. It is he that knits heaven and earth together ; so the angels, because they attend upon Christ first, they become our attendants. Whatsoever we are, whatsoever privileges we have, it is in Christ first. It belongs to us no further than we by faith are made one with Christ. Thus we see whatsoever we have from God, it is by promises. And these promises are not abstracted from love, for they are the fruits of love ; and this love is seated in Christ, who hath satisfied God's justice. We have promises, and promises in Christ.

Obs. 3. In the third place, *the apostle saith that all the promises of God in him are yea.* They are constant and sure in him ; they shall be performed.

All promises are either Christ himself, or by Christ, or from Christ, or for Christ. All promises that ever were made to God's people, they were either of Christ himself, when he was promised, or such as were promised for Christ. The promise of Christ himself is the first grand promise, that he should be made man, the promise in his own person. But whatsoever promise was made by the prophets and apostles, they were made by his Spirit, they were made for him, for his sake, and in him, and they were made to those that are in him too. For as God's love is founded in him to those that are in him mystically as the Son of his love, so the promises are made and given over to him of all good. He takes all the promises of good from God for us, and then they are made to us as we are in him.

He himself is the first promise that runs along in all the Scripture ; and all the promises of Christ are ' yea ; ' for whatsoever was promised of Christ before he came, it was fulfilled when he came. For all types were fulfilled in him, and all prophecies, and all promises, they were all accomplished in him.

I. *All types, whether personal or real.*

1. For *personal types*, he was the ' second Adam.' Adam was a type of him. He is the true Adam. He was the true Isaac, the ground of laughter.* He is the true Joseph, advanced now to the kingdom, to the right hand of God. He is the steward of his church, to feed his church here, and bring her to heaven with himself afterward. He is the true Joshua, that brought Israel out of the wilderness to Canaan. He brings us from Moses, from the law, to heaven. He is the true Joshua, that brings us through Jordan, from death and miseries in this world to heaven. He is the true Solomon, the prince of peace.† So all personal types of kings and priests, as Aaron was a type of him, &c., they were yea in him, they were fulfilled in him.

2. And all *real types.*‡ He is the true ' mercy-seat' wherein God would be heard and prayed unto, for he covers the law, the curse of it, as the mercy-seat did. He is the true ' brazen serpent,' that whosoever looks on him with the eye of faith, ' shall not perish, but have everlasting life,' John iii. 15. He is the true ' manna,' the bread of life. That type had its ' yea' in Christ. He is the true sacrifice, ' the passover lamb,' the lamb of God ' that takes away the sins of the world,' John i. 29. If our hearts be sprinkled with his blood, the destroying angel hath nothing to do with us. The passover hath its ' yea' in him. Therefore that which is affirmed of the passover is affirmed of him, ' Not a bone of it shall be broken,' Ps. xxxiv. 20. That is attributed to Christ that was performed in the type. That is applied to Christ that was spoken of the passover ; to signify the identity of the type, and the thing signified. He was the yea of that, and of all comfortable types that were real, and personal, all have their ' yea' in him.

Therefore saith our Saviour Christ, the last words of his almost upon the cross, ' All is finished,' John xix. 30, all the types real and personal.

II. And *all promises and prophecies have their ' yea' in Christ.* The first

* That is, the name Isaac means ' laughter.'—G.
† That is, the name Solomon means ' peace.'—G.
‡ That is, ' typical *things*.'—ED.

promise, what was it but Christ? 'The seed of the woman shall break the serpent's head,' Gen. iii. 15. It was nothing but Christ, it was 'yea' when he was born; and when he died he crushed the serpent's head. 'By death he overcame him that had the power of death, that is, the devil,' Heb. ii. 14. So the promise that was renewed to Abraham, ' In thy seed shall all nations of the earth be blessed,' Gen. xii. 3, that is, in Christ. And so to David, that he should come out of his family. And that particular promise of Isaiah, 'that a virgin should conceive,' Isa. vii. 14. And the Baptist points him out, ' Behold the Lamb of God,' John i. 29. All the particular things that befell Christ in time, they were prophesied of before, and Christ was the 'yea' of all, that is, all had their determinate truth in Christ when he came. This is one reason why St Paul saith, 'All the promises in Christ are yea.' Whatsoever was promised concerning Christ, or foretold, it was 'yea' in him, concerning his birth, and the place of it; concerning his death, and the manner of it; concerning his resurrection and ascension; concerning his offices, all was foretold. As we see in Scripture, in the New Testament, it is the foot of divers verses, that ' it might be fulfilled;' so this that was foretold in the Old, it was fulfilled in the New. So Christ is the first promise, and whatsoever was said of him is 'yea and amen.' Whatsoever was spoken of Christ, it was 'yea' in the Old Testament and ' amen' in the New; it was made to them in the Old Testament and performed in the New.

And what is the Old and New Testament but this syllogism? He is the blessed seed, that is, the Son of the Virgin Mary, born in Bethlehem, that shall come in the end of Daniel's weeks, that shall come when the sceptre shall be departed from Judah, &c. He is the true Messiah, the true Christ, saith the Old Testament. Here is the 'yea.' 'Amen,' saith the New Testament to this. But Christ is the Son of the Virgin Mary, he suffered these things that it might be fulfilled. So all is 'amen' in the New Testament. I say, this is the main reason that all is built on. He in whom all these agree is the true Messiah. But, saith the New Testament, all these are 'amen' in Christ. Therefore Christ, the Son of the Virgin Mary, he is the true Messiah. We see whatsoever was prophesied concerning Christ himself, was 'yea.'

III. And not only so, *but all the prerogatives and good things that come by Christ are ' yea.'* They are undoubted in Christ, and they were 'yea' before he was. He profited before he was. He was 'yea' to Adam. Because, however he that was the seed of the woman came not till the latter end of the world, till four thousand years after the beginning or thereabouts, yet the faith of Adam and of Abraham made him present. Abraham ' saw Christ's day, and rejoiced,' John viii. 56. There was a virtue from Christ to all former ages. They all had benefit by Christ, as it is proved at large, Heb. xi. And in Acts xv. 11, ' We hope to be saved by Christ, as well as they,' insinuating that they hoped to be saved by Christ as well as we. So he was 'yea' for comfort to all that were before him, as well as now. All the promises were 'yea,' even to the patriarchs and prophets.

Even as if a man should undertake three or four years hence to pay a debt that is due by one that is subject to be carried to prison, and on that condition that this man shall be freed. I undertake at such a time to pay such a debt. So though the debt be paid three or four years hence, he is let go free that was obnoxious to go to prison for the debt, though it be to be paid after. So it was with Christ. He, the second person in the Trinity, undertook, being so appointed by God the Father. The blessed Trinity stab-

lished this, that Christ should pay the debt by death ; the debt to divine
justice should be satisfied by the cursed death of the cross, that those that
before should have gone to hell else for the debt, should be all freed that
had any part and interest by faith in Christ, who should pay the debt afterwards.   Christ undertook at such a time to be incarnate, and to pay it for
us.   God the Father to whom we were obnoxious, that was the creditor for
the payment of that, four thousand years after, let them go.   So Christ was
yea to them, they had benefit by Christ's death.

Hereupon the prophets spake of him as a thing present, ' To us a Son
is born, to us a child is given,' Isa. ix. 6.   Faith mounts over many years,
six hundred years before Christ in the prophet it mounted, and made the
time of Christ's coming and his death to be present ; because they had
benefit by him as if he had been present.   Only with this difference, in the
time present when Christ came in the flesh they had some comfortable enlargement of grace.   When he. came in the flesh, I say, there was a new
world as it were, there was grace poured out in abundance.

So you see that all the promises concerning Christ, they were performed ;
they were ' yea and amen,' and the good things by Christ.   St Paul saith
excellently, Heb. xiii. 8, ' Christ yesterday, to-day, and the same for ever.'
Yesterday to the patriarchs, to-day for the present time he is ' yea,' and for
the time to come he is ' yea,' the same alway.

He is yea to all ages.   He is yea to us as well as to those that were in
Christ's time.   Christ is then crucified to thee, when thou believest in
Christ crucified.   If we now by faith look to Christ, crucified and sent
from his Father to take our nature on him, we have as much benefit by
Christ as those that beheld him crucified.   As they before looked for-
wards by the eye of faith, so we look backward.   We have benefits by
Christ.   He is ' yesterday, to-day, and the same for ever.'   ' All the promises are yea in him,' that is, they are constantly ' yea' for all ages.   The
promises of Christ, as the spirits in the body, they run through all ages of
the church.   Without him there is no love, nor mercy, nor comfort from
God.   As I said before, God cannot look on our cursed nature out of
Christ ; therefore whosoever will apprehend anything merciful in God,
must apprehend it in Christ the promised seed.   ' All the promises in him
are yea.'

He is called *Logos*, the word.   Why is he so ?   Both actively and passively.   Actively, ' the word,' because how should we ever have known the
mind in the breast of God, hidden and sealed there, unless Christ had been
the *Logos*, the word ?   For a word is expressed from reason, and there is
a word that is essential, that is reason, *Logos ;* and so the word coming
from it, speech, the issue of reason.   So Christ is the essential word, by
nature and by office the word, to discover the inward will and purpose of
God to us.   All the promises of God are discovered by Christ, as the Angel
of the covenant.   And passively he is the word, *Logos*, of whom all the
prophets spake, as Peter saith, Acts iii. 18, who was fore-signified by all the
types, as I shewed.   Christ he is truly all in all.

Use. It is a comfortable way to study Christ this way ; to see him foretold in the Old Testament, and to see the accomplishment in the New ; to
parallel the Old and New Testament.   It is an excellent way of studying
the gospel.   For we know men are delighted to know divers things at once.
When a man's knowledge is enriched divers ways at once, it delights him,
as when a man knows the history of a thing, and the truth with it ; when
he knows a promise, and the truth ; a type, and the truth, how doth it

delight! When a man sees the type in the Old, and the truth in the New, the history there, the promise and the accomplishment here, it is a wondrous delightful thing. For why doth proportion delight the eye, but because it is an agreement of different things, a sweet harmony of different things? Why doth music so please the ear? Because it is a harmony of different things. When we see a type different from the truth performed, and a promise different from the performance, and yet a sweet agreement, from agreement a man is delighted. A man is not delighted with colours as colours, but as they hold proportion with the rest of the body; he is not delighted with a limb as a limb, but as it holds proportion with the man; if there be no proportion and comeliness, it delights not. So in this case it is good to consider both together. God therefore for this end and purpose would have truths conveyed in the Old Testament, by way of types, and prophecies, and promises, that it might delight us now to hear them, and to study them the more; for, as I said, when we know many things at once, it is delightful.

That is the reason why comparisons and allusions are so delightful, because we know the comparison, and the thing to which it is compared. And that is the reason why our Saviour Christ, besides types and figures, and promises and prophecies, is set out by whatsoever is excellent in nature in the Scriptures. There is nothing in nature that is excellent, but there is something taken from it to set forth the excellency of Christ. He is the 'Sun of righteousness;' he is the 'water,' he is the 'way,' he is the 'bread,' he is the 'vine,' he is the 'tree of life.' Whatsoever is excellent in nature, either in heaven or earth, it serves to set forth the excellency of Christ. Why? To delight us, that we may be willing and cheerful to think of Christ; that together with the consideration of the excellency of the creature, some sweet meditation of Christ, in whom all those excellencies are knit together, might be presented to the soul. When we see the sun, oft to think of that blessed Sun that quickens and enlivens all things, and scatters the mists of ignorance. When we look on a tree, to think of the Tree of righteousness; on the way, to think of him the Way; of life, of him that is the true Life. When we think of anything that is excellent, think of God's love in Scripture to set out Christ, that he would shadow him in all; for he is the true Sun. All creatures must vanish ere long, and whatsoever is excellent in the creature; and what will stand then? Only he in whom all these excellencies are comprised in one. ' All the promises in him are yea and amen.'

If this be true then, that the promise of Christ himself, who is the chief good promised, is in the New Testament 'amen,' all of him is ' yea and amen,' then comes this as a deducted truth, all other promises must needs be ' yea and amen.' For God, he that performed the grand promise in giving Christ in the fulness of time, will for Christ's sake perform all other promises. Therefore the incarnation, the life, the death, and resurrection of Christ our blessed Saviour, it is a pawn and pledge to us of the performance of all things to come.

God promised to the Jews that they should come out of Babylon, he promised that he would deliver them from the enemy; and he usually prefixeth this promise, ' A virgin shall conceive and bear a son,' Isa. vii. 14; and ' to us a child is born, and a son is given,' Isa. ix. 6; to signify, that therefore they should have deliverance, because God would give them a better thing than that. He would give them Christ, in whom all the promises are ' yea and amen;' and because Christ should come of that people, they should not miscarry in captivity under their enemies; for then how should Christ come of them ?

Therefore because ' a virgin should conceive,' and because ' a Child shall be born, and a Son given,' therefore you shall have outward deliverance. All other things are ' yea and amen' for Christ, as St Paul divinely reasons, ' If he spared not his only begotten Son, but gave him to death for us all, how shall he not with him give us all things else ?' Rom. viii. 32. All other promises are made in Christ and performed for him. And since the grand promise itself is now ' amen,' that Christ is come, it is a pledge of all other things that are to come. Is Christ come in the flesh according to the promise ? Hath he done all and suffered all according to the prophecies, as it was written of him ? Then why shall we not look for the accomplishment of all that are to come, on the same ground ? Have we not a pledge ? Why shall we not look for the resurrection of the body, for the day of judgment, for the second coming of Christ ? Is not his first coming a pledge of it ?

When God is become man, and was mortal, why should we doubt that man being mortal should be immortal ? Is not the greater performed already ? Is it not a greater matter for God to become man, and to die in our nature, than for we that are mortal to become immortal by Christ ? Why should we not expect that which is to come, since the greater is done ? Why should we doubt that we shall be taken up to God, since he is come down to man ? Therefore, since it is upon the same ground, let us look for the performance of all to be ' yea and amen.'

Since the coming of Christ, many promises have been performed in the church, and many yet remain. Some have been performed, as the calling of the Gentiles, and the discovery* of antichrist foretold by St Paul, and the consuming of him in part. There is somewhat unfulfilled : the conversion of the Jews, the confusion of antichrist, the resurrection to glory with Christ, &c. Why should we doubt of them that are to come, having such a pledge of truth of God and Christ in the real performance of that which is past ? Let us not doubt of it ; for in Rev. xvi. 17, *et alibi*, when he speaks of the destruction of antichrist, ' It is done, it is done,' saith the angel. As Christ said when he was on the cross, all was finished, so it is as true of his adversaries, all is done ; it is as sure as if it were done already.

Therefore the church and people of God should comfort themselves for the time to come, in the destruction of the implacable, malicious enemies of the church, that glory in the flesh, that set up an outward religion that is opposite to the power of Christ, that the time shall come that all shall be done to them, and that all other promises shall be finished. For as in the first coming of Christ all was finished for the working of our salvation, so in his second coming there will be a time when it will be said, all is finished, for the accomplishment of that which was done in his first coming. Therefore let us stablish our souls in the expectation of the blessed promises, for ' all the promises in Christ are yea and amen,' and shall be for ever.

All the promises are infallibly true, as God and Christ himself is true. Christ shall as soon fail, and God shall as soon fail, as any promise that we have made us in the gospel, if we apprehend it in Christ, and believe it in Christ.

Use 1. Then here you see for the direction of our judgment, what to think of a rotten opinion that some have that are unacquainted with divine truth, and the all-sufficiency of Christ, and the mercy of God in Christ, that consider

* That is, ' manifestation.'—G.

not the vileness of our nature, and the infinite majesty of God. They will have the Gentiles saved by the light of nature, and the Jews by the law of Moses, and Christians by the gospel of Christ ; as if there were some other means now to come to heaven, and to the favour of God, than by Christ. Whereas now all that we have must be by promises, and all the promises we have are in Christ. They are all yea in him. Without him there is no intercourse between the majesty of God and us. Therefore ' there is no name under heaven whereby we can be saved, but by the name of Jesus,' Acts iv. 12 ; which not only confutes the devilish opinion and conceit that some have, but also the charitable error of others, that think the heathens that never heard of Christ shall be saved. I leave them to their Judge. We must go to the Scriptures. All the promises are in Christ, in him they are ' yea,' in him they are made ; in him they are ' amen,' in him they are performed. Out of him we have nothing, out of the promises in him we have nothing.

Use 2. How we are *to magnify God that we live in the sunshine of the gospel,* that in Christ we have precious and rich promises! A precious Saviour we have, and precious faith to lay hold on him, and precious promises ; all precious, both promises to be believed, and our Saviour in whom they are apprehended. He is ' a precious stone,' 1 Pet. ii. 6 ; and the faith that lays hold on him is ' precious,' 1 Pet. i. 7. How are we to bless God that we have these advantages ! that we have Christ laid open, and precious and rich promises, whereby we may have precious faith to lay hold on these precious promises ? We are much to bless God for it.

Use 3. Again, are all the promises of God in Christ, and in him yea and amen ? *This should direct us in our dealing with God, not to go directly to him, but by a promise ;* and when we have a promise, look to Christ in whom it is performed. Go to God in the blessed promises that we have for Christ's sake, that he would perform all. ' If we ask anything of God in Christ's name, we shall receive it,' 1 John v. 14, because the promises are in him. If we thank God for anything, it must be in Christ, for that we have in him.

What a comfort is this, that we may go to God in Christ, and claim the promises boldly ; because we see out of the love he bears to Christ, he loves us, and hath made us promises in him, and as verily as he loves him, so he loves us, and will perform all his gracious promises to us ? If we lay fast hold on Christ, I say, he can as soon alter his love to Christ as to us ; for he loves us with the same love that he loves Christ with, he loves us in his beloved. He hath ' blessed us with all spiritual blessings in him,' Eph. i. 3, he hath made us sons in him that is the natural Son ; and as his love is unchangeable to his Son, so it is to us in Christ.

If a prince's love to any man be founded and grounded upon the love he bears to his son, if he loves his son he loves such a man, because his son loves him. Surely he may have great comfort that it will hold ! Because his affection is natural and unalterable, he will alway love his son. Therefore he will love him whom his son loves alway. Now Christ is the Son of God, he loves us in his Son ; he hath given us rich promises in his Son. He hath given him the first promise, and all other promises of forgiveness of sins, and life everlasting in and through him. As long as he loves Christ, he will love us, and as sure as he loves Christ, he will love us.

Nothing in the world can separate his love from his own Son, and nothing in the world can separate God's love from us, because it is in his Son. Christ loves his mystical body as well as his natural body ; and God loves the mystical body of Christ as he loves his natural body. He hath advanced that to glory at his right hand, and will he leave his mystical body the church? Will he not advance that? Doth he not love whole Christ? Yes! God loves whole Christ. Our nature that he hath taken to him, it is the chief thing, the most lovely thing in heaven or earth, next to God; and he loves all that are in him, his mystical body. For indeed he gave us to Christ. He hath sealed and anointed him. He is anointed by God the Father for us.

Upon what an unchangeable, eternal ground is the love of God built, and the faith of a Christian! How can the gates of hell prevail against the faith of a Christian, when it carries him to the promises, and from the promises to the love of God, and from thence to Christ, upon whom the love of God is founded? Before the faith of a Christian can be shaken, the promises must be of no effect, they must be 'yea and nay,' and not 'yea.' And if the promises be shaken, the love of God must be uncertain, and Christ uncertain. Heaven and earth must be overturned to overturn the faith of a Christian. There is nothing in the world that is so firm as a believing Christian, that casts himself on the promises, that are alway 'yea;' and to make them 'yea,' they are founded on Christ, the Son of God's love.

Well, these promises, coming from such love, may be ranked into divers ranks. I will touch some of them, to shew how we are to carry ourselves, to make comfortable use of this, that 'all the promises are yea and amen in Christ.'

(1.) There are some universal promises, for the good of all mankind; as that God would never destroy the world again. Or (2.) promises that concern more particularly his church. And those are promises either of outward things, or of spiritual and eternal things, of grace and glory.

Now, for the manner of promising, they admit of this distinction: all the promises that God hath made to us, either (1.) they are absolute, without any condition. So was Christ. God promised Christ, let the world be as it will, Christ did and would have come. And so the promise of his glorious coming, he will come, let men be as they will. There will be a resurrection. Some promises (2.) be conditional in the manner of propounding, but yet absolute in the real performance of them. As, for example, the promises of grace and glory to God's children. The promise of forgiveness of sins,—God will forgive their sins if they believe, if they repent. They are propounded conditionally, but in the performance they are absolute, because God performs the covenant himself; he performs our part and his own too. For since Christ, though he propounded the promises of the gospel with conditions, yet he performs the condition; he stirs us up to attend upon the means, and by his Spirit in the word he works faith and repentance, which is the condition. Faith and repentance is his gift.

He 'writes his law in our hearts,' Jer. xxxi. 33, and teacheth us how to love. So, though they be conditionally propounded (for God deals with men as men by way of commerce,—he propounds it by way of covenant and condition), yet in the covenant of grace, which is truly a gracious covenant, he not only gives the good things, but he performs the condition, by the Spirit working our hearts to believe and to repent.

Again, there are promises not only propounded conditionally, of grace and comfort, but of outward things. All outward things are promised conditionally, as thus: God hath promised protection from contagious sicknesses, from war, and troubles. General promises there are of protection everywhere. 'God will be a hiding-place,' Ps. xci. 2, and he will deliver his children. There are private promises, and then positive promises, that he will do this and that good for them; but these are conditional, so far forth as in his wise providence he sees it may serve spiritual good things, grace and the inward man. For God takes liberty in our outward estate, and in our bodies to afflict them, or to do them good, as may serve the main.

For do what we will, these bodies will turn to dust and vanity, and we must leave the world behind us; but God looks to the main state in Christ, to the new creature. Therefore as far as outward blessings may encourage us, and as far as deliverances may help the main, so far he will grant them, or else he denies them. He takes liberty in outward things.

Therefore that sort of promises they are conditional, with exception of necessary affliction. For we cannot have the blessings of this life positive or privative, we cannot be delivered always, and have blessings, but our corrupt nature is such, that except we have somewhat to season them, we shall surfeit of them: we cannot digest them, and therefore they are all with the exception of the cross.* As Christ saith, he that doth anything for him, he shall have 'an hundredfold here,' Mat. xix. 29, but with affliction and persecutions; he shall be sure of that; whatsoever else he hath, let him look for that. All the crosses we have in the world are to season the good things of this life. Many other distinctions and differences we might have to lay open the kinds of promises in Scripture; but this shall suffice to give you a taste. Now, all these are made in Christ, and performed in Christ, so far forth as is for our good.

Use. Are all the promises, of what kind soever, spiritual or outward, temporal and eternal—are they all made to us in Jesus Christ, and are they certain, yea and amen in him? Then make this use of it, *let us renew our former exhortation, get into Christ by all means;* for out of him we have nothing savingly good.

Obj. But you will say, Doth not God do many good things to them that are out of Christ? Doth not the rain fall upon the ill as well as the good? And doth not he 'fill the bellies of the wicked with good things?' Ps. xvii. 14.

Ans. Yes, he doth, he doth! But are they blessings? No! they are not. But as God saith to Moses, if you do this and this ill, 'I will curse you in your dough, I will curse you at home and abroad, I will curse you in your children,' &c., Deut. xxvii., xxviii. They are cursed in their blessings, Mal. ii. 2. There is no man that is a carnal, brutish man, but though he live and have revenues and pleasures, he is cursed in his blessings. For what? Is he made for this life only? No! he is but 'fatted on to the day of destruction;' they are 'snares' to him, Josh. xxiii. 13. How do you know they are snares? Because they make him secure and careless of the worship of God; they make him profane, they make him despise the power of religion. A man may see by his conversation they are snares. They are not promises in Christ, for then they would come to him out of God's love. Therefore get into Christ, rest not in anything abstracted from Christ. Let us not rest in any blessing except we have it in God's love in Christ.

And I may know that I have anything in this world, any deliverance from ill, or any positive good thing from God's love in Christ, if I have it with a heart wrought on to the best things, to value Christ, and to account all dung in comparison of him. When I esteem my being in Christ above all beings, above being rich, or honourable, or in favour, alas! this I know

* That is, the cross is to be always on the other side of the balance.—ED.

is fading; but my being in Christ is 'yea and amen,' that will stand by me when all these beings will fail. This is comfortable, if I can do this, and have other things, I have them with the love of God and Christ. Let us get into Christ therefore.

For this purpose, *attend upon the means of salvation*, that the word may be effectual, by his Spirit accompanying his own ordinance, to open the excellencies of Christ to us, to make us love him, and get our affections into him. How are we in Christ? By knowing him; and then knowledge carries our hearts. For our wills cleave to that that we know to be excellent and necessary. Christ is discovered as excellent and necessary, and so the will cleaves to him as a good so discovered; and the affections follow the will. When the will cleaves to Christ as excellent and necessary, then I love him, then I rest on him, then I have peace in him. I may know that I am in Christ, upon my knowledge of him and cleaving to him, and finding peace in my conscience. For he that is in Christ hath rest. Faith in Christ hath a resting, stablishing power. If I be in Christ, my soul rests; for I know that all is 'yea and amen in him.' My soul rests in him. Whatsoever I find in the world to unsettle me; things are amiss, and otherwise than I would have them; but I rest in the love of God in Christ. Let us get into Christ by knowledge; let the will follow that, and our affections follow that; and then we shall find the rest and peace that will secure us that indeed we are in Christ.

Alas! what is a man out of Christ? As a man in a storm, that hath no clothes to hide his nakedness, to cover him from the violence of the storm: as a man in a tempest, that is out of a house to hide him: as a stone out of the foundation, that is scattered here and there as neglected: as a branch out of the vine, out of the root, what shape is in such a branch? It will be cast into the fire afterwards. A man out of Christ, that is not clothed with him, that is not built on him, and settled on him, and planted in him, he is a man destitute. We pity such men's cases in the world; but if we had spiritual eyes to look on these men, on profane civil wretches, that pride themselves in a little morality, and have scarce that perhaps, and neglect grace, and the mystery of Christ, such a man deserves pity. There is but a step between him and hell, if he be out of Christ, and live and die so; and at the day of Christ he will account him so.

Oh! saith St Paul, Philip. iii. 8, 'I account all dung and dross in comparison of Christ, not having my own righteousness, but to be found in him,' having the righteousness of God in Christ. O happy man in death, and at the day of judgment, that is found in Christ, and not in himself, not in his own righteousness; though that there must be, not to give us title to heaven. The best thing is to be found in Christ, to have his righteousness and obedience. That is so excellent that St Paul accounted all 'dung and dross' in comparison of that, to be found in that. Get into Christ by all means; for in him all the promises are 'yea and amen;' not out of him.

Use. If so be all the promises be 'yea and amen' in Christ, then here again see the stability of a Christian's estate, that hath promises to uphold him. Compare it with a man that hath present things only, with an Esau that hath the things of this life, Heb. xii. 16. The men of this world, as the psalmist calls them, they have present things, they have performance; he gives them their portion here, as he saith to Dives, 'Thou hadst thy good,' Luke xvi. 25; that which thou caredst for, thou hadst it here; and Lazarus had pain, and misery, and poverty here. Now the case is altered: he is advanced, and thou art tormented.

A Christian, as a Christian, he hath a great many promises. Some of them are performed; for God is delivering him, and comforting him, and protecting him, and speaking peace to his conscience; but the greatest part are yet to be performed, the perfection of grace and glory to come. He is a child of the promise, a son of the promise, here is his estate. Another man hath present payment, and that is all he cares for; he hath something, and he swells in the conceit of that, that he is somebody. What is the difference? what hath the one but a great deal of nothing? what saith Solomon, that had tried all the world? ' All is vanity and vexation of spirit,' Eccles. i. 2. All is uncertain, and we are uncertain in the use of them, if we have no better life than the life of nature. But the promises they are ' yea,' they are certain, they contain undoubted certain good things, that will stick by us when all else will leave us.

A Christian, take him, and strip him in your thoughts from all the good things in the world, he is a happier man than the greatest monarch in the world out of Christ. Why? He hath nothing but present things, with a great deal of addition of misery: and his greatness makes him more sensible of his misery. It makes him more tender and apprehensive than other men. The other he wants many comforts of this life, he wants the performance; he is rich in bills and bonds. God is bound to him, he hath promised he ' will not forsake him,' Deut. iv. 31; but he will be his God in life, to death, and for everlasting. He hath title to all the promises, ' Godliness hath the promises of this life, and of that which is to come,' 1 Tim. iv. 8. Happy man! he hath so much performance for the present, as is useful for his safe conduct to bring him to heaven! He shall have daily bread: he that will give him a kingdom, will not deny him bread; he that will give him a country, will give him safe conduct. And besides that he hath here by performance, he hath rich and precious promises, and they are all ' yea and amen,' they are certain.

His life is uncertain, his estate in the world is changeable here, his life is as a vapour; and the comforts of life are less than life. When life itself, the foundation of these comforts, is but a vapour, so uncertain, what are all the comforts of life? yet a Christian hath comfort here, the promises are invested into him, and lodged in his heart, and made his own by faith.

Faith hath a wondrous peculiarising virtue. It makes a man own that which is generally propounded in the gospel. Now faith making the promises his own, and they are certain. A Christian, take him at all uncertainties, he hath somewhat to build on, that is ' yea and amen,' that is undoubtedly constant and certain, that will stick by him when all things fail him.

I speak this, to commend the estate of a believing, repentant Christian, to make you in love with it. In all the changes and varieties in this world, a Christian hath somewhat to take to. And likewise in all the dangers of this life, he hath a rock to go to, a hiding-place. God hath chambers of providence, as it is, Isa. xxvi. 20, he bids the church ' come into thy chambers.' God hath a hiding-place, and secret rooms to hide children in, when it is good for them, in the time of pestilence and war, in the time of public disturbance; when there is a confusion of all things, ' come into thy chambers.' God is a resting-place and a hiding-place. He is styled so everywhere in the Psalms: Ps. xviii. 2, ' my rock and my shield,' as if David had said, I have many troubles in the world, but in God is my defence; for he is my rock, my shield, and all. Whatsoever is defensive, I have it in him.

What a comfort is this in all dangers! a Christian knows either he shall be safe here or in heaven ; and, therefore, he doth rest. 'He dwells in the secret of the Almighty,' Ps. xci. 1, that is, in the love and the protec-tection of God Almighty ; and as Moses saith, 'Thou art our habitation from everlasting to everlasting,' Ps. xc. 1, that is, God is a dwelling-place for him that builds on his promise ; for God and his word are all one. 'Thou art our dwelling-place,' &c. He saw they dropped away in the wilderness by the wrath of God, as we do now by the pestilence,* and Moses made that psalm. He took occasion to meditate of the frailty of man's life. We are as grass, as a tale that is told ; but what is our estate in God, in the promises ? 'Thou art our habitation from everlasting to everlasting,' Ps. xc. 2. We dwell not long in the world, sickness may come and sweep us away, but 'thou art our habitation.' We dwell in God when we are dead, when we are out of the world ; we dwell in God in Christ for ever. Our estate in Christ is an everlasting estate. Therefore in Psalm cxii. 7, the Psalmist saith ·of the righteous man there, 'that he is not troubled for ill news.' He is not senseless, he is very sensible ; but yet notwithstanding he is not shaken from his rest, from his rock and stay for no ill news or tidings, why ? The Psalmist gives the reason, 'his heart is fixed.' Upon what foundation ? Upon the promises and providence of God. God hath promised to provide for him. He is his Father ; and, therefore, he is not afraid of ill tidings.

What a blessed estate then is it to be in Christ, and to have promises in Christ to be protected and preserved here, so as is for our good, and to have such a state in God, for him to be our habitation and hiding-place from everlasting to everlasting ! If our hearts be fixed here, let us hear of ill tidings, of war, of this sickness and contagion, let it be what it will, if our hearts be fixed, blessed men are we. But if we have nothing to take to when trouble comes, we are, as I said before, as a man in a storm with-out a hiding-place. Now every word of God, saith the Psalmist, 'is a tried word, as silver tried in the fire,' Ps. xii. 6. The promises are tried promises that we may rest on them, and as we are Christians, what are we but men of promise ? The best is behind, and what is our comfort in this world ? God lets down his love to us in gracious promises ; and he gives us a taste of the performance. As children have somewhat of their inheritance in their nonage to keep them, so somewhat of heaven to comfort our souls we have, but the main is to come, and the performance is left till then ; therefore we cannot too much consider of this comfortable point. Consider how many promises we have in the word ; the certainty of them, that they are 'yea and amen ;' and in whom they are founded, in him that is 'Amen' himself ; for Christ is 'Amen, the true and faithful witness,' Rev. iii. 14. These are comfortable considerations.

Are the promises of God in Christ 'yea and amen ? Let us divide men who may make any use of them. All men, they are either such as are in Christ, or such as are not in Christ.

Quest. All the promises being made in Christ, what comfort or what good can those that are not yet in Christ have by the promises ?

Ans. I answer, till they be in Christ, none at all ; for a man out of Christ is out of the favour of God. God cannot look on such a man but as the object of his wrath, and as fuel for his vengeance ; and, therefore, there is no hope for such a man till he be in Christ. All other things in the world cannot comfort such a man ; for, alas ! his being in the world,

* In the margin, 1625. See note *r*.—G.

his being rich, his being in favour with such or such, what are they? Fading beings that fail, and himself with them. He stands on the ice. They slip and he slips with them. What are all beings in death, if a man have not a more stable being in Jesus Christ.

Quest. What comfort is there then for such a man by the promises in Jesus Christ?

Ans. This, that while there is life, there is hope to get into Christ, and so to get interest in the promises; for the promises are free, the word is *evangelia,**** free promise. It is not a promise on this or that condition; but a free promise out of mere love, a mercy. Then though thou be yet in the state of corruption in old Adam, yet the promise is free.

Obj. But I have no worthiness in me, thou wilt say; I have no faith, no grace in me at all.

Ans. But remember the promise is free, the condition is only if thou wilt receive Christ, which is not properly a condition of worth in thee. It is not propounded by way of condition of any worth, but thou must come with an empty hand, with a receiving hand; as a man must let fall what he hath, before he can hold and take anything. A man must let go other things, he must let go his hold of the creature; he must not be so proud of the creature, and so confident in it as he was; he must see the emptiness of the creature, and of all things in the world; thou must see that, if thou be not in Christ, thou art a wretched, damned creature. The hand of thy soul must be empty, and then a sight of thy unworthiness is all that is required before thou come to Christ, and the promises, a sight of thy unworthiness and a coming to grasp with Christ and the promises; for what is faith but a beggar's hand, empty of all things, coming to receive a benefit? They are most unworthy † that find themselves most unworthy.

Obj. But you will say, the promise is made to the poor in spirit, and to those that hunger and thirst.

Ans. It is true, but it is by way of preventing an objection of these men that are cast down in the sight of their unworthiness. As if Christ had said, you think these men the unworthiest men in the world, that are poor, and hungry, and thirsty, you think you are destitute and have nothing; but you are 'blessed,' you have interest in Christ, and in the promises, they are for you. Let no man therefore be discouraged, the promises are free. Therefore be not rebellious, stand not out against God's command. God lays a command upon thee. Though thou be not in Christ, and hast no right to the promises, he lays a command on thee to believe.

Quest. Thou wilt ask, what ground, or title, or right hast thou to believe, to claim Christ and the promises?

Ans. This right thou hast, thou hast the offer of God's love in Christ. And thou hast not only God's offer, but his command. God commands thee to do it. As St John saith, 1 John iii. 23, he hath commanded us to believe in his Son Christ, as well as not to commit adultery, or murder. And thou art guilty if thou break this command, as if thou break the other of murder or adultery. And men that live under the hearing of the gospel, they shall be damned more at the day of judgment for disobeying this command, for not receiving of Christ, than for the other; for the breach of all other commands may be forgiven if this were obeyed. Therefore there is an offer of Christ, with a command to receive him, and a promise if thou

---

* That is, εὐαγγέλια. But Sibbes appears to have quoted from memory; for the word in the text is the cognate and nearly synonymous one ἐπαγγέλια.—G.

† Qu. ' worthy?'—G.

receive him all shall be well, all thy sins shall be forgiven; is not here encouragement enough?

And then there is an invitation, 'Come unto me, all ye that are weary and heavy laden,' Matt. xi. 28. And put case thou hast nothing, yet notwithstanding, 'come and buy without silver,' saith the prophet, Isa. lv. 1. If thou say thou hast nothing, yet all is free here, 'Come whosoever will, and drink of the water of life.'

And he threatens damnation if thou wilt not, the wrath of God hangs on thee if thou do not come in.

Aye, but I am a sinner.

But where sin hath abounded, 'Grace shall more abound,' Rom. v. 20. So if a man stand out of Christ, and come not in to him, there are many encouragements for him to come, and terrible denunciations of wrath if he come not. 'The wrath of God hangs over his head,' John iii. 36. For if he be not in Christ, he sinks into hell when this short life is ended.

So there is this to encourage a man, there is God's command, and his sweet invitation, 'Come unto me.' And add to that his beseeching, 'We are ambassadors in Christ's name, to beseech you to be reconciled to God,' 2 Cor. v. 20, to come to Christ, to come out of the state of nature, and out of the curse of God that you are under, to come out of the uncertain condition that the world affords. We beseech you to be reconciled to God, to cast away your weapons whereby you are enemies to God; he seeks to you for your love. And if you have nothing, come and buy without money; have you a will to come? If you be besotted, and will continue in your estate, then be damned, and rot in your estate; but if you will, 'come and drink of the waters of life freely,' Rev. xxi. 6.

Let none be discouraged: Christ and the promises are open to all. Therefore how will God's vengeance be justified at the day of judgment, when these courses have been taken, and yet men will not come in? As Christ said to the Jews, 'You will not believe in me, that you might have life,' John v. 40. Men will not. Men are in love with the profits and pleasures and fading things: they will not embrace the promises that are 'yea and amen.' It is nothing but wilful rebellion that keeps men off, that rather than they will leave their sins, and come under the government of Christ, they will reject the offers of mercy; if they cannot have Christ with their sins, away mercy. If they can have him to lead them to hell, to swear, and cozen, &c., then welcome Christ: if he will come on those terms, he is welcome; but rather than they will have him upon his own terms, they reject him.

So there is great reason for God to justify the damnation of wretched hard-hearted persons, that rather than they will alter their course, they will reject mercy, and Christ, and all. If they may have half Christ, they will. They will have him with mercy to forgive them, but they will not have whole Christ as a King to govern them. So there is ground for those that are not yet in the state of grace to come to Christ. If they will receive him upon his own terms, to take him as a King as well as a Priest, to take him as a King to rule them, as well as a Priest to reconcile them to his Father. Nay, God, as I said, in the ministry entreats them to receive Christ, to cast away the weapons of their rebellion, to come under his government, and all shall be well with them.

But for them that are in Christ, that have embraced and clasped him in some comfortable measure, what comfort is it for them that all the promises in Christ are 'yea and amen?'

I answer, when we are once in Christ, and believe in Christ, all the Scripture speaks comfort to us. If we come in, and receive him as he is offered, upon his terms, to be our governor, our king, our priest, and prophet, then all the promises are ' yea and amen' to us.

As for instance, forgiveness of sins : if we receive Christ, God will forgive us our sins, and be reconciled to us for Jesus Christ's sake. ' We have an advocate with the Father, and he is the propitiation for our sins,' 1 John ii. 2. ' The blood of Christ shall cleanse us from all sins,' 1 John i. 7. These promises shall be ' yea and amen' to thee ; if thy sins trouble thee, they shall be done away. How many promises to this purpose have we of the forgiveness of sins !

Again, if so be thou find want of grace, all the promises in Christ are ' yea and amen.' He hath promised his Holy Spirit to them that ask him, Luke xi. 13. There is a promise shall be ' yea and amen,' if thou beg it. He hath promised the fundamental graces. ' He will put his fear in our hearts, that we shall never depart from him,' Jer. xxxii. 40. ' He will teach us to love one another,' John xiii. 34. You are taught of God to love one another. He hath promised private blessings in this kind, ' to circumcise, and cut off the foreskin of our hearts,' Jer. iv. 4. If a naughty and stony heart vex thee, ' he will take away that and give thee an heart of flesh,' Ezek. xi. 19, a tender heart. So these promises in Christ shall be ' yea and amen,' if we apply and believe them, to take away our corruption, and subdue that ; and to give and plant graces,—he hath promised to do this. Therefore make use of them, not only of the promises of pardon and forgiveness of sins, but of grace necessary.

Art thou sensible of thy imperfections, that thou canst not go about the duties of religion, and of thy particular calling ? What saith Moses ? ' Who gives a mouth ?' Exod. iv. 11. Is it not God that gives a mouth ? And, ' Be not afraid,' saith Christ, ' you shall have speech,' Mark xiii. 11, and a spirit given you that all shall not be able to withstand. Be not afraid, God that calls us he will enable us.

You have a promise of sufficiency of gifts. ' If any man lack wisdom, let him ask it of God,' James i. 5. If any man lack wisdom, to manage his affairs, to bear crosses and afflictions, let him ask it of God ; a rich promise in that kind.

And so, art thou doubtful for the time to come what shall befall thee ? God in Christ Jesus hath made a promise, that where he hath begun he will make an end, ' He that hath begun a good work will finish it to the day of the Lord,' Philip. i. 6. Christ is ' Alpha and Omega,' too, Rev. i. 8 ; and ' What shall separate us from the love of God in Christ ? Neither things present, nor things to come, nor anything else,' Rom. viii. 35, seq. Why ? Because it is the love of God in Christ. God's love is founded in Christ, and he will love thee eternally. There is a ground of perseverance. Therefore be sure to take in trust the time to come, as well as the present : he will be thy God for the time to come, as well as for the present ; he will be thy God to death. Jesus Christ ' is yesterday, to-day, and to-morrow, and the same for ever,' Heb. xiii. 8. ' He was, and is, and is to come,' Rev. i. 8. He was good to thee before he called thee ; he is good to thee now in the state of grace, and he will be for ever. Why shouldst thou stagger for the time to come ? Take in trust all that shall befall thee for the time to come, as well as for the present ; for he is ' yea and amen' himself, and ' all his promises are yea and amen.' Christ is ' Amen,' the true witness. ' Thus saith Amen,' Rev. i. 18, and all his promises are like himself, ' amen.'

Obj. Oh but I may fall away, my grace is weak, I stagger often! But are the promises founded upon thee? No! the promises are founded in Christ. Christ receives grace for thee, and he is a King for ever, and a Priest for ever, to make intercession for thee, and he is faithful. He is beloved for ever, and as long as he is beloved, thou shalt be beloved, because thou art in him. God is in Christ, and thou art in Christ, how canst thou miscarry? God is in Christ for ever, and thou art in Christ. Will he lose a limb? Will he lose a member? No! the promises in him are 'yea and amen,' and not in thee. They are in thee 'yea and amen,' thou hast the benefit of them, because they are in him 'amen' first.

Aye, but for the troubles of this world, for afflictions, and crosses, what promises have we to build on for them?

God in Christ is 'yea and amen' to us; and the promises are 'yea and amen' in that kind, in all things necessary for this life. 'Let your conversation be without covetousness: for he hath promised he will not fail thee nor forsake thee,' Heb. xiii. 5. It is taken along from Joshua's time. It was a promise made to Joshua, and is enlarged to all Christians. He hath promised, he will not fail thee, nor forsake thee.' Therefore 'let your conversation be without covetousness,' insinuating the reason why men are covetous, because they do not trust that promise, 'I will not fail thee, nor forsake thee.'

For if men in their calling, as they should do, would trust in God, without putting forth their hands to ill means, their conversation would be without shifting and covetousness. Therefore covetous men are faithless men. They believe not the promise, that God will not fail them nor forsake them; for then they would not live by their wits and by their shifts, but by faith in this very promise, which is 'yea and amen' to all that believe it.

'God is a sun and shield,' Ps. lxxxiv. 11, 'and no good thing shall be wanting to those that lead a godly life.' Would you have more? He is a sun, for all good; he is a shield, to keep from all ill. 'I am thy buckler, and thy exceeding great reward,' saith God to Abraham, Gen. xv. 1. 'I am thy buckler,' to keep thee from all ill; 'and thy exceeding great reward,' to bestow all good. Having these promises, why should we stagger? They are 'yea and amen' in Christ; God is all-sufficient in Christ.

For the issue in our labours, Oh! what will become of it? We take pains to no purpose, we rise early, and go to bed late, what will become of all in the issue? What saith St Paul? 1 Cor. xv. 58, 'Be constant, alway abounding in the work of the Lord: be ye abundant in the work of the Lord, knowing that your labour is not in vain in the Lord.' Therefore abound you in the work of the Lord: let the issue go to God, you have a rich promise, 'Knowing this, that your labour is not in vain in the Lord.' Therefore you know, when Peter had fished all night, and had caught nothing, when Christ bids him cast the net into the sea, saith he, 'We have fished all night, and catched nothing,' Luke v. 5, to what purpose should I cast it? yet in thy word, in thy command I will cast it. He obeyed, and he drew so many, that the net brake again with the fish. So, I say, it is thy command, Lord, that I should go on in the duties of my calling, that I should do that that belongs to me; and in welldoing to commit myself to thee 'as to a faithful Creator,' 1 Peter iv. 19, and a gracious Redeemer, and to cast myself on thy promises, do what thou wilt: you shall see then, as the apostle graciously speaks, 'Your labour shall not be in vain in the Lord,' 1 Cor. xv. 58. 'Cast your care on him; for he cares for you,' 1 Peter v. 7.

Aye, but when we have done, there are so many imperfections cleave to that we do, that they discourage us. Why, look, the promise is ' yea and amen' for acceptance, 'a cup of cold water is accepted,' Mat. x. 42. Offer that thou doest in the mediation of Christ, God will pardon that which is faulty, and accept that which is good. So we have promises of acceptance in Christ, ' God will pardon, and spare us as a father spares his child,' Ps. ciii. 13. Doth not a father accept the endeavour of his poor child, and pardon his weakness, when he cannot do as he would? God looks on us as a father on his children. Therefore let us not fear this. We have a promise of acceptance of what we do, though it be weak, and maimed, and lame obedience. If we cannot do as much as others, yet bring ' two turtles,' Lev. v. 7. They that could not bring an ox, a great sacrifice, a less was accepted, two pigeons. If thou canst not do as much as others, a little sacrifice shall be accepted.

Oh! that we had faith! we might run through all the passages of our life, justification, sanctification, perseverance for the time to come; the duties of our calling, the issue of our labours, whatever you can imagine. There is no passage of our life but our souls would be supported, if we could think that these promises are ' yea and amen' in Jesus Christ. There is no estate that we are in but there are promises made to it. We want no good, but we have a promise of supply; we are under no ill, but we have a promise, either for the removal of it, or for the sanctifying of it, which is better.

We may enlarge it likewise to posterity. If the promises in Christ be ' yea and amen,' that is, true to us, and to them that succeed us; for as I said, Christ ' is yesterday, to-day, and the same for ever.' He was yesterday to our ancestors, to-day to ourselves, to-morrow to our posterity. Therefore saith Peter to the believing Jews, Acts ii. 39, ' The promise is made to you, and to your children;' your children are in the covenant, and God is the ' God of thee and of thy seed;' for the ' promises in Christ are yea and amen,' they are constant to us, and to our children, to the end of the world.

It is a comfort to parents that can leave their children no inheritance: they leave them God in covenant, and he is a good portion. ' I will be thy God,' Jer. vii. 23; for the grand promise is the promise of the Father, Son, and Holy Ghost. God hath promised to be a Father, and the Father gives his Son, and the Father and Son give the Holy Ghost. Well then! God is the God of us and of our children; he is the Father of us and of our children; Christ is the Christ of us and them; the Holy Ghost is the Spirit that sanctifies us and them. Is not this a comfort to those that can leave their children nothing else, that they leave them God in covenant?

And this is a comfort for children, if they have good parents, that they may say when they pray, ' O God of my father Abraham,' Gen. xxiv. 12. And as David, Ps. cxvi. 16, ' I am thy servant, and the son of thy handmaid;' I am thy servant myself, and the son of one that was thy servant. Is not this a comfort to a Christian to say, I am thy servant, and the son of thy servant, therefore there is a double bond why thou shouldest respect me? I cast myself on thee, and I am the son of a believing father, of a believing mother. Oh! it is a blessed thing to be in covenant with God, that those that can leave their children little else, can leave them a place in the covenant by their own goodness and faith.

Wicked parents are cruel. They damn their own souls, and they are cruel to posterity. Jeroboam hurt his posterity more than all the world besides. For his sin God cursed his posterity. ' They walk in the ways of Jeroboam,' 1 Kings xv. 34. God many times will not punish men themselves, but their posterity. Wicked kings, God spares them themselves sometimes, but he punisheth their posterity. Jeroboam was spared for his own life, but his posterity was punished. When wicked men die, others applaud their wisdom. They die thus and thus, &c., and their posterity applaud their wisdom. God therefore curseth their posterity, walking in their ways. Jeroboam's children, I say, had cause to curse their father. They had a prejudice in his example. They thought him a very wise man, that by setting up the calves he could make such a rent, but it turned to their destruction. I say, parents are cruel to posterity; for God revengeth their sins on their posterity. Let this be a strong motive to men to believe in Christ, that they may leave a good posterity, a posterity in covenant with God.

Men are very atheists in this point; for they are more careful a great deal to leave them rich, to leave them great, than to leave them good; and so they leave them a little goods perhaps, but they leave the curse and vengeance of God with it. I beseech you, therefore, enlarge this comfort, that the promises of God concerning all good things are made in Christ, they are yea and amen to ourselves, and to all ours, to our posterity.

Thus I have laboured to lay open a little to you the promises. You may enlarge them yourselves. Therefore take this course:

First, consider your present estate, if you would make use of this portion. It is our portion. Our best inheritance are the promises, and indeed they are a good child's portion. Though the world take all from us, though God strip us of all, if he leave us his promises, we are rich men. Therefore the psalmist calls them his portion, and his inheritance; and indeed so they are: because they are so many bonds whereby God is bound to us; they are so many obligations.

And if a wretched exacting man think himself as rich as he hath bonds, though he have not a penny in his purse; he that hath a thousand pounds in bonds, thinks himself richer than he that hath a hundred pounds in money, and he thinks he hath reason to be so, because he hath good security; certainly, a Christian that hath rich faith in the rich promises, he is a rich man, because he hath many bonds; and when he pleaseth he can sue his bonds, and God is well pleased with it. Therefore indeed there is little difference between a Christian in poverty and a rich Christian; only the one hath more for the present, but God is the riches of the other. As for a worldling, he hath but a cistern when he hath most; the other hath the spring, he hath God in covenant, and God's promises.

Let us therefore consider every day the exigents* we are in, whether in want of grace, or want of assistance and necessaries, or want of comfort; and according to that, let us consider what we are to do. Are we at our wits' end now? Is there no hope for this in Israel? Yes! God hath left us rich and precious promises. Let us look to them.

In the next place, then, *from our wants look to the promises, and proportion the promises to our wants;* rank the promises. It were a good work. Oh, that we should have so many promises, and yet have them to seek when the devil besiegeth us. He layeth siege to shake our consciences, and we are to seek in the time of temptation. Let us remember the promises answerable to our necessities.

If we be troubled with sin, call to mind the promise of forgiveness. If

* That is, ' exigencies.'—G.

we be troubled with want, call to mind the promise of supply. If we be troubled with fear for the time to come, call to mind the covenant of grace, the marriage for everlasting. ' God, whom he loves, he loves to the end,' John xiii. 1. God loves us in Christ. He loves Christ for ever. Therefore he will love us for ever. So, as I said before, suit the promises to our present estate.

And from the promises have a higher rise yet : *go to him in whom they are made.* They are rich promises indeed, good promises ; but how shall I know they shall be performed ? In whom are they made ? In whom ? God loves thee in Christ. What is he ? God and man. He is God, and therefore able to perform them : he is man, and therefore he loves thee as his own flesh, and therefore he will perform them. He is ' the Son of God's love.' God for his sake, as Mediator, will perform them. Heaven and earth shall conspire for thy good, rather than thou shalt miss of the performance of the least promise. Therefore from thy wants go to the promises, and from the promises go to Christ, and consider him. He is anointed of God for thee. He is anointed that he might be thy Christ, and thy Jesus, that he might be thy Saviour, ' Immanuel, God with us,' Isa. vii. 14, that he might reconcile God in us, that in office he might be so, that he might bring God and us together. Consider him.

And then go *to God, and consider what relation in Jesus Christ God hath put upon him.* In Christ God is a Father, and what can a father deny to his adopted son in Christ, whom he looks on in his natural Son Christ ?

Yea, and to settle our minds the more, let us consider *the relations that God and Christ have put upon them, and the relations we stand in;* and the many promises we have in Christ, who is anointed and sealed by God the Father to be our Saviour, and to bestow good upon us. God is become our Father. What a world of promises is in that word Father ? What will a father deny to his son ? What if God had not left particular promises in Scripture, if he had left but the relation of a father, it had been promise enough. What can a father deny his child ?

And then Christ, what relation hath he taken on him ? He is our husband. What a world of promises is there in that ? What can a loving husband deny his spouse, that he hath given himself for ?

He hath taken upon him to be our head. What want of influence can there be from such a head, that hath taken all upon him for the body ? The head sees, and hears, and doth all for the body ; so Christ hears, and sees, and doth all for us. What a world of promises is in this relation of a head, if there were no particular promise ?

Again, Christ styles himself sweetly our brother. What a world of promises are in these relations ! God the Father is ours, Christ is ours. Here is the grand promise, ' I will be your God,' and will give you my Son.

And then, in the third place, he hath promised his Spirit. He will ' give his Spirit to them that beg him,' Luke xi. 13. What a world of promises is in that promise of the Spirit ! It is a comforting Spirit, a sanctifying Spirit, a quickening Spirit, a strengthening Spirit, all is in the Spirit. As our soul doth all that the body doth, so it is by virtue of the Spirit, all the grace, and all the comfort we have. God hath promised himself, and Christ, and the Spirit, the whole Trinity. There is the grand promise : I will be your God, Christ shall be your Christ, and I will give you my Spirit. If we had not other promises, what a world of comfort have we in these !

Now in what relation stand we to these? We are children, we are heirs, we are 'temples of the Holy Ghost,' &c., 1 Cor. iii. 16. Put case our memories do not serve to call to mind particular promises, in the time of trouble, consider in Christ how God loves thee: he is thy God in Christ; how Christ loves thee: he hath taken thy nature on him to be thy husband; he makes love to thee, and desires thee to be reconciled. And the Spirit is given thee by Christ; he hath promised to give him if thou ask him: the Holy Spirit is the 'Spirit of promise,' Eph. i. 13. Think therefore of the general, of the covenant of grace, and these relations that have the force of promises; for sometimes particular promises may not come to our mind perhaps, and these will stablish a man against the gates of hell, and against all particular temptations.

This course we ought to take, then, to feed our thoughts with the promises. The promises are the food of faith. Let not our faith languish and famish for want, for want of meditations of God and Christ, what relations they have put upon them: and for want of meditating on particular promises in all kinds. How well-thriving might our faith be, if we would oft think of these things?

And to make us the more to think of these things, consider that all other things, alas! what are they, when we have not a promise of them in Christ? They are all vain, fading things; they will all come to nothing. That which we have by promise, grace, and comfort, and glory, they are ours for ever. God is ours for ever, Christ is ours for ever, the Spirit is ours for ever, the relations we are in are for ever. All other things are nothing, they will come to nothing ere long. This course we ought to take, then, that we may have comfort by the promises.

Again, in the next place, if we look to the kinds of the promises, whether to the promises for this life, or the promises of grace.

1. If they be promises of this life, take heed *we abuse not ourselves in them.* There have been gross miscarriages even from the beginning of the world, and will be to the end of the world, in the false application of outward promises. We see the Jews cried, 'The temple of the Lord, the temple of the Lord,' Jer. vii. 4, as if God had tied himself to that by a perpetual promise. 'Trust not to lying words,' saith the prophet, Jer. vii. 4. You think you are God's people, and that he will always keep you out of captivity; challenge not temporal promises without reservation and subjection to God's will, as he shall see good. Babylon saith, 'I sit as a queen, and I shall for ever.'

So mystical Babylon in the Revelation saith, 'I sit as a queen,' Rev. xviii. 7, till her judgment and destruction come in one day; because she trusted to her present temporal estate. Let no man promise himself that that God doth not promise in his word, immunity from the cross; for whatsoever promise of protection and provision we have, all is with the exception of the cross; remember therefore to construe the promises aright.

2. Then again, another rule about the promises is, *that it is usual with God to perform them in a wonderful manner,* that men know not how. He doth perform them notwithstanding. Take that for a rule. How is that? As Luther was wont to say, God's carriage is by contrary means; he performs them wonderfully.

He promised Abraham a child, but his body was dead in a manner first, and Sarah's womb. He promised Joseph to raise him up so high; but alas! the iron entered into his soul first. He promised that Christ should come, but all was desperate first, 'The sceptre was departed from Judah,' Gen.

xlix. 10. So he hath promised, that we shall rise from the dead, but we must rot in our graves first. He hath promised forgiveness of sins, that he will be merciful to us, but he will waken our consciences to see our desperate estate, that we are forlorn creatures first, and unworthy of any respect from him. He hath promised us happiness. We that are Christians are the happiest creatures in the world, yet in the sense and eye of the world for the present we are the most forlorn creatures that are. Yet he performs his promise with comfort here, and at last will fully manifest his love to us. So at the last his promises shall be wonderfully performed.

God doth not perform his promises according to human policy ; he will not do thus, because we look he should do thus and thus. He will cross our expectation, and yet perform his promise. St Paul looked to come to Rome, Rom. i. 15, but he thought not of coming to Cæsar by whipping, and peril, and shipwreck. Moses knew he should come to see Canaan, did he think to have such a conflict in the wilderness ? Alas ! he thought not of it. God doth wondrous strangely perform his promises by contraries ; he crosseth our imaginations and conceits directly, and yet he is true of his promise.

3. Another branch of this is, that though God's promises be 'yea and amen' in his time, *yet he usually defers his promises for a time*, and why ? Among many other reasons, to mortify self-confidence, to fit us for his blessings! for except he deferred them, we should not be fit for them. He defers them, that we may be fitted for them long before they come ; that we might mortify self-confidence, to see that he immediately and graciously performs his promise. And in the mean time, to exercise faith and repentance, and desire, and prayer, therefore he defers them ; but they are amen at last, though he defer.

God's time is better than ours, he knows better than we. The physician knows his time better than the patient. Hereupon comes a duty consequently upon this dispensation of God. If he perform his promises wondrously, and unexpectedly, and perform them in delay ; let thy duty be answerable to his dealing, *wait, wait upon God*, tie him not to such and such courses. He can transcend, and go beyond thy imagination, and do more than thou art able to conceive, as the apostle saith. Therefore wait his good time, ' He that shall come will come,' Heb. x. 37, stay God's leisure, prevent him not, run not before him.

And as he doth things by contraries, so when thou art in contraries look for contraries. When thou art in sin, and feelest it on thy conscience, believe that he is made righteousness to thee. He hath promised it. It is ' yea and amen' in Christ. When thou shalt be turned to dust in the grave, believe that he will raise thy body. This promise is ' yea and amen,' and as a pledge of it Christ is gone to heaven. When thou art miserable, remember the promise, thou shalt be glorious with Christ as he is glorious. ' All his promises are yea and amen.' In contraries believe contraries; because in contraries he performs contraries ; and say as Job doth, 'Though he kill me, yet will I trust in him,' Job xiii. 15. I know thou canst not deny thyself, and thy ' promises are yea and amen.'

In the worst estate that befalls us, let us learn to wrestle with God in the promises, and implead his promises. Why ! Lord, thou hast promised forgiveness of sins to them that ask it ; thou hast promised grace, and mercy, and favour ; remember thy promise, thou canst not deny thyself, thou canst not deny thy gracious promise, thy word is thyself, thou art Amen, and thy word is ' yea and amen,' only give me grace to wait thy good leisure ; yet I will not let thee depart without a blessing, I will hold thee till I have received a gracious answer, as Jacob wrestled with him till he had the blessing, Gen. xxxii. 24, *seq.* Let us labour to answer the promise with our faith, and labour to bring our souls to be like his promises. They are 'yea and amen.' Though they be not presently performed, let us constantly believe a constant promise, let us cleave to God, let us have an 'amen' for God's 'amen.' Are the promises amen? Amen let the soul say. Lord, 'So be it,' so it shall be, I will seal thy amen in thy promise, with my amen in my faith. So let us have an amen for Christ's amen. They are all, and will be all amen in Christ in fit time; all the gracious promises will be 'yea and amen;' let our souls echo, and say, Amen. For our faith must answer the promises. Faith and the promises be correlatives ; for the promise is not except it be applied. Let faith answer the promise. Let us labour to be established in the promises in God's word.

Shall we have certain promises, and *shall we waver and stagger?* Therefore let us complain, Lord, thy promises are sure and certain as thou hast said, what is the reason I cannot build on them? Oh my unfaithful heart! Let us condemn our unbelieving, our lying hearts, that call the truth of God into question, and make that which is 'yea and amen' to be 'yea and nay.' We make truth a lie, and do rather believe our own lying hearts than God's immutable and unchangeable promises. Therefore let us see the fulness* of our hearts, and complain of them to God, and desire him to cure it and redress it, and he will do it.

This is *to give glory to God indeed.* We cannot honour God more than to believe his promises, and build on him. This will breed love, when we feel the comfort of the promises. Foolish men think to honour God by compliments, by dead performances. Silly men consider that the principal honour in the world. To God, [it] is to seal his truth, that thou shouldst not make him a liar. Hath he promised all things in the world? Get faith. That will honour him, and he will honour thy faith.

What makes God honour faith so much? He that believes he will bring him to heaven. Faith honours him. It gives him the glory of his truth, the glory of his goodness, of his mercy, of his truth, &c. As it honours him, he honours it.

The believer shall come to heaven, when the idle fashionable Christian shall vanish with his conceits, that thinks to serve God with empty vain shadows. Honour God with the obedience of faith, man. Cast thyself upon him, trust in him, in life and death, and then thou givest him the honour that he requireth at thy hands. For as the honour of his mercy is the greatest honour he will have in this world, more than that in the creation, so thou honourest him more in the gospel, to cast thyself on him for forgiveness of sins, and life everlasting, and for the guidance of thy daily course of life ; thou honourest him more than by looking on the creature, or by doing him any service. He is honoured more by faith in Christ than by any other way. Let faith go to him ; as faith honours him, so he will honour it, 'Let it be according to thy faith,' Mat. xv. 28.

Let not all be lost, let us bring vessels for the precious promises, the vessel of a believing heart. Shall all this be lost for a vain heart that will not lodge up these promises? Shall we have a rich portion, and neglect it? Shall we have so many promises, and not improve them, and make use of them?

* Cf. Ezek. xvi. 49.—G. Qu. 'foulness?'—ED.

Therefore I beseech you, let it be our practice continually every day, of all portions of Scripture make the promises most familiar to us ; for duties follow promises. If we believe the promises with our heart, they are quickening promises. We will love God, and perform other duties. 'Faith works by love,' Gal. v. 6. If we believe, love will come kindly off. Therefore he saith here, 'All the promises are yea and amen,' insinuating that all is included in the promises.

Let us empty our hearts of confidence in anything, and fill them with the promises in Christ that are 'yea and amen.' Let us stablish our hearts with the promises, let us warm, and season, and refresh our hearts every day with these.

In these times of infection, what do we ? Those that are careful of themselves, that go abroad in dangerous places, they have preservatives, they take something to preserve their spirits, and to strengthen them against the contagion abroad ; and it is wisdom so to do, it is folly to neglect it, and to tempt God, not to be careful in this kind : it is very well done. But what is this, if thou do not fence thy soul and thy spirit, and take a draught of the promises every day afresh ? Let us take out our pardon of course every day, of the forgiveness of sins. We sin every day, let us go for our pardon. 'If we sin, we have an Advocate with the Father, Jesus Christ, and he is the propitiation for our sins. And the blood of Jesus Christ shall purge us from all sin,' 1 John ii. 1. And he is in justifying us still every day, he is acquitting our souls ; and there is a pardon of course to be taken out every day. Let us renew and refresh our hearts with the promises of pardon and forgiveness of sins every day. Let us strengthen our souls with renewing the promises of grace for that day to walk comfortably before God, that he will keep us by his Spirit from sin, that he will be a shield and a sun to us, that he will give us wisdom to carry ourselves as we should ; and he will give us his Holy Spirit if we beg it.

Let us every day take these promises to be cordials in these dangerous times ; and then come life, come death, all shall be welcome. Why ? Because we are in Christ, and have embraced the promises and Christ ; and all in Christ is 'yea and amen :' it shall go well with us. What a wondrous comfortable life would a Christian's life be, if he could yield the obedience of faith answerable to the promises ! What a shame is it, that having such rich promises we should be so loose, so changeable, that we should be cast down with crosses, and lift up with prosperity ? It is because we believe not the promises of better things, therefore we are proud of present things, and cast down with present crosses, and are fast and loose. Now we have good things for the present, afterward the devil comes between us and the promises, and makes us let go our hold. Religion stands on this, which makes me to press it the more. If this were well taken to heart and digested, we should know what religion means ; if we know Christ and the promises, all other things will come off. All others are but formalities. They will never comfort without the consideration of knowing God in Christ, and the rich promises to us in Christ.

Likewise, if this be so, that the promises of God in Christ are 'yea and amen,' this teacheth us how *to make use of all former examples of others, and of all former goodness to ourselves.* Was God merciful to Abraham and to David ? 'Our fathers trusted in thee, and were not confounded,' Ps. xxii. 4. Therefore he reasons, if I trust in God I shall not be confounded ; for the 'promises are yea and amen.' They are true to one as well as another. And 'whatsoever was written afore, was written for our comfort,' Rom. xv..4.

And this is a singular good use we may make of reading of the stories of the Scripture, and of holy men, that the same God he lives for ever, ' his arm is not shortened, he that was, is, and is to come,' Isa. lix. 1 ; and therefore we should read histories with application. Did God make sure his promises to them ? Surely he will make sure his promises to us. Had David forgiveness of sins upon his confession ? Surely so shall we. ' Abraham believed, and it was accounted to him for righteousness,' Gal. iii. 6, and so it shall to us if we believe. It is alleged for that end. And St Paul prefixeth his example to all posterity, ' God was merciful to me, and not so only, but to all that believe in him,' 1 Tim. i. 16.

This is an use that we may make likewise of the story of our own lives, as well as the story of others ; for, consider the former times, why, Lord, thy promises heretofore have been ' yea and amen,' thou hast delivered me from such and such dangers, thou hast been so good, and so good to me, thou art not changed. Let us store up experience out of the story of our own lives. God is ' Yea and Amen,' and ' his promises are yea and amen,' constant to all his children, and to their children ; and they are alike in all ages ' from generation to generation,' as Moses saith, Ps. xc. 1, ' Thou art our God from generation to generation for ever.'

Thus we see how to make use of the promises ; for promises, we must know, are either directly to particular persons, or implied. A promise made to any directly, to any in particular, is an implied promise to me in the general equity in matter of grace, and glory, or the removal of some true misery. What was made to Joshua, is applied to all the church, Heb. xiii. 10, *seq.* ; that which was directly promised to him, is an implied promise to all that will make use of that example.

Again, if so be that all the promises of God be ' yea and amen,' that is, certain and constant in Christ, this should comfort us *when men deal loosely with us, and fail in their promises*, whereon perhaps we have builded too much, when men deal falsely with us. And indeed, there is nothing that makes an honest heart wearier of this wicked world, than the consideration of the falsehood of men in whom they trust. Oh ! it is a cruel thing to deceive him, that unless he had trusted he had never been deceived by thee. It is a treacherous thing, but this world is full of such treacherous dealing, that a man can scarce trust assurances, much less words. But there are things thou mayest trust, if thou have a heart concerning the best good, there are promises that are ' yea and amen ;' there is a God that keeps covenant. It is his glory to do so from generation to generation. Here is the comfort of a Christian, when he finds falseness in the world, to retire to his God, and hide himself there.

And in the uncertainty of all things below, in all changes, as this world is full of changes—now poor, now rich ; now in favour, now out of favour— why, what hath a Christian to cast himself on ? The promises of God in Christ, they are ' yea and amen ;' they are promises that never fail. They that know thy name will trust in thee, Ps. ix. 10. What is the reason ? It follows, ' Thou never failest those that trust in thee.' Therefore in the vicissitude and intercourse of all earthly things under the moon, that are like the moon, changeable, let us stablish our souls upon that which is un-changeable, and that will make us unchangeable, if we build on it, ' For the word of the Lord endures for ever,' Isa. xl. 6, which is alleged by Peter, 1 Peter i. 25, ' All flesh is grass, and as the flower of the grass,' that is, it fades as the grass, and as the flower of the grass ; all the excellency of wit and learning, it is but as the flower of the grass, but ' the word of the

Lord endures for ever.' How doth the word of the Lord endure for ever? St John expounds it, 1 John ii. 17. A true Christian endures for ever by the word of the Lord. He that believes in the word, he endures for ever, because his comforts endure for ever; they are 'yea and amen.' His grace endures for ever. God's love endures to him for ever. Therefore by building upon that which is certain, we make ourselves certain too. When the word is ingraffed (it is St James his phrase), when it is ingraffed into our hearts, it turns our hearts to be like itself, it is eternal itself, and it makes us eternal. 'He that doth the will of the Lord abides for ever, saith St John. 'The world passeth, and the lust thereof, but he that doth the will of the Lord abides for ever,' 1 John ii. 17. And 'the word of the Lord abides for ever,' as it is in another place, 1 Peter i. 25. The one expounds the other, that is, we, by believing, and doing the word of the Lord, abide for ever.

To stir us up to rely constantly upon this word, the promises, and the grace of God brought to us by the promises. As I said before, shall we have certain promises of God that never lie, and shall we not build on them? What is there in the world to build on, if we cannot build on this? And yet the froward heart of man will believe anything rather than God's truth. The merchantman he commits his estate, his goods, to the sea. He hath no promise that they shall come again. It is only in the providence of God. He hath made no promise for it. The husbandman commits his seed to the ground, though he have nothing left of his seed; and though he sow in tears, yet he commits all to the earth in hope of a return; and yet he hath no promise for this, but God's ordinary providence, that may sometimes fail.

Are we in such hope when we commit our seed to the ground, and when we commit our goods to the sea, to the waves, and yet have not a promise for this, but God's ordinary providence, which ofttimes fails, having not bound himself that it shall be alway so, because God will shew himself the God of nature, that he can command nature? And shall we not trust him when we have his providence and his promise too? when he is bound by his promise, when he hath made himself a debtor to us? when the free God, who is most free, hath made himself a debtor by his promise, and hath sealed his promise by an oath and by sacraments?

Alas! God hath made all things faithful to us. Therefore we trust them. But we trust not him that hath made other things so, and is so faithful to us. Therefore let us build on these promises in Jesus Christ.

Now to direct us a little further, to train ourselves up to make use of the promises of God in Jesus Christ,

1. Observe every day, *how God fulfils his promises in lesser matters.* Parents train up their children by education, that they may trust them for their inheritance. So God trains us up to believe his providence, that he will provide for us, without cracking our consciences by ill means. Will we believe his promises for these things, and will we not believe him for life everlasting? No! certainly we cannot. Therefore let us exercise faith to believe the promises for provision, that 'he will not fail us, nor forsake us,' but be with us in our callings, using lawful means for the things of this life.

2. Sometimes again take another method. When faith begins to stagger for the things of this life, quicken it *with the grand promises.* Will God give me life everlasting? and hath he given me Christ? are his promises in him 'yea and amen?' will he give me the greater, and will he not give

me the less? Sometimes by the lesser, be encouraged to hope for the greater; sometimes quicken our deadness and dulness in believing the lesser, with the undoubted performance of the great. Will God give me life everlasting, and will he not give me provision in my pilgrimage till I come there? undoubtedly he will. 'Fear not, little flock, it is your Father's will to give you a kingdom,' saith Christ, Luke xii. 32. They were distrustful for the things of this life. Do you think, saith he, that he will not give you the things of this life, that keeps a kingdom for you? 'Fear not.'

3. Again, when we hear any promise in the word of God, *turn it into a prayer*, put God's bond in suit, as it were. His promises are his bonds. Sue him on his bond. He loves to be sued on his bond; and he loves that we should wrestle with him by his promises. Why, Lord, thou hast made this and this promise, thou canst not deny thyself, thou canst not deny thine own truth; thou canst not cease to be God; thou canst as well cease to be God, as deny thy promise, that is, thyself. So let us put the promises into suit, as David, Ps. cxix. 49, if it be his (*www*), 'Lord, remember thy promise, wherein thou hast caused thy servant to trust,' as if God had forgotten his promise; 'Lord, remember thy promise,' I put thee in mind of thy promise, 'wherein thou hast caused thy servant to trust.' If I be deceived, thou hast deceived me. Thou hast made these promises, and caused me to trust in thee, and 'thou never failest those that trust in thee.'

What makes a man faithful? Trust to a man makes him faithful. So when God is honoured with our trusting of him, it makes him faithful. Let us therefore put in suit his promises of provision and protection every day in the way of our calling; and for necessary grace and comfort, that he will not fail us in any necessary grace to bring us to heaven, considering that he hath filled our nature with all grace in Christ.

4. Again, let us take this course, when we hear of rich and precious promises that are made, *labour to know them*. What? shall we have an inheritance, a portion, and not labour to know it? Let us labour to know all our portion, and to know it of those that search the word of God, to be glad to hear anything concerning the privileges and prerogatives of a Christian. Those that dig the mines of the Scripture, which is the office of the ministers, let us labour to know all our privileges.

Let not Satan rob us of one privilege. Every promise is precious. They are rich promises. Yet they are no more than God thought necessary for us. He thought all little enough to stablish our faith. Let us not lose one. We cannot be without one. Let us labour to know them.

And when we know them, work them upon our hearts by meditation, and shame ourselves upon it: say, is it true, are these promises so? Is it true that God hath revealed these things in his word? To whom hath he made them? to angels or to beasts? No! to men, to sinners, to men in the world to comfort them. They are their provision, their inheritance, as David saith, Ps. cxix. 57, 103, 'Thy word is my inheritance, and my portion; they are sweeter than the honey and the honeycomb.' Are they so? Do I believe this, or do I not believe it? Yes! I do. If I do, can I believe them, and be so uncomfortable? Let us shame ourselves. Do I believe the promises of life everlasting, the promises of perseverance, the promise that God will hide me in danger, that he will be my habitation and my hiding-place? and do I look to unlawful means? Do I live without God in the world, as if there were no promise? What a shame is this! There is a weakness in my faith certainly. When a branch withers, there is a fault in the root. So there is a defect in the radical grace, that it draws not juice out of the promises as it should. There is a defect in my faith. Therefore I will look where the defect is, and strengthen my faith.

Thus we should shame ourselves. Can I hear these promises, and be no more joyful, and be no more affected? Can I use indirect means, and yet believe that God is all sufficient to me in the covenant? Certainly I cannot.

Therefore let us come to the trial, to some few evidences, that a man doth believe in the promises.

He that believes the promises of God in Christ to be ' yea and amen,' doubtless he will be affected, answerable to the things promised. Saith David, ' Thy statutes they are the joy of my heart,' Ps. cxix. 11.

1. The promises *will be the joy and rejoicing of our heart*. He that can hear of promises, and not be affected, certainly he believes them not. When a man thinks of his inheritance, and of his evidences, that they are clear, that he shall enjoy it without suit, or trouble, it comforts him, he cannot think of it without comfort. Cannot a man think of a little pelf of the earth without comfort, when he knows he hath assurance to it? and shall we think of heaven and happiness, and not rejoice? Will not these be the joy of a man's heart? Certainly they will affect him. When good things are apprehended by faith, will they not work upon the affections? Certainly they will.

2. Again, where the promises are believed, they will *quicken us to all cheerful obedience*. Certainly, if God will assist me with strength and comfort if I go on in his ways, and in the end of all give me life everlasting, this will quicken me to all obedience. Therefore those that go so deadly and dully, as if they had no encouragement here, nor promise of glory after, they believe not the promises. For God doth not set us on work as Pharaoh set the children of Israel to make brick without straw; but when he bids us do anything, he promiseth us grace, and gives us his Spirit, and after grace he gives glory. If men did believe this, they would go about God's work without dulness and staggering. So far as we are dull, and stagger in the work of God, so far our faith is weak in the promises of God.

3. Again, as they quicken in regard of comfort, *so they purge in regard of holiness;* for they make men study mortification and sanctification, 2 Cor. vi. 18, and the beginning of the viith, ' Having these promises, let us purge ourselves from all filthiness of flesh and spirit, perfect sanctification in the fear of God.' ' Having these promises.' So that the promises, as they have a quickening, so they have a purging power; and that upon sound reasoning. Doth God promise that he will be my Father, and I shall be his son? and doth he promise me life everlasting? and doth that estate require purity? and no unclean thing shall come there? Certainly these promises being apprehended by faith, as they have a quickening power to comfort, so they purge with holiness. We may not think to carry our filthiness to heaven. Doth the swearer think to carry his blasphemies thither? Filthy persons and liars are banished thence: there is ' no unclean thing.' He that hath these promises purgeth himself, ' and perfecteth holiness in the fear of God.' ' He that hath this hope purifieth himself, as he is pure,' 1 John iii. 3. So these promises affect, and quicken, and purge.

4. And then the promises *they do settle the soul*, because they be ' yea and amen:' they make the soul quiet. If a man believe an honest man on

his word, he will be quiet; if he be not quiet, he doth not believe. So much faith, so much quiet. ' Being justified by faith, we have peace with God through Jesus Christ our Lord,' Rom. v. 1. So much faith, so much peace. ' In nothing be careful, but let your desires be known to God in prayer, supplication, and thanksgiving,' Philip. iv. 6 ; and when you have done this, ' The peace of God which passeth all understanding, shall preserve your hearts and minds in Christ Jesus,' ver. 7. So where there is prayer, and thanksgiving, and doing of duty, the peace of God which passeth all understanding, will keep the mind in Christ; and where there is not quiet and péace to preserve the heart and mind, there is neglect of duty before, not committing ourselves to God's promises to build on them.

5. Again, where there is a believing the promises, there is not only a staying of the soul in general, *but when all things are gone, when all things are contrary.* That is the nature of faith in the promises. Put the case, that a Christian that is of the right stamp, have nothing in the world to take to, only God's word and promises ; surely he knows they are ' yea and amen.' It is the word of God all-sufficient; he is Jehovah ; he gives a being to his word, .and to all things else ; therefore he hath the name Jehovah. Therefore thinks the soul, though I have nothing, yet I have him that is the substance of all things. All other things are but shadows ; God the Father, Son, and Holy Ghost, are the substance that give all things a being ; and therefore I will cast myself on God. Here now is the triumph of faith. When there is nothing else to trust to, nay, when all things else are contrary, when it is faith against faith, and ' hope against hope ;' when there is such a conflict in a man, that he sees nothing but the contrary ; here faith will shut the eye of sense, and not look to present things too much. Though I see all things contrary, though I see rather signs of anger than otherwise, yet I will hope and believe in God, for this or that. Here is the wisdom of a believing Christian that believes the promises—he will shut his eyes, and not look on the waves, on the troubles. They will carry him away, and dazzle him. But he looks to the constant love of God in Christ, and to the constant promises of God. His nature is constant, and his truth is as his nature. He cannot deny himself and his own word, when he hath made himself a debtor by his promise, and bound himself by his word.

Therefore in contraries say as Job, ' Though he kill me, yet will I trust in him,' Job xiii. 15. True faith when it is in strength will uphold a man when all fails ; nay, it will hold a man when all is contrary. This our Saviour Christ, in whom ' all the promises are yea and amen,' did excellently teach us by his own example. For when all was contrary, and our blessed Saviour felt the wrath of God, which made him sweat drops of blood, and made him cry out, ' My God, My God, why hast thou forsaken me ?' Mark xv. 34 ; yet here faith wrestled with ' My God, my God,' still, even under the wrath of God. He brake through the seeming wrath of God, into the heart of God.

Faith hath a piercing eye. It will strive through the clouds, though they be never so thick, through all the clouds of temptation. Christ had so piercing a faith, it brake through all. He saw a Father's heart under an angry semblance. So a Christian triumphs by faith in oppositions to faith. When all is contrary to faith, yet notwithstanding he can say ' My God' still. This is an evidence of a strong faith in the promises.

6. Again, an evidence of faith in the promises is *faithfulness in ourselves, in our promises to God;* for surely the soul that expects anything of God,

that he should be faithful, it studies to be faithful in the covenant, Ps. xxv. 10, ' All the ways of God are mercy, and truth.' All his dealings to his children are mercy and truth, ' to them that keep his covenant.' For you know, the promises have conditions annexed ; and where God fulfils his promise, he gives grace to perform the condition, to walk before him, to allow ourselves in no sin. For if we allow ourselves in any sin, we perform not the covenant on our part. Now God will give grace to perform the covenant where he will perform his own. Therefore those that are unfaithful in their covenant, and yet think God will be faithful to them, it is presumption.

When we come to the communion, we think we do God a great deal of service ; but we must consider we enter into covenant with God, as well as he binds himself to us. He gives us Christ, and all his blessings. He reacheth forth Christ with all in him, if we will receive him. Aye, but we bind ourselves to God, to lead a new life, and to be thankful, and to shew it in obedience. And so in baptism ; we do not only receive in the sacraments, but we yield, we bind ourselves to God. And we must be careful of what we promise to God, as well as expect that which he promiseth to us. If we expect his truth, we must be faithful, and careful of performing our covenants to him.

Quest. Oh, but how shall I do that ? saith the distressed soul. I have no grace.

Ans. God knows that well enough ; therefore he that promiseth, he promiseth grace to perform the condition ; that is one part of the covenant, to give grace to fulfil the covenant. For he that saith, If we believe and repent, &c., he will give us hearts to repent, if we ask them ; he hath promised to circumcise our hearts, to give us new hearts, and to give us his Holy Spirit if we ask him. Why, Lord, thou knowest I have no grace in myself to fulfil the covenant ; no, but thou must perform both parts ; thou givest the grace, and good thing promised, and grace to keep the covenant too ; therefore let none be discouraged.

Many things are required, it is true ; but the things are promised that are required, if in the use of means we depend on him by prayer. For the promises are legacies as well as promises. What is the difference between a legacy and a covenant ? A covenant is with condition, with stipulation ; a legacy is an absolute thing, when a man gives a thing freely without any condition. So, though the promises be propounded by way of covenant, with stipulations to and fro in the passages of them, as a covenant ; yet in regard of God's gracious performance, to them that depend upon him, all the promises are legacies.

Therefore God's promises, and God's covenant they are called a testament, as well as promises. They are called a will. A will, shewing what God will give us freely in the use of means, as well as what our duty is in the covenant. Therefore our estate is happy in Christ, if we depend upon God in the use of means. He will give us all things that are necessary that he hath promised ; nay, he will give grace to fulfil the covenant, if we beg it.

If a man be careless and live in sins against the covenant, he cannot perform the covenant ; and let him not allege this, that he cannot, for God will give grace to them that are careful to fulfil it. Let such a man as neglects the performance on his part, expect no good from God while he is so, let him expect vengeance ; *for all the threatenings of God* are ' yea and amen,' *as well as his promises,* to them that live in sins against conscience. Those that will not expect grace to serve him for the time to come, all the threatenings are 'yea and amen.' There is no comfort for such.

I beseech you therefore consider, it is a terrible thing to live in a state without God, and without Christ; to have no care of the performance of that that we have bound ourselves to God by the sacrament, and in our particular vows; for his threatenings are effectual as well as his promises. In Zech. i. 5, there he tells the Jews of the prophets that had threatened many things. The prophets are dead, saith he, that threatened your fathers; but for all that, the threatenings lighted on them. 'The prophets, where are they?' They were but men, but when they were gone, the threatenings lighted on your fathers. Jeremiah died, but the captivity that he threatened, it did not die; they were carried captive seventy years. So we threaten the vengeance of God on obstinate sinners, that will not come in to the gospel; we are not 'yea and amen' in regard of our being, we die; but our threatenings are 'yea.' If they be not reversed by repentance, the threatenings are 'amen,' as well as the promises. It is an evidence therefore we do not believe, if we have not care to make good the covenant on our part.

7. Again, another evidence of a child of the promises, of a man that believes the promises, *it is inward opposition of the flesh, and hatred of fleshly men;* for as it is, Gal. iv. 29, 'The son of the bondwoman persecuted the son of the freewoman.' A true, downright believer is a son of the freewoman, a son of promise; and the flesh in us opposeth it, like Ishmael, like Job's wife, and like Sarah, that laughed when the promise was made. We have an Ishmael and a Sarah in us. Aye, can this promise of life everlasting when I am rotten, and this promise of forgiveness of sins, and that goodwill, be good to me if I crack not[*] my conscience? If I take this and that course, shall these promises be performed? Here is opposition. We cannot believe the promises without much opposition.

So carnal men, 'they mock and deride the counsel of the poor,' as the psalmist saith, Ps. xiv. 6. The children of the promise that depend upon God's mercy in Christ, they are persecuted by fleshly justiciaries, and they that look to be saved by themselves without a promise, they will not be beholden to God so much. Their proud, swelling hearts rise against Christians that honour God by trusting in his promises, and will be saved by promises.

A proud popish person, his heart riseth against a holy Christian that is a son of the promise; he scorns him. You intend to be saved by the righteousness of another. No! we will not be so much beholden to God, we will satisfy for ourselves; we will merit heaven ourselves. God shall not be beholden to us to trust in him, we will bring somewhat ourselves, we will buy it out. Can these men have humble hearts? Nay, can they have any other than malicious, persecuting hearts against humble, believing Christians, that honour God by trusting in his promises?

You know Isaac was 'a son of the promise.' How was he born? Not according to the course of nature. Sarah's womb was dead. Christ was the Son of the promise. How was he born? Not according to the course of nature, for his mother was a virgin. So a Christian is a son of the promise. He is begotten where there is nothing in the course of nature likely, where there is breeding for sin, no works, no righteousness, then he believes in Christ. Isaac was a notable type of Christ and a son of promise. He was begotten besides the course of generation. So a Christian is not

* Qu. 'crack?'—ED.

begotten as a proud justiciary, by works; but he shews himself therein to be a true believer. He is begotten against the course of nature when he sees a barren heart, and sees as little disposition in his heart to be a Christian as was in the virgin's womb for Christ to be born.

How was the promise made to the virgin? She could not conceive how this should be since she knew not man. It was replied again, 'The Holy Ghost shall overshadow thee,' Luke i. 35. Her heart closed with that speech, and Christ was conceived then. So the barren heart of a Christian if it can believe, his sins shall be forgiven, and he shall have life everlasting,—if he can honour God in believing that he will keep him in life and death. Let the heart close with these promises, and a Christian is begotten. He is a son of the promise.

As for the proud justiciary that will have something in himself to vaunt of, and will persecute others that are true Christians, he relies on no promise. A Christian when he sees nothing to rely on but the promise, he closeth with the promise, and Christ is begotten in him at that very instant. To name no more evidences, you see how we may examine ourselves whether we trust in and cast ourselves upon the promises of God or no. If we do, we shall find them 'yea and amen.'

Consider it therefore, and be glad of these promises; and when you have them, go to God in Christ for the performance of them. Take the counsel of that blessed man, that in these latter times brought the glorious light of religion to light, Luther, I mean (to whom we are beholden for the doctrine of free grace more than any other divine of later times). Go to God in Christ in the promises. Christ is wrapped up in the promises. The promises are the swaddling-clothes wherein Christ is wrapped, as he saith (*xxx*). We must not think of God out of Christ. There is, saith he, God absolute in himself; so, he is 'a consuming fire,' Heb. xii. 29. But there is God incarnate, go to God incarnate, to God making good his promises in Christ incarnate; go to Christ sucking his mother's breast, lying in the manger, living humbly, talking with a sinful woman, inviting sinners to come to him, conversing with sinful creatures, altering and changing their natures, that never refused any that came to him.

Go not to God absolute. He is a 'consuming fire.' Go to Christ incarnate, God-man; go to him abased, and there is sweet converse for thy faith; for 'all the promises are made in him yea and amen.'

I beseech you, therefore, be acquainted with the mystery of Christ more and more. We have the promises in him. And you must know besides, that the Father and the Holy Ghost, they have a part, a hand in Christ's abasement; for Christ did all by his Father's appointment, and therefore it is as much as if the Father had been abased; for Christ was anointed to be so. Therefore think, that God the Father allures and invites you when Christ doth it, because he is anointed to invite you. Think that the Father is as peaceable as Christ was, because Christ was so by his Father's appointment, by his anointing. See all the three Persons, the Father, Son, and Holy Ghost in Christ. See God incarnate making all the promises before, and as the ground of all that is made good to us. See the wondrous love of God incarnate. And then go and see Christ raising that flesh that he was abased in; see him ascended into heaven, and sitting in it at the right hand of God. Then think of God in Christ glorious, think of Christ a public person, and we all in him. So as Leo saith, 'Only Christ was he that died, in whom all died; he was crucified, in whom all were crucified; and he rose again, in whom all rise, he being a public person; other particular men died, and themselves died only.'* Let us look upon God incarnate, and see ourselves in him, see God in Christ, see Christ a public person; for therefore the second Person took the manhood, that he might be a public person.

Christ took not our persons, but our nature; that our nature being knit to the second person, he might be a public person; as Adam was a public man for all mankind. Therefore think of all the promises in Christ as God-man, that he was the man Christ, made man for us. This is wondrous comfortable, let us solace ourselves with it.

Take away Christ, and the promises in Christ, and what is there in the world? Nothing but idolatry and superstition, staggering and wavering, and darkness and blindness, and popery and devilishness. Who reigns in the world but the devil and antichrist, heathenism and paganism, and all filthiness? Take away Christ, the sound knowledge of Christ incarnate, and the sound knowledge of the promises, the clear, settled promises in Christ, and what is the life of man but a horrible confusion, even a hell upon earth? Where Christ is not known, what are the lives of men, the utmost quintessence of them, but only projecting for an estate here in this world, and then to slip into hell? To live a civil life, as morality perhaps may fit a man for that, and then to be cast into hell.

Out of Christ there is no salvation, no certain comfort, no life, no light, nothing to be reckoned on out of Christ, and the promises in Christ. Therefore let us love them, and build on them, and make much of the truth we have, and get into Christ; for 'all the promises in him are yea and amen.' God hath no commerce with us immediately but by Christ the mediator, through whom he looks on us, and in whom he conveys all good to us.

The Scripture is termed a paradise. It is like a paradise, wherein we have the streams of the water of life, and the tree of life, Jesus Christ, and wherein we have the promises of life; and there is no angel to keep the door, or gate, or entrance of this paradise, but rather we are allured to come to it to refresh ourselves. There is God himself walking, there is Christ himself the tree of life. Therefore, we should make the Scriptures wondrous familiar to us, especially single out the promises, make use of them. Learn what it is to live by faith in the promises, for 'all the promises in Jesus Christ, in him are yea and in him amen.'

'*To the glory of God by us.*' The end of all this, that God will engage himself by promises, that he will stablish these promises so sure in Christ Jesus the Mediator, God and man, that he will make them 'yea and amen' in him, it is for his own glory, and 'to the glory of God' by us ministers; for we preach these promises to the people, and people believe them, and they believing give glory to God.

Obs. God's glory is manifested in the gospel, especially when it is believed in the promises.

What wondrous glory hath God in the promises in Christ! More a great deal than in the creation. In the creation man was made according to God's image. Now, in the gospel we are created according to Jesus Christ, God-man. There God added light to light, comfort to comfort. He made man good, and would have continued him good. But here is the glory of his mercy and goodness in Christ. Here he doth good to sinners. He raiseth a sinner to mercy. He doth not add light to light, but he brings light out of darkness. In the gospel mercy strives with

* See the passage from Leo, in foot-note, vol. I. page 369.—G.

misery, and strives with sin, and overcomes all our ills. It is God's will in the gospel to do good to sinners. Mercy is added to sinful men, contrary against contrary, God's goodness triumphing over the misery of man.

The righteousness that Adam had, it was the righteousness of a creature, of a man ; but the obedience we have in Christ, it is the obedience of God-man. Therefore, that being imputed to us, it is a more exquisite righteousness. It brings us to God and entitles us to heaven. It is infinitely more than Adam's was. God manifests greater glory than in the creation. There is greater love, and greater mercy, and greater goodness manifested in the gospel than to Adam in innocency.

Our estate in Christ is more perfect. His estate was not ' yea and amen,' for it was ' yea ' to-day and ' nay ' to-morrow. He stood but a while. But in Christ the ' promises are yea and amen.' He had no promise, we have. Our estate by promises in Christ is better than ever Adam's was, as we are in a better root than he, for he was not in Christ the Mediator. We by faith are united to Christ, Mediator ; and by virtue of the promise, God, where he begins, he will make an end ; where he is Alpha, he will be Omega. What a glory is this to God, that he can repair man to a better estate than ever he had at the first, as God's mending is ever for the better. The state of grace and glory is better than ever the state of nature was ; spiritual is better than natural. Therefore, it is much for the glory of the wisdom of God that he can in Christ reconcile justice and mercy, and shew more mercy than ever he did in making man out of the dust of the earth, and all is to the glory of God. These attributes especially are glorious in the promises in Christ.

His justice is glorious in punishing sin in Christ. There sin is odious in the punishing of Christ, God-man ; if we speak of justice, there is justice.

If of mercy, to put it upon our surety, for God to give his Son for us, there is transcendent mercy and transcendent justice in the punishing of our sin. How could it be punished greater ?

And then the glory of his wisdom, to bring these together, infinite mercy and infinite justice, in Christ.

Infinite power, for God to become man, and, without sin, to be so far abased ; a humble omnipotency, to descend so low that God could be mortal, and then to raise himself again.

And then the glory of his truth, that whatsoever was promised to Abraham, to David, to the prophets, all was performed in Christ, all the types. Here is glory by Christ of mercy, justice, wisdom, truth ; for all are ' yea and amen ' in Christ. Therefore, he may well say all this is ' to the glory of God.'

Therefore, consider how the glory of God shines in the face of Jesus Christ, as the apostle saith. If you would see God, see him shining ' in the face of Jesus Christ,' 2 Cor. iv. 6, see his mercy shining in Christ, and his justice in the punishing our sin in Christ ; see his truth, his power, his wisdom, shining in Christ, and shining more than in the creation, or in anything in the world besides.

Can you honour God more than in believing the gospel ? Can you dishonour him more, than to call his truth into question, that is ' yea and amen ?' If you believe the gospel, you ' set to your seal that God is true,' John iii. 33. What an honour is this, that God will be honoured by you ! In setting to your seal that he is true, you give him the glory of all his attributes. In not believing, what a dishonour do you do to God ! You deny his mercy, his wisdom, his justice, his truth, you deny all his attributes, ' you make God a liar,' 1 John v. 10. What a horrible sin is unbelief!

Therefore fortify your faith. The devil layeth siege to our faith above all other things. If he can shake that, he shakes all: for holy life goes when faith goes. Who will love God, or obey God, when he knows not whether he be his God or no? Let faith flourish, and it will quicken life in the heart. Let the promises grow in the heart, and the word be grafted in the heart, and all will flourish in a Christian's life. All will come off clearly and freely. Obedience will be cheerful and free, when we see God reconciled in Christ. Then love will be full of devices. When I see God's love to me, what shall I do to shew love again, to shew thanks to God? Where is there any that for God's sake I may do good unto? How shall I maintain the truth, and resist all opposers of the truth? Can I do too much for him that hath done so much for me? Love quickens. The devil knows if he can shake faith he shakes all. Let us fortify faith, and we glorify God more than by anything else. He is glorious in the gospel, and how shall he be so by us, except we set our hearts to believe him? Therefore let us seal God's truth by our faith, and ' set to our seals that God is true.' God vouchsafes to be honoured by weak sinful men believing of him: and that faith that honours him he will be sure to honour.

' By us.' By us ministers. How? When the gospel is preached, God is carried in triumph, as it were, and his banner is set up, and the promises displayed, and sinners called unto him; and God is glorified by the discovery of these things, and faith is wrought in people to whom they are discovered; and they glorify God when they believe: they bless God that ever they heard these tidings. So every way God is glorified.

The ministers they open, as it were, the box of sweet ointment, that the savour of it may be in the church, and spread far. They lay open the tapestry, the rich treasure of God's mercies: they dig deep, and find out the treasure. Therefore these promises in Scripture being so made and performed in Christ, they tend to God's glory, but by us, by our ministry. God, to knit man and man together, will convey the good he means to convey by the despised ministry.

The enemies, therefore, of the ministry of the gospel, what are they? Here is a double prejudice against them: they are enemies of the glory of God, and of the comfort of God's people, for they glorify God in the sense of his mercy. When it is unfolded to them, God gets glory, and they comfort.

What do we think then of Popish spirits, that feed the people only with dead and dull ceremonies? But let them go. I go on to the next verse, having dwelt somewhat long on this.

VERSE 21.

' Now he that stablisheth us with you in Christ is God, who hath anointed us,' &c. As the riches of a Christian consisteth in the promises of God, which, as we have heard, in Christ ' are all yea and amen;' so unless he be stablished and built upon this strength, all is nothing. What if a man stand on a rock, if he be not built on it! What if the foundation be never so strong, if he be not stablished thereon! It is not sufficient that the promises be stablished, but we must be stablished upon them. The promises of God are indeed ' yea and amen,' might the soul say, but what is that to me ? Therefore the apostle addeth, He that gives the promises, will stablish us upon the promises.

' *Now he which stablisheth us with you in Christ is God.*' The first thing that I will observe, before we come to the particular handling of the words, shall be only this in the general, from the connection and knitting together of this verse with the former, viz.,

Obs. That there must be a double amen.

1. There is an amen in the promises. They are in themselves true. There must be an amen likewise in us. We must say amen to them, that is, we must be stablished upon them. There must be an echo in a Christian's heart unto God ; that as God saith, these and these things I promise, and they are all amen ; so the soul by faith must echo again, these things are for me, I believe them.

For, as we say in the schools to good purpose, there is a double certainty, a double firmness ; a certainty of the object, and a certainty of the subject ; there is a firmness of the promises in Jesus Christ ; and there must be a firmness in us upon those promises. It is no matter what the certainty of the thing be that we are to build upon, if there be not a certainty in the person, if there be not a building on that thing. God shall lose the glory of his truth, and we the comfort, unless we be certain, as well as the promises are certain. It is no matter what the garment be, if it be not put on. It is no matter, as I said before, how firm the rock be, if we plant not ourselves upon it ; and therefore besides the writing of God's word on tables, unless he write it likewise in our hearts, unless our hearts be stablished on that truth that in itself is certain, that it may be certain to us, all is to no purpose.

You see therefore, *the absolute necessity of the application of the soul unto those truths which are certain and sure in themselves.* There must be a stablishing of us, as well as a stablishing of the promises. There is a necessity of the application of the promises to ourselves, that they be true to us. Christ is a garment. We must put him on then. He is the robes that we appear glorious before God in ; but we must put him on by faith. Christ is the food of life. He is so indeed, but then he must be digested. Meat, except it be applied, except the stomach work nourishment out of it by application, and so digest it to all the parts, the body hath not nourishment from it.

Christ is the foundation of his church, aye, but there must be application. We as living stones must be built on him. Let the foundation be never so strong, if the stones be not laid on the foundation, the stones cannot stand. Though Christ be the spouse of the church, and be never so rich, there must be application and consent ; we must strike up the bargain and match between Christ and us. There must be our consent to tie ourselves to him, to give up ourselves to him. So look to all the comfortable relations that our blessed Saviour hath taken upon him in the book of God, they all enforce application.

The ground, I say, is this, that though there be never so much certainty in the thing, yet if there be not a certainty in the person to found application upon, all is to no purpose.

These two therefore must go together, and they are sweet relatives, promises on God's part, and faith on our part. The promises and Christ are nothing without faith. For there must be a touch to draw virtue. If faith have never so little touch of Christ, it will draw virtue ; but there must be a touch, there must be application.* Christ is nothing without faith, and faith is nothing without Christ and the promises.

For what is the difference between faith and presumption? Presumption is an empty, groundless, fruitless conceit. Faith builds on the promises of the word; we can allege the promise. It is nothing for a madman to assume himself to be king of another country. Why? He hath no promise. He that made account that all the ships that came to the haven were his, it was but a frantic part of him, and so he was accounted. So a man that thinks his estate is good, and builds not himself upon the promise, that hath no ground for it out of God's word, it is but a presumptuous frantic conceit. The promises are nothing without faith, and faith is nothing without the promises. There must be application. This I thought good to observe first in the general. To come now more particularly to the words themselves.

' He that stablisheth us with you,' &c. In the words you have, *first*, a gracious act of building, or stablishing.

Secondly, the basis, the foundation of that stablishing or building, and that is Christ.

Thirdly, the author of this stablishing—God.

Lastly, the persons who are built and stablished on that foundation ' with you.' ' He that stablisheth us with you in Christ is God.'

The first thing *is the act* ' stablishing.'

The point is this, first, that,

Obs. Stablishing, settling grace is necessary.

It is necessary that there be a stablishing, confirming grace. It is not sufficient that we be brought out of the kingdom of Satan; for when we are gotten out of his hands and strength, he pursues us with continual malice. Therefore there must be the same power to stablish us still in grace, that first brought us into the state of grace. For as providence is a continual creation, so stablishing grace is the continuance of the new creature; the same grace that sets us in the state of the new creation in Christ, the same sta̓lisheth us. Stablishing grace is necessary. It is necessary many ways. Man of himself is an unstable creature. Take him at the best, but a creature. God found no stability in the angels. Take the best of creatures, even as creatures they are unstable. For God will have a creature as a creature to be a dependent thing upon the Creator, who is a being of himself, Jehovah. There is no stability in any creature. Man in his best estate was an unstable creature. Since, we are very unstable, ready to be carried away in our judgment to the wind of any false doctrine, ready to be blown over with every little temptation. Nay, now in the state of grace, in ourselves we are very unstable, ready to fly off presently; and therefore we have need to be established of God.

Reason 1. It is necessary in regard *of the indisposition of our nature to supernatural truths.* We are an unprepared subject for them in ourselves. The law indeed, we have some principles of it; but of the gospel there are in us no seeds at all of it; and that is the reason there are so many heresies against the gospel: there are none against the law. And therefore divine truths being contrary to our disposition, as there must be a supernatural beginner, so there must be a supernatural strengthener. He that is Alpha must be Omega. As there must be a mighty subduing of the heart to be a vessel to receive these truths, an almighty power to lay the soul on this foundation, because of the contrariety of the truth to the natural heart of

* Cf. Mark v. 25–34.—G.

man, so there is need of no less than of a divine and supernatural stablishing. Our natures are very inconstant, and unsettled, and wayward. Take us at the best, before the fall, you see how soon we fell, being left to ourselves, and having no stablishing grace. Much more now since the fall is there a necessity of divine stablishing. When we come to know the truth, we are subject to fall away. Like little children, that are ready to sink, if they be not upheld by their parents or nurse, God must uphold and prop us, and shore us up: we presently sink else. Moses was but in the mount a while, and we see how soon the Israelites fell to idolatry. Paul did but leave the Galatians a little, and they were removed presently from Christ to false teachers, Gal. iii. 1. The nature of man is wonderful unstable, very loose and unsettled. Divine truths are supernatural. We have need of stablishing therefore.

2. Again, stablishing grace is necessary, *in regard of those oppositions that are made against us after once we be in Christ.* For with what malice doth Satan pursue a Christian, when he is once taken out of his kingdom! And the world runs a clean contrary bias in the several examples thereof. How many scandals do there arise daily even in the very church itself! How many things are in our natural disposition joining with them! All which will make a man fly off, and unsettle him, if he be not stablished in grace.

And indeed what is the difference between one Christian and another that lives in the bosom of the church? between a temporiser and another? The difference is but in their radication, in their stablishing. For all have the general knowledge of the truth. But here is the difference,—the true Christian is radicated and rooted in the truth, a false Christian is not. And thereupon when temptations come, either from within, from conscience, or from without, from Satan and the world, he falls away, because he is not rooted; but the other holds on, because he is established.

3. And the best of us all have need of stablishing; for there *be degrees of truths, degrees of faith, in all the parts of faith.* There is conjecture, a certain suspicious knowledge; and there is opinion, which is with fear of the contrary; and there is knowledge; and there is faith, which is founded upon the authority of the speaker: and yet this faith, though it be founded upon the word of God, it may receive further and further strength in all the parts of it. In assent, there may be a higher degree; in affiance, there may be a higher degree, &c.; and therefore the best of us all have need of strengthening.

But where shall we have it?

Christ is the basis, the foundation, of all our stability. Now, in the covenant of grace, we are stablished in him, not in ourselves. The point is this, that

Obs. Christ is the ground of our firmness.

As all the promises are made to us in Christ in regard of the execution, so God he brings us Christ. All is conferred to us in Christ. As the promises are made, so they are executed. God stablisheth us in Christ. He draws us to Christ. 'None come to me, but God the Father draws,' John vi. 44. Therefore God doth reveal Christ to us in our conversion, and our stablishing is in him. Therefore our salvation is so certain, because it is laid upon one that is so certain in himself, Jesus Christ.

And happy it is, that we are stablished in him that loves us so well, that is both a low high priest, that will pity us; and a great high priest, equal with God, able to do all things to God for us, and between God and us. Adam, we know, had his strength in his own keeping, and being left to himself, we see what became of him. The angels had their strength in their own keeping, and we know how soon they fell. But since the fall, we are founded and bottomed upon a surer foundation. Now we stand not by our own strength, but we are established in Jesus Christ. We are surer than the angels were before they fell, surer than Adam was in paradise ; for now we are stablished in Christ the Mediator, God and man. And because we could not keep our stability in ourselves, we are stablished in him that wrought it for us, and that possesseth it for us in heaven, and that keeps it for us ; and as it is laid up and kept for us, so we are kept for it. ' You are kept by the power of God to salvation,' 1 Pet. i. 5. And, therefore, as there be many differences which advance the state of grace above the state of nature, so this is one, that our state in grace is more stable and firm, as being stablished upon a better ground, even upon Jesus Christ the second Adam. God never mends, but he mends for the better ; and he never restores, but he restores for the better. The new heaven and the new earth shall be better than the first, so the new creature, the new Adam, is more glorious than the first ; and as that which we recover in Christ is more and better than that we lost in Adam, so the certainty and security of our estate in grace, is far beyond the other, this being stablished in Christ.

But what in us is stablished in Christ ? and in Christ how considered ?

1. First of all, *our judgment*, that is stablished in evangelical truths, concerning the natures and the offices of Christ, concerning the privileges that we have by him ; and this is the ground of all other stablishment. We cannot firmly cleave to that with our will and affections, which we do not clearly apprehend with our understandings. When we have a clear and judicious apprehension of things, then follows a firm affection to them. The adhering and cleaving of the will and affections, it comes from the discerning of the understanding ; and, therefore, as we say of the first concoction, if that be naught, all is naught ; and if that be good and sound, it makes way for all concoctions after ; so if things be well digested in the judgment, if there be a sound illumination and apprehension of divine truths, it makes way for a constant and firm adhesion ; therefore the first stablishing is of our judgments.

2. Secondly, as our judgments, *so our wills* are stablished in cleaving unto Christ, making choice of him above all things in the world ; that as he became man to sue unto us for our love, and to become our husband, so we then marry him, when upon judging what an excellent person he is, and how fit for us, we choose him and cleave unto him constantly without all separation, for better, for worse, in our joy, in our love and delight. For, indeed, he is the only excellent object, and most fittest for our affections to be placed on. Whatsoever other things besides, we place our affections on too much, they make us worse than ourselves. Only he can advance us to a better state than we are in, that can raise us higher.

3. In a word, the whole soul, judgment, will, *and affections*, and all the inward man, for so the apostle takes it in that latitude, Eph. iii. 16, is stablished in Christ, and this carries the outward man with it. We are stablished in Jesus Christ, not in ourselves.

Now when we are stablished in Christ, whatsoever Christ hath, or is, is ours. It is a most excellent condition to be in Christ, and to be stablished in him ; for to be established in Christ, is to be in a firm estate, in an everlasting estate. Once Christ's, and for ever his. It is a glorious state, for he hath conquered over all enemies whatsoever, and his conquest is ours.

Well then, we see the foundation of the church, and of every parti-

cular Christian, Christ Jesus. Whence comes the stability and firmness
of the church, 'that the gates of hell shall not prevail against it'? It is
built upon the rock, upon Christ. So all the stablishing that a Christian
hath, it is from this rock, his being built upon Jesus Christ. If we were
built upon man, we could not stand; if we were built upon angels, we could
not stand; if we were built upon anything in the world, we could not stand;
but being built upon Jesus Christ, who is 'all in all' to a soul that is
stablished in him, there must needs be an everlasting stablishing.

It is a fond* objection of some, and unlearned, against the principles of
divine truth, that we may fall, as well as Adam in paradise, as well as the
angels in heaven; as if there were not a wide and broad difference between
the state of grace and the state of nature. A Christian hath more strength
than the angels in heaven, or than Adam in paradise ever had; he hath a
more firm consistence, because he stands by grace. 'By grace we stand,'
as the apostle saith, Heb. xiii. 9. A Christian hath promises of perseverance, Adam and the angels had none. And, therefore, to fetch a reason of
falling away from grace, from the proportion we have to that condition, is
a mere sophism, not rightly discerning the disparity. It is not alike with
the angels, and Adam, and us, for we stand by grace, out of ourselves, being stablished in one another.†

We have not only a promise of happiness, as the angels and Adam had
happiness and a blessed estate, but they had no promise to stand and be
confirmed. A poor weak Christian hath a promise to be stablished and
confirmed. Therefore those proud sectaries that are between us and the
papists, and join rather with them than us, that trouble the church so much,
they make an idle objection concerning falling away from grace, to say,
Did not Adam fall away? What is that to the purpose? Was Adam under
the same covenants as we are now in Christ? Is there not a new promise
made to us in Christ, better than ever Adam could attain to?

Besides, we are founded upon a better Adam, upon the 'second Adam,'
God-man. We have not only a better foundation, but better promises,
that Adam and the angels themselves wanted. And, therefore, the covenant of grace is said to be 'an everlasting covenant.' 'I will marry thee
to myself for ever,' Hosea ii. 19.

A Christian is not to be considered abstractively, or alone; for then, indeed he is a weak creature, as weak as other men are; but consider him in
his rock on whom he is built; consider him in his husband to whom he is
united and knit; consider him in his head, Christ; look upon him as he is
thus founded and stablished, Oh he is an excellent person!

See him in the difference betwixt him and others. Those that are not
stablished by a firm judgment, and will, and affection, and so by faith in
Jesus Christ, what confidence, what stability have they? Those who have
the firmness they have in the favour of men, it is but vanity; those that
have the firmness they have in riches, what are they? how soon do they
leave it all? those that have the firmness they have in dependence upon
any creature, be it never so great, alas! they are nothing, they are all
vanity. Both we ourselves in depending, and the things we depend upon,
are vanity. Therefore we are vanity, because we fasten upon that which is
vanity. Things have no more firmness than that hath upon which they
lean. Those that have but a weak prop to support them, when that falls,
they fall together with it. Now those that are not founded upon Christ by
knowledge and love, and united to him by faith, alas! what standing have

* That is, 'foolish.'—G.   † Qu. 'in another?'—ED.

they, when all things else besides God are vain! For nothing hath a being but God, and a Christian so far as he leans upon God. Were not all things taken out of nothing? and shall not they all turn to nothing? must not this whole world be consumed with fire?

There must be a new world, ' a new heaven and a new earth,' 2 Pet. iii. 13; but this and all the excellencies in it, as they were raised out of nothing, so they shall come to nothing. God, he is, ' I am that I am,' saith he, Exod. iii. 14; and Christ he is ' yesterday, to-day, to-morrow, and the same for ever,' Heb. xiii. 8. A man cannot say of any creature in the world, that it was yesterday, and shall be to-morrow and for ever. We may say it of Christ, ' he is Alpha and Omega, the first and the last, he was, and is, and is to come,' Rev. i. 8; and, therefore, those that are founded upon him, that have their happiness in him, they are firm as he is firm; and those that build upon any other thing, they vanish as the thing vanisheth. There is nothing in the world hath such a being, but it is subject in time not to be. It is only a Christian that is in Christ, who is as firm as Christ is; and Christ can never be but that which he is; for of necessity God must be always like himself. He is Jehovah, ' I am, I am ' at all times; and Christ he is Jehovah. A Christian therefore, and none but a Christian, hath a firm stablishing in Christ. Without this stablishing in Christ, what are we? what are wicked men? Chaff, that the wind blows away! They are grass, &c., things of nothing, carried away with every blast. But a Christian is a stone, a rock, built upon Christ Jesus.

But to come to the person, who is it that stablisheth? ' He that stablisheth us in Christ, is God.'

Wherein we may consider these two branches:

God must stablish.

God will stablish.

Can none stablish the soul upon Christ but God?

No! For God is the only maker of the marriage between Christ and the church. The same God that brought Adam and Eve together in paradise, brings the church and Christ together. And as he gives Christ to the church, and hath sealed and appointed him to be ' wisdom, righteousness, sanctification, and redemption,' 1 Cor. i. 30 (being made of God unto us for that purpose, as the apostle saith), so he works the consent of the church, a consent in heart and spirit to take and embrace Christ. Now it is God only that can work the heart to Christ. ' None can come unto me, except God the Father draw him,' John vi. 44. It is God that gives Christ to be the husband of the church, and that brings the spouse, the church, to Christ.

1. For first, it is God by his Spirit that discovers *to the soul its hideous, desperate, and woful estate without Christ; and by the Spirit in the ministry of the word, lays open the riches and excellency that is in Christ, and the firmness and stability that is to be had in him;* and so draws us with the cords of a man, with reasons, discovering an absolute necessity of getting into Christ, and of having him to be our husband, except we will lie under the wrath of God and be damned; and, withal, discovering the fulness and excellency that is in Christ.

2. Again, it is God only that must *stablish the soul, all the parts of it, both judgment and conscience.* For, I beseech you, what can any human creature, what can anything under God, work upon the soul? I mean so firmly as to stablish it; and, therefore, our controversy with the papists is just and good.

We say the reason and ground of our believing the word of God to be the word of God must not be the testimony of the church and the authority thereof; for, alas! what can the judgment of man, what can the judgment of the church, do? It may incline and move the will by inducing arguments, and so cause a human consent; but to establish the soul and conscience, and to assure me that the word of God, which is the ground of my faith, is the word of God, it must be God by his Spirit that must do it; the testimony of the church will never do it. The same Spirit that inspired holy men to write the word of God, works in us a belief that the word of God is the word of God. The stablishing argument must be by the power of God's Spirit. God, joining with the soul and spirit of a man whom he intends to convert, besides that inbred light that is in the soul, causeth him to see a divine majesty shining forth in the Scriptures, so that there must be an infused establishing by the Spirit to settle the heart in this first principle, and indeed in all other divine principles, that the Scriptures are the word of God.

3. And, to go on a little further, this is a fundamental error in our practice; *for what is the reason we have so many apostates?* What is the reason so many are so fruitless in their lives? What is the reason that men despair in death, but even this, because men are not built and stablished aright? God's Spirit never stablished their souls in divine truths. For, first, concerning apostasy, ask them what is the reason they are of this or that religion, they will say they have been taught so, they have been brought up to it, the company with whom they have conversed have been devout men, and have been always led with this opinion, and they see no reason to thwart it.

Is that all? Hath not the Spirit wrought these things in thy heart? hath he not given thee a taste of them? hath he not convinced thee in thy judgment that it is so? hast thou not found the power of the Spirit working upon thy soul, changing of thee, raising of thee, drawing of thee out of the world nearer to God? hast thou not, I say, felt the power of the Spirit this way?

No; but thus I was catechised, and thus I have been bred, and thus I have heard in the ministry. And no otherwise? Alas! it will never hold out, there will be a falling away; for when a man believes not that which he believes from the Spirit of God, he will be ready, when dangerous times come, when there is an onset made by the adversaries, to fall, and to fall clean away, as we see it was in the time of popery; for whatsoever is not spiritual, whatsoever knowledge is not divine and from the Spirit of God, never holds out. Therefore, I beseech you, what is the reason that you have many illiterate men that set upon the truth and hold out to the end, and, on the contrary, many great seeming scholars, that are skilful in school-learning and in other authors, do not? The reason is, the one hath the truth from the Spirit, discovering all the objections that the heart of man can make against it, and the strength that is in the truth to answer and silence all those objections. The other man hath only a discoursing knowledge, an ability to gather one thing from another, and to prove one thing by another, by strength of parts. But the Spirit of God never discovered the sleights and the corruptions of his heart, never fastened and settled his heart upon the truth, he never had experience of the truth. For, indeed, nothing doth stablish so much as the experience of the truth on which we are stablished.

4. Again, what is the reason of that *unfruitfulness that is amongst men*, but because truths were never settled in the soul by the Spirit of God?

That which men know out of the word of God concerning Christ and the privileges by him, they were never persuaded of it in their hearts; therefore, they come not to a fruitful conversation. It is impossible but that men should be abundantly fruitful that have spiritual apprehensions of divine things, of evangelical truths. Hence comes all our unthankfulness and undervaluing of the gospel. The gospel of itself is an unprized thing. However we esteem of it, God values it highly. We value it not, because our apprehensions of it are customary and formal, gotten by breeding, and education, and discourse, and not by the Spirit; we feel not the spiritual and heavenly comforts of those truths we think we know.

5. How comes likewise *despair in time of temptation, and in death*, but only because men want this stablishing by the Spirit of God? Men go on in evil courses, trusting to a formal, dead, human knowledge, gotten by human means, and not settled in them by the Spirit of God, that hath not sealed the truth in their hearts; and hereupon, when sharp trials come, they despair, because they have no feeling of the truths of the gospel; and so when conscience is awakened and smarts, it clamours and cries out upon all their formal and human knowledge. For they having not a spiritual sense of the mercies of God in Christ, and the persuasions of comfort are not so near to support the soul, as the temptations, and vexations, and torments are, how can they but despair? Now who can still the conscience, but the Spirit of God? Why now, if the knowledge that men had were spiritual and heavenly, in all accusations of conscience, it would set conscience down and still it. I am a sinner indeed, I am this and this, but I have felt the sweet mercies of God in Christ; God hath said to my soul, 'I am thy salvation,' Ps. xxxv. 3; he hath intimated to my spirit, by a sweet voice, 'Son, thy sins are forgiven thee,' Mark ii. 5. Where there is, I say, a knowledge and an apprehension of these evangelical truths wrought by the Spirit, it sets down conscience and stills it, though the heart rage at the same time. There are thousands in the very bosom of the church that miscarry because of this, resting in a literal, outward, formal knowledge, gotten only by discourse, and by reading, and commerce with others, and never labour to have their hearts stablished in Christ by God's Spirit.

You see here, then, a necessity of God's writing his truth in our bowels. He saith in the covenant of grace, 'I will write my law in their inward parts,' Jer. xxxi. 33, that is, I will teach their very hearts: that knowledge that they have shall be spiritual.

For, beloved, the knowledge that must save us must not only be of divine things, but it must be divine; it must not only be of spiritual things, but it must be spiritual. The light that we have of spiritual things must be answerable to the things; we must see them by their own light. We cannot know spiritual and heavenly things by a human light; but as the things themselves are spiritual, so we must have the Spirit of God, that by it we may come to know spiritual things spiritually.

Desire God therefore to vouchsafe us his Spirit, that it may teach us, and convince us of the truth of those things which we read and hear. God must do it, he must persuade and bow the heart, and will, and affections; and so he will do it, and doth it to those that rely upon him. And this is the second branch.

Obs. As God must do it, so God will do it.

What is the reason of that?

1. It is this: he will do it, *because he is constant.* Where he 'begins a

good work, he will finish it to the day of the Lord,' Philip. i. 6. He will do it, because in the covenant of grace he hath undertaken both parts, both his own and ours. He undertakes his own part, which is to give us eternal life, and to give us Christ ; and he undertakes our part too, which is to believe, and to cleave unto Christ, &c. He makes this good himself. He works this in the heart by the Spirit ; for therefore it is called the covenant of grace, because God himself is graciously pleased to do both parts, which must be comfortably remembered against an objection that flesh and blood will make. I might indeed come to God and Christ, but I am an unworthy, empty creature, I have no faith.

Come and attend upon the means ; the gift of application, and confirming, and stablishing, is part of the covenant. The covenant that God makes with thee, is not only to give thee life everlasting and glory, but to give thee grace likewise. ' Faith is the gift of God.' He that stablisheth us, and confirms us upon that which is certain in itself, is God.

Lay it up against a time of temptation for a pillar and ground of your faith, that here God doth both. He gives us promises, and gives us Christ whereon the promises are founded ; and likewise establisheth us, and seals us, &c. He doth all. So that as none can stablish the soul, but God by his Spirit, so he will do it. It is an excellent reason of the apostle in Rom. v. 10, ' If when we were enemies, God gave us his Son to reconcile us, how much more now shall we be saved ! ' If we were saved by the death of Christ when we were enemies, much more shall we be preserved by his life, he now living in heaven ! So I say, if God, when there was nothing in us, but we were in a clean opposite estate, did begin spiritual life in us, much more will he stablish that which he hath begun in us.

And this stablishing, as well as the beginning of grace, comes likewise from God ; for take grace in the whole latitude and extent of it, take all that can be in grace, all comes graciously from God : the offer of it, the beginning of it. This manner of it, that it should be strong, the strengthening of grace, it comes from God. He strengtheneth us in grace, as well as begins it. So that grace itself, and this *modus*, this manner, that it is strong and firm, that it should hold out, all comes from God.

A Christian needs not only converting grace, but stablishing grace. God that converted him must stablish him, and build him up, and confirm him. Peter was in the state of grace, and yet when God did not stablish him, you see how he fell. So David was an excellent man, but when God did not stablish him, you see how he fell. The weakest, with the stablishing grace of God, will stand : and the strongest, without the stablishing grace of God, will sink and fall.

The apostle doth not say, he hath done, but he doth ' stablish' us. This must be considered, that the life of a Christian is a perpetual dependent life : not only in his conversion he lives by faith, he hath his first life ; but ever after he lives by faith, that is, dependence on God for assistance, and protection, and strength in the whole course of his life.

The ignorance of this makes us subject to fail ; for when we trust to grace received, and do not seek for a new supply, we fall into Peter's case, ' Though all men forsake thee, yet will not I,' Mat. xxvi. 35. Hereupon Peter fell foully. He had too much confidence in grace received.

Therefore God is fain to humble his children, to teach them dependence ; and usually therefore in Scripture, where some special grace is given, he hath somewhat joined with it, to put them in mind that they do not stand by their own strength. In the same chapter where Peter makes a glorious confession, 'Thou art the Son of the living God,' Mat. xvi. 16, and he was honoured of Christ by that confession ; yet Christ calls him Satan in the same chapter, ver. 23, and he forsakes his Master. A strange thing! to teach us, that we stand not of ourselves. When we are strong, it is by God ; when we are weak, it is by ourselves.

Jacob wrestled, and was a prevailer with God, but he was fain to halt for it. He was struck with halting all the days of his life : though he had the victory, and overcame God, taking upon him, as I said before, the person of an enemy to strive with him. Yet God, to put him in mind that he had the strength whereby he prevailed from him, and not of himself, he made him limp all his days. We need perpetual dependence upon God.

Therefore let us set upon nothing in our own strength, as Hannah saith comfortably, 1 Sam. ii. 9, 'No man is strong by his own strength.' God is all our sufficiency. Man's nature doth affect a kind of divinity; he would be a god to himself: but God will teach him that he is not a God, but a dependent creature. He affects a divinity. Thus he will set upon things in confidence of his own wisdom, without prayer, and thinks to work things with the strength of his own parts, to compass things with his own wit, to bring things to a good issue. O no! it will not be so. In Prov. iii. 6, 'Acknowledge God in all thy ways,' that is, acknowledge him in thy enterprises in anything; acknowledge him in the progress, that thou needest stablishing grace ; acknowledge him in the issue, that thou needest his blessing upon all thy endeavours ; acknowledge God in all our ways.

Therefore, what do we but make ourselves gods, when we set upon business, especially weighty, without invocation and dependence ? A Christian is wondrous weak, a man is vanity in himself; but take him as he is built upon the promises, and as he is in the love of God and Christ, he is a kind of almighty man; then 'I can do all things in Christ that strengtheneth me,' Philip. iv. 13. A Christian is omnipotent if he depend upon the promise, and commit his ways to God ; but he is impotent and weak in himself. It is God that must stablish us. A man that is vanity, he makes him firm ; a man that is weak, he makes him strong ; a man that is unsettled, he settles him. The word is a firm thing, and God that builds us on the word is as firm ; and Christ in whom we are built is as firm. Peter when he built on the word he was wondrous firm, he was a rock too. A man that stands on a rock is firm. Now in believing the gospel, and in being built on the gospel, upon the prophets and apostles, upon apostolical truth, now we that are weak in ourselves are firm.

The weakest creatures have the strongest shelters ; and weakness is turned by God to be a help ; for conscience of weakness makes us seek for strength out of ourselves. You know the conies, as Solomon saith, 'they hide themselves in the rock,' Prov. xxx. 26, they flee to their burrows. The birds, because snares are laid for them below, they build their nests on high, to secure themselves that way. We see the vine, a weak plant, it hath the elm to prop it. Weak things must have a strong support. So man, being weak in himself, weak in judgment, weak in affections, he is stablished by God, God herein triumphing in our weakness over strength. For when we have strong adversaries, and we are weak, Satan is a strong enemy. God himself puts upon him the vizor of an enemy sometimes, as in Job's case, and Christ's on the cross; when God personates an enemy, and the devil is a real enemy; and the devil's instruments, heretics and seducers, are strong, strong in wit and parts every way, and we are weak to encounter with God, to wrestle with him ; and we are weak to encounter with ' principalities and powers,' Eph. vi. 12, and with men of stronger parts, that are besotted and intoxicated with Satanical temptations, and labour to draw all into the snare of the devil with themselves.   Now when God in weakness shall triumph over strength, here is glory to God, in stablishing us.   It is God that must stablish us.

And as God must only do it, so he is ready to do it ; for in the covenant of grace it lies upon him.   God hath promised there to confirm it ; and therefore the apostle, 1 Thess. v. 24, binds it with the faithfulness of God, ' Faithful is he that hath promised, who also will do it.'   God is content that our confirmation should lie upon his faithfulness ; and therefore when he accepts us into the covenant of grace, he performs our part as well as his own.   ' God is faithful,' saith the apostle, 1 Cor. i. 9, ' who hath called us to the fellowship of Christ,' who will confirm us to the end.   He is content to hazard his reputation, as it were, and to be counted unfaithful else ; so that strengthening grace is of God.   He hath bound himself by his faithfulness to confirm and to stablish those that are his.

Mark here by the way, before I come to handle the doctrine of perseverance, what an invincible argument you have to prove that a man that is once in Christ can never fall away.

Say they, indeed, God for his part is ready to maintain us, to do this ; but we for our part are subject to fall away : as if the carrying of us along in the course of grace to salvation did not lie upon God and Christ.   God is faithful to confirm us to the end.   We being once in the covenant of grace, he doth our part and his own too : how can those then that are in the state of grace ever finally fall away ?

Now God doth confirm us, by working such graces in us by his Spirit, by which we are stablished.   As for instance, ' I will put my fear into their hearts, that they shall never depart from me,' Jer. xxxii. 40 ; he stablisheth us by fear.   ' Make an end of your salvation with fear and trembling, for it is God that works in you both the will and the deed,' Philip ii. 12. He puts a spirit of jealousy into a man over his corruptions ; and a reverential filial fear, which keepeth him from presuming.

And likewise he preserveth us by wisdom, as it is, Prov. ii. 10, 11. ' When wisdom entereth into thy heart, discretion shall preserve thee, and understanding shall keep thee.'

And by faith, ' you are kept,' saith the apostle, ' by the mighty power of God through faith to salvation.'

And by peace of conscience, which is wrought in the heart by the Spirit. ' The peace of God which passeth all understanding shall guard (for so the word signifieth) your hearts and minds,'* that is, a true believer that is once in Christ, he finds such joy in the Holy Ghost, such inward peace of conscience, as preserves and guards him from despair, from the temptations of Satan, from the seeming wrath of God.   So that God as he stablisheth us, so he stablisheth us as it becometh Christians, as it becomes men, by sanctifying our understandings, by working grace in our hearts, the grace of fear, of wisdom, of faith, of peace, &c.   So that a Christian now cannot presume, save in a holy kind of presumption, that God will finish his own good work.   But of this, I say, I shall have fitter occasion to speak hereafter.

To conclude therefore—God you see must stablish, and God will stablish.   It is a point of great comfort every way ; comfort from the foundation and root in whom we are stablished ; and from him that hath taken

* Cf. note *k*, vol. I. p. 334.—G.

upon him to stablish us, God by his Holy Spirit.   If a Christian should fall, God must be unstable ; or Christ the foundation must be unstable; or the Holy Spirit by which we are stablished must be unstable ; but it were blasphemy to think thus.

I come now to the last thing, the subject, or the persons that are stablished, ' us with you.'

' He that stablisheth *us with you*.'   We should have honourable conceits of all Christians.   There is an ointment runs down upon the very skirts of Aaron's garment, Ps. cxxxiii. 2.   There is not the lowest Christian, but he receiveth something from Christ the head.   Perhaps thou hast one grace in an eminent manner.   It may be he hath another more eminent than thou hast.   Thou mayest have more knowledge, he may have more humility; thou mayest have more strength of judgment, he may have more sense of his own wants.   There is somewhat in every Christian that is valuable, that is estimable and precious, not only in the eye of God, who valued him so as to give his Son for him, but should be so also in the eye of stronger Christians.   Therefore St Paul here, a strong Christian, out of the sweetness of his spirit, joins ' us with you.'   He saith not, you with us, but as if they were as firmly set in Christ as himself, he saith, ' us with you ;' he puts them together with himself; for indeed, all of us, one with another, weak Christians and strong Christians, fetch all that we have from one fountain, draw all from one spring, are led all by one Spirit.

You have here also the character of a sound Christian ; he loves and values all Christians.   A carnal man may value excellent Christians, that have excellent parts, of whom he hopes for kindness in some peculiar regard, but he loves not all the saints.   Love to all Christians as they be Christians, because they have some anointing of the Spirit, some earnest, somewhat they have to be valued, is a note of a good and sound Christian.

Another reason why he joins ' us with you,' is, to shew that the working of the Spirit it is not in the members severed from the body, but as they are in the body.   The Spirit works in us, but in us with you, and in you with us ; that is, as all the spirits come from the head and heart to the several members of the body, so they must be united, they must be in the body, before they can have the benefit of the spirits.   There must be an union with Christ the head and with the rest of the members before we can have the Spirit to strengthen us and anoint us.   Those that rend themselves from the body, cannot hope for stablishing from the head.

This should be a bond to tie us to the communion of saints.   We have all that we have in the body ; we all grow in the body ; we are all stones in one building, whereof Christ is the foundation; therefore as stones in an arch strengthen one another, so should we.   Let us look for grace to be given in the communion of saints.   It is an ill sign when any man will be a solitary Christian, and will stand alone by himself.   As we are knit to Christ by faith, so we must be knit to the communion of saints by love. That which we have of the Spirit is had in the communion of saints.   It is worth observing, the better to cherish Christian lovingness.

Thus you see the parts of this sentence in which we have the grace itself here spoken of, ' stablishing.'

In whom we are stablished—' In Christ.'   *By whom ?*—' By God.'   And *who those are that are stablished*—' Us with you.'

To make now some application of all.

Use. If it be God that stablisheth us, let us make this use of it, *let God have the glory of our stablishing*.   If we have it in dependence upon God by prayer, let us return all by praise and thanksgiving. All comes of his mere grace, let all return to his mere glory. 'Not unto us, but unto thy name give the praise,' Ps. cxv. 1. It is the song of the church on earth, and the song of the church triumphant in heaven, that all glory be to God in all the whole carriage of salvation. The promises are his, stablishing is his, that he would make a covenant, it is his; that he will perform his covenant to us, it is his; that he will enable us to perform the covenant, it is by his strength; all is his. Therefore both the church here, and the church in heaven, our song should be, Great, and gracious, and merciful is the true God, that is so gracious and righteous in all his promises.

Let us labour, I beseech you, for stablishing, especially in these times. Is it not a shame that we have gotten no more ground now than we had threescore years ago? Nay, that we rather call principles into question? The pope hath been antichrist; and traditions hath been accounted traditions, and not equal with the word. What shall we now stagger in the foundation? Is here our progress? Oh, beloved, labour to be stablished in the present truth, that you may not be a prey for every subtle man.

And here especially I would speak to the younger sort, that they should labour for this stablishing betimes, before they be engaged in the world, and before other businesses possess them over-deeply; for falsehood hath more correspondency, and suits better with our corruption, specially if it be forced from subtle wits. It prevails much with unstable dispositions. Those that are uncatechised and ungrounded, they are soon led away; and, therefore, with other studies we should study the truth, and remember that our best calling is to be a Christian, and our best honour to be able to stand for the truth we profess.

Labour to have fundamental graces established, and then all will be stablished. If the root be strengthened, the tree stands fast; radical graces must be strengthened.

First, *Humility.* The foundation of religion is very low, and humility and abasing is in all parts of religion. Every grace hath a mixture of humility, because our graces are from God; they are dependencies. Now humility is an emptying grace, and acknowledgeth, that in myself I am nothing. Spiritual poverty with humility acknowledgeth that I in myself am a dependent creature. If God withhold his influence, if God withdraw his grace, I shall be as other men, as Samson when his hair was cut. Our strength is in God altogether. Let us pray that we may be humble; 'God gives grace to the humble,' James iv. 6. 'When I am weak,' saith blessed St Paul, 'then I am strong;' that is, when I am humble, and feel, and acknowledge my weakness, 'then I am strong,' 2 Cor. xii. 10; or else a man is not strong when he is weak, but when he feels and acknowledgeth his weakness. Therefore let us labour to grow in humility and self-denial, and we shall grow in strength.

2. Then again, another radical grace to be stablished is *Faith.* Depend upon God altogether; for considering our strength is out of ourselves, and faith being a grace that goes out of ourselves, and lays hold of that that is out of ourselves, faith is necessary to our stablishing, 'Believe, and ye shall be stablished,' saith the prophet, 1 Pet. v. 10.* Though the promise be sure in itself, yet we must be established by faith. How doth God stablish us? By working a spirit of faith; therefore strengthen faith, strengthen all other graces. All have their issue from faith.

3. And faith comes from *sound knowledge;* knowledge therefore hath the

* Qu. 'Isa. vii. 9?'—ED.

name of faith. ' This is eternal life, *to know thee*,' 1 John v. 20 ; strengthen and increase knowledge. Historical faith is nothing but knowledge ; when we know the word of God to be as it is ; and that is the ground of justifying faith and dependence. For the more I know God in covenant as he hath revealed himself, and the more I know the promise, and the more I know Christ, the more I shall depend upon him, and trust in him. ' They that know thy name will trust in thee,' Ps. ix. 10.

Therefore let us labour for certainty of knowledge, that we may have certainty of faith. What is the reason that our faith is weak ? Because men care not to increase their knowledge. The more we know of God, the more we shall trust him. The more we know of a man that we have bonds from, that he is an able man, and just of his word, we shall trust him more, and the more our security upon his promise and bond is increased. So the more we know of God as he hath revealed himself in his word, and his voluntary covenant he hath made with us, and performed in the examples of Scripture, the more we know him, the more we shall trust him.

And this must be a spiritual knowledge ; not only a bare, naked reading, but it must be spiritual, like the truth itself. We must see and know spiritual things in their own light. To know them by their own light is to know them by the Spirit. You know the Spirit dictated the Scripture to the prophets and apostles, the Spirit did all : they wrote as they were acted by the Spirit. Now the same Spirit must inform our understanding, and take away the veil of ignorance and infidelity, I say, the Spirit must do it : we must know spiritual things in their own light.

Therefore a carnal man can never be a good divine, though he have never so much knowledge. An illiterate man of another calling may be a better divine than a great scholar. Why ? Because the one hath only notional knowledge, discoursive knowledge, to gather by strength of parts one thing from another. Divinity is a kind of art, and as far as it is an art to prove one thing by another ; so a natural man may do wonders in it, and yet know nothing in its own spiritual light. That is the reason the devil himself knows nothing. He is a spirit of darkness, because he knows nothing spiritually and comfortably ; therefore as there must be humility and faith for our stablishing, so there must be spiritual knowledge.

It is said here, that God stablisheth us. The same God that stablisheth us, must give us faith whereby we are stablished, and he must give us knowledge. Beg of God that he would vouchsafe us his Spirit. When we read the Scriptures, beg of God that he would open our understanding by his own Spirit, that as there is light in the Scriptures, so there may be in us.

You know an eye must have light before it can see the light. Light is full of discovery of things in itself. I can see nothing except there be light in my eye too. There must be a double light. So there must be a Spirit in me, as there is a Spirit in the Scripture before I can see anything. God must open our eyes, and give us spiritual eye-salve, to see, and then the light of the Scripture, and our light together, is sufficient to found a saving faith, as stablishing faith, on.

What is the reason that a Christian stands to his profession, though he be weak, when the greatest learned men in the world flinch in persecution ? The knowledge of the one is spiritual and heavenly : he hath light in him ; the other hath no divine, spiritual light. When light is joined with light, the light in the soul with the light in the Scripture, it makes men wondrous confident.

1. To this end, labour *to be acquainted with God's word*. Study the Scrip-

tures and other treatises of that kind, that you may be able to hold fast the truth, that it be not wrung from you upon any occasion. And in reading, it is a good course to observe the main, principal, undeniable truths, such dogmatical truths as are clear and evident, and to lay them up ; and oft make queries to ourselves, Do I understand this or no ? Yes, I do, this I know is true. Build on it then, and bottom the soul upon it. And so if it be matter of promises ; these promises are undeniable true, I will stay my soul upon them. And so when we meet with plain evidences in the Scriptures that cross our corruptions, that meet with our known sins, then consider of those places as jewels, and lay them up that you may have use of them as occasion serves.

All things have not an equal certainty in Scripture to us ; some things we may have an implicit faith in ; but the main we must have a clear apprehension of. There are some things that concern teachers more to know than others, by reason of their standing in the church. It is sufficient that in preparation of mind we be ready to embrace further truths that shall be discovered ; but in fundamental truths it is not so. We must have our hearts stablished upon them, that as they are certain in themselves, so they may be certain to us. And often let us examine ourselves, would I die in this, and for this ? would I stand in the defence of this against any ? This will make us make much of so much truth as we know, and labour to grow in truths in that kind.

2. And *take no scandal* * *to hear that any shrink from the profession of the truth, and the maintaining of it, that are of great reputation.* Was Christ the worse for Judas betraying of him, and for Peter's denying of him ? was Paul's truth the worse because he had many enemies, Elymas the sorcerer and others ? Is the truth the worse because there are many that have carnal outward dependence, that seem to shrink when they should stand out ? The truth is not the worse. It is the same truth still. Truths are eternal in themselves, and in the good they bring, if they be believed. The word of God endures for ever. It is not variable, as man is. And therefore be not discouraged, though men discountenance it ; remember whose truth it is, and for whose good it is given. The word of God, it is a soul-saving truth.

3. And *retain the truth in love.* Love is an affection with which we should receive the truth ; or else God will give us over to uncertainties. They in 2 Thess. ii. 10, had the truth, ' but because they received not the love of the truth,' therefore God sent them ' strong delusions,' that they should believe a lie. Oh, how lovely is the truth ! The certainty of our estate in Christ ; the glorious privileges that come by him ; that the gifts of God are without repentance ; that God looks on us, not for foreseen faith or works, but such as he had decreed to work himself,—how comfortable ! how lovely are these truths, being the word of God, notwithstanding some seek to shake them ! These very truths should be retained in love. And indeed, the truth is not in its own place, till it be fixed in the heart and affections, and in a good conscience, which St Paul makes likewise the vessel of the truth ; and those that care not for that, they make shipwreck of the truth.

4. And what truths you know, *labour to practise*, and then you shall be stablished. ' If any man do the will of my Father,' saith our Saviour, John vii. 17, ' he shall know of the doctrine, whether it be of God, or whether I speak of myself.' Be true to known truths ; be not false in disobeying

* That is, ' offence,' = let it not be a stumbling-block.—G.

them. ' To him that hath shall be given,' Matt. xiii. 12. We have a little
stablishing; by an uniform obedience to the truth we shall have more;
God will increase it. I say, let us be faithful to the truths we have, and
not cross them in any sinful course; let us not keep the truth prisoner to any
base affection; as those in Rom. i. 21, *seq.*, that had but the light of nature,
yet because they imprisoned it, and held it in unrighteousness, and lived
in sins contrary to that light that God had kindled in them, though I say
it were but the light of nature, God gave them up to sins not to be named;
much more will he do to us if we withhold the light of the gospel. Take
heed therefore that we enthral not the truth to any base lust whatsoever,
and that is a means to be stablished in the truth.

5. And *be oft in holy conference with others.* Conference, if it be rightly
used, is a special means to stablish. That is most certain, which is certain
after doubting and debate; because that which is doubted of at the first,
we come to be resolved of at the last, comparing reason with reason,
remembering always that of St Ambrose, that there must not be striving
for victory, but for truth (*yyy*). And then when we have tried all, we
must keep that which is good, and not be always as the iron between two
loadstones, haled this way and that way, always doubting and never
resolved; there must be a time of resolution. This the apostle observes
to be an excellent way of stablishing, oft to confer of things doubtful.

6. And labour *to get experience of the truth in ourselves;* nothing stablisheth ⸢more than experience. Our Saviour Christ, in John vi. 68, when
many left him out of dulness, not understanding the spiritual things that he
taught (as many whose wits will serve for matters of the world, and to make
them great amongst men, but when they come to heavenly things they have
no understanding, they cannot apprehend them) he asks his disciples,
' Will you go away also?' John vi. 67. Peter, who had his heart opened by
the Spirit of God, saith he, ' Lord, whither shall we go? thou hast the
words of eternal life;' insinuating, that the experience that he had of the
power of that truth that Christ taught, did so establish him in the present
truth, that with a holy kind of indignation at the question, he replies,
' Whither shall we go? thou hast the words of eternal life.' I have found
thy words to have a spiritual life in them. So when we come once to have
an experimental knowledge of the truths we learn, then our hearts are
stablished. Indeed, then it is an ' ingraffed word,' as St James saith, i. 21,
then the word is true leaven, when it altereth and changeth the soul. In
such a case there is no separating from fundamental truth, when it is one
with ourselves, and digested into us.

7. And *pray to God oft,* as David did, Ps. lxxxvi. 2, *seq., to knit our
hearts to fear his name.* Lord, my heart is loose and ready to fall off of
itself, Oh, knit my heart! It is unsettled, Oh, settle my unsettled heart!
settle my judgment and affections. This should be our meditation.

8. And because it is God that stablisheth, *alway maintain spiritual poverty
in the soul,* that is, a perpetual dependence upon God. See the insufficiency
that is in ourselves, that we cannot stand out. What is the reason that
God suffers great men to fall from the defence of the truth, and from the
profession of it in their lives, as we see it in the case of Peter? To shew,
that we stand not by our own strength. Therefore we should be always in
this temper of spiritual poverty, to know that as Samson's strength was in
his hair, so our strength is in God. God is my strength, of myself I have
no strength. And therefore upon every new defence of the truth, when we
are called to it, we should lift up ejaculations, and dart up strong desires to

God, that God would strengthen and stablish our souls, that we may not be traitors to the truth, but that we may stand to it; for in his own strength shall no man be established.

9. And *grow every day more and more in detestation of a lukewarm temper.* Your *Ancipites,* as Cyprian calls them (*zzz*), your doubtful flatterers of the times, that have their religion depending upon the state and the times, that are neither fish nor flesh, bats, as we say, that are neither mice nor birds, but of a doubtful religion, that out of carnal policy are fit to entertain anything; Oh, this is a devilish temper! Howsoever we, in our lukewarm disposition, value the truth, God values it highly. It was purchased by Christ's blood, and sealed by the blood of martyrs, and shall not we transmit it to our posterity, as safe and as firm, and retain it, come what will? Let us grow into dislike of this temper, a temper that we should as much hate as God hates it; such a temper as is in popery, they are in an *adiaphorisme** temper in religion, a lukewarm, cold temper, a temper of religion according to reasons of flesh and reasons of policy; this will make us be spued out of God's mouth at the last. Do we think to lose religion alone? Oh no; never think to part with religion alone. It came with peace and prosperity, and if we keep not this *depositum,* this truth delivered to us, God will take it away, and that which we betray it for, peace and plenty.

Use 1. Let us labour, therefore, *to be radicated in our judgment, in our affections, in our love, in our faith, in our whole inward man, in the truth revealed.* To be stablished in the truth, it is our best inheritance, it is that will stand by us when all leaves us.

What consistence hath a man out of the truth? Are you rich or honourable? Death will drive you out of all your riches and honours in the world, and strip you of all. What stablishing hath any man but in Christ, in the truth? Take a man that is not bottomed, that is not fastened on Christ, he is the changeablest creature in the world, he is vanity, he is nothing.

Oh! love this state, that we may say, though I be variable here, though I be not so rich as I was, or have not that favour of great ones that I have had; or it is not with me as it hath been, but in all changes I have somewhat that is unchangeable; my soul is settled upon Christ, and upon the truth in him, which is certain. As it is a glorious being to be found in Christ, so it is an eternal and an everlasting being: once Christ's, and for ever his; he will never lose a member. Labour we therefore to be stablished in Christ in all the changes and alterations in the world, and then we shall have something that is unchangeable to fix and stay ourselves upon, even in the hour of death.

Use 2. Again, in the second place, to make an use of examination, I beseech you, *examine yourselves whether you find this stablishing in your hearts or no?* whether your hearts be thus settled or no by the Spirit of God? For, beloved, it is worth the labour and pains to get this grace, and to be assured that you have it. Stablishing in Christ is most necessary, and we stand in need of a great deal of spiritual strength. Do we know what times may come? If dangerous times come, if we be not stablished, what will become of us? Oh! it is a happy estate, a Christian that is stablished in the sound knowledge and faith of Christ! I beseech you therefore consider of it. To give you an evidence or two whereby you may discern whether your hearts be settled and stablished.

1. A man hath the grace of stablishing, and confirmation, *when it is upon the word,* when God doth stablish him upon the promises.

* That is, = 'adiaphorous,' from ἀ?ιαφορος, indifferent.—G.

2. And then, again, *by the effect of it.* A man is stablished by the Spirit of God when his temptations are great, and his strength little to resist, and yet notwithstanding he prevails. Satan is strong. If we prevail against Satan's temptations, we are stablished. God is strong, too strong for us. If we can break through the clouds when he seems an enemy, as Job, ' Though thou kill me, yet will I trust in thee,' Job xiii. 15 : here is a prevailing, a stablished faith. In great afflictions, when clouds are between us and God, when we have faith that will break through those clouds, and see God through them shining in Christ, here is a strong, a stablished faith ; because here is mighty temptations and oppositions.

The strength is known by the strength of the opposition, and the weakness of the party. In the times of martyrdom, there was fire and faggot, and the frowns of cruel persons ; who were the persons that suffered ? Children, women, old men sometimes, all weak. Children, a weak age ; women, a weak sex ; old men, a withered, melancholy, dry age, fearful of constitution. But when the Spirit of God was so strong in young ones, in weak women, in old withered men, as to enable them to endure the torment of fire, to enable them to endure threatenings, and whatsoever, as we see, Heb. xi. 35–37, here was a mighty work in weak men. A man may know here is stablishing grace, because, except there were somewhat above nature, where were a man in such a case ? Then a man may know especially that there is stablishing grace, when he sees somewhat above nature prevailing over the temptation, and confirming the weak nature of man. That is the best evidence we have of God's stablishing grace. Sometimes, them that are stronger at some times are weaker at other times ; but, as I said before, that is to teach them that they have their strength from God.

Use 3. Again, if your hearts be soundly bottomed and founded and grounded on Christ, and the promises of God in him, then *you will be freed at least from all victory and thraldom to base fears, and to base cares, and base sorrows, and base passions.*

A man that hath no settled being on Christ, he is tossed up and down with every passion : he is full of fears and cares for the world, which distract the soul upon every occasion, full of unseasonable and needless sorrows and griefs, which vex and perplex the soul continually. Oh ! how he fears for the time to come ! what shall become of me if such a thing happen ? how shall I be able to live in such a time, &c. ? If he were settled upon God in Christ, that he were his Father : if he were stablished upon the promises of God in Christ, ' I will not fail thee nor forsake thee,' Heb. xiii. 5. ' Fear not, little flock, it is the Father's will to give you the kingdom,' Luke xii. 32 ; and ' Why do you fear, O you of little faith ?' Matt. vi. 30. And, ' He that provides for the birds of the air, for the sparrows, for the lilies of the field, for the poorest creature, will he not much more for you ?' Matt. vi. 25, *seq.* If, I say, we were thus stablished upon Christ, and the promises, there would be no disquietness. Those [are the] fears and griefs that usually perplex and enthral the minds of men ; but where there are these distracting cares, and vexing sorrows, and needless fears, it argues a heart unsettled, though perhaps there may be some faith notwithstanding.

Let us often examine ourselves in this particular : how it is with us when such thoughts arise ? what if trouble should come ? what if change and alteration should come ? He that hath truly settled his heart will say, If they do come, I am fixed, I know whom I have believed ; I know I am a member of Christ, an heir of heaven, that God is reconciled to me in his Son ; I know God hath taken me out of the condition I was in by nature, and hath advanced me to a better condition than I can have in the world ; and when the world shall be turned upside down, I know, when all things fail, I shall stand.

He that his heart can answer him thus, is firm. A good man, saith the psalmist, ' shall not be afraid of evil tidings,' Ps. cxii. 7. Why? His heart is fixed, trusting in the Lord ; and again, in ver. 8, ' His heart is stablished, therefore he shall not be afraid.' If our hearts be established, then we shall not be afraid of evil tidings, nor afraid of wars, nor of troubles, nor of loss of friends, nor of loss of favours, or the like. A righteous man is afraid of no evil. He that hath his heart stablished in Christ, and that hath peace of conscience wrought by the Spirit of God in the promises, his heart is fixed. In all alterations and changes, he hath somewhat that is unchangeable. Even when he ceaseth to be in this world, he hath a perpetual, eternal being in Christ. If he die, he goes to heaven. He hath his being there, where he enjoys a more near communion with Christ than he can have in this world. So that all is on the bettering hand to him that is stablished in Christ ; for it is not an act of one day to be stablished in Christ. God doth it more and more till death, and then comes a perfect consummation of this stablishing. ' We shall be for ever with the Lord,' saith the apostle, 1 Thess. iv. 17. A man then that is stablished in Christ, he is fixed, he is built on a rock ; come what can come, he is not afraid.

Alas ! others that are not so, they are as wicked Ahaz, in Isa. vii. 2 : he was boisterous out of trouble, but in trouble he was as fearful. His heart shook ' as the leaves of the forest,' as the leaves of the forest when the wind comes. They are shaken, because they are not seemly knit to the tree, because they have no stability.

All those whose hearts are not firmly settled in the knowledge of Christ, and the excellent prerogatives that come by him, when trouble come, they are as the leaves of the forest ; or, as you have it in Ps. i. 4, ' As the chaff that the wind driveth to and fro ;' because it hath no consistence, it is a light body, or as ' the dross,' Ps. cxix. 119. ' God shall destroy the wicked as dross.' See how the Scripture compares men, not only for their wickedness, but for their misery, that have no certain being, but on earthly things, though they be never so great, and, as they think, deeply rooted, when troubles come, they are as dross, they are as chaff that hath no firmness before the wind ; when the wind of judgment comes, they are as stubble presently wasted and brought to nothing.

I beseech you therefore, without deceiving of our own hearts, let us enter into our own souls, and examine, for our knowledge first, and then for our boldness.

What dost thou know in religion that thou wouldst die for, or die in ? We are stablished in no more to purpose, than we would die for. Are those truths thou knowest so firmly wrought in thee by the Spirit of God ? Hast thou such experience of them, such spiritual sense and taste of the goodness of them, that thou wouldst be content to part with thy life, rather than to part with them ? Thou art stablished then by the Spirit of God in Christ. I do not speak of every little truth. It needs not that a man should die for that ; but I speak of fundamental truths. Canst thou prove them so out of the Scripture ? and dost thou find the testimony of Jesus Christ witnessing to thy heart that they are true ? Then thou art confirmed and stablished in these truths. I beseech you, let us often examine upon what grounds, and how firmly we know what we know. For, have we not many that, if the adversaries should come, would conform to popery, and join themselves to Rome, because they cannot back their principles with Scriptures, and because they have not a spiritual understanding and apprehension of divine truths? Now he that is stablished stands firm against temptations and against arguments; he will not be won away from his faith, but remains unmoveable.

Therefore, I say, let us often examine ourselves in this particular. I believe this and this against the papists and others. Aye, but how shall I stand out for this? If trials should come, am I able to prove this from the Scriptures so clear as if it were written, as he saith, 'with a sunbeam?' The temptation and assaults of the devil, by men's subtle wits and arguments, will shake our judgments, will hurt more, and if time should come, try us better than fire and fagot. Those spies that brought an evil report upon the land of Canaan, we see that though the land, when it was won, was fruitful enough, and the conquest of it honourable, &c., and therein those spies discovered their own weakness; yet when they had made that shrewd oration, and brought subtle arguments to the eye of flesh and blood, we see, I say, how the people were discouraged, and how they staggered, Num. xiii. 33, *seq.* So a man that is not stablished, he may sometimes have shrewd men to deal withal, perhaps atheists, papists, Jesuits, and the devil joining with them to unsettle men; and they will prevail if men be not well settled and stablished before.

4. And so *for the course of our life and conversation amongst men, we should examine how we are stablished in that;* for we are not only to stand firm in cases of religion, but for causes of honesty. John Baptist was as good as a martyr, though the cause he died for was not religion, but a bold telling of Herod, when he thought he took an unlawful course in keeping his brother's wife, Mark vi. 18.

An honest man may die and suffer much for civil matters. Therefore examine yourselves in this. I have undertaken this cause, upon what ground? in what confidence? how far would I willingly go in it? could I be content to lose the favour of great ones? to die in the quarrel if need be? So far as a man is stablished by God's Spirit, so far is he settled also in this.

You have had heathen men, that would stand out firmly even to the death, against all disfavours, against all losses and crosses for evidence of civil truths, as you have it storied of Papinian, an excellent lawyer, that in the defence of right stood forth to the loss of his life (*aaaa*); and many other the like examples have been. But much more doth the Spirit of God stablish men. This I understand, this is good, this I will stand in, come what will, when I am called to it.

Let us oft call ourselves to an account, what we believe, and upon what ground; what we do, and upon what ground we undertake it; whether on grounds of conscience, or out of spleen and passion. When a man undertakes things on natural grounds, in great temptations, if God do not assist him, he will sink. Take the strongest courages that are, if they have no more but nature, though they may stand out sometimes, to the shame of Christians, yet in some cases they will shew themselves to be but mere natural men.

And therefore labour for the Spirit to stablish us. It is not necessary that we should enjoy our wealth, nor the favour of men, nor our life itself;

but it is necessary that we should keep a good conscience, it is necessary that we should be saved, it is necessary that we should look upon our Judge with confidence at the day of judgment.

It becomes Christians who, besides the light of nature, have the Spirit to stablish them, to be settled in their courses, to look that the conscience be good, the cause good, the aim good. If such a one give over when the cause is clear and good, it is a sign that his heart is not stablished by the Spirit of God in Christ. He hath either corrupt aims, or else he is weak, and understands not the grounds of religion, and the vanity of this life as he should do.

There are none that flinch and give over in a good quarrel, but either it is from hypocrisy, that he pretends to believe in Christ, and life everlasting, and yet he doth not; or else it is from extreme and wonderful weakness, which, if he belong to God, he shall recover, as Peter did, and shall stand more strongly another time.

It is but a forced, a false encouragement and stablishing, when a man that hath not the Spirit of God shall set light by death, though perhaps he die in a good quarrel, and with some comfort. For when a man shall know that after death there is a judgment, and that God hath many things to lay to his charge, when his conscience shall tell him that he is guilty of a thousand deaths, if he be not in Christ, and his pardon sealed by the Spirit of God in the blood of Christ: is it not madness to be courageous in that which he cannot conquer? It is good for a man to be courageous in time of conquest. It is a dastardly thing for a Christian to be cowardly, because he hath death and hell conquered, and everything is made serviceable to help him to heaven. But for another man to set light by these things, it is mere madness. No man but a Christian can be stout and courageous, except it be from a false spirit; especially in things that are above man's natural power, as death, it is eternal, and what man can stand out against the eternal wrath of God?

And therefore those that put on a Roman stoutness and courage, though they seem to have strong spirits, it is but false; either they are besotted with sensuality, or else with a spirit of pride. When they look before them, and see eternity, and see their sins, and that they must all appear at the day of judgment, they cannot be strong. Let us labour therefore to have our hearts stablished by the Spirit of God; and try ourselves often, by propounding queries, how we do things? With what minds and upon what grounds?

5. Again, another evidence whereby we may know that we have spiritual strength and stability in Christ wrought in us by the Spirit of God, is this, *when it makes us desire the coming of Christ;* when it makes us think of death, and of the time to come with joy and comfort; and that for the present it gives us boldness to the throne of grace in extremities. He that in extremity can go to God in Christ, it is a sign his heart is established.

Hypocrites in extremity fly to desperate courses, as Saul and Ahithophel did; but in extremity the soul that is stablished goes to God. ' My God, my God,' saith Christ, Mark xv. 34; so Job, ' Though he kill me, yet will I trust in him,' Job xiii. 15. I say, it is an evidence of a soul stablished upon Christ by the Spirit of God, to have ' boldness to the throne of grace,' Eph. iii. 12, in extremity; nay, when God seems to hide himself, which is the principal extremity of all, as in divine temptations, when God seems to be an enemy. Then for a man to fight and wrestle with God, and tug with the temptation, and not to let God go, though he kill him, this is a true Israel, a conqueror of God ; this is a heart fortified by the Spirit.

It is an argument of a heart established, when, besides for the present, for the time to come, he can cheerfully and boldly think how it will be with him when death shall come, that he shall go to Christ, that the match shall be fully made up that is begun by God between Christ and him (for the contract is in this world, but the nuptials are celebrated in heaven), and in confidence hereof can say, ' Come, Lord Jesus, come quickly,' Rev. xxii. 20.

A heart that is not stablished saith, Oh ! come not. ' Wherefore art thou come to torment us before our time ?' Mat. viii. 29, say the devils to Christ ; so an unstablished heart, at the hour of death, is afraid it shall be tormented before the time : and therefore Come not, come not, saith such a soul. But the soul that is stablished upon Christ, and upon the promises in Christ of forgiveness of sins, and life everlasting by the Spirit of Christ, that saith, ' Come, Lord Jesus, come quickly.'

I have been larger upon this point than I intended. These unsettled times moved me to speak a little more than ordinary, that we might labour to have our hearts stablished, that whatsoever comes, we may have somewhat that is certain to stick to ; that our estate in Christ may be sure, whatsoever becomes of our state in the world otherwise.

VERSE 22.

' *Who hath anointed us, and also sealed us, and given the earnest of the Spirit in our hearts.*' The apostle having formerly laid open the riches of a Christian, in this verse he cometh to shew his strength. His riches consisteth in the promises of God in Christ ; his strength, in being stablished upon those promises. Now that which he had spoken of more generally in the word ' stablishing,' he unfolds in three borrowed terms, ' anointing,' ' sealing,' ' earnest,' implying therein the manner of the Spirit's establishing a Christian. ' He who stablisheth us,' how is that wrought ? By the Spirit ' anointing,' by the Spirit ' sealing,' and by ' the earnest of the Spirit ;' which three terms do all argue assurance. For you know, that in the old law, kings, priests, and prophets were anointed, that is, they were authorised and confirmed in their places. And for sealing, writings among ourselves are ' sealed ' for security. And an ' earnest ' secures contracts and bargains. So that whatsoever may serve to strengthen a Christian's faith and assurance, is here laid down. God, to help our souls by our senses, fetcheth it from human affairs, applying words borrowed from earthly commerce, by a heavenly anagogical* sense to spiritual things.

First, the sure estate of a Christian is set down in the general, by ' stablishing ;' and then in particular, we are ' anointed and sealed,' and have ' the earnest of the Spirit.'

God, in the covenant of grace, doth our part and his own too. He gives faith, and strengthens faith, and seals us. He gives us promises, he doth stablish us upon those promises, and works our hearts to an embracing of them. He anoints us, and seals us, and gives us ' the earnest of the Spirit.' All in the covenant of grace depends upon the faithfulness of God ; and not upon ours, but upon ours dependently, as he is faithful in stablishing us. Now, because the holy apostle would have us settled in the excellency of

* That is, ' ascending.'—G.

the state of a Christian in the covenant of grace, you see how large-hearted he is.   He useth four words implying one and the same thing, ' stablishing,' ' anointing,' ' sealing,' and giving ' earnest;' all of them words used in ratification amongst men.

God is pleased to stoop to speak to us in our own language ; to speak of heavenly things after an earthly manner ; and, therefore, he sets down the certain estate of a Christian by borrowed speeches.   This is a gracious condescending of God, stooping, as it were, lower than himself; and, indeed, so he always abaseth himself when he deals with man, coming down far below himself.

To come to the words in particular.

' *And hath anointed us.*'   This word hath a double reference.   The Holy Ghost carries our minds, first, to the relation and proportion that is between the graces of the Spirit of God, and the ointment with which in former times they were anointed in the Jewish polity.   And it hath reference likewise, and relation, to the persons that were anointed.   The persons were kings, priests, and prophets.

Now God hath anointed us in Christ.   The order is this :

First, Christ himself, as Mediator, is ' anointed with the oil of gladness above his fellows,' Ps. xlv. 7, but *for* his fellows.   The ointment is first poured on the head of spiritual Aaron, and then it runs down to all the skirts of his garment, that is, to the meanest Christian.   Even as the least finger and toe is actuated, and enlivened, and moved by the soul and spirits, that the head and the chief vital parts are ; so every Christian, though he be but as the toe or the foot, yet all have communicated by the Spirit, from Christ the head.   So that the third person, the Holy Ghost, that sanctified the human nature of Christ, that filled and enriched it with all grace, and anointed Christ ; the same Spirit enricheth all his mystical members.   As there is one Spirit in Christ, and that sacred body he took on him ; so there is in the mystical body but one Spirit quickening and enlivening, and moving the head and the members.   He is a head of influence, as well as a head of eminence.   ' Of his fulness we have all grace for grace,' John i. 16.   He is first anointed, and then we are anointed in him.

We will first speak of it as it hath reference to anointment ; and then, as it hath reference to the persons anointed.

In the *first* place then, why are graces here called anointing ?

I answer, they are called ' anointing,' from reference to that composed ointment in Exod. xxx. 22, *seq.*, where you have the composition of the holy oil laid down.

But in particular, you may observe these five particulars in which the relation standeth.

1. *First*, ointment *is a liquor supereminent :* .it will have the highest place, it will have the eminency, and be above all other liquors, and in that respect it is a royal liquor.   So the graces of God's Spirit, they are of an eminent nature.   Spiritual gifts are above the gifts of nature ; and spiritual blessings are above earthly things.   The grace of God is a supereminent, a royal thing.   It will be above all, even above our parts of nature.   If a man have by nature a strong wit, grace will subdue his wit, so that he shall be only witty* to salvation, he shall be only strong to defend the truth, and to do nothing against it : he will subjugate and subordinate his parts and whatsoever excellency he hath by nature to grace, cast all at Christ's feet, ' count

* That is, ' wise.'—G.

all as dung, in comparison of the excellent knowledge of Christ,' Philip. iii. 8. And so again, grace is above corrupt nature, above all our corruptions. It will bring them under, it will subdue corruptions, temptations, afflictions ; any thing, what you will, that is either natural or diabolical ; for grace is spiritual, and that which is spiritual is above all that is below. Grace is of an invincible nature. It will bear sway by little and little. It is little in quantity, but it is mighty in operation. And it is above any outward excellency whatsoever. If a man be a king, if he have this anointing, it makes him better than himself. He is better in that he is a Christian, that he hath this sacred anointing, than for any other created excellency under heaven whatsoever, yea, though he were an angel. Grace hath its derivance* and influence from Christ, who is higher than all, and will be above all ; and so will grace. That is the first. Other liquors, the best of them will be beneath, but oil, it will be above all.

2. It is compared to ointment in the *second* place, because that ointment *is sweet and delightful.* So was the ointment that was poured upon our Saviour by the woman in the gospel. Therefore the spouse in Cant. i. 3, speaking of Christ, ' Because,' saith she, ' of the savour of thy good ointments, thy name is an ointment poured forth, therefore do the virgins love thee.' The graces that are in Christ are so sweet, that they draw the virgins, they draw all believers after him. So grace in a Christian, it makes us sweet ; it sweetens our persons and our actions. It sweetens our persons to God. God delights in the smell of his own graces. It makes us delectable for Christ and his Holy Spirit to lodge in our souls as in a garden of spices. It makes us sweet to the church, to the communion of saints. A gracious man, that hath his corruptions subdued, is wondrous sweet. His heart is as fine silver, every thing is sweet that comes from him. When the woman poured the box of ointment upon Christ, the whole house was filled with the smell thereof, John xii. 3 ; so the whole church is filled with the savour of the graces of good men, that either do live in the present times, or have left their graces in writing to posterity.

A wicked man is an abomination to God, and so are all his actions. He that is in the flesh ' cannot please God,' Rom. viii. 8. A civil man that hath not this anointing, all that he doth is abominable to God. ' All things are unclean to the unclean,' Rom. xiv. 14 : even their best actions have a tincture of defilement from their corruption. Without this ointment we are not sweet, neither to God nor to others. Therefore the Scripture terms men in the state of nature, swine and goats, stinking creatures ; and so indeed they that have not this anointing, they are stinking goats, and shall be set at Christ's left hand, except they have grace to sweeten their understandings and affections, and to draw them higher than nature can.

Likewise grace is full of sweetness to a man's self. It sweeteneth our nature and our actions to ourselves. A ' good conscience' being privy to itself of the work of grace, ' is a continual feast,' Prov. xv. 15. The conscience of a Christian, once renewed by grace, enlargeth the soul, and fills it with sweet peace and joy in believing.

3. Thirdly, the graces of the Spirit are called anointing, *because anointing strengthens.* Therefore, usually warriors and combatants, among the heathen, that were to encounter, were first anointed. So there is a spirit of strength in all those that are true Christians, which they have received from God, whereby they are able to do that that worldlings cannot do. They are able

* That is, ' derivation.'—G.

to deny themselves, to overcome themselves in matters of revenge, &c., they are able to want and to abound, to bear crosses, to resist temptations, and, as the apostle saith, 'able to do all things,' Philip. iv. 13. Nothing can stand in the way of a gracious man, no, not the gates of hell. He that is in him, grace is stronger 'than he that is in the world,' 1 John iv. 4. The least measure of grace, though it be but as a ' grain of mustard seed,' is stronger than the greatest measure of opposition, though strengthened with all the power of hell.

4. In the fourth place, ointment *makes the joints of the body nimble.* So this spiritual anointing it oils the joints of the soul, as I may say, and makes them nimble and ready to serve God ' in newness of Spirit, and not in the oldness of the letter,' Rom. vii. 6. God's people are called ' a willing people,' Ps. cx. 3, and a cheerful people, ready to every good work. And there is good reason for it ; for they have an inward spiritual anointing, that makes them active and nimble in everything they do. That Spirit that sanctifieth them, that spirit telleth them what Christ hath done for them, that ' there is no damnation to them,' Rom. viii. 1, that God is reconciled to them, that they are freed from the greatest dangers, that all is theirs, and so their joy and nimbleness is from good reason, and there is a spirit of love in them unto God and Christ, which makes them nimble. When a man is without grace, he goes lumpishly and heavily about the service of God. He is drawn and forced to prayer, and to hearing, and to conference and meditation : he is dead and dull, and frozen to good works. But when a man hath received this sweet anointing of the Spirit, his heart is enlarged to all duties whatsoever, he is prepared to every good work.

5. Again, *oil makes cheerful.* So doth grace. It makes cheerful in adversity, cheerful in death, cheerful in those things that dismay the spirits of other men ; so much grace, so much joy. For even as light and heat follow the fire, so the spirit of joy doth follow this spiritual anointing. Conscience of the interest he hath in the favour of God in Christ, and the evidences of grace stamped upon his heart, and an assurance of a better estate in the world to come, wonderfully enlarge the soul with spiritual joy. That which makes a man lumpish, and heavy, and earthly, is not the Spirit of God. The Spirit of God is a Spirit of joy, and it puts a gracious cheerfulness in the heart of a Christian. If there be mourning, it is that it may be more cheerful ; for ' light is sown to the righteous,' Ps. xcvii 11, sometimes in mourning. ' God loves a cheerful giver,' 2 Cor. ix. 7, and a cheerful thanksgiver ; all must be sweetened with cheerfulness. Now this comes from the Spirit of God ; and he that is anointed with the Spirit, in some measure partakes of spiritual joy and cheerfulness.

6. Again, ointment, you know, *is of a healing nature,* as balm and other sweet ointments have a healing power and virtue. The Scripture makes mention of the ' balm of Gilead,' Jer. xlvi. 11 ; so grace hath a healing power. Repentance ! That is of a purging, spiritual joy, of a healing nature. There must, you know, be first a cleansing, and then a healing and strengthening ; so some graces are purgative and cleansing, some again are strengthening and healing. Repentance is a good purgation. It carries away the malignant and evil matter. But the cordial that strengthens the soul is joy. ' The joy of the Lord is your strength,' Neh. viii. 10. And so the grace of faith and love tend to cherish and corroborate the soul, so that, I say, these graces, this balm of the Spirit, hath a special sovereign power to heal us, to heal us both from the guilt of sin, and from the

dominion, and rule, and filthy stain of sin. It hath both a purging and a cordial virtue.

Thus you see, that upon good grounds the graces of God's Spirit that he communicates to the elect, and only to them that are in Christ, they are called 'anointing;' and they will have the effect of an ointment in us, if we receive this anointing.

Let us therefore try ourselves by these, whether we be anointed or no. What cheerfulness is there? What joy? What strength? What nimbleness to that which is good? What sovereignty hath grace in our hearts? You have a company that profess religion, but make it serve their own turn, that make heaven to come under earth, that make the service of God to stoop to other ends. Beloved! grace it is a superior thing, and religion makes all subordinate. Grace, and religion, wheresoever it is in truth, is of a ruling nature; and so it is sweet, and it is strong wheresoever it is. It is curing, and purging, and cleansing wheresoever it is. Therefore, I beseech you, let us not deceive ourselves.

I need say no more of the point; you may enlarge it in your own meditations. I come to the persons.

As this anointing hath reference to the ointment, so it hath relation to *the persons that were anointed.*

Now the persons anointed were first dedicated by anointing; they were consecrated to God, and separated from the world. And as they were dedicated and separated, so they were dignified by this anointing. It raised them above the common condition. And likewise with this anointing God gave them qualifications suitable.

You have three eminent persons that were anointed, and so raised above the common condition of other men.

Prophets, to teach the people.

Priests, to offer sacrifice.

Kings, to govern them.

Now Christ is principally all these. He is the principal Prophet of his church, 'the Angel of the covenant,' Gen. xxxii. 24, 25–29. He is 'Logos,' the Word, John i. 1, because as the inward word, the mind of a man, is known by the outward word, so Christ is called the Word, because, as a Prophet, he discovers his Father's mind, and makes known his Father's will unto us.

And he is the great High Priest. He makes atonement between God and us; he stands between his Father and us.

And he is the great King of his church, that rescues it from all its enemies, to protect and defend it.

But as Christ hath received this anointing primarily, and 'above his fellows,' Ps. xlv. 7, yet, as I said before, he hath received it *for* his fellows. Every Christian hath his anointing from Christ's anointing: all our graces and all our ointment is derived from him. 'He,' saith the apostle, Rev. i. 5, 'hath loved us, and washed us in his blood.' He loved us first, which is the cause of all, and then he washed us in his blood. He did not only shed his blood for us, but he 'washed us in his blood.' He hath applied his blood to our souls, and by applying that and sprinkling it upon our souls, 'he hath made us kings and priests to God his Father,' Rev. i. 6. And indeed, the great King of heaven and earth, he is and will be attended upon by none but kings and priests. He hath no servants but such as are anointed. He is followed of none but eminent persons, such as are separated from the world, and dignified above all other people; for the glory of his followers tends to his honour.   Therefore those whom God chooseth to be his attendants, he qualifies them, gives them the hearts of kings, royal qualifications, and the hearts of priests, and the hearts of prophets. But this in the general.

To shew it therefore in particulars.

A Christian is *anointed :* he is a person severed from the world, dedi‑ cated to God, and dignified above others, and that from good reason, be‑ cause God hath given him an inward qualification, which is the foundation of all.

1. And first, he is a *true prophet*, for he hath received ' the anointing' of the Spirit, 1 John ii. 27, whereby he is enabled to discern of things.   He knows what is true honour, to be the child of God ; he knows what is true riches, grace ; he knows what is true nobility, to be ' born of God,' 1 John ii. 29 ; what is true pleasure, ' peace of conscience, and joy in the Holy Ghost,' 1 Thess. i. 6 ; he can discern between seeming and real things, and only he that hath received this ' anointing of the Spirit.'

And again, as a prophet, he knows not only the things, but the doing of the things.   He hath with the anointing of the Spirit ability to do that which he knows.   The grace of God teacheth him not only the duty, that he should live ' justly, and soberly, and godly,' Tit. ii. 12, but teacheth him to do the things.   For God writes his laws in his bowels, that is, in his affections.   He can love and joy in God, and hate sin, and overcome re‑ venge, &c.   The Spirit sheweth him divine things by a divine light.   He sees heavenly things with a heavenly light ; and divine and spiritual know‑ ledge is a working knowledge, of the same nature with the things known. The poorest Christian in the world, having this anointing, sees good things with such a convincing light, and evil things with such a convincing hatred, that he is doing and acting ; whereas a Christian that hath not the Spirit, he may know heavenly things by a natural light, by a discoursive know‑ ledge.   He may know what he should do, and so perhaps he may talk, but he cannot do ; he may talk of death, but he cannot die ; he may talk and discourse of suffering, but when it comes, he cannot suffer ; he may speak much of patience, but he cannot act patience when occasion is.   A true Christian hath the knowledge of doing things.

And likewise he is able ' to speak a word in due season,' 2 Tim. iv. 2, to reprove, to admonish, to comfort.   Every member in the communion of saints hath some qualification in regard of knowledge, when he is put to it.

But especially he hath received this anointing as a priest and a king.

2. As a *priest*, to stand before God, and to offer up prayers for himself and others.   Every Christian is a favourite in heaven.   He hath much credit there.   He hath God's ear open at all times, and he improves it for the good of the church, for the good of others as well as for his own.   And as to pray for ourselves and others, so to bless ourselves and others, that was one part of the priest's office, and so, as the Scripture saith, we are called unto blessing ; and therefore those that are given unto cursing are not priests.

And again, a Christian that hath received this anointing as a priest, he keeps himself ' unspotted of the world,' James i. 27.   You know, the priests were to touch no unclean thing, nor to defile themselves with any manner of pollution.   So every Christian in some measure is enabled to abstain from the common pollutions of the times, to hate ' even the garment spotted with the flesh,' Jude 23.   He is not carried with the stream of the times ;

he will not converse amiably with those that may stain him, but as his calling leads him, lest he contaminate his spirit.

And likewise a Christian hath his heart always as the ' holy of holies,' that so he may offer up thanks and praise to God. There is a disposition in him always to praise God. As the fire in the sanctuary must never go out, so the fire that is kindled by the Spirit of God in the heart of a Christian, it never goes out. The Holy Ghost maintains it continually. He is ready to praise God upon all occasions ; ready to offer up himself unto God as a sacrifice. The sacrifices of a Christian are a broken heart ; and as in the law, the sacrifices for sin must first be killed, and then offered, so now in the gospel, it is the work of every Christian, to mortify, to kill, and slay those beasts, those corruptions that are in him contrary to God. A Christian must not offer himself to God as a sinner, but he must first slay his corruptions. He must mortify his sins, and then offer up himself slain to God.

Therefore our care must be to mortify every corruption, every faculty of the soul, and every part of the body. We must circumcise our eyes, that they behold not vanity ; and our ears, that they hear not, and delight not in unchaste things ; and our thoughts and every part, our wills and affections, and then offer up soul and body as a living sacrifice unto God, that all may be dedicated and sanctified unto him : and then it is a sweet sacrifice. Then, when a Christian hath dedicated himself to God, it is an easy matter to give him his goods when he calls for them, then he will be ready to let all go, as the apostle saith of the Corinthians,* ' they first gave themselves to God, and then to others,' 2 Cor. viii. 5. Other sacrifices will follow when we have first given ourselves to God. Therefore the first sacrifice is to kill our corruptions, to offer ourselves to God, and then we shall be ready to offer our estates, and to have nothing but at God's disposing. O Lord ! of thy hand I have my body and my life, and my goods and all, I give them unto thee ; if thou wilt have me to enjoy them, I do ; but if thou wilt have them sacrificed, I am a priest, I am willing to offer myself as a burnt-sacrifice to thee even to the death, and all other things when thou shalt be pleased to call for them ; and, indeed, all other sacrifices of our goods, and thankfulness in words, they will easily come off when we have offered ourselves, as I said before.

What is the reason that men will not part with a penny for good uses ? They have not given themselves as sacrifices unto God ; therefore in the Scripture we are pressed to give ourselves unto God first ; and it useth arguments to that purpose ; as that ' we are not our own, but bought with a price,' &c., 1 Cor. vi. 20.

And so for the kingly office.

3. Every Christian by this anointing *is made a king*, Rev. i. 6, ' He hath loved us, and washed us, and made us kings,' &c.

But how are we kings ? To take away an objection that ariseth in the hearts of carnal men. Oh, say they, they talk that they are kings, when perhaps they have not a penny in their purse ; they talk they are kings, when in the mean time they are underlings in the world. Here are kings indeed, think profane, conceited persons.

Indeed, all other things are but shadows ; these be realities. This is a kingdom to purpose. Thou livest by sense and by fancy, or else, if thou hadst the spiritual eye-salve, if thou hadst thine eyes open to see the dignity of a Christian, thou wouldst judge him to be the only king in the world ; and,

* The ' Macedonians,' not Corinthians.—G.

therefore, I do not enlarge the point to set colours upon matters, but indeed I rather speak under. There is no excellency that we can think of in this world that riseth high enough to set out the state of a Christian; he is indeed a king.

For, I beseech you, what makes a king? Victory and conquest, that makes a king. Is not he a conqueror that hath that in him that conquers the world and all things else? Others, that are not Christians, they are slaves to lusts and pleasures. A Christian is chief conqueror in the world, he conquers the world in his heart, and all temptations are inferior to him; he sees them as things that he hath gotten the mastery of; he subdues the principal enemy. A Christian fears not death, he fears not judgment, he fears not the wrath of God. He knows God is reconciled in Christ, and so all things are reconciled with him. God being at peace, all things else are at peace. So he is a conqueror. He hath a kingdom in himself. Others have kingdoms out of themselves, and in themselves they are slaves. He is such a king as hath a kingdom in himself. He hath peace and joy, and rest from base affections and terror of conscience.

Is not he a king that is lord and master of all things? A Christian is master of prosperity. He conquers it, he can make it serve his turn—to be thankful to God, to be ready to distribute. He is master of adversity. 'I can want and I can be abased, I can do all things through Christ that strengtheneth me,' saith blessed Paul, Philip. iv. 12, 13. He is an omnipotent king in some sense, ' he can do all through him that strengthens him.' He hath conquered the king of fears—death. That that makes the greatest monarch in the world to shake and tremble, a Christian can think of with comfort. He can think of God's wrath with comfort appeased in Christ, staunched with his blood. He can think of the day of judgment with comfort, that then his Saviour shall be his judge, and that he shall stand at the right hand of God. He can think of afflictions with comfort; he is sanctified to all things, and all things are sanctified to him, and ' all things shall work for his good,' Rom. viii. 28 ; ' nothing shall be able to separate him from God's love to him in Christ, neither things present nor things to come,' Rom. viii. 38. That which amazeth the Belshazzars of the world, and makes their knees smite one against another, as that handwriting did him ; that which makes others quake to think of, a revenging God, before whom they must appear, and answer for all their miscarriages, and their neglect of precious time, and abuse of their places, they can think of with joy and comfort.

He hath conquered himself and his own heart : he can subdue the carnal part of him, and bring it under the Spirit. All others, though kings, if they be not Christians, are slaves to some reigning lust or other.

He is a king likewise in regard of possession, which is a second thing which makes a Christian an excellent person. As he is a great conqueror, so he is a great possessor ; for ' all is yours,' saith the apostle, ' things present and things to come, life and death, afflictions and crosses, and all is yours,' 1 Cor. iii. 22. How ? To help him to heaven. Things present are his ; comforts are his, if they be present ; afflictions are his, to purge him and fit him for heaven ; things to come are his, heaven is his, and terrors to come, all serve him. Even evil things are his in advantage and success. Though in disposition they be not his, but have an hostile disposition in them, they are all overpowered by the love of God ; and Christ, the king of heaven and earth, overrules all to the good of his. And so all good things are his, though not in civil possession, but as far as the great governor of all things sees fit. What a king is this ! And, therefore, the word is not too great, to say a Christian is a king. He is indeed the most excellent person in the world.

And he hath likewise a kingly spirit, that is, he doth things with love and freedom of spirit that others do upon compulsion, for he hath the royal law of love, as the apostle saith, written in his heart, James ii. 8. What is that ? The royal law of love is this, when a man doth that which he doth from love and from a princely spirit,—when he is not compelled. That which others do not at all, or by force is wrung from them, he doth out of a princely spirit that is in him, because his spirit is enlarged and anointed by the Spirit of God to every good work.

These things might be enlarged, but a taste of them is sufficient, and they are very useful to raise our hearts to consider that there is another manner of state than the world thinks of. There are spiritual and excellent kings and priests ; and this will stand by us when all other excellencies fail, ' All flesh is grass, and as the flower of the grass,' 1 Peter i. 24. But this dignity, this anointing which we have by the Spirit and by the word of God, it endures for ever, and abides to all eternity.

Now, not to go on in more particulars, but to make some use of this. Surely this is true in some degree of every Christian, that he is a prophet, ' to discern of things that differ,' Heb. v. 14 ; and he hath a supernatural, heavenly light answerable to the things, a spiritual light to judge of spiritual things. And he is a priest, to stand before God continually ; and he is a king, by conquest, by possession, by qualification. I say this undoubtedly is true of all spiritual persons, that are anointed. As it is said of Saul, that when he was anointed he had another spirit, 1 Sam. x. 11, so God never makes a Christian but he gives him the spirit of a Christian. God's calling is with qualification. It is not a mere titular anointing, but there is another spirit goes along with this anointing than there was before calling. Though men be trained up from their infancy in the truth, yet when they are anointed by the Spirit of God there will another manner of spirit appear in them than ever was in them before, or than that which is in the world.

I beseech you therefore,—for dignity prepares and stirs up to duty ; a man never so carries himself in his place and condition, as when he thinks of his condition,—oft think of the excellent estate we are advanced to in Christ. It will put us in mind of a qualification and disposition answerable ; that as the apostle oft presseth it, we may ' walk worthy our calling,' Eph. iv. 1, that we may walk worthy of this dignity.

When we are tempted therefore to sin, and to base courses, let us say as good Nehemiah when he was moved to flee, ' what, shall such a man as I flee ?' Neh. vi. 11. So should we say to any temptation to base courses of life, what! shall such a man as I do this ? Why ! if I be a Christian, if I be not only a titular Christian,—which is only sufficient to damn me, and not to do me good,—but if I be a real Christian, I must be a priest, I must keep myself unspotted of the world, and undefiled, and not touch any unclean thing ; I must be in a state and condition to pray to God, ' Shall I regard iniquity, that God should not hear my prayer ?' Ps. lxvi. 18.

If I be a Christian, I am a king ; shall I debase myself ? shall I cast my crown in the dirt ? God hath raised me, and made me an heir of heaven, shall I abase myself to sins, and to base lusts, so that I cannot rule my own members, and yet profess myself to be a king? For a Christian that is a king, that hath a guard of angels about him, that is the most excellent creature in the world, for him to abase himself to the world; he that is bred from heaven, for him to have no higher thoughts than the things below, to have an earthly mind, and earthly thoughts, it is a shrewd presumption that he is but only a titular Christian, and hath not received this inward and spiritual anointing. It was a speech of the martyrs in the primitive church, when they were asked their names, they gave this answer, *Christianus sum*, I am a Christian (*bbbb*), and that satisfied all questions. So when we are basely tempted to courses unbefitting our dignity, answer them from our baptism, I am baptized into Christ, and so am become a Christian, and this is unbeseeming the profession of Christianity.

I beseech you let us remember our calling. We are called to be prophets, kings, and priests, and not only here, but in the world to come we shall be so. We must not think to be kings in heaven, except we begin it here.

It is with a Christian, as it was with David. He was anointed many years before he was actually a king upon the throne, 1 Sam. xvi. 13. While Saul lived, he did not enjoy the kingdom. So we are anointed in this world, in part we are kings while we are here; kings over ourselves, and over the world. A Christian sees all under him that is worldly, he treads the moon under his feet. But our anointing hath then especially its effect when we are in heaven, as David's anointing, it had its special effect when Saul was dead. We must now carry ourselves as those that shall be kings. Those that are not kings here, shall never be kings hereafter; those that are not priests here, shall never walk with Christ in heaven in long white robes for ever. Eternal life is begun here, in all the parts of it.

And therefore I beseech you, if our memories be so shallow that we cannot remember other bonds, let us remember our baptism, let us read our duty in our baptism. What are we baptized into? Into Christ, that is, to take the name of Christ upon us, to be Christians; which name implies these three, to be a king, priest, and prophet. What do we then when we sin? We reverse our baptism in some sort. Let it be an aggravation then when we are tempted to sin; it is treason to God, I shall leave my Captain, under whose banner I have vowed to fight against 'the devil, the world, and the flesh;' and to forsake my colours is the greatest treachery. Yea, it is sacrilege. And so God accounts it, when thou profanest thine eyes and thine ears in seeing and hearing of vanity, as you do when you frequent playhouses and the like. I say, it is sacrilegious. Kings and priests were dedicated persons, and to employ dedicated things about any other business, than to God, is sacrilege; it is a committing of folly with thy soul. Men have slight conceits of religion, and scarce a tincture of it. If they did deeply consider what religion is, that it seizeth upon the soul, that it alters and changeth it, that whosoever will have benefit by the promises, he must have an inward qualification, and be anointed with the Spirit, they would have better conceits of it than they have; and hence it is therefore that men make so little conscience of giving liberty to their ears and eyes to hear and see vanity, and defile themselves in evil courses, and cleave to the occasions of sin.

Let us oft, I beseech you, be stirred up to think of our high prerogatives, with high admiration. What love! what love! hath God shewed, 'that we should be called the sons of God,' 1 John iii. 1, that we should be made kings and priests to God the Father. And if ever you hope to have comfort by religion, you must find this anointing in yourselves, raising you above other men to holy duties, to be kings, and priests, and prophets.

' *Who hath anointed us, and sealed us,*' &c. You see then, a Christian is stablished this way in Christ, because he is anointed by the Spirit of God; he is dedicated and consecrated to God. Hence, before I go on to that which followeth, in that the apostle coupleth anointing, and sealing, and earnest to the promises, observe this briefly,

None have interest in the promises of mercy, none can find comfort by them, but such as find some change in themselves.

The promises of God, as I have often said, are the riches of a Christian, and his inheritance. Take all from him, you must needs leave him this. You cannot take this from him. And as an usurer thinks he is a rich man, though he have not twopence in his house, but all that he hath is in bills and bonds; so a Christian, though happily he have not much in actual possession, yet he is rich in that he hath God's bonds in the promises. But now a man cannot say that he is interested in the promises, that he can lay claim to them, if he be an unfruitful man, an unhallowed man, that hath not the sweet ointment of the Spirit, changing of him, as it is said of Saul, into another man; for God wheresoever he reconciles himself, and gives any promise of favour and mercy, there he works a qualification. Of necessity it must be so, because he is reconciled to amity. Now in friendship there must be a correspondent similitude of disposition and sympathy. Now as long as we are in our natural estate, and remain unhallowed and defiled, we are in such terms as God and we cannot meet in amity; and therefore wheresoever the promises of the favour of God and reconciliation are of force, there must be a change. God, when he intends to shew favour to any, he alters and changeth them, that they may be such as he may have content, and complacency and delight in.

We see then there is a necessity of examining ourselves in this point. If thou be anointed, examine thyself, what inward power of grace thou hast, what sweet work of the Spirit; whether thou find in thee a principle above corruption, that makes thee rule above that which the world is inthralled unto. Undoubtedly as our title to heaven it is out of ourselves, by the promises we have of salvation and reconciliation in Christ; so the evidences must be found in ourselves; there must be anointing, and sealing, and the earnest of the Spirit. Therefore I beseech you, think seriously of what I have delivered of that point before. But we shall have occasion in the particulars after to speak more of this. I go on therefore to the second word,

' *Who hath sealed us.*' The same God that anoints us seals us. Anointing and sealing go both together; both are to secure us our estate in Christ, both wrought by the Spirit of God.

Now Christ is the first sealed, John vi. 27, ' Him hath God the Father sealed.' Christ is sealed to be our redeemer, that is, God hath set apart Christ from others, hath distinguished him, and sealed him, and set a stamp upon him to be the Messiah; sealed him to the great work of redemption, first by the graces of the Spirit; for he is full of them, having received ' the Spirit above measure,' John iii. 34; and not only so, but he sealed him by many miracles, by the resurrection from the dead, by which he was declared to be the Son of God; by the calling of the Gentiles, and by many other things.

Christ being sealed, he sealed all that he did for our redemption with his blood ; and for the strengthening of our faith, he hath added outward seals, the two sacraments, to seal our faith in this blood, and in him who is sealed of the Father.

But here in this place is meant another manner of sealing ; for here is not meant the sealing of Christ, but the sealing of us, that have communion with Christ. The same Spirit that sealed the Redeemer, seals the redeemed.

What is our sealing ?

Sealing we know hath this use.

1. *First* of all, *it doth imprint a likeness of him that doth seal upon the wax that is sealed ;* as when the king's picture or image is stamped or sealed upon the wax, everything in the wax answers to that in the seal, face to face, eye to eye, hand to hand, foot to foot, body to body. So we are said to be sealed, when we carry in our souls the image of Jesus Christ ; for the Spirit sets the stamp of Jesus Christ upon every Christian, so that there is the likeness of Christ in all things ; understanding answers understanding, in proportion. As a child, you know, answers the father; it hath limb for limb, foot for foot, finger for finger, but it is not in quantity, but in proportion and likeness ; so it is in the soul that is sealed by the Spirit, there is a likeness to Christ, something of every grace of Christ. There is understanding of the same heavenly supernatural truths ; there is a judging of things as Christ judgeth ; and the affections go as Christ's do ; he loves that which Christ loves, and he hates that which he hates ; he joys in that which Christ delights in. Every affection of the soul is carried that way that the affections of our blessed Saviour are carried in proportion. Everything in the soul is answerable to Jesus Christ ; and there is no grace in Christ, but there is the like in every Christian in some small measure. The obedience of Christ to his Father even to the death, it is in every Christian. The humility whereby Christ abased himself, it is in every Christian. Christ works in the soul that receiveth him, a likeness to himself.

And this is an undoubted character of a Christian. The soul that believes in Christ doth not only believe in him for his own sake, to be forgiven of his sins ; but together with believing, feeling the forgiveness of his sins, and that Christ hath so loved him, and done such things for him, he is ambitious to express Christ in all things ; and it stirs him up with desire to be like him ; for, thinks he, is there such love in Christ to me ? and is there such grace and mercy in God to me ? and was Christ so good as to do and to suffer such things for me ? Oh ! how shall I improve things for him ! Oh ! that I might be like him ! lovely in his eyes ! This, I say, must needs be so. These desires are undoubtedly universally in the souls of all those that partake of Christ. It is the nature of the thing to be so. We shall desire to be transformed more and more to Christ; every way to bear the image of the ' second Adam,' who is, as the apostle saith, from heaven, heavenly ; and so shall we be heavenly-minded as he was heavenly-minded on earth, talking and discoursing of the kingdom of heaven, and fitting people for the kingdom of heaven, and drawing others from this world to meditate of a better estate. There is a likeness to these in the soul of every believer ; and that is the reason that Christ's offices are put together in all those that he saves, that look, whosoever he is a priest to, to die for their sins —to them he is a prophet to teach them, and a king to subdue their corruptions, and to change them, and alter them, and to rule them by his Spirit.

You have carnal men in presumption, which leads them to destruction ; they sever things in Christ. They will take benefit by Christ, but they care not for his likeness ; they will have him as priest, but they respect him not as a king. Now all that are Christ's have the stamp of the Spirit upon them. There are desires wrought in them by the Spirit of God to that purpose ; and a Spirit of sanctification that makes them every way like Christ in their proportion.

And that is an evidence of the sealing of such a soul, because the soul of itself hath no such impression : for the soul of itself is a barren wilderness, a stone that is cold and incapable of impression. When, therefore, the soul can command nature, being stiff, and hard, and dead, we see an impression of a higher nature, a man may know that undoubtedly the Spirit of God hath been in his soul ; for we see a loving spirit, an humble spirit, a gracious, a believing, a broken spirit, an obedient spirit to every commandment of God, the soul can yield itself wholly to the will of God in all things. Certainly, I say, the Spirit of God hath been here, for these things grow not in a natural soul. A stone, you know, is cold by nature, and if a man feel a stone to be hot, a man may undeniably gather, certainly, the sun hath shined upon this stone. Our hearts are very cold by nature ; undoubtedly, when they are warmed with the love of God, that they are made pliable to duties, the Sun of righteousness, Christ, hath shined on this cold heart. God's Spirit can work on marble, can work on brass, as Jeremiah saith, Jer. vi. 28. It was the commendations of one of the fathers that he could work on brass. God can work on our souls, which are as brass, and make an impression of grace there ; and therefore when a man sees an impression upon such hard metal, certainly he may know that the finger of God's Spirit hath been there. So that the work of sanctification is an undoubted seal of the Spirit of God.

2. A second use of a seal is *distinction*. Seals are given for distinguishing ; for, you know, sealing is a stamp set upon some few out of many. So this sealing of the Spirit, it distinguisheth Christians from others, as we shall see more at large afterwards.

3. Then again, a seal, it serves for *appropriation*,' for men seal those things that are their own. Merchants seal those wares that they either have or mean to have a right unto. Men seal their own sheep and not others, and stamp their own wares and not others. God here stoops so low as to make use of terms that are used in human matters and contracts : and by sealing he shews that he hath appropriated his own to himself, chosen and singled them out for himself to delight in.

4. Again, sealing further serves *to make things authentical, to give authority and excellency to things.* Magistrates and officers go with their broad seal, and deliver things that they would have carried with authority sealed, and the seal of the prince is the authority of the prince. So that a seal is to make things authentical, to give validity to things answerable to the value and esteem of him that seals.

These four principal uses there is of sealing. Now, God by his Spirit doth all these : for God by his Spirit sets the stamp and likeness of Christ upon us ; he distinguisheth us from others, from the great refuse of the world ; he appropriates us to himself, and likewise he authoriseth us and puts an excellency upon us to secure us against all. When we have God's seal upon us we stand against all accusations. ' Who shall separate us from the love of God ?' Rom. viii. 35. We dare defy all objections and all accusations of conscience whatsoever. A man that hath God's seal, he stands impregnable, it so authoriseth him in his conscience; for it is given us for our assurance, and not for God's. God seals not because he is ignorant; he ' *knows* who are his,' 2 Tim. ii. 19.

But what ? Is the Spirit itself this seal, or the graces of the Spirit, or the comforts of the Spirit ? What is this seal ? for that is the question now, whether the Spirit itself, or the work of the Spirit, or the comfort and joy of the Spirit ?

I answer, Indeed, the Spirit of God where it is is a sufficient seal to us that God hath set us out for his: for whosoever hath the Spirit of Christ is his, and whosoever hath not the Spirit of Christ is none of his ; but the Spirit is the author of this sealing, and the sealing that is in us is wrought by the Spirit, so that except you take the Spirit for that which is wrought by the Spirit, you have not the right comprehension of sealing : and so the Spirit, with that which the Spirit works, is the seal, for the Spirit is alway with his own seal, with his own stamp. Other seals are removed from the stamp, and the stamp remains, though the seal be gone ; but the Spirit of God dwells and keeps a perpetual residence in the heart of a Christian, guiding him, moving him, enlightening of him, governing him, comforting him, doing all offices of a seal in his heart, till he have brought him to heaven, for the Holy Ghost never leaves us. It is the sweetest inhabitant that ever lodging was given to. He doth all that is done in the soul, and he is perpetually with his own work in joy and comfort. Though he seems sometimes to be in a corner of the heart, and is not discernible, yet he alway dwells in us ; the Spirit is always with the stamp it sets upon the soul.

What is that stamp, then ? to come to the matter more particularly, what is that that the Spirit seals us with, especially,—what is that work ?

I answer, The Spirit works in this order, for the most part, and in some of these universally :

1. *First*, the Spirit doth, together with the word, which is the instrument of the Spirit, the chariot in which it is carried, *convince us of the evil that is in us, and of the ill estate we are in by reason thereof.* It convinceth us that we are sinners, and of the fearful estate that we are in by sin. This is the first work of the Spirit on a man in the state of nature,—it convinceth us of the ill that is in us, and of the ill due unto us, and thereupon it abaseth us. Therefore, it is called ' the Spirit of bondage,' Rom. viii. 15, because it makes a man tremble and quake till he see his peace in Christ.

2. When the Spirit hath done that, *then it convinceth a man by a better, by a sweeter light, discovering a remedy in Christ,* who is sealed of God, to reconcile God and us. And as he enlighteneth the soul, convinceth it of the all-sufficiency that is in Christ, and the authority that he hath, being sent and sealed of God for that purpose, so he works on the affections, he inclines the heart to go to God in Christ, and to cast himself on him by faith.

Now, when the soul is thus convinced of the evil that is in us, and of the good that is in Christ, and with this convincing is inclined and moved by the Holy Spirit, as, indeed, the Holy Spirit doth all, then upon this the Spirit vouchsafeth a superadded work,—as the Spirit doth still add to his own work,—he adds a confirming work, which is here called ' sealing.' That seal is not faith, for the apostle saith, ' *After* you believed, ye were sealed,' Eph. i. 13. So that this sealing is not the work of faith, but it is a work of the Spirit upon faith, assuring the soul of its estate in grace.

But what need confirmation when we believe ? Is not faith confirmation enough, when a man may by a reflect act of the soul know that he is in the state of grace by believing?

It is true, as the natural conscience knows what is in a man, as the natural judgment can reflect, so the spiritual understanding can reflect; and when he believes, he knows that he believes, without the Spirit, by the reflect act of the understanding, except he be in case of temptation. What needs sealing then?

This act of ours in believing, and the knowledge of our believing, it is oft terribly shaken; and God is wondrous desirous, as we see by the whole passage of the Scripture, that we should be secure of his love. He knows that he can have no glory and we can have no comfort else. And, therefore, when we by faith have sealed to his truth, he knows that we need still further sealing, that our faith be current and good, and to strengthen our faith, for all is little enough in the time of temptation. And, therefore, the single witness of our soul by the reflect act, knowing that we do believe when we do believe, it is not strong enough in great temptations, for in some trials the soul is so carried and hurried that it cannot reflect upon itself, nor know what is in itself, without much ado; therefore, first the Spirit works faith, whereby we seal God's truth, John iii. 33, ' He that believes hath put to his seal that God is true.' When God by his Spirit moves me to honour him by sealing his truth, that ' whosoever believes in Christ shall be saved,' John iii. 18, then God seals this, my belief, with an addition of his Holy Spirit. So that this sealing is a work upon believing; and as faith honours God, so God honours faith with a super-added seal and confirmation.

But yet we [are] not come particularly enough to know what this seal is. When we honour God by sealing his truth, then the Spirit seals us; certainly then the Spirit doth it by presence, by being with us in our souls. What then doth the Spirit work when we believe? How shall we know that there is such a spiritual sealing?

I answer, the Spirit in this sealing works these four things:

First, a secret voice or witness to the soul, that we are ' the sons of God.'

Secondly, a voice or speech in us again to God, causing us to have access to the throne of grace ' with boldness.'

Thirdly, a work of sanctification.

Fourthly, ' peace of conscience, and joy in the Holy Ghost,' Rom. xiv. 17.

By these four ways we may know the sealing of the Spirit after we believe, and that our faith is a sound belief, and that we are in the state of grace indeed.

1. *First,* I say, *the Spirit speaks to us by a secret kind of whispering and intimation,* that the soul feels better than I can express. ' Be of good comfort, thy sins are forgiven thee,' saith he to the soul, Matt. ix. 2, ' I am thy salvation,' Ps. xxxv. 3. There is, I say, a sweet joining, a sweet kiss given to the soul. ' I am thine, and thou art mine,' Cant. vi. 3. God by his Spirit speaks so much. There is a voice of God's Spirit speaking peace to his people upon their believing.

2. And then, *Secondly, the Spirit of adoption stirs up the speech of the soul to God, that as he says to the soul, Because thou believest, now thou art honoured to be my child; so the Spirit stirs up in the soul a spirit of prayer to cry, ' Abba, Father.'* It can go boldly to God as to a Father; for that ' Abba, Father,' it is a bold and familiar speech.

There are two things in a prayer of a Christian that are incompatible to any carnal man : there is an inward kind of familiar boldness in the soul, whereby a Christian goes to God, as a child when he wants any thing goes to his father. A child considers not his own worthiness or meanness, but goeth to his father familiarly and boldly : so, I say, when the Spirit of God speaks to us from God, and tells the soul, ' I am thine,' ' I am thy salvation,' ' thy sins are forgiven thee, be of good comfort : ' and when the soul again speaks to God, when it can pour forth itself with a kind of familiar boldness and earnestness, especially in extremity, and in time of trouble, and can wait in prayer, and depend upon God,—this spiritual speech of God to the soul, and of the soul to God, it is a seal of the Spirit that indeed we are true believers, because we can do that that none can do but Christians. God speaks to our souls, he raiseth our souls, and by his Spirit he puts a spirit of supplication into us, and helps our infirmities ; for we know not what to ask, but he helps our weakness, and enables us to lay out the wants of our souls to God. These are evidences of the presence and of the seal of the Spirit.

3. In the third place, this sealing of the Spirit after we believe, is known *by the sanctifying work of the Spirit :* for, as I told you before in the unfolding of the point, the Spirit seals our spirits by stamping the likeness of the Spirit of Christ on us. So that when a man finds in his soul some lineaments of that heavenly image of Christ Jesus, when he finds some love, he may know by that love that he is ' translated from death to life,' John v. 24 ; when he finds his spirit subdued, to be humble, to be obedient, when he finds his spirit to be heavenly and holy as Christ was ; when he finds this stamp upon the soul, surely he may reason, I have not this by nature ; naturally I am proud, now I can abase myself ; naturally I am full of malice, now I can love, I can pray heartily for mine enemies, as Christ did ; naturally I am lumpish and heavy, now in afflictions, I can joy in the Holy Ghost ; I have somewhat in me contrary to nature, surely God hath vouchsafed his Spirit, upon my believing in Christ, to mark me, to seal me, to stamp me for his, I carry now the image of the second Adam, I know the Holy Ghost hath been in my heart, I see the stamp of Christ there. ' Know you not that Christ is in you, except you be cast-aways ? ' saith the apostle, 2 Cor. xiii. 5. So upon search, the Christian soul finds somewhat of Christ always in the soul to give a sweet evidence that he is sealed to the day of redemption.

4. The fourth evidence that the Spirit of God hath been in a man's heart, *is the joy of the Holy Ghost and peace of conscience.* Sanctification is the ordinary seal that is always in the soul : this is an extraordinary seal, peace and joy. When the soul needs encouragement, then God is graciously pleased to superadd this, to give such spiritual ravishings which are as the very beginnings of heaven, so that a man may say of a Christian at such times that he is in heaven before his time, he is in heaven upon earth. But especially God doth this when he will have his children to suffer, or after suffering, after some special conflict, after we have combated with some special corruption, with some sinful disposition, with some strong temptation, and have got the victory : ' To him that overcometh will I give of the hidden manna, and a white stone, and a new name that none can read it, but he that hath it,' Rev. ii. 17, that is, he shall have assurance that he is in the state of grace, and the sweet sense of the love of God, and that sweet heavenly manna that none else can have. Thus God dealt with Job. After he had exercised that champion a long time, at the last he discovered

himself in a glorious manner to him. So it is usually after some great cross ; or in the midst of some great cross, when God sees that we must be supported with some spiritual comfort, we sink else. Then there is place and time for spiritual comfort, when earth cannot comfort. Thus St Paul in the midst of the dungeon, when he was in the stocks, being sealed with the Spirit, he ' sang at midnight,' Acts xvi. 24, *seq.* Alas! what would have become of blessed Paul ? his spirit would have sunk if God had not stamped it with ' joy in the Holy Ghost,' Rom. xiv. 17 ; and so David, and the ' three young men' in the fiery furnace, and Daniel in the den. God doth then, even as parents, smile upon their children when they are sick and need comfort : so above all other times God reserves this hidden sealing of his children with a spirit of joy when they need it most, some-times in the midst of afflictions, sometimes as a reward when they come out of their afflictions ; sometimes before. So our Saviour Christ had James and John with him upon the mountain to strengthen them against the scandal of suffering after. So God when he hath a great work for his children to do, some suffering for them to go through, as an encouragement beforehand, he enlargeth their spirits with the joy of the Holy Ghost. And sometimes also after a holy and gracious disposition in the ordinances of God, God doth add an excellent portion of his Spirit, a seal extraordinary : for indeed, God thinks nothing enough for his children till he have brought them to heaven, seal upon seal, and comfort upon comfort ; and the more we depend upon him in the means of salvation, and the more we conflict with our corruptions, the more he increaseth the sweet comforts and the hidden manna of the Spirit.

Thus we see how the Spirit seals ; I beseech you, therefore, let us exa-mine ourselves by that which hath been spoken : after we believe, God seals those that do believe. We honour him by believing, he honours us by sealing us with his Spirit. Hath God spoken to thy soul by the wit-ness of the Spirit, and said, ' I am thy salvation,' ' thy sins are forgiven thee ?' doth God stir up thy spirit to call upon him, especially in extre-mity ? and to go with boldness and earnestness to him ? Surely this bold-ness and earnestness is an evidence of the seal of the Spirit ; for a man that hath no seal of the Spirit, he cannot go to God in extremity. Saul in extremity he goes to the witch ; and Ahithophel and Judas in extremity go to desperate conclusions. A man that hath not the Spirit of God speak-ing peace to his conscience, to whom God hath not given the spirit of adoption to cry, ' Abba, Father,' in all manner of exigents, he sinks as lead to the bottom of the sea. So heavy is the soul that is not raised by the Spirit of God, he hath no consistence till he come to the centre, to hell. Did you ever feel the sweet joy of the Spirit after conflict with corruptions, and getting ground of them, and in holy duties, &c. ? It is a sign that God hath sealed you.

But you will say, How can that be a seal that is not always ? A seal continues with the thing. God's children find not peace always. The joy of the Spirit comes after the work of the Spirit : how then can this be a seal ?

I answer, Yes ; for howsoever it be or not alway sensible, yet it is alway a seal. Though we have not always the joy of the Spirit, yet we have the spirit of joy. A Christian hath not the joy of the Spirit at all times, for that is moveable ; but he hath always the spirit of joy, which spirit, though it be not known by joy, yet it is known by operation and working. There is the work of the Spirit, where there is not always the

joy of the Spirit ; and therefore when that fails, go to the work of sanctification, and see what stamp and resemblance of Christ there is ; see if thy
heart be humble and broken, if thou have a loving disposition in thee like
to Christ, that thou hatest that which Christ hateth, that thou seest a
division in thyself. I say, when the joy of the Spirit ceaseth, go to the
work of the Spirit, and to this work of the Spirit, viz., the voice of the
Spirit,—canst thou cry to God with prayer and supplication ? and if thou
canst not pray with distinct words, canst thou mourn and groan to God ?
This sighing and groaning is the voice of God's Spirit, and God knows
the voice of his own Spirit. But for the question propounded : the soul of
a Christian knows that when it finds not extraordinary comfort from God's
Spirit, that God's love is constant. It can reason thus : though I find not
the comfort of the Spirit, yet I have the spirit of comfort, because I had
the Spirit in former times, and God's Spirit is unchangeable, and therefore
though it be not with me now as in those ravishings of the Spirit, yet the
love of God is the same, though my feeling be not the same ; because,
though I be off and on, and my feelings ebb and flow, yet His love is not
so ; and hereupon the extraordinary feeling of the Spirit, which is super-
added as an extraordinary seal, it may be a sound seal of comfort from the
constancy of God who gave it ; and he gave it for this end, that we might
have recourse, and retire back in our thoughts, and argue it was thus and
thus with me. Then we remember the times of old, as David saith, Ps.
lxxvii. 6, and help ourselves with our former feelings. He that alway hath
life, is not always alike stirred. Christ may be begotten and live in us, but
he stirs not always alike. So though the Spirit of sanctification be in us,
and stir in us, yet his stirring is not alike so sweet ; and the stirring of
the Spirit, though it be not alway, yet the Spirit is alway there. So the
soul may have recourse to that which is unchangeable and constant, even
God himself, and his love is as himself.

But to take a Christian in his worst time, in the worst and greatest
afflictions, how shall he know then that he is sealed of the Spirit ? When
corruption, temptation, and affliction meet together in the soul ; when
temptation is joined with our corruption, and afflictions yield ground to
temptations (for Satan useth the afflictions we are in as temptations to
shake our faith), canst thou be a child of God, and be so exercised ? Is
this grace ? So affliction is a weapon to temptation, for Satan to help his
fiery darts with. Now how shall a man know that God hath any part here ?

1. He may know that he is sealed by the Spirit of God, *if he have a
spirit to thwart these,* if he row against the stream, if he go contrary to all
these ; if he find a spirit resisting Satan's temptations, and raising himself
above afflictions, and standing against, and combating with his corruptions,
and checking his carnal soul when it is drawing him down. ' Why art
thou discomforted, O my soul ? ' saith David, Ps. xlii. 11 ; xliii. 5. He
found corruptions, and afflictions, and Satan's temptations working with
them, depressing his soul downwards ; hereupon, having the Spirit in him,
saith he, ' Why art thou disquieted within me ? Trust in God.' He first
chides his soul, ' Why art thou so ? ' and then he lays a charge upon it,
' Trust in God.' So I say, when this is in the soul in the greatest extremity,
when I can check my soul, ' Why art thou thus ? yet trust in God ;'
whatsoever there is in the world, yet there is hope in heaven, though there
be little comfort upon earth ; this is a sign that I am sealed with the Spirit
of God : and thus in the worst temptations that can come, and so in the
worst times, a man may know that he is in the state of grace.

2. One use of a seal, I told you before, was to distinguish. If a man, therefore, find in himself *a distinguishing from the errors of the times* [he may know that he is ' sealed ']. ' Many walk,' saith the apostle, ' of whom I have told you oft, their end is damnation, their belly is their god, they mind earthly things,' Philip. iii. 18, 19. But what did St Paul in the mean time ? what did the Spirit work in him ? ' But our conversation is in heaven,' saith he. The whole world was overspread with a deluge of sin; but what was Noah and his family ? God by his Spirit distinguished them ; they went a contrary course to the world ; and Lot in Sodom. So a man may know that he is sealed, when the Spirit leads him another way, that he is not led with the errors of the times.

Thus we have unfolded to you the sealing of the Spirit ; and you see the Spirit of God not only anoints, but seals. Now we should labour to have our hearts thus sealed by the Spirit. Can we desire and never be at quiet till our instruments be sealed, till our acquittances, till our charters be sealed ? and shall we be patient not to have our souls sealed ?

Let us labour by all means to have the image and likeness of Christ stamped upon our souls especially. That is wondrous comfortable when we can find somewhat in us like to Jesus Christ.

To encourage us to this, let us consider, that death and judgment will come, and God will set none at his right hand but his sheep that have his mark. Those that he sets his stamp and image upon, those he will set on the right hand in the day of judgment.

And how comfortably in the hour of death can the soul commend itself to God, when it sees itself stamped and sealed by the Spirit of Christ ! when he can say to Christ, ' Lord Jesus, receive my soul,' Acts vii. 59, that thou hast redeemed by thy blood, that thou hast sealed by thy Spirit, and that thou hast set thine own stamp upon, acknowledge thine own likeness, though it be not as it should be ; what a comfort, I say, hath the sealed soul at the hour of death ! And so in all other extremities, and in times of trouble and danger, those in whom God sees his own image and likeness, he will own, and to those he will always shew a distinct and respective love in hard times.

What a difference is between that soul and others in the time of affliction, as in the time of pestilence and war. The soul that is sealed knows that he is marked out for God, for happiness in the world to come, whatsoever befalls him in this world ; and he knows that God in all confusion of times knows his own seal. Those that are sealed, God hath a special care of, I say. Therefore in Ezek. ix. 6, they are said to be marked in their foreheads ; not that there was any visible mark on them, but it is a phrase to signify what special care God had of his people, specially in times of destruction : God will as it were set them out in those times, and make special provision for them. Thus Josiah was taken away from the evil to come ; and Lot was taken out of Sodom when fire and brimstone was to come from heaven ; and Pella, a little village, was delivered when the general destruction came upon Jerusalem (*cccc*). So that, I say, God hath a special care of his little ones in this life ; and if he take them away, yet their death is precious in his sight. He will not part with them but upon special consideration ; he sees if they live it will be worse for them ; he sees it is better for them to be gathered to himself, and to ' the souls of men made perfect in heaven.'*

* Cf. with Catlin's reflections on the death of Sibbes himself. Appendix to Memoir, A. vol i. pp. cxxxix-xli.—G.

And as he hath a special care of them in regard of outward miseries and calamities, so in regard of spiritual contagion and infection, as Rev. vii. 3, *seq.* There God's holy ones were sealed, so many of such a tribe, &c., which is to signify to us, that God hath always some that he will keep and preserve from the universal infection and contagion of Antichrist in the worst times. God hath always a church in the worst times, in the obscurest age of the church, eight or nine hundred years after Christ, especially nine hundred years [after], when Egyptian darkness had overspread the world, and there was little learning and goodness in the world,* God had always sealed ones, marked ones, that he preserved from the danger of dark times ; and so he will always have a care of his own, that they be not led away with that soul-hurting error, popery ; another manner of mischief than men take it for. The Scripture is more punctual in setting down the danger of those, especially in lighter times of the church, that are carried away with that sin, than any other sin whatsoever ; they have a contrary mark. Those that have the mark of the beast, it is contrary to the mark of Christ : it is far from being the mark and seal of the Spirit, that implicit bloody faith. Theirs is the bloody church, pretend what they will, and they stand out to blood in the defence of all their cruel, superstitious, and bloody decrees. Those persons, I say, that are deeply dyed in popery, that have the mark of the beast, they are in a clean opposite condition to those that are marked with the Spirit, that Christ marks for his.

Let us not fear therefore, I say, if we have the Spirit of God stamped upon us, though in a little measure : if it be true, let us not fear death ; Christ knows his own mark even in death, and out of death. And let us not fear afflictions nor evil times, Christ will know his seal. He hath a book of remembrance for those that are his, Mal. iii. 16 ; for those that mourn for the sins of the times, and when he gathers his jewels, those shall be his. He will gather his jewels as a man in his house gathers his jewels ; he suffers his luggage to burn in the fire. So God in common calamities, he suffers luggage, wicked men to go to wreck, but he will free his own.

Let us labour therefore for this seal, to have our souls stamped with the Spirit of God, to have further and further evidence of our state in grace, that in the time of common calamity we may be free from danger, free from error and destruction.

But you will say, What shall I account of it, if there be but a little sign of grace ?

Be not discouraged, when the stamp in wax is almost out, it is current in law. Put the case the stamp of the prince be an old coin (as sometimes we see it on a king Harry groat†), yet it is current money, yea, though it be a little cracked. So, put the case the stamp of the Spirit be, as it were, almost worn out, it is our shame, and ought to be our grief that it is so, yet there are some evidences, some pulses, some sighs and groans against corruption : we mourn in our spirits, we do not join with corruption, we do not allow ourselves in sin. There is the stamp of the Spirit remaining, though it be overgrown with the dust of the world that we cannot see it.

Sometimes God's children, though they have the graces of the Spirit in them, yet they yield so much to their corruptions, that they can read nothing but their corruptions. When we bid them read their evidences, they can see nothing but worldliness, nothing but pride and envy, &c. Though there be a stamp on them, yet God holds the soul from seeing it, so that they can see nothing but corruption. This is for their negligence. God gives

* That is, the ' Middle or Dark Age,' so-called.—G.   † That is, Henry VIII.—G.

them up to mistake their estates, because they will not stir up the graces of the Spirit, because they grieve the Spirit, and quench the Spirit, by doing that which is contrary to the Spirit.

Let us therefore, that we may have the more comfort, preserve the stamp of the Spirit fresh, by the exercise of all grace, and communion with God, and by obedience, and by faith. Honour God by believing, and he will honour thee by stamping his Spirit on thee more and more. And let this be our work every day to have the stamp of the Spirit clear. Oh! what a comfort it is to have this in us at all times! If a man have nothing in him better than nature, if he have nothing in him in regard of grace, if he have not Christ's image upon his soul, though he be a king, or an emperor, yet he shall be stript of all ere long, and be set on the left hand of Christ, and be adjudged to eternal torments.

It is the folly of the times come up of late, there is much labouring for statues, and for curious workmanship of that kind, and some pride themselves much in it, and account it great riches to have an old statue. Alas! alas! what a poor delight is this in comparison of the joy that a Christian hath by the seal of the Spirit? and what is this to the ambition of a Christian, to see the image and representation of Christ stamped in his soul? that he may be like the ' second Adam,' that he may be transformed more and more by looking on him, and seeing himself in him, to love him, considering that he hath loved us so much (for we cannot see the love of Christ to us, but we must love him the more, and be transformed into him). Now this transforming ourselves into the image of Christ is the best picture in the world; therefore labour for that every day more and more.

There is besides the common broad seal of God, his privy seal, as I may call it. It is not sufficient that we have the one, that we have admittance into the church by baptism, but we must have this privy seal which Christ sets and stamps upon the soul of the true Christian. Alas! for a man to build only on the outward seals, and outward prerogatives, (which in themselves are excellent, yet) the standing upon them betrays many souls to the devil in times of distress.

It is another manner of seal than the outward seal in the sacrament that will satisfy and comfort the conscience in the apprehensions of wrath at the hour of death or otherways. It must be this privy seal, and then comes the use of those public, open, known seals, the broad seals; then a man with comfort may think upon his baptism, and upon his receiving the communion, when he hath the beginnings of faith wrought in him by the Spirit of God. When a man finds the beginnings of faith in him, then he may make use of the broad seal to be a help to his faith.

We must not be so profane as to think slightly and irreverently of God's ordinances. They are of great and high consequence; for when Satan comes to the soul, and shakes the confidence of it, and saith, Thou art not a Christian, and God doth not love thee; why! saith the soul, God hath loved me, and pardoned my sins; he hath given me promises, and particularly sealed them in the sacrament; here is the excellency of the sacrament, it comes more home than the word, it seals the general promise of God particularly to myself. I am sealed in the sacrament, and withal I find the stamp of the Spirit in my heart; and therefore having the inward work of the Spirit, and God having fortified the inward work, and strengthened my faith by the outward seal, I can therefore stand against any temptation whatsoever. They are excellent both together, but the special thing that must comfort, must be the hidden seal of the Spirit.

Let us labour therefore to be sealed inwardly, and observe God's sealing-days, as we use to speak, which though it may be every day if we be in spiritual exercises, yet especially on the Lord's day ; for then his ordinance and his Spirit go together.

Now as there is a sealing of our estates that we are the children of God, so there is of truths, and both are in the children of God ; as for instance, this is a truth, ' Whosoever believes in Christ shall not perish, but have everlasting life,' John iii. 16. Now the same Spirit that stirreth up the soul to believe this, seals it in the soul, even to death, and in all times of temptation ; and likewise there is no promise but upon the believing of it ; it is sealed by the Spirit upon the soul ; for those truths only abide firm in the soul which the Spirit of God sets on.

What is the reason that many forget the comforts and consolations that they hear ? Because the Spirit sets them not on, the Spirit seals them not. What is the reason that illiterate men stand out in their profession to blood, whereas those that have a discoursive kind of learning they yield ? The reason is this, the knowledge of the one is sealed by the Spirit, it is set fast upon the soul, the Spirit brings the knowledge and the soul close together ; whereas the knowledge of the other is only a notional swimming knowledge ; it is not spiritual.

Those therefore that will hold out in the end, and not apostatise, those that will stand out in the hour of death against temptation, and those that will hold out in the time of life against solicitations to sin, they must have a knowledge suitable to the things they know, that is, they must see and know heavenly things by a heavenly light, spiritual things by the Spirit of God.

And therefore when we come to hear the ministers of God, we should not come with strong conceits, in the strength of our wit ; but with reverent dispositions, with dependence upon God for his Spirit, that he would teach us together with the ministers, and close with our souls, and set those truths we hear upon our souls ; we shall never hold out else. And it must be the Holy Ghost that must do this ; for that which must settle and seal comfort to the soul, must be greater than the soul, specially in the time of temptation, when the terrors of the Almighty are upon us, and when the hell within a man is open, when God lays open our consciences, and ' writes bitter things against us,' Job xiii. 26, and our consciences tell us our sins wondrous near ; they are written as it were ' with a pen of iron, and the point of a diamond, upon our souls,' Jer. xvii. 1 ; now I say, those truths that must satisfy conscience that is thus turmoiled, must be set on by that which is above conscience. The Spirit of God who is above our spirits, can only set down our spirits, and keep them from quarrelling and contending against the truth, and quiet the conscience ; and this the Spirit doth when it sets the truth upon the soul.

And therefore when our souls are disquieted and troubled, and we hear many comfortable truths, let us lift up our prayers to God, let there be ejaculations of spirit to God. Now Lord, by thy Holy Spirit set and seal this truth to my soul, that as it is true in itself, so it may be true to me likewise.

This is a necessary observation for us all. Oh, we desire all of us in the hour of death, to find such comforts as may be standing comforts, that may uphold us against the gates of hell, and against the temptations of Satan, and terrors of conscience ; why ! nothing will do this but spiritual truths spiritually known ; nothing but holy truths set on by the Holy Spirit of God.

But what course shall we take when we want comfort ? when we want joy and peace ?

In the first [Epistle] of John, v. 7, 8, there are ' three witnesses in heaven, and three in earth,' to secure us of our state in grace, and the certainty of our salvation. The three witnesses upon earth are ' the Spirit, the water, and the blood, and these three agree in one;' and the ' three that bear witness in heaven,' are ' the Father, the Word, and the Holy Ghost;' and the three on earth, and these three in heaven agree in one (*dddd*).

Now the Spirit is the feelings and the sweet motions of the Spirit. The water may well be that washing of the Spirit, sanctification. The blood is the shedding of the blood of Christ, and justification by it. When therefore we find that part of the seal, that extraordinary seal that I spake of before, the joy of the Spirit of God, that it is not in us, what shall we do ? Shall we despair ? No ; go to the water. When we find not spiritual joy and comfort, when the witness of the Spirit is silent, go to the work of the Spirit in sanctification.

Aye, but what shall we do if the waters be troubled in the soul, as sometimes there is such a confusion in the soul that we cannot see the image of God upon it in sanctification, we cannot see the stamp of God's Spirit there, there is such a chaos in the soul ? God can see somewhat of his own Spirit in that confusion, but the spirit itself cannot.

Then go to the blood of Christ ! There is always comfort. The fountain that is opened for ' Judah and Jerusalem' to wash in is never dry. Go therefore to the blood of Christ, that is, if we find sin upon our consciences, if we find not peace in our consciences, nor sanctification in our hearts, go to the blood of Christ, which is shed for all those that confess their sins, and rely on him for pardon, though we find no grace. For howsoever as an evidence that we are in Christ, we must find the work of the Spirit; yet before we go to Christ it is sufficient that we see nothing in ourselves, no qualification ; for the graces of the Spirit they are not the condition of coming to Christ, but the promise of those that receive Christ after. Therefore go to Christ when thou feelest neither joy of the Spirit, nor sanctification of the Spirit ; go to the blood of Christ, and that will purge thee, and wash thee from all thy sins.

This I only touch for a direction what to do when our souls want comfort, when perhaps we cannot see the seal of the Spirit in sanctification so clearly.

To go on now to the next.

' *And given us the earnest of the Spirit.*' Here is the third word borrowed from human affairs, to set out the work of the Spirit in our souls. ' Anointing' we had before, and ' sealing'; now here is ' earnest.'

The variety of the words shews that there is a great remainder of unbelief in the soul of man, that the Spirit of God is fain to use so many words to express God's dealing to the soul to bring it to believe, to be assured of salvation. And indeed so it is, howsoever we in the time of prosperity, when all things go well with us, we are prone wondrously to presume, yet in the hour of death, when conscience is awakened, we are prone to nothing so much as to call all in question, and to believe the doubts and fears of our own hearts, more than the undoubted truth and promise of God. Therefore God takes all courses to stablish us. He gives us rich and precious promises, he gives us the Holy Spirit to stablish us on the promises, he seals us with his Spirit, and gives us 'the earnest of the Spirit,' and all to settle this wretched and unbelieving heart of ours.

So desirous is God that we should be well conceited of him, he loves us better than we love ourselves. He so much prizeth our love, that he labours by all means to secure us of his love to us, because except we know his love to us, we cannot love him again, and we cannot joy in him, &c. But that only in the general.

Here is earnest, and 'the earnest of the Spirit,' that is, in plain terms, he gives us the Spirit with the graces and comforts of it, which doth in our hearts that which an earnest doth amongst men.

But what is the Spirit an earnest of?

It is an earnest of our inheritance in heaven, of our blessed estate there. We are sons now, but we are not heirs, invested into the blessed estate we have title to. God leaves us not off in the mean time while we are in our pilgrimage. He keeps not all for heaven, but he gives us somewhat to comfort us in our absence from our Husband, from our Lord and King, Christ. He gives us the earnest of the Spirit, that is, he gives the Holy Ghost into our hearts, which is the earnest of that blessed, everlasting, glorious condition which we shall have in heaven hereafter. That is the meaning of the words.

In what regard is the Spirit called an 'earnest?'

1. *First of all*, an earnest is for *security of bargains and contracts*. So the Holy Ghost assures the soul of salvation, being present with his graces and comforts ; the Holy Ghost is given for security.

2. *Secondly*, an earnest is *part of the whole bargain*. Though it be a very little part, yet it is a part ; and so the Spirit of God here, and the work of the Spirit, and the graces and joy of the Spirit, it is a part of that full joy and happiness that shall be revealed. The Spirit dwells not fully in any one. He dwelleth no further than he sanctifieth and reviveth. But that is an earnest for the time to come, that the Spirit shall be all in all, wherein we shall have no reluctancy, nor nothing to exalt itself against the sure regiment* of the Spirit.

3. *Thirdly*, an earnest is *little in comparison of the whole bargain*. So the work of the Spirit, the comforts, the joy, the peace of the Spirit, it is little in comparison of that which shall be in heaven, in regard of the fulness of the Spirit which we shall have there. An earnest, though it be little in quantity, yet it is great in security and assurance. A shilling may secure a bargain of a thousand pounds perhaps ; so the Spirit, it is little in quantity it may be, but it is great in assurance. And as we value an earnest, not for the bigness of the piece ; for, alas! it may be it is but little ; but we value and esteem it for that which it is an earnest of. So the work of the Spirit, the joy and peace of the Spirit, the comforts of the Spirit, though they be little, yet they are great in security, and are to be prized according to that excellent bargain and possession, of which they are an earnest.

4. *Fourthly*, an earnest is given *rather for the security of the party that receives it, than in regard of him that gives it ;* so God gives 'the earnest of the Spirit,' grace and comfort ; this is not so much in regard of God, for God meaneth to give us heaven and happiness. (He hath passed his word, and he is master of his word, he is 'Jehovah,' that gives a being to his word as well as to every other thing.) But, notwithstanding, having to deal with doubtful, mistrustful persons, he doth it for our security, he regards not himself so much, but us. He works answerable to his own

* That is, 'government.'—G.

greatness, strongly ; bnt he speaks according to our weakness ; and therefore here is the term of ' earnest' borrowed for this purpose.

5. And *lastly*, an earnest *is never taken away, but it is made up with the
bargain.* So it is with the Spirit of God ; the graces and comforts of it are
never wholly taken from a Christian, but accomplished in heaven. ' I will
leave you the Comforter,' saith our Saviour Christ, ' that shall abide with
you for ever,' John xiv. 16.

So that in these and such like other respects, the Spirit of God by itself,
together with the graces of it, and the comforts it bringeth, for they go both
together, are called an ' earnest.'

Hence then, having thus cleared the words, we may observe some particular doctrines. As first, I observe from the first property of an earnest,
that it secures the whole bargain, this, that

Obs. A Christian ought to be, and may be assured of his estate in grace.

Because, as I said before, an earnest is given for security, and that not
so much for God's sake, as for our sakes ; this then must needs follow, either
none have this earnest, or those that have it may be assured, or else God is
fickle and plays fast and loose with his children, which is blasphemy to
affirm. If none have this earnest, then the apostle speaks false, when he
saith here, he ' stablisheth us, and gives us the earnest of his Spirit, and us
with you,' both together. Ordinary Christians as well as grand ones, as
well as Paul, may be assured of their salvation. And if this be so, then
either those that have this earnest, this seal of the Spirit, they may be assured or no ; and if not, where is the fault ? Doth not God mean in good
earnest to them when he gives them this ? Undoubtedly he doth. And
why is it given but for assurance ? He is desirous that we should be persuaded of his love in all things, and therefore God's children they may and
they ought to be assured of his love in this world.

It is a point that we have often occasion to meet with in other portions
of Scripture. I speak it therefore here only as a ground out of this place,
in that the Spirit of God, together with the graces and comforts, are called an
' earnest,' I say therefore from hence, *that we may be assured of our salvation.*

I beseech you, what is the aim of the Epistles to the Romans, to the
Ephesians, of the Epistle of St John, but a stirring of them up to whom
they wrote to be persuaded of God's love to them, and to shew what excellent things we have by the love of God in Christ ? And St John's
Epistle* it is for nothing else, in respect of the substance of it, but to give
evidences how we may know that we are the sons of God. Wherefore did
God become man ? Wherefore was Christ himself sealed by the Father,
Son, and Holy Ghost to his office, when he was baptised ? And wherefore
did he die and rise again ? And wherefore doth he make intercession in
heaven ? That we should doubt of God's love, when he hath given us that
which is greater than salvation, that which is greater than all the world,
his own Son ? Would we have a greater pledge of his love ? Is not all
this, that we should not doubt of his love to us, if we cast ourselves upon
him by faith ? Christians may, and ought, and have had assurance.
These here had assurance, and the Scripture speaks of such as had it.
They have had it, we may have it, because the Spirit is a seal and an earnest ;
and we ought to have it, because God hath framed both his word and his
sacraments, and all his dealing to man so as to persuade us of his love.

Caution. Yet add this caution, *that Christians have not at all times a like
assurance of their salvation ;* neither all Christians at all times have it not,

* That is, the 1st Epistle.—G.

nor the best have it not at all times. For there is an infancy of grace, when we know not our own estate and condition ; and there is a time of temptation after infancy, when likewise we stagger in our assurance. There be times likewise of desertion, when God, to make us look better to our footing, leaves us a little, as if he would forsake us, when indeed he leaves us to draw us after him, to cleave more closely to him; for this shaking is to settle us deeper. So there be times and seasons wherein though we be assured, yet we cannot then know our own assurance. And this assurance differeth in Christians ; for some have more, some less ; even as the constitution of the body, some are of a melancholy constitution, that helps Satan in his temptations, and they are subject to fearing and misdoubting : and so as there is a difference in regard of tempers, some are more hardly brought to be persuaded than others, so there is a difference likewise in care and diligence ; for those that use more care and diligence have more assurance. There is a difference likewise in growth and continuance in Christianity, some are fathers, and some are babes. Answerable to the difference of constitution, and of care and diligence, and of age and growth in Christianity, so is the difference of assurance.

Nay, it is possible that for a long time God's child may want this act of assurance, for there is a double act of faith.

(1.) An act whereby the soul *relies upon God as reconciled in Christ*, and relies upon Christ as given of God, and relies upon the promise. And then ;—

(2.) There is a *reflect act*, whereby, knowing we do thus, we have assurance. Now, a man may perform the one act and not the other. We may do that deed that may found our assurance, if the waters of the soul were not troubled ; that is, we may believe and yet want assurance, because that is another distinct act that followeth upon our casting of ourselves upon God. And so, many of the dear children of God, sometimes they can hardly say that they have any assurance, but yet, notwithstanding, they can say, if they do not belie themselves and bear false witness against themselves, that they have cast themselves upon God's mercy, they have performed the first act of faith, and this faith is not fruitless altogether.

Now, there be many things that may hinder this other act, viz., that act of faith whereby I am assured of my state in grace. Sometimes God, together with my believing, will present such things to the soul as wholly take it up, so that a man cannot have definitive thoughts upon that that God would have him think of. As when God will humble a man for his boldness in adventuring upon sin, he takes not away the spirit of faith, but God, to humble him throughly, he sets before him his anger, sets before him terror, even hellish terrors, that will make him in a state little different from a reprobate for the time, so that he is far from saying that he hath any assurance at that time ; yet, notwithstanding, he doth not leave off, he casts himself upon God's mercy still. Though God ' kill him, yet he will trust in him,' and yet he feels nothing but terror. And this, I say, God doth to school him, and to humble him, and to prepare him for the feeling of assurance after.

These things we must observe, that we give not a false evidence of ourselves, that though we have not such assurance as we have had and as others have, yet, I say, alway there is some ground in us, whereupon we may be assured that we are God's, if we could search it. Such ought to labour for assurance, and such will in time come to assurance. And, therefore we should be far from allowing that· doctrine, which is as if a man should light a candle before the devil, as we use to say, to help him against our hearts by a doctrine of doubting, as if our naughty hearts were not ready enough of themselves to doubt.

It is the profaneness of the world—they will not use the means that God hath appointed to this end ; nay, they had rather stagger, and take contentment and assurance in their own ways.   If God will love me in a loose course, so it is ; but ' to give diligence to make my calling and election sure,' 2 Peter i. 10, I had rather believe the popish doctrine that I ought to doubt, and only to be of a good hope; whereas we ought constantly to labour to be assured of our state in grace, that God may have more honour, and that we may have more comfort from him again, and walk more cheerfully through the troubles and temptations that are in the world.

A carnal, proud person, he swells against this doctrine, because he feels no such thing, and he thinks what is above his measure is hypocrisy.   He makes himself the measure of other Christians, and therefore he values and esteems others by his dark state ; for a carnal man's heart, it is like a dungeon.   A man in a dungeon can see nothing, because he hath no light, but he that hath the light, he can see the dungeon.   The heart of a Christian hath a light in it,—there is the Spirit in him,—and therefore he can see his own estate, and he can tell what is in him upon due search.   Now, in a carnal man all is dark.   He sees nothing, because his heart is in a dungeon, his eye is dark, his heart is full of darkness ; all is alike to him, he sees no difference between flesh and Spirit, and therefore he holds on in a doubting hope and confused disposition and temper of soul.   But a Christian that labours to walk in the comforts of the Holy Ghost, he is not content with such a confused state ; and therefore we ought to abhor that doctrine by all means, and to justify this doctrine, that we ought, and that we may, have assurance of salvation in this world.*

The *second* thing which I observe, and which I join to the former, is *the doctrine of perseverance.*   An earnest, you know I told you, is made up with the bargain, but it is never taken away, so that the point is this, that God's children, as they may be assured of their salvation, so

Obs. They may be assured that they shall hold out to the end.

I think many of you think these two points to be so clear that it is unnecessary to divide them ; for if we be assured of our salvation, there must needs be perseverance to the end, for what kind of assurance is it to be in the state of grace to-day, and not to be to-morrow ?

But if you ask some degenerated followers of Luther, that leave him in his sweet and comfortable doctrines, and take up some errors of his, and some others that would divide these, hot they are against the papists for denying the doctrine of assurance of salvation ; but when they come to perseverance, they hold that a Christian may fall away altogether.   These things cannot stand together, for undoubtedly it is most sure and just and right that these truths follow one the other, assurance of salvation and perseverance.   And, therefore, if they maintain that we ought to be assured of salvation, and not doubt of God's love, surely then they cannot, with the same spirit and the same ground, doubt that God, that hath begun a work, will finish it to the day of the Lord.   There is no question but that the one follows the other, because an earnest, as it assures us of salvation, so it assures of perseverance.   Herein an earnest differs from a pawn or pledge. A pledge, it is given, but it is taken away again; but an earnest, when it is once given, is never taken away again, but as it is a part of the bargain, so it is

* Cf. Richard Blachynden's exhaustive treatise, ' Whether a Certainty of being in a State of Salvation be Attainable,' &c. 1685.—G.

filled and made up with the bargain. So grace is a part of glory, and is never taken away, but made up with perfection of glory.

From this we see, then, that he that is in the state of grace is undefeasible, he perseveres to the end, because he hath the earnest of the Spirit. If God should take away his Spirit from him, he should take away his earnest, and if he takes away his earnest, he takes away that for which he gives it, assurance of salvation, and so should overthrow all. But God never repents of his earnest. Man ofttimes repents of his earnest, and wisheth he had not made such a fruitless bargain ; but God never doth, but where he gives the first-fruits, he makes up the harvest ; where he lays the foundation, he makes up the building ; where he gives earnest, he makes up the bargain ; where he begins a good work, he finisheth it to the day of the Lord ; once his, for ever his. We cannot be so sure of anything as we may be of God's love for the time to come. We have a common speech amongst us, I know what I have, but what I shall have I know not. It is an ill speech. Thou knowest not what thou hast, for these worldly things, a man hath them so to-day as they may take to themselves wings and be gone to-morrow, for they are but vanity. I may be as rich as Job in the morning, and as poor as Job at night. So that a man knows not what he hath ; but for the time to come for grace and glory he may say, Though I know not what I have, or how long I shall have it, I know what I shall have, ' I know that neither things present, nor things to come, shall be able to separate me from the love of God in Jesus Christ,' Rom. viii. 38.

So that you see here a foundation of the sweet and comfortable doctrine of perseverance. Grace is the earnest of glory, and it doth but differ in degrees. The beginning of glory is here in grace, the consummation of it hereafter. We are anointed kings here, we shall be kings in heaven. We are sons here in this world, we shall be heirs in heaven. We shall be adopted there in soul and body, here we are adopted in soul. For in this life Christ's first coming was for the soul, his second coming is for body and soul. Therefore the resurrection is called the ' day of regeneration,' Mat. xix. 28, because then it shall be perfected : then regeneration is only begun.

So that in respect that the work of the Spirit, the graces of the Spirit are called an ' earnest,' we may know and be assured of perseverance in grace, and that that which we have now in the beginning shall be accomplished. *

O ! how should this set us upon desires to have the blessed work of the Spirit upon us, to have the Spirit to set his seal upon us, to be Christ's, to have this earnest, and to get more and more earnest till we have the full bargain accomplished in heaven.

Thirdly, I told you that an earnest is part of the whole : they therefore that have not the earnest cannot look for the bargain. The observation hence is, that—

Obs. Those that look to be happy, must first look to be holy.

This point I mean to touch very briefly. I am loath to pass it by, though it be not the principal thing I aim at, because it may serve *for a kind of trial, whether a man have any right to heaven or no.*

It is the ordinary presumptuous error of common Christians, to think to go to heaven out of unclean courses, with ' Lord, have mercy upon us ; ' but miserable wretches are they that have not this ' earnest ' of the Spirit in them, an earnest of heaven beforehand, in grace, and peace, and joy. We must all read our happiness in our holiness ; and therefore it is that

* Cf. Stafford Brown's ' Truth on both Sides ; or, Can the Believer Finally Fall.' 1848. 12mo.—G.

happiness in heaven and holiness here, which is happiness inchoate, have both one title, to shew that we cannot have the one without the other. We must enter into heaven here in this life.

The stones, you know, they were hewed before they were brought to the building of the temple, they were all made and fitted beforehand ; and so all that shall be stones in heaven, they must be hewed, and prepared, and fitted here ; there must be no knocking and fitting of them there.

So then you see these three things touched, that the Holy Spirit, together with the graces and comforts of it, are called an ' earnest,' and therefore that it is a part of the whole, an assurance of the whole, and that it shall never be taken away.

Now for the fourth, that an ' earnest ' is little in regard of the whole ; (and indeed the holy apostle aims at this partly as well as at any other thing else) an earnest is little, perhaps we have but a shilling to secure us of many pounds. So then the point is this, that—

Obs. Howsoever we may be assured of our estate in grace, and likewise that we shall hold out, yet the ground of this assurance is not from any great measure of grace, but though it be little in quantity, it may be great in assurance and security.

As we value an earnest not for the worth that is in itself, but because it assures us of a great bargain ; we have an eye more to the consummation of the bargain, than to the quantity of the earnest : so it is here, grace is but an earnest ; yet notwithstanding though it be little as an earnest is, yet it is great in assurance of validity, answerable to the relation of that it hath to assure us.

There is nothing less than a ' grain of mustard-seed,' but there is nothing in the world so little in proportion, in a manner, that comes at length to be so great, as the graces of God, and the work of the Spirit is. The crocodile, a huge creature, comes of an egg, and the oak, it riseth to that greatness from an acorn. But what are these to the wondrous work of the new creature, to be the ' heir of heaven,' rising from so little, despised beginnings, from a little light in the understanding, from a little heat in the affections, from a little strength in the will, compared for the littleness thereof to a grain of mustard-seed !

Indeed, grace grows, a man knows not how. As Christ saith of the seed sown in the earth, it grows up first ' to a blade, and then to a stalk, and then to an ear, and then to be corn,' Mark iv. 28, but a man cannot tell how ; so it is with the work of grace and the comforts of the Spirit : when the Spirit together with the word works upon the soul, there is a blade, a little, and then a stalk, and then corn.

First a babe in Christ, little at the first ; and as it is little, so it is much opposed. As we see the sun when it is weak in the rising in the morning: there gather a great many vapours to besiege the sun, as it were, as if they would put out the light of it, till it comes to fuller strength, and then it spends them all, and gloriously shines in heaven. So it is with the work of the Spirit of grace. When it first ariseth in the soul, there gather about it a great many doubts and discomforts ; the flesh riseth and casteth up all the dirt and mud it can, to trouble the blessed waters of grace, till it have gotten fuller and fuller strength to spend them all, as it is when a man comes to be a strong Christian. But yet as little as it is, seeing it is an ' earnest,' and ' the first fruits,' as the apostle saith, which were but little in regard of the whole harvest, yet it is of the nature of the whole, and thereupon it comes to secure. A spark of fire is but little, yet it is

fire as well as the whole element of fire ; and a drop of water, it is water
as well as the whole ocean.　When a man is in a dark place,—put the
case it be in a dungeon,—if he have a little light shining in to him from a
little crevice, that little light discovers that the day is broke, that the sun
is risen.　Put the case there be but one grape on a vine, it shews that it
is a vine, and that the vine is not dead.　So, put the case there be but the
appearance of but a little grace in a Christian, perhaps the Spirit of God
appears but in one grace in him at that time, yet that one grace sheweth
that we are vines, and not thistles, or thorns, or other base plants, and it
shews that there is life in the root.

The Spirit of God appears not in all graces at once, it appears some
time or other in some one grace.　We see in plants, the virtue of them
appears diversely.　In winter the virtue of them lies in the root ; in the
spring-time, in the bud and the leaf ; in the summer, in the fruit : it is
not in all parts alike.　So it is with the Spirit, as it is an ' earnest,' it
appears not in all graces in a flourishing manner at the first.　Sometimes
it appears in the root, in humility, sometimes in faith, sometimes in love,
sometimes in one grace, sometimes in another.　Though the Spirit be in
every grace, yet in appearance to a man's self and others, it appears but
in one.　An ' earnest ' is little, especially at the first.

Weak Christians therefore should not be discouraged.　' Despise not the
day of little things,' Zech. iv. 10.　There is cause of mourning.　We that
have received the ' first-fruits ' of the Spirit, we mourn because we have but
the first-fruits, and we would have the full harvest ; but as there is cause
of mourning because we have but the first-fruits, so there is cause of comfort, because it is the first-fruits.　It is an ' earnest ' only, and not the
whole bargain, therefore we have cause of mourning that it is so imperfect,
that it is so weak as it is ; yet there is cause of comfort, because though
it is not the whole, yet [it] is a part, and secures us of the whole.

And therefore Christians should labour to mingle duties, and let one
grace qualify another ; for indeed a Christian is a mixed creature, his comforts are mixed, and his mourning is mixed.　With a carnal man it is all
otherwise, if he mourn he is all a mort,* because he hath no goodness ; if
he joy, he is mad, his mirth is madness.

A Christian joys indeed, sometimes he hath ' joy unspeakable and glorious,'
1 Peter i. 8, because he looks to his hope, and the accomplishment of it,
and yet he mourns, because he hath but the ' earnest,' because he hath but
the beginnings, because he hath but the first fruits here.

Use 2. And therefore again, as it should comfort us, if we have anything ;
so it should exhort us to examine rather the truth, than the measure of any
grace.　We have examined the truth, it is the truth of this ' earnest,' the
truth of grace and comfort.　It is an excellent speech of our Saviour
Christ, in Rev. iii. to the church of Philadelphia, in verse 8, ' Because thou
hast a little strength, and hast kept my word, and hast not denied my
name.'　There is a great promise made to the church of Philadelphia ; and
why ?　' Because thou hast a little strength.'　How is that discovered ?
' Thou hast kept my word, and hast not denied my name.'　So then, if
that little be true, God respects not that little as it is little in quantity, but
as he means to make it ere long.　He looks upon the ' earnest,' as he
means to make up the bargain ; he looks upon the foundation, as he means
to rear up a goodly building ; he looks upon the first-fruits, as he means
to add the harvest ; and therefore, Eph. i. 4, and other places, ' We are

　　* That is ' dead,' = ' deeply sunken'.—G.

elected to be holy and blameless in his sight.' So Eph. v. 27, ' He purgeth the church, that she may be presented to him without spot.' So Christ looks upon his Church as he is purging and washing, till he have made it holy in his sight. We are elected, not to ' earnest,' not to ' first-fruits,' but to be ' unblameable ; ' we are elected to perfection. It is the comfort of Christians, that God looks upon his, not as they are imperfect here, but as they are in beginning, and as they are growing, and as he intends to bring them to perfection afterwards. For all things are present, we know, to him, the time to come, what we shall be ; he considers us as if we were in heaven already ; we are in our degree, and in our faith. So now ' we sit in heavenly places,' Eph. i. 3 ; therefore as he looks on us as we shall be, so faith answers his looking, when we are framed by the Spirit to comfort ; faith looks not upon the weak ' earnest,' the poor beginnings, but as we shall be after in heaven, ' without spot and wrinkle,' Eph. v. 27.

Aye, but how shall we know the truth of his ' earnest,' that it is true, though it be little ? To speak a word or two of that for trial.

Where the Spirit of God is, with the relation of an ' earnest,' he is an earnest' by way of grace and comfort ; for those two ways the Spirit discovers himself in us, to sanctify our nature, or by comfort, and peace, and joy, and such like.

1. Then it doth stir up the soul *to mourn that* [it] *is but an ' earnest,'* as I said before, and to wait for the accomplishment, as the apostle saith in Rom. viii. 23, ' We that have received the first-fruits of the Spirit, mourn in ourselves, that it is no better with us than it is ;' and withal.

2. ' *We wait for the redemption of the sons of God,*' the adoption of the sons of God, we wait for the accomplishment hereafter. It is the nature therefore of the Spirit of God, as it is an earnest, to stir up the spirits of God's children to mourn something, and likewise,

3. To *wait patiently, to wait for the full accomplishment hereafter ;* and as a fruit of their waiting, to endure quietly, patiently, and comfortably that which is between the earnest, and the accomplishment of it. And therefore God gives them the grace of hope and constancy, and of perseverance, till all be accomplished ; for there is the tediousness of time, between which is irksome, hope deferred, and a tediousness of deferring, and besides many afflictions withal.

Now God's children that have the earnest of the Spirit, they have a spirit likewise to wait ; and that they may be strengthened to wait, they have,

4. The *spirit of constancy,* a spirit of patience to endure trouble, and to persevere, and to hold out in regard of the tediousness of the time. So that they may not give over religious courses, though they have it not fully here, but go on still, and wait. And likewise those that have the earnest of the Spirit, that have the Spirit, as it hath this qualification upon it of an earnest, it stirs them up,

5. To *frame themselves, answerable to the full accomplishment ;* for ' He that hath this hope,' saith the apostle, ' purgeth himself,' 1 John iii. 3. He that finds some little beginnings of grace and comfort, the beginnings of heaven upon earth, he frames himself to the perfect state in heaven ; for it is the nature of faith and hope, wheresoever they are, to frame the disposition of the person in whom those graces are planted by the Spirit, to the condition of that soul that believes and hopes, for it is in the nature of the thing it should be so. For doth not hope in any man that hopes to appear before some great person, make him alter his attire, and fashion his carriage and deportment, as may be plausible before the person whom

he goes to ? and doth not faith and hope of better things, where they are in truth, fashion and dispose every man to be such as may be fit for heaven ? The title to heaven we have indeed by Christ; but the soul knows there must be a qualification, ' No unclean thing shall enter into heaven,' Rev. xxi. 27; and therefore where the ' earnest' is, there is a continual desire to be better, a continual relinquishing of corruption more and more, a perfecting of the work of mortification, and the work of grace more and more ; for the same Spirit that is an earnest, and gives us any beginning of a better life, it likewise stirs us up, it fits and prepares us for that state that is kept for us. It is impossible it should be otherwise. In what strength the ' earnest' is, in that strength sanctification and mortification are ; and therefore persons that live in sins against conscience, that defile their tongues, and defile their bodies, let them talk what they will, it is but a presumptuous conceit. It is not the voice of God's Spirit, but of carnal presumption ; for wheresoever the Spirit is an ' earnest' of heaven, it is always preparing and fitting the soul for that glorious and happy estate. And wheresoever likewise this earnest of the Spirit is, wheresoever this grace is begun in truth,

6. There *is a desire of accomplishment*, an earnest desire of the coming of Christ to finish all, to finish the bargain. Rev. xxii. 17, ' The Spirit and the spouse say, Come ;' that is, the spouse by direction of the Spirit, where the spouse is guided by the Spirit ; and so far as the spouse is guided by the Spirit, she saith, ' Come, come, Lord Jesus, come quickly,' Rev. xxii. 20.

Cautions. Except in two cases, (1.) Except the Christian *hath grieved and wounded his conscience, grieved the Spirit*, and then it is loath to go hence. (2.) Unless likewise the spirit of a Christian *be careless, and would settle things in better order before he go to Christ;* for this is the fruit of presumption, and carelessness, that it grieves the Spirit of God, and the Spirit being grieved, grieves them. He makes that which should be their comfort, their going to Christ by death, he makes it terrible ; for as we see a weak eye cannot endure the light, so a galled guilty conscience trembles to think of Christ's coming. Though the ' earnest' be there ; yet if the soul tremble, that the soul be wounded, stay a while, ' O stay!' saith the psalmist, ' before I go hence, and be no more seen.' When the wife hath been negligent, she would have her husband stay ;＊ but when she hath been diligent, then the wife is willing her husband should come ; but perhaps things are not settled as they should, and therefore she doth not desire his coming as at other times.

But take a Christian in his right temper, he is willing to die ; nay, he is willing, and glad, and joyful to go to Christ. Then he knows the earnest shall be accomplished with the bargain ; then he knows what God hath begun, he will perfect ; then he knows, all the promises shall be performed, when all imperfection shall be removed, and all enemies shall be conquered, &c. A carnal man doth not say as the Spirit in the spouse speaks, ' Come, Lord, come ;' but stay, Lord, stay ;† and as the devil that possessed that person, ' What have we to do with thee ? Art thou come to torment us before our time ?' Mat. viii. 29. They think of it with quaking. For otherwise they that have the earnest of the Spirit, have joyful thoughts of it, and wishes answerable to those thoughts.

7. Again, wheresoever this earnest is in truth, the earnest of the Spirit, *there is growth;* for it is the nature of things imperfect to come to their per-

＊ and † That is, ' stay *away*.'—G.

fection, that they may encounter with whatsoever is contrary to them, and that they may do their functions that they are fitted by for God.

Now God having fitted the new creature to serve him, and to go through all the impediments in this world, and all the crosses, where he hath begun this work, it will labour to come to perfection. As in the natural body we are not content to live; but when we have life, we desire health; and when we have health, we are not content with that, but we desire strength; not only health, but strength to perform that we should do. So where the spiritual life is begun, the living soul is not content to live, to find an ' earnest,' a little beginnings, but if he have that, he would have health, he would not have any spiritual disease to lie on the soul, that might hinder it in the functions of it; and together with health, it desires fuller and fully strength, because it hath many temptations to encounter with, many corruptions to resist, many actions to do, many afflictions perhaps to bear, all which require a great deal of strength. Wheresoever grace is in truth, it is always with a desire of growth, and answerable to that desire will be the use of all the means of growth. Again, to name one or two more, and so end:

8. Wheresoever the Spirit is as an ' earnest,' it doth as the seal doth, spoken of before, that as it hath a quieting power, an assuring power, *it quiets the soul*. Wheresoever it is, it is given to stay the soul, to comfort it, that the whole shall be performed in time; and therefore the soul that hath the ' earnest of the Spirit,' so far forth as he hath this ' earnest,' it quiets and stays the soul. A man may know true faith from false, and true earnest from presumption by this, as we know other things; I say, it stills and quiets the soul, and

9. *It will endure the trial.* We say of alchemy* gold, *it is counterfeit*, it will not strengthen the heart. True gold hath a corroborating power to strengthen the heart (whether it be so or no, let the alcumists look to it); but it is true, that true ' earnest,' the beginnings of faith, though it be but in a little measure, it hath a quieting, a stilling, a strengthening power, to strengthen and corroborate the soul, for it is given for that purpose. And a man that hath the least grace will endure the search, as true gold will endure the touchstone, the false will not. And it is a sign that a man hath true grace in him, although it be with much imperfection, that desires *to be searched in preaching :* hearing searching sermons, and desiring to be searched in conference, and that doubts not his conscience, but would be searched throughly. When men fret at the searching of their sins, they will not be searched, and are content to go on in presumptuous courses, and think all is well, it is a sign there is not so much as an ' earnest.' But not to go further, that in the Revelation shews the truth of a little grace; what saith he? ' Thou hast a little strength.' What doth that little strength move the church of Philadelphia to do? ' Thou hast kept my word, and hast not denied my name.'

10. Where there is a little strength, *there will be a keeping of the word in obedience*, a keeping of it in conversation; where is not a regard to God's word, a moulding of the soul into it in obedience of it, there is not so much as a little strength of grace, and therefore those that live in rebellious courses, have not so much as an earnest to them; yet, ' Thou hast kept my word,' and withal, ' thou hast not denied my name.'

11. Where a little strength is, there they will not deny Christ's name, *they will hold out* in the profession of the truth, and confess it if occasion

* Spelled ' alcumy,' and a little onward ' alcumists.—G.

serve. And therefore where any are slight in their profession, that give in
if they be ready to dash upon any displeasure of any one ; if they be to venture their estates or so, then they are ashamed of Christ, and that profession
which they took upon them ; they deny his name, at least they do not own
it, they have not so much as a little strength, if they do not recover. Peter
was in such a temptation, but he recovered his strength, and got more
strength, and a firm standing upon it : the shaking of Peter was for the
rooting of him.

So God to shame his children, suffers them sometimes to have dastardly
spirits, but they recover themselves, they are ashamed of it. But those
that are common politicians in this kind, that will not stand out in a good
cause to maintain their truth and profession, when God thrusts his cause
into their hands, specially at such times when God saith to them,
'Who is on my side ? who ?' 2 Kings ix. 32, now is the time to appear
then. If they have not a word for God, they will not own the quarrel and
cause of God and religion, they have not a little strength ; for they that
have a little strength here, keep the word and have not denied the name.
Those therefore that can fashion themselves to all religions, to all companies, they will have a religion mutable and flexible to their occasions ;
where is the earnest of the Spirit ? The Spirit, as much as he is, is strong
and vigorous, and powerful. These men have not so much as a little
strength, that are as water which is fashioned to the vessel it is in, like to
the Samaritans, as Josephus* the historian of the Jews writes of them (eeee).
When the Jews prospered, oh ! then they would be Jews ; when the Jews
had ill success, then they were great enemies to the Jews ; so you have
many that are no friends to the afflicted, to the disgraced truth ; but
as long as the cause of religion is carried out with the countenance of the
State, with the favour of great ones, so far they will own it ; but if Christ
once comes to be abased, they will not know Christ, nor his cause.

I beseech you, let us take notice of it. It is a sign there is no grace at
all, where there is such an habitual disposition without shame or grief, or
repentance ; for God's children sometimes may be overtaken with a spirit
of dastardliness, which afflicts them sore afterwards, that they gather more
strength. A man may know if he be God's child in such a state ; for it is
universally true, God's children are never overtaken with a spirit of coward-
liness and fear, but they regain it, and grow more strong upon it ; as we see
in Cranmer and others (ffff). God purposeth sometimes to let them see
what they are in themselves without his support and strength; but afterwards
they gather new resolutions, new purposes to stick firmer to the truth than e'er
before. I might add many other things, but I go on to that which follows.

You see here now how we may try, if we have any true ' earnest' in us
at all or no.

Now I beseech you, let us labour *to have this ' earnest,'* if we have it
not, to have this assurance especially. Let me desire those of the younger
sort to labour to have the seal of this Spirit, and the ' earnest' before they
be further and further engaged into the world, and before they be so hardened
that they will not receive a contrary stamp to their corruptions. It is a
wondrous advantage that gentlemen, and others that are young, before the
world hath soiled them, and before their understandings be darkened, and
their affections are crooked, and carried away much with the stream and
errors of the time, they have much advantage above others, for they have
spirits fitter for grace, fitter to receive the impression of this seal of the Spirit,

* Spelled ' Joseph.'—G.

and fitter for the ' earnest.' Let us labour for this earnest betimes. What a comfortable thing will it be to carry along with the ' earnest' an assurance of a better estate from our youth to our age, and from our age to our old age, and so to heaven with us ! What a deal of comfort do young ones deprive and rob themselves of, that will not be gracious betimes ! Let us labour to have the stamp of the Spirit set on us in our prime time, in the strength of our years. But I will press the point, if the time will give leave, afterwards.

Now we must know, that God gives this earnest *not for himself, but for us*, to secure us ; and that is one reason why it is called an earnest.

There is besides bargaining another state and condition that ' earnest' is applied unto, which perhaps the apostle aims at, as marriage ; whatsoever was before the consummation of the marriage, was a kind of *Arrah*,* a kind of ' earnest,' to assure the affection of the contracted person and persons that loved one another, till the consummation of the marriage.

So Christ now contracts us on the earth, and having love to us, and taking our nature on him, that he might woo us in our own flesh, and in our own nature, taking upon him the ' earnest' of our flesh, he gives us the ' earnest' of his Spirit ; and to assure us that he loves us, and that he means to make up the bargain afterwards, he sends us love tokens, graces, and comfort and joy. Even as Isaac when he was to marry Rebecca, he sent by his servants bracelets and jewels, and such things, to secure† her of his love, Gen. xxiv. 53.

So Christ in heaven intending the consummation of the match, he sends us here graces and comforts of the Spirit, and all to secure us : all is for us, I say, which I observe the rather, because I would raise your hearts to hate unbelief and distrust exceedingly, because God labours to undermine it by all means possible.

Wherefore doth he use so many terms here, of ' sealing,' ' anointing,' and ' earnest,' with words and sacraments, and all whatsoever may confirm you ? The Holy Ghost applies it to us. All this is that we may not doubt of the favour of God : and therefore when we find any goodness in us, let us account that to give false witness against ourselves is a horrible sin; it is to make God a liar. God stands upon his credit; and therefore take heed what we say (specially if we have found the work of grace in former time, any ' earnest '), that we have no grace. God doth this for our assurance. All his dealing of word and sacraments, of earnest and oath, and all that may be to assure us ; and therefore we should not cross the good-ness of God, so as to cherish such a disposition as is most contrary to him, that he labours to undermine by all means.

And, therefore, here is the poison of popish religion, that it maintains doubting, and leaves men doubting. Indeed they do well to maintain it in their doctrine, for indeed they false-found a man upon satisfaction, they false-found him upon purgatory and merits, and the foundation they have of a Christian soul is uncertain ; and therefore they may well teach doubt-ing: it suits with the course that they take. But I say it is very corrupt, for God useth all means that we should not doubt ; and therefore it is idly objected, God for his part will, but for our part we have reason to doubt. Why ! he in all things stoops to us, he labours to secure us ; and there-fore in the covenant of grace he doth his part and ours too.

* That is, ἀῤῥαβών = earnest, pledge. The Scotch ' *arles*,' or earnest-money seems to preserve this, and is a curious example of an unexpected etymology.—G.

† That is = assure, make her certain of.—G.

But I hasten to that which follows, because I would end with the time. To touch that a little distinctly by itself, that the Spirit doth all, the ' earnest of the Spirit :' for indeed, though Spirit be not added to stablishing, yet the Spirit stablisheth by Christ, and the Spirit anoints, and the Spirit ' seals to the day of redemption,' and ' the earnest of the Spirit.'

So it is the Holy Ghost doth all. Here you have the three Persons in the Trinity. We have three grand enemies, ' the world, the flesh, and Satan.' Now here are the three Persons in the Trinity stronger than all our enemies. ' He which stablisheth us, is God the Father, by his Spirit :' upon whom ? upon Christ, ' in Christ,' and gives ' us the earnest of his Spirit.' You have, I say, the three Persons of the Trinity here. But why doth the Spirit give us the earnest ? why doth the Spirit give us grace and comfort, seal us, and doth all, and stablish us ?

1. I answer, first of all, because now since the fall *we have no principles of supernatural good*, and therefore it must be a principle above our nature to work both grace and comforts in our barren hearts.

2. Again, as there is no principle to that which is supernaturally good, *so there is opposition to that which is supernaturally good ;* and therefore there must be somewhat to overpower the corruptions of our nature.

(1.) But why the Spirit, rather than the Father and the Son ? *He comes from both ;* and proceeding from both he is fit to witness the love of both. For the Holy Ghost is in the breast of the Father and the Son, and proceeds from both, and he knows the secret love of the Father to us, and the love of Christ Jesus Mediator to us.

Now the Spirit knowing the secrets of God, as a man's spirit, saith the apostle, knows his own secrets, he knows his love, and he knows whom he loves ! So the Spirit of God knowing the affection of the Father, and the affection of Jesus Christ to us, is fit to be an ' earnest,' fit to be a ' seal.'

Indeed all things are wrought by the Spirit in grace for application ; the desert* is from the Son, originally from the Father ; but in regard of application of what is wrought by the Son, all is by the Holy Ghost. Both graces and comforts the Holy Ghost takes from Christ ; for if grace be wrought, it is with divine reasons from the love of God in Christ. If grace be wrought, it is from the wondrous love of God reconciled in Christ, wherein heaven is opened, hell is vanquished. It is by reasons fetched from Christ ; and so ' he takes of mine,' as Christ saith, ' He shall take of mine, and give to you,' John xvi. 15. He takes reasons from Christ,—the Holy Ghost,†—whereby he makes all. The application is altogether by the Spirit.

(2.) And it must be by the Spirit again, because the Spirit of God, and no less than the Spirit, *can quiet our spirits.* For when the soul is distempered, it is like a distempered lock that no key can open : so when the conscience is troubled, what creature can settle the troubled conscience ? can open the ambages‡ of a troubled conscience in such perplexity and confusion ? and therefore to settle the troubled conscience aright, it must be somewhat above conscience ; and that which must quiet the spirit, must be such a Spirit as is above our spirits. This is excellently set down in this epistle, in the third chapter, the work of the Holy Ghost in this kind. But I cannot stand upon it now at this time. I go on.

* That is, ' merit.'—ED.
† That is, ' He, the Holy Ghost, takes reasons from Christ.'—G.
‡ That is, ' winding-passages,' = subterfuges, evasions.—G.

Likewise in the first Epistle to the Corinthians, the second chapter, and 11th verse, that one place shall stand instead of all. ‘ What man knows the things of a man, but the spirit of a man that is in him ? So the things of God no man knows but the Spirit.’

Now, ‘ We have received the spirit, not of the world, but the Spirit of God, to know the things that are freely given us of God.’ If our spirits were in the heart and soul of another man, in the breast of another man, we should know what another man thinks. If a man had a spirit in another man’s spirit, surely he would know all his thoughts and all his affections.

Now the Holy Spirit of God is in the breast of the Father, and the Son, and he knows our spirits better than we know our own spirits ; he searcheth, he is a ‘ searcher,’ as the word is in the original (*gggg*). The Spirit is a searcher. He searcheth our own hearts, and he searcheth the secret love of God to us, that is, the Spirit must stablish us.

Well then, if the Spirit doth all, how shall we know then that we have this Spirit ? A note or two, and so go on.

1. If we have this Spirit of God to seal us, and to be an earnest (I will not speak all that may be, but a little ; for indeed all comes from the Spirit), even as in our souls, how may a man know that he hath a soul ? *by living and moving, by actions vital,* &c., so we may know a man hath the Spirit of God by those actions that come only from the Spirit, which is to the soul, as the soul is in the body : for as all beauty and motion comes from the soul to the body, so to the soul from the Spirit, all comes of the Spirit, and therefore every saving grace is a sign that the Spirit is in us.

2. In a word, the Spirit is in us in the nature of fire, as in other things, so in this, *in transforming.* Wheresoever the Spirit dwells, he transforms the soul, he transforms the party like himself holy and gracious. Those therefore that find the Spirit transforming and changing them in the use of the ordinance of the word, they may know that they have the Spirit sealing them, and being an earnest to them.

3. They may know likewise, that they have it wrought by the Spirit, for every one grace, you may know spiritual graces are *with conflict ;* for what is true, is with a great deal of resistance of that which is counterfeit.

Comforts and graces that are not the earnest of the Spirit, are with little conflict ; but where there are true comforts and graces of the Spirit wrought by the Spirit, it is with much conflict with Satan and with himself; for there is a great deal of envy in the devil against the man that walks in the Spirit. Thinks he, what ! such a base creature as this is to have the ‘ earnest’ of heaven, to walk here as if he were in heaven already, and to defy all opposite powers ! Nay, I will trouble his peace, he shall go mourning to heaven, if he go there. This is the reasoning of the cursed spirit, and hereupon he labours to shake the assurance and persuasion; and the grace and comfort of a Christian,—it is with much conflict and temptation, not only with Satan, but with his own heart.

Our hearts misgive us, when we are guilty of some sins, as always there is guilt on the soul,—so much guilt, so much doubt. Till the soul be free from guilt, it will never but be casting of doubts; and therefore there is always resistance in us, and there must be a higher power than the heart and soul of a man to set the heart down and quiet it; it is always in conflict.

4.* And the graces and comforts of the Spirit wrought by the Spirit, are

* In margin, ‘ By supernatural obedience.’—G.

always in the use of means, holy means; and it carries a man *above the strength of nature*, it carries a man to the practice of that which he could not do by nature, to pardon his enemies, to pray for them, to overcome revenge, and to enjoy prosperity without pride, in a comfortable measure; and it enables him to practise the last commandment, that he shall be content with his estate, and not lust after others; and the first commandment. The graces of the Holy Spirit enables a man to love God, and to rejoice in him above all as his best portion. It makes his joy spiritual, and it makes him delight in all connatural things that are like the Spirit; as whatsoever is spiritual is connatural to the Spirit.

If a man have the graces of the Spirit, he joys in spiritual company, he joys in the presence of God, he hates sin as being contrary to the ' earnest of the Spirit,' he hates terror of conscience, and the way unto it. He will look on good things as God looks on them, and as the Spirit looks on them, and everything that is spiritual he relisheth, ' he favours the things of the Spirit,' Mark viii. 33.

Now because I will not detract* your thoughts, there are some six or seven properties of the Spirit in one chapter, that you may have them all together in Rom. viii. I will not name all, but such as are easy.

5. First of all, it is said in the 9th verse, that the Spirit where it is, *it dwells* as in a house. Now, wheresoever the Spirit is, he is dwelling and ruling; for the Holy Ghost will not be an underling to lusts, and he repairs and makes up the breaches of the soul. Where the Spirit dwells, all the breaches are made up. Ignorance to knowledge, he begets knowledge, and affection, and love; he prepares all, he prepares his own dwelling, and it is familiar and constant to the Spirit. A dwelling implies familiarity and constancy. He is not in us, as he is in wicked men that have the Spirit. As Austin saith, ' The Spirit of God knocks at their hearts, but he doth not dwell there' (*hhhh*).

To go on, that is the first. The Spirit dwells in us, if we have the Spirit.

6. And then the Spirit *doth subdue the contrary;* for the Spirit, when it comes into a man, it pulls down all the ' strongholds,' it makes way for itself; and, therefore, it is said to ' mortify the deeds of the flesh,' ver. 13. If you mortify the deeds of the flesh by the Spirit, you are led by the Spirit. Those, therefore, that by the help of the Spirit, by spiritual reasons, subdue their corruptions, they are led by the Spirit; those that cherish corruptions, or mortify them, not by spiritual reasons, but out of civil respect, to carry authority among men, and, therefore, they would be free from aspersions, as might disable their reputation, they have not the Spirit.

7. Thirdly, as many as are led by the Spirit, *are the sons of God;* the Spirit *leads them.* As the angel that went before the Israelites from Egypt unto Canaan; so the Spirit of God, like the angel, goes before us, and leads us the way, and removes the lets.† It doth lead us, I say, sweetly, and not violently, as the devil leads his that are possessed with his spirit. So that those that have the Spirit working grace and comfort in them, sweetly he leads them, and yet strongly too; for it is strongly, because it is against corruption and opposition from without; but yet sweetly, preserving the liberty and freedom of the soul. We by nature are like children or blind men; we cannot lead ourselves, and, therefore, the Spirit leads us. Those therefore that have the Spirit, it leads them, they submit themselves to the guidance and leading of the Spirit. That is another evidence.

* Qu. ' distract'? or perhaps = divert, turn aside.—G.
† That is, hindrances. Cf. note *d*, vol. I. p. 101.—G.

8. A fourth is this, That *it is a spirit of adoption.* It assures us that we are the sons of God ; it gives us assurance of our adoption, that we are the sons of God. The same Spirit that sanctifieth us, it witnesseth to us, it makes us holy. It witnesseth to us that we are the sons of God.

9. And then again, the Spirit *stirs up* ' sighs and groans that cannot be expressed,' Rom. viii. 26, when we are not of ourselves *able to pray.* This is an evidence of the ' earnest' of the Spirit, when we can send our sighs and groans to God. I say, God will hear the groans, the voice of his own Spirit. For whence come those sighs and groans to God ? Why ! should we not rather sink in despair in troubles, but because the Spirit is in us ? Those therefore that in extremity, having nothing to comfort them, and yet are able to send forth sighs and groans to God, they may certainly know that they have the Spirit.

10. And, likewise, the Spirit makes us *mourn and wait for the adoption* of the ' sons of God.' Those that mourn and wait, have the evidence of the Spirit ; for a worldling doth not mourn for his imperfections, for his corruptions : he doth not mourn that he is absent from his Saviour, neither doth he wait for the accomplishment of that that shall be bestowed on saints, because he hath his portion here. Therefore, those that can mourn for their corruptions, for those things which the world is not able to tax them for, because they cannot serve God with enlargement of the Spirit as they would ; and they wait also without despair, or without discouragement, till God have finished their course, they are led with a better Spirit than the world.

Though I should name no more, what a many sweet evidences are here to manifest a soul truly acted, and guided, and led by the Spirit. But these shall be sufficient for this time.

Well then, if the Spirit doth all, if the Spirit anoint and seal, and give ' earnest' of grace, and comfort, and all, till he bring us to heaven, being Christ's Vicar (for Christ hath no other vicar on earth but his Spirit) ; if the Spirit doth all, as indeed he doth all for God to us, and from us to God (whatsoever God doth to us it is by the Spirit ; he anoints, and seals, and sanctifieth by the Spirit ; and whatsoever we do to God, it is by the Spirit, or else it is not acceptable ; we sigh and groan in the Spirit, we pray in the Holy Ghost, saith Jude, ver. 20, and that God doth to us immediately from the Spirit, and all that we do to God, is in the Spirit). Is this so, then is it an undoubted truth, oh then ! we should labour by all means for this Spirit of God. To give some directions in a word, and so to end.

1. Labour, I say, to have the Spirit, and to groan in the Spirit ; and to this end, because the word is the chariot of the Spirit, in which the Spirit is carried, *attend upon the ordinances of God, and use all kind of spiritual means,* wherein the Spirit is usually effectual ; for the Spirit will only work with his own means. All those bastard inventions and devices fetched from the Church of Rome, human devices in God's service, they are naught. God's Spirit will not be effectual with popish devices ; and, therefore, Rome is ' the habitation of devils,' Rev. xviii. 2. God's Spirit hath nothing to do there, because they have set up a worship contrary to God's worship, they have set up a covenant contrary to Christ's covenant, they have set up the covenant of works, and deny, in a manner, a covenant of grace. Christ is not taught as he should be there.

Now, wheresoever the Spirit is, it is with the clear teaching of the gospel. ' Received you the Spirit by hearing of the law, or of faith preached ? '

Gal. iii. 2. Therefore, let us attend upon the unfolding of Christ Jesus in the gospel ; for the Spirit is given with a clear and true unfolding of Christ; and omit no spiritual means, wherein the Spirit is effectual, as meditation, reading, &c.

For as a man working in a garden, though he think not of it, perhaps he draws a sweet scent of the flowers, there is a tincture from the air that is round about him.

So the word of God being indited by the Spirit of God, we being in holy company, being led by the same Spirit, a man shall either by reading of the word, or in holy company, or conversing in good books, he shall draw a spiritual sweetness from the word, or from those that he hath to deal with.

The spirit of a man is like water that runs from minerals. As we see baths have their warmth from minerals that they run through, they have a tincture from them to be hot in this or that degree, in this or that quality; so it is with the soul, when it runs through holy things, when it hath to deal with good books, and good company, &c., it draweth a spiritual tincture. And, therefore, if we would have the Spirit of God to guide us, let us be much in those things that the Holy Ghost hath sanctified us for that end, at all times, when we have liberty from our callings.

2. And withal, take heed that *we grieve not the Holy Ghost any way*, if we will have the Spirit to ' seal' us, to increase our earnest.

How do we grieve the Holy Ghost ?

(1.) By *cherishing contrary affections, and lusts, and desires*. And resist not the Holy Ghost ; as now when you hear the word of God, if you shut your resolutions, if you shut your hearts, and resolve not to give way to any instruction that shall be delivered, this is a resisting of the Holy Ghost. God now knocks at the hearts of those that are here, by his word and Spirit ; and therefore we should ' open the everlasting doors, and let the King of glory come in,' Ps. xxiv. 7, 9.

We should lay open all to the Spirit. Oh, when the Spirit, when Christ is so willing to give the Spirit, it cannot be any but our fault, if we be no more spiritual than we are ; for indeed there is nothing in a manner required to be spiritual, but not to resist the Spirit.

The Holy Ghost presseth upon us in the word such reasons of heavenly-mindedness, of despising of earthly things, of purging ourselves from the corruptions in the world, such reasons to be good, that indeed none are damned in the bosom of the church, but such as set a bar against the Spirit of God in their hearts, with a cursed resolution that they will not be better, that they will not part with their cursed lusts. Therefore they are damned, because they will be damned, that, say the preachers by the word, and Spirit, what they will, they think it better to be as they are, than to entertain such a guest as will mar and alter all that was there before. Take heed therefore of resisting of the Spirit, and of grieving of the Spirit by any thing in ourselves, or by conversing with company that will grieve him.

He that hath the Spirit of God in him, cannot endure carnal company ; for what shall he hear, what shall he draw in at his senses ? but that which will be vexation of spirit to him. Therefore it is said of Lot, ' His righteous soul was vexed with the unclean conversation of the Sodomites,' 2 Pet. ii. 7. It is an undoubted sign of a man that hath no grace, not to care for his company that hath grace.

(2.) Likewise *yield all obedience and subjection to the Spirit*, and to all the motions of the word and Spirit ; bring our hearts into subjection, lay

H h

ourselves, as it were, before the Spirit, suffer ourselves to be moved, and fashioned, and framed by it; for God gives his Holy Spirit to them that obey him.

(3.) And *beg the Spirit* also as the principal thing. ' God gives the Spirit,' saith Christ, ' to them that ask him,' Luke xi. 13; and by Christ's manner of speaking there, he insinuates, as if he should say, What can I give you better than the Holy Ghost? and yet this will I give you, if you ask him, that is the good thing that God gives; for indeed, that is the seed of all graces, and of all comfort; and therefore a world of promises are included in that promise, that he ' will give the Spirit to them that ask him.'

Labour by these and such like means for the Spirit; and then if you have the Spirit, the ' earnest' of the Spirit, and the ' seal' of the Spirit, then mark what will come of such a temper of soul. That will go through all conditions whatsoever, come what will; for the Spirit is above all, and the comforts of the Spirit are above all earthly comforts; and the graces of the Spirit are able to encounter with all temptations.

So that a man that hath the Spirit, stands impregnable. The work of grace cannot be quenched, because it is the effect and the work of the Spirit. All the powers of all the devils in hell cannot stir it. God may hide his comfort for a time, to humble us; but to quench the work of the Spirit once wrought in the heart, all the power of all the devils in hell cannot quench the least spark of saving grace. It will carry us through all opposition whatsoever.

Let a man never baulk or decline in a good cause, for anything that he shall suffer; for the ' seal' and the ' earnest' of the Spirit is never more strong than when we have no other comfort by us but that: when we can draw comfort from the well-head, from the spring; therefore we should labour for the earnest of the Spirit; for it will fit us for all conditions whatsoever.

What makes a man differ from himself? What makes a man differ from another? Take a man that hath the ' earnest' of the Spirit, you shall have him defy death, the world, Satan, and all temptations. Take a man that is negligent in labouring to increase his earnest, you shall have him weak, and not like himself.

The apostle Peter, before the Holy Ghost came upon him, the voice of a weak damsel astonished him; but after, how willing was he to suffer any thing! Therefore let us not labour much to strengthen ourselves with the things of this life, or to value ourselves by our dependence upon others. If thou hast grace, thou hast that that will stand by thee when all other things fail; for all other things will be taken away, but the Comforter shall never be taken away; it goes along with us continually.

1. First, *it works ' earnest' in us*, and then it stamps upon us his own mark; and then it leads us from grace to grace; and in the hour of death, then especially it hath the work of a Comforter, to present to us the fruits of a good and holy life, and likewise the joys of heaven. When we are dead the Spirit watcheth over our bodies, because they were ' the temples of the Holy Ghost,' and at the day of judgment the same Spirit shall knit both body and soul together, and after, the same Spirit that hath done all this, shall be all in all to us in heaven for ever, and then our very bodies shall be spiritual, whereas now our souls, even the better part of them, is carnal. Even as the fire when it possesseth a piece of iron, it is all fire; so our bodies shall be all spiritual.

What a blessed thing is this, to have the Spirit! What are all friends to the Holy Ghost, which will speak to God for us! The Spirit will make request with sighs and groans, and God will hear the voice of his own Spirit.

What prison can shut up the Spirit of God? Above all, labour to have more of the Spirit of God. This will make us more or less fruitful, more or less glorious in our profession, more or less willing to die. Labour to increase this ' earnest,' that the nearer we come to heaven, the more we may be fitted for it.

Consider but this reason, if you want this, alas! we can never be thankful to God for anything, if by the Spirit we have not assurance that our state is the state of grace. For otherwise we might think that God gives us all in anger, as a carnal man, he always fears that God fats him as an ox to the slaughter. What a fearful case is this, that a man cannot be thankful for that he hath!

2. Labour for the Spirit, *that we may be thankful to God for everything,* that we may see the love of God in everything, in every refreshing we take; that that love of God that fits us for heaven, and that fits heaven for us, it gives us daily bread. The earnest of the Spirit will make us thankful for everything.

3. Again, labour for the ' earnest' of the Spirit, *that we may be joyful in all conditions.* How can a man suffer willingly, that knows not that he is sealed with the Spirit; that knows not that God hath begun a good work in him? Alas! he is lumpish and heavy under the cross.

What makes a man bear the cross willingly, but this assurance? what makes him deny himself in temptations, and corruptions? Oh! saith the child of God, the work of the Spirit is begun in me, sealing me up to life everlasting, shall I grieve and quench this Spirit for this base lust? But a man that hath not the Spirit, saith, I had as good take this pleasure, as have none at all; for aught I know, I shall have none; he sees no greater pleasure than the following of his lust.

So that none can resist temptations, but he that hath the Spirit giving him earnest in a comfortable measure; and it is a good sign when we resist temptations for spiritual reasons, that the Spirit works it.

4. Again, unless we have this earnest of the Spirit in our hearts, we can never *be content to end our days with comfort.* He that hath the earnest of the Spirit is glad of death when it comes. There shall be then an accomplishment of all the bargain. Then the marriage shall be consummate, then shall be the year of Jubilee, the Sabbath of rest for ever. Then is the triumph, and ' then all tears shall be wiped from our eyes,' Rev. vii. 17.

But now let a man stagger and doubt whether he be the child of God or no, that he cannot find any mark of the child of God in him, that he cannot read the evidences of a Christian state in his soul, they are so dim, he sees nothing but corruption in him, he sees no change, no resistance of corruption, he hath no earnest. Alas! what a miserable case is such a man in when he comes to die! Death, with the eternity of misery after it, who can look it in the face, without hope of life everlasting, without assurance of a happy change after death? Therefore we should labour for the Spirit, that howsoever we grow or decay in wealth and reputation, let God alone with that; but above all, beg of God that he would increase in us, and renew the earnest, and the stamp of the Spirit, that we may have somewhat in our souls, wherein we may see the evidences of a Christian estate.

I might add many things to this purpose, but this is sufficient to any judicious Christian, to encourage us to labour for the Spirit above all things in the world. All other are but grass, but fading ; but grace and glory, grace, and peace, and joy, nay, the very ' earnest ' of the Spirit, is better than all earthly things ; for the earnest of it is ' joy unspeakable, and glorious, and peace that passeth all understanding,' 1 Pet. i. 8.

If the promise and the earnest here be so, I beseech you, what shall the accomplishment of the promise be ? If the promises, laid hold on by faith, so quicken and cheer the soul, and if the giving a taste of heaven lift a Christian's spirit above all earthly discouragements, what shall it be when the Spirit shall be all in all in us, if the earnest be so comfortable ? But I go on to the next verse.

VERSE 23.

' *Moreover, I call God to record upon my soul, that to spare you, I came not yet to Corinth.*' In this verse the apostle labours to remove suspicion of levity and inconstancy. There were jealousies in the minds of the Corinthians, which were also fomented by some vain-glorious teachers amongst them, that laboured to undermine St Paul in the hearts of the Corinthians, as if he had not loved the Corinthians so well as they did. Therefore he is so careful to clear himself in their thoughts, from suspicion of inconstancy, and want of love to them ; because suspicion grounded upon the lightness in his carriage, might reflect upon his doctrine.

He knew well enough the malice of man's nature, and therefore he is very curious, and industrious, to make a clear passage for himself into the hearts of these Corinthians by all means possible, as we heard in part out of the 17th verse.

' *Moreover, I call God to record,*' &c. St Paul is here purging himself still, to clear himself.

First, he labours to clear himself from the suspicion of inconstancy, and want of love to them in not coming.

Secondly, he sets down the true cause why he did not come : ' I came not, to spare you.'

You were much to blame in many things, and among the rest of the abominations among you, you cherished the incestuous person, and many of you doubted of the resurrection. I should have been very severe, if I had come, therefore ' I came not, to spare you,' hoping that my letter would work upon your spirits, so that I need not be severe to you ; therefore do not suspect that for any ill mind I came not, for it was to spare you, that I might not be forced to be severe.

Then the *third* thing is, the sealing of this speech with a serious oath, ' I call God for record upon my soul, that I came not, to spare you.' So here is the wiping away of suspicion, and the setting down the true cause why he did not come, and the ratifying and confirming it by an oath : he makes his purgation here by an oath. These three things I will briefly touch.

First of all, you see here he *avoids** *suspicion of lightness* which the Corinthians had of him, partly by the false suggestion of proud teachers among them, who fomented their suspicious dispositions, because they would weaken St Paul's esteem among the Corinthians. They had a conceit he

* That is, 'frees himself from.'—G.

was an uncertain man : he promised to come, and did not ; now here he declines that suspicion.

Where, first, observe these two things briefly.

First, that the nature of man is inclined to suspicion.

And *secondly,* that it is *the duty of men to avoid it as much as may be, and to wipe it away, if it cannot be avoided.*

Obs. Man's nature is prone to suspicion.

Man's nature is prone to suspect ill of another, though never so good. Christ could not avoid it. Because he conversed sociably with other men, he was thought to be a ' wine-bibber,' 'a companion of sinners.' And God himself was suspected of Adam in innocency. The devil is so cunning, that he calls God himself into question, as if he had not meant so well to him. What will that impudent spirit do, that will bring the creature in suspicion of him that is goodness itself ? ' God knows that when you eat, your eyes shall be open, and you shall be as gods, knowing good and evil,' Gen. iii. 5. Do you think that he intends you any good, in forbidding you to eat, &c. ? He did not spare Christ, innocency itself, clothed with man's flesh ; and will he spare to bring uncharitable suspicions upon others ? Surely he will not. And then man's nature of itself is prone to suspect and think ill of another, from many grounds—

1. Sometimes, out of experience of *the common infirmities* that men meet with in the world; out of the experience of the falsehood of men, they are many times prone to suspicion.

2. But most commonly it is *out of guiltiness* that men think ill of others, because others have cause to think ill of them. None are so prone to suspicion as those that are worst themselves, because they judge others by their own hearts.

The better sort of people think of others as they are, and as they deserve themselves ; but others, because they are naught, they think others are so. Because they deserve ill, they think others have deserved an ill opinion of them. So many times it comes of guilt, because we are not as we should be.

Then again, it ariseth from a guilty conscience in another respect. We think, because men have cause, though they have no wrong to themselves ; yet because our own hearts tell us we are ill, we suspect them. So from an uncharitable disposition, and guiltiness of conscience, it ofttimes comes.

3. Then again, sometimes from *the concurrence of probabilities*, the suiting of circumstances that makes things somewhat probable, whereupon suspicion may be fastened. Sometimes when there is a concurrence of probabilities of the likelihood of things, their suspicion is prone to rise ; for suspicion is not a determining of a thing, it is but a slight kind of conceit. It is more than a fear, and less than judgment of a thing. It is more than fear ; for he that fears, suspects not. Suspicion is a degree to judgment. It doth not fully judge, for then it were not suspicion. It is more than fear ; suspects not, but fears. It conceives slightly that such a thing should be done, and yet he dares not say it is done.

Suspicion is nothing else but an inclination of the soul to think and imagine ill of another ; a looking curiously under a thing, or person. As we use to say, envy pries into things. An envious person searcheth. So, a suspicious person looks under to see if he can see matter of ill to fasten his ill soul upon. So it inclines the soul to think ill upon slight grounds. Now this ofttimes ariseth, and is fed with seeming probability. Christ conversed with wicked men. Here was some colour for them to conjecture him so.

We say, things have two hands, a right hand, and a left. Now suspicion takes hold of the left hand always. If things will admit of a double construction, suspicion alway takes hold of the worst, suspicion takes hold of the ill part. That is the nature of a diseased soul, to take things by the wrong hand. We see then it is a disposition that we are subject unto naturally; and it is cherished by Satan, and Satan's instruments, wicked men.

And why doth the devil so cherish suspicion, and a jealous disposition? Oh, it hath been wondrous instrumental to Satan! I daresay, there is no disposition or frame of soul that hath been the occasion of more bloodshed, of more injustice in the church and state from the beginning of the world, than a jealous disposition, especially in great ones. Therefore the devil labours, as to breed jealousies of God, so of God's church and children from the beginning. Was it not ever the disposition of ill-minded men to put jealousies into the hearts, especially of those that were in authority concerning men far better than themselves? Was it not Haman's policy? when the Jews had angered him, oh, they are a people that care not for the laws, &c. Perhaps they were more obedient than himself. Had it not been the occasion of their ruin, if God had not been more merciful?

Herod had a jealousy and suspicion, that Christ when he was born would turn him out of his kingdom; and all Jerusalem was in an uproar, Mat. ii. 3. Alas! Christ came to give a heavenly kingdom, and not to take away earthly; yet this jealousy cost the lives of the poor infants.

So in the primitive church, there were wicked men put jealousies concerning the Christians, into the heads of the emperors, when alas! they reverenced the emperors, next God, above all. Yet alway there were wicked instruments that sought to domineer, and have their own ends under the emperors. They conveyed jealousies; and thence came so much bloodshed. In later times in popish countries, if a man read the stories, whence came that bloodshed? This was one chief cause, jealousies, and suspicions cast into the heads of popish princes by wicked men about them, set on work by Satan himself. O! they are such as will turn you out of your state; a people that are rebellious, and unquiet.

This was the policy among us in former times. We may consider of later times; to see the disposition of a man, that was a great statesman in his time, and a man of great parts and learning, but of a very fierce and cruel disposition; I mean Stephen Gardiner.* The chief hurt that was done in that magnanimous prince's time,† it was done by him. And how? By jealousies, as appears by his letters, &c. Oh, if these things prevail, this and that will come! He cast such jealousies that did affright that great prince. Oh, other princes will fall out with you, if you maintain not these things, they will break with you! And so upon his death-bed; this doctrine of justification, if the people once know it, all is gone.

God shows, that all these jealousies are but follies; for all that he feared came to pass. In good Queen Elizabeth's time, religion that he was so jealous of, was established: and she cared not for princes' correspondency, that were of other religions, further than might stand with reasons of state; and did not she flourish, and her people in quiet all her time, notwith-

* Cf. note *ss*.—G.

† That is, Henry VIII. It is curious to find Sibbes anticipating the eulogy of Froude.—G.

standing all former jealousies, as if religion established could not stand with peace ?   So that the event proved what kind of jealousies these were.*

Do we think then that a great deal of hurt is not done among particular persons, when in states there is such a world of hurt done by Satan, and his instruments ?   Well ! let us take notice therefore of our disposition, and of the inclination of men this way, that we may the better prevent it, and that will appear in the second thing, that,

Obs. We should labour by all means to avoid suspicion, and to decline it as much as we can.

It should be the care of ministers, and others (it generally belongs to all Christians), to free themselves from any ill suspicion in the hearts of others as much as they can ; as St Paul did here the suspicion of inconstancy, and lightness, and want of love to them that he did not come among them.

Suspicion is a canker that eats into the soul where it is, and it will consume and waste all love.   It is the very venom of love and friendship.   A little thing will breed it, but will not work it out.   Therefore we ought first of all to take great heed that we give no ground of suspicion at all ; or if we do, that we be careful to get it out as soon as we can ; for usually where it takes place, it boils till it break out into words, and then words when they are discovered, breed strangeness, and that breeds other inconveniences.

And the rather we should labour to avoid it, because, *quod suspectum,* &c., that which is suspected, is made unprofitable ; for a man when he unwarrantably suspects another thing, it is unprofitable to him.   We take little good by those that we suspect are ill, or ill-affected to us, and then we do little good to them ; for love is much daunted by the ill conceit we have taken against them.   A man cannot do that good that he might, when he is suspected.   There lies a bar in the way ; ill suspicion in the other party, which is an obstruction between him, and the good he might do.   Therefore even for the love of others we ought to avoid suspicion as much as may be, that they may receive good from us.

As we ought not uncharitably to suspect others, that we may do good to them ; so we ought to avoid by all means suspicion from them, lest it be a bar for that good we might do towards them.   Let us labour to clear ourselves from all suspicion of want of love, and ill carriage what we may, that so there may be nothing between our spirits and theirs that may hinder the good that might come from us to them, but that all may pass clear.   You see how curious holy men have been in all times, to avoid suspicion as much as they could.

Even God himself,—we cannot have a more glorious pattern,—what course hath he taken from the beginning of the world with mankind ?   He hath condescended, and stooped to man's weakness, to clear himself of suspicion of unkindness to man, that man might not cherish suspicion that he doth not love him.   For there is that poison in the cursed nature of man, that do God what he can, he will lay imputations upon God, to bear himself out in stubborn courses, as if God delighted not in him, nor regarded him.   And as you have it in Ezek. xviii, 2 *seq.*   I am punished for other folks' sins, God deals hardly with me, and brings the sins of my fathers upon me ; and, 'the fathers have eaten sour grapes, and the children's teeth are set on edge.'   God knows the cankered disposition of man since the fall.   Satan lies upon the disposition of man, and broods upon it, to make it like him-

---

* Cf. Sir Philip Sidney's famous Letter to Elizabeth on her fears of isolation in Europe.   It will be found in ' Life' of Sidney, by Bourne, and by Lloyd, both recently issued.—G.

self, malicious even against God himself. God, as it were, puts himself to his purgation, even with no less than an oath. ' As I live, saith the Lord, I will not the death of a sinner,' Ezek. xviii. 23. You think I am severe to you; and men they will rather impute it to God's severity, than their own sin. That is the pride of man's nature.

A sinner is wondrous proud till he come to destruction itself, and the book of conscience be opened. Sin will have something to shelter itself with : sin is a proud thing. God purgeth himself by an oath. ' As I live, saith the Lord, I will not the death of a sinner.' If you die, you may thank your own sins. Though you be so bad, if you will repent, ' I will not the death of a sinner, but rather that he return, and live.' Yet notwithstanding, man to countenance himself in sin, he will fly perhaps to the decree of God. God perhaps doth not delight in me. Whereas the rule of our life is, ' He hath shewed thee, O man, what is good,' Micah vi. 8, to do good, and abstain from evil, and then that question will be out of question, whether thou be God's or no. But man will force upon himself, that God doth not regard him, that he may sin with more freedom.

As the unfaithful servant, ' I knew thou wert a hard master, that exactest that that thou hadst not given,' Mat. xxv. 24,—and therefore I hid my talent. The bad servant forceth upon himself hardness in his master, when he was not so,—that he might be idle. So men force upon themselves somewhat in God to be hard ; God's dealings to be so and so, that they may take more liberty. For if God be so loving, and so gracious, as he hath discovered himself to be, their hearts would melt, they would never live in such courses, but rather put all to the venture, than to clamour upon God's justice. Therefore God himself purgeth himself from a disposition of unkindness, and unmercifulness. ' As I live, saith the Lord, I will not the death of a sinner.' So his whole course is to shew that he loves us.

And what is our Saviour Christ's whole course, but to free men from suspicion of want of love ? Did he ever turn any back from him, but those that went away of themselves ? Did he not shed tears for those that shed his blood, so merciful and gracious was he ? If so be that holy men of all times have laboured to clear themselves to others, we ought not to rage against the ill dispositions of men. If we were as good as God, and as Christ, men would have false suspicion of us. It is no innocency in the world that will free a man from suspicion ; the wicked, poisonful disposition that the devil stirs up against him. Therefore rage not against it, but bear it with a spirit of moderation.

And let us decline as much as we can, and free the hearts of people from evil suspicion ; and if we cannot avoid it, yet to bear it without discontent, considering it is the lot of God's children to be suspected, as we see here St Paul was.

' *To spare you, I came not to Corinth.*' St Paul besides his labouring to remove suspicion, he sets down here the true cause of his not coming to them. It was not lightness and inconstancy, it was ' to spare you.' They had many abuses among them, and amended they must be, that was a conclusion. But the question is *de modo*, whether by gentle means, by writing an epistle, and staying a while, or afterwards by coming, and telling them their sin to their face, and by being severe, and terrible among them ? Now he concludes, I came not among you, for this very cause, that I might not be so severe, and terrible among you, as by office I should have been, if you had not amended before I came ; as indeed they did, for they cast out the incestuous person, and reformed other abuses comfortably. They prevented St Paul's severity, with their reformation. They had not at the first cast out the incestuous person, and they had factions among them; they had atheists among them that doubted of the resurrection, many abuses were crept in among them. St Paul wrote a former epistle upon a desire to reform those, and there was a blessed reformation wrought. St Paul did not delight in austerity ; therefore he deferred his coming, that he might have more joy and contentment than sorrow.

' To spare you, I came not.' Before I come to the points, take this for a ground,

Obs. Sin must be judged and censured when it is committed.

It must be undone by repentance, or by eternal punishment in hell. It must be censured here or hereafter.

For it is against God's nature and God's word. ' The soul that sinneth shall die,' Ezek. xviii. 4. It must be repented of, of necessity, or eternally punished in hell. Censured it must be, one way or other, it is of such a contrary nature, so opposite to the holiness of God. That is a ground.

Now this being laid as a ground, the question is, What is the best way to take away sin, whether by means gentle or severe ? By gentle means, it may be ; if not, then by severe. St Paul would not have spared them, if he had come, if they had not amended. So the points are two.

First of all, that the best way for the redressing of sin, *is by gentle means, if it may be.*

Secondly, if that will not, *then by severe,* if men would not have men damned.

' I came not, to spare you,' because I desired that gentler courses might prevail. So I say, the first point is this, that

Doct. If gentler courses will prevail, they ought especially, and in the first place, to be taken.

It should be the care both of ministers, and of all those that deal with others, first of all to use mild, and winning, and gaining courses.

Now to prove this.

Reason 1. First, *they are more suitable to the nature of man ;* for the nature of man is best wrought on by rational courses suitable to his nature, suitable to his principle. Man is a reasonable creature, therefore rational courses will prevail with a rational man, a course of persuasion and discovery. A man that is not beast-like, tell him but the danger of his sin, tell him the peril of it in gentle words, and he will amend, if so be he be not hardened by God to destruction ; or if God do not reserve him to a more severe redress. Gentle courses ought first to be used, because they are agreeable to the nature of man.

2. Again, *they suit most to God's disposition ;* for ' God is love,' 1 John iv. 8, and his course to man is love. If he take any course contrary to love, it is not his own work ; as he saith, to punish man it is not his own work, he is forced to that alway. To shew love and mercy, that is his work, that that comes from his own principle, from his mercy, ' he is love.' He doth not say, he is justice, or rigour, but he is love. It agrees with the nature of God to deal mercifully. If he deal otherwise, it is forced from us.

3. *It suits with the whole carriage of our salvation,* these courses of love, and gentleness first of all; for we are saved by a manner of love. We are saved by God giving his Son, and by his Son giving himself. We are saved by a course of entreaty. The ministers of God are ambassadors to

desire us to be 'reconciled to God,' 2 Cor. v. 20. God having saved us by a manner of love, he will have us taught by a manner of love, in the gospel especially; because God's aim is to gain our love, and which way can that be, but by a way of love?

For the nature of man is such, that it will never love till it know it be loved first. Therefore God stoops to a way of love, because he would have our love; which he would never have by other courses, because they are contrary to our nature.

4. *It is the practice of God.* His custom is answerable: for first, he deals by gentle means always, and then after, if those will not prevail, he goes to severe means, and in severe means he takes degrees; first less, and then more violent, and then violent indeed. God would never descend to sharper courses, if milder would serve the turn. You know he bade his own people, before they set in hostile manner upon any, to give them fair warning, to give them conditions of peace: so it is his course to offer conditions of peace. So he did to the old world, and so he doth to us. Before he corrects, he offers conditions of peace. You see how sparing Christ was, and how full of love, 'O Jerusalem, Jerusalem,' &c., Mat. xxiii. 37.

5. Again, *they are courses that promise best success ordinarily:* for the proud nature of man will raise itself up, and will harden itself against severe courses. Man naturally, as I said, will be led, and not forced. His nature will rise against forced violent courses, therefore for the event itself it is the best.

6. Again, *they are courses that are more lasting.* That that is gained by love, is constant; that that we prevail with men for by reason, it will hold. Other courses are not so faithful, they will not hold. What we gain on men by fear, there is shame in it, that a man should be forced to anything, and nature will break out; but it will hold best, that is gained by way of love and reason.

Use. Therefore *let us imitate God in this*, when we are to deal with any, not to take violent courses in the first place, but to deal with men as men, deal with them by love and reason, and not stand upon our own stomach and greatness, and take delight, as it were, in the commanding of others; that we have a destructive power, a power that can quash, and crush men, and shew it to the utmost, and pride ourselves in it. If God should deal so with such, where were those proud creatures? If God were not a forbearing, indulgent, sparing God?

Therefore you may see what disposition those are of, that all are for fire, for violent courses, rigorous courses. That is not the way that God useth. It is not the way that Christ used. It is not the way that ministers do use that have the Spirit of God.

You have some kind of people, that if a man be not always in matters of damnation, his sermon is nothing. So you have some that in their courses are so violent, that they know nothing that is moderate, (and yet perhaps they are good too, but) they cherish too much a violent disposition. Now St Paul, though he were a very zealous, holy man, yet notwithstanding he would not put himself upon violent courses but when there was great necessity. He is rather a butcher than a physician, that loves to torment his patient. You see what course is first to be taken. I need not be long in so clear a point; therefore I will spend no more time in it, but come to the second, that is more generally useful. Because indeed men are so, that gentle means will hardly prevail with them, what must be done then? 'not spare them.'

Doct. When gentle means will not serve the turn, then we must not spare.
St Paul came not, that he might ' spare them.' Now, if they had not amended, what would have St Paul have done, think you? Would he have suffered them to have cherished the incestuous person among them? that wicked person that had committed that which was intolerable amongst the heathen? Would he have cherished proud factious men amongst them, that would disgrace St Paul's doctrine, to win authority to themselves? Would not he have told them to their face the danger of their sin, and have made them ashamed? Undoubtedly he would : he would [not] ' have spared.' So I say, if gentle means will not prevail, men must not be spared; neither minister nor magistrate must spare; especially in dangerous courses that are prejudicial to the souls of others.

Why?

Reason. We must spare none, that God may spare all. We that are ministers must spare no sin, that God may spare all. ' Lift up thy voice like a trumpet,' saith God, ' and tell Israel of their sins,' Isa. xviii. 58. If gentle means will not reform them, ' lift up thy voice like a trumpet.' Cast out Jezebel with her painted face. Though sin paint and colour itself, it must be cast out. Jonah must out of the ship, the ship will perish else. Achan must be stoned. We must tell men of their danger, not with hatred of their persons, but to prevent an eternal punishment.

You know well that preventing justice is better than executing justice. Is not discipline better than execution? Is it not better to hear of our faults roundly, when other means will not prevail, than to cherish that that will be for our eternal destruction? Is not searing and cutting better than killing? Is it not better that a limb be seared and cut, than that all be clear cut off, and the whole body perish? Is not the pain of chirurgery, or physic that makes a man sick for a while, better to be endured than the pains and terrors of death itself? These preventing courses are the best courses : therefore we must spare none, but tell them of their danger faithfully.

Only, liberty of speech must not be a cover for boisterousness, or a cover for the venting of evil humours, as sometimes it is. For flesh will never prevail with flesh. Flesh, and pride in the speaker, will never prevail with pride in the hearer ; but it must be a spiritual kind of severity, discovering the danger to them we speak to, with a spiritual holy affection, and a spirit of love, though with severity : for there is a severity of love and gentleness, it will prevail when it comes from such a spirit. But if there be a discovery of flesh, not only in ministers, but in those that deal with others, flesh will rise against flesh. A man may sometimes find fault with another with greater corruption than the thing he finds fault with in another ; he may be more to blame for his dealing than the other for his fault. ' I came not, to spare you.'

Use. Therefore, when ministers are plain in discovering the danger of the times, the danger of the persons, and places where they are to deal, *people must hear them as they love their own souls.* If they have any quarrel, let them quarrel with their master ; for what we speak is from the word of God. We come as his ambassadors and servants, and should be considered as ambassadors. Therefore, considering whose message we bring, they must take it in good part to be told of their sins in a good manner. As St Austin saith very well. Christ, saith he, speaks to the sea, and it was quiet : Christ said, ' Be still,' the sea heard, and the waves were still ; but he speaks to us in the ministry to stay our violent courses in sin, and we puff and swell when we are told of our faults (*iiii*). Is this good, think you? No. If we do so, it is a sign that God intends to seal us to destruction. As we know, Eli's sons, when they did not hearken to their father, God had appointed them to destruction. Those that will not hearken to ministerial reproof, it is a sign that God hath sealed them over to destruction.

If we would not have either ministers or others to be severe in telling us, let us be severe to our own sins first. Men are like to children; first they foul and defile themselves, and they cry when they are washed: so men soil themselves with sins, and cry when they should be purged from them. If we cannot endure to be told of our faults, how shall we endure to be tormented for our faults in hell? Those that are so tender, that they will not endure a word contrary to their dispositions, how will they endure that sentence, ' Go ye cursed,' when they shall be turned into hell? Consider what will come of it, if we live in sin.

I beseech you therefore, suffer the word of exhortation at our hands. Our salvation lies upon it. If we discover not the danger of the sins of people to whom we speak, if we discern them, we shall perish for it, because we are unfaithful in our embassage. Therefore for your own souls; and likewise that we may discharge our duty as we should, patiently and quietly sit under exhortation and reproof, not only public, but private, if occasion be.

O beloved! at the latter day it will be a matter of vexation that we were cherished too much in our courses. Do you not think that the damned spirits in hell wish, O! that we had been told! O, that we had been dealt with violently, that we had been pulled out of this flame! There is an excellent place in Jude's epistle, ' Have *mercy* upon some.' Use some gently that are of tractable dispositions; and pull ' some out of the fire with fear,' with threatening eternal damnation, with terrible courses, that they may have cause to fear; first with admonitions, and if that will not prevail, with suspension, with further censure; and if that will not prevail, with excommunication, cast them out of the church, as this incestuous Corinthian, ' that their souls may be saved in the day of the Lord,' verse 23.

There is a threefold correction, or finding fault, that are gradual one after another, and they should be of vigour in the church in all times.

1. *First, a friendly telling of a fault*, between man and man, if we see any thing dangerously amiss.

2. Then, *when a man takes another man before company*, when he takes him before those that he respects, when privately he will not amend. Then

3. *Correction*, if admonition of friends will not do, ' *tell the church*,' Mat. xviii. 17, rather than suffer his soul to perish.

These steps and degrees were observed in the best times of the church, and if they were observed now, many souls would be saved. This is that that St Jude speaks of, ' Save some, pulling them out of the fire,' that is, snatch them out by violent means, by excommunication, that ' their souls may be saved in the day of the Lord.' Those that are in hell wish that they had been pulled out with fear, with violent courses. O! that we had been told of our filthy courses, of our swearing, of our injustice, that we had had violence offered us rather than to have come into this place of torment. O! those will bless God another day for that gracious violence. And those that are let alone will curse all another day; ministers, friends, and parents, they will curse all, that there were not more violent courses taken with them, to stop them in their way to hell: to deal plainly with them. It is the best mercy that can be shewed, to be faithful in this kind.

Therefore while it is time, suffer the word of exhortation, and reproof; the time will come else that you shall condemn yourselves that you were so impatient, and shall wish, O! that we had had those that would have dealt more violently with us! It is cruel pity as can be in ministers, to be flatterers, and to daub; or in parents and governors of others, to dissemble with them in their courses, and not to tell them of it. It is the most cruel pity of all; it is betraying of them to eternal torments. For sin, as I said, it must be judged and censured here, or hereafter; if it be not here, there is more reserved for the time to come, when God will open the treasures of his wrath. We put into his treasury fast enough; and the time will come of opening all the treasuries of his vengeance, when he will pour out the vials of his wrath upon sinners that are not reformed. So much for that point.

'*I call God for a record upon my soul.*' St Paul to purge himself from suspicion, seals all this with an oath. Herein he doth shew his great love to them, and his care over them, that he would so seriously purge himself to gain their love, and good opinion of him. It was an argument of the great esteem he had of them. He was willing they should think he was very desirous of their love, and of their good opinion, for whose sake he would swear, and clear himself by an oath. As God esteems man's love much, when he will condescend so far as to seal his love, and promise with an oath; God would have us to think that he values, and esteems our respect very much, so St Paul would have them think he esteemed them much, that he would make such a solemn oath for their sakes. Now to speak of an oath a little.

An oath, as we know, is either in judgment before a magistrate; or in particular cases between private persons. And it is either assertory of a thing past, or promissory of a thing to come. Now this oath of St Paul's is an assertory oath of a thing that was past, to secure them that he did not come to them upon this ground, that he had a mind to spare them. It was no promise of anything to come, but an assertion of a thing that was past. An oath is either an assertion or a promise, with a calling of God to be a witness and a judge; to be a witness of the truth, or a judge if he say false. You have the description of an oath in this text. I say, it is either an assertion of a thing past, or a promise of a thing to come, a sealing of this by calling God to witness of the thing we say, and to avenge the falsehood if we say false. As St Paul here, 'I call God to record,' that what I say is true, 'and upon my soul,' if I say false.

Many conclusions concerning an oath might be raised out of the text.

1. *First of all*, concerning the person that makes an oath, *he should indeed be a gracious, a holy, and a good man.* As St Paul saith, 'I call God to witness, whom I serve in my spirit,' Rom. i. 9. A man is scarce fit to swear, which is a part of God's worship, that is not good otherwise. Will he care for the religion of an oath, that hath no religion in him? He whose oath should be taken, should be such a man as St Paul, in some degree, whose oath should be taken. The Turks are careful of this,—to the shame of Christians,—they will not take an oath of an ordinary swearer. It must be a man that hath somewhat in him, that shall have his oath regarded.

2. Again, we see *by whom an oath should be taken:* by the name of God. We ought not to swear by creatures, but by God himself; nor to swear by any idol, as the mass, and by Mary, and such like. It is a taking God to witness. An oath is a part of God's service, a part of divine worship, as it

is, Deut. xxix. 12, and other places. Now we ought to serve God only; therefore we ought not to use the name of any creature in an oath. He that we swear by must know the heart, whether we speak true or no. Now who knows the heart but God? therefore we must swear only by the name of God. These things are easy, therefore I do but name them.

3. We see here again, *the two grand parts of an oath;* besides assertion, or promise of the truth, there must be a calling God to witness, and imprecation. Though these be not always set down, they are implied. Sometimes the Scripture sets down the one part; but always the other is implied. There is imprecation in every oath. Sometimes imprecation implies both, as God do so and so. Sometimes there is a calling God to witness without imprecation, yet it is always implied. For whosoever swears, calls God to witness of the truth, and if it be not true, that God would punish him.

These three go together in an oath. God that can discover it, he knows my heart whether I say true or no. And he is judge, and thereupon a revenger. In an oath, God is considered not only as *judex,* but as *judex* and *vindex;* not only as a discoverer, but as a judge and revenger, if it be false. Therefore it is a part of divine worship, because it is with prayer; and imprecation is alway implied, if it be not expressed. So we see in this text what an oath is, and by whom it is to be taken, and the parts of it.

4. Again, we see here in the text, *that an oath ought to be taken in serious matters.* The rule of an oath is excellently set down by Jeremiah, iv. 2. I know no one place of Scripture more pregnant, and therefore I name it. ' Thou shalt swear,'—how?—' The Lord liveth, in truth, in judgment, and in righteousness.'

(1.) We must swear *in truth,* that is, that not only the thing be true that we swear; we must look to that, but we must think it so too. The thing must be true, and we must apprehend it so. ' We must swear *in truth.*'

(2.) And then *in judgment,* that is, with discretion. We must understand throughly the matter whereof we swear, and what an oath is. Therefore persons under years ought not to take an oath, because they cannot swear in judgment, to know what the weight and validity of an oath is; and when it is a fit time to take it. It must be taken in serious business, as St Paul here to clear himself to the souls of the Corinthians whom he laboured to edify; when he saw their ill conceit of him hindered their edification, therefore he clears himself by an oath.

(3.) Thirdly, it must be *in justice,* that is, we must not bind ourselves by an oath to anything that is ill : it is a rule a long time past. Herod bound himself by an oath in that kind, Mat. xiv. 9. But an oath must never be a bond of injustice, but it must be taken in righteousness.

Therefore here is condemned the equivocation and reservation of the papists. They will swear before a magistrate, but with equivocation. This is not in righteousness; for it is a rule that an oath must be taken in that sense as he to whom we swear takes it; that is a constant rule among all divines, because it is to persuade him of the truth that we swear. It is for his and others' sakes; and as he and others take it, so it must be took. Therefore equivocation with absurd reservations are wicked, because they are absurd if they be expressed. He will swear that he is not a priest : he means after the order of Melchizedec. It is a mocking and profaning of an oath, it is not to swear in justice and righteousness. But it is so foul and abominable a course, that it is not fit to be spoken of almost; and they are ashamed of it themselves. St Paul's oath was all this. He sware in truth ; he was truly persuaded of the truth of his own affections toward them. And then in judgment ; it was done in discretion ; for being not able otherwise to clear himself, having no witness in earth, he goes to heaven for a purger, he goes to God himself for a witness ; he fetcheth strength from heaven. There was none on earth that knew St Paul's affection, but the Spirit of God and his own spirit ; and he thought his own spirit was not sufficient. My own spirit tells me that ' I came not, to spare you ;' but if you would know my mind better, ' I call God to witness,' and to be a revenger, if I speak false, that I came not, for this end, that I might spare you, to prevent the rigour and severity that I should have used toward your sin.

An oath should be true and weighty ; but that is not enough, it must be in matters indeterminable. For if a thing may be determined without an oath, we should never use it. The end of an oath is to end controversies ; for if St Paul could have persuaded them of his gracious and loving heart, that he stood affected as he did, he would not have used an oath ; but having no other means to do it, he goes to heaven for a witness.

It were but misspending of time to shew that an oath is lawful. Have we anabaptists among us, that call this into question ? No ! we have many atheists. It is dangerous atheism in the anabaptists to question whether they may take an oath. We have the example of St Paul, we have the example of God himself ; shall we think it unlawful when God himself swears, and the angel swears, and Christ swears, and the apostle swears ?

Where it is forbidden that we should not swear, it is meant that we should not swear in our ordinary talk, where we need not seal every light speech with the solemnity of an oath. Men will not put on their best apparel every day ; so men ought not to use solemn matters upon every occasion, but only upon holy and grand occasions.

Our Saviour Christ forbids swearing, first by the creature at all, and swearing in ordinary talk at all. ' Whatsoever is more than yea and nay,' in ordinary talk, is sin, Mat. v. 37. Therefore, considering that St Paul doth it in a serious matter, we ought to learn not to swear, except it be in great matters : when we are called before a magistrate, or when we are to purge ourselves from evil suspicion of our Christian friends ; as we see here St Paul doth to the Corinthians : he calls God to witness against his soul, if it were not true.

Obj. But you will say, Men will not believe me except I swear, and therefore I swear so oft.

Ans. Then live better for shame, that men may believe thee for thine honest life. If thy honest life be not better than thy oath, they will not believe thee for swearing ; for he that swears oft swears false, and ' in many words there cannot want iniquity,' Prov. x. 19, much more in many oaths there cannot want iniquity ; and he that swears much, out of doubt he oft forswears.

Obj. Oh ! it is my custom, and I cannot break a custom.

Ans. Use that apology to a judge. Though malefactors be none of the modestest creatures, will any of them say, It is my custom to rob and steal ? Will not the judge say it is his custom to cut them off ? Thou sayest it is thy custom. It is God's custom to damn such persons. Therefore that is an aggravation of thy sin.

But here we that are ministers may take up a complaint, that when we have to deal with the wretched disposition of men in things concerning their souls and a better life, do what we can, we cannot prevail with them to leave that that they have no profit nor no good by; they are not put upon it by any fear. It is only out of superfluity of pride and malice against God, out of the abundance of profaneness.

Can we think to prevail with men to deny themselves in greater matters, to forsake their unlawful gains, or to venture the suffering ill for a good cause, and to renounce pleasures that are lawful, do we think to gain upon men for these things, when we cannot for superfluities that they are not forced to by any violence, that they have no gain nor credit by, except it be among a company of debauched men like themselves? Yet it is our case; we deal in the world with a company of persons to leave that that they have no gain by, except it be the wrath of God, and yet we cannot prevail.

Obj. Oh, but you will say, I live with such company that I must swear.

Ans. What a shame is it for thee that carnal company should prevail more with thee than the vengeance of God, and the authority of God in the ministry! What a heart hast thou that a base person like thyself should move thee to do that that God himself and the authority of his ordinance cannot move thee to forbear! It is an argument of a base nature. How darest thou look God and Christ in the face another day, when for his sake thou wilt not leave a superfluous, profane oath? Thou regardest a wicked companion more, because thou wilt not be mocked of him; thou wilt swear for company, or because thou wilt please him, that he may think thee to be so and so, a companion fit for him; to please him, thou wilt displease God and Christ, before whom thou shalt be judged ere long. If people were not mad and sold to destruction, they would consider these things.

Indeed, these things are so clear, and so odious in themselves, that we need not press them. We should spend that little time we have to preach of more sublime matters than to come to dissuade men from swearing. Alas! under the glorious gospel that we have lived so long, have we gained so little that we are forced to spend our time to dissuade men from swearing? We should look to the mysteries of religion, and draw men to further perfection; but such times we are fallen into, and we must be content with it, and I would we could gain anything by discovering the danger of these things.

An ordinary course of swearing, it argues a very vile heart wheresoever it is: bear it out as boisterously as they will. It argues this venom in the heart: Well! I cannot offend against the second table, but the laws of the kingdom will hamper me! I cannot steal, or murder, but somewhat I can do in despite of God himself, and the worst that can come, it is but a trifling matter. What venom is in the hearts of men, that where there is but the least damage, they will be restrained; and here, because there is not present execution upon a sinner in this kind, they profane and abuse the glorious name of God!

1. When God's name is abused by swearing and blasphemy, usually the original of it, among other things, *is atheism.* If we thought that God were so as the Scripture shews, we would not dally so much. They that lead others into bad courses, it is from the height and depth of atheism. Make the best of it, it is a great degree of irreverence to the glorious Majesty of God. For when God shall say, 'He that takes my name in vain, shall not carry it away guiltless,' Exodus xx. 7: What will he do, think you, to him that swears idly, and profanely, when the vain taking of God's name in vain without an oath, the vain trifling with the name of God, shall not

escape ? When men do not reverence and fear an oath, as it is, Eccles.
ix. 2, it argues much irreverence.

And, indeed, it is worse in the principle than in the thing itself.
Though the words be heinous, yet the principle whence it ariseth is worse,
that is, infidelity and atheism, and alway irreverence and want of fear of
the glorious Majesty of God, this ground makes it more odious. Therefore, those that are subject to it, if they would amend it, let them remove
the ground.

2. Sometimes, again, *it is cherishing too much passion.* So, because
they cannot be sufficiently revenged upon their poor brethren, God must
smart for it; they will tear his glorious name that never did them wrong.
What a mad passion is this; hath God done them any wrong? Therefore,
I say, let us labour to remove the ground of it; and labour to plant the
contrary in our hearts, the true fear of God, that we may fear an oath.
Let us labour to subdue unruly passion.

3. Again, in some others *affectation is the cause.* Many of the frothy
sort, they think it a thing commendable to fill up their discourse with these
parentheses, with oaths; which perhaps doth them a service to knit their
wounded discourse together. So this foolish and sinful affectation is one
cause. Men desire to be thought to be somebody, by swearing. They
would have the world to think that they are valorous men, that can be so
bold with God himself; therefore let other men take heed how they meddle
with them, when God smarts for it, as if he that could swear most, had
most courage.

4. And in many *it is out of a sinful shame,* because they will hold correspondence with the company, and they are afraid to be thought to be
strict; and that they may be thought to be free from suspicion of overmuch conscionableness* in their ways, they will not let the world see that
they shall not think that they are men that make any conscience of strictness, but they can be bold with the name of God: so, because they
would have others think that they are men that do not stand upon terms
of conscience and strictness, they will swear they are men for the world,
they are serviceable for any purpose. Men that make conscience of anything, make conscience of all ; but a man that makes conscience of an oath,
or any such thing, he is a stiff man, he is not serviceable, he is not for the
turn. Now, because men would be thought of others not to be of that
strain, to make any conscience, hereupon they break out to the profaning
of the name of God. How shall such persons, that out of sinful weakness
labour and apply themselves more to satisfy sinful men, than the great
God, how dare they look God in the face? Jesus Christ saith, ' He
that is ashamed of me before men ;' he that is ashamed to own religion, nay, to own justice, to own even common good behaviour, rather
than he will offend others : he that is ashamed of me in such mean things
as these, ' I will be ashamed of him before my Heavenly Father,' Mark
viii. 38.

If other reasons will not move us to leave this sin, let the love of the
state and kingdom we live in do it. Jeremiah saith, ' for oaths the land
shall mourn,' Jer. xxiii. 10. Indeed, there is a mulct for this, but that men
slight it. And God, I hope, will be merciful to the state, for the censure
of the state upon profanation, it is a very worthy act *(jjjj)*. But if that
be not executed, or men grow not to make more conscience, the land will

* That is, ' conscientiousness.'—G.

mourn for it; because where the magistrates cease to do their office, God will do his office. Where sin is punished, God will not punish. Where the magistrate spares, God will not spare. He will punish. Therefore this sin where it is not censured and punished, the land shall mourn for it.

If the care of the kingdom will not move them, yet the care of their own houses and families should. In Zech. v. 1, the prophet speaks of a flying book of judgments that should come upon the house of the swearer, and consume the posts of his house. And the wise man saith in Ecclesiasticus (though it be apocryphal), ' The plague shall not depart from the house o the swearer,' iii. 11.* God's vengeance accompanies even the very family and house of the swearer.

And, for avoiding of this, I would there were more conscience made of those oaths that border upon gross oaths. I will not dispute the matter. Take it for granted they be no oaths, but asseverations, as to call their truth in question, and their confidence in matters of religon ; who will lay a thousand pound to pawn for a matter of sixpence ? Who, if he be discreet and considerate, will lay his faith and religion to pawn for every trifle in common talk ? Faith is the most precious thing in the world : for a man to lay a great matter for a twopenny or sixpenny debt, it is odious among men. Certainly, it is idle at the best among men, to lay asseverations of religion without ground, upon every trifle. He that will avoid danger must not come near it; he must avoid all that borders upon it. I would therefore more care were had, even of these.

I will only add one thing more. Whereas he calls God ' for a record upon his soul,' that those that are overmuch given to rash calling upon the name of God, to rash swearing, let them know this, as I said, that there is an imprecation implied in every oath : they do as it were curse themselves. If the thing be not true, their damnation is sealed under a curse : they call God to record upon their souls against themselves.

Let us so live that our life may be a kind of oath : the life of a Christian should be so. An oath is a calling God to witness, a calling God to curse if it be not so. A Christian should live so, as he may call God to witness for every action he doth ; to bring himself to an oath, under a curse oft-times, as it is in Ezra, and oft in Scripture, ' If I do not so and so,' vii. 23, &c. Because our nature is unstable, it starts† from holy duties, we should bring ourselves to duties with an oath, under a curse.

It is an excellent thing when we can live as in God's presence ; to do all we do in the presence of God. God is a witness whether we call him or no. Therefore we should so carry ourselves, that we might call God to witness the sincerity of our aims, and whatsoever we do. He is a witness, and he will be our judge : therefore, whether we formally in the manner of an oath call him or no, that is not the matter, but let us know and think that he is, and will be so.

I beseech you consider the sweet comfort that will arise out of it, that he that will live and think and affect,‡ and speak in the presence of God, that he may call God to record of the sincerity of his intentions, of all that he speaks, and thinks, and doth ; how comfortably shall he live, and give his account to God, that hath lived as in the presence of God all his days ! He that hath presented to his soul, as it were, the bar of Christ in his life-time, that hath lived as one that could give an account and reckoning,

---

* Cf. footnote, vol. II. page 351.—G.   ‡ That is, ' choose, love.'—G.
† That is, ' turns aside.'—G.

when he comes to the point that he must give up his account, how joyfully and comfortably will he do it! So much for that verse. I come now to the last verse of the chapter.

VERSE 24.

' *Not that we have dominion over your faith, but are helpers of your joy; for by faith ye stand.*' St Paul is yet in his clearing, he is yet in his apology. ' Not that we have dominion over your faith,' &c. I do not tell you, I came not yet to ' spare you,' as if I meant to domineer over your faith when I came. Because those words, ' I came not yet, to spare you,' might seem to carry some highness, some lordliness with them, as if the apostle would have taken much upon him; therefore he corrects those words in this verse, ' Not that we have dominion over your faith,' &c. So that in these words he removes a suspicion of spiritual tyranny over them. Because he had said before, ' he came not, to spare them,' they might think, What would he have done if he had come? would he have enforced us? Oh no! Indeed your reformation hath spared me a labour, and you a chiding; but if I had reproved you sharply, it should have been for your good. Then he sets down the true cause, ' We are helpers of your joy.' If I had come, and told you of your faults, if I had not spared you, it should have been to help your joy; and now I come not to you, it is to help your joy: my scope in all is to be a furtherer of your joy. So these words are a reason of the former, why he did not come to domineer over their faith, ' For by faith ye stand.' You stand by faith, and you stand out by faith against all oppositions whatsoever; therefore your faith must not lean on me; I must not domineer over that you stand by; if your faith should rely on me, I am but a man. Faith must rely on God. It must have a better pillar than myself. You must stand upon Divine strength: therefore ' you stand by faith;' and if you stand by faith, we have no reason to have dominion over your faith.

These words are declined by many interpreters (*kkkk*). They know not what the dependence is: but this is the best dependence of the words, ' We domineer not, or rule not over your faith;' because by faith you stand as upon a bottom; you stand against all adverse power by faith. Therefore you had need to have it well founded, you had need to plant your faith well, by which you stand against all opposite power, and against all human authority. For a man may be a liar, and do good in many things. A man hath a deceitful nature, as far as he hath a corrupt principle in him. He may deceive, and yet be a good man too; in particular cases he may shew himself a changeable creature. But there must be no falsehood nor uncertainty in faith; for it is a grace that must have truth and certainty: it must have immoveable and unchangeable truth to build on. Therefore we domineer not over your faith. God forbid we should do so; for faith is the grace whereby you stand; if you should build upon us as men, you could not stand alway. The point is clear, that,

Doct. No creature can have dominion over the faith of another.

The faith of a man is only subject to the Spirit of God, to God, and to Christ. And by the way, St Paul taxeth* those false apostles and false teachers, that laboured to creep into the consciences of people, to have higher place in the hearts of people than they should have, that so they might rule the

* That is, ' chargeth, accuseth.'—G.

people as they list. Now that should not be the scope of the minister, to have dominion over the faith of others ; for the ministry is a ministry, not a magistracy. A minister, so far as he is a pastor, he is a minister ; that is, he is to deliver things from God that may stablish the soul, not to domineer over men's faith, as if he would prescribe what men should believe.

Now to unfold this point, I will first shew what it is to have no dominion over men's faith. And then what it is to have dominion and rule over other men's faith, and who are guilty of this.

1. Not to have dominion over another man's faith, it is not when a church doth force prescribing * to the articles of religion. That is not to have dominion over the faith of others, to draw people to conformity of the same religion in the substantials of it (as some that [seek extravagant liberty, lay that imputation perhaps). It is used in all churches.

2. Again, it is not to domineer over faith, to suppress that that they call of late in neighbour-countries, a liberty of prophesy (*llll*), to suppress a liberty of preaching when men list; that men should have an unbridled licence. We see in Poland, † and other countries, what abundance of heretics there are, where there is more liberty to preach, and to publish what men list. Those countries are like Africa‡, where, they say, there are alway new monsters. Or like to Egypt ; when *Nilus* overflows it leaves a slime behind, and when the sun works upon that slime it breeds many imperfect strange creatures. So those countries where there is liberty of religions, there are always some strange novel opinions, some monsters. Experience of foreign countries shews it too true ; therefore to hinder that extravagant liberty is not dominion over faith.

Nay, to force men to the means of faith, it is not to domineer over faith. St Austin himself was once of this mind, that people were not to be forced (*mmmm*). It is true. But they may be compelled to the means, though they cannot be compelled to believe. Men may be compelled to the means by mulcts, and other courses of state. And it is a happy necessity when people are forced to the means, under which means, by God's blessing, they may be reduced to a better habit and temper of soul.

Therefore it is cruelty to neglect this care, to leave people to their own liberty to attend upon the means, or not to attend on them. Therefore our State is, and may be justified well, for those violent courses to recusants. And many of them after, bless God they have done it, and they have cause. For there is a majesty in the ordinances of God. If people were brought under the means, God's Spirit would make the means effectual. And there is not a greater snare of the devil, whereby he holds more in the Romish church in perdition, than by persuading them that it is a dangerous thing to come to our prayers, and to attend upon the means of salvation ; whenas in our liturgy there is nothing that may justly offend. Therefore to force to the means, it is not to domineer over faith ; because it is only a drawing from outward inforcement to the use of means.

3. Again, it is not a ruling over faith, nor a base slavery, when men hear the word of God opened directly and clearly, when men shall persuade others according to their own judgment, that this is so, and when others shall yield. There is some faith that may be called in some degree implicit faith and obedience, that is not sinful, but good and discreet. As when men by their standing in the church, and by their experience and holiness of life, are thought to be men that speak agreeable to the ground

---

* That is, ' subscribing, subscription.'— G.   ‡ Spelled ' Africk.'—G.
† Spelled ' Polonia.'—G.

of Scripture, though they have not a direct rule and place of Scripture for it, other men's conscience may follow what they say. I have been directed by such men at such times, that by reason of their calling have opportunity to advise.

But this frees it from base service, that it must be with reservation, till it appear otherwise by some place of Scripture, or till better counsel may be yielded. Obedience to others with reservation, and counselling with others, this is no domineering, because it is with reserving ourselves to a further discovery, and a further light. That, the moralists use to call the opinion of an honest man. Where the law speaks not, it is much to be esteemed; especially an honest discreet Christian, when the law of God speaks not directly. Then he that speaks out of conscience, and some light, he may persuade another man, with this reservation, till further light be discovered; this is no domineering over faith.

I might take away many things that might breed a suspicion, as if we domineered over the faith of others when we do not.

But to come to shew you this positive truth, what this tyranny over the faith of others is, and where it is practised.

1. Those tyrannise over the faith of others *that do equalise men's traditions, some canons of their own, with the word of God*, and press them with equal violence, perhaps more; because they are brats of their own brain. Those that will devise a voluntary worship of God, and so entangle people, and tell them, This you must do, when there is no ground for it in the word of God; it is will-worship. God loves willing worship, when we worship him willingly; but he loves not will-worship, when it is the device of our own brain how we will serve him. As if a servant or a slave must devise how his lord will be served; what impudency is this, if we consider what God is! They tyrannise over people's consciences, that equalise their own dotages, though they account them witty devices, and their own inventions with the worship of God; that jumble all together, as if conscience were equally bound to any device of their own, as to God's word.

2. Again, those do tyrannise over the faith of others, *that think they can make articles in religion to bind conscience*. Those that think to free themselves from the danger of error, as if what they said were infallible, they tyrannise over others. Those that for trifles excommunicate whole churches, because they hold not correspondency with them in their errors, they tyrannise over the faith of others: those that withhold the means of knowledge, that so in a dark time all their fooleries may be more admired. As we see masks, and such like overly* things, they must have the commendation of some light that is not so glorious as the sun to win admiration of men; so those that would win admiration of their fooleries, they shut people, as much as they may, in darkness, that they may have their persons, and all other things in admiration. This is to tyrannise over faith, and to hinder them from that that is the means to reform them better.

Quest. But who are guilty of all this?

Ans. We see what church especially is guilty of this of domineering over the faith of others, that is, the church of Rome.

1. The Council of Trent equaliseth traditions with the word of God. They divide the word of God into the written and unwritten; and under a curse they pronounce that all must be received with the same reverence.

2. And then they have devised a will-worship of their own, and follow,

* That is, 'over-lying,' = concealing, disguising.—G.

and force their will-worship with greater violence, than the worship of God ; and they set God's stamp upon all their fooleries, to gain authority under the name of Christ's church, and the word of God : they carry all.

3. Again, you know, they hold the church to be infallible. They hold the judgment of the pope, the ' man of sin,' to be infallible, he cannot err ; and hereupon whatsoever he saith, it must bind conscience, because he is in his chair and cannot err ; whatsoever he saith is the scope of God's word, infallible. And this is a fundamental error, as we call it, a first lie, a leading lie. This is moving to error, this is the mover that moves all other errors under it.

For whereupon is all the abominations of popery justified ? They are justified by this, though they seem ridiculous, gross, and blasphemous, they came from the church, and the church is virtually in the pope. An absurd position, that the whole church should be virtually in one man ; yet that is the Jesuitical opinion ; and the church cannot err : therefore it is good, because these tenets come from him whose judgment is infallible. That is the error that leadeth to, and establisheth all other errors under it : it is the first lie. And in lies, there is a leading, one goes under another, they never go alone ; so this is the leading lie of all popery, that the pope cannot err ; by this means they domineer over the faith of others, and make the people even beasts indeed.

But to see the indignity of this, that the pope cannot err, it is the greatest error of all, and the prevention of all amendment on their side. Do you think that they will ever amend their opinion, when they hold this that is a block in the way of all reformation, that the pope can err ? for deny that, and you call all the fabric of their religion in question ; and grant that, it stops all reformation on their side. What reformation may we hope for on their side that hold this position, that they cannot err ? Hence come all their treasons, and rebellions ; they have some dispensation from the pope, and he cannot err, though he prescribe rebellion and treason.

4. Another opinion they have, *that the church is the judge of all contro-versies*, in which the faith of men must be resolved at last ; but it is the pope that the Jesuits mean. Now this is indeed to domineer over the faith, to make a man of sin to be a judge over all points of faith, and faith to be resolved at last into that, into the judgment of the church.

The church hath an inducing power, a leading power, persuading to the belief of the Scriptures, and to hear what God saith in his word, but after, there is inward intrinsical grounds in the word, that make us to know the word without the church. Now they would have the authority of the word depend upon the church, and so overrule men's consciences in that case. Whereas all that the church hath, is a leading, inducing, persuading to hear the word, under which word and ordinance we shall see such light and majesty in the Scriptures, that from inward grounds we shall be persuaded that the word of God is the word of God. Therefore the church is the first inducer to believe the word of God, not the last object to which all is resolved. For they themselves cross it in their tenets when they speak discreetly. Is this opinion so, and so ? The church holds it. But what authority hath the church to maintain it ? Where is the authority of your church ? Then they bring some place of Scripture ; ' I will be with you to the end of the world,' Mat. xxviii. 20. And, ' he that heareth you, heareth me,' &c. Luke x. 16. I do but a little discover to you the danger of this error. They make the word of God to be believed, because the church saith so ; they make truth to be believed, because their man of sin, whom they depend upon, saith so.   Do we believe the Trinity, or that Christ is our Redeemer, because the church saith so ?   Should we not believe it except the church say so ?   What if the church teach the ' doctrine of devils,' 1 Tim. iv. 1, as they do ?   They cannot shake it off.   We must believe because the church saith so.   So upon equal grounds they shall teach the doctrine of devils, and the doctrine of Christ, because the church saith so.

As it was said anciently, he that believes two things, the one for the other, he believes not two, but one in effect ; because he believes the one for the other.   So in effect they believe nothing but the church ; that is, themselves believe the truth to be divine, because they say so ; so they may believe any devilish error, because they say so ; so any treason, or rebellion must go current, because they say so, because they cannot err.   You see how they domineer over the faith of others ; shall not Christ be Christ, nor God be God, nor the devil be the devil, except the church say so ?

5.   Again, *in the very matters themselves, in the points that themselves do not urge,* the church of Rome domineers, and tyranniseth over the souls of people. For example, they hold that *the intention of a minister in the sacrament makes it effectual.*   What a fear doth this breed in the souls of men, that they know not whether they be baptized or no, because it must be in the intention of the minister ?

And then *in confession,* they must confess all.   What a tyranny is this to the souls of people, when perhaps there is somewhat that they have not confessed, and so their confession is of no worth ?

And *in satisfaction,* perhaps I have not made satisfaction enough by their injunction laid on me, and therefore I must satisfy in hell ; what a rack is this to conscience ?

So, what a rack to conscience is that opinion, that the pope cannot err ; when I cannot tell, perhaps, whether he be the right pope or no.   If he came in by simony, or is not *in cathedra* (*nnnn*), and many conditions they have to solve that point.   If any of those conditions be not observed, he is not the man he should be ; what tyranny do they force upon people over their faith ?   Therefore they are called in the Revelations, ' scorpions,' Rev. ix. 3, 10 ; indeed they are spiritual scorpions, that sting the soul of God's people.

The devil is the king of darkness ; and is not he the prince of darkness that maintains ignorance of the word of God, that all his old tenets and opinions may have the better sway, that he may sit in the blind and dark consciences of people ?   It is said that he ' sits in the temple of God,' 2 Thess. ii. 4, that is, in the church ; nay, he labours to have another temple, to sit in man's soul, which is the temple of the Holy Ghost.   It is not sufficient for him that is the man of sin to have any other place, he must sit in the very souls and consciences of men.

Satan hath a special malice to sit in the place of God.   Since he was turned out of heaven, and cannot come thither, he will come to that place, if he can, upon earth where God should be ; and where will God be ?   God will especially be in the hearts of his people, in the souls and consciences of his people.   Conscience is God's throne.   Satan being thrust out of heaven, labours to stablish his throne there.   Now they that are Satan's vicars, led with his spirit, they are of the same mind.   Let them be what kind of great ones they will, they desire to sit in God's throne, in the conscience ; and if a man will not tie his conscience to them, he is nobody to them.   This is the property of antichrist in the highest degree ; as far as any are addicted to this, that they will not be satisfied, but the consciences of men must be tied to them, they must deny all honesty, and justice, and law, and all to please them, and to gratify them with particular kindness; so far they are led with the spirit of antichrist, and of the devil himself, who labours to sit in God's throne, that is, in the hearts and consciences of people. And therefore, as I said, they labour to keep people in darkness for this very purpose, that people may let them into their consciences, and rule them as they please.

As Samson, when they had put out his eyes, they led him to base services; so do they with God's people, they put out their eyes, and then they lead them to grind in the mill, to all the base services they can, Judges xvi. 21. It is not to be spoken of the brutish slavery and ignorance that is in Spain and other countries where that devilish inquisition reigns, which is a great help to popish tyranny.

What should I speak of the state of the Romish Church? Indeed the main scope of it is to subdue all to them, to subdue all kings and kingdoms to them. That is the grand scope of the greatest of them. Others have their particular scope for their bellies and base ends; but those among them that have brains, that are governors, their scope is to bring all under their girdle; and how shall they do this? They cannot bring their persons, but they must bring their consciences; for where the conscience is, the person will follow presently. Therefore they labour to lay a tie upon the conscience of prince and people, upon all, that so they may domineer and rule over their consciences. And for that end, they labour to nourish them up in blindness; for by blindness they rule in the conscience; and ruling their conscience, they may rule their persons and kingdoms. This is their main scope, this hath been their plot for many hundred years.

So that the Romish religion indeed is nothing but a mere carnal devilish policy, to bring others to be subject to them; and to make not only kings and princes, but to make God, and Christ, and the Scriptures, whatsoever is divine or human, to make all to serve their aims. What do they with Christ, but under the name of Christ serve themselves? What do they with the church, but under the name of the church, carry their own ends? What do they with the names of saints and angels, Peter, Mary, &c., but under a plausible pretence carry their own ends, and set up a visible greatness in this world, answerable to the Cæsarian monarchy? This is plain and evident to all that will see, that it is so; and one main way to attain their ends is to·rule over the conscience.

And that they may help all the better forward, they have raised in the church a kind of faith which they call an implicit and infolded faith, that people must believe what the church teacheth, though they know not in particular what the church teacheth, and so they lead people hoodwinked whither they please themselves.

To make some use of it briefly.'

Use. Let us labour *to bless God that hath freed us from this spiritual tyranny.* O! beloved! it is a great tyranny when conscience is awaked, to be racked and tormented, and stung by scorpions; to have conscience tormented with popish errors; as in the point of satisfaction, the most of them, if their eyes be open, they die with terror. O! it is a blessed liberty that we are brought out of antichristian darkness, that we know we believe, and upon what terms we believe; and are taught to submit our conscience only to the blessed truth of God; that the soul it is the bed, as it were, only for Christ, and his Holy Spirit to dwell in, and to lodge in; and that no man may force the conscience with any opinion of his own, further than it is demonstrated out of the word of God. What a sweet enlargement of spirit do we live in now! and our unthankfulness perhaps may occasion God to bring us in some degree of popish darkness again.

I beseech you, let us stand for the liberty of Christ, and the liberty of our consciences against the spiritual tyrant of souls. Let us maintain our liberty by all we can, by all laws and execution of laws; by all that may uphold our spiritual liberty; for there is no bondage to that of the soul. Do but a little consider the misery of the implicit faith that the popish sort are under, that infolded, inwrapped faith, wherein they are bound to believe, without searching, what the church determines. Hereupon they swallow in all doctrines that tend to superstition, that tend to rebellion, that tend to treason. They swallow up all under this implicit faith, as if God had set an ordinance and ministry in the church against himself; as if he had advanced any ministry against his own ordinance.

When you think of popery, consider not so much particular dotages, as about images, and transubstantiation, and relics, &c., but consider the very life and soul of popery in this opinion, the leading error of all others, the tyranny over souls of people, and holding them in blindness and darkness. It is not a device of mine. Do but read the Council of Trent in some editions. There the late Pius Quartus that sat there daily, he made more articles than the [apostles, distinct, not proved by Scripture; he made articles of his own to be believed. People were tied upon the necessity of salvation to believe them, and to believe them with that faith that is due to Scripture (*oooo*).

And it is a common tenet among them, Every man is bound to be under the authority of the church of Rome, under peril of damnation. There is the grand error, that it is a matter necessary to salvation to be under their tyranny.

Hereby they excommunicated all the Eastern churches, and all former times wherein they were not under the Roman tyranny, for that is but of late, six hundred years since. They condemned St Cyprian's time, and other times. And they made articles of religion, and established them with this censure, that upon pain of damnation men must believe these things as well as the articles of the creed, as transubstantiation, invocation of saints, purgatory, and such things. They are so many articles, indeed, as I say, they have more articles than the twelve articles of the apostles.*

We say, an error in the foundation, it is not mended after: and the first concoction, if it be naught, all after are naught; if there be not good concoction in the stomach at the first, the blood is naught, and all is naught. So this is a fundamental error, and a ground of all errors, that they hold they cannot err; and hereupon they come to tyrannise over the consciences and souls of people.

Therefore, I say, let us bless God that hath set our souls in spiritual liberty, that now we see God in the face of Christ, now we see the means of salvation. We see the bread of life broken to us, we see Christ unveiled, we see what to found our consciences upon. We cannot be sufficiently thankful for this. Thankful we may be for the peace of the kingdom that we have so long a time enjoyed, and for the outward prosperity we have so long had; but, above all, be thankful for the peace of religion, for the peace of conscience, for the liberty of soul, that we enjoy. And, as I said, if anything move God to strip us of all, it will be our unthankfulness, and our

* The reference here and above, is to ' The Creed,' which is commonly called the Apostles'. Cf. Nichols' Pearson, (8vo, 1854).—G.

practice witnessing our unthankfulness, by valuing no more the blessed estate of the gospel we enjoy.

' *Not that we have dominion over your faith.*' This disposition to domineer over the faith of others, from abominable grounds it ariseth :

Partly from pride and tyranny, that they would set themselves in the temple of Christ, where he should rule in the hearts of his people.

ꜰ And partly out of idleness. They raise the credit of their own traditions, that they may not be forced to take the labour of instructing the people. Therefore, they fasten a greater virtue upon outward things than there can be, only to avoid the labour of instruction.

And then it riseth partly from guilt. They are so in their lives, especially if they be looked inwardly into, as that they cannot endure the knowledge of people. They are afraid that people should know much, lest they know them too well, and their courses and errors. So, partly from pride, and partly from idleness and sloth, and partly from guilt, they domineer over the faith of God's people.

' *But are helpers of your joy.*' The end of the ministry is not to tyrannise over people's souls, to sting and vex them, but to minister comfort, to be helpers of their joy ; that is, to help their salvation and happiness, which is here termed joy, because joy is a principal part of happiness in this world and in the world to come. Now, the end of the ministry is to set the people's hearts into a gracious and blessed liberty, to bring them into the kingdom of grace here, and to fit them for the kingdom of glory, to help forward their joy.

This is the end, both of the word and of the dispensation of the word, in the ordinances of salvation, in the sacraments, and all, that our joy may be full ; as our blessed Saviour saith, ' These things have I spoken, that your joy may be full,' John xv. 11. It is the end of all our communion with the Father, Son, and Holy Ghost, and with the ministry, and one with another ; as it is, 1 John i. 4, ' These things have I written that your joy may be full ;' you have communion with the Father, Son, and Holy Ghost, and with us, ' that your joy may be full.' All is for spiritual joy.

' We are helpers of your joy.' The meaning is, we are helpers of your faith, from whence joy comes more especially ; for he doth not repeat the word again, ' We have not dominion over your faith, but are helpers of your faith ;' but, instead of that, he names joy, as that that doth accompany true faith.

The points considerable in this clause are these :

1. *That joy is the state of Christians, that either they are in, or should labour to be in*, because the apostle names it for all happiness here. All that have given their names to Christ should labour to rejoice. Either they do rejoice, or they should labour to come to it. That is supposed as a ground. I will be the shorter in it.

2. The second is, *that the ministers are helpers of this blessed condition.*

3. The third is, *they are but helpers*. They are helpers, and but helpers. They are not authors of joy, but helpers. ' We are but helpers of your joy,' saith the apostle. These three things I will speak of briefly out of these words. First,

Doct. 1. *Joy is that frame and state of soul that all that have given their names to Christ either are in, or should labour to be in.*

For this doctrine is fetched from the principle of nature. We do all with joy. All in our callings is done with joy. What do men in their trades, but that they may have that that they may joy in when they have it? It is an old observation of St Chrysostom, 'We do all, that we may joy.' Ask any man why he doth take so much pains, and be a drudge in his place? It is that he may get somewhat to rejoice in in his old days. So, out of the principle of nature, this ought to be the scope of all, to joy.

Now, those that are Christians, God requires it at their hand as a duty, 'Rejoice alway, again I say, rejoice,' Philip. iv. 4. And he doth prepare and give them matter enough of joy, to those that are Christians.

(1.) For whether we consider *the ills they are freed from*, the greatest ills of all. They are freed from sin and the wrath of God, they are freed from eternal damnation, they are freed from the sting of death, from the greatest and most terrible ills.

(2.) Or whether we regard *the state that God brings them in* [to] *by believing:* being in the favour of God, they enjoy the fruits of that favour, 'peace and joy in the Holy Ghost,' Rom. xiv. 17. And then for the life to come, they are under the 'hope of glory.' The state of a Christian is a state of joy every way, whether, I say, we regard the ill he is freed from, or the good he is in for the present, or the hope of eternal good for the time to come. A Christian, which way soever he look, hath matter of joy. God the Father is his, Christ is his, the Holy Ghost is his Comforter, the angels are his, all are his, life or death, things present or things to come, all are his, 1 Cor. iii. 22. Therefore, there is no question of this, that every one that hath given his name to Christ is in a state of joy, if he answer his calling, or he should labour to be in it; he wrongs his condition else.

Why should they labour to be in that state?

Reason 1. Among many reasons, one is, that God that gives them such matter of joy, may have glory from them. For what should the life of a Christian be, that is freed from the greatest ill, and advanced to the greatest good? His life should be a perpetual thanksgiving to God; and how can a man be thankful that is not joyful? Joy is, as it were, the oil, the anointing. It makes a man cheerful, it makes the countenance of his soul to be cheerful.

Reason 2. It makes him active in good, when he is anointed with the oil of gladness. Now every man should have a desire to be good, to be diligent and expedite* in all that is good. Therefore we should labour for this spiritual anointing, that we may be ready for every good work, 'Vessels of mercy prepared for every good work,' Rom. ix. 23.

Reason 3. And then for suffering, we have many things to go through in this world. How shall a man suffer those things that are between him and heaven, with joy, unless he labour to bring himself to this temper of joy?

Reason 4. And then for others, every man should labour to encourage others. We are all fellow-passengers in the way to heaven. Therefore even to bring on others more cheerfully, we ought to labour to be in a state of joy. Those that do not rejoice, they bring an ill report upon the way of God, as if it were a desolate, disconsolate way. As the spies brought an ill report upon the land of Canaan, whereupon the people were disheartened from entering into it; so those that labour not to bring their hearts to spiritual joy, they bring an ill report on the ways of God, and dishearten others from entering into those ways. Which way soever we look, we have reasons to encourage us to joy, that God may have more glory, and that we may do him more service; that we may endure afflic-

* That is, 'active.'—G.

tions better, and encourage others, and take away the reproach of religion from those that think it a melancholy course of life ; which indeed do not understand what belongs to the state of a Christian, for the state of a Christian is a state of joy.

And if a Christian do not joy, it is not because he is a Christian, but because he is not a Christian enough, because he favours the worse principle in him, he favours himself in some work of the flesh.

God in the covenant of grace is all love and mercy. He would have us in our pilgrimage to heaven to ' finish our course with joy,' Acts xx. 24 ; and he knows we can do nothing except we have some joy. It is the oil of the soul, as I said, to make it nimble and fit for all actions, and for all sufferings. It gives a lustre and grace to whatsoever we do. Not only God loves a cheerful performer of duties, but it wins acceptance of all others, and makes the worker himself wondrous ready for any action. This I mention only as a ground. A Christian that hath given his name to Christ, is either in a state of joy, or else should labour for it.

The second, which is the main, is that—

Doct. 2. *The word of God, as it is unfolded, is that that helps this joy.*

' We are helpers of your joy,' we ministers. St Paul spake of himself as a minister. The word of God is a helper of joy, especially as it is unfolded, considered as it is dispensed in the ministry. You know the word of God it is called 'the word of reconciliation,' 2 Cor. v. 18, because it doth unfold the covenant between God and us. It is called ' the word of the kingdom,' the ' word of life,' &c., which all are causes of joy ; therefore the word breeds joy, Ps. xix. One commendation of the statutes of God is, that ' they comfort the heart,' Ps. xix. 8, and refresh the heart. He follows the commendation of the word at large, ' The statutes of God are perfect, converting the soul ; the testimonies of God are sure, making wise the simple,' Ps. xix. 7, 8, 9. And among the rest of the commendations, as a commendation issuing from the rest, ' The statutes of God are right, rejoicing the heart.' The word of God is a cordial, especially to refresh and solace the heart.

St Paul, Rom. xv. 4, makes it the scope of the word : ' Whatsoever was written aforetime, was written for our learning, that we, through patience and comfort of the Scriptures, might have hope,' So likewise, ' He that prophesieth speaketh to men to edification, to exhortation, and to comfort,' 1 Cor. xiv. 3, 4. ' He that prophesieth,' that unfoldeth the word, ' he speaketh to men to edification, to exhortation, and to comfort.' So the end of the word, and the end of prophesying, the ministry of the word, is to help our joy, our comfort, to support us against all ills either felt or feared, by greater arguments than the ill is. For that is to comfort and rejoice, to make any to joy. It is to support the soul against all grievance, either spiritual or outward, either felt or feared, and that from stronger arguments than the grievances are. If they be equally poised, it is no comfort ; if the comfort be inferior, it is no comfort.

As the heathen man complained of those comforts he had, I know not how it is, but the physic I have to cure the grievance of my mind, it yields to the malice of the disease, the disease is above the cure. So it is true of all philosophical comforts, that are fetched out of the shop of nature, the physic yields to the disease ; the malady or disease exceeds the remedy, therefore there is no comfort. Comfort is, when the inward support is greater and stronger than the grievance is, whatsoever it be.

Now such comfort must only be fetched out of the word. The Scripture is a common treasury of all good and comfortable doctrines ; but especially as it is dispensed in the ministry, as it is divided by the ministers of God ; thereafter as they see the necessity of God's people, and the exigents* they are brought to, accordingly they should draw comfort out of this common treasury. Thereupon that that Christ saith of himself, ' Thou hast given me the tongue of the learned, to speak a word in season to the weary soul,' Isa. l. 4, it is true of all the true ministers of Christ, that have that spiritual anointing, that have the same Spirit that Christ had. ' God hath anointed them, that they might speak a word in season ' to poor distressed souls. God hath given them the tongue of the learned, for this very end and purpose. God hath given them a healing tongue for a wounded soul. Indeed, they carry physic in their tongues ; and the very leaves, the very words, have a medicinal force.

When those that are true ministers speak a word in season to a wounded, distressed soul, the Spirit goes with the word, and it hath wondrous efficacy for the comfort and raising up of the soul. Experience shews this.

Now to give a few instances how it is done, how the ministers do it, how they are ' helpers of our joy.'

1. They do it *first* of all, *by acquainting people with the ill estate they are in;* for all sound comfort comes from the knowledge of our grief, and freedom from it. They acquaint people with their estate by nature, that they are in the state of damnation, that they are under the ' curse' of God, under the ' wrath of God,' that they are in a ' spiritual bondage ;' they labour that they, together with the spirit of bondage, may make people to see their state of bondage. For they must plough before they sow, and the law must go before the gospel. The law shews the wound, but the gospel heals the wound. Now they must know the wound ; the commanding part, all the threatening part of the word. They must know what they are, before they can know their comfort. Therefore John Baptist he came before Christ, he made way for the sweet doctrine of Christ that came with blessing in his mouth, ' Blessed are the poor in Spirit ;' ' Blessed are they that hunger and thirst ;' ' Blessed are those that suffer persecution,' &c., Mat. v. 3, 6, 10. Even as to Elias there was a strong wind came before the still voice, 1 Kings xix. 12, so there must be somewhat to rend, and to open the heart, before this oil of comfort can be poured in. Now that is the first thing, the ministers help people to comfort, by helping them to understand themselves, what they are in the state of nature. They labour to search the wound first, to cure the soul as much as they can of all guile of spirit, that the soul may not be guileful to misunderstand itself.

2. And when they have done this, then they breed joy, *by propounding, and shewing the remedy which is in Jesus Christ;* then they open the riches of God's love in Christ, then open the sweet ' box of ointment' in Christ, they shew to man his righteousness. As you have an excellent place in Job, chap. xxxiii. 14, *seq.,* of the whole force of the ministry ; it is followed at large what the minister doth to bring a man to joy. He begins, verse 14, ' God speaks once and twice, but man perceives it not ; in visions and dreams by night, when deep sleep falls upon them ; then he opens the ears of man, and seals instruction,' &c. ' He chastiseth him with pain upon his bed, and the multitude of his bones with strong pain ; so that his life abhors bread.' He speaks of a man, that is brought down by the sight of sin. ' His flesh is consumed away, it cannot be seen, his bones stick out,' &c.

* That is, ' exigencies:' Cf. footnote, vol. I. p. 412.—G.

A strange description of a man in a disconsolate estate. His ' soul draws near to the grave, and his life to the destroyers.' What of all this? what is the way to bring him out of this? 'If there be a messenger with him, an interpreter, one of a thousand, one that hath the tongue of the learned, to shew a man his righteousness, then God is gracious to him, and delivers him from going to the pit. I have found a ransom,' &c. The messenger, ' one of a thousand,' the man of God, that hath ' the tongue of the learned,' he hath showed him where his ransom is to be had, he hath shewed him his righteousness.

Thus did St Peter, after he had brought them to ' Men and brethren, what shall we do to be saved?' Acts ii. 37, 38; then he points them out to Jesus Christ. Therefore the ministry is called ' the ministry of reconciliation,' 2 Cor. v. 18, and the 'ministry of peace,' Eph. ii. 17; they are called ' messengers of peace.' You know joy comes from reconciliation with God in Christ, joy comes from peace. Now the ministers they are messengers of reconciliation, and messengers of peace, and therefore messengers of joy, ' They bring glad tidings of joy,' Luke i. 19. You see how ministers are helpers of joy, by shewing to man his ill, and then by shewing to man his good, and comfort in Jesus Christ; they shew, that ' where sin hath abounded, grace abounds much more,' Rom. v. 20. They dig the mine, to let people see what riches, what treasure they have in the word of God, and what comfort they have there.

3. And then in the continual course of life, they are ' helpers of joy.' For what do ministers, if they be faithful in their places, but *advise in cases of conscience what people should do?* so their office is to remove all scruples, and hindrances, and obstacles of spiritual joy, by advising them what to avoid, and what to do (*pppp*).

We know that *light* is a state of joy. The ministry of the gospel is light. It sets up the light of God's truth. It shews them the way they should go in all the course of their life; and thereupon it rejoiceth them. The word of God is a lanthorn, especially in the ministry.

Spiritual liberty, and freedom, that doth make people joyful. But the end of the ministry is to set people more and more at liberty; both from the former estate that I named, and likewise daily by office, to set them at liberty from corruptions, and temptations, and snares; to bring them to an enlarged estate.

Victory, and triumph is a state of joy. Now the ministers of God teach God's people, how to fight God's battles, how to handle their weapons, how to answer temptations, how to conquer all, and at length how to triumph. Therefore in that regard they are helpers of their joy. They encourage them against discouragements, against infirmities and afflictions, against Satan's temptations, shewing them grounds of joy out of the Scriptures.

4. Then they are ' helpers of their joy,' by *forcing it as a duty upon them*, ' Rejoice evermore, and again I say, rejoice,' saith St Paul, Philip. iv. 4. They are as guides among the rest of the travellers, that encourage them in the way to heaven, ' Come on,' let us go cheerfully. As the apostles in all their epistles, they stir up to joy and cheerfulness; so should those do that are guides to God's people. Travellers they need refreshments of wine, &c. Now thus the ministers of God help the people of God in their spiritual travel to heaven. If the people of God faint at any time, then as it is, Cant. ii. 5, they refresh them with ' apples and wine,' with the comforts of the Holy Ghost. They are ready to support and comfort them in all their spiritual falls, when they are ready to sink.

We see by experience in all places where the ministry of the word is established, how comfortably people live, and die, and end their days above other people ' that sit in darkness, and in the shadow of death,' Mat. iv. 16. So we see this is true, that the ministers help joy, because they help that that breeds joy, not only at the first, but continually help the joy of the people of God, even to death.

5. And then *in death itself*, the end of the ministry is to help joy, to help them to heaven, to help them to a joyful departure hence, to give them a good and comfortable loose* out of this world, drawing comfort out of the word for this purpose ; for whatsoever the minister doth, it is by drawing comfort out of the word, shewing them that the sting of death is taken away, that now death is reconciled, and become a friend to us in Christ ; that it is but a passage to heaven, that now it is the end of all misery, and the beginning of all happiness, ' Blessed are those that die in the Lord,' Rev. xiv. 13. So they assist, and help them in those last agonies.

There is special use of the dispensation of the word in all conditions while we live, and at the hour of death. You see it is clear, I need not further enlarge the point, that the ministers by reason of the word, which indeed is the main thing that comforts, they are helpers of the joy of God's people.

Obj. But you will say, They help God's people to sorrow, and they vex and trouble them ofttimes.

Ans. Indeed, carnal men think so, as the two witnesses in the Revelations, it is said, ' They vexed the men upon the earth,' Rev. xi. 10. So indeed, the faithful witnesses of God, they vex the earthly-minded, base men ; as Ahab said of Elias, ' Thou art he that troubleth Israel,' 1 Kings xviii. 17. He accounted him as one that troubled Israel, when it was himself that troubled Israel. These ministers, they are accounted those that mar all the mirth in the world ; that a man that is given to pleasures and delights, he trembles at the sight of them, as men opposite to his delights and carnal course : he cannot brook the very sight of them ; so it is with a carnal man.

But we may make an use hence, to judge of what spirit they are that judge and think so, they are not true believers; for there is no man that hath given his name to Christ, and makes it good by his life that he is a good Christian, but he accounts the ministers ' helpers of his joy.' Those that do not so, are in an ill course ; and which is worse, they resolve to be in an ill course.

Therefore, let us make much of the ordinances of God, as that which is the joy of our souls ; not only make much of the word of God, but of the word of God in the ministerial dispensation of it ; for ofttimes we find that comfort by the opening of the word of God, that our own reading and private endeavours could never help us to : experience shews that. We see when the eunuch was to be converted, it was he that read, but Philip was sent to open the word to him, and then ' he went away rejoicing,' Acts viii. 39. And so the poor jailer, when the word was opened and applied to him, then he rejoiced, Acts xvi. 33. Therefore, as we intend our own comfort, let us regard the ministry.

Obj. Many object that, that Naaman the Assyrian did, I can have as much comfort by reading.

Ans. I would they were so well occupied. But God gives a curse to private means, when they are used with neglect of the public. And joy comes

* That is, ' loosening,' = departure. Cf. note *a*, vol. I. p. 350.—G.

from God's Spirit. God will not attend our pleasure to give us joy and delight in what we single out, but in his own course and way. And if Naaman the Assyrian,* that thought the rivers of Damascus were as good as Jordan, and, therefore he thought it a fond† thing to wash there ; if he had not yielded to the counsel of his servants, he had gone a leper home as he came ; but he was wiser, 2 Kings. v. So those that cavil at the ordinance of God, they may live and die lepers for aught I know, except with meekness of spirit they attend upon the ordinance.

Obj. But you will say, Those that are true Christians and good men, they are ofttimes cast down by the ministry, and brought to pangs of conscience ; therefore, what joy can there be ? how are they ' helpers of their joy ? '

Ans. If they do so, yet it is that they might joy. St Paul did bring the Corinthians here to sorrow, but he brought them to sorrow that they might joy ; as you have it excellently set down. ' For though I made you sorry with a letter, I do not repent, though I did repent,' 2 Cor. vii. 8. I was sorry that I was forced to be so bitter against you ; for I perceive that the same epistle made you sorry, though but for a season ; ' now I rejoice, not that you were made sorry ' (here is a sweet insinuation), but that you were sorry to repentance ; ' for you were made sorry after a godly manner, that you might receive damage by us in nothing.' So the sorrow that is wrought by the ministry in the hearts of the people, it is a sorrow to repentance, a sorrow tending to joy.

We say of April, that the showers of that month dispose the earth to flowers in the next ; so tears and grief wrought in the heart by the ministry, they breed delight in the soul ; they frame the soul to a delightful, joyful temper after.‡ And that is part of the scope of this very text, ' we are helpers of your joy,' and, therefore, if I had not spared you, but had come in severity, all had been for joy : so whether the minister open comfort or direction, it is for their joy. If they see them not in a state fit, then [it is their office] to discover to them their sin and danger, and to tell them that they must be purged by repentance, before they can receive the cordial of joy ; but all is for joy in the end.

A physician comes, and he gives sharp and bitter purges ; saith the patient, I had thought you had come to make me better, and I am sicker now than I was before. But he bids him be content, all this is for your health and strength, and for your joyfulness of spirit after ; you will be the better for it. So in confidence of that, he drinks down many a bitter potion. So it is with those that sit under the ministry of God, though it be sharp and severe, and cross their corruptions, yet it is medicinal physic for their souls, and all will end in the health of the soul, in joy afterwards.

Obj. It will be objected again, The word of God, and the dispensation of it, it is for doctrine, ' to teach and to instruct,' and not especially to joy : that should not be the main end ; for we see in Rom. xv. 4, ' Whatsoever was written, was written for our learning.' So in 1 Cor. xiv. 3, he that speaks, speaks to ' edification and exhortation,' as well as to comfort.

Ans. It is true ; but all teaching, and all exhortation, and all reproof, they tend to comfort : even doctrine itself tends to comfort. For as it is with divers kinds of food, they have both a cherishing virtue in them to strengthen, and a healing virtue to cure. So it is with the word of God,

---

* That is, ' Syrian.'—ED.   † That is, ' foolish.'—G.

‡ See this comparison beautifully stated by Adams (Practical Works, vol. III. p. 299).—ED.

the doctrinal part of it hath a comforting force. And, indeed, doctrine is for comfort; for what is comfort but a strengthening of the affections, from some sound grounds of doctrine imprinted upon the understanding, whereof it is convinced before? The understanding is convinced thoroughly, before the soul can be comforted thoroughly. Therefore the Scripture tending to doctrine, that being one end of it, tends likewise to comfort, because that is the issue of doctrine; for what is comfort, but doctrine applied to a particular comfortable use?

As in plants and tree, what is the fruit of the tree? nothing but the juice of the tree applied and digested into fruit; so, indeed, doctrine is that that runs through the whole life of a Christian, and the strength of doctrine is in comfort. Comfort is nothing but doctrine sweetly digested and applied to the affections. He will never be a good comforter, that doth not first stablish the judgment in some grounds of doctrine, to shew whence the comfort flows. So that howsoever there be many things in Scripture that are doctrinal, yet in the use of them those doctrinal points tend to joy and comfort. As, I said, in meat there is the same thing, something* that both nourisheth and likewise refresheth, as a cordial; so the word of God both nourisheth the understanding, and is as a cordial to refresh and comfort; and it is a kind of joy to the soul, to have it stablished in sound doctrine: that is the ground of comfort. So that notwithstanding any thing that can be objected, the end of the word of God, especially in the dispensation of it, is to joy and comfort.

Use. Which should teach people to regard the ministry in this respect, that it is a helper of their comfort, that they do not grieve those that help their comfort; for what is the end of a minister, as a minister, but to make others joy? that both God in heaven, and the angels, and ministers, and all may rejoice together in the conversion of a Christian.† Now, for people to vex those that, by virtue of their calling, labour to help forward their joy, is very unkind usage; yet it was the entertainment that our blessed Lord and Master himself found in the world; and St Paul himself saith, ' The more I love you, the less I am loved of you,' 2 Cor. xii. 15.

And then it should move people to lay open the case of their souls to their spiritual physicians upon all good occasions. People do so for the physicians of their bodies; they do so in doubtful cases for their estates. Is all so well in our souls that we need no help nor comfort? no removing of objections that the soul makes, no unloosing of the knots of conscience? Is all so clear? Or are men in a kind of numbness, and deadness, and atheism, that they think it is no matter that they put all to a venture, and think all is well? It were better for the souls of many if they had better acquaintance with their spiritual pastors than they have; for their calling is to help the joy of the people; and how can they help it except they lay open their estates to them upon good occasion? What do they herein but rob themselves of joy? They are their own enemies.

I pass to the third,

Doct. 3. They are helpers of joy, and but helpers.

They do but utter and propound matter of joy, grounds of joy from the word of God; but it is the Spirit of God that doth rejoice the heart, ' The fruit of the lips is peace,' Isa. lvii. 19. It is true, but it is when the Spirit of God speaks peace to the soul together with the lips, ' God creates the fruit of the lips to be peace,' saith Isaiah. The fruit of the lips is peace,

---

* Misprinted ' sometime.'—G.

† That is, ' of a sinner converted *into* a Christian.'—G.

but God creates it to be so. So the ministers are comforters, but God saith, ' I, even I, am thy comforter,' Isa. li. 12. We speak matters of comfort and grounds of comfort, but God seals them to the heart by his Holy Spirit. God is the comforter himself, ' He is the Father of comfort, and the God of all consolation,' Rom. xv. 5. And the Spirit is called ' the Comforter,' to shew unto us that however in the ordinances the materials of comfort be set a-broach* to God's people, yet notwithstanding that that speaks peace to the heart, and sets on those comforts to the soul and conscience, it is the Spirit of God, God himself. So there is the outward preaching and the spiritual preaching. He hath his chair in heaven that teacheth the heart, as St Austin saith (qqqq). St Paul speaks, but God opens the heart of Lydia ; he hath the key to open the heart.†

Therefore, you have all attributed to the Spirit of God. In John xvi. 5, seq., ' I go hence, but I will send you the Comforter,' the Holy Ghost ; and what shall the Comforter do ? ' He shall convince the world of sin, of righteousness, and judgment.' Do not pretend, therefore, your own inability, that you are unable to comfort, or to cast down, or to seal unto people their righteousness ; do you that that is your duty, propound grounds of direction, and casting down, and of righteousness, and of judgment, of holy life after ; and then the Holy Ghost shall go with you ; the Comforter shall do this to the hearts of people ; the Holy Ghost shall convince. ' What is Paul, or what is Apollos, but ministers ? ' ' Paul may plant, and Apollos may water ;' but if God give not the increase, what is all ? 1 Cor. iii. 6.

Therefore, Christ promiseth his disciples, that the Holy Ghost should accompany their teaching. They might have objected, Alas ! we shall teach the world, that they are Gentiles, that they are obstinate persons, hardened in superstition. Do not fear, saith he, ' I will send the Holy Ghost.' He shall fall upon you and furnish you. Now when the Holy Ghost was in them, and the Holy Ghost in their auditors too, together with the word inspired by the Holy Ghost : when the Spirit meets in these three, there are wonders wrought. When the Spirit of God is in the teacher, and the Spirit of God in the hearers, and the Spirit of God in the word : I say, when there is one Spirit in the teacher, and in the hearers, and in the word, there are wonders wrought of conversion and comfort.

It is the Spirit that must do all. We are nothing but ministers. ' Let a man conceive of us as ministers and dispensers of the gospel,' 1 Cor. iv. 1. Ministers of comfort we are, and but ministers ; just so we are ' helpers of your joy,' but we are but helpers. Those that account us not helpers of joy, know not our calling ; and those that account us more, that we are able to comfort people by the word, they turn the preaching of the word to magic, to a charm. We can speak the word ; but God must speak to the heart at the same time.

As it is with physical water ; there is the water, and there are many strong things in it. What ! doth the water cure or purge ? It is a dead thing, it hath no efficacious quality, but to cool, &c. Whence comes the efficacy ? There are some cool herbs, some strong things in it, and then it doth wonders. So what is the infusion of the word but water, but aqua vitæ, water of life, the dew of heaven, rosa solis? Whence is it so ? As water ? No ; but there is a divine influence and vigour in it, that refresheth and

---

* That is, ' broached ' = opened.—G.

† ' Lydia's Heart Opened,' is the title of one of Sibbes's minor writings.—G.

quickeneth the soul. It doth not do it of itself, but it hath a divine influence of the Spirit.

So we see, though ministers be helpers of joy, they are but helpers. They are but the conduits that convey that that comes from the Spirit of God. They are instruments of the Spirit.

1. You see it clear then, *that God only speaks comfort*; because the Spirit of God only knows our spirits thoroughly. The Spirit of God can only comfort, because he knows all the discomforts of our hearts, he knows all our griefs, all the corners of our hearts. That the minister cannot do. The minister may speak general comforts ; but the Spirit of God knows all the windings and turnings of the heart, and all the disconsolate pangs of the heart and soul ; every little pang and grief, the Spirit of God knows it. Therefore, the Spirit of God is the Comforter. He strikes the nail, and seals the comfort to the soul : we are but helpers.

2. Then again, the Spirit of God must do it, *because the soul must be set down with that that is stronger than itself.* It must be so convinced and set down, that it must have more to say against the grief or temptation, than can be alleged by the devil himself. The soul, before it be comforted, it must be quieted and stilled. Now who is above the soul, and Satan that tempts the soul ? Let Satan be let loose to tempt the soul, and the soul hath a hell in itself, if God let it alone. Who is above those unspeakable torments of conscience, if they be not allayed by the Spirit of God ? Who is above the soul, but the Spirit of God ? Will the soul allay itself ? No, it will never. Therefore the Spirit of God, that is stronger and wiser than the soul, and is the Spirit of light and strength, it must set down, and quiet, and calm the soul, that it hath nothing to say against the comfort it brings, but quiets itself, and saith, I must rest, I must see this is from heaven, I am quiet. This the Spirit doth.

Use. Therefore make this use of it, that in all our endeavours to procure peace to our consciences, and spiritual balm to the wounds of our souls, *let us go to this heavenly Physician :* not depend overmuch upon the ministry, or reading, or any outward task ; but in the use of all things lift up our hearts to God, that he would comfort us by his Spirit, that he would send the Comforter into our souls.

Though the disciples had comfort upon comfort by Christ, yet till the Comforter came, whose office it was to do it, to seal his word to their souls, alas ! they were dead-hearted people ; but after the resurrection, when the Comforter came, and refreshed their memories, and convinced their understandings, then they could remember all the sweet comforts that our blessed Saviour had taught them before. So it is with us,—we hear many sweet comforts day after day out of God's book, comforts against sin, comforts against trouble, outward, and inward, and all ; but till the Comforter come, till God send his Holy Spirit, we shall not make use of them. Therefore let us labour to have more communion with God before we come to hear the word ; and after we have heard it, let us have communion with God again, that he would seal whatsoever is spoken to our souls, and make it effectual to us.

Therefore we must learn to give the just due to the ordinance of God, and not to idolize it ; to make it the means of comfort, not to make it the chief Comforter, but the Spirit of God by it. What is Paul or Apollos ? what are we but ministers of faith ? and by consequent, ministers and helpers of comfort, but not the authors of comfort.

Oh ! if I had such and such here, I should do well, I should be so and so.

Alas ! all is to no purpose, unless thou hast the Holy Ghost, the Spirit of God. That can help by weak means. Therefore we must not tie comfort and joy to this or that means ; but in all means look to the ground of comfort, and the spring of all, the Holy Ghost.

The reason why men do not profit more, that they are not more cheered and lift up with the ministry of the word (which is a word ' of reconciliation,' and of joy and comfort), it is because they are more careful in the use of means, than in going to God for his Spirit to bless the means. Now these must go together : a care of using the means, and a care to pray to him that he would give us wisdom, and strength, and blessed success in the use of all means. Then if we would join religiously and conscionably* these two together, the use of all means conscionably, and in the use of all to lift up our hearts to God to bless them, we should find a wondrous success upon the ministry, and all other good means likewise. So much for that. I go on to the last clause of the chapter.

' *For by faith ye stand.*' Why doth the apostle vary the word, ' We have not dominion over your faith, but are helpers of your joy,' whereas the consequence, it seems, might run thus : ' We do not domineer over your faith, but are helpers of your faith ? ' He puts joy instead of faith ; and afterward he brings in faith again : ' for by faith ye stand.'

This is one main reason : because joy riseth from faith, therefore he names it instead of faith ; for the Holy Ghost is not curious of words, but when the same Spirit works both, he names that which he thinks will fittest suit the purpose.

Obs. Faith breeds joy.

How is that ?

1. Because faith, first of all, doth shew to us the freedom from that that is the cause of all discomfort whatsoever, *it takes away all that may discourage.* For it takes away the fear of damnation for our sins ; it shews our reconciliation in Jesus Christ. Faith shews liberty and deliverance ; and so discovering deliverance by a Mediator, it works joy. Is not a prisoner joyful when he is set at liberty ?

2. Then likewise faith discovers to us the face of God shining to us in Jesus Christ : *it shews not only deliverance, but favour.* It shews us the ground of all, the righteousness and obedience of our Saviour, whereby we are delivered, and brought into favour.

Now from this comes peace : from the knowledge of our deliverance and acceptance with God, founded upon the obedience of God-man, a Saviour, there comes in peace, and peace breeds joy ; because faith discovers all these, the ground of reconciliation with God in Jesus Christ, and thereupon peace, therefore it causeth joy.

For this is the pedigree and descent of joy, as the apostle hath it, ' The kingdom of God is in righteousness, and peace, and joy,' Rom. xiv. 17. There must be righteousness first, of a Mediator, to satisfy the wrath of God, and procure his favour. From righteousness comes peace, peace with God, peace of conscience. From peace comes joy. There is no joy without peace, no peace without righteousness.

And this whole pedigree of joy, as it were, is excellently set down, ' Being justified by faith, we have peace with God through Jesus Christ our Lord,' Rom. v. 1, and have access to the throne of grace, by which grace we stand, and not only so, but rejoice. So there is justification by the

* That is, ' conscientiously ' = with conscience.—G.

righteousness of Christ, and thereupon peace with God ; and from peace, boldness and access to God, and thereupon joy. So wo see how faith brings in joy, because it shews the spring of joy whence it comes, it shews peace, and peace riseth from reconciliation, and reconciliation from [the] righteousness of Christ, Mediator, whereupon we are delivered from all that we may fear, and set in a state of true joy, God being our friend. When God is reconciled, all is reconciled, all is ours ; have we not cause of joy then ? Therefore the apostle saith, ' The God of peace fill you full of joy in believing,' Rom. xv. 13, shewing that faith is the cause of all spiritual joy. And the same you have in 1 Pet. i. 8, ' In whom ye rejoiced, after ye believed, with joy unspeakable and glorious.' In whom, after ye believed, that is, in Christ, ' you rejoiced with joy unspeakable and glorious.' And therefore you see the apostle might well substitute joy instead of faith, because it springs and riseth from faith in Jesus Christ, the Mediator.

Use. Hereupon we may come to make this use of trial, how we may know whether our joy be good or no. Among many other evidences, this is one.

1. That spiritual joy is good, *if it spring from the word of faith ;* if it spring from the ordinance of God unfolded in the word, shewing us the ground of believing. For he that truly joys, can shew the ground of his joy.

Herein joy differs from presumption, from presumptuous swelling conceits. True joy, that is, not the joy of an hypocrite, it doth shew from whence it comes, it riseth from grounds out of divine truth.

2. Then again, this joy *doth more immediately spring from faith in the word,* from assurance that God is ours, and that Christ is ours ; that God is at peace with us, and that we are at peace with him. It ariseth from peace that is wrought by faith.

3. Then again, this joy, if it be sound, it is such a joy as St Peter saith is an unspeakable and glorious joy. Joy arising from the word of God, and from faith and peace, *it is above discouragement,* because we have in the word of God matter of joy above all discouragements and all allurements whatso ever. It is a joy above the joy of riches, or pleasures, or profits. Why ? Because the word shews matter of joy above all these. The prophet David rejoiced in the word of God above gold and silver, ' as one that had gotten great spoils,' Ps. cxix. 162. You see how oft he repeats it. ' It was sweeter to him than the honey and the honeycomb,' Ps. xix. 10. It puts his soul out of taste with all other things. This joy of the Spirit, it puts such a relish in the soul that it makes it undervalue all other things whatsoever. The price of other things falls down when a man joys in the Holy Ghost, because it ariseth from the grounds of faith, from peace and righteousness.

And, likewise, if it look forward, from the hope of life everlasting and the favour of God, the ground of all, it riseth from things that are above all other contentments, ' the lovingkindness of the Lord ' (that faith apprehends, that is the ground of joy), ' it is above life itself,' Ps. lxiii. 3. Now, life is the sweetest thing upon earth ; but the lovingkindness of God is better than that.

Therefore, those that lose their souls in base contentment, and joy in the dirty things of this life, that are not fit for the soul to fasten on, to place contentment in, but are only to be used as those that take a journey to refresh them ; but those that are swallowed up in these things, they know not what spiritual joy is, that ariseth from the word of God, from divine truth, that ariseth from faith ; for if they did, this joy would raise them higher, above all earthly contentments whatsoever.

4. Then again, where this joy is, this spiritual enlargement of soul, which is called joy, it is from true grounds, *it is with humility;* for the same word that discovers matter of joy, discovers matter of humility and grief in ourselves, by reason of the remainders of sin and of our own deservings. So true joy, it is a tempered and qualified joy. It is not joined with pride and swelling, because it riseth from those grounds that teach us what we are in ourselves. Alas ! such, that we need not be proud in ourselves, but if we will glory, ' we must glory in God,' 1 Cor. i. 31. Well! it is not that that I mean principally to stand on, but only I speak of it because it is placed here for faith, as it springs from faith. ' We are helpers of your joy.' To hasten, then, to that that follows.

' For by faith ye stand.' This principally depends upon the first words, ' We have not dominion over your faith,' because faith is such a grace as you stand by in all conditions. Now, what you stand by must be firm, it must be on a good bottom ; and what is firm must not be human, but divine. Therefore, we have no dominion over your faith, ' for by faith ye stand.'

Standing is a military word (*rrrr*). ' By faith ye stand,' that is, first of all faith gives a standing, a certain standing, before any conflict. It gives a standing in Christianity, it sets the soul in a frame, in a standing.

Nay, faith helps us ; we stand by faith, not only in a frame of Christianity, and furnished with spiritual strength, but then we are fit to encounter opposition. By faith we stand to it, and stand against all opposition. We stand, and stand to it, by faith.

And standing likewise implies continuance in managing Christianity, and opposing all enemies whatsoever. By faith we stand, and continue standing; we hold out in all opposition.

Standing likewise, in the next place, implies a kind of safety, together with victory at length. ' By faith ye stand.' You stand so as you are not wounded to death ; you stand so as you are kept safe, especially from mortal wounds, and altogether safe so far as you use faith as a shield, till you have got perfect victory, and faith end in triumph. So faith is that grace whereby we stand, whereby we are in a frame of religion fit to stand, and whereby we, so standing, encounter oppositions, and continue so encountering, and preserve ourselves safe, till victory be obtained. This is the full expression and comprehension of the word, ' By faith ye stand.'

Quest. Now, why is it by faith that we have this standing ?

Ans. Because faith, it is that grace in the new covenant that makes the soul go out of itself. It empties the soul of all things in itself, and goes out to somewhat else, whereupon it stands. For in the new covenant, since Adam's fall, all our strength is in the ' second Adam,' our Head ; we fetch it there.* And faith is the hand of the soul.

Now, because faith in the new covenant is an emptying grace, and likewise because, as it is a grace that empties the soul, so it fastens upon another thing, whereupon it relies ; for faith is an uniting grace as well as an emptying grace. Now, faith emptying and uniting, so it makes us stand.

And likewise faith as it draws. It hath a drawing virtue, an attractive force. It is a radical grace. It is like a root ; when it knits to Christ, it sucks out and draws virtue from him. Every touch of faith draws

* That is, ' thence.'—ED.

spiritual strength and virtue; so it causeth us to stand by the attractive virtue it hath.

And then it is the force of faith, likewise, to make things present; for therein it differs from hope. Hope looks upon things as absent. Now, the things that hope looks on as things remote and distant in time and place, faith makes them present; therefore, it is said to be ' the evidence of things not seen,' Heb. xi. 1. Now, that that makes the soul to be strong and able to stand, it must be somewhat present. However the full possession of things be reserved, not for faith, but for vision, for comprehenders in heaven, where faith ends and determines, yet notwithstanding faith draws so much for the present. It sets things to come so far present with such evidence and force, as it upholds the soul and makes it stand. ' It is the evidence of things not seen;' and thereupon it hath a kind of omnipotent power to make things that are not, to be. Heaven, and glory, and happiness, they are not for the present; but faith, looking on them in the authority of God and the divine promises, faith makes them present by a kind of almighty power that it hath, laying hold on an Almighty power; and hereupon it upholds the soul, it is the prop and stay of the soul, as in Heb. xi. i. *seq.*, it signifies to stay up, to hold up as a pillar; even from this virtue it hath to make things to come present.

You see, then, what it is to stand, and how faith is fitted for this purpose, because, as I said, it is the grace of the new covenant emptying us and drawing us to Christ, from whom we draw all virtue, and because it makes things to come as present.

By faith we are set in a right frame and condition again, as by want of faith we fell. The same grace must set us right, for want of which we fell.

How came we to fall at the first? You know Adam hearkened to his wife Eve, and she hearkened to the serpent. They trusted not in God, they began to stagger at the promises, to stagger at the word of God. Satan robbed them of the word. He observes, and continues the same art still, to take the word from us, and to cause us to stagger and doubt whether it be true or no. He comes between us and our rock, the word of God. So Adam fell. Now we must be restored by the contrary to that we fell. We fell by unbelief and distrust, by calling God's truth in question; we must learn to stand again by the contrary grace, by faith. Thus you see the terms something unfolded. ' By faith ye stand.'

To clear it a little further. There be four degrees of assent that the soul hath to anything.

1. The *first* is *a slight assent*, that we call opinion, that is, with some fear that it may be otherwise. That is a weak, a pendulous * assent. It is a wavering assent, it yields not a certain assent. Opinion is a weak thing: it may be so: aye, but it may not be so. It is with a fear of the contrary.

2. The *second* degree of assent is that that hath a better ground, *that is the assent to grounds of reason.* A man hath reason to yield and assent to, and those reasons satisfy the soul, and rest the soul something † thereafter as the strength of them is. And that assent we call knowledge, science. ‡ This is founded upon grounds of reason.

3. There is a *third* kind of assent and yielding that the soul hath, *that we call believing*, which is merely upon the credit of him that speaks, though we know no reason why the thing should be so; but only the person, it may

* That is, ' swaying.'—G.   † That is, ' somewhat.'—G.

‡ Cf. Dan. i. 4, and 1 Tim. vi. 20.—G.

be, is a person of credit, and wisdom, and knowledge ; and thereafter as we conceive well of him, thereafter we fasten our faith and assent to his authority ; so that assent to the authority of the speaker, we call belief.

4. The *fourth* degree of assent is, when we do not only assent to the thing because we have reason so to do, and arguments, or because we have some man to confirm it by authority ; but because we feel it to be so *by experience and by taste*. As a man assents that fire is hot, and that sweet things are so, not from reason altogether, or from the speech or rehearsing of another man, but because he feels it so indeed ; he assents to it from experience.

Now you will say, How come we then to stand by faith ?

As faith especially relies upon the authority of God, upon God's word, so we stand by faith, because it assents to an authority. But God's word gives reasons too ; therefore faith assents to the authority of God's word first ; and then we see divine reason enough too, when we once believe God.

And then experience in divine things too. After we believe there is an incredible sweetness in divine things, there is a knowledge with a particular taste. There is never a divine truth but it hath an evidence in it, when a man believes it once, that a man may say, 'I know whom I have believed,' 2 Tim. i. 12, from experience. Let the speakers of the things be what they will, let them apostatize from that that they have spoken ; after a man believes, he will see the things themselves have divine reason in them, as well as divine authority stablishing of them.

Some divine truths are altogether upon divine authority. We see no other reason but that God hath said it ; but some truths are both credible and intelligible. Credible, because God hath said it, and there is reason to prove it ; as a man may prove by divine reason, that ' all shall work for the best,' Rom. viii. 28. Why ? The apostle saith, ' We love God, and God hath called us according to his purpose,' Rom. viii. 28. Therefore all things shall work for them that God hath called, to them that answer his divine call. There is both reason and comfort. So it is credible as it hath divine truth, and intelligible as it hath comfort. There are homogeneal reasons with divine authority. God doth not only press us with authority, but he gives us reasons.

Besides this, there is experience ; for the doctrine of divine providence, and of the corruption of nature, and the doctrine of comfort in the Mediator Christ altogether, the doctrine of faith, the doctrine of the issue of all troubles for good, we find these by experience. However the teacher that teacheth them, perhaps, may have no sense of them himself, let him apostatize and do what he will, our faith stands upon them, partly because God saith so, that is the chief ; and because there is reason for them ; and because we find it so by experience. In many divine things, these three, both reason, authority, and experience, concur in faith. But to come a little further.

Quest. What doth faith itself stand most on, by which we stand ? That which we stand on must stand itself. Let us examine a little what faith itself stands on, by which we stand.

Ans. I shewed you before partly : by divine authority and experience, which gives some light to it ; but we will follow it a little further. That faith by which we stand must stand itself ; therefore it cannot be opinion, it must be faith. It must not be bare science neither, it must be science that hath faith ; faith must come in. Now faith looks to divine revelation especially, it looks to truth revealed from God. Now faith looking to the word of God, it builds, and pitcheth, and bottoms itself upon divine truth, divine authority, divine revelation, which we call the first truth, the first verity.

And not only so, but faith, that it may stand the better, hath, together with the word of God, the seals ; for God hath added sacraments as seals to the word, that helps the word. To us at least, God's word is true enough of itself in regard of him ; but he condescends to us, and therefore that faith may stand the better, that we may build upon his word, there are his sacraments. There are seals together with his word, and his oath too.

Again, that his word may be the better foundation for faith, it is conceived under the manner of a covenant, the evangelical part of it, the covenant of grace, wherein God in Christ promiseth to forgive our sins, to accept us to life everlasting, if we believe in Christ. It is a gracious covenant. God condescends to make a covenant that faith may stand ; shall not I believe him that hath made a covenant, and bound himself by covenant that he will do so ? Nay, in the covenant of grace, faith lays hold upon this, that he will fulfil and perform both conditions himself, both his part and our part. For the same truths that are a covenant, are a 'testament' too in the gospel. A testament bequeaths things without a covenant, and therein it differs from a covenant. A testament is, I bequeath, and give this. Now, whatsoever Christ in the covenant requires, because that in the gospel he makes good, the covenant, is* a testament, 'If we believe and repent,' John iii. 36. Now he hath promised to give repentance and belief in the covenant of grace to all that attend upon the means, and expect the performance of the covenant from him.

For we can no more perform the conditions of the covenant of grace of ourselves than the covenant of the law. Nature cannot do it, because it must be done by the Spirit altogether. Now here is a foundation for faith to stand on. God so far condescends, as he gives his word, and his seal, and his oath with his word, to convey that word by way of a covenant, and to make that covenant a testament and will to us, that he will do this: and to seal that will with his own blood : for ' a testament is of no force till the testator be dead,' Heb. ix. 17. His own blood hath sealed the testaments. You see here what ground there is for faith to stand upon.

Then, again, the sweet relation that God hath taken upon him in Christ. He is our Father. Faith builds not on naked God, divested of his sweet relations (for then he is a ' consuming fire,' Heb. xii. 29) ; but upon God a Father in Christ. What a sweet thing it is to consider God a Father! In Christ the nature of God is fatherly to us, and our nature is sweet to him. We are sons in Christ. His nature is sweet to us, and ours to him. He will surely perform his relations. For in Christ he is a Father, not in creation only, but in the covenant of grace. Faith relies upon the word of God, upon the covenant, and testament, and upon God himself, altered and changed in the covenant of grace to be a sweet Father.

But what is a further ground of this ? The nature of God himself who is a Father : for if God himself were not clothed with properties that might satisfy faith, and satisfy the soul fully, though he were a Father, it were not a sufficient ground for faith. But now who hath taken the relation of a father upon him ? God, who is infinitely good, infinitely merciful above all our sins. It must be infinite mercy. Faith would not have footing else. For the soul will so upbraid in the sense of sin, that if God

* Misprinted ' as.'—G.

were not a Father, and a Father infinite in mercy, nothing but infinite mercy will satisfy the soul when conscience is awaked, and infinite power to subdue all enemies, and infinite wisdom to go beyond the reach and subtlety of all the devils in hell. God is such a Father, as in his nature is of infinite mercy, and wisdom, and power. Here is a foundation for faith to lay hold upon indeed, to have a Father, and such a Father that is Jehovah. There we must rest in his essence; he is ' Jehovah, I am ;' he is eternal and immutable, an eternal being of himself, and he gives being to all; and all things have their dependence upon him. The devils in hell, and wicked men, he can quell them all, and subtract their being, and turn them to their first nothing from whence they came.

You see if we resolve all to ' Jehovah, I am,' to the eternity of God ; and then to his nature, clothed with power, and wisdom, and mercy ; and then to his relation of a Father : and then how he condescends to convey himself sweetly by way of covenant and testament, I beseech you, is not here a foundation for faith to build upon in the word of God, when God hath thus opened himself to us ? You see what this standing is, and how by faith we stand, and what faith stands on, and may well stand on. To come to some observations, then,

First of all, observe hence, that,

Obs. The foundation of faith must be out of a man's self.

That bottom that a man must lay his soul upon, must be out of himself : it must be divine, it must be God. For the soul rests not till it come to God.* And if the word were not God's word, it would not rest on that. God must open himself by his word. It must be divine revelation that the soul must stand upon, and at last resolve to pitch, and build, and rest there. It must not be human authority, therefore, not the authority of any creature that the soul must stand on ; because that that the soul stands on, must stand itself. Now nothing hath a firm consistence, but that which is divine : which I prove thus, there is no creature, but though it be true and good, yet it is changeably true, and may be otherwise than it is, and yet be a creature still, and a good creature. There is no man but he is changeable, and is changeable as a creature, and as a creature severed from the consideration of sin he is changeable. The very angels are changeable as they are creatures. All things created are mutable. It is the observation of Damascene.†

Now that that is the foundation of faith must not only be true, but infallibly and unchangeably true : there must be no danger of error in that that faith lays itself upon. It is an old rule, falsehood cannot be under faith, because faith must lie upon truth, infallible and immutable truth; and who is so but God? and what revealed truth is so, but divine truth ? Therefore faith only relieth upon the first good, and the first truth, upon God and his truth.

Therefore we may see what to judge of that controversy between us and our adversaries, that would have our faith to be resolved into the authority of the church, and not of the Scriptures, and by consequent, not to the authority of God himself.

The question is, Who hath the best standing, the papists or we ? We say we stand by faith, therefore we stand better than they. They say they stand by faith too, but how ? Their faith is resolved into the authority of the church at length, and there they rest. But I say, even by the confession of themselves, or of any reasonable man, the word of God is more divine than the authority of the church can be. For the authority of the church is therefore infallible and true, because the word of God saith so, that ' he will be with the church,' &c., and save his church. The ground is determined upon the word.

Now the word to which they have recourse, to prove that they cannot err, that must be trusted before them. If they have credit from the word, the word must be believed before them, before men ; for there is no man, if God speak by him, but he speaks by him so far as he understands the Scripture, and builds upon the Scriptures first. Therefore we must first found ourselves upon the Scriptures, and upon men as far as they agree to the Scriptures.

If the Scriptures were not the word of God indeed, they could not be the foundation of faith, we could not stand upon them ; but they are the word of God indeed, for men wrote as ' they were inspired by the Holy Ghost,' 2 Tim. iii. 16. Now that that comes from men it is not infallibly the word of God ; but if they speak anything that is good, it is so far as it is agreeable to the first truth, the word of God.

Indeed, the resolution of their faith is very rotten and unsound, and bewrays what their church is ; for they come at length in the grand point of all, to mere traditions. What is the present church ? The pope is the church virtually. How do they know that he cannot err ? He is Peter's successor ! How do they know he is so ? The Scriptures saith not so. It is tradition. So that the foundation of their religion is mere tradition, a thing from hand to hand, that is questionable and uncertain. That is the foundation of all their religion. What a resolution of faith is this!

We stand upon this against the gates of hell, and against all temptations and trials whatsoever. We believe, and fasten our souls upon this truth. Why ? It is the word of God. How do we know it is the word of God ? Indeed the church first of all hath an inducing, leading power, persuading to read, and to hear the word of God, and to unfold the word by the ministry ; and that is all that the church doth. But when we hear this, there is a divine intrinsical majesty in the word itself, by which I know the word to be the word. How do I know light to be light? From itself. It gives evidence from itself. So divine light in the Scriptures gives light of itself to all those for whom the Scripture was penned. For whom was the Scripture penned ? For God's people. To all that have gracious hearts, the word carries its own evidence with it. As light carries its own evidence, it discovers itself and all things else ; so doth the Scriptures, ' You have a sure word of the prophets,' 2 Pet. i. 19.

Our Saviour Christ himself founds what he teacheth upon the word. Shall not we therefore ground our faith upon the word, when he that was the head of the church brings all to the word in his teaching ? Therefore we have a better resolution for our faith than they have.

For indeed to say the truth, as we may say of their kind of prayers, when they pray to saints, &c., ' They worship they know not what,' John iv. 22. So we may say of their faith, they believe they know not what, they believe in a sinful man ; for the present pope is all their church, which is an ignorant man, many times, in the Scriptures, perhaps he never read them ; and he must determine controversies, and get into the chair, and judge that that shall judge him ere long. He must judge the Scripture that must be his judge, and the judge of all mankind. I list not to be large in this point ; a little discovery is enough.

I hasten to something more practical. We see then that faith hath an establishing power; to stand by faith. Then hence we may see these truths, which I will but touch.

1. *First*, that faith *is certain*. It is a certain thing, and makes the soul certain. It is not a weak apprehension.

2. Again, in that it is said here, ' By faith ye stand,' we see here *the perseverance of faith*.

But you will say, that faith whereby we stand is changeable, and therefore we may fall. No; St Peter makes a comment upon this place. ' We are kept by faith to salvation ; ' and ' receiving the end of your faith, the salvation of your souls,' 1 Pet. i. 5, 9. We are kept through faith to salvation. So God by his power keeps that faith that keeps us. There is a divine power that keeps faith, that faith may keep us ; so we stand by faith, and that faith stands to salvation, because it hath a firm bottom to stand on, and because it is kept by God himself. ' We are kept by the power of God through faith to salvation.' Mark how it runs along to salvation. Salvation is not only certain in itself, but that faith that lays hold on salvation is sure. ' By faith we stand ; ' not only for the present, but we continue by faith, and stand even to the death.

3. Again, in the *third* place, which follows from the other, *faith is a certain thing in itself*, and we are assured of our continuance. We are assured that we shall be saved ; he that believeth may be assured that he shall be saved. First, faith is a certain thing in itself, laying hold upon a strong foundation, the word of God. And it is sure to continue, it builds upon the rock. Therefore a man may believe, and he may know that he shall be saved ; he may know that he shall continue in a sure faith. There is a latitude, a breadth in faith ; and sometimes there is doubting, and sometimes faith, but yet there is always faith, more or less. There is a little and a great faith, but there is always faith. ' By faith we stand.' These things need no further enlargement. I only shew how they spring from this text.

4. In a word, hence we learn, *that it is by faith that we stand, and withstand all opposition whatsoever ;* for faith is our victory. ' That is your victory, even your faith,' 1 John v. 4. By faith we overcome the world, by it we stand, and stand against all opposition whatsoever.

To make it a little clear.

The reason is, partly because faith *doth present to the soul greater good than the world can*, therefore nothing on the right hand can shake the soul of a believing Christian. Shall pleasures, and profits, and the honours of the world draw a Christian from his faith, when faith presents better honours, better pleasures at the right hand of God, ' pleasures for evermore ' ? Ps. xvi. 11. No, they cannot ; for there is nothing in the world, but there is better in religion, incomparably better. There is no comparison of the pleasures of religion and of the world ; between the honour of being a child of God, and the honours that the world can give. Therefore there is nothing on the right hand in the world that can overcome the faith of a Christian, but he can stand against all, though it be a kingdom. ' Moses refused to be called the son of Pharaoh's daughter.' Why? Faith presented him greater honours in the church of God. He accounted the very ' reproach,' the worst thing in the church, better than the best thing in the world, ' the reproach of Christ better than the treasures of Egypt,' Heb. xi. 26.

Let discouragements be offered to faith by Satan and the world, let them come with all the terrors and threatenings they can, faith is victorious, and triumphant against them all, it stands against them all ; because it sets before the soul greater good than the ill that the world can inflict ; and sets before the soul greater ills if it apostatise than the world can inflict. Saith the world, If you do not thus and thus, you shall be cast into prison, or perhaps you shall lose your life. O ! but saith the soul, if I yield to the temptations of Satan, and my own vile corruptions, I shall be cast into hell ; is not that worse ? There can nothing be presented to the soul that is terrible, but faith will present to it things more terrible ; therefore if there be faith in the soul, it will stand against all those terrors whatsoever. 'Fear not them that can kill the body, when they have done their worst ;' if you will needs fear, I will tell you whom you shall fear, 'Fear him that can cast both body and soul into hell,' Mat. x. 28.

So, if we be forced to suffer the loss of any thing that is good in the world, or be cast into any ill condition, what saith St Paul ? 'The troubles and afflictions of the world are not worthy of the glory that shall be revealed,' Rom. viii. 18. Let us set that glory before us, and that will prevail against all that the world can threaten, or take from us. What is all to it ? Nothing. Therefore, 'by faith we stand,' we keep our own standing, and withstand all oppositions whatsoever.

Quest. Oh ! but what if there come more subtle temptations, and the Lord himself seems to be our enemy : that we have sin, and God is angry ; and we see he follows us with afflictions that are evidences of his anger ; how shall we stand now, and keep ourselves from despair ?

Ans. This is a fiery dart of Satan, when a man hath sinned, and conscience is awakened, to make him sink in despair. O, but faith will make the soul to stand in these great temptations against those fiery darts ; faith puts a shield into the hand of the soul, to beat back all those fiery darts. For faith will present Christ to God. Indeed I have been a sinner, but thou hast ordained a Saviour, and he is of thine own appointing, of thine own anointing, a Saviour of thine own giving, and thou hast made a promise, that 'whosoever believeth in him shall not perish, but have everlasting life,' John iii. 36. I cast myself upon thy mercy in him. Hereupon faith comes to withstand all such fiery temptations whatsoever, nay, against God himself: Lord, thou canst not deny thine own Saviour, thou seemest to be an enemy, and though I be a sinner, and have deserved to be cast into hell, yet I come to thee in the name of thy Son, that is at thy right hand, and pleads for me by virtue of his blood shed for me ; I come in his name, thou canst not refuse thy own Son. For all temptations, when a man hath faith in him, it will send Satan to Christ to answer for him. Go to Christ, he is my husband, he hath paid my debts, he hath satisfied for my sins. So that whatsoever the temptation be, make it as subtle as you will, there is a skill in faith to stand against it, and to beat back all the fiery darts of Satan.

Therefore, to end all, we see here *what an excellent estate a Christian is in above all others*, that he hath a better standing than others have ; not only a better standing in religion than the papists have, but in the profession of religion, he hath a better standing than common professors. Why ? He stands by faith, by sound faith. He stands not upon opinion, or because he hath been bred so ; he stands not upon his wit, because he sees reason for it ; he stands upon faith, and faith stands upon divine authority. He stands partly upon his own experience, that seconds faith.

Those then that care not for religion, what standing have they ? Those that stand only in pleasures and profits, and in the favour of great men, what standing have they ? They stand, as the psalmist saith, 'in slippery places,' Ps. lxxiii. 18. There is no man, but if he have not faith he stands slippery; though he be never so great, if he be a monarch, alas ! what is it to stand a while ? All these things are but uncertain. Though they yield present content, they are but uncertain contentments. The wise man saith, they are but 'vanity,' Eccles. i. 2. They are like 'the reed of Egypt,' 2 Kings xviii. 21, that will not uphold. They will not sustain the soul in the time of trouble. There is nothing that a man can stand upon, and fasten his soul upon, if he be not religious, that will hold scarce the fit of an ague, that will hold in the pangs of death, even in the entrance of it, that will hold in terrors of conscience.

How little a trouble will blow away all those that stand on so weak a foundation as an earthly thing is ! For they have but an imaginary good to speak of, and that imagination is driven out by the sense of the contrary. Let contrary troubles come, and all their fools' paradise, and their happiness they had before, is at an end; it goes no deeper than imagination.

All the things in this world stablish not the heart. Those that do not stand by faith in the favour of God in Christ, let their standing be what it will, it will soon be overturned by any temptation ; they can stand out against nothing.

Therefore let us labour, above all things in the world, to have that faith strengthened by which we stand ; and let us often be encouraged to strengthen our faith by all means, that we may stand the better upon it ; and try our faith, before we trust it. It is that that we must trust to, and stand to in life and death.

Therefore let us often think, Is my faith good ? is it well built ? Let us oft put this query to our souls, I believe the religion I profess, but upon what grounds ? I believe the truths in the word of God, but upon what grounds ? Have I a clear understanding of them, because they are divine ? Doth the Spirit of God open them, and shew a light in the Scripture that is divine ? Doth the Spirit of God give me a relish of the Scriptures above all the pleasures in the world ? Do I find God speaking to my heart in the word ? Do I find the Spirit of God with his ordinance ? Then my knowledge and my faith will hold out, I can stand by that faith in the word that is wrought by the Spirit, and fastened upon the word with the Spirit. But if I believe the religion I profess only because the State doth so ; and if the king and State should do otherwise, I would change my religion ; or if it be because my parents were so, or my friends and patron is of that religion, whom I depend upon ; or because I see greater seeming reason for this than for the other ; I can hold argument for this, and n)t for the other. Alas ! this will not hold. But labour to know the truth of the word of God by experience as much as we can, and by the Spirit of God giving evidence to our souls, from the inward grounds of Scripture, that it is the word. 'I know whom I have trusted,' 2 Tim. i. 12. I know the promises are good ; I have felt them in my soul ; the Spirit hath reported them to my soul ; they are sweeter than all the things in the world. It is a sure word ; I bottom upon it ; I have found the comfort of it before, therefore I will build upon it.

We can never stand, unless we can make our knowledge spiritual. It is but acquisite* knowledge else.

We fall in three things vilely, [unless] we labour that our knowledge of

* That is, 'acquisitive' = acquired.—G.

religion be spiritual, and fetched divinely out of the word of God, together with the Spirit.

1. We fall into sin from this very ground; for why do men fall into sin? Because at that time they stand not upon the word of God, revealed by conscience to be the word of God. Ask them why they swear? if they did believe the truth, the word saith, ' I will not hold them guiltless that take my name in vain,' Exod. xx. 7. But I am not convinced by the Spirit assuring my soul that it is the word of God. If men did believe it, would men bring a curse upon themselves?

And so whoremongers. The word of God saith, ' Whoremongers and adulterers God will judge,' Heb. xiii. 4. Would men, if they did believe this truth, live in these sins? But they have only an opinion of these things, I hear that these things are divine, perhaps they are not so, and the knowledge that we have is not divine ; faith is not mingled with the Spirit.

2. Then again, from sin, we fall into despair for sin at last. Why? Because our knowledge of divine truths is not spiritual, nor from inward grounds of Scripture felt by experience, the Spirit sealing the Scripture to my heart by some spiritual experience ; and thereupon men fall into despair for sin at length. For Satan plies them with temptations from their own guilty conscience. The grounds of their fears are present, and the grounds of their terrors are present to their souls ; for they are there, as it were, sealed, and branded in their very souls ; but their comforts are overly,* the promises are overly, the word is not rooted in their hearts by faith, it is not sealed there by the Spirit of God, the sanctifying Spirit never brought the word and their souls together. Hereupon they fall into desperation, when their terrors are present, and their comforts are overly.

If a man had never so sound a foundation, if he stand not, but float upon it, he may fall, and sink. If a man be never so weak, if he lie on a rock, the strength of the rock is his. So in our temptations, if we have a strong foundation, if we do not rest on it, the foundation will not uphold us. Now how can those rest on it that stagger in it? that were never convinced by the Spirit that these things are so? and that have had no spiritual experience? Satan draws thousands of souls to perdition, because their terrors are present, and their comforts are overly. They are not built upon divine truth by the Spirit of God.

3. Again, for apostasy, in the times of the alteration of religion ; why do men alter as the State alters? They are ready to have every month a new faith, if the times, and government alter. Why? Because they were never convinced by the Spirit of God of divine truths. They had it from foreign arguments. The former state of things countenanced this way, now another state countenanced another opinion, therefore I will be of the safest. This is because the soul was never convinced of the truth.

Therefore I beseech you, labour to have arguments from the experience of the power of the word in your souls, and arguments from the Spirit of God to your spirits that it is the word of God. I will stand to divine truth, I find such a majesty, such a humbling, pacifying, satisfying power in it to all my perplexities and doubts, that it cannot but be the word of God, it stays my soul in all oppositions, in all temptations, and corruptions : it gives a stay and foundation to my soul, that no truth in the world else can do. When the soul is brought to such a frame, such a soul will not fall into gross sins while it is in such a frame, much less will it despair for sin ; and if there be altering of religion a thousand times, it stands as a rock

* That is, ' lying over, superficial.'—G.

unmoveable, because it knows from inward grounds, from the word of God itself, sealed by the Spirit to my spirit, that it is the word of God. Such a soul will hold out, and only such a soul.

We should labour therefore by all means to have our faith strengthened ; and amongst other means, by the use of the sacrament, whereby God sweetly conveys himself to us, by way of a banquet strengthening our faith in Christ. He presents Christ to us as the food of our souls to refresh us, even as the bread and wine doth. Our blessed Saviour is wiser than we. He knows what we stand in need of, that we have need to strengthen our faith. For we have need to strengthen that that must be our strength, which is faith. And what is the ordinance of God to strengthen faith, is it not the sacrament ? The proper use of the sacrament is to strengthen faith ; which the sacrament doth, being a visible sermon to us ; for here we see in the outward things Christ's body broken, and his blood shed. It is a lively representation, a visible crucifying of Christ, a breaking of his body, and pouring out of his blood. And withal here is an offer of Christ to us in the elements, sealing of what it represents to our souls, if we come prepared.

God feeds us not with empty signs, but together with the outward things themselves, he gives the spiritual to the soul that is a worthy receiver.

Therefore come with a humble stooping to God's wisdom in appointing these ordinances to this end, to strengthen faith. And come with a desire to have faith strengthened. That will uphold us against all temptations to sin, or to despair for sin.

Oh, beloved ! if we knew what good our faith must do us ere long, we would labour to have it strengthened by all means. What will become of us in the hour of death, and in great temptations ? We shall be as chaff driven with the wind. If we have no consistence, and stability in divine truth, if our souls be not built on that, if we have not faith whereby our souls may be rooted in Christ, we shall be but a prey for Satan. Therefore considering that faith is of such wondrous consequence, it is the root of all other graces whatsoever ; as the apostle saith here, ' By faith ye stand.' He doth not say, by patience, or by hope, or the like. They are drawn from faith. Strengthen that, and strengthen all other that are infused from it.

As a tree, we cast not water on the branches, but on the root. All the branches are cherished by the root. So strengthen faith. We strengthen love, and hope, and all, if we strengthen faith, and assurance of God's love in Christ. Thus I have at length gone over this fruitful portion of Scripture.

TRIN-UNI DEO GLORIA !

NOTES.

(a) P. 9.—' As a proud critic said, " I would they had never been men that spake our things before we were, that we might have had all the credit of it."' This seems to be a kind of paraphrase of the saying, 'Pereant qui ante nos nostra dixerunt,' which, if I err not, belongs to the younger Scaliger.

(b) P. 9.—' And so in the Acts of the Apostles, xvii. 28, he quotes a saying out of an atheist.' It may be well to give here the original . . . ὡς καί τινες τῶν καθ᾽ ὑμᾶς ποιητῶν εἰρήκασιν Τοῦ γὰρ καὶ γένος ἐσμέν. Γένος οὖν ὑπάρχοντες τοῦ Θεοῦ. . . . The quotation has been traced to two of the Greek poets, viz.,

(1) Aratus. Phenomena, 5. Τοῦ γὰρ καὶ γένος ἐσμεν = For we are also his offspring.

(2) Cleanthes. Hymn to Jupiter. Ἐκ σοῦ γὰρ γένος ἐσμεν = For we are thy offspring. Cf. 'The New Testament Quotations collated with the Scriptures of the Old Testament, in the original Hebrew, and the Version of the LXX; and with other writings, Apocryphal, Talmudic, and Classical, cited or alleged so to be. By Henry Gough. 8vo. 1855.' The whole of this masterly and standard work is valuable; but the division headed 'Quotations from Greek Poets,' with the relative 'Notes,' is of the last interest.

(c) P. 11.—' Corinth. . . . But Augustus Cæsar afterwards repaired it.' For a very full and vivid description of ancient and more modern Corinth, I would refer readers to Conybeare and Howson's 'Life and Epistles of St Paul,' in any of its editions. Cf. also Alford, Webster and Wilkinson, Hodge and Stanley, in their respective introductions to the 'Epistles.' Dr Stanley will especially reward. Dr Smith's 'Dictionary of the Bible,' and Herzog, contain much excellent elucidation of the topography.

(d) P. 16.—' Salute him not.' For the significance of the Eastern 'salutation' cf. Rom. xvi. 5, 7, 10, 11, 13, 16, 21, 22; and the present Epistle (2 Corinthians), xiii. 13. Also with another reference, 2 Kings iv. 29. One of the few post-apostolical traits preserved of John, represents him in the well-known anecdote as refusing to reciprocate the 'salutation' of a heretic who had met him in the public baths.

(e) P. 19.—' Grace is the begetter of joy; for they both have one root in the Greek language.' That is, χάρις is grace, favour, and χάρμα is joy, delight. There is here the same root for favour and for joy.'

(f) P. 28.—' By Father, which is a kind of Hebraism,' &c. The original is ὁ πατὴρ τῶν οἰκτιρμῶν, on which consult Dean Stanley, in loc. (2d ed. 1858). Webster and Wilkinson prefer 'Orientalism' to 'Hebraism.' Cf. in loc. (Greek Testament, vol. ii., 1861.)

(f*) P. 39.—' We see by many that have recovered again, that have promised great matters in their sickness, that it is hypocritical repentance, for they have been worse after than they were before.' For startling illustrations of this, consult ' The Prison Chaplain : a Memoir of the Rev. John Clay, B.D., late Chaplain of the Preston Gaol, &c. &c. By his son, the Rev. W. L. Clay, M.A. Cambridge (Macmillan). 8vo. 1861;' also his 'Annual Reports,' and other occasional publications. Of 'reprieved' criminals who, in the shadow of the gallows, had manifested every token of apparent penitence and heart-change, the number whose subsequent career gave evidence of reality is as 1 to 500, perhaps as awful a fact as recent criminal statistics reveal.

(g) P. 40.—' We must not do works of mercy proudly.' Lowell has finely put this :—

' Not that which we give, but what we share,
For the gifts without the giver is bare :
Who bestows himself with his alms feeds three,
Himself, his hungering neighbour, and me.'
The Vision of Sir Laurifal.

(g*) P. 41.—' What a cruel thing is it . . . without Church,' &c. This touching expression of Sibbes's feeling for the neglected ' masses,' the home-heathen, deserves a place beside the excellent Alleine's and Baxter's like-minded early setting forth of the claims of the foreign heathen. Consult Stanford's 'Joseph Alleine,' pp. 207–208.

(*h*) P. 47.—' St Chrysostom, an excellent preacher, yields me one observation upon this very place.' This seems to be a very vague recollection of the father's sentiment in his ' Homily ' on the Epistle, under the verse. Nor have I met with anything nearer elsewhere in his writings.

*** Having omitted a letter of reference to the following in its place, I add it here :—

P. 66, line 4th from bottom.—' As St Cyprian saith, ' We carry as much from God as we bring vessels.' The original is ' Nostrum tantum sitiat pectus et pateat. Quantum illuc fidei capacis afferimus, tantum gratiæ inundantis haurimus."—*Epist. I. ad Donatum.*

(*i*) P. 71.—' If any man be overtaken . . . . set him in joint, as the word is,' Gal. vi. 1. The word is καταρτίζω = to refit, mend. Cf. Liddell and Scott, and Robinson, *sub voce.*

(*j*) P. 83.—' There were three put in, and there was a fourth, which was Christ, the Son of God.' Cf. Daniel iii. 25. Our English version with its capitals has placed this among the *memorabilia* of Scripture, and of Christian experience. Few texts are oftener used to cheer the afflicted, while in the ' *furnace* of affliction.' It is perhaps allowable as an accommodation to do so, but the original does not seem to warrant our interpreting the ' *fourth*,' as THE Son of God = the Lord. As in the case of the ' den of lions,' Jehovah sent his ' angel,' in Scripture phrase ' *a* son of God,' Job. xxxviii. 7.

(*k*) P. 92.—' So that now the fire is our friend, the stone,' &c. Compare Thomas Adam of Wintringham's very remarkable ' thanks ' to God for ' the stone,' in his ' Private Thoughts,' than which few modern books contain so much uncommon and suggestive thinking. Bishop Wilson has worthily edited the priceless little volume.

(*l*) P. 95.—' So St Justin Martyr saith when he saw Christians suffer,' &c. His words are worth giving (Apolog. ii. 12), ' I myself, when I took pleasure in the doctrines of Plato, and heard the Christians slandered, seeing them to be fearless of death, and of everything else that was thought dreadful, considered that it was impossible that they should live in wickedness,' &c. &c.

(*m*) P. 97.—' The blood of the martyrs is the seed of the church.' This familiar apophthegm originated with Tertullian ; but runs more literally, ' Blood is the seed of Christians.' *(Apologeticus adversus Gentes,* c. 1.) The original is ' Plures efficimur quoties metimur a vobis ; semen est sanguis Christianorum.'

(*n*) P. 98.—' Some Greek copies,' &c. Cf. Alford, *in loc.* (Greek Testament, vol. ii.)

(*o*) P. 99.—' It is an excellent speech, solus Christus.' For the passage, see vol. I. footnote. page 369.

(*p*) P. 100.—' It is read in the margin, and most go that way,' &c. Cf. Alford, as in note *n.*

(*q*) P. 104.—' A man need not to whip himself, as the Scottish papists do.' The reference is probably to the *over*-zeal of the Scottish papists at the period contemporary with Sibbes, which manifested itself in a morbid observance of the extremest austerities of popery.

(*r*) P. 108.—' When he hears of any calamity of the church, whether it be in the Palatinate, in France, in the Low Countries,' &c. Sibbes, as stated in our Memoir, took the deepest interest in the ' foreign ' Protestants, and especially in the persecutions in the Palatinate. Cf. ' Memoir,' c. vii., and ' Sword of the Wicked, vol. I. pp. 115, 116.

(*r**) P. 114.—' It were offensive to name what distasteful things they will take to do them good.' In Stehelin's ' Rabbinical Literature ; or, the Traditions of the Jews, contained in the Talmud and other mystical writings, &c. &c. (2 vols. 8vo, 1748) ; Dr Wotton's ' Miscellaneous Discourses relating to the Traditions and Usages of the Scribes and Pharisees in our Blessed Saviour Jesus Christ's Time ;' &c. &c, (2 vols. 8vo, 1718), and scattered throughout Lightfoot's ' Talmudic,' and other ' Illustrations,' will be found many singular confirmations of the text of Sibbes in relation to Scripture ; while Timothy Bright's ' Treatise, wherein is declared the ' Sufficience of English Medicines for cure of all Diseases' (1615). preserves, with all the quaint wit of his ' Melancholie ' (the prototype of Burton's great book), the ' distasteful things' to which Sibbes's contemporaries submitted. Consult also the various histories of the early ' Materia Medica.'

(*s*) P. 117.—' A learned Hebrician Capne,' &c. John Reuchlin, one of the foremost names of Germany, alike in relation to the Reformation and the Restoration of Letters, has recently received the splendid eulogium—enriched with accumulated 'testimonies'—of Sir William Hamilton. Consult his 'Discussions on Philosophy and Literature,' &c. &c. (2d edition. 1853), pp. 212, *seq.*, 216, 237, 239, *seq.* His student-visitors will remember how Sir William was wont to exhibit, as one of the greatest prizes of his collection, the interesting holograph letter of Reuchlin, first published in above; and with what glowing appreciation he expatiated upon its writer. Sibbes calls him by his later name of Capne. He translated, in the fashion of the day, his guttural German into the more euphonious Greek,—both signifying the same thing, viz., 'smoke' (*Der rauch* and καπνος), as Philip Schwartzerde became Philip Melancthon. He was born at Pforzheim, 1450; died, 1522. He was the preceptor of Melancthon; and Luther acknowledged to him that 'he only followed in his steps,—only consummated his victory, with inferior strength, indeed, but not inferior courage, in breaking the teeth of the Behemoth.' Epist. ad. Reuchl., lib. ii., sig. C. iii., and in De Wette's Luther's Briefe, i. 196.

(*t*) P. 121.—'The word is very significant in the original,' &c. The expression is intensive, ἐξαπορηθῆναι = to be utterly at a loss, or absolutely without a way (πόρος) of escape. Cf. Dr Charles Hodge, *in loc.*

(*u*) P. 121.—'The schoolmen say,' &c. Query, Aquinas? He speaks of the ' Magnitudo doloris Christi' as arising from his body being 'optime complexionatus.' Leigh, in his 'Body of Divinity,' so cites it, and gives as the reference ' Aq. Part 3. Quæst. 46., Art. 6.'

(*v*) P. 129.—' As the heathen man could say,' ' There is not the oldest man but he thinks he may live a little longer, one day longer.' The 'heathen man' is Cicero, who says, ' Nemo enim est tam senex, qui se annum non putet posse vivere.' De Senectute, c. vii. § 24.

(*w*) P. 133.—' They renounce their own religion at the hour of death, as Bellarmine did.' The authority for this statement is Bellarmine's own work on Justification, lib. v. c. 7. After defending the Romish doctrine on this subject in opposition to the Protestant Evangelical, he makes this concession, which speaks more for his piety than his consistency : ' Propter incertitudinem propriæ justitiæ et periculum inanis gloriæ, tutissimum esse in sola misericordia Dei et benignitate fiduciam suam reponere.' If I err not, a like confession is made in his ' Last Will.'

(*x*) P. 134.—' Coster saith, and saith truly, if Christ be not there, we are the greatest idolaters in the world.' Cf. Note *p*, vol. II. p. 434.

(*y*) P. 137.—' Saith St Austin, ' I dare say, and stand to it, that it is profitable for some men to fall ; they grow more holy by their slips.' The sentiment will be found in the following quotations :—

(1.) ' Audeo dicere, superbis continentibus expedit cadere,' &c.—*De Divers. Serm.* cccliv. cap. ix, tom v. col. 1378. Bened. ed. fol. Par. 1679 *sqq.*

(2.) ' Audeo dicere, superbis esse utile cadere in aliquod apertum manifestumque peccatum, unde sibi displiceant, qui jam sibi placendo ceciderunt.'—*De Civ. Dei.* xiv. 13.

Cf. footnote vol. I. 324, and Jeremy Taylor, ' Sermon on Lukewarmness and Zeal; or Spiritual Fervour.' Edition of Works by Eden, iv. 149.

(*z*) P. 138.—' As the heathen man said, that great emperor, " I have been all things, and nothing doth me good now," when he was to die. " Omnia fui, nihil expedit' is ascribed to the emperor Septimus Severus on his deathbed (A. D. 211).

(*aa*) P. 149.—' St Bernard, a good man in evil times,' saith he, ' I consider three things in which I pitch my hope and trust, *charitatem adoptionis,* the love of God in making me his child ; and *veritatem promissionis,* the truth of God in performing his promise,' &c. Sibbes paraphrases the following: ' Tria igitur considero, in quibus tota spes mea consistit, charitatem adoptionis, veritatem promissionis, potestatem redditionis.'—Sermon iii., *de panibus,* 8.

(*bb*) P. 154.—' It is a seizon, as a piece of earth,' &c. Sir William Blackstone (' Commentaries,' b. ii. c. 20.) explains this : ' This livery of *seisin* is no other than the pure feodal investiture, or delivery of corporeal possession of the land or tenement; which was held absolutely necessary to complete the donation.'—Cf. also Richardson, *sub voce.*

(*cc*) P. 170.—' Deliverance is promised upon ill terms; that they may redeem their lives if they will, by denying God and religion—an ill bargain.' The 'persecutions' of the early Christians furnish many illustrations of the text. They were called merely to ' sprinkle a little incense on the altar' (*i. e.*, of the gods), and a free pardon would ensue. The stern ' Covenanters' of Scotland, under Charles II. and James II., were repeatedly offered their ' lives,' if they would say, ' God save the king.' Neither earlier nor later was the ' ill bargain' acceded to.

(*dd*) P. 170.—' That they carry not themselves uncomely in troubles, but so as is meet for the credit of the truth which they seal with their blood.' The pleasant message of the proto-martyr of the Reformation, John Rogers, to Hooper—who was confined in another apartment—on the night before his death, is perhaps the most striking illustration of the text in English history. There is abundant evidence of the ' credit' his stout-hearted bearing brought to ' the truth.' Rogers' most recent biographer observes : ' To the other condemned preachers still in prison, the news of Rogers' constancy came like a sudden burst of sunlight from a heavy cloud. If they wavered under the doom that threatened them, they did so no longer. He had set them an example worthy of imitation, and whither he had led the way, they could now more confidently follow. We find Bradford, in a letter to Cranmer, Ridley, and Latimer, written four days after Rogers' death, rejoicing that their ' dear brother' had ' broken the ice valiantly.' Ridley writes thus to Bradford : ' I thank our Lord God and Heavenly Father by Christ, that since I heard of our dear brother Rogers' departing and stout confession of Christ and his truth, even unto the death, my heart, blessed be God, so rejoiced of it, that, since that time, I say, I never felt any lumpish heaviness in my heart, as I grant I have felt sometimes before.'— Cf. Chester's ' Life of John Rogers,' pp. 213–14. 8vo. 1860.

⁎ P. 182.—' As St Austin saith well, God hath made the rich for the poor, and the poor for the rich : the rich to relieve the poor, and the poor to pray for the rich ; for herein one is accepted for another.' The words are, ' Fecit Deus pauperem, ut probet divitem ; et fecit Deus divitem, ut probet illum de paupere.' In Psalm cxxiv. *Enarrat in fine.*

(*ee*) P. 184.—' That great divine Paulus Phagius, who was a great Hebrecian,' &c. Paulus Fagius was born 1504, died 1550. The words quoted by Sibbes form part of his "Concio valedictoria," which will be found both in German and Latin, in Melchior Adam's Lives of German Theologians, page 209. The German begins thus, ' Ihr jungen bittel Gott,' &c. The Latin thus, ' Vos juniores orate Deum. Forte enim vos facilius exaudiet quam qui plus peccatorum admiserunt.'

(*ff*) P. 191.—' Therefore you know the Grecians accounted that a chief blessing.' Sibbes probably refers to the many praises of ὑγίεια, and to the axiomatic summary of every ' blessing,' ἡ περὶ το σῶμα καὶ την ψυχὴν ὑγίεια, (Isocrates, 234 B) which has passed into the Latin (*mens sana in corpore sano*), and all other civilized languages. Hygieia, the goddess of health, received abundant ' worship.'

(*gg*) P. 208,—' The original word in the Old Testament that signifies the heart, it is taken for the conscience.' Cf. Gesenius, *Thesaurus* (preferable to his ' Lexicon'), under לֵב and its synonymes, with Liddell and Scott, and Robinson, under καρδία and συνείδησις.

(*hh*) P. 209.—' Therefore the name for conscience in the Greek and Latin signifies a knowledge with another.' That is συνείδησις = a knowing with one's self, consciousness ; and *conscientia* (con-scio) = joint knowledge. Cf. Note *gg* above.

(*ii*) P. 209.—' It is a knowledge with a rule, with a general rule,' &c. See this principle brought out with power and pungency, by Professor Sewell of Oxford, in the following remarkable pamphlet, now unhappily ' out of print,' and only to be met with at an extravagant price, ' The Plea of Conscience for seceding from the Catholic Church to the Romish Schism in England. . . . A Sermon preached before the University of Oxford, Nov. 5. 1845. To which is added an Essay *on the Process of Conscience.* Oxford : J. H. Parker. 1845. Pp. xxvii. and 53.

(*jj*) P. 214.—' Cursed is he, saith the Council of Trent, that doth not equalize those traditions with the word of God.' Cf. History of the Council of Trent, by L. F. Bungener (1853. Crown 8vo.) ; Tradition, book ii. pp. 83, 88, 89, *et alibi ;* also Memoirs of the Council of Trent, &c., &c., by Joseph Mendham, M.A. (1834. 8vo) ; and Buckley's ' History,' (1852.)

(*kk*) P. 217 —' So holy St Austin, what saith he to a Donatist that wronged him in his reputation,' &c. The reference is to the following, ' Senti de Augustino quidquid libet, sola me in oculis Dei conscientia non accuset.' *Lib. Secund. contra Manich.*

(*ll*) P. 229.—' So it is in the original, "in the *simplicity* and sincerity of God." The word is ἀπλότης = *singleness* of mind, the opposite of duplicity. Cf. Deans Alford and Stanley as to the *readings.*

(*mm*) P. 234.—' Christ made as though he would have gone further,' &c. The Evangelist is *describing the attitude* of the Lord *as he appeared to the ' two disciples.'* He was '*going on* ' (προσεποιεῖτο). Assuredly he *would* have gone on had he *not* been solicited to 'abide.' His 'going on,' or 'remaining,' was contingent on their request, . . . only a lesser operation of the great law of all our spiritual 'blessings' being contingent upon prayer, upon our 'asking.' It seems somewhat perilous then to concede with Sibbes and our translators, that the Lord made a 'show to do' what he did not 'mean' to do. He *was* 'going on,' intended to 'go further,' but was '*constrained*' to 'abide,' (ver. 29). This explanation is surely more satisfactory than Sibbes's concession, and than that which resolves it into a 'speaking after the manner of men.' Jeremy Taylor and others, 'he *pretended*,' is exceedingly unguarded.

(*nn*) P. 234.—'Saith Tertullian very well, There is no necessity of sin to them, upon whom there lies no other necessity but not to sin.' The passage is in the treatise *De Coronâ Militis*, as follows :—'Nulla est necessitas delinquendi, quibus una est necessitas non delinquendi.'

(*oo*) P. 238.—'Thou shalt be uncased.' One of Thomas Adams' most wonderful 'sermons' is entitled 'The White Devil ; or, The Hypocrite *Uncased*,' (*i.e.*, Judas). See 'Practical Works' in the present series, II. p. 221, *seq.*;

(*pp*) P. 251.—'Comb-downes,' as we say. The Rev. Dr Bonar of Kelso kindly informs me that he met with the word 'comb-downe' in an old English poet as = sky-fort. That is, 'comb or coomb,' old English and Scotch for sky (coomb-ceiled = sky-roofed, *i. e.*, arch-roofed, concave) and down = dun, *i. e.*, fort or castle. According to this, 'comb-downe' resolves itself into our 'sky-castles = castles in the air.' I regret that Dr Bonar has not been able to recover the reference. I venture to query if in 'comb-downe,' we have not the origin of our word, '*down-come*' or '*come-down*' = great fall, as from prosperity to poverty.

(*qq*) P. 267.—'As we see in Spira,' &c. Consult Gribaldus. 'Historia Francisci Spiræ' (1548), which, translated into English by Aglionby, as follows : 'A notable and maruailous epistle concerning the terrible judgment of God upon hym that for feare of men denyeth Christ and the knowen veritie ; being the case of Francis Spera or Spira, an Italian, with a preface of Dr Caluine' (1550), has ever since been a popular chap-book.

(*rr*) P. 268.—'Curse God.' &c. Cf. Rev. A. B. Davidson's 'Job' *in loc.*, (vol. i. 1862). He says, '*Renounce* בָּרֵךְ, the usual word in these chapters. Some prefer taking the word here, however, in its usual sense. *Bless* (with sarcastic intonation and in irony), bless this God of yours (i. 21) again, and die ! &c. &c. (page 28).

(*ss*) P. 269.—'Stephen Gardiner's letters.' &c. There does not appear to be any collected edition of the 'Letters' of this notorious Prelate : but various were published singly, and others are met with in collections. Nearly all are in the library of the British Museum ; and also among the MSS. there.

(*tt*) P. 271.—'As St Austin hath a good speech, "Lord, free me from myself, from my own devices and policy."' This is a reminiscence of an often-recurring apophthegm of the 'Confessions.'

(*uu*) P. 274.—'Therefore Luther was wont to say, 'Good works are good, but to trust in good works is damnable.' This is a frequent saying of the Colloquia Mensalia, which in the great folio of Captain Henrie Bell (1652), was a special favourite with the Puritans. Our copy bears the autograph of the famous 'Puritan' worthy and statesman Sir Nathaniel Barnardiston, a presentation copy to his son, 'Ex dono T. B. meo filio.' Sibbes seems to have derived the greater number of his Luther quotations from the 'Colloquia Mensalia.'

(*vv*) P. 275.—'Graces, not as habits, as it was the proud term of the philosophers to call it.' The reference appears to be to the Greek term ἦθος, a custom, but taken to signify a virtue—hence *ethics*. So also the Latin term *mos*.

(*ww*) P. 284.—'It was a proud term . . . . . *as I said*.' Cf. page 275, and note *vv* as above.

(*xx*) P. 288.—'Saith the heathen man Tully, "I thought myself wise, but I never was so."' This must be a vague recollection of Cicero. I have not been able to trace it.

(*yy*) P. 209.—'As that wretch said himself, when he came to die, "That he had provided for all things but for death."' See note *z* above.

(*zz*) P. 301.—'For I think not that he means his former epistle,' &c. Modern scholarship agrees with Sibbes. Cf. Deans Stanley and Alford.

(*aaa*) P. 302.—'As you know in a war of theirs with the Turks, the story is well known,' &c. The Turk was Amurath. He made a treaty of peace for ten years with Ladislas, king of Hungary. Julian, the pope's legate, persuaded Ladislas to break the peace, absolving him from his oath. Amurath was engaged in another war, and was thus taken at a disadvantage. A battle was fought at Varna, 10th November 1444. At first the victory inclined to the side of the Christians ; upon which Amurath, seeing his great danger, plucked from his bosom the treaty which had thus been broken, and holding it in his hands, with eyes upraised to heaven, made the following appeal : ' Behold, thou crucified Christ ! this is the league that thy Christians in thy name made with me ; which they have without any cause violated. Now, if thou be a God as they say thou art, and as we dream, revenge the wrong now done unto thy name and me, and shew thy frown upon thy perjured people, who by their deeds deny thee their God.' An attack was immediately made, and the battle, which was almost lost to the Turks, was restored. The Hungarian king was killed, and his head placed upon a spear. Two-thirds of the Christian army perished ; and yet the Turks lost 20,000 men, so dreadful was the slaughter. I find above abstract of Sibbes's reference, in the Life of the great Huniades of Hungary, who was taken prisoner in this battle, and who afterwards became regent during the minority of Ladislas, the successor of Ladislas IV.

(*bbb*) P. 302.—' The old principle of Isidore is constantly and everlastingly true, " Conceive," ' &c. Isidore (Hispalensis) died 636. ' Quacunque arte verborum quis juret, Deus tamen, qui conscientiæ testis est, hoc accipit sicut iste cui juratur intelligit.'—Libri duo Synonymorum, lib. ii.

(*ccc*) P. 306.—' That hope should stir up some endeavour to pray for them, seeing their estates are not desperate,' &c. Cf. note *c*, vol. I. page 171. In a long, very characteristic (unpublished) letter of John Newton, addressed to the late Professor Lawson of Selkirk, in our possession, the following paragraph occurs, and is a beautiful commentary upon Sibbes's counsel. He is speaking of the sudden death of Robinson of Cambridge, in the house of Dr Priestly, and says :—' I think Dr Priestly is out of the reach of human conviction ; but the Lord can convince him. And who can tell but this unexpected stroke may make some salutary impression upon his mind ? *I can set no limits to the mercy or the power of our Lord, and therefore I continue to pray for him. I am persuaded he is not farther from the truth now than I was once.*'

(*ddd*) P. 327.—' " That you might have a second benefit," saith the last translation.' ' The last translation ' was our present or King James's version, first issued in 1611. We find ' benefit ' in the text, and ' grace ' in the margin, as described by Sibbes.

(*eee*) P. 331.—' Therefore St Austin doth well define predestination ; it is an ordaining to salvation. and a preparing of all means tending thereto.' The original is as follows :—' Hæc est Prædestinatio sanctorum, nihil aliud ; præscientia scilicet et præparatio beneficiorum Dei, quibus certissime liberantur, quicumque liberantur.' —De Dono Perseverantiæ, o. xxv.

(*fff*) P. 340.—' Saith St Ambrose, " Et nobis malus," ' &c. I have failed to discover the saying in Ambrose. Sir Philip Sidney uses it with great effect (without naming Ambrose), in his memorable Letter to Elizabeth, dissuading her from her proposed marriage.

(*ggg*) P. 350.—' Cave, time, &c., saith the holy man St Austin.' One of the *memorabilia* of the ' Confessions.'

(*hhh*) P. 354.—' Isidore saith, " An oath is to be esteemed as he," ' &c. Cf. note *bbb*.

(*iii*) P. 357.—' " Our word, our preaching," as it is in the margin.' See note *ddd*. The word is ὁ λογος, probably of purpose indefinite, so as to embrace both his personal communications and his ' preaching.'

(*jjj*) P. 357.—' " As God is true," it is in our translation, but in the original it is, " God is true." ' The original is πιστὸς δε ὁ Θεος, ὅτι ὁ λόγος ἡμων, &c., which Dean Stanley thus puts, ' So true as it is that God is faithful, so true is it that my communications are not variable.' Cf. xi. 10 ; Rom. xiv. 11.

(*kkk*) P. 359.—' The oracles of Apollo . . . . . . true one way, and false another.' Consult Schmitz's article on ' Oracles,' in Smith's Dictionary of Greek and Roman Antiquities,'(2d edit. 1859, 8vo).

The following paragraph, from *Horne's Introduction*, gives a clear view of the matter :—

. . . . . When no means of evasion remained, the answers given by the heathen oracles were frequently delusive, and capable of quite contrary interpretations; and the most celebrated of them concealed their meaning in such ambiguous terms that they required another oracle to explain them. Of this ambiguity several authentic instances are recorded. Thus, when Crœsus consulted the oracle at Delphi relative to his intended war against the Persians, he was told that he would destroy a great empire.—Κροισος 'Αλυν διαβὰς μεγάλην ἄρχην καταλυσει. This he naturally interpreted of his overcoming the Persians, though the oracle was so framed as to admit of an opposite meaning. Crœsus made war against the Persians, and was ruined ; and the oracle continued to maintain its credit. The answer given as to Pyrrhus, King of Epirus, many ages after, was of yet more doubtful interpretation, being conceived in terms so ambiguous, that it might be either interpreted thus :— *I say that thou, son of Æacus, canst conquer the Romans. Thou shalt go, thou shalt return, never shalt thou perish in war ;* or thus, *I say that the Romans can conquer thee, son of Æacus. Thou shalt go, thou shalt never return, thou shalt perish in war.*

Aio te Æacida Romanos vincere posse :
Ibis redibis nunquam in bello peribis.

Pyrrhus understood the oracle in the former sense ; he waged an unsuccessful war with the Romans, and was overcome ; yet still the juggling oracle saved its credit. Another remarkable instance of the ambiguity of the pretended prophets occurs in 1 Kings xxii. 5, 6. Jehoshaphat, king of Judah, and Ahab, king of Israel, having united their forces against the Syrians, in order to recover Ramoth-Gilead, the latter monarch gathered the false prophets together, about four hundred men, and said unto them. " Shall I go up against Ramoth-Gilead to battle, or shall I forbear ?" And they said, " Go up, for the Lord shall deliver [it] into the hands of the king." It is to be observed that the word *it* is not in the original, and that the reply of the pseudo-prophets is so artfully constructed, that it might be interpreted either *for* or *against* the expedition ; as thus.—the Lord will deliver *it* (Ramoth-Gilead) into the king's (Ahab's) hand ; or, the Lord will deliver (Israel) into the king's hand ; that is, into the king's hand, that is, into the hands of the King of Syria. Relying upon this ambiguous oracle, the monarchs of Judah and Israel engaged the Syrians, and were utterly discomfited.—*Horne's Introduction*, vol. i. ch. iv. sec. 3, pp. 274–5 (10th ed. 1856).

This subject is well treated by Henry Smith, in his " God's Arrow against Atheists."

(*lll*) P. 361.—' Man is changeable, because he is a creature, as Damascene's speech is.' The speech is the following :—πᾶν γαρ γενητὸν, τρεπτόν ἐστιν. ὧν γὰρ ἡ ἀρχὴ της γενέσεως ἀπὸ τροπῆς ἤρξατο, ἀνάγκη ταῦτα τρεπτὰ ἔιναι. Damasc. De Fide Orthodoxa, cap. xxvii.

(*mmm*) P. 364.—' St Austin. . . . . . He wrote a book of retractations of his former opinions.' This father's magnanimous ' retractations ' are found in all the collective editions of his works.

(*nnn*) P. 365.—' If only yea be true, then that which is contrary to it must needs be false.' All Sibbes's hits at popery have long formed the commonplaces of the controversy, and are introduced into all the standard works *pro* and *con*.

(*ooo*) P. 366 —' The pope he makes Garnet, a traitor, and Thomas of Becket, saints.' Henry Garnet was a ' priest,' notorious as having been ' privy ' to the ' Gunpowder Plot.' He was born 1555, and was executed May 3. 1606. His plea for not revealing the infamous ' Plot ' was that it had been made known to him in ' confession,' an extenuation that intensified the national abhorrence of the whole system of popery. Sibbes speaks of the pope making him a ' saint.' While going to the block, he was told by his friends that he would be regarded as a ' martyr ;' but exclaimed, ' Me martyrem! O qualem martyrem !' Concerning Becket, it is only necessary to refer to ' Becket, Archbishop of Canterbury ; a Biography. By J. C. Robertson. 1 Vol. 8vo. 1859. (Murray.)

(*ppp*) P. 367.—' It is somewhat uncertain whether ever Peter were at Rome.' For a full and scholarly examination of this matter, consult ' The Question, " Was St Peter ever at Rome ?" Historically Considered. By Augustus Scheler.' (1 Vol. 12mo. 1849. Nisbet.) Scheler's conclusive treatise, which returns a negative to the question, is at once an expansion of the ' Ist Petrus in Rom und Bischof der römischen Kirche gewesen,' and a gathering together of data scattered through the writings of Scaliger, Salmasius, Spanheim, Bost, and Malan.

(*qqq*) P. 373.—' But as Cyprian saith well, " It must be consent in the truth." ' Perhaps the following may be the passage referred to : ' Quare si solus Christus audiendus est, non debemus attendere quid alius ante nos faciendum esse putaverit, sed quid qui ante omnes est, Christus prior fecerit. Neque enim hominum consuetudinem sequi oportet, sed Dei veritatem.'—Ep. 63, Ad Cœcilium de Sac. Dom. Cal (*rrr*) P. 374.—' It sets him down that he can say nothing, but that it is divine truth, because he finds it so.' On the force of personal 'experience' as an 'evidence' of the truth of Christianity, consult the excellent treatise of Wardlaw thereupon— worthy son of a worthy sire.

(*sss*) P. 375.—' How we may know that our church was before Luther's time or no.' Cf. Note *d*, vol. II. p. 248. I take this opportunity of giving the exact title-page of Logie's rare tractate :—' Cum Bono Deo. Raine from the Clouds upon a Choicke [*sic*] Angel : or, A returned Answere to that common Quæritur of our Adversaries, Where was your Church before Luther ? Digested into several Medita-tions, according to the difference of Points, Extorted off the Author, for stilling the incessant and no lesse clamorous coassation of some Patmicke Frogges, against the lawfulnesse of our Calling. Aberdeene. Imprinted by Edward Raban, Dwelling upon the Market-place, at the Townes Armes, 1624, cum privilegio.' 4to. 1634, in Note *d*, vol. II. is a misprint for 1624. A copy of this singular tractate is preserved in Peterborough Cathedral Library ; and I have to acknowledge the kindness of the Rev. Thomas Hutton, M.A., Rector of Stilton, in securing to me unrestricted access to its treasures, of which privilege after-volumes will shew the benefit.

(*ttt*) P. 377.—' The most of the points of popery, wherein they differ from us, nay, not any of them, were never established by a council till the Council of Trent, except transubstantiation, by the Council of Lateran, which was a thousand years after Christ.' The Councils of Lateran were held in the Basilica of the Lateran, at Rome. Of these Councils, there were five. The 'fourth,' on church affairs gene-rally.—attended by 400 bishops and 1000 abbots—was held in 1215. Innocent III. presided.

(*uuu*) P. 379.—' Luther saith, If they [the papists] live and die peremptorily in all the points professed in the Tridentine Council, they cannot [be saved].' Cf. Note *uu*.

(*vvv*) P. 382.—' There is some diversity in reading the words.' Cf. Alford *in loc.*

(*www*) P. 412.—' As David, Ps. cxix., if it be his.' Consult S. F. Thrupp's 'In-troduction to the Study and Use of the Psalms' (2 vols. 8vo, 1860). He accepts Bishop Jebb's suggestion of Daniel being the author of this the most splendid tribute to the Word of God anywhere to be found. See vol. II. pp. 244–256.

(*xxx*) P. 417.—' Take the counsel of that blessed man . . . Luther, I mean, . . . Go to God in Christ, in the promises.' From the 'Colloquia Mensalia.' See Note *uu* concerning this storehouse of quotable sayings.

(*yyy*) P. 436.—' Remembering always that of St Ambrose, that there must not be striving for victory, but for truth.' See note *fff*.

(*zzz*) P. 437.—' Your *Ancipites*, as Cyprian calls them, your doubtful flatterers of the times.' Cyprian seems to employ the vivid word in its etymological sense of having two heads, two natures, double = undecided, changeable. Lucan speaks of 'ancipites animi' (9, 46).

(*aaaa*) P. 440.—' As you have it storied of Papinian, an excellent lawyer.' For an interesting notice of Papinian, consult Mr Long's article in Dr Smith's 'Diction-ary of Greek and Roman Biography and Mythology ;' also Dio. Cass., lib. lxxvii., with note from Spartianus, Caracc. c. viii.

(*bbbb*) P. 451.—' They gave this answer, *Christianus sum*, I am a Christian.' This is recorded in all the early 'Apologies,' *e. g.*, Justin Martyr, Tertullian (Apolog. c. ii.).

(*cccc*) P. 460.—' Pella, a little village, was delivered when the general destruction came upon Jerusalem.' Pella was the place whither the Christians fled before the destruction of the 'Holy City.' Cf. Eusebius H. E. iii. 5 ; Epiphanius de *Mens. et Ponder*, p. 171 ; Reland, Palaestina, p. 924 ; also Croly's 'Salathiel.'

(*dddd*) P. 464.—' 1 John v. 7, 8.' With reference to the 'Three Witnesses' of the present passage, it is only necessary to refer to Orme's admirable and well known 'Memoir' of the 'Controversy' (1830, 12mo) ; and to the works of Travis, Bur-gess, Middleton, and Wiseman in favour of, and Porson, Marsh, and Turton against, the retention of the disputed clause. It is now usually enclosed in our Greek Testa-ments in brackets ; and perhaps it were well if it were similarly marked in our English Bibles. Cf. Webster and Wilkinson *in loc.*, and Tregelles in Horne, iv., c. xxxvi. (10th ed., 1856).

(*eeee*) P. 475.—' Like to the Samaritans, as Josephus, the historian of the Jews, writes of them. When the Jews prospered, oh ! then they would be Jews,' &c. The passage will be found in the 'Antiquities,' Book ix., c. xiv. § 3, 'When they [the Cutheans or Samaritans] see the Jews in prosperity, they pretend that they are changed, and allied to them, and call them kinsmen, as though they were derived from Joseph, and had by that means an original alliance with them; but when they see them falling into a low condition, they say they are no way related to them, and that the Jews have no right to expect any kindness or marks of kindred from them, but they declare that they are sojourners that come from other countries.' Cf. also xi. c. viii. ⸹ 6, and xii. c. v. 5.

(ffff) P. 475.—' As we see in Cranmer and others.' The good Archbishop's early faltering, and subsequent recantation and martyr-death, are historic.

(gggg) P. 478.—' The Holy Spirit searcheth. . . . He is a " searcher," as the word is in the original.' Cf. 1 Cor. ii. 10 The verb is ἐρευνάω, = explore; *i.e.*, accurately and thoroughly know. Hodge, and Webster and Wilkinson, *in loc.*, will reward consultation.

(hhhh) P. 479.—' As Austin saith, " The Spirit of God knocks at their hearts but he doth not dwell there." ' This is a frequently-recurring saying of the ' Confessions ' and *De Civitate*, with varying phraseology, as all readers of this father are aware is common with him.

(iiii) P. 491.—' As St Austin saith very well. Christ. saith he, speaks to the sea, and it is quiet,' &c. Cf. Augustine on Mark iv. 39. It is found also in Theophylact.

(jjjj) P. 497.—' God, I hope, will be merciful to the state; for the censure of the state upon profanation, it is a very worthy act.' There were multiplied ' proclamations ' at this period against '*profaneness*,' as also during the reign of Charles II. The rigidness of the 'laws,' and the laxity of the practice, suggest much.

(kkkk) P. 499.—' These words are declined by many interpreters.' Consult Hodge, Dean Stanley, and Webster and Wilkinson *in loc.*

(llll) P. 500.—' It is not to domineer over faith, to suppress that that they call of late in neighbour countries a *liberty of prophecy*.' Cf. Bishop Jeremy Taylor's magnificent vindication of this ' liberty ' in his ' ΘΕΟΛΟΓΙΑ ᾽ΕΚΛΕΚΤΙΚΗ ; or, A Discourse of the Liberty of Prophesying, with its just Limits and Temper : shewing the Unreasonableness of prescribing to other men's faith, and the iniquity of persecuting differing opinions.' (Works, ed. 1849, by Eden. V. pp. 339–605)

(mmmm) P. 500.—' St Austin himself was once of this mind, that people were not to be forced.' His words are, ' Ad fidem quidem nullus est cogendus invitus.' *Contra Ep. Petiliani Donatistæ*, lib. ii. c. lxxxiii.

(nnnn) P. 503.—' If he came in by simony, or is not *in cathedra*.' Ranke supplies abundant examples of the former, and the latter denotes that the pope is infallible only while he acts in his official character, *e.g.*, propagating a bull or making a decision. *Extra cathedram*, or as a *private* man, he is held by papists to be liable to err.

(oooo) P. 505.—' Council of Trent and Pius IV.' Cf. note *jj*, and Ranke under Pius IV. and Trent.

(pppp) P. 510.—' Ministers . . . . advise in cases of conscience.' Sibbes's contemporaries, and indeed the whole of the leading theologians before and after him, occupied themselves with drawing up ' resolutions ' of ' cases of conscience.' It is only necessary to name the great ' Ductor Dubitantium ' of Jeremy Taylor, and the pungent ' Treatise ' of William Perkins.

(qqqq) P. 514.—' He hath his chair in heaven that teacheth the heart, as St Austin saith.' The words are, ' Cathedram habet in cœlo, qui corda docet in terris.' *In* 1 *Epist. St Johan.* Tr. iii. ⸹ 13. Cf. also his *De Disciplina Christiana.*

(rrrr) P. 518.—' Standing is a military word;' *i.e.*, ἵστημι, opposed to φεύγω. Cf. Eph. vi. 13. A. B. G.

ALPHABETICAL TABLE

DIRECTING THE READER TO THE READY FINDING OUT THE PRINCIPAL POINTS

AND MATTERS HANDLED IN THIS BOOK.*

---

* This 'Alphabetical Table,' prepared by Dr Thomas Manton, it has been deemed proper to retain, and accommodate to the pagination of our reprint. It does not furnish those minuter details and references that belong to an Index *proper*, such as will be given with the closing volume of this edition of the Works ; but as the 'Commentary' is extensive, it will prove acceptable as an interim guide to the 'treasures, new and old,' of this Treatise.

This 'Commentary,' it is necessary to observe, is *not* a fragment of an intended Exposition of the entire Epistle, but a Treatise on the 'Apology of St Paul,' complete within itself, according to the design of the author. Cf. page 528, last line.—G.

best known, 259 ; a sound Christian loves and values all Christians, 432 ; Christians are prophets, priests, and kings, how ? 447, *seq.* (See Saint.)

Church.—Whether the church can give authority to the word or Scripture, 9, 10, 523 ; God hath a church in most wicked places, and among most wicked people, 10 ; every Christian ought to be a member of some particular church or congregation, 11, 12 ; the church hath its name sometimes, 1, from the mixture in it, 2, from the better part of it, 12 ; churches not to be left or forsaken for some corruptions in them, 322.

Civil.—A mere civil man, who, 14.

Comfort, Consolation.—Comfort or consolation, what, 44, 45, 86 ; God the God of comfort, how, 44, 45 ; what this title attributed to God implies, 47 ; whatsoever the means of comfort be, God is the spring and fountain of it, 49 ; God can create comfort out of nothing, 47 ; God can raise comfort out of contraries, 47, 48 ; what use to be made of this, that God is the God of comfort, 48, 49, *seq.*; reasons or grounds why Christians are uncomfortable, 50 ; God comforteth his people in all tribulation, 51, 52, 53, 54 ; objection against this answered, 52, 74 ; God applieth comfort answerable to all miseries in this life, 52, 53 ; to comfort what, 54; what use to be made of this, that God is the God of all comfort, who comforteth us in all our tribulation, 54, 55, *seq.*; how to derive comfort from the God of comfort, 55 ; no comfort for such as go on in sin, 56 ; comforts for those that are relapsed, 57 ; general comforts should be had for all kind of maladies and grievances, and which be they, 57, 58 ; means for obtaining of comfort, 57, 59-64 ; to keep a daily course of comfort, how, 59, 60 ; Christ in Scripture is set forth by all terms that may be comfortable, 60 ; means whereby we may be enabled to comfort others, 65, 66, 69, 70; all God's children have interest in divine comforts, why, 66 ; divine comforts are not impaired by being communicated, 66; God conveys comfort to men by men, 67, 68; we should be willing, ready, and able to comfort one another, 67, 68, 69, 75, 76; experience a great help to comfort others, why, 76, 77, 78 ; objections of such as complain of want of comfort answered, 74 ; our comforts and consolations are proportionable to our sufferings, 86 ; greatest comforts follow greatest sufferings, why, 86; what hinders comfort in affliction, 90 ; no comfort for wicked men, 90 ; comfort or consolation abounds by Christ, 91 ; why Christians are no more comfortable, 92; suffering a necessary precedent of comfort, why, 108 ; those that suffer as they should, are sure of comfort, 110.

Commendation—A man may speak in commendation of himself, and in what cases, 204.

Communion.—Bond of communion of saints, 432.

Companion.—Companions in sin shall be companions in suffering, 110.

Conceit.—We should have a good conceit of others, 306, 307 ; it is good to have a good conceit of others, 327. (See Hope, Opinion.)

Confidence.—Certain account of, and looking for death, is a notable means to draw us from self-confidence, 127 ; God's children prone to self-confidence, 128. (See Trust.)

Conformity.—A three-fold conformity with Christ, 110.

Conscience.—Conscience, what, 208, 209, 210, *seq.*; three things joined with conscience, 209 ; God hath set up a court in man, wherein conscience is, (1.) register, (2.) witness, (3.) accuser, (4.) judge, (5.) executioner, 210, 211; consc ence. God's hall, wherein he keeps his assizes, 211 ; judgment of conscience a forerunner of the great and general judgment, 210, 211; conscience beareth witness, 211 ; what manner of witness conscience is, viz., (1.) faithful, (2.) inward, 211, 212 ; how to have conscience witness well, 212-215, *seq* ; an ignorant man cannot have a good conscience, 213 ; why men have bad consciences, 213 ; papists cannot have a good conscience, why, 214; the

witness of a good conscience the ground of joy, why, 215-219; a good conscience breeds joy, (1.) in life, (2.) in death, (3.) at the day of judgment, 216-219 ; a good conscience comforts in all estates and conditions whatsoever, 216-219; why a good conscience doth not always witness comfort, 219, 220 ; means how to joy and rejoice in the witness of conscience, 221 ; nothing worse than a bad conscience, 223-226 ; labour for a good conscience, 226 ; commendation of a good conscience, 226 ; how to have a good conscience, 227; God's children have place in the con-cience of others, 304.

Contraries—God is able to raise comfort out of contraries, 48 ; God carries on the work of our salvation by contraries, why, 137.

Conversation.—Conversation, what, 252 ; Christianity may stand with conversing abroad in the world, 253; religion makes a man converse abroad in the world untainted, 254; a Christian's conversation is best where he is best known, 259.

Corinth.—Corinth a very wicked city, yet even there God hath a church, 10 ; what is now become of the church of Corinth, 10, 11 ; Corinth the metropolis or mother-city of Achaia, 11. (See Achaia.)

Danger.—God suffers his children sometimes to fall into extreme perils and dangers, why, 117, 118, *seq.*

Day.—Christ hath a day, 323 ; there be two special days of Christ, 323 ; the measure of a Christian's joy is, as it will be esteemed at the day of judgment, 324: we should often think of the day of the Lord Jesus, 325. (See judgment.)

Death.—God's children are sometimes very sensible, and much afraid of death, why, 120-122, *seq.*; how and in what respect the saints desire death, 124 ; Christ was afraid of death, and yet thirsted after it, how, 124; God's children are often deceived concerning the time of their death, why, 125 ; death uncertain, how, 125; the time of death uncertain, why, 125, 126 ; certain account of, and looking for death is a means to draw us from self-confidence, and from the world, and to make us trust in God, 126, 127 ; physicians fault in flattering the sick, and feeding them with false hopes of long life at the point of death, taxed, 127 ; affliction called death, 161.

Deliver.—God doth not deliver his children at the first, but suffers them to be brought to a low ebb, to a very sad condition, and why, 161, 162 ; God delivers after he hath done his work, 162; God's time to deliver, when, 163, 164 ; God's children alway stand in need of deliverance, 165 ; God delivers both outwardly and inwardly, 166, 170 ; Christians have deliverance from trouble, 167 ; a double deliverance of God, 168; experience of God's deliverance in time past, a ground of confidence to expect the like for time to come, 162, 168,171; objection against the doctrine of God's delivering his people from trouble answered, 169; deliverance various or manifold, 170, 171 ; God will deliver his people out of all trouble, 171.

Dispense.—No dispensing with God's law, 380.

Dissembling, Dissimulation.—Grounds of dissimulation, 231 ; a threefold dissimulation, (1.) before, (2.) in, (3.) after, the project, 231, 232 ; objection for dissembling answered, 234 ; man naturally prone to dissemble, 231-237 ; dissembling to be avoided and declined, 301 ; a Christian is no dissembler, 301. (See Simulation.)

Dominion—No man hath dominion over another's faith, 499 ; what is no domineering over the faith of others, 500 ; what is domineering over the faith of others, 500 ; who are guilty of domineering over other men's faith, 501 ; the Church of Rome guilty of domineering over the faith of others, how, and wherein, 501 ; grounds from whence this domineering over other men's faith ariseth, 505.

Double.—Doubling a great sin, 234; man by nature

is prone to double, and the grounds of it, 237 ; some persons and callings are more prone to doubling than others, 237 ; a Christian is no doubler, 301.

Earnest.—What the Spirit is an earnest of, 465 ; the Spirit resembled to an earnest in five particulars, 465, 466 ; how to know whether we have the earnest of the Spirit, 470-472 ; how to get this earnest of the Spirit, 480-482 ; motives to labour for this earnest, 482, 483

End.—Holy men work for holy ends, 330.

Equivocation.—Popish equivocation odious and abominable, 233, 354, 494.

Error.—How prophets and apostles were subject to errors and mistakes, and how not, 356. (See Infallible, Mistake)

Experience.—Former experience a ground to expect like mercies for the future, 171, *seq.*

Extremity —God sometimes suffers his children to fall into great extremities, and why, 117-119 ; God's people are sensible of their extremity, 120. (See Afflictions, Sufferings, Tribulations.)

Faith.—Difference between faith and presumption, 422 ; a double act of faith, (1.) direct, (2.) reflect, 467 ; of standing by faith (see Standing) ; to have dominion over the faith of others (see Dominion) ; the foundation of faith must be out of a man's self, 522 ; true faith is built upon the word or the Scriptures, not upon unwritten traditions, 522, 523 ; popish faith not built upon the Scriptures but upon traditions, 523, 524 ; faith sure and certain, 524 ; true faith will persevere and hold out to the end, 523, 524 ; it is by faith that we stand, and withstand all opposition whatsoever, 524 ; faith a Christian's victory, by it he conquers all adversary powers, 524, 525 ; the sacrament a means to strengthen faith, 528.

Falsehood.—Falsehood to be declined, 300, 301.

Father.—God as the Father of Christ to be praised, 26, 27 (see Praise) ; God the Father of Christ, our Father, and the Father of mercies, how, 26, 27 ; why God is called the Father of mercies, 28 ; why not the Father of mercy, but of mercies, 28, 29 ; uses to be made of this title of God, the Father of mercies, 31-34, *seq.* (See Mercy.)

Flesh.—Flesh, what, 262, 346 ; carnal wisdom, why called flesh, 346 ; to purpose and consult according to the flesh, a ground of lightness, 348 ; how to know whether we consult according to the flesh, 349 ; signs whereby to know that we are not led or advised by the flesh, 349, 350 ; how to avoid fleshly wisdom, 350, 351. (See Wisdom.)

Generation.—Prerogatives of Christ's generation, 370.

Gentle.—Gentle courses first to be used, why, 489 ; when gentle means prevail not, severe must be used, 489.

Glory, Glorying—Whether a man may glory of anything in himself ? how he may, and how he may not, 204 ; cautions for glorying in grace, 228 ; God's glory manifest in the gospel, viz., the glory of his, (1.) Justice, (2.) mercy, (3) wisdom, (4.) power, (5.) truth ; 418, 419, 420 ; God's glory is displayed by the ministry, 420 ; grace and glory differ but in degrees, 469.

Good.—God's children do good in every condition, 105 ; what good we get by other's afflictions, 101 ; the sufferings of saints do good to others, how, 101 (see Afflictions) ; God in all outward things that are ill, intends the good of the soul, 142 ; a good man a public good, 258 ; a good man should take occasion to do good, 336 ; the good things the wicked enjoy, are not blessings, but curses and snares to them, 395 ; how to know they are so, 395,396 ; how to know that the good things we enjoy, we have them in love, 396.

Govern, Guide—All inferior creatures are under the guidance and government of some superior, 275.

Grace.—Grace sweetens all a Christian's conversation, 14, 15 ; grace, what, 16 ; Christians, though in the state of grace, yet still need grace, 17, 331, 332 ; how to have continual assurance of grace, 18, 19 ; a man may know his own estate in grace, 221, 222 ; objection against this answered, 223 ; why the apostle names grace, not wisdom, 275, 276 ; grace twofold, 281 ; grace wrought in us described, 281, 282 ; all our wisdom comes from grace, 282 ; every thing necessary to bring us to heaven is a grace, 283, 334, 335 ; all the good we have is of grace, 283 ; God is ready to give us grace, 284 ; signs of being led and guided by grace, 288, *seq.* ; helps or means to be led and guided by grace, 293, 294, *seq.* ; the preaching of the word is a special grace, 330 ; every benefit and blessing is a grace, 283, 334, 335 ; we ought to strengthen radical graces, viz., (1.) humility, (2.) faith, (3.) knowledge, 433, 434 ; we may be assured from a little measure of grace, that we are truly in the state of grace, 470, *seq.* ; how to know whether the little grace we have be true grace, 472, *seq.*

Health —Health is a gift, yea, a great blessing of God, 191 ; all other blessings are uncomfortable without health, 191, 192.

Holy —Holy men are but men, subject to mistake, 355, 356 ; holiness and happiness differ but in degrees, 469 ; those that look to be happy, must first be holy, 469, 470.

Hope —A double efficacy in hope, 111, 113 ; we may stedfastly hope for the performance of divine truths. 113 ; we should hope well of others, 306, 307, 327. (See Conceit, Opinion.)

Hypocrite.—Wherein a true saint differs from an hypocrite, 14, *seq.* ; a Christian no hypocrite, 14, 301 ; profane professors are gross hypocrites, 12.

Jealousy.—Men are wondrous prone to jealousy and suspicion, 339, 485 ; whence jealousy or suspicion ariseth, 340, 485, 486 ; jealousy, what, 485 ; mischief from jealousy, 485, 486 ; we should labour to avoid jealousy, why, 487.

Inconstancy.—Public persons should labour to avoid the just imputation of inconstancy, 342 ; grounds or causes of inconstancy, 343, 344. 345 ; we must not take that for inconstancy which is not, 343; remedies against inconstancy, 345, 346 ; carnal men inconstant, 352.

Indulgences.—Popish indulgences, what, 99 ; popish indulgences confuted, 99. (See Satisfactions.)

Infallibility.—How the prophets and apostles were infallible, and how not, 355, 356. (See Error, Mistake.)

Ingratitude.—Ingratitude a horrible sin, 193 ; a carnal man ungrateful, why, 24.

Joy, Rejoice.—Christians have their joy, or a Christian's estate is a joyful and a rejoicing estate, 205, 206, 506, *seq.* ; a Christian's joy is spiritual, he rejoices in spiritual things, and what these are, 205, 206 ; wicked men dare not reveal their joy, but seek to hide the ground of it, 207 ; a Christian is not ashamed of his joy, why, 207 ; a faithful minister is the joy of the people, why, 317, 506, *seq.* ; the people's proficiency in grace is the minister's joy, 319 ; salvation termed joy, why, 506 ; the end of the ministry is to be helpers of the people's joy, 506, *seq.* ; how ministers are helpers of the people's joy, 509, *seq.* ; objections answered, 511, *seq.* ; joy is that frame and state of soul that Christians are in, or should labour to be in, why, 506, *seq.* ; reasons or motives why Christians should be joyful, 507, *seq.* ; ministers only helpers, not authors of joy, 506 ; God's Spirit alone speaks joy and comfort to the soul, why, 513, 514 ; faith breeds joy, how, 516 ;

signs or evidences whereby to know whether
our joy be good, 517.

Journey.—It is a commendable thing for Christians
to bring one another on their journey, 338 ; our
journey to heaven certain, 357; how St Paul
could be deceived in his journey, and not in his
doctrine, 355, 356.

Judgment.—God's word or the holy Scriptures the
judge of all controversies, 364 ; properties of a
judge, 364 ; judgment of conscience a forerunner
of the great and general judgment, 210, 211 ;
the measure of a Christian's joy is as it will be
esteemed at the day of judgment, 323 ; we should
often think of the day of judgment, 324. (See
Day.)

King.—Christians are kings, how, 448, 449.

Knowledge.—God is known in his (1.) nature, (2)
promises, (3) works, 149 ; if our knowledge be
not spiritual, we fall into, (1.) sin, (2.) despair,
(3.) apostasy, 526, 527.

Legacy.—God's promises are legacies, 415 ; difference between a legacy and a covenant, 415.

Lightness.—Public persons should avoid the just
imputation of lightness, 342; grounds of lightness, 343, 344, 345 ; remedies against lightness,
345, 346 ; to purpose according to the flesh, is a
ground of lightness, 348.

Lie.—All sorts of lies are unlawful, 234 ; a lie, what,
301 ; equivocation is a lie, 301. (See Equivocation.)

Live.—We may not live as we list, if we mean to
die well, 258.

Mercy.—Mercy, what, 30 ; God styled the Father
of mercies, why, 29, 30, 31 ; why not called the
Father of mercy, but of mercies, 30, 31 ; use to
be made of God's mercifulness, or in that he is
the Father of mercies, 31, *seq.* ; against presuming upon God's mercy, 32, 33 ; men are prone
to presume of God's mercy, 32, 33 (see Presumption) ; all God's attributes without mercy are
terrible, 30 ; objections of a poor dejected soul
against the doctrine of God's mercy, or mercifulness, answered, 36 ; to whom God's mercy is
unlimited, viz., to repentant souls, not to presumptuous sinners, 32 ; how to be made fit for,
or capable of mercy, 42 ; how to improve mercy
daily, 42, 43 ; kinds of God's mercies, 31.

Merit.—Against merit, 191.

Minister, Ministry.—Ministers must win by life as
well as by doctrine, 260 ; ministers are joined
with Christ in acceptance and neglect, 317 ; a
faithful minister is the joy of the people, 317 ;
the ministry is a great gift and blessing of God,
318, 329, 330, 331 ; the people's proficiency in
grace is the minister's joy, 319 ; all the good we
have by Christ, is conveyed by the ministry,
372 ; consent of ministers is a help to faith, 373 ;
ministers are to be prayed for by the people.
(See Prayer.)

Mistake.—Holy men are subject to mistakes, 355,
356. (See Error.)

Name.—Men have oft their name and denomination in Scripture, by that which they are ruled
by, 262, 346.

New.—Popery is a new religion, 377, 378.

Oath.—Oath, what, 357, 493 ; an oath lawful, 494,
495 ; kinds of oaths, 357, 493, 494, 495 ; a Christian life is a kind of oath, 498 ; conditions of an
oath, 357, 494, 495 ; an oath is not good unless
necessary, 357, 493, 494, 495 ; qualifications of
an oath, 495 ; none but good men should take
an oath, 493 ; parts of an oath, 493 ; an oath to
be taken only in serious matters, 494, *seq.* (See
Swearing.)

Occasion.—A good man must take all occasions to
do good, 336.

Oil, Ointment.—The Spirit with its graces compared to oil, or ointment, 443, 446.

Old.—Our religion is the old religion, 375, 376, *seq.*;
popery no old, but new religion, 377, 378.

Oneness.—A Christian man is one man, he doth act
one man's part, 301 ; there is but one faith, 375 ;
one catholic church, 375.

Opinion.—It is good to cherish a good opinion of
others, 306, 307, 327. (See Conceit, Hope.)

Partake.—Those that partake in other men's sins,
shall also partake in their sufferings, 110.

Paul.—St Paul's prerogative above other apostles
8 ; St Paul's modesty and humility, 9 ; St Paul
had a good opinion and conceit of the Corinthians, 306 ; how St Paul could be deceived in
his journey, and not in his doctrine, 355, 356 ;
how Timothy is called St Paul's brother, 10 ;
St Paul's course to hold out in holy resolution
to the end, 308.

Peace.—True peace issues from grace, 20.

Persecution.—They that persecute the saints, persecute Christ, 85. (See Affliction, Suffering,
Tribulation.)

Perseverance.—Resolution to persevere, and hold
out in a good course to the end, 307, 308 ; St
Paul's course to persevere in holy resolutions to
the end, 308; God's children may be assured
that they shall persevere and hold out to the
end, 468, *seq.*; he that is in the state of grace,
shall persevere in to the end, 469.

Physician.—Physicians do ill in flattering the sick,
and feeding them with hopes of long life, when
they are at the point of death, 127 ; we should
open the case of our souls to our spiritual
physicians, 513.

Policy.—A Christian should avoid the imputation
of carnal policy, 347 ; not to subordinate religion
to state policy, 279, 280.

Pope, Popery.—Popery crosses the word of God.
365, 36? ; the pope's treasury, what, 99 ; popery
founded upon traditions, 522, 523 ; popery a
rotten and unsound religion, 523 ; popish religion is full of contradictions, 366 ; popish religion is full of uncertainties, 366, 367; how and
wherein popish and protestant religion agree,
and differ, 376, *seq.* ; it is safer to be a protestant
than a papist, 379 ; whether a papist may be
saved, 379, 380 ; popery to be detested, because
it teacheth men to trust to their own works
and satisfactions, 133.

Praise.—God the object of praise, how, 26 ; God
to be praised as he is the Father of Christ, 27;
praise follows prayer; or, after prayer praises
are due, 193 ; the praises of many are grateful
and acceptable to God, 193, 194: how the unreasonable creatures praise God, 195 ; we are to
praise God for others ; for all sorts of men, 195 ;
wherein praise consists, 196. (See more in Bless,
Thankfulness.)

Prayer.—Prayer is a means to convey all good,
and deliver from all ill, 178 ; God's children can
pray for themselves, 180 ; Christians ought to
help one another by prayer, 181 ; people ought
to pray for ministers, 182, 183, 189, 190 ; what
is to be begged of God or prayed for for ministers, 190 ; Christians have not the Spirit
of prayer at all times alike, 182 ; prayer is not
a work of gifts, but of grace, 183 ; divers gifts
in prayer, 183 ; prayer is a prevailing course
with God, and why, 184, *seq.* ; how to know
whether our prayers help the church, 188, 189
it is an ill condition not to be able to pray, 189,
190 ; God will deliver the ministers by the
people's prayers, 190 ; it is a good thing to beg
the prayers of others in sickness, 192 ; the more
eminent men are, the more they are to be prayed
for, 203.

Preach.—Christ is the main object of preaching,
369. (See Ministry, Word.)

Presence.—Personal presence hath a special power,
329.

Presumption.—Against presuming upon God's

mercy, 32, 33. (see Mercy) ; difference between faith and presumption, 422.

Pride.—Pride is a sin against all the commandments, 207, 208.

Priest.—Christians are priests, how, 447, 448

Promise.—God deals with men by promises, 383 ; a promise, what, 384 : all promises made in Christ, 384 ; all the promises are yea and amen in Christ, 388, 389, *seq.* ; several kinds of promises, 394 ; till a man be in Christ he hath no good by the promises, 399 : what right a man out of Christ hath to the promises, 400 ; comfort from the promises to them that are in Christ, 401, 402, *seq.* ; how to make use of the promises, and to have comfort by them, 404, *seq.* ; what to do when in trouble we cannot call to mind any particular promise, 409 ; we should make the promises familiar to us, 409, *seq.* ; signs or evidences of believing the promises, 413, *seq.* ; promises are legacies as well as promises, 415 ; God's promises called a testament, a will, 415 ; necessity of application of the promises to ourselves, 420, *seq.* ; none have interest in the promises but such as find a change in themselves, 452.

Prophets.—How Christians are prophets, 447; prophets and apostles, how subject to error, how not, 355, 356.

Providence.—Providence, what, 167.

Rejoice — See Joy.

Religion.—Not to subordinate religion to State policy, 279. 280 ; religion tends to practice, 280 ; popish religion is a carnal religion, 296, *seq.* ; the most religious men are the best statesmen, 299 ; wherein our religion and the popish agree and differ, 376. *seq* ; popish religion unsound and rotten, 523 ; popish religion is not founded upon the Scriptures, but upon tradition. 522, 523 ; popish religion cross th the word of God, 365, 3 6 ; popish religion is full of contradictions, 366: popish religion is full of uncertainties, 366, 367 ; it is safer to be of the protestant religion than of the popish, 379 ; whether one living and dying in the Romish religion may be saved, 379, 380.

Repentance.—Late repentance (such as is in time of sickness and death) seldom true repentance, 39.

Reproof.—It is a sign of a gracious heart to endure reproof, and to esteem and affect the reprover, 314, 491 ; a minister must not spare to reprove people for sin committed, 491. *seq.* ; a threefold reproof or correction, 492, 493

Resolution—Of good resolutions, 308, *seq.*

Resurrection.—The resurrection is an argument to strengthen faith, 157 ; there will or shall be a resurrection, 157, *seq* ; God raiseth the dead, 157, *seq.*

Rock.—What is meant by rock, Mat xvi. 18, 376.

Saint.—Our love and respect should be carried to all saints, 11 ; God scatters his saints, why, 12 ; all that make profession of religion should indeed be saints, 12 ; professors called saints, why, 12; four things required to make a saint, viz. (1.) Separation, (2.) Dedication, (3.) Qualification, (4.) Conversation, 13, 14 ; how to know a saint from a mere civil man, 14 ; true saints wherein different from hypocrites and formal professors, 14. (See Christian.)

Salvation—Salvation wrought by affliction or suffering, how, and how by Christ, 100, *seq.* ; how afflictions or patience in suffering afflictions helps to salvation, 101, 102, *seq.* ; two ways to obtain salvation, 100. *seq* .

Salutation.—Use of holy salutations threefold, 15 ; salutations should be holy, 15, 16 ; God's name when taken in vain in salutations, 15, 16 ; salutations in what cases to be omitted, 16.

Satisfaction.—Against popish merits and satisfactions for others, 99. (See Indulgences.)

Scripture.—How to know the Scriptures to be the word of God and truly divine, 366, 373 ; whether the Scriptures receive any authority from the church, 9, 10 ; the Scripture is to be believed for itself, not because of the church, 373, 374, 375, *seq.* (See Word)

Seal.—Christ the head is first sealed, and then the members, viz , Christians, 452 ; our sealing, what, 453 ; four uses of a seal, 453, 454 ; the Spirit compared to a seal, wherein, 454, 455, *seq* ; how the Spirit differs from other seals, 455, 456, *seq.* ; how the Spirit seals us, 456, 457, *seq.* ; four things the Spirit works in this sealing, 456 ; how to know the sealing of the Spirit, or that we are sealed by the Spirit, 456, 457, 458, 459 ; objections against the Spirit's sealing answered, 458, *seq.* ; motives to labour to get the Spirit's sealing, or to have image of Christ stamped upon our souls by the Spirit, 460, *seq.*

Simplicity.—Simplicity, what, and how taken, 205, 229, 230 ; why called godly simplicity, or the simplicity of God, 240 ; difference between simplicity and sincerity, 229 ; St Paul's conversation in simplicity, how, 229, 230; to what things simplicity is opposed, 232, *seq* ; directions or means to get simplicity, 237, 238.

Simulation.—Of simulation, 231 ; aggravations of this sin, 232, *seq.* (See Dissembling.)

Sincerity.—Sincerity, what, 240 ; how sincerity differs from simplicity, 228 ; why called godly sincerity, or the sincerity of God, 240 ; a Christian's conversation in the world should be in sincerity, 240, 258 ; sincerity in good actions, how discovered or tried, 241, 242 ; sincerity, how tried or discovered in ill actions, 243 ; sincerity, how tried or discovered in actions indifferent, 244 ; motives to labour for sincerity, 245, 246, *seq.*; means to get sincerity, 247, 248; corruptions and imperfections may stand with sincerity, 250, *seq.*; order in sincerity, how to be kept, 251 ; sincerity extends itself to all the frame of a man's life, 252, 253 ; we must have our conversation in sincerity while we live in the world, 258.

Singularity.—There is a spirit of singularity in many, 9.

Slander.—How to arm and fence ourselves against slander, 340.

Society.—The comfort and benefit of society, 76, 253.

Solitariness—Solitariness very dangerous, 76, 253. (See Alone, Society.)

Son.—Christ the Son of God, how differing from other sons, 370

Soul.—God's Spirit alone speaks comfort and peace to the soul, 514 ; God in all things that are ill intends the good of the soul, 142 ; the soul must have somewhat to trust to, 142 ; people should do well to open the case of their souls to their spiritual physicians, 513.

Spirit.—The Spirit with its graces compared to anointing or ointment (see Anointing, Ointment) ; the Spirit compared to an earnest (see Earnest) ; the Spirit compared to a seal (see Seal) ; why the work of grace is attributed to the Spirit rather than to the Father or the Son, 447 ; why the Spirit is said to seal, and to be an earnest, and not the Father or the Son. 477 ; means to attain or come by the Spirit, 480, 481, 482, *seq* ; how to know that we have the Spirit, 478. 479 ; of our anointing by the Spirit, 442, *seq.* ; of our sealing by the Spirit, 452, *seq.* ; God's Spirit alone seals comfort to the soul, 514.

Stablish—Stablishing grace necessary, why, 422 ; Christ is the foundation of our stability, 423 ; our judgment, will, affections, &c., are stablished in Christ, 424 ; it is only God that can stablish the soul—he must do it, none else can, 426, *seq.* ; as God can, so he will stablish us, 426, *seq.*; God stablisheth us by working in us stablishing graces, viz., (1.) fear, (2.) wisdom, (3) faith, (4.) peace of conscience, &c., 431 ; means of stablishing, or whereby we may come to be stablished, 433. 437 ; signs or evidences of our stablishing, 437, 438, *seq.*

Strength,—How these two may stand together,

We are pressed out of measure above strength, 2 Cor. i. 8 ; and, God is faithful, and will lay no more upon you than you shall be able to bear, 1 Cor. x. 13, 116. 117.

Suffering.—The sufferings of Christ abound in us, or God's saints are subject to many sufferings, why, 78; all Christians suffer, how, 104 ; a threefold suffering in the church since Christ's time, 80, 81 ; the sufferings of Christians are the sufferings of Christ, and why so called, 82, 83 ; Christ's sufferings twofold, 82 ; differences between the sufferings of Christ and ordinary crosses, 83 ; motives to suffer for Christ, 83, 84, 85 ; how the sufferings of saints do good, or are profitable to others, 101 ; God's children partake of the sufferings of others, how, 107 ; suffering must precede comfort, and why, 108, *seq* ; those that suffer as they should are sure of comfort, 108. (See more in Affliction, Persecution, Tribulation.)

Suspicion.—Man's nature is prone to suspicion, 339, 485 ; grounds of suspicion, from whence it ariseth, 340, 485, 486 ; suspicion, what, 340, 485 ; how to arm ourselves against suspicion, 340 ; how to know when suspicion is evil, 341; suspicion is more than fear, less than judgment, 485; suspicion makes the worst construction, 485, 486 ; why the devil cherisheth suspicion, 486 ; mischief from suspicion, 486.

Swearing—What meant by the prohibition, Swear not at all, 357, 494, 495 ; to swear by none but God, 493 ; swearing lawful, 494, 495 ; ordinary swearing condemned, 357, 358. 494, 495, 496 ; objections for common and ordinary swearing answered, 495, *seq.*; original causes for ordinary swearing, 496, 497 ; motives against ordinary swearing, 497, 498 ; means against ordinary swearing, 497, 498 ; ordinary swearers curse themselves, 497.

Thankfulness—It is the disposition of God's people to be thankful for mercies received, 22 ; we are to be especially thankful for spiritual favours, 24 ; means to become thankful, 24, 25, 26, 196, 197; a carnal man unthankful, why, 25 ; motives to thankfulness, 26, 198, 199, 200 ; not only verbal, but real, thanksgiving is required, 200. (See Bless, Praise.)

Tradition.—Popish faith is built upon traditions, 522, 23.

Treasury.—The pope's treasury, what, 99 ; the pope's treasury confuted, 99 ; Christ is the only treasury of the church, 99.

Tribulation.—God's children are subject to tribulation. 52, 65, 79. (See Affliction, Persecution, Suffering.)

Trust.—God's children are prone to trust in themselves, why, 128 ; not to trust in anything but in God, 132, 133, 134, *seq.*; signs of trusting in these outward things, as riches, &c., 129, 130; it is a dangerous thing to trust in ourselves, or in the creature, why, 132 ; popery to be detested, because it teacheth men to trust to their own works, satisfactions, &c., 133 ; we must not trust our own graces, 133 ; creatures may be trusted to subordinately, 135, 136 ; worldlings trust in the creature above God, yea, against God, 135 ; how to cure false confidence, or trusting in ourselves and in the creature, 136, 138 ; to trust in God a lesson hardly learned, 139 ; God, to make ns trust in him, is fain to cast us out of ourselves, 139 ; God is the sole and proper object of trust, 144 ; God in Christ the object of trust, 144 ; it is a man's duty to trust in God, 145 ; trials of trust in God, or signs whereby to know whether we trust in God, 146, 147, 148 ; helps or means to

trust in God, 149 ; trust in God, how to be exercised in great afflictions, 152 ; trust in God, how exercised in the hour of death, 153 ; God, to strengthen our trust, hath given us his, (1.) promise, (2) seal, (3.) oath, (4) earnest, (5) a pawn, (6.) seisin, 154 ; objection against trusting in God answered, 155 ; a Christian may trust or rely on God for the time to come, 168 ; trust what, 305. (See Confidence)

Truth.—Truth may not be spoken at all times, 233, 234 ; God is true and faithful, how, 360 ; objection against this answered, 361 ; how to know the word of God to be true, 366, 373 ; it is a matter of comfort to believe the word of God to be true. 367, *seq.*; the word of God, or evangelical doctrine, is most true and certain, 373.

Vain—Ministers' labour is not in vain in the Lord, 7.

Vehement.—Carnal men are vehement, 353.

Unbelief—The heart of man is full of unbelief, and can hardly be settled in the persuasion of divine truth, 464, 465.

Uniformity.—A Christian is uniform, 301.

Union—There is a threefold union, viz., (1) of Christ and our nature, (2) of Christ and his members, (3.) of one member with another, 108.

Wait.—Grounds of waiting upon God for deliverance from trouble, or motives thereunto, 163, 164, *seq.*, 410.

Way—It is a commendable custom for Christians to bring one another on their way, 338.

Weak.—The weakest creatures have the strongest shelters, 430.

Will.—Every one in his calling placed by the will of God, 8, 9 ; the more will, advisedness, and deliberation in sin, the greater the sin, 236.

Wisdom—Wisdom manifold, 260, 261 ; wisdom, what, 261 ; carnal or fleshly wisdom described, 261, 262, 263 ; why called fleshly wisdom, 261, 262 ; all carnal men have not fleshly wisdom, 261, 262 ; fleshly wisdom is where there is no simplicity nor sincerity, 262 ; God's children not ruled by fleshly wisdom, why, 263, 274, 275 ; mischief of carnal wisdom, 264, 265 ; carnal or fleshly wisdom hinders our joy and comfort, 273, 274 ; popery is founded on carnal wisdom, 522, 523 ; how to avoid fleshly wisdom, 350, 351 ; a Christian needs wisdom, why, 277 ; wisdom may be had, 278 ; we should go to God for wisdom, 278, 279 ; God gives wisdom for the things of this life, 279 ; true wisdom toucheth conversation, 280.

Word.—The preaching of the word, accompanied with God's Spirit, is able to convert and change the most wicked hearts that be, 10, 11, (see Ministry, Preaching) ; it is a matter of consequence to believe the word of God to be true, certain, and immutable, 367, *seq.*; the word of God is the judge of all controversies, 363 ; Christ the Word, how, 390, 446 ; the word of God is most true, certain, and infallible, 373 ; how to know the word of God to be true, 366, 373. (See Scripture)

World.—Christianity may stand with converse in the world, 253 ; religion makes a man converse in the world untainted, 254 ; wicked men called the world, why, 261, 346, 347.

Yea and Nay.—Grounds of yea and nay, 353 ; dissemblers are yea and nay all at once, 354 ; all promises and prophecies are yea in Christ, 388, 389, 390, *seq.*

END OF VOL. III.